Post 9/11 and the State of Permanent Legal Emergency

IUS GENTIUM

COMPARATIVE PERSPECTIVES ON LAW AND JUSTICE

VOLUME 14

For further volumes:
http://www.springer.com/series/7888

Aniceto Masferrer
Editor

Post 9/11 and the State of Permanent Legal Emergency

Security and Human Rights in Countering Terrorism

Springer

Editor
Aniceto Masferrer
Faculty of Law
Comparative Legal History
University of Valencia
Avda. de los Naranjos
Valencia, Spain

ISBN 978-94-007-4061-7 ISBN 978-94-007-4062-4 (eBook)
DOI 10.1007/978-94-007-4062-4
Springer Dordrecht Heidelberg New York London

Library of Congress Control Number: 2012938035

Printed on acid-free paper

Springer is part of Springer Science+Business Media (www.springer.com)

Preface and Acknowledgements

This book is devoted to exploring an age-old problem which touches upon people's lives and requires constant deliberation: the necessity of limiting State power to protect individuals, including non-citizens. Accordingly, it is important to recognize human rights which exist prior to the state. These pre-political or natural rights lie beyond the siren song of sovereignty and are not negotiable whether through legislation, executive power (or otherwise). Protecting these rights, as conceived in law, avoids allowing the excessive exercise of State power, a power which is otherwise neither limited nor restrained.

In countering terrorism, the State is not allowed to exercise unrestrained power. It may not rely on a supposed national or popular sovereignty or even on the legitimacy of the democratic process. While establishing limits on State power and law-making may not completely resolve the complex relationship between national security and the protection of fundamental rights, it may moderate the State's often excessive utilitarian approach which, focusing more on the *quantum* than on *quod*, ignores the pre-political dimension of human rights and trivializes – if not ignores – the dignity of each human being, leaving him/her unprotected from the absolute power of Leviathan.

This collective monograph is the result of a research project which started in 2009 and took an important step forward in the context of an International Workshop on 'Security and Human Rights in Countering Terrorism', celebrated at the University of Valencia in July 7, 2010. Later, many Workshop participants and other distinguished scholars became involved and put this project together. I'm grateful to all of them for their generous co-operation and academic excellence. I also give thanks to the *Fundación Universitas* for its support in partially sponsoring this project (www.fundacionuniversitas.org). Moreover, I wish to express gratitude to Mortimer Sellers and James Maxeiner, the Series Editors in the 'Ius Gentium: Comparative Perspectives on Law and Justice', for allowing the publication of this book in their prestigious Springer's collection.

Valencia — Aniceto Masferrer

Contents

1 Introduction: Security, Criminal Justice and Human Rights in Countering Terrorism in the Post 9/11 Era 1
Aniceto Masferrer

Part I State Power and Legal Responses from an Historical Perspective

2 The State Power and the Limits of the Principle of Sovereignty: An Historical Approach 15
Aniceto Masferrer and Juan A. Obarrio

3 Legal Concepts of Terrorism as Political Crime and International Criminal Law in Eighteenth and Nineteenth Century Europe 53
Karl Härter

Part II Defining Terrorism

4 Civilising the Exception: Universally Defining Terrorism 79
Ben Saul

5 Terrorism: Limits Between Crime and War. The Fallacy of the Slogan 'War on Terror' 101
Mariona Llobet

Part III Keeping Counter-Terrorism Within the Criminal Law Justice?

6 The Impact of Contemporary Security Agendas Against Terrorism on the Substantive Criminal Law 121
Clive Walker

7 **The War on Terror and Crusading Judges: Re-establishing the Primacy of the Criminal Justice System** 153
Francesca Galli

8 **Secret Evidence and Its Alternatives** 179
Kent Roach

9 **Evolution of British Law on Terrorism: From Ulster to Global Terrorism (1970–2010)** 201
Leandro Martínez-Peñas and Manuela Fernández-Rodríguez

10 **Australian Responses to 9/11: New World Legal Hybrids?** 223
Simon Bronitt and Susan Donkin

11 **Democratic States' Response to Terrorism: A Comparative Reflection on the Perceived Role of the Judiciary in the Protection of Human Rights and Civil Liberties** 241
Marinella Marmo

12 **The U.S. Response to Cuban and Puerto Rican Right-Wing Terrorism in the Pre and Post 9/11 Era** 259
José M. Atiles-Osoria

Part IV Counter-Terrorism from an International-Law Perspective

13 **Permanent Legal Emergencies and the Derogation Clause in International Human Rights Treaties: A Contradiction?** 287
Christopher Michaelsen

14 **National Self-Defence in the Age of Terrorism: Immediacy and State Attribution** 315
Mark D. Kielsgard

About the Contributors 345

Contributors

José M. Atiles-Osoria Centro de Estudos Sociais, University of Coimbra, Coimbra, Portugal

Simon Bronitt ARC Centre of Excellence in Policing and Security, Brisbane, QLD, Australia

Susan Donkin ARC Centre of Excellence in Policing and Security, Brisbane, QLD, Australia

Manuela Fernández-Rodríguez Facultad de Ciencias Jurídicas y Sociales, Universidad Rey Juan Carlos, Vicálvaro/Madrid, Spain

Francesca Galli FNRS Post-Doctoral Researcher, Institut d'Etudes Européennes, Université Libre de Bruxelles, Brussels, Belgium

Karl Härter Max-Planck-Institut für europäische Rechtsgeschichte, Frankfurt am Main, Germany

Mark D. Kielsgard City University of Hong Kong, School of Law, City University of Hong Kong, Kowloon Tong, Kowloon, Hong Kong

Mariona Llobet Faculty of Law, Universitat Pompeu Fabra, Barcelona, Spain

Marinella Marmo Studies in Criminal Justice, School of Law, Flinders University, Adelaide, SA, Australia

Leandro Martínez-Peñas Facultad de Ciencias Jurídicas y Sociales, Universidad Rey Juan Carlos, Vicálvaro/Madrid, Spain

Aniceto Masferrer Faculty of Law, University of Valencia, Valencia, Spain

Christopher Michaelsen Faculty of Law, University of New South Wales, Sydney, NSW, Australia

Juan A. Obarrio Faculty of Law, University of Valencia, Valencia, Spain

Kent Roach Faculty of Law, University of Toronto, Toronto, ON, Canada

Ben Saul Sydney Centre for International Law, Faculty of Law, The University of Sydney, Sydney, NSW, Australia

Clive Walker Centre for Criminal Justice Studies, School of Law, University of Leeds, Leeds, UK

Chapter 1
Introduction: Security, Criminal Justice and Human Rights in Countering Terrorism in the Post 9/11 Era

Aniceto Masferrer

Terrorism violates human rights and constitutes a serious challenge for liberal democracies. Not because terrorists can defeat liberal democracies by force of arms, but because their actions can potentially undermine the domestic social contract of the state by undermining its ability to protect its citizens from attack and undermining the ability of democratic process to solve pressing problems. As Audrey Kurth Cronin has noted, 'the greatest danger [for liberal democracies] is not defeat on the battlefield but damage to the integrity and value of the state'.[1] While the events of 9/11 and the subsequent attacks around the world attributed to Islamist terrorists have led to a renewed focus on the threats and challenges associated with terrorism, the phenomenon is not new. Throughout history, states have had to deal with acts of political violence and terrorism. Democracies, perhaps, have been particularly vulnerable to campaigns of terrorism because of their openness, limits on government and restrains imposed by the rule of law. As Paul Wilkinson has observed, 'it is part of the price we must pay for our democratic freedoms that some may choose to abuse these freedoms for the purposes of destroying democracy, or some other goal'.[2]

In the aftermath of the 9/11 attacks on New York and Washington, many commentators claimed that the world had changed 'forever' with international terrorism

---

[1] A. K. Cronin, "Rethinking Sovereignty: American Strategy in the Age of Terrorism," *Survival* 44, no. 2 (2002): 134.

[2] P. Wilkinson, *Terrorism versus Democracy – The Liberal State Response* (London: Frank Cass, 2001), 220–224.

A. Masferrer (✉)
Faculty of Law, University of Valencia,
Avda. dels Tarongers s/n, Edificio Departamental Occidental, E-46022 Valencia, Spain
e-mail: aniceto.masferrer@uv.es

A. Masferrer (ed.), *Post 9/11 and the State of Permanent Legal Emergency*,
Ius Gentium: Comparative Perspectives on Law and Justice 14,
DOI 10.1007/978-94-007-4062-4_1, © Springer Science+Business Media B.V. 2012

constituting one of the defining global security challenges of the twenty first century.[3] The renewed focus on counter-terrorism law and policy also called into question whether the lessons drawn from previous terrorism emergencies are pertinent to the post-9/11 environment. Indeed, to what extent, if at all, are the principles identified for the liberal democratic response to traditional forms of terrorism applicable to a response to contemporary international terrorism? The historical, political and security implications of 9/11 notwithstanding, many scholars and policy-makers appear to agree that the basic tenets of the traditional liberal democratic response continue to apply to responses to contemporary international terrorism.

This volume focuses on four particular aspects of the liberal democratic response to terrorism an era of perceived permanent emergency. Accordingly, it is structured in four parts which provide a historical perspective, address definitional issues in the context of terrorism and examine specific challenges arising in the field of criminal justice as well as in international law.

Part I opens with an analysis of state power and legal responses from an historical perspective. It contains two chapters approaching two different topics related to the crucial theme of how a state counters terrorism without overly encroaching upon the fundamental rights of its citizens. In Chap. 2, Juan A. Obarrio and I explore the notion of sovereignty and the limits of state power in the framework of criminal justice. It is not an easy enterprise to counter terrorism while respecting the rule of law and guaranteeing the security of citizens to the maximum extent possible without violating their fundamental rights. Theoretically, modern constitutionalism emerged to protect citizens from political abuses of power. In practice, however, fundamental rights are not always fully respected since the state is often tempted to exercise its power beyond legal boundaries. To limit the power of the state means to limit its sovereignty. Otherwise, the abuses of power by the state become inevitable. Surprisingly, modern constitutionalism applied limits to the state during an historical period in which sovereignty was regarded, in the realm of political philosophy, as an unlimited notion (Rousseau).

Nevertheless, the notion of sovereignty, being the result of a long development in the Western legal tradition (particularly from the Middle Ages to the sixteenth century), was never regarded as unlimited. The second chapter analyses the limits to the principle of sovereignty in three specific periods. Firstly, in Roman antiquity, when, during the transition between the Republic and the Principality, Cicero weighed the values, principles and institutions of the republic, by resorting to the defence of freedom, the class of the *optimates*, a mixed constitution and to the natural law. Secondly, in the Middle Ages, where, in front of the Emperor, the Papacy, Pact laws

---

[3] See e.g., P. Kelly, "How 9/11 changed the world," *The Australian* (Sydney), 8 September 2006; R. W. Stevenson, "Cheney says 9/11 changed the rules," *New York Times* (New York), 21 December 2005. For thoughtful analysis see, e.g., R. Jervis, "An Interim Assessment of September 11: What Has Changed and What Has Not?," *Political Science Quarterly* 117, no. 1 (2002): 37–52; T. L. Friedman, *Longitudes and Attitudes: Exploring the World after September 11* (New York: Farrar, Straus and Giroux, 2002).

and the observance of natural law became elements to limit the sovereignty of the monarch. Lastly, in the early Modern Age, the notion of sovereignty – and its limits – was notably developed by Jean Bodin in his most famous work, *The Six Books of the Commonwealth.*

This historical survey is an attempt to demonstrate that the challenge of dealing with emergency is not new, and that the lessons of history demonstrate that unchecked power of the sovereign leads to the demise of liberty.

In Chap. 3, Karl Härter gives a fascinating overview of the history of terrorism by analyzing terrorism as a political crime in eighteenth and nineteenth century Europe. At that time 'terrorism' did not merely exist as a separate, specific phenomenon but was considered as a political crime like treason or the 'crimen laesae maiestatis.' Reacting to different forms of political dissidence, revolt and criminal/terrorist action, the European authorities and states slowly shaped the legal concept of terrorism and developed an anti-terrorism legislation which could be extended to various forms of political dissidence and crime. This development was accompanied by the establishment of different new techniques of policing and anti-terrorism measures which were only partially integrated in the legal system or legally controlled. Particularly in the second half of the nineteenth century this development implied not only the modification of domestic criminal law but also affected fundamental rights and civil liberties already established by European constitutionalism.

On the basis of these general developments Härter's chapter explores especially the impact of the legal concepts of terrorism on 'international criminal law'. Political movements, political dissidents, rebels and anarchist could be labeled 'terrorist' and were considered a trans-border threat. This influenced not only the establishment and intensification of trans-border police activities and prosecution of 'terrorists' but stimulated the formation of international criminal law, particularly with regard to legal assistance, extradition, and asylum. The latter practices were modified by new norms like the assassination or the anarchist clause which restricted the granting of political asylum and extended extradition with regard to political crimes and terrorism. In this respect the legal concepts of terrorism affected fundamental rights and civil liberties on the international level and influenced the development of trans-border anti-terrorism measures and the formation of 'international criminal law'.

Based on a historical definition of terrorism, Härter analyses the legal responses to political violence in Central Europe from 1789 to 1914. In this period of the emerging constitutional state (*Rechtsstaat*), authorities responded to various phenomena of political dissidence and violence regarded as political (or even terrorist) crimes by introducing a range of measures including criminal justice, punishment and prevention.

Thus, political violence was used to assert a state of emergency, to legitimise emergency laws and to develop substantial legal elements of political crime, which in the long run gained importance for the legal conceptualisation of 'terrorism' and the implementation of legally based counter-terrorism measures. They concerned the conceptualisation of the 'terrorist' group as 'criminal association' (including the criminalisation of membership, support and participation in concomitant activities), the planning and commission of violent crimes (including the penalisation of preparatory acts and the concept of anticipatory crimes), the control and criminalisation of public activities (press, writings, speeches, assemblies, propaganda) and the transnational level with regard to the restriction of asylum and the extension of extradition. In consequence, the legal responses to political violence facilitated and legitimised extended surveillance, policing and suppression of oppositional groups, dissidents and the labour movement, which could be labelled and criminalised as the breeding ground of political violence or even as 'terroristic'. Härter's chapter demonstrates exemplarily that the legal conceptualisation of terrorism as a political crime could implicate the extension of 'social control' and the constraint of civil rights.

Part II contains two chapters exploring definitional aspects of terrorism. Ben Saul's chapter, analyses, among other questions, whether there is now an accepted definition of terrorism in general international law. His chapter is particularly timely in the wake of a decision by the UN Special Tribunal for Lebanon, which recently declared the existence of an international crime of transnational terrorism.

Saul concludes, however, that there is insufficient evidence of a customary international law definition of terrorism, largely because there is too much inconsistency and divergence in the material sources of law such as international and regional treaties, national laws and judicial decisions, and United Nations resolutions. There are nonetheless good international public policy reasons for defining terrorism, to protect important community values and interests. In Saul's view, those policy reasons can illuminate the proper approach to the technical problem of defining the elements of terrorism, particularly in ways which do not interfere with other important global values, such as human rights and humanitarian law. In this context, the chapter explores the advantages and costs of defining terrorism in certain ways.

In Chap. 5 Mariona Llobet illustrates that a key challenge in contemporary discourses on this subject lies in identifying the limits between terrorism and war. She observes that there appears to be considerable confusion between the concept of terrorism and the concept of war in the post 9/11 era, especially in the context of military action in Iraq and Afghanistan.

Llobet analyses the link between terrorism and war from three distinct but interrelated perspectives. Firstly, terrorist practices are also performed by the armed forces and organised groups of resistance in wartime. However, she argues that, as a phenomenon, terrorism should not be confused with war or warfare guerrilla.

Secondly, Llobet explores whether the threat of contemporary international terrorism is a manifestation of some sort of criminality, or, by contrast, represents a new form of warfare. The chapter considers the consequences of taking into account one or the other approach, as each would lead to the application of two opposite legal models. If it is a crime-focused model, the fight against terrorism should be conducted within the legal mechanisms established by the principles of criminal justice to prevent and punish any kind of crime in peacetime. If it is a war-focused model, the provisions of the law of armed conflict should be applied.

Finally, Llobet questions the premises of our response to the 9/11 events. She asks whether it is admissible to respond to crime (terrorist attacks) with war (such as the events in Iraq and Afghanistan). She argues that to justify legally our response we should consider terrorist violence not as a form of crime but as an armed attack from abroad that legitimises the resort to war.

Part III analyses some specific topics whose common trait is whether it may be possible to confine counter-terrorism within criminal law justice principles, that is, to effectively combat terrorism without diminishing both the rule of law and fundamental rights.

Clive Walker, in Chap. 6 explores three basic questions regarding how the substantive law has been impacted upon by terrorism. In other words, in Walker's view, terrorism presents several severe challenges for the criminal law of any state which must deal with its impact, and his chapter tackles three vital questions, with illustrations primarily from the laws of the United Kingdom.

The first question concerns the appropriate overall role to be served by the criminal law in regard to counter-terrorism as compared to other potentially coercive exercises of state power, such as executive (ministerial) measures. One way or another, governments are not willing to stand impassive while terrorists kill citizens and subvert the proper working of democracy. Indeed, governments are given every encouragement to be energetic in their responses, with UN Security Council Resolution 1373 of 28 September 2001 pronouncing that 'States should … take the necessary steps to prevent the commission of terrorist acts; deny safe haven to those who finance, plan, support, commit terrorist acts …'. It follows that criminal law is part of the weaponry of counter-terrorism. Many governments have seen it as their prime response, some have even relied on criminal law as their exclusive response, but some have mixed criminal and non-criminal responses, such as detention without trial. Reasons are suggested why criminal law responses are ethically superior.

The second and third questions relate to the modes of application of the criminal law within counter-terrorism and, closely-related, how far criminal law may be altered from its 'norm' or paradigm format in the pursuit of those functions and yet retain sufficient recognisable characteristics essential for legitimacy. One may take the articles of the European Convention on Human Rights as authoritative guides for the 'lowest common denominator' of due process.

Within that context, universal standards must contend with six identified adaptations of criminal law to counter-terrorism. First, and most evident in recent years, criminal law can allow for prescient intervention before a terrorist crime is completed. Second, there can be net-widening, so that peripheral suspects can be neutralised. Third, criminal law can reduce obstructive 'technicalities'. Fourth, the criminal law can be used to mobilise the population against terrorism – to force them to assist in counter-terrorism work. Fifth, the criminal law can serve a denunciatory function. Sixth, the criminal law can bolster symbolic solidarity with the state's own citizens and with the international community.

Walker shows that the challenge of terrorism can be the trigger for a variety of rational and effective legal responses within criminal justice and that not all 'special' laws must invariably be viewed as illegitimate. Nevertheless, criminal justice solutions to counter-terrorism are not all without costs to the values of criminal justice. He maintains that the state should not assume that a criminal justice preference in counter-terrorism represents an unquestionable victory for societal values.

In Chap. 7, Francesca M. Galli starts with the common place recognition that, since 11 September 2001, countering terrorism has become one of the biggest priorities of the international community, the common trend among different jurisdictions being the adoption of fierce and authoritarian measures to prevent and suppress the terrorist threat in the name of a widespread call for further security.

In her view, the current changes are to be seen in the broader picture of developments in criminal justice in Western Europe in recent years to address an allegedly mounting insecurity in the need to be tough on crime: the current normalization of extraordinary means and, in particular, the emergence of an "us and them" approach to criminal justice, which German legal writers call *Feindstrafrecht*, (enemy criminal law)

Galli points out that this authoritarian model of preventive criminal law would deny human rights and legal guarantees (the 'citizen's criminal law') to those who are seen as sources of extreme danger because of their suspicious behaviour. She makes some general suggestions as to what could and should be done to counter the existing trends and with a view of re-establishing the primacy of the criminal justice system and limit the recourse to exceptional measures to cope with the terrorism threat.

Kent Roach, in Chap. 8 denounces that the fall-out from 9/11 and the blurring distinctions between secret intelligence about security threats and evidence of terrorist crimes of preparation has placed a focus on the use of secret evidence against terrorist suspects. He affirms that attempts have been made to use secret evidence in a variety of contexts including proceedings at Guantanamo, immigration proceedings resulting in administrative detention in the United Kingdom and Canada and in control order proceedings in the United Kingdom and Australia. All of these uses of secret evidence have been legally and politically controversial.

He maintains that much of the debate about secret evidence has centred on correctives such as the use of security cleared counsel or special advocates to challenge the evidence and the use of active and expert judges to challenge the secret evidence/intelligence. In Canada, reliance on expert judges was found to be constitutionally insufficient in the *Charkaoui* case and a regime of special advocates was created. At the same time, however, reliance on special advocates in British proceedings has been challenged and narrowed by various requirements imposed by the House of Lords and the European Court of Human Rights that require the gist of the allegations to be disclosed.

Roach takes a broader approach to the secret evidence debate in light of these developments. In examining the problem of secret evidence, he notes an increase in the use of secret evidence since 9/11 most notably at Guantanamo Bay and when immigration law has been used against terrorists. He stresses, however, that secret evidence has been both legally and politically controversial. Its use in military commissions has been successfully challenged as has its use in Canadian security certificate immigration detention proceedings.

Roach argues that we should not ignore the political controversies caused by secret evidence and secret trials which invoke images of Kafka's *The Trial*. He cites evidence from Canada that suggests that sympathy may have grown for some terrorist suspects precisely because they were held on secret evidence. He also cites the criticisms of the UN's terrorist listing regime as found in the *Kadi* case from the European Court of Justice and other cases following in its wake.

Roach also argues that there are many more proportionate alternatives to the use of secret evidence. They include not only the use of security cleared counsel or special advocates to challenge secret evidence as is done in the United Kingdom and Canada, but security clearances for lawyers representing terrorist suspects, the use of public interest immunity proceedings to prevent the disclosure of unused intelligence in criminal prosecutions.

More fundamentally, Roach argues that those who collect intelligence must become more willing to live with disclosure even if that requires innovative use of witness protection and adjusting Cold War mentality that suggests that the sources and methods of intelligence should remain secret forever.

Leandro Martínez-Peñas and Manuela Fernández-Rodríguez, in Chap. 9, consider the techniques employed by the United Kingdom as one of the most experienced Western democracies in fighting terrorism. They describe how the UK has faced terrorist threats for over half a century. These threats began with political and religious violence in Northern Ireland in the Ulster counties and thereafter segued into global jihadist terrorism. The authors describe how, in the twenty-first century, the British government has deployed legal formulas and measures that it had applied in the 1970s and 1980s to counter political violence in Northern Ireland and adjusted them to address modern challenges posed by groups linked or inspired by Al Qaeda. Exclusion orders, extended periods of detention or increasing executive powers and usurping judicial review and authority are some of the measures attempted in Britain's contemporary counter-terrorism efforts.

In their view, extending law enforcement or executive authority denigrates individual rights and freedoms unnecessarily and ultimately have a transcendent impact beyond the purpose for which they were created. For example, they show how the use of excessive legislation and anti-terrorism standards to combat jihadist financial backing seriously impeded Icelandic banks that had nothing to do with terrorism.[4]

In Chap. 10 Simon Bronitt and Susan Donkin show how Australia has significantly altered its legal frameworks for responding to terrorism in the decade since 9/11. Although the risk of attack on Australian soil is comparatively remote, the global and local political imperative has led to the creation of a new corpus of terrorism law, with more than one hundred new offences and powers enacted at the federal, state and territory level.

Their chapter explores the historical development of these laws focusing particularly on the normalization of derogations from fundamental tenets of criminal law. These deviations include creating novel offences that criminalise acts perceived to be remotely preparatory or conducive to terrorism, as well as modifications to procedural and evidential rules such as reversing the presumption of innocence. In Bronitt's and Donkin's view, the use of civil regulatory measures relating to the suppression of terrorist financing, preventive detention and control orders are also a feature of this legal response. Although heavily influenced by reforms in the UK, as

[4] For a different view on that matter, see Lennon, G / Walker, C, 'Hot Money in a Cold Climate' [2009] Public Law 37–42.

a New World legal hybrid, they demonstrate that Australia has developed its own distinctive legal response, which reflects its complex federal structure (in which criminal law is divided between Commonwealth, States and Territories) and, some unusually for a liberal democracy, the absence of an entrenched bill of rights.

Marinella Marmo, in Chap. 11 offers an insightful reference to a point in time when Australian senior judges were caught between their perceived role and mission, and what achieved abroad by their colleagues in the field of transnational crimes with special reference to the fight against global terrorism. Her methodology is a combination of interviews with Australian senior judges collected in the years 2005–2006, and primary and secondary sources with the scope to compare and contrast the empirical data. The outcome of this methodology shows that, while the perceived role and rhetoric aim to protect human rights, the results are not as radical as in other international cases.

Even if there is a sense that the Australian sample of senior judges, in the years 2005–2006, are alerted and concerned about reinforced state powers in the fight against terrorism, Marmo's chapter reveals rather conservative self-reflections on the role and function of the judiciary. It is revealing to see that most judges interviewed by her expressed views about their role that are in contrast with the judicial approaches embraced by their counterparts abroad, especially in reference to the US Supreme Court and the House of Lords in the UK during the same time frame.

As a consequence, Marmo argues that there is a transition in visibility of senior judges on the international scene in the area of transnational crimes. And even if Australian judges come across as being more conservative and less dedicated to question new state powers, Marmo discusses a new level of judicial assertiveness, 'a mission that connects judges of different jurisdictions' in the fight against terrorism.

In Chap. 12, José M. Atiles-Osoria explores the United States' response to political violence by Cuban exiles and Puerto Rican extreme right-wing organisations during the pre and post 9/11 era. Grounded in the scholarship on critical studies on terrorism, it takes as a point of departure the fact that studies on terrorism fall short of analysing concepts such as threat of terrorism and political violence within the framework liberal democratic state. He argues that mainstream studies on terrorism have underestimated the role of the state as potential terrorist actor.

The chapter is divided into three sections. The first section traces a depiction of the historical and socio-political conditions that determined the formation of Cubans exiles' organisations in the U.S. The second section provides an outline of some of the terrorist actions perpetrated by these organisations against Puerto Rican independence movements. The third part addresses the positions and responses adopted by the governments of the U.S. and PR in the post 9/11 era. The overall aim of the chapter is to show how counter-terrorist policies implemented by democratic states in pre and post 9/11 are not equally effective or consistent when dealing with actions that contribute to their geopolitical interest and the control of left-wing and independent movements.

In Atiles-Osoria's view, when dealing with situations where the state can be either complicit or supportive of terrorist practices, we are left with a theoretical void. That arises from the treatment of the liberal state as a silent and invisible body.

Atiles-Osoria shows the constant tension between the exercise of state terrorism, the support to terrorist organisation and the guarantee of the human, civil and political rights in the colonial case of Puerto Rico (PR).

Finally, Part IV examines selected international law challenges in the area of counter-terrorism.

In Chap. 13 Christopher Michaelsen focuses on the interpretation and role of derogation clauses in an era of permanent legal emergency. Such derogations can be found in the International Covenant on Civil and Political Rights as well as the European and American Conventions. While the State parties may not derogate from the entire treaty, they may legally suspend their obligation to respect and enforce specific rights contained in the respective convention during times of war or other public emergency. The international treaties do not provide any definition of what constitutes a public emergency. However, the respective monitoring organs, the European Court of Human Rights and the Human Rights Committee in particular, have developed certain requirements that need to be met before a state party can lawfully derogate.

Michaelsen reviews relevant case law and other sources on the matter in order to provide a framework for the analysis of whether, and to what extent, the derogation clauses remain adequate in an era of international terrorism. In the aftermath of the 9/11 attacks, the vast majority of states did not invoke derogation clauses in spite of the fact that, in many instances, anti-terrorism legislation developed to counter the perceived new threat raised serious concerns in relation to their compatibility with international human rights obligations. An exception to this trend was the United Kingdom which derogated from both the European Convention and the International Covenant. These derogations were subsequently challenged in English courts – including the House of Lords – as well as before the European Court of Human Rights in Strasbourg.

It is true that both the House of Lords and the Strasbourg Court confirmed that a public emergency (within the meaning of Article 15 of the European Convention on Human Rights) existed in the United Kingdom. Michaelsen's chapter, however, challenges these findings. He argues that contemporary international terrorism does not qualify as a public emergency for both theoretical and factual reasons. He then discusses the implications of this finding and argues that it may be most appropriate to consider abolishing the derogation clauses altogether. While this may be political not feasible at this stage, honest and detailed discussions on the issue should be initiated in the framework of the Council of Europe.

In the final chapter Mark Kielsgard reviews the current literature and jurisprudence on the legitimacy of the use of military force against terrorism under international law. Kielsgard examines the nature and history of national self-defence in the context of international law and counter-terrorism. He recounts and analyzes state practice, Security Council initiatives, international jurisprudence, and scholarship in order to shed light on the limitations imposed by the United Nations Charter, in particular Article 51. He explores historic trends and specifically addresses the issues of state attribution (or targeting non-state actors) and the degree of immediacy (including anticipatory self-defense) necessary to justify the use of force in self-defence. Moreover, he addresses arguably premature representations that the character of national self-defence experienced organic change in response to the 9/11 attacks.

This chapter shows how the inclusion of non-state actors as legitimate targets for national self-defence further fuels permanent war and how attenuated justifications of preemption provide a 'carte blanche' for states to prosecute the war against terrorism wherever that may take them. Moreover, the copy-cat efforts of other states creates a snowballing effect and exemplify the dangers in this approach as the barriers to the unilateral use o force become increasingly reduced and justified on a rhetorical basis (i.e., fighting terrorism). Kielsgard argues that justifying permanent war on the basis of a self-defeating interpretation of Article 51 only serves to concede the hegemonic authority of powerful states, and law through intimidation. It also serves to circumvent the fundamentally pacific object and purpose of the Charter.

The 9/11 attacks had tremendous impact on modern international law, culture and society. This was a watershed moment politically. Yet, as dramatic as the events were, when viewed in the sober reflection of hindsight, such events seldom permanently shape law, domestically or internationally. Scholars, diplomats and jurists who exaggerate the long-term significance of such events and support measures that in the long run are more devastating than the harm sought to be remedied – or who take advantage in order to advance self-interested national policy agendas – do a disservice to the international community. Kielsgard maintains that most of those who deduce that a general organic change has already taken place are jumping to unjustified conclusions based on unusual facts and circumstances. Indeed, it is only those sources tied to political control, or executive bodies, which jump to extremist responses while the traditionally more deliberate judicial bodies continue to apply basic customary responses.

Historically, the gravest threats to human safety and human rights always take place during armed conflicts. In the determination of state power and appropriate legal responses under international law, UN charter articles 2(4) and 51 reflect the balance between the state's duty to protect its citizens from violence as well as protecting their fundamental human rights. Under domestic law this balance is also struck by national legal instruments. Therefore, expanding article 51 and broadening the states power to wage war are ultimately counter-productive as the only clear result is the victimization of the state's own integrity and values – and this is no less true in the aftermath of 9-11, during the permanent so-called War on Terrorism, then during any other historical epoch.

In conclusion, there is no doubt that state efforts to provide security in countering terrorism in the post 9/11 era will continue to provide the setting for harsh and complex conflicts of values, policies, and practices. Those commentators who emphasise the novelty of the post 9/11 era conflict between collective security and individual rights or indeed the novelty of the threat of terrorism are shown by the historical perspectives presented in Part I of this book to be mistaken and misleading. In reality, terrorism has long shaped the development of states in regard to their institutions and laws, especially those in the criminal law and criminal justice fields, as again demonstrated by the chapters in Part III of this volume. Yet, the longevity of the problem has not given birth to easy or satisfying solutions. There is still endemic uncertainty as to what should be defined as 'terrorism' (Part II). There also remains controversy as to how international law should categorise terrorism and how far it should be tackled as a distinct category (Parts II and IV). As a result of these ongoing normative and conceptual conflicts, perhaps the best one can ask of states is to recognize the broad and informed perspectives taken in this book. Each government must play its part in countering terrorism, but it would be wise to bear in mind that terrorism rarely impacts as an existential phenomenon, that valuable lessons can be learnt from history and comparisons, and that the value of security, when viewed through the prisms of criminal justice and international law, is pursued as much to deliver human security as state security.

This advice underlines why it is so necessary to recognize that human rights exist as a condition of state legitimacy, and that they are not mere "creatures" of the state:

> It is because our rights flow from who and what we are that we may form, re-form, or accept states in order to make our rights more certain and secure. So those who say that our rights depend on or are the creatures of the state have it the wrong way around.[5]

The recognition of the pre-political character of human rights poses objective limits both to the state itself and to the exercise of state authority, precluding in the 9/11 era for all states sooner or later (later for the militarily mighty) counter terrorism tactics which involve unending and capricious derogations from rights or even the setting aside of non-derogable rights:

> If we have some rights, and therefore liberties, that are prepolitical rights which the state is bound to recognize, rights that are there before the state gets down to the business of defining rights, then, like Archimedes with his lever, we have a place to stand, and liberty can move the world. To put it in more traditional language, unless we have natural law, prepolitical rights, liberty is not secure[6]

It is true that establishing limits on executive power and lawmaking may not resolve the complex relationships between the security and the protection of the fundamental rights in countering terrorism. However, states with realistic claims to legitimacy should never conceive the law as a formal passport, affording them powers which are neither limited nor restrained.[7]

---

[5] C. Fried, *Modern Liberty and the Limits of the Government* (New York/London, W.W. Norton & Company, 2007), 72.

[6] C. Fried, *Modern Liberty and the Limits of the Government*, 144–145; on this matter, see also at 80, 84–85, 90–94 and 155.

[7] O. Gross, "Chaos and Rules: Should Responses to Violent Crises Always Be Constitutional," *Yale Law Journal* 112, 1011–1134; see also the review published by D. Dyzenhaus in his edition of the *Civil Rights and Security*. Farnham (UK), Ashgate, 2008, xiv–xvi.

Part I
State Power and Legal Responses from an Historical Perspective

Chapter 2
The State Power and the Limits of the Principle of Sovereignty: An Historical Approach

Aniceto Masferrer and Juan A. Obarrio

It is not an easy enterprise to counter terrorism while respecting the rule of law and guaranteeing the security of citizens to the maximum extent possible without violating their fundamental rights. Theoretically, modern constitutionalism emerged to protect and free citizens from political abuses of power. In practice, fundamental rights are not always fully respected, since the state is tempted to exercise its power in an unlimited way. Counter-terrorism constitutes a paramount example of it. To limit the power of the state means to limit its sovereignty. Otherwise, the abuses of power by the state become inevitable.

Surprisingly modern constitutionalism applied limits to the state during an historical period in which sovereignty was regarded – at least, in the political philosophy – as a limitless notion (Rousseau). It is undeniable that Rousseau significantly contributed to the 'mythicization of the political power'.[1] That was the outcome of the wrong turn which had been taken by previous authors. In this sense, it has been shown the influence of Hobbes' approach to liberty and its negative effect by being "too willing to sacrifice individual liberty to the needs of the state".[2]

---

[1] J. Ballesteros, "Estudio introductorio," in *Itinerarios humanos del Derecho*, ed. S. Cotta (Pamplona: Ediciones Universidad de Navarra, 1974) at 16; on this matter, see also S. Cotta, "Philosophie et politique dans l'oeuvre de Rousseau. Une esai d'interpretation," *ARSP* 49 (1963): 171–189; "Theorie politique et theorie religeuse chez Rousseau. Rousseau et la philisophie politique," *Annales de Philisophie politique* (1965); "La position du probleme de la politique chez Rousseau," *Etudes sur le Contrat Social de Jean-Jacques Rousseau* (Paris, 1964).

[2] C. A. Gearty, "Escaping Hobbes: Liberty and Security for Our Democratic (Not Anti-Terrorist) Age," (January 27, 2010), LSE Legal Studies Working Paper No. 3/2010 (available at http://ssrn.com/abstract=1543121), for whom Hobbes is partly responsible of the fragility of liberties and fundamental rights in the current Western legal culture: "…there is no doubt that Hobbes remains hugely influential (…). Hobbes's residual theory of liberty has proved of immense influence" (at 8).

A. Masferrer (✉) • J.A. Obarrio
Faculty of Law, University of Valencia, Avda. dels Tarongers s/n, Edificio Departamental Occidental, E-46022 Valencia, Spain
e-mail: aniceto.masferrer@uv.es; juan.obarrio@uv.es

A. Masferrer (ed.), *Post 9/11 and the State of Permanent Legal Emergency*, Ius Gentium: Comparative Perspectives on Law and Justice 14,
DOI 10.1007/978-94-007-4062-4_2,

Modern constitutionalism needs to be approached from an historical and comparative perspective in order to better understand the current situation in the fight against terrorism and the fragility of fundamental rights. A comparative approach to the development of the Rule of Law and its limits, that is, the fundamental rights of individuals, reveals the existence of three distinct areas that must be distinguished: (1) International and Constitutional level; (2) the legislative level; and (3) the political, legal-theory doctrinal. An historical analysis of these three areas shows divergent developments and contradictions. While modern constitutional texts include a growing list of principles and fundamental rights, such rights are barely respected by governments whose far reaching executive powers are difficult to limit and control. Moreover, if the progressive weakening of human rights in post-modern thought is added, as much in legal as political philosophy, it is understandable how the state in its response to terrorism appears to be undermining the foundations of democracy and the rule of law.[3]

In the Western legal tradition, notions of sovereignty, which were a long development (particularly from the Middle Ages to sixteenth century), was never regarded as limitless. Although it is difficult to find a concept subject to more discussion,[4] the concept of sovereignty suffers from imprecision and changed meaning over time. That said, in the work of Jean Bodin we find some of the characteristics which are considered to be "essential" for understanding its meaning.[5] Sovereignty, in his view, is the supreme, absolute, independent, original, indivisible and inalienable character of the power of the State. Sovereignty is a part or essence of the unity and of the power of the State. As Jean Bodin holds: "The sovereignty is the absolute and perpetual power of a republic". In reality, this translates to "the right government of various families". However "without the sovereign power which unites all the members and parts of it and all the families and colleges in one body, [it] ceases to be republic."[6]

Once it is admitted that the concept of sovereignty entails a power which possesses the task of making the ultimate decision, it becomes clear the basis and historical development of sovereignty has not been linear. Tension has always existed between those who believed it was necessary for the sovereign to hold monopoly legal and political power, against those who saw it as necessary to limit such powers. There was an effort to harmonise the power of the sovereign, with the power of the community, essentially a harmonisation between the Law and the Power respectively.

---

[3]On this matter, see A. Masferrer, "Legislación anti-terrorista, Estado de Derecho y Derechos fundamentales: una aproximación a los límites del Estado en el constitucionalismo moderno," ed. A. Masferrer, *Estado de Derecho y derechos fundamentales en la lucha contra el terrorismo. Una aproximación multidisciplinar* (*histórica, jurídico-comparada, filosófica y económica*) (Pamplona: Thomson-Aranzadi) at 191–254.

[4]G. Jellinek, *Teoría General del Estado* (Buenos Aires: Editorial Albatros 1954) at 447.

[5]J. A. Maravall, *Teoría del Estado en España en el siglo XVI* (Madrid: Centro de Estudios Constitucionales, 1997) at 15.

[6]J. Bodin, *Los Seis Libros de la República*, I. 2 (Madrid: ed. Tecnos, 1986).

2.1 The Limits of Sovereignty in Roman Antiquity: The Ideal State of Cicero

The concept of sovereignty has been a constant matter for debate in the 'History of Thought'. Twenty one centuries ago, Marcus Tulius Cicero, a Roman paradigmatic and controverter, wrote and reflected on the scope of the state's power. As a pure jurist of classic Rome, Cicero resorted to the theory of political and legal argumentation[7] in propounding the moral duty to intervene in the public life.[8] Such intervention was in the hope of saving the moral values, and for maintenance of the dignity, welfare and legal certainty.[9]

According to Daza,[10] the pinnacle of Cicero's career was 63 B.C., the year of his consulate. This was the moment he warned of the conspiracy of Catiline[11] that fundamentally sought to eliminate the *concordia ordinum* from public life. These were the ethical ideals he had defended, among which was the agreement between large land proprietors belonging to the senatorial and equestrian orders; Catiline wanted to undermine the established order. Such order saw the supremacy of the *optimates*, which was justified not for pleasing the people, but for trying to obtain the social recognition of all good citizens,[12] the survival of peace and civic dignity,[13] of justice and equity – "they are not wild revolutionaries"[14] –. The supremacy of *optimates* was also due to their perception of reality and for their economic prosperity, which made them the defenders of the constitutional *ordo* in front of the intents of the destabilizers of the popularities.[15]

In times of turmoil for the Republic, when the subversive elements challenged the inherited *dignitas*, the task of the *optimates* was the protection of traditions and institutions, not for their own sake, but for the common good.[16] This led to *optimates* begging people to become, like them, devoted to the eternal memory of the *veteres*,

---

[7]A. Viñas, *Teoría del Derecho y experiencia jurídica romana* (Madrid, 2002) at 49.

[8]E. Gómez Royo, *Las sedes históricas de la cultura jurídica europea* (Valencia: Tirant lo Blanch, 2010) at 499. Hovewer, as rightly mentioned S. Mas, "Notas sobre el pensamiento político de Cicerón: imperio ilegítimo," *Gerión* (2009) 27 at 9, the aporetic character of their reflections should be accepted, given that his legal thinking was combined with the political and philosophical one in the Arpinate.

[9]A. D'Ors, *Nuevos papeles de oficio universitario* (Madrid, 1980) at 193–194.

[10]J. Daza Martínez, "*Libertas Populi Romani* (Libertad política, historia y Derecho natural en Cicerón)," *Revista de Estudios Políticos* (1976, July–Oct.) at 163 ff.

[11]J. Bayet, *Literatura latina* (Barcelona: Ariel, 1970) at 145, warns his animosity towards Catilina, Codio, Pisón and Antony.

[12]Cicero, *Pro Sestio* 96.

[13]Cicero, *Pro Sestio* 98; J. C. Pérez, "*Arceriotifinibus* (*Cic. har. 4*), *¿"paz" civil u "ocio" de los jóvenes aristócratas?*," *Estudios Clásicos* 108 (1995) at 57–92.

[14]Cicero, *Pro Sestio* 97.

[15]Cicero, *Pro Sestio* 97.

[16]Cicero, *De Re Publica,* 1.7.

whose task, according to Cicero, is not without its difficulties and dangers.[17] Cicero's forced exile demonstrates this.[18]

Cicero's work as a civil advocate, together with his political and moral convictions, led him to being a self proposed protector and guardian of the *libertas* of Rome.[19] Cicero believed the superior values of the people of Rome were those presided over by the action of the *Patres*, commonly known as the *nosse exempla maiorum*. Out of respect for the past freedoms and institutions of the Republic, he opposed what he considered as the morally degraded present: *quos denique libertas, eaquae dulcissima est, ad salute patriae defendendam excitavit.*[20]

Cicero's conflict with Catiline illustrates his awareness of being a defender of the Republic. By reminding Catiline of his knowledge of underlying plans, he expressed his readiness to face all dangers in order to save the country because, as Cicero stated, it was worth his life.[21] This is symbolised by the *ius* in front of the *vis* in the two figures of the orator, constituting polar opposites. The orator uses the weapon of the persuasion, of the *sapientia* and of the *ius*. The orator is in front of the violent soldier, *horridus miles*, whose weapons are the *ferrum* and the *vis.*[22] According to Notari, both figures go beyond the mere metaphor, symbolising that in ancient times, the resolution of any dispute could only be achieved through two ways. First, as represented in institutions, through a *consensus* able to create the *omnium bonorum*; and secondly, through force, through war.[23]

Cicero believed he did not cause, but merely existed in, this moment of transition. Witnessing the decline of the old institutions led him to vindicate the principle of the liberty, of the good government and of the good Law.[24] Consequently, upon his return from exile, Cicero declared despite looting and loss of his property,[25] he had not been defeated by his unjust exile. As Cicero stated in his speech of gratitude to the Senate, the only thing he did when he was consul, was to defend the common cause,[26] of liberating their homeland from destruction[27] and defending the freedom,

---

[17] Cicero, *Pro Sestio*102.

[18] Cicero, *Pro Sestio* 43 and ff.

[19] Cicero, *Filipicas* 3, 1, 28.

[20] Cicero, *Oratio IV in Catilinam*, VIII, 16.

[21] Cicero, *Oratio I in Catilinam*, XI, 27.

[22] Cicero, *Pro Murena* 30; T. Notari, "La teoría del Estado en Cicerón en su *Oratio pro Sestio*," *Revista de Estudios Histórico-Jurídicos* 32 (2010) (Valparaíso, Chile) at 211.

[23] *Ibidem*.

[24] In this sense, P. López Baraja de Quiroga, *Imperio legítimo. El pensamiento político en tiempos de Cicerón* (Madrid: A. Machado Libros, 2007) especially at 58–80, holds democratic character of republican Rome. An interesting view of a union in L. Labruna, "Algunas reflexiones sobre la reciente historiografía jurídica referente a la llamada «democracia» de los Romanos," *Arsboni et aequi. Festschrift für W. Waldstein zum 65. Geburtstag* (Stuttgart, 1993) at 203–214; A. Duplá, "Interpretaciones de la crisis tardorrepublicana: del conflicto social a la articulación del consenso" *Studia historica Historia antigua* 25 (2007) at 185–201.

[25] Cicero, *Pro Sestio* 53 ff.

[26] Cicero, *Cum senatui gratias egit*, XIV, 34.

[27] Cicero, *De domo sua*, 34.93.

harmony and dignity of the Roman nation.[28] By defending the freedom, he was defending the citizens and the Roman *civitas*.[29] This explains Cicero's faith that liberty was the destiny of Rome. Renouncing such a destiny would be a sacrilege, because Rome was destined by the gods to "rule over all the nations".[30] This is because the Roman civilization, in contrast with other nations, could not fall under the yoke of slavery.[31] By preserving its freedom, Rome became a superior society, whose principles and values were not to be found in other nations.[32]

2.1.1 The Mixed Constitution[33]

To this claim of the liberty as a legacy given by the *maiores*,[34] Cicero added that the freedom of the State could only be guaranteed within the institutions of the Republic.[35] His conception of the State is given in his book *De re publica*, published in 51 B.C., where he emphasises the characteristics of his "Ideal State", of the *optimus status civitatis*, and the State's best men.[36]

According to Cicero, the Ideal State was the Roman *res publica*, understood as a *consocitatio* of the formal and legal nature, the "nation is not only a set of men gathered in any way, but a set of a multitude associated by the same law, which serves everybody equally".[37] *Res publica* was not the work of a singular man, unlike *Minos* in Crete or *Licurgus* in Sparta,[38] but was the result of a long evolution through

---

[28] Cicero, *In C. Verrem*, I. 5.183.

[29] U. Álvarez, *La jurisprudencia romana en la hora presente* (Madrid: Real Academia de Jurisprudencia y Legislación, 1966) at 46.

[30] Cicero, *Phil.* VI.19.

[31] Cicero, *Phil.* X.20.

[32] Cicero, *Harusp. Resp.* 19.

[33] J. Rivera García, "El republicanismo de Cicerón. Retorica, constitución y ley natural en *De Republica*," *Doxa* 29 (2006) at 367–368.

[34] The idea that there is no republic that by its constitution, structure or its regime could be comparable with the one "our fathers received from ancestors and passed it on to us", which we can find in CICERO, *De re publica*, I. 70: *sic ad firmo, nullam omnium rerum publicarum aut constitutione aut description aut disciplina conferendam esse cum ea, quam patres nostril nobis acceptam iam inde a maioribus reliquerunt.*

[35] In this line of thought it could be read in *De oratore*, specifically, in the words of Craso when hewho praises the Law of Rome, because there appears the *civilis scientia*, in which all the most useful institutions of the organising of the internal life are contained, the optimal conditioning and ordination of the life of the State, through which true greatness and dignity is achieved (CICERO, *De oratione* I. 193).

[36] E. Berti, *Il "De re publica" di Cicerone e il pensiero politico classico* (Padova: Cedam, 1963); L. Perelli, *Il pensiero politico di Cicerone* (Firenze: La Nouva Italia, 1990).

[37] Cicero, *De re Publica*, I. 39.

[38] Cicero, *De re Publica*, II. 1–4.

the centuries and over the generations in the itinerary of the *Urbs*,[39] in an *imitatio maiorum*.[40] This organic evolution provided stability and the eternal character of the State which could adapt to its institutions and to the customs of the ancestors.[41]

In light of *Maiore's* legacy,[42] as treated by Panecius, in presence of Polibius, Cicero's Ideal State is constituted by three elements: the congregation of people, the unity of the Law and public security, and the coexistence of these communities of interest that underlie the unification.[43]

From this point of view the *re publica* appears to be linked to the legal concept of People (*populus*), of the "group of men united by the bond of law". [44] From this a *consensus iuris* arises, with the object of the upholding common good, consistent with the possession of the equal rights and duties. This leads to the argument that the *res publica* is independent from the State's form, and by virtue of this, three right forms of State, described by Aristotle in his *Politica*, might occur: the monarchy, the democracy and the aristocracy. Deviation from these forms is tyranny, which appears when all the power is held by one person, whose interest is self serving, and with it, heralds the decline of the *res publica*.

Underlying this line of argument, is Cicero's criticism of low participation rates in public by society. This appears highly illustrative of his political thought, described in his first book *On the Republic*, where after his affirmation that "the stability of the republic requires people to have enough freedom", he says:

> How may be just, I don't say the kingdom, where the slavery is neither dark nor doubtful, but in these republics where everyone is free just in words? There the citizens vote, appoint the judges with a supreme command, participate in elections and in the approval of laws, but give what they have to give although they don't want to, and give to those who ask them things which they themselves don't have; because they are apart from the commandment, from the public government, from judging and from the power to be elected as judges, as this depends on the lineage and the family's fortune.[45]

This thinking reflects Cicero's desire for a democratic tradition, for a more participative society. Cicero warnings of society's degradation, leads him to an idealized defense of the tradition, of the ancient Roman constitution. Consequently, Scipio argues in favor of the most optimal form: the mixed regime, the one in which the best men abound, those in whom the *consilium* forms part of their being.[46]

The Roman constitution is, though with some modifications, the mixed constitution described by Polybios.[47] It is an ideal state, combining the features of different

---

[39] Cicero, *De re Publica*, I. 46.

[40] Cicero, *De tosculanorum disputationum*, I. 2.

[41] Cicero, *De legibus* II. 25.

[42] The idea that the republic is not the result of one man but many, and formed not thanks to just a single generation but to centuries, can be found in Cicero, *De re publica*, II. 2.

[43] Cicero, *De re publica* I. 39.

[44] Cicero, *De re publica* I. 13.

[45] Cicero, *De re publica* I. 47.

[46] López Baraja de Quiroga, P, *Imperio legítimo*, at 241.

[47] J. Daza Martínez, "*Libertas Populi Romani*," at 172.

forms of government. This guarantees both the stability of structure of the State, as well as the freedom of individual and of community, without either interfering with the other.[48] Thus, the personage of Scipio argues that the kings who rule the people well are characterized by parental love; the nobles by their prudence or the government of virtue; and the people by the defense of freedom or of the complete equality of rights.[49]

From Cicero's point of view, while each one of the regimes has its drawbacks, he argues:

> Any of these three forms, if serves to maintain the bond that began to unite men in a public society, is certainly not perfect, none of them, in my opinion, is the best, but tolerable.[50]

In particular, in relation to the monarchy, Cicero argues there is little freedom in kingdoms because citizens are separated from the Law and government, and are consequently subordinated in a substantial proportion[51]; a good king, like Romulus, who tends to the public good, might be succeeded by another cruel and uncontrolled man, like Tarquinius.[52] For these reasons, Romans hated the word 'king'.[53]

Nevertheless, among the all pure forms of government, Scipio, although realising the rule of a monarch could lead to corruption – "becomes the worst of the best… a tyrant" [54]– ultimately favoured the monarchy, concluding that "when the people is deprived of a righteous king, nostalgia slowly seizes the hearts".[55] The reason behind praising the monarchy is found in the origin of Rome. He argued that "the best form of government of the city was the one transmitted to us by our ancestors",[56] the monarchy, in which its transition to the tyranny was not necessary, was not cause and effect.[57] This is because the tyranny is not a political form, but a deviant behavior of a common good, and consequently is unjust, because this implies a lack of dominance over its own instincts and passions.[58] From there, against the tyranny it has to be presented the "other type of the king, good, wise and knowledgeable of what is appropriate and worthy for the city, that is like a tutor and administrator of the republic", because he is "the one who can defend the city with his intelligence and action."[59]

---

[48] T. Notari, "La teoría del Estado en Cicerón," at 213.

[49] Cicero, *De re publica* I. 55.

[50] Cicero, *De re publica* I. 42.

[51] The idea that the fate of people, which depends on the will and talent of one person, is unstable, can be seen in Cicero, *De re publica* II. 50.

[52] The comparison between a tyrant and a beast can be found in Cicero, *De re publica* II.48.

[53] Cicero, *De re publica* II. 52.

[54] Cicero, *De re publica* I. 65.

[55] Cicero, *De re publica* I. 69.

[56] Cicero, *De re publica* I. 34.

[57] Cicero, *De re publica* II. 44–47.

[58] Cicero, *De re publica* II. 45.

[59] Cicero, *De re publica* II. 51.

Cicero's criticisms of political reality are also observed when he analyses shortages of both aristocracy and democracy. In the former system of government, people lack freedom to participate in the public life, while in the latter, the merit and the virtue of the people is not appreciated.

Cicero's study of the different regimes leads him to conclude that when failures of each are exposed, each one tends to become its contrary: the monarch becomes an unjust despot or a tyrant[60]; among nobles the desire to protect the interests of a part of the *res publica* arises; and from the People (or nation) a revolutionary mob lacking any notion of common good appears – *turba et confusio*[61]–. As none of the regimes contain true *iustitia* or *sapientia*, the preferable one "would be the combined and moderated form that composes three types of a republic". This is because,

> there should be something superior and royal in the republic, something imparted and attributed to the authority (*auctoritas*) of the chiefs, and other things reserved to the discretion and will of the crowd.[62]

This inevitably leads to Cicero's *optimus status*, the ideal state of the mixed nature, in which the recognition of the dignity, stability and equality of the rights and duties is possible. This is in addition to *iuris consensus*, a common right serving everyone, because only in this way can the *utilitas publica* be realised, enhanced and strengthened, and the superior State with it. This is what Cicero believed will be able to regain the fundamental values he sees as supreme: *virtus et dignitas.*[63] Without such values, the State would be presided by the *avaritia* – *vitia nostra* – which degrades it and destroys it, and does the same with all other areas of the political life.[64]

From Cicero's point of view, in that particular historical moment, with disruption and inevitable destabilisation of the Republican State, where the structures of the institutions were in turmoil, the strong necessity to faithfully maintain the body of the *maiorum instituta* emerged. For instance, there was the desire to conserve and recover the Roman tradition of the antique constitutional *ordo*. Cicero holds, in Scipio's words, that "a city must be established in a way that results eternal" because "the death is not as natural for a republic as it is for a man, for whom the death is not only necessary, but often also desirable."[65] Despite all this, in Cicero's mixed constitution, the effective power, represented by the *imperium* or in the *auctoritas*,

---

[60] In the book it is present that where the tyranny is imposed, there cannot be found the *res publica* (Cicero, *De re publica* III. 43).

[61] Cicero, *De re publica* I. 59.

[62] Cicero, *De re publica* I. 69.

[63] As points Magris, A, *L'idea di destino nel pensiero antico* (Trieste, 1986) II at 484, the idea of that the *virtus* became the sap of the moral *techne* has been strongly permeated in the Hellenism, with special reference in the Stoicism, and from these philosophical flows became the thoughts of Cicero.

[64] Cicero, *De republica* II. 57; Daza Martínez, J, *Kyriosnomos. De la 'iuris societas' de Ciceron al 'polikos logos' de Marco Aurelio* (Cuenca, 1976) at 15 ff.

[65] Cicero, *De re publica*, III. 3–4.

was left in hands of the ruling class, limiting the power of the People, as noted above. More specifically, the tribunes of people did not represent an alternative to the government of consuls, but represented, on the one hand, restraint upon their power, for their *imperium*,[66] and, on the other hand, they had the crucial task of averting popular revolution. So it was because, according to Cicero, although the power of tribunes were excessive, these two virtues or functions of the representatives of people made them indispensable for maintaining the harmony of the *res publica*.[67]

This conception leads Cicero to affirm the moments of greatest glory for the Republic were when the *auctoritas*,[68] the public prestige or the social recognition of the nobles or senators,[69] prevailed. This is because, from Cicero's perspective, the *vir vere romanus* could obtain relevance and projection in political life only if his behavior and life were based on the combination of moral, intellectual and material elements. Without these elements there was no capacity to carry out a leading role in public life, in the *forum*, an ideal venue to an accreditation, and an establishment as *vir gravis*, as a man of moral and social prestige. But conscious – as it is said in the *De re publica*[70] – that the *virtus* should be translated to *facta*, to actions that give continuity to the last example of the *veteres*, example and pattern of behavior for the *nobilitas*, an ethical-moral reform of the Senate was necessary to guarantee the harmony of the mixed constitution, in which the aristocracy would continue being a social, real and effective body of public life, because, in Arpinate's words:

> …if the senate leads the general politics, if all the citizens support its decisions and if the rest of orders leave the State to be governed by the prudence of the superior order, therefore it is possible to maintain this wise and harmonious equilibrium of the State that arises from a just distribution of the rights among the People, invested with the power, and the senate, invested with the authority.[71]

However, as the Roman philosopher argued himself, this ideal could only be achieved if the *nobilitas* complied with the forms and the precepts that, like an ethical code, were present in the past. This is because only in the wise and balanced guidelines of the *veteres* could safe and sound points of support be found to regain its *auctoritas:*

> Well, just enough to go through history to see that as the leading citizens of the republic were, as was this republic, and that any change that was introduced by majors in their customs, was followed by the People […] I think that a change in the life and behavior of the nobles changes the customs of the citizens. That is why, some bad habits of the majors result particularly harmful for the republic, because they don't only cover them in themselves, but also infuse them into the city. [72]

[66] Cicero o, *De re publica*, II. 58.

[67] A. Rivera, "Crisis de la autoridad: sobre el concepto político de autoridad en Hannah Arendt," *Daimon* 26 (2002) at 94.

[68] On the *autoritas*, see J. Casinos Mora, *La noción romana de auctoritas y la responsabilidad por auctoritas* (Granada: Comares 2000).

[69] Cicero, *De re publica*, II, 56.

[70] Cicero, *De re publica*, II. 59.

[71] Cicero, *De legibus*, III. 112. 38.

[72] Cicero, *De legibus*, III. 111.

2.1.2 The Natural Law[73]

The concept of *nature* was key and determinant in the Greek philosophy, with a special emphasis on the so-called New or Third Academy and, in particular, for the Stoics,[74] whose proposals formed the structural and theoretical basis of the Cicero's thought.[75]

In particular, when Cicero is thinking of a State whose exercise of power is consistent with the Law, which is an eminently moral value for him, he takes as a starting point the analysis of the dialectical work of Carneades of Cyrene.[76] Carneades, as noted by both Lactantius and Arpinate, criticizes Roman war policy in his speeches made before the young men of Rome.[77]

In *Institutions*, Lactantius argues the key idea of Carneades' discourse is that the intimate relations between the politics and the morals implied the old stance of sophists. Sophists warned that the Law was a way for achieving the *utilitas*, for it was a specific Order of every nation, ordered for its interest and its government. By virtue of being transitory, non-permanent and unstable, no one could speak of *ius naturale*, because there was no justice "per se". To the contrary, to hold that such a justice existed according to Carneades, would lead to claims of the most significant necessity any human could imagine; because all the nations were at the apex of power, a situation in which the Roman people should be included, which dominated the Orb, had to return, if they pretended to be just, everything they had ever conquered, and had to go back to their natural borders to live modestly and with dignity.[78]

The plan of Carneades holds an irreducible antagonism between the *ius naturale* and the *ius civitate*. From Carneades' perspective, the *iustitia civilis* does not factor in the authentic *iustitia*, with history showing there cannot be a common agreement that establishes what is "just", given that the justice does not originate in nature but between men. Consequently, the concept of *utilitas* prevails, as does the *sapientia* that allows the hegemony of an individual and of a State over other individuals and States, either to gain wealth or to extend it territorial boundaries. This would go against the superior and true justice that requires the *ius naturale*. Accordingly, when he realizes it was the expansionist policy of Rome, he affirms that calling it just is a mere exercise of cynicism and hypocrisy.[79]

---

[73] E. Bloch, *Derecho natural y dignidad humana* (Madrid: Aguilar 1980) at 2, distinguishes that the knowledge of the stoic natural law natural by Roman jurists, began in 150 B.C., by influence of Panecio, who visited Rome because of invitation of Scipio the Junior.

[74] M. Isnardi Parente, *Introduzione a lo Stoicismo Ellenistico* (Roma/Bari: Laterza, 1993).

[75] O. Robleda, "Filosofía jurídica de Cicerón," in *St. Biondi* (Milano, 1965) II at 467 ff; 'Cicerón y el Derecho romano', (1985) 18–19 *Humanidades* at 33–58; J. Daza Martínez, "Libertas populi romani," at 179; J. Daza Martínez, *Kyrios Nomos*, at 30.

[76] Thus it is testified by Cicero himself, when, in his *De fato*, he mentions that for fighting with the dogmatism of the Stoa, he used, as dialectic weapon, the principle of internal contradiction (Cicero, *De fato*, 30).

[77] Cicero, *De divinatione liber alter* 23.

[78] Lactantius, *Institutionies divinae* V. 16 2–4.

[79] E. Gómez Royo, *Las sedes históricas*, at 507–509.

Against the scepticism of Carneades' Dialectic (argument), Cicero revives the stoic idea of *ius immutable* to assert that the majesty of the Roman State and the supremacy of the moral and eternal law are not separate attributes. *Ius civile*, *ius naturale*, *iustitia*, *sapientia*, *bonorum* and *honestum* were the same reality that the Rome of ancestors embodied in its conception and application – as well in the private life as in the public – the picture of ethic virtues as was the Roman *fides*,[80] the *gravitas* – dignity o social prestige[81] –, the *constantia*,[82] the *virtus*,[83] the *pietas*,[84] the *concordia*,[85] the *humanitas*,[86] the *clementia* and the *mansuetudo*[87] –, virtues that by providing a framework of social ethics – more guarantees and more protection than power –, did not enter into the conflict with the divine, eternal and natural law.[88]

This apologetic argumentation has its base in the harmonious union within the Ideal State, where the *vera iustitia* prevails through the above-mentioned ethical virtues and natural law, a corpus of law that is an objectification of the eternal law – which makes it common to all the nations based on pattern of rational behaviour of a man who is prudent and rules through discerning right from wrong.[89] In this sense we can read in his work *On the Laws* that:

> it is absurd to think that everything determined by the customs and the laws of the nations is just. Perhaps also they are if they are laws of tyrants? … There is only one law that maintains the community of men united, and it is constituted by only one law, the one that is a just criterion that prescribes or prohibits; everyone who ignores it, written or no, is unjust. Because if justice is the observance of the written laws and of the customs of the people, and, as it is said by those who argue it, everything have to be measured by interest, whoever estimates that it must be disadvantageous, will despise the laws and will break them if possible. Therefore results that there is no more justice than the one of nature.[90]

In line with this conception, the *ius* had to take in consideration the *fas*, the Order of world: nothing could exist without being in accordance with the superior order.

---

[80] The *fides populi romani* demanded from Rome, in sense of victorious power, *fides et benevolentia*, protection and help to defeated, that became known as a term in the cornerstone of Roman law (Cicero, *De Officiis*, I. 23).

[81] E. Gómez Royo, *Las sedes históricas*, at 437–438.

[82] In the field of social ethical virtues, *virtus* results in the qualities that characterised the character and the personal of *vir vere romanus*, of right man of the *nobilitas* (Cicero, *Orationes Verrinae* I. 52).

[83] Cicero, *Tusculanae Disputationes*, II. 43.

[84] Cicero, *De re publica*, VI. 16.

[85] Cicero, *De re publica*, I. 45. 69.

[86] The *humanitas*, for Cicero, is human culture, the integral formation of a man in its intellectual dimention – *paideía* – and the moral one – *philanthropía* –, gained through an adequate education (Cicero, *Oratio pro Archia* 16).

[87] Cicero, *De Oficiis*, I. 18.

[88] Perelli, L, *Il pensiero politico di Cicerone*, at 120 ff.

[89] Cicero, *De legibus*, I. 6.18.19.

[90] Cicero, *De legibus* I.42.

This is because, as he tells us in *De Legibus* (*On the Laws*), "the Law is not a product of the human thought, neither is any promulgation of the nations, but something eternal that governs the entire universe through its wisdom for ordering and prohibiting,"[91] "the true law is the just reason in accordance with the nature", because "any attempt to change this law is a sin, nor is permitted to reject any part of it, and it is impossible to abolish it entirely."[92] Accordingly, "the universe obeys God; the seas and lands obey universe; and the human life is subjected to the decrees of the supreme law".[93] In conclusion, "the Law is a distinction between the just and unjust things made in accordance with the first one and the most antique of all the things, the Nature,"[94] resulting in "the Law whose nature I have explained cannot be rejected or repealed."[95]

Under this line of argument, Cicero claims that when the law dictated by the crowd, by the plebs, it will be illegitimate if they oppose the Natural Law. He argues laws approved in the Assembly by "a band of thieves" do not deserve to be called laws.[96] He considered "the most silly notion of all is the belief that everything found in customs or in laws of nations is just,"[97] and to understand that it is not lawful to regard as law any kind of statute,[98] Cicero's proof being that the Senate finally abolished them.[99] This is because, from Cicero's perspective, if the natural law could be disturbed by the mob,[100] it would be possible to conclude that it was lawful too to "order that the bad and evil must be considered good and healthy".[101] Accordingly, he sustains that "the silliest notion of all is the belief that everything found in customs or in laws of nations is just".[102]

From this premises, in his work *De finibus*, Cicero argues that the source from which the Civil law proceeds is *nature*, the same that teaches us that no one has to take advantage of others in business. For this reason, the *ius civile*, in emanating from the *lex naturae*, punishes all malice and fraud committed by those who take advantage from other's ignorance.[103] According to Cicero, this does not happen with the Law of Rome, in which all the *civilis scientia* is collected and where all the most useful institutions are contained for the ordering of the life of the particulars and of the State.[104]

---

[91] Cicero, *De legibus* II. 4.8.

[92] Cicero, *De re publica,* III .22.33.

[93] Cicero, *De legibus* III. 2.4.

[94] Cicero, *De legibus* I. 5.13.

[95] Cicero, *De legibus* II. 5.14.

[96] Cicero, *De legibus* II.5.13.

[97] Cicero, *De legibus*, II. 14.42.

[98] Cicero, *De legibus*, II. 5.13.

[99] Cicero, *De legibus*, II. 5.14.

[100] Cicero, *De legibus*, II. 5.13.

[101] Cicero, *De legibus*, II. 16.44.

[102] Cicero, *De legibus*, II. 14.42.

[103] Cicero, *De finibus*, III. 71.

[104] Cicero, *De oratore*, I. 193.

Hence in Roman law the theory of the *optimus princeps* emerges, of the wise and intelligent governor who is able to govern in accordance with the good and virtue, and not from the tyranny.[105]

This reflection about Natural Law leads Cicero to maintain that in some defined circumstances apparently immoral acts are not such in reality. Accordingly, tyrannicide was not an execrable act, but rather "the most beautiful act out of the fine actions that can be performed", in which "the honesty has reached an agreement with the utility".[106]

To exemplify this theoretical conception, Cicero presents us the assassination of Cesar as a paradigm of his approach. Taking as a reference the method and the system of the Stoics, he argues that "what is honest, as well is useful, and there is nothing useful that won't be honest".[107] Based on his idea that *nature* and the Civil Law form the same reality, as both order the same, Cicero comes to the conclusion that it is unlawful to hurt someone for your personal benefit.[108] However, this is not the case, as he theorizes in *On the Republic*,[109] when what is ordered is not the dominance of the stronger nations over the weaker nations, but the community of the interests between the stronger and the weaker ones – this being not for the benefit of one or another, or even both, but for the whole of humanity. This is why he explains tyrannicide is justifiable, because an apparently immoral action will be justified when it relies on the principle of the Natural Law: one which seeks to promote the welfare of the mankind and not particular interests.

Consequently, in his work *On duties*, Cicero holds that the view of the natural law is the one applied in the antiquity in the Republic, "when the empire of the Roman Empire kept its dominion through benefices, not through injustices". This is a period where the "dominion could be called patronage of the whole world."[110] This legitimate Empire, as it was defined by Cicero, declines in the epoch of Sulla and fundamentally during the tyranny of Cesar, when the Roman dominance becomes illegitimate. As a consequence of this illegitimacy, the Republic loses all its dignity and reason for being. Accordingly, by departing from the ordering rules and principles of the Natural Law, the evolution of history makes Empires falter for giving up its ends, its welfare, promoting private interests, for that the Republic has become illegitimate when the justice, the virtue, the common good, the *utilitas* and the *bellum iustum* were infringed:

> And so, when foreign nations had been oppressed and ruined – the author thinks about Cesar –... I might mention many other outrages against our allies, if the sun had ever beheld anything more infamous than this particular one. Justly, therefore, are we being punished.[111]

---

[105] Isnardi Parente, M, *Introduzione*, at 129 ff.

[106] Cicero, *De officiis*, III. 19.

[107] Cicero, *De officiis*, III. 20.

[108] Cicero, *De officiis*, III. 23.

[109] Cicero, *De re publica*, III. 33.

[110] Cicero, *De officiis*, II. 26.

[111] Cicero, *De officiis*, II. 28.

> The Republic, in reality, we have entirely lost. It is so because we have preferred to be the object of fear rather than of love and affection that all these misfortunes have fallen upon us. And if such were the consequences for their injustice and tyranny, what ought private individuals to expect?[112]

The approval of the tyrannicide, based upon the designs of the Natural Law – that seeks the common good –, can be found in his work *Pro Sestio*. In *Pro Sestio* Cicero holds that those who guide the destinies of the politics, *gobernada viris*, must guarantee a worthy kingdom to the community, with this requiring honourable behaviour. Otherwise, a personal attack is permitted in case of execrable behaviour:

> Which is, therefore, the target at which these pilots of the nave of the State must look and orient their route? The one that is the best and most desirable for all sane, honest and happy men: a peaceful life with honour – *cum dignitate hotium* –. Everyone who desires this is considered *optimates*; the ones who achieve it are the learned and guardians of the State. For it is not convenient for men to seek holding public offices to the point of losing their tranquillity, nor to seek an excessive peaceful life to the extent of avoiding any public responsibility.[113]

For this reason, Cicero is not thinking of a *rector* or a *moderator rei publicae*, of a prince (*princeps*) in a strict sense of the term. He is thinking of the *consulares*, of a figure of the *homo politicus, rector et gobernator rei publicae*, whose assignment is to protect, in any way, the *res publica*, the constitution, the citizens, the union and, fundamentally, the justice. This is because it must be the predominant ideal of the State, as for him it is, a more moral value than legal.[114]

To sum up, Arpinate takes the *imago naturae* as a leading thread, which projects into the soul of man, into the *vir prudens*, an interior process of continuous exam. Through which he does not stop amending himself, in this sense being able to attract other citizens by the brightness of his soul. This leads him to become a "man of Ideal State", for being able to create justice, harmony and union in a city, in a Republic governed from the justice for the general welfare. Without justice, he says through Scipio, the permanence and stability of the State cannot exist.[115]

2.2 Power and Limits of the Medieval Monarchy

2.2.1 *The Princeps-Iudex*

Sovereignty, as an expression of political and legal power, is not alien to late-medieval thought. Over centuries, a crisis of the Roman legal tradition emerged: with the reception of the Roman-canonical Law the theocratic conception of the regal office and the

[112]Cicero, *De officiis*, II. 29.

[113]Cicero, *Pro Sestio* 98. In similar sense in *De oratore* I. 1.

[114]Cicero, *De legibus* III. 3.

[115]Cicero, *De legibus* II. 69.

idea of justice as an image of God – *imago deitatis*[116] – slipped, thereby allowing monarchs to assume all the prerogatives that the Roman Order vested in the Emperor,[117] who represented himself as a supreme holder of the *potestas judicandi.*[118]

Grossi affirms that this conception of the *princeps-iudex*,[119] presented in the thought of Saint Isidore,[120] and afterwards in Thomas of Aquinas,[121] can be found in all medieval thought through the concept of *iurisdictio*, which is understood, in words of Azon, as "the necessity to promulgating the Law and establishing equity".[122] Under this conception, the king enjoys, following the doctrine of the commentators and glossators,[123] the exercise of several faculties of jurisdiction with exclusive character.[124] This means not just a *potestas legis condendae*,[125] but a *potestas iuri dicendi*, as a necessity of pronouncing Law and establishing equity.[126]

---

[116]See also in others, F. Kern, *Derechos del Rey y derechos del pueblo* (Madrid: Rialp, 1955) at 36 ff.; M. García Pelayo, *El reino de Dios, arquetipo político* (Madrid: Revista de Occidente, 1959) at 152 ff.; A. Maravall, "El pensamiento político en la Alta Edad Media," in *Estudios de Historia del pensamiento español* (Madrid: Ed. Cultura hispánica, 1983) I at 33–66; W. Ullman, *Historia del pensamiento político en la Edad Media* (Barcelona: Ariel, 1983) at 21 ff.; E. M. Kantorowicz, *Los dos cuerpos del rey. Un estudio de teología política medieval* (Madrid: Alianza Editorial, 1985), first reference of which can be found in at 57, footnote n. 8, criteria which extend through the chapters III-IV; C. Petit, "Iustitia, e Iudicium en el reino de Toledo. Un estudio de teología jurídica visigoda," in *Giustizianell'alto Medioevo*. Settimane di Studio del Centro Italiano di Studi sull'alto Medioevo (Spoleto, 1995) at 843–932; S. M. Coronas González, *Estudios de Historia del Derecho público* (Valencia: Tirant lo Blanch, 1998) at 11–13.

[117]Diego de Covarrubias y Leyva, *Opera Omnia. In regula Peccatum, de regulis iuris Libro Sexto* (Genevae, 1762), VI *De regulis iuris* 4. II. *Caput* 9, num. 6.

[118]A. Marongiu, "Un momento típico de la Monarquía medieval. El rey juez," *AHDE* 23 (1953) at 677–715; F. L. Pacheco Caballero, "Reyes, leyes y Derecho en la Alta Edad Media castellano-leonesa," in *El Dret comú i Catalunya* (Barcelona: Fundació Noguera, 1996) at 165–206; F. L. Pacheco Caballero, "Potestad regia, justicia y jurisdicción en el Reino de Aragón (Edades media y moderna)," in *El Dret comú i Catalunya* (Barcelona: Fundació Noguera, 1997) at 119 ff.

[119]P. Grossi, *El Orden jurídico medieval* (Madrid: Marcial Pons, 1996) at 140.

[120]St Isidore, *Etymologiarum* (Madrid, 1982), *Liber* 9, num. 3, 5.

[121]Thomas of Aquinas, *Summa theologiaea* (Romae, 1588), *Secunda Secundae,quaestio* 58, art. 1, *ad. totum.*

[122]In relation to this term, see F. Calasso, "Iurisdictio nel diritto commune classico," in *Scritti di Francesco Calasso* (Milano, 1965); as well as in *Annali di storia del diritto* (1965) 9 at 100; P. Costa, *Iurisdictio. Semantica del potere político nella publicistica medievale (1100–1433)* (Milano, 1949) at 99–101; see also J. Vallejo, *Ruda equidad, ley consumada. Concepción de la potestad normativa (1250–1350)* (Madrid: Centro de Estudios Constitucionales, 1990) at 40 ff. and 314; P. Grossi, *El Orden jurídico*, at 144.

[123]Bartolus de Saxoferrato, *In primam Digesti Veteris partem commentaria* (Venetiis, 1570), Book 1, tit. 1, *lex* 9, *quaestio* 1, num. 3; Baldus de Ubaldis, *Commentaria in primam Digesti Veteris partem* (Lugduni, 1585), Book 1, rub. *De iustitia et iure*, *lex* 9, num. 20.

[124]Azo, *Summa Super Codice. Corpus Glossatorum Juris Civilis*. III (Reed., 1965), Rúbrica *De iurisdictione omnium iudicum et de foro competenti.*

[125]Pedro Belluga, *Speculum Principum ac iustitiae* (Paris, 1530), rubric 2*, De inventione Curia*, num. 7; similarly, see J. Vallejo, *Ruda equidad*, at 100 ff.; F. L. Pacheco Caballero, 'Potestad regia' at 215.

[126]This idea of king-judge can be found in the Espéculo 2, 1, 5: *Et los santos dixeron que el rey es puesto en la tierra en lugar de Dios para cumplir la justicia e dar a cada uno su derecho.*

Once the jurisdictional supremacy of the monarch is recognized, the king additionally enjoys the power to create law. As Accursius states, this power is transmitted to the monarch by the community, *transferendo de populo ad principem.*[127]

The normative power of the prince has its textual base in the Digest (1, 4, 1) and in the Code (14, 12, 3). The text, which grants to the king the power to create law, provides, from the thirteenth century onwards, a strong support to the concept of the *princeps* as *conditor legum.* This means the king is responsible for the legislative power within its own kingdom, either with absolute power, through the assistance of the notables of the city,[128] or through delegation.[129] This proposition, presented equally in the scholasticism,[130] as among canonists[131] and commentators,[132] is underlined by the development of the formula *the king does not recognize the emperor in his kingdom.* This formula, widely analyzed by Calasso,[133] heralded the end of the conflict between the emperor and the kings for the control and creation of the Law. As Bartolus stated, the reception of the Roman Law as Imperial Law was determined by the tacit recognition of the superiority of the emperor (over the kings), as well as of the binding force of the imperial laws.[134] From a legal perspective, the comparison of both powers came through the decretal *Through the venerable – Per venerabilem –*, of Innocence III in 1213, by which it was affirmed that the king who does not recognize any superior in secular matters should be considered as the emperor in his own kingdom.[135]

---

[127] J. A. Obarrio Moreno, *De iustitia et iure regni Valentiae: la tradición de las fuentes jurídicas romanas en la doctrina valenciana* (Madrid, 2005) at 25.

[128] Bartolus de Saxoferrato, *In Primam Digesti Veteris Partem*, Rub. *De legibus, lege Omnes populi*, num. 9; I. de Maino, *In Primam Digesti Veteris Partem Commentaria* (Lugduni, 1530), Rub. *De constitutionibus principium, lege* 1, num. 1.

[129] Bartolus and Nicholas de Tudeschi admitted that such power was delegable given to the technical difficulty in the lawmaking process (Bartolus de Saxoferrato, *In Primam Digesti Veteris Partem.* D. 1, 1, 9, num. 20); Tudeschis, N de, *Commentaria ad Quartum et Quintum Libros Decretalium* (Augustae Taurinorum, 1577).

[130] Thomas of Aquinas, *Summa*, II II, *quaestio* 50, num. 1.

[131] c. 10, X, 1, 2; Hostiensis (Henricus de Segusio), *Summa Aurea* (Venetiis, 1537), *Proemium*, n 18: *Quid potest constitutionem facere ... Imperator in temporalibus ...*; Tranensius, G, *Summa super titulis decretalium* (Lyon 1519, reed. Aalen, 1992), Rubric *De constitutionibus*, num. 5.

[132] Bartolus de Saxoferrato, *In Primam Codicis Partem* (Venetiis, 165), VII. Ad. C. 1,14,11; Baldus de Ubaldi, *Ad Tres Priores Libros Decretalium Comentaria* (Lugduni, 1585, reed. Aalen, 1970), Rubric *De constitutionibus*, Cap. 1, num. 31.

[133] F. Calasso, *I Glossatori e la teoria della sovranità* (Milán, 1957) at 39–83; in the same manner, his influence was pointed in different peninsular kingdoms by A. Otero Varela, "Sobre la plenitudo potestatis y los reinos hispánicos," *AHDE* 34 (1964) at 141–163; J. Egea i Fernández, and J. M. Gay i Escoda, 'Eficàcia de les normes a la tradició jurídica catalana des de la Baixa Edat Mitjana fins al Decret de Nova Planta' (1979) 78.2 RJC at 9.

[134] Bartolus de Saxoferrato, *Commentaria in Secundam Digesti Novi Partem* VI (Venetiis, 1615), *Ad* D. 49,15,24; Checchini, 'Impero papato e comunità particolari nelle dottrine dei glossatori' in *Atti del convegno internazionale di studi accursiani. Bologna, 21–26 Ottobre 1963* (Milano, 1968) at 117–130.

[135] c. 13,X,4,17.

Recognition that the law of each kingdom must be considered as the Imperial Law in its territory, and that its power lies upon the monarch, was readily accepted in different Spanish kingdoms. For instance, in the Crown of Castile this criterion had an early reception, from both a legal perspective in *Partidas* 2, 1, 8, and from a doctrinal basis.[136] Certainly, Diego of Covarrubias accepted the monarch as a source of Law, basing his view upon his recognition of the war – that was used against the Saracens –, upon the right of prescription or upon the custom.[137]

2.2.2 *The Prince Is Not Bound by the Law: The Clauses Non Obstante, Ex Certa Scientia, Ex Plenitudine Potestatis*

The idea of the monarch as a source of Law, as *conditor legum*, was admitted by the *doctores legum*, assuming that both the judicial and the normative power belonged to the prince.[138]The more specific application of this argument is exemplified in the inclusion of the formulae *non obstante*, *ex certa scientia*, and *plenitudine potestatis*. Recognition of the legal supremacy of the prince, as well as his normative power beyond the limits established by the Legal System,[139] *conditor legis*, *ea non obligatur*,[140] can be implicitly found.

The generic recognition of the prince as *legibus solutus* is recognised by the late-medieval doctrine, which consequently admitted the *potestas absoluta* of the monarch, for his condition as *princeps supra legem.* According to the aforementioned formulae, the king was not subjected to the law of the kingdom, because if the prince had dictated the law without the mediation of parliament, it would be valid by virtue of application of the general clause '*non obstante*'.[141]

2.2.2.1 The Judgements of the Princes

A specific consequence of this conception was the idea of the normative value of the judgements pronounced by the prince.

[136]Salón de Paz, *Ad leges Taurinas in signes comentarii* … (1568), *Prooemio*, ns. 32–35 and 143–144.

[137]Diego de Covarrubias, *Opera Omnia. In regula Peccatum de regulis iuris libro* sexto. VI, *Pars* II, 9, num. 9.

[138]In this sense, Baldus said that his power is absolute and supreme: Baldus de Ubaldis, *In Primum Codicis Librum Praelectiones* (Lugduni, 1556), Book 1, Tit. 14, 1.4, pr: *suprema et absoluta potestas.*

[139]U. Nicolini, *La propietá*, at 168; E. Cortesse, *Norma giuridica*, II at 81–96; Pacheco Caballero, FL, "*Non obstante. Ex certas cientia. Ex plenitudine potestatis*. Los reyes de la Corona de Aragón y el principio princeps a legibus solutus est," in *El Dret Comú i Catalunya. Actas del VII Simposi Internacional. Barcelona, 23–24 de maig de 1997* (Barcelona, 1998) at 91–127.

[140]P. Belluga, *Speculum*, rub. 11, vers. *Restat*, num. 1.

[141]P. Belluga, *Speculum*, rub. 2, num. 5.

The first textual reference recognising the normative character of the royal judgements is found in the Justinian Constitution (contained in *Codex* 1, 4, 12), where it is affirmed that judgements dictated by the emperor in a judicial process turned into a law and became a legal precedent. This explains, in last instance, the royal normative power, his position of *conditor legum.*[142] The principle is reiterated in the text of Ulpian (Digest 1, 4, 1) which states that judgement dictated by emperor as a judge is actually law, as the emperor, by words of Accursius, actuates giving the *definitivam sententiam.*[143]The same recognition can be seen among civilians and canonists from the thirteenth to fifteenth centuries. Consequently, if the value of precedent of the papal judgement is affirmed in the *ius canonicum* context, as it is laid down in the decree *in causis* of Innocentio III,[144] the glossators and commentators admitted and considered the royal judgement as *ius generale.*[145] This was irrespective of whether it was a final or interlocutory judgment.[146] This led authors such as Jason of Maine to sustain the nullity of judgements that violate the law and judgements of the prince.[147]

2.2.2.2 The Letters of the Princes

The late medieval doctrine questioned whether the answer of a sovereign to a specific doubt or issue could be considered law (*lex*).[148] As a textual base, the doctrine took the *Corpus Iuris Civilis*, especially in the *Codex* 1, 14, 12, and the text of Ulpian collected in the Digest 1, 4, 1, 1 where it is established what the emperor grants by a letter *legis vim obtinere*.

The passages of the Justinian *Corpus* led the commentators of both *corpora iuris* to a wide controversy over whether the answers given by the emperor or the Pope

[142]C. 1, 14, 12; it should be noticed, from the point of view of Accursius, *Codicis Iustiniani Sacratissimi Principis Imperatoris Augusti*. IX, *gl.* C. 1, 14, 12*vv. Si imperialis*, as the law mentions, it is only applicable to the cases not solved by laws.

[143]Accursius, *Digestum Vetusseu Pandectarum Iuris Civilis*. I. *gl.* 4, 4, 1*v. Decrevit.*

[144]c. 19, X, 27, 19; Fransen, G, 'La valeur de la jurisprudence en droit canonique' in *La norma en el Derecho Canónico* (1979) I at 201, where c. 22, X, 1, 6 is cited; Vallejo, J, *Ruda equidad*, at 180, fn 7.

[145]Azo, *Summa Super Codicem*, rub. *De legibus et constitutionibus*.

[146]The exclusion or non exclusion of the normative value of an interlocutory statement depends to a certain extent on its inclusion in the *Corpus Iuris*; Accursius, *Digestum Vetus*, *gl.* D. 1,4,1, *vv. Interlocutus est*; Bartolus de Saxoferrato, *In Primam Codicis Parte Commentaria*, rub. *De legibus*, *lex* 11, num. 1; Baldus de Ubaldis, *In I, II et III Codicis Libros Commentaria* (Venetiis, 1615), Rub. *De legibus*, *lex* 2, num. 2; Albericus de Rosate, *Commentarii in Primam Digesti Veteris Partem*, rub. *De constitutionibus principum*, *lex* 1, num. 5.

[147]Maino I de, *In Primam Digesti Veteris Partem Praelectiones*, Rub. *De feriis*, nums. 23–24.

[148]J. López de Palacios Rubios, *Opera varia* (Antuerpiae, Apud Ioannem keerbergium, 1616), *Repetitio* rub., num. 11, where is mentioned that the legal issues solved in a rescript only affected to the foral Law, not to the Imperial one.

triggered a juridical effect only *inter partes.* This was sustained by, among other jurists, Bartolus,[149] Godofredus of Trane,[150] Decius,[151] and Paulus de Castrus.[152] Conversely, that its legislative power could extend *inter omnes*, was claimed by jurists such as Azzo,[153] and later Jason de Maine,[154] Abbas Parnomitanus,[155] and Feline Sandeo.[156]

In respect to the literature of the different Spanish kingdoms, it became known, as a general rule, that *rescriptum Principis legis habet vigorem* always when it does not attack the Law of the kingdom or the public utility.[157]

2.2.3 *The Limits to the Power of the Monarch*

2.2.3.1 The Medieval Dualism: The Fight of the Investitures

As García Marín rightly outlines, sovereignty was the result of a "long and rough way" that a late medieval king as well as jurists had endured to achieve the desirable *plenitudo potestatis.* Through this, the so called fight of the investitures interposed, with the Church, at face of the Roman Pontiff, vindicating the right to represent the continuity of imperial power. As a result, the Pope, who at first assumed the title of the *Vicar of Christ*, also claimed the *plenitudo potestatis*, the plenitude that is not confined to the *auctoritas sacrata* above the royal power, but comes to the royal power, the one that decides about the right use of the coercive power, and that gave birth to both the doctrine of the indirect power – *potestas indirecta* – and the theory of two swords. In accordance with this conception, the Pope could dispose of the princes and dissolve the fidelity bond of feudalism. This pronouncement, as Innocent III

[149] Bartolus de Saxoferrato, *Commentaria in Primam Codicis Partem.* Rub. *De legibus*, *lex* 2, num. 1.

[150] G. Tranensius, *Summa Super Titulis Decretalium*, Rub. *De rescriptis*, num. 2.

[151] P. Decius, *Lectura Super Decretales* (Venetiis, 1523), Rub. *De rescriptione*, num. 1.

[152] P. de Castro, *In Primam Digesti Veteris Partem Patavinae Praelectionis* (Lugduni, 1550), Rub. *De constitutionibus principum*, *lex* 1, num. 1.

[153] Azo, *Summa Super Codicem*, rúb. *De legibus.*

[154] I. de Maino, *In Primam Digesti Veteris Partem Praelectiones* (Lugduni, 1545), Rub. *De feriis*, nums. 23–24.

[155] N. de Tudeschis, *Commentaria Secundae Partis in Primum Decretalium Librum* (Lugduni, 1586), Rub. *De filiis presbyterorum ordinandis vel non*, cap. 9, num. 2.

[156] F. Sandeus, *Comentaria ad V Libros Decretalium Pars Prima* (Lugduni, 1587), rub. *De rescriptione*, num. 1.

[157] See, for example, L. Matheu y Sanz, *Tractatus de regimine urbis et regini Valentiae* (Lyon, 1704), book 1, chapter. 3, part 3, nums. 24–25; F. J. de León, *Decisiones Sacrae Regiae Audientia Valentinae* (Matriti, 1620), book 1, *decisio* 113, num. 3; book 2, *Decisio* 144, nums. 3–4; N. Bas y Galcerán, *Theatrum Iurisprudentiae forensis Valentinae, romanorum iuri mirifici accomodatae* (Valencia, 1690), *Pars* 1, *praeludium*, num. 108.

manifested, was not issued conforming to the political criteria, but *ratione peccati*, that is, by reasons of the moral and spiritual nature, and always by logic of the subordination of the kings – vassals – to the Pope – feudalists –.[158]

There is no doubt the Roman Pontiff's doctrine of the *plenitudo potestatis* shaped an authentic theory of the sovereign's limited temporary power. It was not intended to become a true *potestas directa*, by understanding that upon the Papacy two swords were relied. This was not for the common exercise of the temporary power, but for the salvation of the men and of the world.[159]

Regarding power, the doctrine emphasized the superiority of the spiritual over the temporary.[160] This supremacy was secured through the Law converting the temporal power into a spiritual, granting to the Pope the right to instruct and remove the kings. These faculties meant that Pope's sovereignty was based upon the primate of the sacral (spiritual) over the earthy (temporary).[161]

2.2.3.2 The Pactist Character of the Law

Despite recognising the Monarch's normative power, he did not retain exclusive ownership of his sovereignty which was, as Bartolus notes, subject to the proper community, *civitas sive princeps*. This was the foundation of the link between sovereign and popular power, originating the complexity of the late medieval legal system. The Law was settled by its pactist character and the *universitas civium* began converting to the legislator.[162] This conception is seen in the work of Petrus Belluga, a Valencian jurist, in his *Speculum Principum*[163] where he summarises the relevant ideas concerning the pactism.[164]

158 J. H. Burs, *The Cambridge History of Medieval Political Thought* c.350-c.1450 (Cambridge, 1991) at 300–305; W. Ullman, *Principios de gobierno y política en la Edad Media* (Madrid: Ediciones de la Revista de Occidente, 1971) at 23 ff.; Ullman, W, *Historia del pensamiento político en la Edad Media* (Barcelona: Ariel,, 1983); W. Ullman, W, *Escritos sobre teoría política medieval* (Buenos Aires: Eudeba, 2003) at 201.

159 G. H. Sabine, *Historia de la teoría política* (Madrid, F.C.E., 1994).

160 A. Black, *El pensamiento político en Europa, 1250–1450* (Cambridge: Cambridge University Press, 1996) at 65.

161 W. Ullman, *Principios de gobierno*, at 72–86.

162 Lalinde Abadía, "El sistema normativo valenciano," *AHDE* 2 (1972) at 305–330; J. Vallet de Goytisolo, "Valor jurídico de las leyes paccionadas en el Principado de Cataluña," at 80; J. Lalinde Abadía, "El pactismo en los Reinos de Aragón y de Valencia," in *El pactismo en la Historia de España* (Madrid, 1980), particularly at 126–127.

163 On this matter, we use the accurate translation of R. García-Gallo, *Antología de fuentes del antiguo Derecho. Manual de Historia del Derecho Español II* (Madrid, 1979) at 97–103; see also A. Marongiu, 'Lo 'Speculum principum' del valenzano Pere Belluga' (1970) 8.II *CHCA* at 53–65; J. Vallet de Goytisolo, 'Valor jurídico de las leyes paccionadas en el Principado de Cataluña' at 80; J. Lalinde Abadía, "El pactismo en los Reinos de Aragón y de Valencia," at 126–127.

164 J. Lalinde Abadía, 'El pactismo en los Reinos de Aragón y de Valencia' at 126.

From Belluga's perspective, the essence of the pactism was already reflected in the Roman Law,[165] through the *Codex* affirming the political and legislative power were transmitted by the people to the emperor. Consequently, he also issued laws respecting the advice of the *proceres*, the senators and the judges.[166]

This conception continued through the majority of late medieval legal systems, but not as a requirement for Justice.[167] Its continued existence was the result of custom, as the monarchs, under the advice of the *proceres* summoned in the *Curia*,[168] created laws and pragmatic sanctions. This demonstrates the legislative function did not fall only to the king, but in a formally constituted assembly. These laws are said to emanate from the *Curia*, acquiring legal value when the community granted money for their promulgation. This legally converted them into a contract,[169] into pactist and irrevocable laws,[170] for the prince as well as for his successors.[171]

The prevailing value of the pactist laws,[172] assumed by the glossators and – although with refinements – by canonists,[173] is ratified when Belluga upheld that the prince, with the council of the proceres, could create laws that violated the private Law.[174] Belluga's understanding was that if these laws sought public utility or the common good, it was lawful to create norms that could violate private rights or individual interests'.[175]

Underlying this argument is the understanding that although the pactist concept of Law did not imply the violation of the principles *quod Principi placuit, legis habet vigorem* and *Princeps legibus solutus*,[176] it determined clear limitations, given that the bond of the monarch to the normative pact limited his legislative power in favour of the justice and common good.[177]

In our view, Belluga in his *Speculum* intended to harmonise the aforementioned Ulpian principle with the will of the kingdom. It was hoped this would limit and regulate the Law making powers by subjecting the prince himself to the authority of

---

[165] P. Belluga, *Speculum*, rubrica 2, num. 1.

[166] P. Belluga, *Speculum*, rubrica 47, versículo *Sciencum*, num. 1.

[167] This conception is found in the number 4 when Belluga holds that if it is appropriate for the kings to create laws, then as well it is to create them with the council of the *proceres*, not because of the necessity, but because of their humanity.

[168] P. Belluga, *Speculum*, rubrica 2, num. 2.

[169] P. Belluga, *Speculum*, rubrica 9, num. 28.

[170] P. Belluga, *Speculum*, rubrica 11, vers. *His igitur*, num. 2.

[171] P. Belluga, *Speculum*, rubrica 2, num. 3.

[172] Accordingly, see P. Belluga, *Speculum*, rubrica 2, num. 4.

[173] P. Belluga, *Speculum*, rubrica 2, num. 3.

[174] P. Belluga, *Speculum*, *rubrica* 9, num. 26.

[175] P. Belluga, *Speculum*, *rubrica* 9, num. 25; num. 23.

[176] J. Vallet de Goytisolo, "Valor jurídico de las leyes paccionadas en el Principado de Cataluña," at 90–91.

[177] P. Belluga, *Speculum*, *rubrica* 11, num. 8.

the laws, although, in expression of Bartolus, the king accepted it *de voluntate* and not *de necessitate.*[178]

In this sense, the Valencian lawyer maintains that although the power of making laws vested in the prince, people could approve laws for themselves as long as they did not contradict the royal laws. This idea, along with the Gaius' fragment of the *lex omnes populi,*[179] enabled Belluga to assert that the civil law (private law), as it is established by each people for itself,[180] may enter into its own sphere of a *civitas*, with no necessity of requesting the authorisation or approval of the prince.[181]

The heterogeneity of legal reality of the late medieval law is made evident by Belluga, who recognized in the figure of the monarch, not only a *princeps conditor legum,*[182] responsible for making the law, but of an *iudex ordinarius et superior*, capable – *in omni tempore* – to administer justice and to consider society and the kingdom with a sufficient normative power.[183] This allows Belluga, at last instance, to identify the prince and the king as convergent realities in the exercise of the normative power (or in making laws).

2.2.3.3 The Limits of the Law: Honest, Just, Destined to the Common Good and to the Natural Order

The legal doctrine of Thomas Aquinas defines the law as the ordination of the reason destined to the common good, promulgated by the one who cares for the community.[184]The law appears, following the scheme of the *Summa Theologiae*, as a suitable instrument for which the *princeps*, as *conditor legum*, is subjected, not to the impulses of one's will, but of reason and intellect.[185] Otherwise, there is no *lex* but *iniquitas*.[186]

Admitting the idea that the law does not belong to the province of will but to that of reason, the legal literature, following a passage of the Gratian Decree,[187] coming at its turn from the *Etymologies* of Isidore of Seville,[188] establishes the fundamental elements that define the law: honesty, justice, and in accordance with nature.[189]

[178]Bartolus de Saxoferrato, *In Primam Codicis Partem Praelectiones* (Venetiis, 1615), rub. *De legibus*, *lex* 4, num 4.

[179]D. 1,1,9.

[180]P. Belluga, *Speculum*, part 2, num. 6.

[181]P. Belluga, *Speculum*, part 2, num. 7.

[182]P. Belluga, *Speculum*, part 2, see *De inventione curia*, nums. 4–5.

[183]P. Belluga, *Speculum*, part 11, see, *Ac Iusticiae*, num. 1.

[184]Thomas of Aquinas, *Summa Theologiae,* I-II, *quaestio* 90, num. 4.

[185]Thomas of Aquinas, *Summa Theologiae*, I-II, *quaestio* 91, art. 1, c.

[186]Thomas of Aquinas, *Summa Theologiae*, I-II, *quaestio* 90, art. 1, c.

[187]I, d. 4, c. 2.

[188]I. St Isidore, *Etymologiarum*, Lib. 5, num. 6, see, for example, Butrio, A de, *Super Prima Primi Decretalium Commentarii* (Venetiis, 1578), rub. *De constitutionibus*, Cap. 4, num. 13.

[189]Gómez, *Ad legem Tauri commentaria* (Matriti, 1780), *Ad legem* I, num. 5.

Lex Honesta

Under the natural-law principle *Honeste vivere*,[190] the authority of a text is consolidated: the one that establishes the law is a measure of rectitude, a right, honest and useful rule.[191] As Aquinas affirms, this is contrary to any immoral precepts.[192] This principle was assumed by the doctrine of *ius commune*, which affirmed that no precept could abolish the rule that sustains that the norms must be directed by the reason.[193]

Lex Iuxta

The second requirement of the law is that, it must be just. This is because justice, as Accursius says, must precede the Law.[194] Accordingly, if the law should be obeyed by everyone, it has to be just; otherwise, it would contradict one of the elements that shape the foundation of the law.[195] As Baldus and Covarrubias, among others, say, the law may be rigid, but it cannot be unjust, *Lex potest durum continere, sed non injustum.*[196]

Upon the understanding that *legem iustam esse debere*, that it, justice is the essence of the law, late medieval doctrine holds that the reason that could justify the suppression of a precept could be its iniquity. Following the Thomist distinction,[197] this may occur *ex defectu potestatis* (when the legislator acts at a margin of the

[190] *Decretalia, prooemium*, II,1; on the reception of the Ulpian text in the Middle Ages, see Calasso, *Medio evo*, at 470–473.

[191] A de Rosate, *Commentarii in Primam Digesti Veteris Partem*, rub. De *iustitiaetiure*, *lex* 8, num. 6.

[192] Thomas of Aquinas, *Summa Theologica*, I-II, *quaestio* 90, art. 1. Con anterioridad, Cicero, *De legibus*, II, 5, 11.

[193] Azo, *Summa Super Codicem*. Part *De legibus et constitutionibus principum et edictis*; Placentinus, *Summa institutionum* (Ed. *Corpus Glossatorum Juris Civilis*, 1973), Rub. *De iustiticia et iure*; Bartolus de Saxoferrato, *In Primam Digesti Veteris Partem Commentaria, De iustitia et iure, lex IX, Omnes populi*, num. 26; *In Primam et Secundam Codicis Partem Commentaria* (Venetiis, 1570), Part *Si contra ius, vel utilitatem publicam, lex* 6, num. 2.

[194] Accursius, *Digestum Vetus seu Pandectarum Iuris Civilis*. I., Tit. 1, part. *De iustitia, etiure, lex* 1, *v. Iustitia*; Rosate A de, *Commentarii in Primam Digesti Veteris Partem*, Rub. *De iustitia et iure, lex* 1, num. 7.

[195] Bartolus de Saxoferrato, *In Primam et Secundam Codicis Partem Commentaria*, Part *Si contra ius, vel utilitatem, lex* 6, num 6; Rosate A de, *Commentarii in Primam Digesti Veteris Partem*, Part *De legibus et senatusconsultis, et longa consuetudine*, num. 2; Butrio, A de, *Super Prima Primi Decretalium Commentari*, Part *De constitutionibus*, Ch. 4, num. 13.

[196] Baldus de Ubaldis, *Ad Tres Priores Libros Decretalium Commentaria*, part *De constitutionibus*, Ch. 6, num. 1; Diego de Covarrubias y Leyva, *Relectio Regulae c. Possessor. Opera Omnia*. I, *Pars* 2, Ch. 6, num. 3, p. 541.

[197] Thomas of Aquinas, *Summa Thologica*, I-II, *quaestio* 96, art. 4, c. Its influence to the posterior doctrine can be seen in Albericus de Rosate, *Commentarii in Primam Digesti Veteris Partem*, Part *De legibus*, num. 4.

limits of his jurisdiction),[198] *ex defectu finis* (when the law does not tend to the common good but to particular or merely accidental interests),[199] and also *ex defectu formae debitae* (when the norm does not distribute proportionally the loads between the subjects of the community), since it was understood that the *lex non solum esse justa in substantia, sed etiam in proportione*.[200]

Pro communi Civium Utilitate Conscripta

Admitting that the law should be just and honest, it is further added that the intention of the legislator should be to enact law for the sake of common good, or, as Accursius said, in favour of the common utility.[201] The requirement that the law serves the common good and not for the private interest led scholarly doctrine to reflect upon its scope, validity and nature of that concept, namely the common good.[202]

Particularly, the doctrine said that no norm could be based on love or hate of a particular thing, but on God and on the right reason,[203] by being its vicar;[204] hence the civil law, in pursuit of the common good, would tend to order what was just in the ambit of the virtues, and to prohibit what violates the honesty and the justice.[205] As a result, for both canonist[206] and civil-law doctrine,[207] individual prejudice was lawful when the norm conformed in benefice to the common good. As Accursius explains, as the norm's aim was public utility, it was lawful to attack the private interest. As such, it was understood that the law tending to the private interest converted to a private norm,[208] to a privilege, a *privata lex*.[209]

---

[198] Albericus de Rosate, *Commentarii in Primam Digesti Veteris Partem*, Part *De legibus*, num. 47.

[199] Albericus de Rosate, *Commentarii in Primam Digesti Veteris Partem*, Part *De legibus*, num. 51.

[200] Albericus de Rosate, *Commentarii in Primam Digesti Veteris Partem*, Part *De legibus*, num. 51.

[201] Accursius, *Digestum Vetus*, *gl. ad* D. 1,3,1, *see Lex est*.

[202] I. de Maino, *In Primam Digesti Veteris Partem Commentaria*, part *De legibus*, *s. lexest*; Gregorio López, *Las Siete Partidas del Rey D. Alfonso, glosadas por el Licenciado Gregorio López ... Los Códigos Españoles* (Madrid, 1848), II, Gl. to Partida I, tit. 1, law 9; A. Gómez, *Ad legem Tauri commentaria*, Leg. 1, num. 5.

[203] Gregorio López, *Las Siete Partidas*, Gl. *Partida* 1, 1, 9, v. *A pro comunal*.

[204] St Isidore, *Etymologiarum*, Liber V, num. 3, 3–4.

[205] Thomas of Aquinas, *Summa Theologicae*, I-II, *Quaestio* 96, 2.

[206] In favour of its validity, see St Isidore, *Etymologiarum*, Liber V, num. 21; c. 18, X, 3, 31.

[207] For which the execution of fraud should be appealed or alleged, except when the reasonable causes are given in sake of the common good. Thus, Tudeschis, N de, *Commentaria Primae Partis in Primum Decretalium Librum* (Venetis, 1605), Tit. 1, part 2, num. 2; Maino, I de, *In Primam Digesti Veteris Partem Commentaria*, part *De legibus*, law 6, num. 4.

[208] Accursius, *Digestum Vetus*, *gl. ad* D. 1, 3, 1, part *De legibus*, *v. lex est*.

[209] G. Durandus, *Speculum iudiciale. Illustratum et repugatum a Giovanni Andrea et Baldo degli Ubaldi* (Basel, 1574, reed. Aalen Verlag, 1975), book 2, *particula* 2, part 11 *De impugnatione privilegii*, num. 4; book 2, *particula* 3, part 6; Bartolus de Saxoferrato, *Commentaria*, part *De mandatis principum*, *lex* 2, num. 3; Castro, A de, *De potestate legis poenalis libri duo*

Secundum Naturam

The late medieval jurists reaffirmed the idea that neither royal sovereignty, nor the laws could be contrary to the Natural law[210] because this was the ultimate fundament and the immutable base the State.[211]

For this historical period, two basic texts about natural law require mention: the *Lectura Institutionum* of Petrus de Bellaperticus, and the *Summa Theologiae* of Thomas of Aquinas.

In the *Lectura Institutionum*, Petrus de Bellaperticus draws the distinction between natural law and secular law. Natural law is immutable, referring to the universal principles that any man may find through conscious reflection – you shall not kill, you shall not steal. The secular law (or civil law), by contrast, is the instantiation of natural law for the purpose of regulating particular situations, for which the law ceases to be immutable, as it is imposed to deal with the necessities or circumstances of each moment.[212]

Under this distinction, Petrus de Bellaperticus maintained that when a solution was just, on the earth its compliance was obliged, and morally its observance was obliged, because both laws (natural law and positive law) were included.

However, the assumptions regarding political laws were different. To oblige compliance, the political laws had to be in accordance with the strict principles of the natural law. They also had to be useful and acceptable to the community they affected.[213] The same was applicable to the obedience of political power in general, which obliged compliance as long as they did not violate the criteria of right reason and just nature.

(Salmanticae, 1550, ed. facs. Madrid, 1961), Book 1, ch. 1; Barbosa, A, *Collectanea in Codicem Justiniani, Tomus primus* (Lugduni, 1679), book 1, tit. 14, part *De legibus, lex* 6, num. 1; in the canonical doctrine, see Papiensis, B, *Summa Decretalium*, book 5, tit. 28 *De privilegiis*, num. 1; Tranensius, G, *Summa super titulis decretalium*, part *De privilegiis et excessibus privilegiatorum*, fo. 224; Hostiensis, *Summa Aurea*, book 4, part *De privilegio et excessibus privilegiatorum*, nums. 1–2; Tudeschis, N de, *Comentaria in Decretalium Libros*, book 5, part *De verborum significatione*, num. 7.

[210] On the contrary, such authors as Accursius warned of the possibility that the Natural Law could be, in cases, modified or altered by the Civil Law (Accursius, *Digestum Vetusseu Pandectarum Iuris Civilis*, *gl. ad.* D. 1,1,4, *v. Nascerentur*); taking the view of Accursius, Udalricus Zassius, *Opera Omnia* (Lyon, 1550, reed. Aalen, 1964), Part *De iustitiaetiure, l. Iusciviile. L. Iusautem.L. Nam etipsum*, nums. 6–19.

[211] Cicero, *De legibus*, I,8,28; Thomas of Aquinas, *Summa Theologica*, I-II, *Quaestio* 94, *ad* 4–5; I-II, *quaestio* 100, art. 8 *ad* 2; II-II, *quaestio* 104, art. 4 ad 2; *Decretum* D. 21, c. 4; c. 11,X,1,4; Baldus de Ubaldis, *Ad Tres Priores Libros Decretalium Commentaria*, part *De constitutionibus*, Ch. 1, num. 26; Diego de Covarrubias y Leyva, *Reguale Peccatum, De Regulis Iuris, libro sexto, Relectio. Opera Omnia*, II, *Pars* 2, Cap. 11, num. 3.

[212] F. Carpintero Benítez, *Del derecho natural medieval al derecho natural moderno: Fernando Vázquez de Menchaca* (Salamanca: University of Salamanca, 1977) at 99–116; F. Carpintero Benítez, "The natural laic law of the Medieval Age," *Persona y Derecho* 7 (1981) at 67–69; F. Carpintero Benítez, *Historia del Derecho Natural. Un ensayo* (Méjico: Universidad Nacional Autónoma de México, 1999) at 330–332.

[213] F. Carpintero Benítez, *Del derecho natural medieval…*, at 99–116.

In the *Summa Theologiae*, the law is a rational principle of practical order, adjusting the norm to the exigencies with an aim proposed by reason.[214] The law, inasmuch as it is a statement of a practical reason,[215] turns out to equate with the rule of good moral acts. That is, what grounds its binding force,[216] so the obligatory observance of the law is not a consequence of existence of a will or of a superior sovereign, but the requirement of norms adjusted to the promoted social end. The obligatory character of the law derives from the just equilibrium between the imperativeness of the act and the social end to which it tends.[217] In short, natural law is the rule of reason, just and right.[218] Accordingly, the positive laws and the mandates of sovereigns are to be measured against the rationality of Natural Law. This is because Natural Law not only allows man his intimate relation with God, but also constitutes the way through which God speaks to people.[219]

Under this line of argument, Thomas of Aquinas, through defining the law as the "ordination of the reason to the common good, promulgated by the one who takes care of the community", [220] sustained that only the law created by men would be just, and therefore, observed, if it derived of the natural Law, light of the right natural reason.[221] Consequently, only the law adjusted to it possessed the power of the law – *ratio legis* – and obliged in conscience; if it did not, it was not the real law, but *legis corruptio*, hence it did not oblige in conscience.[222]

According to Solari, this all-embracing spirit of the Natural Law becomes the ethic law by excellence, in the supreme norm. It regulates human behaviour in all its manifestations: moral, legal and political.[223] It becomes a law that limits and restricts the sovereignty of the governors to prevent them circumventing their ruling principles, since rulers, in last instance, acted as mediators of the *lex aeterna* or divine law,[224] law to which the sovereigns were subjected.[225]

---

[214]Thomas of Aquinas, *Summa Theologiae*, I-II, *Quaestio* 57, a. 5 ad 3.

[215]E. Gilson, *El espíritu de la filosofía medieval* (Madrid: Rialp, 1981) at 309.

[216]Thomas of Aquinas, *Summa Theologiae*, I-II, *Quaestio* 96, 2.

[217]Thomas of Aquinas, *Summa Theologiae*, I-II, *In sent.* II. d. 41, q. 1. a. 1. ad 4.

[218]Thomas of Aquinas, *Summa Theologiae*, II, 1, *Quaestio* 95, 2.

[219]H. Welzel, *Introducción a la Filosofía del Derecho. Derecho natural y justicia natural* (Madrid, 1972) at 52 and 55.

[220]Thomas of Aquinas, *Summa Theologiae*, I-II, *Quaestio* 90, 4.

[221]Thomas of Aquinas, *Summa Theologiae*, I-II, *Quaestio* 95, 2.

[222]M. Grande Yáñez, *Justicia y ley natural en Baltasar Gracián* (Madrid: Universidad Pontificia Comillas, 2001) at 231.

[223]G. Solari, *Filosofía del Derecho privado* (Buenos Aires: Depalma, 1946) I at 9.

[224]R. Gómez Pérez, *La ley eterna en la historia. Sociedad y derecho según San Agustín* (Pamplona: Ediciones Universidad de Navarra, 1972) at 71–74; E. Díaz, *Sociología y filosofía del Derecho* (Madrid: Taurus, 1980) at 268–270.

[225]E. Gilson, *El espíritu de la filosofía medieval*, at 302.

2.3 The Limits to Sovereignty by Bodin

When Bodin sustains "*the Republic is a right government of some families, and of what is common to them with sovereign power*",[226] he offers a new formulation on the conception of the authority of the prince.[227] He liberates the prince from the ties that subjected him to the custom and law of his predecessors,[228] allowing the sovereign will of the State to, according to Meinecke, get rid of some "medieval links", that is, the Parliament or estates that impeded the development of a superior sovereign.[229]

Detached of such links, according to Bodin, the prince's power became one of absolute character, which needed to be limited. This leads authors, such as Sabine and Toucharda, to sustain that, with introduction of limits, Bodin "did not escape of a certain degree of contradiction between the absolutism of the sovereignty and its limitation by the natural law",[230] whereas García Marín asserts this contradiction was only an "absolutism of transition" away of the old concept of *legibus absolutes.*[231]

From the authors' perspective, Bobbio's view is more appealing. Bobbio proposes that "Contrary to what is thought commonly, the absolute power does not mean at no point the unlimited power; only means that the sovereign, being holder of the power of making laws valid for all the country, is not subjected to these laws, because it is not possible to order to oneself".[232] This being deduced from Bodin's thinking, "for whom – in words of Maravall – the sovereignty must be absolute in what it is in essence, but perfectly limited in its orbit".[233]

---

[226] J. Bodin, *Los Seis Libros de la República*, I.1.

[227] F. H. Hinsley, *El concepto de soberanía* (Barcelona: Editorial Labor, 1972) at 109.

[228] F. Meinecke, *La idea de la razón de Estado en la Edad Moderna* (Madrid: Centro de Estudios Políticos y Constitucionales, 1997) at 64.

[229] F. Meinecke, *La idea de la razón de Estado en la Edad Moderna*, at 61; similarly, J. A. Maravall, "Introducción," in *Jean Bodin en la historia del pensamiento,* ed. Pierre Mesnard, (Madrid: Instituto de Estudios Politicos, 1962) at 23: "This modern absolute State pretends, through the monopoly of the political power, overcome on the Earth the social power of lords and unions ...".

[230] J. Touchard, *Historia de las ideas políticas* (Madrid: Tecnos, 1990) at 229; similarly, G. H. Sabine, *Historia de la teoría política*, at 319–321, sustains that the argumentation of the sovereign power in Bodin "contained important confusions", given that the exercise of the sovereign power was not that limited as suggested its definitions, "and its result is the existence of restrictions that created much confusion in his theory".

[231] J. M. García Marín, *Teoría política y gobierno en la Monarquía Hispánica* (Madrid: Centro de Estudios Políticos y Constitucionales, 1998) at 85, who sustained: "the Bodin's thesis of the sovereignty of the State personificated in the absolute monarch with power to create laws and untied of its compliance, in reality was no other thing but an absolutism of transition, the previous and immediate step to the true absolutism".

[232] N. Bobbio, *La teoría de las formas de gobierno en la historia del pensamiento político* (México: Fondo de Cultura Economica, 2000) at 325.

[233] A. Maravall, "Introducción," in *Jean Bodin en la historia del pensamiento*, ed. Pierre Mesnard, at 29–30.

2.3.1 Divine Law and Natural Law

When discussing the distinct limits of the sovereign or the unlimited power of the prince, it is important to highlight that Bodin never doubted that the sovereign was limited by the law of God or of Nature. As Meineke points out, Bodin, differing from Maquiavelo, believed Law was the starting point from which one should try to grasp the essence of the Modern state.[234] Consequently, as the sovereign power must not be arbitrary, it could also not be unlimited. It possessed an absolute character within the framework of the limits of natural law and the divine law.[235]

Particularly, in eighth chapter of his first book, Bodin conceives the Law as a divine gift, as an emanation of the goodness and prudence of God. Accordingly, the attribution of the governor is not the *vis* but the political power. Because this power is submitted to the natural law, *ius* and *lex* are distinguished: "The absolute power does not mean other thing but the possibility of derogation of the civil laws, without being allowed to violating the law of God."[236]

This leads Bodine to divide the law into the natural and the human. The Natural is equitable and just, while the human would only be equitable and just if it anchors to the natural law. This means the law mandated by the prince does not become the only source of law. It is merely a way for the sovereign to achieve justice: for which "it is important that the law of the prince is made as the law of God". Otherwise the prince's mandate would be arbitrary and not obligatory on the internal forum, in the conscience of the subjects.[237] This recognition of a superior legal order is assumed as the logical subordination of the perpetual and unlimited power of the sovereign to the law of God, or to the natural law:

> ...all princes of the Earth are subjected to them and do not have power to contradict them... the absolute power of the princes and sovereign lords does not extend, in any way, to the laws of God and of the nature... The sovereignty granted to a prince with burdens and conditions does not constitute proper sovereignty, not the absolute power, except if the imposed conditions derive from the divine or natural laws. [238]

As he concludes, "This power is absolute and sovereign, because it is not subjected to other condition than the one of what the law of God and of Nature orders". This means the sovereign has an absolute and perpetual power, because it is not subjected to any temporal law, but to the law of God and of the nature: "If we say that the absolute power is held by the one who is not subjected to any laws, we

---

[234] F. Meinecke, *La idea de la razón de Estado*, at 59.

[235] D. Wyduckel, "The Sovereignty in the History of the German Dogmatism," in *Soberanía y constitución*, núm. 1 (*Fundamentos* I), *Cuadernos monográficos de Teoría del Estado, Derecho Público e Historia* Constitucional (Oviedo, 1998) at 9.

[236] P. Bravo Gala, "Introduction," to *Los Seis Libros de la República* (Madrid: Editorial Tecnos, 1986) at LII-LIII.

[237] J. Bodin, *Los Seis Libros de la República*, I. 8: "There is a great difference between the right and the law. The right implies the equity only; the law leads command. The law is no other thing but the command of the sovereign who uses his degree to the laws of the Greeks...".

[238] J. Bodin, *Los Seis Libros de la República*, I. 8.

would not find any sovereign prince in the world, given that all the princes are subjected to the laws of God and of the nature, and to certain human laws common to all peoples". Accordingly, Bodin concludes "that the prince is exempt of the authority of the laws", as it is of other subjects, because these "only depend on its pure and true will". However, the prince is not immune from the divine and natural laws, "and do not have power for contradicting them".

However, some authors see a contradiction between the power of the sovereign, of an absolute character, and the link to Natural Law. This is a result of the fact Bodin's thinking tends to secularise the power, moving away from the Divine Law, from all ecclesiastic guardianship.[239] According to Conde, he moves to empty all its content, reducing it to a common denominator, to a *minimum*.[240] This possible contradiction is solved in Bodin's *Colloquium Heptaplomeres*, where he asserts that the absolute sovereign power is still subject to certain limits. These limits form a secondary frame in respect to the liberty of thought, or to the real exercise of the tolerance, of an ambit of common discussion where the different opinions could coexist. In this sense, one of the protagonists, Salomon, at the end of the work, sustains: "What is looked for is the radicalisation of the perspective of each one, with no impediment, but on the contrary, enhances the coexistence."[241]

Following this line of argument, Conde comments on a letter of Bodin to Bautru des Matras. In this writing, dated around of 1563, Bodin sincerely expresses his religious feelings, and his belief in a natural religion. This leads Bodin to admit that society cannot survive without justice and, consequently, one cannot exist without any religion, or without a fear to a Superior Being. Conde states such arguments "had decisive importance in affirming the idea of the modern State: the liberty of conscience and the religious tolerance". They provided the context in which certain conditions attaching to the sovereign power can be observed; namely, absolute sovereignty is subject to limits imposed by the law of God or by the law of nature. These same limits lead to open spaces of tolerance and coexistence among the subjects.[242]

2.3.2 *The Foundational Laws and the Ones of the State*

Importantly, Bodin asserted: "In respect to the laws that appertain to the State and foundation of the kingdom, the prince cannot derogate them for being attached and incorporated to the crown, as it is the salic law"; in the event that he did derogate, "the successor could always nullify everything that had been done in prejudice of the

---

[239] F. Meinecke, *La idea de la razón del Estado*, at 63–65; G. H. Sabine, *Historia de la teoría política*, at 327–319.

[240] F. J. Conde, *Teoría y sistema de las formas políticas* (Madrid: Instituto de estudios políticos, 1944) at 177.

[241] J. Bodin, *Coloquio de los siete sabios sobre arcanos relativos a cuestiones últimas (Colloquium Heptaplomeres)* (Madrid: Centro de Estudios Políticos y Constitucionales, 1998), Book VI.

[242] F. J. Conde, *Teoría y sistema de las formas políticas*, at 177.

real laws, upon which the sovereign majesty is founded".[243] From this text it may be deduced that the sovereign power is not only conditioned by divine or natural Law, but also by the laws attached to the State. To admit, recognise and submit to these norms, those which founded the Kingdom, was so obvious for the prince, that to reject it would be the same as rejecting its own existence. Consequently, the modification or derogation of these founding norms is beyond the scope of the prince.

2.3.3 Private Property

To complete the enumeration of these limits or restrictions to the sovereignty, it is important to show the concurrent respect to private property. Sabine demonstrates that the right to private property constitutes for Bodin, something more than a mere moral limitation to the sovereign power:

> If the sovereign prince does not tend power to pass the confines of the natural laws of God, from which is the image, neither could he take the alien goods without reasonable and just cause, that is to say, by buying, barter or legitimate confiscation, or else for making peace with enemy when it may only be achieved by this mode.

Considering these premises, Bodin declares: "Once the said causes cease, the prince cannot take nor give the foreign goods without consent of their owner… the property is so sacred that the sovereign cannot touch it without consent of the owner."[244] In the view of Maravall, under these limitations Bodin position may be summarised thus:

> It would be an anachronism to say that the republic of Bodin, although in case of achieving the most perfect type of sovereignty, which is the real monarchy, would be a State of Law; but it should be recognised as a State of laws, in which the prince … is obliged to govern by laws and not by individual, isolated and arbitrary determinations.[245]

2.4 Some Concluding Considerations

If, according to Bodin's view, the essence of sovereignty is the power to create law,[246] and sovereignty, primarily, consists of the sovereignty of the law,[247] it becomes clear that on such sovereignty limits should be imposed; otherwise, laws may turn

---

243 J. Bodin, *Los Seis Libros de la República*, I. 8.

244 G. H. Sabine, *Historia de la teoría política*, at 320.

245 J. A. Maravall, "Introducción," in *Jean Bodin en la historia del pensamiento*, ed. Pierre Mesnard, at 30.

246 A. Arnaiz Amigo, *Soberanía y potestad. De la potestad del Estado* (México: Universidad Nacional Autónoma de México, 1971), II at 26.

247 "Sovereign will is the antithesis of subjective will. And since the expression of this will takes the form of law, sovereignty in reality means the sovereignty of law"(M. Loughlin, *The Idea of Public Law*, (Oxford: Oxford University Press, 2003) at 87).

against the individual, denying a person's rights, which would not be protected because the one body or institution who should recognize and protect them, does not see beyond the strictly political-juridical sphere.[248]

It would probably prove beneficial to return to a traditional political philosophy which starts with Cicero, the defender of *lex naturalis* and of *ius gentium*,[249] moving to the Modern times to recover the limits and the sense of moderation, in which the people was considered to be the *consensus iuris et comunitas utilitatis*.[250] The popular sovereign, in the political sphere, enjoyed the legitimacy inasmuch as it was faithful to the Law and in accordance with the general interest.

It is important to overcome the illusion of believing that democracy can guarantee, by itself, freedom. This idea is one which the course of European History strikingly belies. Indeed, the last two centuries of the recent history demonstrate that a sovereignty without limits, based exclusively on the democratic legitimacy, cannot guarantee freedom to individuals, but rather tends to undermine it. And this problem continues to be present, although occasionally may emerge in a less apparent and more subtle manner.[251]

---

[248] Gearty, 'Escaping Hobbes: Liberty and Security for Our Democratic (Not Anti-Terrorist) Age', at 12, shows the negative effects of the current Hobbes' influence: "But his [Hobbes] well-known vision of the government of a state as the location of absolute sovereignty, of power the exercise of which could not be gainsaid by those subject to it, was inevitably agreeable to those who, in subsequent generations, were to feel the need to act against a variety of perceived threats to the security of the state. Hobbes provides an important backdrop to the attacks on liberty in the name of security that have been such a feature of the democratic era, supplying that thread to the discussion which says security matters above all and (recalling our second point above) that security does not infringe liberty: that not only are those who do not notice repressive laws free, but so too are those coerced by fear into sullen obedience" (at 10). Later on, referring to the English context, he adds: "By the end of the 19th century, it is clear that Hobbes's security-state with a residual model of liberty, but without any strong notion of pre-political inalienable rights, is firmly in place".

[249] On this matter, see J. A. Obarrio, "Cicerón y los límites del poder," in *Estado de Derecho y Derechos fundamentales ante la lucha contra el terrorismo. Una aproximación histórica y jurídico-comparada,* ed. A. Masferrer (Pamplona: Aranzadi-Thompson, 2011); see also R. Domingo, *The New Global Law* (Cambridge: Cambridge University Press, 2010) at 6–8; on the relation between *ius naturale* and *ius gentium*, see J. Waldron, "Foreign Law and the Modern Ius Gentium," (November, 2005) 119, No. 1, *Harvard Law Review* at 129–147 (available at http://www.trinitinture.com/documents/waldron1.pdf); J. Waldron, "Ius Gentium: A Defense of Gentili's Equation of the Law of Nations and the Law of Nature," (November 2008), NYU School of Law, Public Law Research Paper No. 08–34 (available at http://ssrn.com/abstract=1280897).

[250] M. T. Cicero, *De Republica*, 1, 8 (quoted by J. Ballesteros, *Repensar la paz*, Navarra, EIUNSA, 2006, at 113, where another reference can be found, A. P. D'Entreves, *Teoría del Estado*, Spanish trans A. Fernández Galiano (Madrid, 1970) at 93 ff. and 233 ff.); on this matter, see also J. A. Obarrio, "Cicerón y los límites del poder,", already cited.

[251] C. Fried, *Modern Liberty and the Limits of the Government* (New York/London: W.W. Norton & Company, 2007) at 165: "But that is my point. In modern, liberal, welfare-administrative democracies, the impositions on liberty are likely to be gentle, marginal. But we must be vigilant, recognize them for what they are, or we will lose our grip on what liberty is, coming to confuse it with comfort, a generalized decency, or just democracy itself–a confusion that lovers of the state would be glad to foist upon us. But liberty is not the same as democracy".

It is necessary to again emphasise that the limits of the State may defend individual rights from the abusive exercise of public power. Otherwise, by adopting such a paternalistic attitude, the state pretends to exercise power without restraint, relying on a supposed national or popular sovereignty and on a democratic legitimacy. Accordingly, it is necessary to recognize human rights which exist prior to the state, and not mere "creatures" of the state,[252] that is, pre-political or natural rights over which any state should not dispose or legislate at its will,[253] avoiding thus conceiving the law, as a formal passport, which allows the State an excessive exercise of power, a power which is neither limited nor restrained.[254]

It is true that establishing limits on state power and lawmaking may not solve the complex relation between the security and the protection of the fundamental rights in countering terrorism. However it may moderate the State's often excessive utilitarian approach which, focusing more on the *quantum* than on *quod*, ignores the pre-political dimension of human rights and trivializes – if not ignores – the dignity of each human being, leaving him/her unprotected from the absolute power of Leviathan.

Bibliography

Álvarez, U. 1966. *La jurisprudencia romana en la hora presente*. Madrid: Real Academia de Jurisprudencia y Legislación.

Arnaiz Amigo, A. 1971. *Soberanía y potestad. De la potestad del Estado*. México: Universidad Nacional Autónoma de México.

Ballesteros, J. 1974. Estudio introductorio. In *Itinerarios humanos del Derecho*, ed. S. Cotta. Pamplona: Ediciones Universidad de Navarra.

Ballesteros, J. 2006. *Repensar la paz*. Navarra: EIUNSA.

[252]C. Fried, *Modern Liberty and the Limits of the Government*, at 72: "It is because our rights flow from who and what we are that we may form, re-form, or accept states in order to make our rights more certain and secure. So those who say that our rights depend on or are the creatures of the state have it the wrong way around". This raises a problem which Fried does not overlook and describes as follows: "What we cannot get to on our own, without laws and so without a state, is the content and detail of those rights. And rights without content are empty. Liberty means honoring our rights, and if the content of our rights is only what the state says it is, then while the *general idea* of rights, and the *general idea* of liberty may be secure against the state, the *substance* of each depends entirely on the state after all".

[253]C. Fried, *Modern Liberty and the Limits of the Government*, at 144–145: "If we have some rights, and therefore liberties, that are prepolitical rights which the state is bound to recognize, rights that are there before the state gets down to the business of defining rights, then, like Archimedes with his lever, we have a place to stand, and liberty can move the world. To put it in more traditional language, unless we have natural law, prepolitical rights, liberty is not secure"; on this matter, see also at 80, 84–85, 90–94 and 155.

[254]O. Gross, "Chaos and Rules: Should Responses to Violent Crises Always Be Constitutional," *Yale Law Journal* 112 (2003) : 1011–1134; see also the review published by D. Dyzenhaus in his edition of the *Civil Rights and Security* (Farnham: Ashgate, 2008), xiv–xvi; on this matter, see also D. B. Goldman, *Globalisation and the Western Legal Tradition: Recurring Patterns of Law and Authority* (Cambridge: Cambridge University Press, 2007).

Bayet, J. 1970. *Literatura latina*. Barcelona: Ariel.

Berti, E. 1963. *Il "De re publica" di Cicerone e il pensiero politico classico* (Padova: Cedam); Perelli, L. 1990. *Il pensiero politico di Cicerone* (Firenze: La Nouva Italia).

Black, A. 1996. *El pensamiento político en Europa, 1250–1450*. Cambridge: Cambridge University Press.

Bloch, E. 1980. *Derecho natural y dignidad humana*. Madrid: Aguilar.

Bobbio, N. 2000. *La teoría de las formas de gobierno en la historia del pensamiento político*. México: Fondo de Cultura Economica.

Bravo Gala, P. 1986. Introduction. In *Los seis Libros de la República*. Madrid: ed. Tecnos.

Burs, J.H. 1991. *The Cambridge history of medieval political thought c.350-c.1450*. Cambridge: Cambridge University Press.

Calasso, F. 1954. *Medioevo del Diritto*. Milano: Giuffrè.

Calasso, F. 1957. *I Glossatori e la teoria della sovranità*. Milán: Giuffrè.

Calasso, F. 1965. Iurisdictio nel diritto commune classico. In *Scritti di Francesco Calasso*. Milano; as well as in *Annali di storia del diritto* (1965) 9 at 100.

Carpintero Benítez, F. 1977. *Del derecho natural medieval al derecho natural moderno: Fernando Vázquez de Menchaca*. Salamanca: University of Salamanca.

Carpintero Benítez, F. 1981. The natural laic law of the Medieval Age. *Persona y Derecho* 7: 67–69.

Carpintero Benítez, F. 1999. *Historia del Derecho Natural. Un ensayo*. Méjico: Universidad Nacional Autónoma de México.

Casinos Mora, J. 2000. *La noción romana de auctoritas y la responsabilidad por auctoritas*. Granada: Comares.

Checchini, A. 1968. Impero papato e comunità particolari nelle dottrine dei glossatori. In *Atti del convegno internazionale di studi accursiani. Bologna, 21–26 Ottobre 1963*, ed. G. Rossi, 117–130. Milano: Giuffrè.

Conde, F.J. 1944. *Teoría y sistema de las formas políticas*. Madrid: Instituto de estudios políticos.

Coronas González, S.M. 1998. *Estudios de Historia del Derecho público*, 11–13. Valencia: Tirant lo Blanch.

Costa, P. 1949. *Iurisdictio. Semantica del potere político nella publicistica medievale*, 1100–1433. Milano: Giuffrè.

Cotta, S. 1963. Philosophie et politique dans l'oeuvre de Rousseau. Une esai d'interpretation. *ARSP* 49: 171–189.

Cotta, S. 1964. La position du probleme de la politique chez Rousseau', *Etudes sur le Contrat Social de Jean-Jacques Rousseau* (Paris).

Cotta, S. 1965.Theorie politique et theorie religeuse chez Rousseau. Rousseau et la philisophie politique. *Annales de Philisophie politique*.

D'Entreves, A. P. 1970. *Teoría del Estado* (Spanish trans.: A. Fernández Galiano) Madrid: A.P.

D'Ors, A. 1980. *Nuevos papeles de oficio universitario*. Madrid: Rialp.

Daza Martínez, J. (1976, July–October). *Libertas Populi Romani* (Libertad política, historia y Derecho natural en Cicerón). *Revista de Estudios Políticos*.

Daza Martínez, J. 1976. *Kyriosnomos. De la 'iuris societas' de Ciceron al 'polikos logos' de Marco Aurelio*. Cuenca: Jesús.

Díaz, E. 1980. *Sociología y filosofía del Derecho*. Madrid: Taurus.

Domingo, R. 2010. *The new global law*. Cambridge: Cambridge University Press.

Duplá, A. 2007. Interpretaciones de la crisis tardorrepublicana: del conflicto social a la articulación del consenso. *Studia Historica. Historia Antigua* 25: 185–201.

Egea i Fernández, J. and J. M. Gay i Escoda. 1979. Eficàcia de les normes a la tradició jurídica catalana des de la Baixa Edat Mitjana fins al Decret de Nova Planta," *Revista Jurídica de Cataluña* 78.2.

Fransen, G. 1979. La valeur de la jurisprudence en droit canonique. *La norma en el Derecho Canónico* I.

Fried, C. 2007. *Modern liberty and the limits of the government*. New York-London: W.W. Norton & Company.

García-Gallo, R. 1979. *Antología de fuentes del antiguo Derecho. Manual de Historia del Derecho Español II.* Madrid, Alfonso 97–103.
García Marín, J.M. 1998. *Teoría política y gobierno en la Monarquía Hispánica.* Madrid: Centro de Estudios Políticos y Constitucionales.
García Pelayo, M. 1959. *El reino de Dios, arquetipo político.* Madrid: Revista de Occidente.
Gearty, C. A. January 27, 2010. Escaping hobbes: Liberty and security for our democratic (Not anti-terrorist) age. , *LSE Legal Studies Working Paper* No. 3/2010. available at http://ssrn.com/abstract=1543121.
Gilson, E. 1981. *El espíritu de la filosofía medieval.* Madrid: Rialp.
Goldman, D.B. 2007. *Globalisation and the western legal tradition: Recurring patterns of law and authority.* Cambridge: Cambridge University Press.
Gómez Pérez, R. 1972. *La ley eterna en la historia. Sociedad y derecho según San Agustín.* Pamplona: Ediciones Universidad de Navarra.
Gómez Royo, E. 2010. *Las sedes históricas de la cultura jurídica europea.* Valencia: Tirant lo Blanch.
Grande, Y.M. 2001. *Justicia y ley natural en Baltasar Gracián.* Madrid: Universidad Pontificia Comillas.
Gross, O. 2003. Chaos and rules: Should responses to violent crises always be constitutional. *Yale Law Journal* 112: 1011–1134.
Grossi, P. 1996. *El Orden jurídico medieval.* Madrid: Marcial Pons.
Hinsley, F.H. 1972. *El concepto de soberanía.* Barcelona: Editorial Labor.
Isnardi Parente, M. 1993. *Introduzione a lo Stoicismo Ellenistico.* Roma/Bari: Laterza.
Jellinek, G. 1954. *Teoría General del Estado.* Buenos Aires: Editorial Albatros.
Kantorowicz, E.H. 1985. *Los dos cuerpos del rey. Un estudio de teología política medieval.* Madrid: Alianza Editorial.
Kern, F. 1955. *Derechos del Rey y derechos del pueblo.* Madrid: Rialp.
Labruna, L. 1993. Algunas reflexiones sobre la reciente historiografía jurídica referente a la llamada «democracia» de los Romanos. *Arsboni et aequi. Festschrift für W. Waldstein zum 65. Geburtstag,* Stuttgart, 203–214.
Lalinde Abadía, J. 1972. El sistema normativo valenciano. *AHDE* 2: 305–330.
Lalinde Abadía, J. 1980. El pactismo en los Reinos de Aragón y de Valencia. *El pactismo en la Historia de España.* Madrid: Jesús.
López Baraja de Quiroga, P. 2007. *Imperio legítimo. El pensamiento político en tiempos de Cicerón.* Madrid: A. Machado Libros.
Loughlin, M. 2003. *The idea of public law.* Oxford: Oxford University Press.
Magris, A. 1986. *L'idea di destino nel pensiero antico.* Trieste: Aldo.
Maravall, A. 1962. Introducción. In *Jean Bodin en la historia del pensamient*, ed. Mesnard Pierre. Madrid: Instituto de Estudios Politicos.
Maravall, A. 1983. El pensamiento político en la Alta Edad Media. In *Estudios de Historia del pensamiento español*, I, 33–66. Madrid: Ed. Cultura hispánica.
Maravall, A. 1997. *Teoría del Estado en España en el siglo XVI.* Madrid: Centro de Estudios Constitucionales.
Marongiu, A. 1953. Un momento típico de la Monarquía medieval. El rey juez. *AHDE* 23: 677–715.
Marongiu, A. 1970. Lo 'Speculum principum' del valenzano Pere Belluga. 8.II *CHCA* at 53–65.
Mas, S. 2009. Notas sobre el pensamiento político de Cicerón: imperio ilegítimo. *Gerión* 27.
Masferrer, A. 2011. Legislación anti-terrorista, Estado de Derecho y Derechos fundamentales: una aproximación a los límites del Estado en el constitucionalismo moderno. In *Estado de Derecho y derechos fundamentales en la lucha contra el terrorismo. Una aproximación multidisciplinar (histórica, jurídico-comparada, filosófica y económica)*, ed. A. Masferrer, 191–254. Pamplona: Thomson-Aranzadi.
Meinecke, F. 1997. *La idea de la razón de Estado en la Edad Moderna.* Madrid: Centro de Estudios Políticos y Constitucionales.
Notari, T. 2010. La teoría del Estado en Cicerón en su *Oratio pro Sestio. Revista de Estudios Histórico-Jurídicos* 32, Valparaíso, Chile.

Obarrio Moreno, J. A. 2005. *De iustitia et iure regni Valentiae: la tradición de las fuentes jurídicas romanas en la doctrina valenciana*. Madrid.
Obarrio Moreno, J.A. 2011. Cicerón y los límites del poder. In *Estado de Derecho y Derechos fundamentales ante la lucha contra el terrorismo. Una aproximación histórica y jurídico-comparada*, ed. A. Masferrer. Pamplona: Aranzadi-Thompson.
Otero Varela, A. 1964. Sobre la plenitudo potestatis and los reinos hispánicos. *AHDE* 34: 141–163.
Pacheco Caballero, F. L. 1996. Reyes, leyes y Derecho en la Alta Edad Media castellano-leonesa. In *El Dret comú i Catalunya*, 165–206. Barcelona.
Pacheco Caballero, F. L. 1997. Potestad regia, justicia y jurisdicción en el Reino de Aragón (Edades media y moderna). In *El Dret comú i Catalunya*. Barcelona.
Pacheco Caballero, F. L. 1998. *Non obstante. Ex certas cientia. Ex plenitudine potestatis*. Los reyes de la Corona de Aragón y el principio princeps a legibus solutus est,, In *El Dret Comú i Catalunya. Actas del VII Simposi Internacional. Barcelona, 23–24 de maig de 1997*, Barcelona, 91–127.
Pérez, J.C. 1995. Arceriotifinibus (Cic. har. 4), ¿"paz" civil u "ocio" de los jóvenes aristócratas? *Estudios Clásicos* 108: 57–92.
Petit, C. 1995. Iustitia, e Iudicium en el reino de Toledo. Un estudio de teología jurídica visigoda. In *Giustizianell'alto Medioevo*. Settimane di Studio del Centro Italiano di Studi sull'alto Medioevo, 843–932. Spoleto.
Rivera, A. 2006. Crisis de la autoridad: sobre el concepto político de autoridad en Hannah Arendt. *Daimon* 26: 87–106.
Rivera García, J. 2006. El republicanismo de Cicerón. Retorica, constitución y ley natural en *De Republica*. *Doxa* 29: 367–368.
Robleda, O, 1965. Filosofía jurídica de Cicerón. In *St. Biondi*. Milano, II.
Robleda, O. 1985. Cicerón y el Derecho romano. *Humanidades* 18–19: 33–58.
Sabine, G.H. 1994. *Historia de la teoría política*. Madrid: F.C.E.
Solari, G. 1946. *Filosofía del Derecho privado*. Buenos Aires: Depalma.
Touchard, J. 1990. *Historia de las ideas políticas*. Madrid: Tecnos.
Ullman, W. 1971. *Principios de gobierno y política en la Edad Media*. Madrid: Ediciones de la Revista de Occidente.
Ullman, W. 1983. *Historia del pensamiento político en la Edad Media*. Barcelona: Ariel.
Ullman, W. 2003. *Escritos sobre teoría política medieval*. Buenos Aires: Eudeba.
Vallejo, J. 1990. *Ruda equidad, ley consumada. Concepción de la potestad normativa (1250-1350)*. Madrid: Centro de Estudios Constitucionales.
Viñas, A. 2002. *Teoría del Derecho y experiencia jurídica romana*. Madrid: Dykinson.
Waldron, J. November 2005. Foreign law and the modern Ius Gentium. *Harvard Law Review* 119, no. 1: 129–147. Available at http://www.trinitinture.com/documents/waldron1.pdf.
Waldron, J. November 2008. Ius Gentium: A defense of gentili's equation of the law of nations and the law of nature. NYU School of Law, Public Law Research Paper No. 08-34. Available at http://ssrn.com/abstract=1280897.
Welzel, H. 1972. *Introducción a la Filosofía del Derecho. Derecho natural y justicia natural*. Madrid: Hans.
Wyduckel, D. 1998. The sovereignty in the history of the German dogmatism. In *Soberanía y constitución*, núm. 1 (*Fundamentos* I), *Cuadernos monográficos de Teoría del Estado, Derecho Público e Historia* Constitucional. Oviedo.

References (Literature, 13th–19th Centuries)

Accursius. 1598. *Codicis Iustiniani Sacratissimi Principis Imperatoris Augusti*. Venetiis.
Accursius. 1598. *Digestum Vetus seu Pandectarum Iuris Civilis*. Venetiis.
Albericus de Rosate. 1585. *Commentarii in Primam Digesti Veteris Partem*. Venetiis.
Azo. 1965. *Summa Super Codice. Corpus Glossatorum Juris Civilis*. III, Reed.

Baldus de Ubaldis. 1556. *In Primum Codicis Librum Praelectiones.* Lugduni.
Baldus de Ubaldis. 1585/1970. *Ad Tres Priores Libros Decretalium Commentaria.* Lugduni/reed. Aalen.
Baldus de Ubaldis. 1585. *Commentaria in primam Digesti Veteris partem.* Lugduni.
Baldus de Ubaldis. 1615. *In I, II et III Codicis Libros Commentaria.* Venetiis.
Barbosa, A. 1679. *Collectanea in Codicem Justiniani. Tomus primus.* Lugduni: Laurentius Arnaud.
Bartolus de Saxoferrato. 1570a. *In Primam Digesti Veteris Partem Commentaria.* Venetiis.
Bartolus de Saxoferrato. 1570b. *In Primam et Secundam Codicis Partem Commentaria.* Venetiis.
Bartolus de Saxoferrato. 1584. *In primam et secundam Codices partem commentaria.* Augustae Taurinorum.
Bartolus de Saxoferrato. 1615a. *Commentaria in Secundam Digesti Novi Partem* VI. Venetiis.
Bartolus de Saxoferrato. 1615b. *In Primam Codicis Partem Praelectiones.* Venetiis.
Bartolus de Saxoferrato. 1996a. *Codex.* Tomus VII, Roma: Ed. Instituto giuridico Bartolo da Sassoferrato. Il Cigno Galileo Galilei.
Bartolus de Saxoferrato. 1996b. *Commentaria cum additionibus Thomae Diplovatii excellentissimorum doctorum.* Tomo III. Ed. Istituto giuridico Bartolo da Sassoferrato. Il Cigno Galileo Galilei. Roma.
Bartolus de Saxoferrato. 1996c. *Digestum Vetus.* Tomus I, Rome: Ed. Instituto giuridico Bartolo da Sassoferrato. Il Cigno Galileo Galilei.
Bas y Galcerán, N. 1690. *Theatrum Iurisprudentiae forensis Valentinae, romanorum iuri mirifici accomodatae.* Valencia: Laurentii Mesnier.
Bodin, J. 1986. *Los Seis Libros de la República.* Madrid: Editorial Tecnos.
Bodin, J. 1998. *Coloquio de los siete sabios sobre arcanos relativos a cuestiones últimas (Colloquium Heptaplomeres).* Madrid: Centro de Estudios Políticos y Constitucionales.
Butrio, A de. 1578. *Super Prima Primi Decretalium Commentari.* Venetiis.
Castro, P de. 1550. *In Primam Digesti Veteris Partem Patavinae Praelectionis* Lugduni.
Castro, A de. 1961. *De potestate legis poenalis libri duo.* Salmanticae, 1550, ed. facs. Madrid.
Cicero, M. T. 1950. *Pro Murena.* Madrid.
Cicero, M. T. 1961a. *De domo sua.* Cambridge.
Cicero. M. T. 1961b. *Orationes, Cum senatui gratias egit.* Cambridge.
Cicero, M. T. 1961c. *Orationes Verrinae.* Cambridge.
Cicero, M. T. 1965. *In C. Verrem.* Oxford.
Cicero, M. T. 1975. *De officiis.* Cambridge.
Cicero, M. T. 1976. *Tusculanae Disputationes.* Stuttgart.
Cicero, M.T. 1977. *De re publica.* Cambridge: Harvard University Press.
Cicero, M. T. 1986a. *De divinatione.* Barcelona.
Cicero, M. T. 1986b. *De fato.* Barcelona.
Cicero, M. T. 1989. *Oratio pro Archia.* Madrid.
Cicero, M. T. 1994. *Filipicas.* Barcelona.
Cicero, M. T. 2002. *De oratore.* Madrid.
Cicero, M. T. 2005. *De tosculanorum disputationum.* Madrid.
Cicero, M. T. 2006. *Pro Sestio.* Oxford.
Cicero, M. T. 2009. *De legibus.* Madrid.
Cicero, M. T. 2010a. *Harusp. Resp.*Madrid.
Cicero, M. T. 2010b. *Oratio IV in Catilinam.* Madrid.
Decius, P. 1523. *Lectura Super Decretales.* Venetiis.
Diego de Covarrubias y Leyva. 1762. *Opera Omnia. In regula Peccatum, de regulis iuris Libro Sexto.* Genevae.
Durandus, G. 1574/1975 *Speculum iudiciale. Illustratum et repugatum a Giovanni Andrea et Baldo degli Ubaldi.* Basel/reed. Aalen Verlag.
Goffredus Tranensius. 1519/1992. *Summa super titulis decretalium.* Lyon/reed. Aalen.
Gómez, A. 1780. *Ad legem Tauri commentaria.* Matriti.

Gregorio López. 1848. *Las Siete Partidas del Rey D. Alfonso, glosadas por el Licenciado Gregorio López ... Los Códigos Españoles.* Madrid.
Hostiensis (Henricus de Segusio). 1537. *Summa Aurea.* Venetiis.
Lactantius. 1977. *Institutionies divinae.* Stuttgart.
León, F. J. de. 1620. *Decisiones Sacrae Regiae Audientia Valentinae.* Matriti.
López de Palacios Rubios, J. 1616. *Opera varia.* Antuerpiae: Apud Ioannem keerbergium.
Maino, I de. 1530. *In Primam Digesti Veteris Partem Commentaria.* Lugduni.
Maino, I de. 1545. *In Primam Digesti Veteris Partem Praelectiones.* Lugduni.
Matheu y Sanz, L. 1704. *Tractatus de regimine urbis et regini Valentiae.* Lyon.
Papiensis, B. *Summa Decretalium.* Ratisbonae.
Pedro Belluga. 1530. *Speculum Principum ac iustitiae.* Paris.
Placentinus. 1973. *Summa institutionum.* Ed. *Corpus Glossatorum Juris Civilis.*
Salón de Paz, M. 1568. *Ad leges Taurinas in signes comentarii ... .*
Sandeus, F. *Comentaria ad V Libros Decretalium Pars Prima.* Lugduni.
St Isidore, H. 1982. *Etymologiarum.* Madrid.
Thomas of Aquinas. 1588. *Summa theologiaea.* Romae.
Tranensius, G. 1519/1992. *Summa Super Titulis Decretalium.* Lyon/reed. Aalen.
Tudeschis, N. de. 1577. *Commentaria ad Quartum et Quintum Libros Decretalium.* Augustae Taurinorum.
Tudeschis, N de. 1586. *Commentaria Secundae Partis in Primum Decretalium Librum.* Lugduni.
Tudeschis, N de. 1605. *Commentaria Primae Partis in Primum Decretalium Librum.* Venetis.
Udalricus Zassius. 1550/1964. *Opera Omnia.* Lyon/reed. Aalen.

Chapter 3
Legal Concepts of Terrorism as Political Crime and International Criminal Law in Eighteenth and Nineteenth Century Europe

Karl Härter

The terrorist attacks of 9/11 seem to have strongly proven that terrorism constitutes a phenomenon of modernity and globalisation and is, by no means, comparable to other examples of political violence in history. Referring to a 'state of emergency' (*Ausnahmezustand*) many states enacted new counter-terrorism laws, resorted to numerous preventive and security measures and extended transnational prosecution. However, despite some exceptional reactions – the 'war on terrorism' and the application of military law and torture in Guantanamo, for example – the responses of the vast majority of concerned states have not transcended their respective legal systems. While existing legal provisions were altered and extended to a certain degree, with regard to prosecution and punishment, most states applied existing criminal law, especially those provisions concerning political crimes.[1]

Although there is an ongoing debate as to whether terrorism should be defined more thoroughly as a distinct crime within criminal law, up to the present day no generally accepted comprehensive legal definition of terrorism exists. As a result, violent terrorist acts, such as assassinations, bombings or kidnappings, are regularly dealt with from within existing criminal law provisions. However, in many countries, preparatory acts, as well as participation in 'terrorist' activities which are not directly part of a violent criminal act such as the distribution of terrorist propaganda, support of conspiracies (e.g. providing places of concealment, financing, money laundering, etc.) or the attendance of terrorist training camps, have been criminalised. The applicability of such regulations is often based on the concept of an organised terrorist group (association, alliance), legally defined, for instance, in

[1] Cf for example V. V. Ramraj, ed., *Global Anti-terrorism Law and Policy* (Cambridge: Cambridge University Press, 2005); P. A. Fernández Sánchez, ed., *International Legal Dimension of Terrorism* (Leiden: Martinus Nijhoff, 2009); M. Polaine, et al., *Counter-terrorism Law and Practice: An International Handbook* (Oxford: Oxford University Press, 2009).

K. Härter (✉)
Max-Planck-Institut für europäische Rechtsgeschichte,
Hausener Weg 120, 60489 Frankfurt am Main, Germany
e-mail: haerter@rg.mpg.de

A. Masferrer (ed.), *Post 9/11 and the State of Permanent Legal Emergency*,
Ius Gentium: Comparative Perspectives on Law and Justice 14,
DOI 10.1007/978-94-007-4062-4_3, © Springer Science+Business Media B.V. 2012

France as *association de malfaiteurs en relation avec une entreprise terroriste* or in Germany as *Terroristische Vereinigung*. These respective laws penalise the foundation, fellowship, support and promotion of such groups and distinguish (in particular, with regard to punishment) between leadership/ringleaders, members and supporters; only sometimes discrete terrorist groups are proscribed. Concerning criminal justice, some states like Germany, Italy or France have created special courts and modified legal procedures, especially with regard to investigative, pre-trial or incommunicado detention. Moreover, a plethora of additional laws has extended the power of police forces and condoned the use of various measures meant to counter and prevent terrorism, as is well-seen in public surveillance, eavesdropping and the control of communication/disclosure of information. In addition, an increasing number of international agreements, as well as some domestic laws, have enhanced transborder prosecution (via the European Arrest Warrant), extradition and mutual legal assistance, thus creating a considerably large body of soft law dealing with international terrorism.[2]

A close examination of such counter-terrorism laws and provisions reveals that despite the impact of 9/11, many of our 'modern' legal concepts and counter-terrorism measures are historically grounded in experiences with and past reactions to political violence and crime. In this regard, terrorism can hardly be described as a totally new phenomenon. Recent studies have traced manifestations and elements of modern terrorism as far back as to ancient times or at least to the early modern period,[3] starting the history of modern terrorism with the English gun powder plot of 1605[4] or, most often, with the French Revolution. Indeed, the term *terreur* was coined by the revolutionary French government to circumscribe the severe and violent measures of the state against the enemies of the nation and the constitution.[5] From the nineteenth century onward the terms 'terror' or 'terrorism' were occasionally used by authorities and governments to attribute political opposition and dissident groups, some of them who were involved in propagating or resorting to political violence.[6]

---

[2] See: C. Walker, *Terrorism and the Law* (Oxford: Oxford University Press, 2011); N. McGarrity, et al., eds., *Counter-terrorism and Beyond. The Culture of Law and Justice after 9/11* (London: Routledge, 2011); with regard to Germany: M. Volz, *Extraterritoriale Terrorismusbekämpfung* (Berlin: Duncker & Humblot, 2007); K. Wolny, *Die völkerrechtliche Kriminalisierung von modernen Akten des internationalen Terrorismus unter besonderer Berücksichtigung des Statuts des Internationalen Strafgerichtshofs* (Berlin: Duncker & Humblot, 2008).

[3] W. Laqueur, *A History of Terrorism, with a new Introduction by the Author* (New Brunswick: Transaction, 2008); G. Chaliand and A. Blin, eds., *The History of Terrorism. From Antiquity to al Qaeda* (Berkeley: University of California Press, 2007); D. Venner, *Histoire du terrorisme* (Paris: Pygmalion, Watelet, 2002).

[4] D. Onnekink, "“Gunpowder, treason and plot”. Aspecten van religieus en politiek fanatisme in vroegmodern Engeland," in *Terroristen en hun bestrijders vroeger en nu*, eds. I. Duyvesteyn and B. de Graaf (Amsterdam: Boom, 2007), 13–27.

[5] B. Lerat, *Le terrorisme révolutionnaire, 1789–1799* (Paris: Ed. France-Empire, 1989).

[6] R. Walther, "Terror, Terrorismus," in *Geschichtliche Grundbegriffe. Historisches Lexikon zur politisch-sozialen Sprache in Deutschland*, vol. 6, eds. O. Brunner et al. (Stuttgart: Klett-Cotta, 1990), 323–444.

For instance, in reaction to the Revolution of 1848, an order of the Prussian Ministry of Justice stated that the judicial officers did not show enough support in stemming 'terrorism' and should not hesitate to apply the criminal laws, particularly concerning crimes against the state.[7] A few years later the official comment to the Bavarian Criminal Code of 1861 pointed out that the prerequisite of high treason directed against the state could require 'terrorism' against the ruler, his family or the legislative.[8]

The historically varying uses of the terms 'terrorism' and 'terroristic' points to the problem of a working historical definition of terrorism that can encompass the different groups and actions linked to political violence.[9] Although historians have not agreed on a common historical definition of terrorism, most authors indicate that the following elements are essential for historical analysis:

- a discernible group/association, sometimes partially formed as a 'secret' or conspiratorial group, comprising leaders, a core group of activists and supporters;
- political motives, 'doctrine' and/or ideology that aims to induce a radical change to the established order and justifies the use of violence against the state or the ruling elite; for example, the ideologies of 'direct action', 'propaganda by deed' or the 'philosophy of the bomb';
- systematic violence as a political strategy and central method of operation, which includes planned and targeted acts of severe violence, like bombing, political murder, assassination or armed assaults, mostly directed against representatives of the 'system', the 'order' or the state; eventually, violence against indiscriminate 'masses' and 'innocent' thirds may be condoned to help reach their goals. In this regard, political violence is often conceived as a symbolic public act which helps to bring attention to the group's cause, as well as to cause ubiquitous fear – terror in its original sense – and provoke repressive responses from the authorities; and, finally;
- the symbolic and communicative dimension of violent political crimes, or acts of terrorism respectively, requires publicity in order to spread fear, destabilise or debunk the 'system', as well as mobilise supporters and induce a public debate on issues such as 'the order', 'the state', 'repression', etc.[10]

These elements have appeared across different historical periods and societies in varying constellations and could be used to ascribe a variety of different activists,

[7] *Deutsche Chronik für das Jahr 1848* (Berlin: Hayn, 1849), 177.

[8] M. Stenglein, *Commentar über das Strafgesetzbuch für das Königreich Bayern und das Gesetz über die Einführung* [...], vol. 2 (München: Kaiser, 1862), 5.

[9] See I. Duyvesteyn, "The Role of History and Continuity in Terrorism Research," in *Mapping Terrorism Research: State of the Art, Gaps and Future Direction*, ed. M. Ranstorp (London: Routledge, 2007), 56–57.

[10] See Laqueur, *History of Terrorism*, 3–20, 84; Chaliand and Blin, eds., *History of Terrorism*, 1–11; A. Merari, "Terrorism as a Strategy of Insurgency," in *History of Terrorism*, eds. Chaliand and Blin, 12–51; J. Dillinger, *Terrorismus* (Freiburg iB: Herder, 2008), 9–20.

groups and forms of political violence as 'terrorist'. As many violent political crimes in history were committed by single activists who did not belong to an organised group or who were only loosely connected to such groups, a historical analysis also has to include acts of individual terror. On the whole it seems difficult (or nearly impossible) to distinguish terrorism from other forms of political violence 'from below' during the nineteenth century or even in pre-modern times.[11] However, recent historical studies on political crime have bestowed significant consideration to terrorism as a crucial manifestation of violent oppositional political crime, especially if one takes into account the diverse responses of political and legal systems to such political violence and crime, sometimes attributed as 'terroristic'.[12] In following this view, this study comprehends terrorism as a historically variable concept of violent oppositional political crimes, which has been defined by various legal systems and was attributed to different manifestations of political dissidence, opposition and violence. This perspective allows terrorism to be studied by using the approaches of criminal justice history or the history of crime, such as the 'labelling approach', the 'process of criminalisation' and the 'process of juridification' (*Prozess der Verrechtlichung*) or 'social control'. Consequently, the following historical analysis does not deal with the political, social or cultural history of terrorist groups, their ideologies or their various activities[13] but rather focuses on legal responses to political violence within the concept of political crime.[14] Terrorism was (and is) not merely regarded as a conventional crime but situated and dealt with within the framework of political crime and its legal concepts: organised, secret criminal groups, associations or conspiracies, violent deeds, like assassinations or bombings, crimes against the state (*Staatsverbrechen*) and the maintenance of public/internal security.[15]

From the French Revolution onward, states and authorities have responded to various expressions of political dissidence and violence regarded as political (or even terrorist) crimes – which, through their aims to destabilise or create radical change, have presented a fundamental threat to order and security – with criminal justice,

---

[11] Laqueur, *History of Terrorism*, VIII.

[12] J. I. Ross, *The Dynamics of Political Crime* (Thousand Oaks: Sage, 2003), 62–77.

[13] For such an approach see: M. Burleigh, *Blood and Rage. A Cultural History of Terrorism* (London: HarperPress, 2010).

[14] See: B. L. Ingraham, *Political Crime in Europe. A Comparative Study of France, Germany, and England* (Berkeley: University of California Press, 1979); D. Blasius, *Geschichte der politischen Kriminalität in Deutschland (1800–1980). Eine Studie zu Justiz und Staatsverbrechen* (Frankfurt am Main: Surkamp, 1983); F. Colao, *Il delitto politico tra ottocento e novecento. Da "delitto fittizio" a "nemico dello Stato"* (Milano: Giuffrè, 1986).

[15] F.-C. Schroeder, *Der Schutz von Staat und Verfassung im Strafrecht* (München: Beck, 1970); J. Coleman, *Against the State. Studies in Sedition and Rebellion. Introduced by Brian Redhead* (London: BBC Books, 1990); Y.-M. Bercé and E. Fasano Guarini, eds., *Complots et conjurations dans l'Europe moderne* [...] (Rome: Publ. de l'École Française de Rome, Palais Farnèse, 1996); Ross, *Dynamics of Political Crime*; K. Härter, "Security and 'gute Policey' in Early Modern Europe: Concepts, Laws and Instruments," *Historical Social Research* 35 (2010): 41–65.

punishment, criminal law and preventative measures. Thus, political violence was used (as it has also been used in modern times) to assert a state of emergency (*Ausnahmezustand*) and to legitimise legal provisions in the field of political crime, internal security and prevention.[16] Consequently, the following analysis focuses on laws and legislation, juristic discourses, trials and punishment, as well as the numerous police activities only observed in relation to normative developments and concepts related to violent political crimes. While the main focus is on Central Europe, some examples are also drawn from the French legislation and the transnational level. The time span is limited to the long nineteenth century (1789–1914), the period which saw a significant development and proliferation of 'modern' legal concepts of political crime related to political violence. The many revolutions of the long nineteenth century were not only accompanied by various manifestations of violence or 'terror' used as a means to achieve further political goals, they also saw the exportation of revolutionary ideology and methods to other countries. The French Revolution of 1789 caused the first mass exodus of political fugitives, the noble *émigrés*, who established for the first time an organised political exile, and resorted to violence (even setting up an insurrection army) as a strategy and means to fight the revolution from abroad, thus creating a blueprint for cross-border political violence.[17]

Besides the various forms of politically motivated spontaneous mass violence and social upheaval, political dissidents, revolutionaries and radical activists used deliberate acts of violence to attack the representatives of the political order or 'system'.[18] In 1800 a bomb attack on Napoleon, with a so-called 'infernal machine', failed. In 1819 the student Karl Ludwig Sand, a member of a German oppositional student fraternity, killed the Russian consul and writer August von Kotzebue in a knife assault that was staged as a public and symbolic political act against a representative of the 'political system'. Since the first half of the nineteenth century such bomb attacks and symbolic attempts against representatives of the 'system' have gained a more important role and can be characterised as an emerging form of politically motivated 'terrorist' violence.[19]

---

[16] W. Hetzer, *Rechtsstaat oder Ausnahmezustand? Souveränität und Terror* (Berlin: Duncker & Humblot, 2008).

[17] See: *L' émigration politique en Europe aux XIXe et XXe siècles. Actes du colloque organisé per l'École Française de Rome* [...] (Rome: Ecole Francaise de Rome, 1991); K. Härter, "Asyl, Auslieferung und politisches Verbrechen in Europa während der "Sattelzeit": Modernität und Kontinuität im Strafrechtssystem," in *Dimensionen der Moderne. Festschrift für Christof Dipper*, eds. U. Schneider and L. Raphael (Frankfurt am Main: Lang, 2008), 481–502.

[18] For an overview see: W. J. Mommsen and G. Hirschfeld, eds. *Social Protest, Violence and Terror in 19th- and 20th-Century Europe* (London: Macmillan Press Ltd., 1982).

[19] See, for instance: I. Hernon, *Assassin! 200 Years of British Political Murder* (London: Pluto Press, 2007); C. Levy, "The Anarchist Assassin and Italian History, 1870s–1930s," in *Assassinations and Murder in Modern Italy. Transformations in Society and Culture*, eds. S. Gundle and L. Rinaldi (New York: Palgrave Macmillan, 2007), 207–221; F. L. Ford, *Political Murder. From Tyrannicide to Terrorism* (Cambridge, MA: Harvard University Press, 1985).

Moreover, many political dissidents and activists formed groups and organisations which often acted secretly and from foreign territory. The German opposition of the *Vormärz* (1819–1848), the arising workers' movement organisations, communist groups or national liberation movements formed secret associations, some of them propagating violence as a strategy of change. A few of these groups actually resorted to violent acts, including cross-border insurrections or the setting up of liberation armies. One of the first groups operating across borders was *Young Europe*. Founded in 1834 by the Italian refugee Mazzini in Berne, this group comprised activists from other countries and planned cross-border violent insurrections.[20]

Especially after the failed Revolutions of 1848/1849 some dissident groups and single revolutionaries gradually adopted the strategy of terrorist violence to destabilise the political system and to instigate revolutionary or political change. In 1849 the German refugee Karl Heinzen published an article (reprinted several times) in which he not only legitimised violent acts, like assassinations or bombings, against representatives of the 'old order', but suggested the use of weapons of mass destruction against the 'forces of repression'.[21] The strategy of terroristic political violence was also adopted by Russian dissident groups like the *Narodnaya Volya* (The *People's Will*) – one of the first 'modern' terrorist groups – and some national independence movements and nationalist-separatist groups, most notably in Ireland (*Irish Republican Brotherhood/Fenian Dynamiters*) and in the Balkan countries. Moreover, the flourishing anarchist groups that were spreading in France, Italy, Spain (*Mano Negra*) and Germany during the second half of the nineteenth century developed and adopted the so-called 'propaganda by deed' ideology.[22]

'Propaganda by deed' barely constituted a consistent terrorist ideology, but was put into practice by anarchist groups and single perpetrators of terrorist acts through several assassination attempts against representatives of the state (or the 'system') in different countries. The (largely successful) attempts against Kaiser Wilhelm (1878), Czar Alexander (1881), the French President Carnot (1894), the Spanish Prime Minister Canovas (1897), the Empress Elizabeth (1898) and the Austrian Archduke Ferdinand in 1914, are not only prime examples of political violence, but

---

[20] C. A. Bayly, and E. F. Biagini, eds., *Giuseppe Mazzini and the Globalisation of Democratic Nationalism 1830–1920* (Oxford: Oxford University Press, 2008).

[21] See the reprint: K. Heinzen, *Murder and Liberty (Printed for the first time in 1853 as a contribution for the "Peace-League" of Geneva)* (Indianapolis: H. Lieber, 1881); cf Laqueur, *History of Terrorism*, 26–27.

[22] For an overview see: I. Land, ed., *Enemies of Humanity: The Nineteenth-Century War on Terrorism* (New York: Palgrave Macmillan, 2008); A. V. Borcke, "Violence and Terror in Russian Revolutionary Populism: The Narodnaya Volya 1879–1883," in *Social protest, violence and terror*, eds. Mommsen and Hirschfeld, 48–62; W. L. Bernecker, "The Strategies of 'Direct Action' and Violence in Spanish Anarchism," in *ibidem*, 88–111; P. Alter, "Traditions of Violence in the Irish National Movement," in *ibidem*, 137–154; A. R. Carlson, "Anarchism and Individual Terror in the German Empire, 1870–1890," in *ibidem*, 175–200; U. Linse. "'Propaganda by Deed' and 'Direct Action': Two Concepts of Anarchist Violence," in *ibidem* at 201–229; furthermore: O. Hubac-Occhipinti, "Anarchist Terrorists of the Nineteenth Century," in *History of Terrorism*, eds. Chaliand and Blin, 113–131.

they were perceived by the authorities and the media as symbols of the growing international threat of terrorist acts. The 'terrorist' aspect of anarchism was amplified by the fact that some groups propagated and used bombings and dynamite regardless of the fact that persons other than the actual target would also suffer damages.[23] In comparison to modern terrorism, only a few innocent people were actually killed by such attempts, but, nonetheless, the violent action and propaganda of anarchists and other political radicals caused widespread fear of 'terrorist threats'. I do not suggest that all of these groups and their activities can be directly equated with modern terrorism or that a linear history of terrorism leading, at least, to 9/11 can be found. However, it is notable that the authorities regarded or labelled such groups and activities as violent political and sometimes 'terroristic' crimes, and responded with legal provisions and measures based on the assertion of a state of emergency caused by a 'terrorist' threat. Relevant examples are the Carlsbad Decrees, reacting to the assassination of Kotzebue, the laws from 1832/1833, responding to the July Revolution of 1830 and the *Wachensturm* of 1833, or the emergency laws which France and Germany enacted in 1878 and 1893/1894. After two assassination attempts against Emperor Wilhelm I in 1878 the German *Reichstag* passed the Anti-Socialist Law entitled 'Law against the hazardous attempts of the Social Democrats against public security' (*Gesetz gegen die gemeingefährlichen Bestrebungen der Sozialdemokratie)*[24] and, likewise, France enacted the *Lois Scélérate* in 1893 and 1894 in reaction to assassination and bombing attempts.[25]

These laws not only influenced the legal conceptualisation of political crime but also stimulated (or legitimised) the extension of police activities and preventative terrorism measures, as well as transnational penal prosecution with regards to extradition, mutual legal assistance and the granting of political asylum. However, many counter-terrorism measures were only gradually defined and controlled by law, and sometimes authorities used violent incidents and 'terrorist' threats as a mere pretext to extend surveillance, policing and the suppression of opposition and dissidence. In this respect, the ambivalent legal responses to the early terrorism threatened to impair the often fragile civil rights and constitutions that many European countries had – often reluctantly – established from the nineteenth century onward.

Though most European countries frequently applied their existing penal laws to political violence, some states responded with new (emergency) legislation or modified the existing legislation, arguing that such changes were necessary to fight or

---

[23] G. Chaliand and A. Blin, "The 'Golden Age' of Terrorism," in *History of Terrorism*, eds. Chaliand and Blin, 175–196; Laqueur, *History of Terrorism*, 11–16; Venner, *Histoire du Terrorisme*, 24–29.

[24] J. Wagner, *Politischer Terrorismus und Strafrecht im deutschen Kaiserreich von 1871* (Heidelberg et al., v. Decker, 1981); K. Felske, *Kriminelle und terroristische Vereinigungen – §§ 129, 129a StGB, Reformdiskussion und Gesetzgebung seit dem 19. Jahrhundert* (Baden-Baden: Nomos, 2002).

[25] G. Loubat, *Code de la législation contre les anarchistes. Contenant le commentaire de la Loi du 28 juillet 1894 ayant pour objet de réprimer les menées anarchistes suivi du commentaire des Lois du 12 décembre 1893 modifiant la loi sur la presse, du 18 décembre 1893 sur les associations de malfaiteurs, du 18 décembre 1893 sur la fabrication et la détention des explosifs* (Paris: Chevalier-Maresq, 1895).

prevent 'terrorism'. At the end of the Ancient Regime, the laws of most European countries offered a wide range of legal concepts which could be used to prevent, prosecute and punish (violent) political crimes, for example: lese majesty, (high) treason, conspiracy, rebellion, sedition, 'breach of peace' (*Landfriedensbruch*). Additional legal provisions aimed at prevention and control, such as the ability to prosecute individuals for speech and press crimes, censorship, prohibition of assembly, secret societies and the likes.[26] These provisions included, to a certain extent, the prosecution and punishment of preparatory acts and the planning of violent crimes, which, in fact, could be extended to such indictable deeds as 'imagining the king's death' and allowed for flexible, or even arbitrary, use.[27] Some German states had established a rough and inconsistent concept of crimes against the state. The Austrian code of 1787 and the Prussian code of 1794 defined them as 'voluntary acts of a citizen through which the state or its head are directly injured',[28] focusing on the state and the public order as prime objects of a politically motivated crime *and* legal protection. With regard to perpetrators, some laws and court practices used the concept of organised criminal groups with political motives, referring to 'secret societies' and conspiracies, which were often considered to involve foreign powers as instigators or masterminds of a plot or an assassination attempt.[29]

On the whole, however, the penal code of 1532 was still in force in the Holy Roman Empire of the German Nation and the *ius commune* comprised various political crimes, but hardly a systematic legal concept. All in all the penal law of most European countries did not provide a stringent, systematic legal definition of political crimes with regard to the deeds, the motives or the legally protected good. The French Revolution brought considerable change, not only coining the term 'terrorism' in the sense of 'state-terror', but also including a new legal definition of political crimes in the penal code and in related legal provisions. With the Constitution of 1793, the National Assembly declared its intention to grant political asylum to all enemies of tyranny (i.e. all dissidents committing a violent political crime and seeking refuge in France) and, subsequently, it established the principle that political crimes should be treated differently than conventional crimes. The privileging of political crimes, which implied political asylum and the non-extradition of political offenders, was adopted by many European states in the first half of the nineteenth century, thus helping to foster the transborder activities of political dissidents or

[26] See: Ingraham, *Political Crime*, 18–36; Coleman, *Against the State*; M. Sbriccoli, *Crimen laesae maiestatis. Il problema del reato politico alle soglie della scienza penalistica moderna* (Milano: Giuffrè, 1974); K. R. Minogue, "Treason and the Early Modern State: Scenes from a Mesalliance," in *Die Rolle der Juristen bei der Entstehung des modernen Staates*, ed. R. Schnur (Berlin: Duncker & Humblot, 1986), 421–435; L. Steffen, *Defining a British State. Treason and National Identity, 1608–1820* (Basingstoke: Palgrave, 2001); D. Cressy, *Dangerous Talk. Scandalous, Seditious, and Treasonable Speech in Pre-modern England* (Oxford: Oxford University Press, 2010).

[27] J. Barrell, *Imagining the King's Death. Figurative Treason, Fantasies of Regicide 1793–1796* (Oxford: Oxford University Press, 2000).

[28] Ingraham, *Political Crime*, 49.

[29] B. Coward, and J. Swann, eds., *Conspiracies and Conspiracy Theory in Early Modern Europe. From the Waldensians to the French Revolution* (Aldershot: Ashgate, 2004).

political exiles. Concerning the legal definition of political crimes, the French criminal codes from 1791 to 1795, and especially the Napoleonic penal code (1810), established for the first time a thorough and systematic concept of political crimes (crimes et délits contre la chose publique), which focused on the nation, the constitution and public security as the pivotal legally protected goods, and distinguished between internal and external politically motivated threats, and internal and external political crimes (*crimes et délits contre la sûreté extérieure de l'état, crimes contre la sûreté intérieure de l'état, crimes et délits contre les constitutions de l'Empire;* Art. 75–131), respectively.

While the code did not mention 'terrorism', it defined, nevertheless, substantial elements of the legal conceptualisation of political violence, many of which are still relevant in today's legal responses to terrorism. Concerning the different manifestations of violent political crimes, the code differentiated between systematic assaults (*attentat*) against the ruler as well as attempts (*attentat*) and plots (*complots*) to destroy or change the government, exciting civil wars and armed conflicts or "to carry devastation, massacre, and pillage into one or more communes" (*porter la dévastation, le massacre et le pillage dans une ou plusieurs communes*, Art. 91). With regard to such crimes, the code threatened severe (capital) punishment not only to perpetrators but extended the culpability of assassination attempts to preparatory acts and to the formation of a criminal group, defined as a conspiracy or complot constituted by at least two or more participants: *'Il y a complot dès que la résolution d'agir est concertée et arrêtée entre deux conspirateurs ou un plus grand nombre, quoiqu'il n'y ait pas eu d'attentat'* (Art. 89). Furthermore, the code criminalised propaganda, public speeches and the distribution of prints against the state as political crimes, which could foster or instigate political violence.[30]

Overall the French penal code of 1810 established the modern concept of political crimes as 'crimes against the state' and defined substantial elements for the further conceptualisation of violent political crimes and terrorism, enabling severe punishment as well as preventative measures, but also raising the issue of asylum and the extradition of political criminals (or 'terrorists'). The French penal code influenced nearly every European criminal code in the nineteenth century. Drawing on the French code, Germany and the German states gradually developed their conceptualisation of violent political crimes, often in reaction to actual incidents which were perceived (or labelled) as violent or terroristic threats.[31] The partial adoption of the French penal code into Germany's diverse legislation was paralleled by legal responses to political violence, and the spreading of revolutionary ideas, since the French Revolution also evoked legal responses to the cross-border revolutionary threat and the *expansion révolutionnaire*. In 1793 the Imperial Diet passed several imperial laws concerning the suppression of revolutionary ideas, censorship,

---

[30] *Code pénal* (Paris 1810); English translation: *The Penal Code of France, translated into English with a preliminary dissertation and notes* (London 1819, online: http://www.napoleon-series.org/research/government/c_code.html). Cf Ingraham, *Political Crime*, 63–84.

[31] C. Brandt, *Die Entstehung des Code pénal von 1810 und sein Einfluß auf die Strafgesetzgebung der deutschen Partikularstaaten des 19. Jahrhunderts am Beispiel Bayerns und Preußens* (Frankfurt am Main: Lang, 2002).

emissaries, speeches, gatherings, symbols, secret societies, student associations, social upheaval and the criminalisation of dissident groups – the so-called German Jacobins. Moreover, several German states issued their own laws establishing or intensifying preventative measures concerning revolutionary activities, criminalising them as political crimes (especially as high treason) aimed at the state or intending to invoke change of the political order.[32]

After the foundation of the German Confederation, the Federation Act of 1815 (*Bundesakte*) declared the maintenance of internal and external security as the Federation's main purpose. Nevertheless, the German states could not agree on a mutual penal code. In the following years, only a few states issued their own criminal codes, which, like the Bavarian criminal code of 1813 and the Prussian criminal code of 1851, often adopted elements of the French penal code.[33] Once more, it took a violent incident to evoke new legal responses to political crime: the assassination of August von Kotzebue by the student Carl Sand in 1819, which bore similarities to a 'terroristic' suicide assassination. Sand murdered Kotzebue as a representative of the 'system', and shortly afterwards he tried to commit suicide in public, handing over a prepared piece of writing to a bystander beforehand. This incident, along with a second assassination attempt in the same year, helped Metternich to attain the Carlsbad Decrees, four laws enacted by the Diet of the German Confederation. There is no doubt that Metternich used these assassinations as a pretext for the intensification of repression; beyond that, the deeds also evoked broad media response and caused a vague public fear of political violence. The Carlsbad Decrees were built on the provisions of 1793 and renewed or extended the control of the press and universities, prohibited student-associations and fraternities (*Burschenschaften*) and established an extraordinary investigative commission (*Central-Untersuchungs-Commission*) which conducted 'a joint investigation, as thorough and extensive as possible, of the facts relating to the origin and manifold ramifications of the revolutionary plots and demagogical associations directed against the existing constitution and the internal peace both of the union and of the individual states; of the existence of which plots more or less clear evidence is to be had already, or may be produced in the course of the investigation'.[34]

---

[32] Ingraham, *Political Crime*, 85–87; K. Härter, *Reichstag und Revolution 1789–1806. Die Auseinandersetzung des Immerwährenden Reichstags zu Regensburg mit den Auswirkungen der Französischen Revolution auf das Alte Reich* (Göttingen: Vandenhoeck & Ruprecht, 1992), 287–377.

[33] K. Härter, "Die Entwicklung des Strafrechts in Mitteleuropa 1770–1848: Defensive Modernisierung, Kontinuitäten und Wandel der Rahmenbedingungen," in *Verbrechen im Blick. Perspektiven der neuzeitlichen Kriminalitätsgeschichte*, eds. R. Habermas and G. Schwerhoff (Frankfurt aM/New York: Campus, 2009), 71–107; D. Klippel, "Legal Reforms: Changing the Law in Germany in the Ancien Régime and in the Vormärz," in *Great Britain and Germany 1750–1850*, eds. T. C. W. Blanning and P. Wende, 43–59 (Oxford: Oxford University Press, 1999).

[34] E. Huber, ed., *Dokumente zur deutschen Verfassungsgeschichte, Bd. 1: Deutsche Verfassungsdokumente 1803–1850* (Stuttgart: Kohlhammer, 1961), 90–95, 105–107; English translation: J. H. Robinson, ed., *Readings in European History*, vol. 2 (Boston: Ginn, 1906), 547–550. http://history.hanover.edu/texts/carlsbad.html, online: [10.06.2011]; also see: E. Weber, *Die Mainzer Zentraluntersuchungskommission* (Karlsruhe, C.F. Müller, 1970).

Consequently, the first legal responses to political crime and individual terrorist acts in the German Confederation aimed primarily at surveillance, suppression and policing, especially via the establishment of a political police agency which was tasked with collecting and distributing information on suspect groups or the planning of political crimes.[35] The use of such information, as well as actual prosecution and punishment, was left to the single states, which relied mainly on their own criminal law that still contained traditional elements, particularly the harsh punishment of lese majesty and/or high treason.

Once again, incidents which were considered to be revolutionary threats and violent political crimes – for example, the July Revolution of 1830, the *Hambacher Fest* of 1832 and the storming of the Frankfurt guardhouse in 1833 (*Fran kfurter Wachenstum*) – triggered legal responses anew, which further developed criminal law concerning political crimes and their prevention. In 1832, 1833 and 1836 the Federal Diet enacted several emergency laws that dealt with preventative measures, such as surveillance, censorship and the prohibition of public assemblies or speeches. To some extent the laws adopted elements from the French penal code and for the first time extended the scope of prosecution to transborder provisions.[36] The ten Articles of 1832 determined the general prohibition of all associations with a political purpose, threatening punishment to the initiators as well as to the participants (Art. 2). Beyond the actual perpetration of a political crime, Article 6 also criminalised participation in seditious activities and plans (*Theilnahme an aufwieglerischen Planen*) through public speeches, writings or other acts (*Reden, Schriften oder Handlungen*) and prescribed the transborder prosecution of all secret associations, conspiracies and involved individuals threatening the security of the state (*staatsgefährlicher geheimer Verbindungen und der darin verflochtenen Individuen*). This included the surveillance of all suspect foreigners or German citizens operating in other countries who tried to enter the German Confederation in order to plan or commit political offences or crimes. To ensure transborder prosecution and punishment, the ten Articles obliged all German states to extradite refugees, suspects and political criminals or to punish their nationals themselves. The federal law of 1833 (*Bundesbeschluß wegen eines gegen den Bestand des Deutschen Bundes und die öffentliche Ordnung in Deutschland gerichteten Complotts*) renewed the political police and assigned the Federal Central Agency to the task of investigating and

[35] H. Liang, *The Rise of Modern Police and the European State System from Metternich to the Second World War* (Cambridge: Cambridge University Press, 1992); W. Siemann, '*Deutschlands Ruhe, Sicherheit und Ordnung*'. *Die Anfänge der politischen Polizei 1806–1866* (Tübingen: Niemeyer, 1985); C. Emsley, "Political Police and the European Nation State in the Nineteenth Century," in *The Policing of Politics in the Twentieth Century: Historical Perspectives*, ed. M. Mazower (Providence: Berghahn, 1997), 1–25.

[36] 'Sechs Artikel' 28.6.1832, 'Zehn Artikel' 5.7.1832, 'Bundesbeschluß wegen eines gegen den Bestand des Deutschen Bundes und die öffentliche Ordung in Deutschland gerichteten Komplotts' 30.6.1833, 'Bundesbeschluß über Bestrafung von Vergehen gegen den Deutschen Bund und Auslieferung politischer Verbrecher auf deutschem Bundesgebiete' 18.8.1836 in Huber, ed., *Dokumente, vol. 1* and online: http://www.verfassungen.de/de/de06-66/bundesbeschluss24.htm [05.06.2011].

collecting all relevant information (also using court files) on seditious plots, conspiracies or associations, including initiators, participants and/or supporters, and to initiate prosecution or criminal proceedings. In 1836 a further law (*Bundesbeschluß über Bestrafung von Vergehen gegen den Deutschen Bund und Auslieferung politischer Verbrecher auf deutschem Bundesgebiete*) penalised every act against the existence, integrity, security or constitution of the German Confederation as an act of high treason and renewed the obligation to extradite every individual suspect of instigating, committing or supporting such crimes or being a member of a group involved in such deeds.

The federal laws of 1832, 1833 and 1836 covered crucial legal issues of violent political crimes adopting, on the one hand, several provisions of the French penal code, but reacting, on the other hand, to political developments and actual incidents which the German Confederation (or its states) perceived as fundamental threats to the political order. Though the single states of the Federation had to individually enforce the laws, they gained importance for the surveillance of dissident groups and the prosecution of political crimes. The Federal Central Agency accumulated a vast body of information and was involved in more than 2,100 state trials concerning political crimes, many of them conducted by non-public special courts and commissions using inquisitorial procedures against citizens from nearly all social classes.[37] In this regard, the legal response of the German Federation to political violence – which can be characterised as emergency legislation – initiated and legitimised widespread political policing, surveillance and prosecution, implying a significant constraint on liberal rights and the emerging *Rechtsstaat*.

After the failed Revolution of 1848/1849 some provisions of the federal laws were partially adopted by the newly enacted criminal codes of some states such as Prussia or Bavaria, the latter comprised a section on high treason (Art. 101) which not only proscribed the use of violence in general but also 'terrorism as a threat' (*als Drohung wirkender Terrorismus*).[38] The Prussian code of 1851 – strongly influenced by the French penal code – extensively dealt with political crimes and crimes against the state, ranging from high treason and lese majesty to riots and seditious offenses like speech and press crimes. Of particular importance was the legal definition of anticipatory crimes, preparatory acts, attempts and conspiracy, i.e. criminal association with regards to participation and support.[39]

---

[37] [F. M. von Wagemann], *Darlegung der Haupt-Resultate aus den wegen der revolutionären Complotte der neueren Zeit in Deutschland geführten Untersuchungen: auf den Zeitabschnitt mit Ende Juli 1838* (Frankfurt am Main: Bundes-Präsidial-Druckerei, 1839); L. F. Ilse, *Geschichte der politischen Untersuchungen, welche durch die neben der Bundesversammlung errichteten Commissionen, der Central-Untersuchungs-Commission zu Mainz und der Bundes-Central-Behörde zu Frankfurt in den Jahren 1819 bis 1827 und 1833 bis 1842 geführt sind* (Frankfurt am Main: Meidinger, 1860). Cf W. Siemann, "Der Vorrang der Staatspolizei vor der Justiz," in *Akten des 26. Deutschen Rechtshistorikertages* [...], ed. D. Simon (Frankfurt am Main: Klostermann, 1987), 197–209.

[38] Stenglein, *Strafgesetzbuch*, 164.

[39] *Strafgesetzbuch für die Preußischen Staaten* (Berlin 1851, new edition 1856), §§ 61–210.

The German Penal Code of 1871 (*Reichsstrafgesetzbuch 1871*) adopted nearly all sections of the Prussian Code concerning political crimes (§§ 80–145) and confirmed the legal definition of elements such as the criminal association, preparatory acts and preventative provisions. The section on political crimes started with Articles (§§ 80, 81) on political murder, assassination, violent attempts to change the constitution (i.e. revolt/revolution) and high treason. The subsequent sections (§§ 82–86) not only criminalised the actual 'undertaking' (*Unternehmung*), including 'attempt' (*Versuch*) and 'completion' (*Vollendung*) of such acts of political violence, but separately penalised the preparation and conspiracy remote from the actual undertaking, as well as all public instigation of treasonable violent crimes through speech, press, placards, etc. ('*öffentlich vor einer Menschenmenge, oder wer durch Verbreitung oder öffentlichen Anschlag oder öffentliche Ausstellung von Schriften oder anderen Darstellungen zur Ausführung einer nach §. 82. strafbaren Handlung auffordert*'); such acts were threatened with severe penal servitude (*Zuchthaus*) of no less than 5 years. Within the category of political offenses (§§ 125–131) the code even broadened the more traditional concept of 'conspiracy' and transformed it into the modern concept of the 'criminal association', thereby criminalising participation in secret societies (*geheime Verbindung*) or associations acting against the state, the administration or the law enforcement (*gesetzwidrige Vereinigung*), as well as penalising the formation of and/or participation in armed groups or crowds. Furthermore, the code proscribed public assemblies, violent crowds and riots – differentiating between ringleaders/instigators and followers/seduced – and penalised the public threat of hazardous crimes (*Androhung eines gemeingefährlichen Verbrechens*). Finally, in section 139 the code proscribed an obligation of disclosure and threatened punishment to anyone who had credible knowledge of the planning of a treasonable crime but refrained from informing the authorities, the police or the targeted person at a time in which the prevention of the felony would have been possible.[40]

The German Penal Code conceptualised substantial elements of legal responses to political violence and terrorism – the criminal association, the preparatory acts, the propaganda/public activities – but from the perspective of the German government (and Bismarck) it lacked provisions allowing for a wider range of preventative measures, surveillance and policing, especially with regards to the growing labour movement and the communist and socialist parties.[41] Two assassination attempts on Emperor Wilhelm I in 1878 (the latter harming him seriously) gave Bismarck the occasion to introduce the Anti-Socialist Law (*Gesetz gegen die gemeingefährlichen*

[40] "Strafgesetzbuch für das Deutsche Reich 1871," *Deutsches Reichsgesetzblatt* 24 (1871), 127–205. English version: G. Drage, *The Criminal Code of the German Empire. Translation with prolegomena and a Commentary by Geoffrey Drage* (London: Chapman and Hall, 1885, reprint: Clark, NJ: Lawbook Exchange, 2005). Cf Ingraham, *Political Crime*, 187–193; and in general S. Kesper-Biermann, *Einheit und Recht. Strafgesetzgebung und Kriminalrechtsexperten in Deutschland vom Beginn des 19. Jahrhunderts bis zum Reichsstrafgesetzbuch von 1871* (Frankfurt am Main: Klostermann, 2009).

[41] Cf Wagner, *Politischer Terrorismus*, 327; Felske, *Kriminelle und terroristische Vereinigungen*, 79–86.

Bestrebungen der Sozialdemokratie), which was legitimised and designed as a temporary emergency law. Bismarck – like Metternich before him – used the assassination attempts as a pretext to 'persuade' the *Reichstag* to enact the law, aiming to repress the socialist political party. However, it is also possible to interpret them as a legal response to political violence and terrorism, because both attempts were committed by two radicals (Hödel and Nobling, neither of whom belonged to any socialist party) as individual acts of terror and they caused a somewhat indefinite fear, not at least through the intense media coverage. Not only Bismarck, but also a majority of the *Reichstag* and a considerable portion of the public suspected the activities of socialists to be a breeding ground for revolution and political violence. Thus, the constraints on socialist speech, writings, press, gatherings, etc., was thought to be an effective measure to prevent political violence and the use of the public for purposes of radical or even 'terrorist' propaganda. As one member of the *Reichstag* put it: 'The abolishment of the press and the assemblies [of the socialists] meant, in effect, the abolishment of terrorism' (*eine Beseitigung der Presse und der Versammlungen bedeutet vor allem die Beseitigung des Terrorismus*).[42]

The main purpose of the Anti-Socialist Law was the suppression of the Socialist Democratic Party through the prohibition of all groups 'which aim at the overthrow of the existing order of government or society by social democratic, socialist, or communist efforts', and the extension of surveillance and policing – especially concerning the extended responsibilities of the police to ban meetings, associations, press and printings. However, the purview of the law reached even further. It could be characterised, in fact, as *polizeiliches Ausnahmegesetz*: an emergency law covering the interface between criminal and police law, allowing the extension of preventative measures, surveillance and policing, as well as criminalising new offences affiliated with political violence.[43] Though the law was rigorously enforced against the Social Democrat Party and was accompanied by a noticeable restriction on liberal rights, it failed to diminish the influence of the Social Democrats and eliminate them as a political power. The law was, however, more successful in stemming political radicalism – especially the growing anarchist movement. For a number of years, the law's provisions worked as a legal response to political terrorism and legitimised the extension of surveillance and the activities of the political police.[44]

Although the anarchist movement in Germany on a whole never gained menacing dimensions,[45] a few bomb attempts in the 1880s caused general fear of violent

[42] Cit. Wagner, *Politischer Terrorismus*, 357; cf Ingraham, *Political Crime*, 196–199; C. Dietze, 'Terrorismus im 19. Jahrhundert: Politische Attentate, rechtliche Reaktionen, Polizeistrategien und öffentlicher Diskurs in Europa und den Vereinigten Staaten 1878–1901' in *Politische Kriminalität, Recht, Justiz und Polizei zwischen Früher Neuzeit und 20. Jahrhundert*, ed. K. Härter and B. de Graaf (Frankfurt am Main: Klostermann, 2012), 179–196.

[43] Wagner, *Politischer Terrorismus*, 357–359.

[44] See Wagner, *Politischer Terrorismus*, 376–378; Blasius, *Kriminalität*, 55–66; Emsley, "Political Police", 17; Carlson, "Anarchism and Individual Terror", 175–200.

[45] A. R. Carlson, *Anarchism in Germany. Vol. 1: The early movement* (Metuchen: Scarecrow Press, 1972).

terrorist attacks and triggered new legal responses. Adhering to the ideologies of 'direct action' and 'propaganda by deed', a small German anarchist group planned violent bomb assaults using dynamite 'to kill as many as possible'.[46] An explosion in a Frankfurt police station and several bombings in Elberfeld in 1883 caused only minor damages but alarmed the government and the public. In 1884 a bomb attempt on Wilhelm I at the dedication of the Niederwald monument failed, but the incident and the subsequent trial caused enormous media hype and fuelled fear of anarchist/terrorist violence. Bismarck and the government used the bomb attempts and the public fear to prompt the *Reichstag* to prolong the Anti-Socialist Law, claiming that the anarchist threat had produced a state of emergency.[47]

In addition, the *Reichstag* passed a new Dynamite Law modelled on the English *Explosive Substance Act* (1883). This law criminalised the possession, distribution and actual use of explosives with regard to criminal intents or activities, aiming clearly at political crimes in general and the anarchists in particular. Since the intended killing of persons with explosives not only implied the death penalty (§ 5), but also participation in a conspiracy, the planning of crimes with explosives was penalised with penal servitude of no less than 5 years, regardless of whether or not the deed was actually committed (§ 6). Likewise, the law penalised any public statement inciting or seducing somebody to commit or participate in such crimes; merely praising or depicting such acts as laudable deeds was prosecutable (§ 10). Finally, the law proscribed an obligation of disclosure, threatening punishment to anyone who chose not to inform the authorities or the police if they had credible knowledge of such crimes.[48] Insofar, the *Sprengstoffgesetz* responded to two elements of terrorism: the use of explosives and bombing as a form of targeted as well as random violence and the propaganda of political violence, be it for the purpose of legitimising the deeds or spreading fear.

Whether the *Sprengstoffgesetz* actually prevented new bomb attempts may be disputable, but it was used to extend surveillance and the activities of the police against the social democrats and labour organisations, and it helped to nourish the fear of a permanent terrorist threat. Though Bismarck had used agent provocateurs and double agents to 'stimulate' the anarchist movement, in the 1880s and 1890s the wave of assassination attempts and violent assaults in other European countries seemed to assert that the terrorist menace was more dangerous than ever, especially with regards to cross-border activities and organisational structures. Violent political crime and anarchism in particular emerged as a prototype of international crime and the first manifestation of international terrorism – or it was perceived as such.[49]

The German government responded again in 1894/1895 – nearly in parallel to the French *Lois Scélérate* 1893/1894 – with a new legislation called the Overthrow Bill

---

[46] Carlson, "Anarchism and Individual Terror", 190.

[47] Wagner, *Politischer Terrorismus*, 369–376; Carlson, "Anarchism and Individual Terror", 189–191.

[48] "Gesetz gegen den verbrecherischen und gemeingefährlichen Gebrauch von Sprengstoffen, 9. Juni 1884," *Deutsches Reichsgesetzblatt*, 17 (1884), 61–64; cf Wagner, *Politischer Terrorismus*, 378–389.

[49] P. Knepper, *The Invention of International Crime. A Global Issue in the Making, 1881–1914* (London: Palgrave Macmillan, 2010), 128–158; cf Hubac-Occhipinti, "Anarchist Terrorists"; Chaliand and Blin, "The 'Golden Age' of Terrorism"; Blasius, *Geschichte*, 67.

(*Umsturzvorlage*). This Bill was designed to modify the section of the penal code that dealt with political crimes and crimes against the state. The rational behind the Bill was the alleged transnational threat of anarchism as well as the growing amount of anarchist and socialist propaganda, which was thought to foster political violence, endanger the state, seduce the people and spread hate and fear. The provisions extended the penalisation of public activities (press, writings, speeches, assemblies, etc.) with regards to the instigation of criminal acts, the incitement of the people (*Volksverhetzung*), insults against the state and its representatives and the 'justification' and 'praise' of political crimes. Furthermore, the concept of 'criminal association' was extended to all conspiracies or organisations attempting (or propagating) an 'overthrow' (*Umsturz*), extending the punishment to 15 years of penal servitude (*Zuchthaus*). The Bill was not only aimed at international anarchism and terrorism, it also was conceived to substitute the already expired Anti-Socialist Law. On the whole, the provisions of the Bill restricted several civil liberties – especially freedom of speech and press – and caused controversial public reactions as well as controversy within the *Reichstag*, as many politicians and parties expressed their apprehensions and objections to its provisions. In the end the Bill failed to pass; the majority was not willing to conjoin the suppression of the social democrats with counter-terrorism legislation that would substantially impair civil rights and the *Rechtsstaat*.[50]

In this regard the German *Rechtsstaat* seemed to prevail against the government's demands to further restrict liberal rights in favour of counter-terrorism. Nevertheless, on the transnational level the threat of political violence and transnational anarchism had evoked legal responses which affected a principle established during the French Revolution: the political asylum and the non-extradition of fugitives (or political criminals from the perspective of the prosecuting state). [51] In 1856 Belgium responded to the failed assassination attempt against Napoleon III with the Belgian *attentat* or assassination clause (*Attentatsklausel*). This legal provision exempted refugees from the privilege of non-extradition and restricted the granting of political asylum if they had murdered or attempted an assassination upon the life of a ruler or his family (and later other state officials). This principle was adopted in many extradition treaties, as well as by several national penal codes, which, in some cases, extended the restriction of asylum and non-extradition to all murderous/terrorist political crimes committed, and this especially applied to criminals suspected to be members of cross-border operating groups like the anarchists. In September 1892 the Institute of International Law adopted a resolution which condensed these developments and recommended that 'extradition be inadmissible for purely political crimes or offenses', especially if they are connected with unlawful acts like 'murder, manslaughter, poisoning, mutilation […], explosion or flooding'. Moreover, the resolution excluded 'criminal acts directed against the bases of all social organisation,

[50] Cf Felske, *Kriminelle und terroristische Vereinigungen*, 87–112; Wagner, *Politischer Terrorismus*, 389–394.

[51] K. Härter, "'Die Formierung transnationaler Strafrechtsregime: Auslieferung, Asyl und grenzübergreifende Kriminalität im Übergang von gemeinem Recht zum nationalstaatlichen Strafrecht," *Rechtsgeschichte* 18 (2011), 36–65.

and not only against a certain State or a certain form of government' from the privileged political offenses, aiming at anarchist (or terrorist) violence.[52]

The anarchist-clause (*Anarchistenklausel*) and the attentat clause were further developed by the first International Anti-Anarchist Conference (*International Conference of Rome for the Social Defence Against Anarchists*), held shortly after the assassination of Empress Elisabeth of Austria (by the Italian anarchist Luigi Lucheni on 10 September 1898 in Geneva, Switzerland) in November and December in Rome. The secret meeting of police officers and state officials discussed legal responses to anarchism and violent crimes as well as appropriate police measures and referred to the resolution of the Institute of International Law by defining anarchism as any act 'having as its aim the destruction, through violent means, of all social organization.' With regards to asylum and extradition, the conference also referred to the attentat clause and approved the extradition of persons who had attempted to kill or kidnap a sovereign, head of state or state official. The further resolutions of the conference concerned legal provisions on the possession, distribution and use of explosives, the distribution of propaganda and the support of anarchist groups and violent acts, as well as several proposals on transnational police co-operation, the exchange of relevant information and the tracing of political criminals via the *portrait parlé*, a complex method of identification.[53]

Besides the question of the actual enforcement and effectiveness of the international discussions, the resolutions and recommendations clearly influenced the legal responses to political violence up to the League of Nations Convention for the Prevention and Punishment of Terrorism (1937), which was never put into force, but defined terrorism for the first time in international law as 'criminal acts directed against a State and intended or calculated to create a state of terror in the minds of particular persons or a group of persons or the general public'.[54]

In summary, we can conclude that Germany and many European countries developed substantial legal elements and concepts in response to political violence over the course of the long nineteenth century, which, in the long run, gained importance for the legal conceptualisation of 'terrorism' and the implementation of legally based counter-terrorism measures; namely legal provisions that concern:

- the conceptualisation of the 'terrorist' group,
- the planning and commission of violent crimes and the methods of operation,
- the communicative/public dimensions and preventative measures, and
- the restriction of asylum and extradition.

[52] J. B. Scott, ed., *Resolutions of the Institute of International Law Dealing with the Law of Nations: With an Historical Introduction and Explanatory Notes* (New York: Oxford University Press, 1916), 103; cf R. Bach Jensen, "The International Campaign Against Anarchist Terrorism, 1880–1930s," *Terrorism and Political Violence* 21 (2009): 89–109; Härter, "Formierung," 60–61.

[53] Cit. M. Deflem, "'Wild Beasts Without Nationality': The Uncertain Origins of Interpol, 1898–1910," in *The Handbook of Transnational Crime and Justice,* ed. Ph. Reichel, 275–285 (Thousand Oaks: Sage Publications, 2005), 278; cf R. Bach Jensen, "The International Anti-Anarchist Conference of 1898 and the Origins of Interpol," *Journal of Contemporary History* 16 (1981): 323–347; Bach Jensen, "International Campaign".

[54] Convention for the Prevention and Punishment of Terrorism, 19 League of Nations O.J. 23 (1938), League of Nations Doc. C.546(I).M.383(I).1937.V (1938) (16 November 1937).

Concerning the conceptualisation of the 'terrorist' group, Germany, France and Italy established the 'criminal association': *staatsfeindliche/staatsgefährdende Verbindung* and *geheime Verbindung, le association de malfaiteurs, l'assiciazione per delinquere*. The Italian *Codice Zanardelli* (1889) added *l'assiciazione per delinquere* to the codified political crimes and in 1894 a new emergency legislation criminalised 'subversive' associations/parties or writings as political crimes allowing for massive prosecution which involved not only anarchists but socialists as well.[55] Among the French *Lois Scélérate* was the *lois du 18 décembre 1893 sur les associations de malfaiteurs*, which integrated and broadened the concept of the criminal association in the penal code as a crime *'contre la paix publique'*, i.e. as a political crime committed by a dissident group.[56] The criminalisation of such groups differentiated between instigators/leaders (ringleaders), members and supporters, also penalising the mere participation/membership/support of such groups – remote from the actual completion of a violent crime – and empowered the authorities (especially the police) to take pre-emptive action. This concept prevailed and is still used with regard to 'modern terrorism'. For instance, the French law of July 22, 1996 specified in the current penal code the *'association de malfaiteurs en relation avec une entreprise terroriste'* (criminal association in relation to a terrorist undertaking), and in 1976 the German legislation modified the criminal association (*kriminelle Vereinigung, Strafgesetzbuch 1951*), implementing the *terroristische Vereinigung* (terrorist association), which was largely based on the previous legal concept of the *staatsfeindliche Verbindung* (subversive association) and the *Geheimverbindung* (conspiracy).[57]

Concerning the methods of operation and the commission of the criminal act the legislation of the nineteenth century criminalised not only attempt and completion, but also the conspiracy, planning and support of violent political crimes, notably using the concepts of the preparatory act and the participation in concomitant activities (propaganda, support etc.). In addition, many countries reacted to bombing attempts – regarded or labelled as a true terrorist method of operation – and enacted laws proscribing and regulating the possession, distribution and use of explosives, as seen in Britain (1883), Germany (1884), Austria (1885), Belgium (1886) and Switzerland (1894). They threatened not only heavy penalties, but aimed at preventative control and penalised public statements/activities that legitimised bombing attempts or used them as a menace to spread fear. To curb the 'propaganda by deed' and the 'philosophy of the bomb' ideologies, many countries enacted more specific laws penalising public support for anarchism and the incitement to commit violent political crimes.[58]

---

[55] R. Minna, *Crimini associati, norme penali e politica del diritto. Aspetti storici, culturali, evoluzione normativa* (Milano: Giuffrè, 2007), 37–39; Levy, "Anarchist Assassin", 209–210.

[56] Loubat, *Code de la législation contre les anarchistes*, 177–179; P. Truche, *L' anarchiste et son juge. A propos de l'assassinat de Sadi Carnot* (Paris: Fayard, 1994), 70–73.

[57] Felske, *Kriminelle und terroristische Vereinigungen*; J. Grässle-Münscher, *Kriminelle Vereinigung. Von den Burschenschaften bis zur RAF* (Hamburg: Europäische Verlagsanstalt, 1991).

[58] Cf Bach Jensen, "International Campaign".

Since the French Revolution, the control and criminalisation of propaganda, public support/activities, assemblies, speeches, writings, press or incitement associated with political violence and anarchism constituted a main field of legislative activities. Although the German governments responded to violent or 'terrorist' activities regarded as an actual threat and arousing widespread ubiquitous fear, they also used violent incidents as a pretext to claim a state of emergency and to enact emergency laws, as seen in the case of the Anti-Socialist Law. Similar patterns can be observed in other European countries like France (the *Lois Scélérate)*. Moreover, the cross-border activities of dissidents and the 'international anarchist conspiracy' were perceived (or imagined) to be a transnational political violence threat evoking legal responses on a transnational level. They ranged from police co-operation to the extension of extradition and the restriction of asylum via the soft law of transnational treaties and agreements, implying the formation of transnational prosecution regimes and a further constraint of civil liberties.

International soft law and emergency legislation constituted the main pattern of legal responses to political violence in nineteenth century Europe and influenced the criminal law and the penal codes. The legal conceptualisation of political crimes incorporated substantial elements of the legal responses to political violence and 'terrorism' concerning the 'criminal association', preparatory acts, anticipatory crimes (*Vorverlagerung der Strafbarkeit*) and the control of the public, the extention of penalisation and prevention. Consequently, this facilitated and legitimised extending surveillance, policing and the suppression of oppositional groups, dissidents and, in particular, organisations or parties of the labour movement, which the authorities could label and criminalise as the breeding grounds of political violence or even as 'terroristic'. Thus, a historical analysis of the legal responses to political violence in nineteenth century Europe demonstrates that the legal conceptualisation of terrorism as a political crime could implicate the extension of 'social control' and the constraint of civil rights.

References (Bibliography)

Alter, P. 1982. Traditions of violence in the Irish national movement. In *Social protest, violence and terror*, eds. W. Mommsen and G. Hirschfeld, 137–154. New York: St. Martin's.

Bach Jensen, R. 1981. The international anti-anarchist conference of 1898 and the origins of interpol. *Journal of Contemporary History* 16: 323–347.

Bach Jensen, R. 2009. The international campaign against anarchist terrorism, 1880–1930s'. *Terrorism and Political Violence* 21: 89–109.

Barrell, J. 2000. *Imagining the king's death. Figurative treason, fantasies of regicide 1793–1796.* Oxford: Oxford University Press.

Bayly, C.A., and E.F. Biagini (eds.). 2008. *Giuseppe Mazzini and the globalisation of democratic nationalism 1830–1920.* Oxford: Oxford University Press.

Bercé, Y.-M., and E. Fasano Guarini (eds.). 1996. *Complots et conjurations dans l'Europe moderne [...].* Rome: de l'École Française de Rome, Palais Farnèse.

Bernecker, W.L. 1982. The strategies of 'Direct Action' and violence in Spanish anarchism. In *Social protest, violence and terror*, ed. W. Mommsen and G. Hirschfeld, 88–111. New York: St. Martin's.

Blasius, D. 1983. *Geschichte der politischen Kriminalität in Deutschland (1800–1980). Eine Studie zu Justiz und Staatsverbrechen*. Frankfurt am Main: Suhrkamp.

Borcke, A.V. 1982. Violence and terror in Russian revolutionary populism: The Narodnaya Volya 1879–1883. In *Social protest, violence and terror*, ed. W. Mommsen and G. Hirschfeld, 48–62. New York: St. Martin's.

Brandt, C. 2002. *Die Entstehung des Code pénal von 1810 und sein Einfluß auf die Strafgesetzgebung der deutschen Partikularstaaten des 19. Jahrhunderts am Beispiel Bayerns und Preußens*. Frankfurt am Main: Lang.

Burleigh, M. 2010. *Blood and Rage. A cultural history of terrorism*. London: HarperPress.

Carlson, A.R. 1972. *Anarchism in Germany*, vol. 1, *The early movement*. Metuchen: Scarecrow Press.

Carlson, A.R. 1982. Anarchism and individual terror in the German empire, 1870–1890. In *Social protest, violence and terror*, ed. W. Mommsen and G. Hirschfeld, 175–200. New York: St. Martin's.

Chaliand, G., and A. Blin (eds.). 2007. *The history of terrorism. From antiquity to al Qaeda*. Berkeley: University of California Press.

Chaliand, G., and Blin, A. 2007. The 'Golden Age' of terrorism. In *History of terrorism*, ed. G. Chaliand and A. Blin, 175–196. Berkeley: University of California Press.

Code pénal. 1810. Paris; English translation: *The Penal Code of France, translated into English with a preliminary dissertation and notes*, London 1819, online: http://www.napoleon-series.org/ research/government/c_code.html.

Colao, F. 1986. *Il delitto politico tra ottocento e novecento. Da "delitto fittizio" a "nemico dello Stato"*. Milano: Giuffrè.

Coleman, J. 1990. *Against the state. Studies in sedition and rebellion. Introduced by brian redhead*. London: BBC Books.

Convention for the Prevention and Punishment of Terrorism, 19 League of Nations O.J. 23 (1938), League of Nations Doc. C.546(I).M.383(I).1937.V (1938) (16 November 1937).

Coward, B., and J. Swann (eds.). 2004. *Conspiracies and conspiracy theory in early modern Europe. From the Waldensians to the French revolution*. Aldershot: Ashgate.

Cressy, D. 2010. *Dangerous talk. Scandalous, seditious, and treasonable speech in pre-modern England*. Oxford: Oxford University Press.

Deflem, M. 2005. "Wild Beasts Without Nationality": The uncertain origins of interpol, 1898–1910. In *The handbook of transnational crime and justice*, ed. Ph Reichel, 275–285. Thousand Oaks: Sage Publications.

Deutsche Chronik für das Jahr 1848. 1849. Berlin: Hayn.

Dietze, C. 2012. Terrorismus im 19. Jahrhundert: Politische Attentate, rechtliche Reaktionen, Polizeistrategien und öffentlicher Diskurs in Europa und den Vereinigten Staaten 1878–1901. In *Vom Majestätsverbrechen zum Terrorismus: Politische Kriminalität, Recht, Justiz und Polizei zwischen Früher Neuzeit und 20. Jahrhundert*, eds. K. Härter and B. de Graaf, 179–196. Frankfurt am Main: Klostermann.

Dillinger, J. 2008. *Terrorismus*. Freiburg: Herder.

Drage, G. 1885. *The criminal code of the German Empire. Translation with prolegomena and a commentary by Geoffrey Drage*. London: Chapman and Hall. Repr., Clark, NJ: Lawbook Exchange, 2005.

Duyvesteyn, I. 2007. The role of history and continuity in terrorism research. In *Mapping terrorism research: State of the art, gaps and future direction*, ed. M. Ranstorp, 56–57. London: Routledge.

Emsley, C. 1997. Political police and the European nation state in the nineteenth century. In *The policing of politics in the twentieth century: Historical perspectives*, ed. M. Mazower, 1–25. Providence: Berghahn.

Felske, K. 2002. *Kriminelle und terroristische Vereinigungen – §§ 129, 129a StGB, Reformdiskussion und Gesetzgebung seit dem 19. Jahrhundert*. Baden-Baden: Nomos.

Fernández Sánchez, P.A. (ed.). 2009. *International legal dimension of terrorism*. Leiden: Martinus Nijhoff.

Ford, F.L. 1985. *Political murder. From tyrannicide to terrorism*. Cambridge, MA: Harvard University Press.

Grässle-Münscher, J. 1991. *Kriminelle Vereinigung. Von den Burschenschaften bis zur RAF*. Hamburg: Europäische Verlagsanstalt.

Härter, K. 1992. *Reichstag und Revolution 1789–1806. Die Auseinandersetzung des Immerwährenden Reichstags zu Regensburg mit den Auswirkungen der Französischen Revolution auf das Alte Reich*. Göttingen: Vandenhoeck & Ruprecht.

Härter, K. 2008. Asyl, Auslieferung und politisches Verbrechen in Europa während der "Sattelzeit": Modernität und Kontinuität im Strafrechtssystem. In *Dimensionen der Moderne. Festschrift für Christof Dipper*, eds. U. Schneider and L. Raphael, 481–502. Frankfurt am Main: Lang.

Härter, K. 2009. Die Entwicklung des Strafrechts in Mitteleuropa 1770–1848: Defensive Modernisierung, Kontinuitäten und Wandel der Rahmenbedingungen. In *Verbrechen im Blick. Perspektiven der neuzeitlichen Kriminalitätsgeschichte*, eds. R. Habermas and G. Schwerhoff, 71–107. Frankfurt am Main/New York: Campus.

Härter, K. 2010. Security and "gute Policey" in early modern Europe: Concepts, laws and instruments. *Historical Social Research* 35: 41–65.

Härter, K. 2011. Die Formierung transnationaler Strafrechtsregime: Auslieferung, Asyl und grenzübergreifende Kriminalität im Übergang von gemeinem Recht zum nationalstaatlichen Strafrecht. *Rechtsgeschichte* 18: 36–65.

Heinzen, K. 1881. *Murder and liberty (Printed for the first time in 1853 as a contribution for the "Peace-League" of Geneva)*. Indianapolis: H. Lieber.

Hernon, I. 2007. *Assassin! 200 years of British political murder*. London: Pluto Press.

Hetzer, W. 2008. *Rechtsstaat oder Ausnahmezustand? Souveränität und Terror*. Berlin: Duncker & Humblot.

Hubac-Occhipinti, O. 2007. Anarchist terrorists of the nineteenth century. In *History of terrorism*, ed. G. Chaliand and A. Blin, 113–131. Berkeley: University of California Press.

Huber, E. (ed.). 1961. *Dokumente zur deutschen Verfassungsgeschichte, Bd. 1: Deutsche Verfassungsdokumente 1803–1850*. Stuttgart: Kohlhammer.

Ilse, L.F. 1860. *Geschichte der politischen Untersuchungen, welche durch die neben der Bundesversammlung errichteten Commissionen, der Central-Untersuchungs-Commission zu Mainz und der Bundes-Central-Behörde zu Frankfurt in den Jahren 1819 bis 1827 und 1833 bis 1842 geführt sind*. Frankfurt am Main: Meidinger.

Ingraham, B.L. 1979. *Political crime in Europe. A comparative study of France, Germany, and England*. Berkeley: University of California Press.

Kesper-Biermann, S. 2009. *Einheit und Recht Strafgesetzgebung und Kriminalrechtsexperten in Deutschland vom Beginn des 19. Jahrhunderts bis zum Reichsstrafgesetzbuch von 1871*. Frankfurt am Main: Klostermann.

Klippel, D. 1999. Legal reforms: Changing the law in Germany in the Ancien Régime and in the Vormärz. In *Great Britain and Germany 1750–1850*, eds. T.C.W. Blanning and P. Wende, 43–59. Oxford: Oxford University Press.

Knepper, P. 2010. *The invention of international crime. A global issue in the making, 1881–1914*, 128–158. London: Palgrave Macmillan.

L'émigration politique en Europe aux XIXe et XXe siècles. Actes du colloque organisé per l'École Française de Rome [...]. Rome: Ecole Francaise de Rome, 1991.

Land, I. (ed.). 2008. *Enemies of humanity: The nineteenth-century war on terrorism*. New York: Palgrave Macmillan.

Laqueur, W. 2008. *A history of terrorism, with a new introduction by the author*. New Brunswick: Transaction.

Lerat, B. 1989. *Le terrorisme révolutionnaire, 1789–1799*. Paris: Ed. France-Empire.

Levy, C. 2007. The anarchist assassin and Italian history, 1870s to 1930s. In *Assassinations and murder in modern Italy. Transformations in society and culture*, ed. S. Gundle and L. Rinaldi, 207–221. New York: Palgrave Macmillan.

Liang, H. 1992. *The rise of modern police and the European state system from Metternich to the Second World War*. Cambridge: Cambridge University Press.

Linse, U. 1982. 'Propaganda by Deed' and 'Direct Action': Two concepts of anarchist violence. In *Social protest, violence and terror*, ed. W. Mommsen and G. Hirschfeld, 201–229. New York: St. Martin's.
Loubat, G. 1895. *Code de la législation contre les anarchistes. Contenant le commentaire de la Loi du 28 juillet 1894 ayant pour objet de réprimer les menées anarchistes suivi du commentaire des Lois du 12 décembre 1893 modifiant la loi sur la presse, du 18 décembre 1893 sur les associations de malfaiteurs, du 18 décembre 1893 sur la fabrication et la détention des explosifs*. Paris: Chevalier-Maresq.
Merari, A. 2002. Terrorism as a strategy of insurgenc. In *History of terrorism*, ed. G. Chaliand and A. Blin, 12–51. Berkeley: University of California Press.
McGarrity, N., et al. (eds.). 2011. *Counter-terrorism and beyond. The culture of law and justice after 9/11*. London: Routledge.
Minna, R. 2007. *Crimini associati, norme penali e politica del diritto. Aspetti storici, culturali, evoluzione normativa*. Milano: Giuffrè.
Minogue, K.R. 1986. Treason and the early modern state: Scenes from a mesalliance. In *Die Rolle der Juristen bei der Entstehung des modernen Staates*, ed. R. Schnur, 421–435. Berlin: Duncker & Humblot.
Mommsen, W.J., and G. Hirschfeld (eds.). 1982. *Social protest, violence and terror in 19th- and 20th-century Europe*. London: Macmillan Press Ltd.
Onnekink, D. 2007. "Gunpowder, treason and plot". Aspecten van religieus en politiek fanatisme in vroegmodern Engeland. In *Terroristen en hun bestrijders vroeger en nu*, eds. I. Duyvesteyn and B. de Graaf, 13–27. Amsterdam: Boom.
Polaine, M., et al. 2009. *Counter-terrorism law and practice: an international handbook*. Oxford: Oxford University Press.
Ramraj, V.V. (ed.). 2005. *Global anti-terrorism law and policy*. Cambridge: Cambridge University Press.
Ross, J.I. 2003. *The dynamics of political crime*. Thousand Oaks: Sage.
Sbriccoli, M. 1974. *Crimen laesae maiestatis. Il problema del reato politico alle soglie della scienza penalistica moderna*. Milano: Giuffrè.
Schroeder, F.-C. 1970. *Der Schutz von Staat und Verfassung im Strafrecht*. München: Beck.
Scott, J.B. (ed.). 1916. *Resolutions of the Institute of International Law dealing with the law of nations: With an historical introduction and explanatory notes*. New York: Oxford University Press.
Siemann, W. 1985. *'Deutschlands Ruhe, Sicherheit und Ordnung' Die Anfänge der politischen Polizei 1806–1866*. Tübingen: Niemeyer.
Siemann, W. 1987. Der Vorrang der Staatspolizei vor der Justiz. In *Akten des 26. Deutschen Rechtshistorikertages [...]*, ed. D. Simon, 197–209. Frankfurt am Main: Klostermann.
Steffen, L. 2001. *Defining a British state. Treason and national identity, 1608–1820*. Basingstoke: Palgrave.
Stenglein, M. 1862. *Commentar über das Strafgesetzbuch für das Königreich Bayern und das Gesetz über die Einführung [...]*, vol. 2. Kaiser: München.
Strafgesetzbuch für das Deutsche Reich. 1871. *Deutsches Reichsgesetzblatt* 24: 127–205.
Strafgesetzbuch für die Preußischen Staaten. 1851. Berlin (new edition 1856).
Truche, P. 1994. *L' anarchiste et son juge. A propos de l'assassinat de Sadi Carnot*, 70–73. Paris: Fayard.
Venner, D. 2002. *Histoire du terrorisme*. Paris: Pygmalion, Watelet.
Volz, M. 2007. *Extraterritoriale Terrorismusbekämpfung*. Berlin: Duncker & Humblot.
von Wagemann, F.M. 1839. *Darlegung der Haupt-Resultate aus den wegen der revolutionären Complotte der neueren Zeit in Deutschland geführten Untersuchungen: auf den Zeitabschnitt mit Ende Juli 1838*. Frankfurt am Main: Bundes-Präsidial-Druckerei.
Wagner, J. 1981. *Politischer Terrorismus und Strafrecht im deutschen Kaiserreich von 1871*. Heidelberg et al.: v. Decker.
Walker, C. 2011. *Terrorism and the law*. Oxford: Oxford University Press.

Walther, R. 1990. Terror, Terrorismus. In *Geschichtliche Grundbegriffe. Historisches Lexikon zur politisch-sozialen Sprache in Deutschland*, vol. 6, eds. O. Brunner et al., 323–444. Stuttgart: Klett-Cotta.

Weber, E. 1970. *Die Mainzer Zentraluntersuchungskommission*. Karlsruhe: C.F. Müller.

Wolny, K. 2008. *Die völkerrechtliche Kriminalisierung von modernen Akten des internationalen Terrorismus unter besonderer Berücksichtigung des Statuts des Internationalen Strafgerichtshofs*. Berlin: Duncker & Humblot.

Part II
Defining Terrorism

Chapter 4
Civilising the Exception: Universally Defining Terrorism

Ben Saul

4.1 Introduction

The struggle to give legal form and content to 'terrorism' has preoccupied states, international organisations, and lawyers for more than 80 years, since the League of Nations first considered terrorism as a transnational legal problem.[1] Originally confronted within the framework of domestic extradition law, the powerful terminology of 'terrorism' soon took on an international life of its own, with calls for its more deliberate regulation. The subsequent great difficulties in defining terrorism are typically portrayed as an unfortunate failure of the international community to confront a virulent species of transnational crime.

In one sense, that dominant critique is understandable because the failure to reach agreement has hindered the highest possible level of international cooperation against terrorism. Countries cannot fully cooperate against 'terrorism' without knowing the scope of the phenomenon against which they would be required to impose legal sanctions. Some of the disagreement between states has stemmed from negotiating positions which have sought to confer unprincipled impunity on certain preferred political actors. Attempts to carve out exceptions for one's own side of international politics have damaged inter-state confidence.

In a different sense, however, the failure to define terrorism can also been viewed as a kind of messy success. Some states have resisted efforts to define terrorism for more principled reasons – for instance, because defining terrorism in a certain way would jeopardize other international public policy interests such as political freedom, asylum, or human rights. That some states have held out against pres-

[1] See B. Saul, "The Legal Response of the League of Nations to Terrorism," *Journal of International Criminal Justice* 4 (2006): 78.

B. Saul (✉)
Sydney Centre for International Law, Faculty of Law, The University of Sydney,
Law Building F10, Sydney, NSW, Australia
e-mail: ben.saul@sydney.edu.au

A. Masferrer (ed.), *Post 9/11 and the State of Permanent Legal Emergency*,
Ius Gentium: Comparative Perspectives on Law and Justice 14,
DOI 10.1007/978-94-007-4062-4_4,

sures to conform to particular definitional proposals is an achievement of sorts, for it has stalled the destructive slide towards overly-punitive responses to terrorism which has tempted many states. Having no definition of terrorism is better than having a definition which criminalises legitimate politics or dissolves freedoms. Meanwhile, practical cooperation against particular forms of terrorism has not only been possible but effective, through various means including transnational crime treaties.

Given the protracted and often acrimonious disagreements among states about defining terrorism, it surprised many to learn that the United Nations Special Tribunal for Lebanon identified a customary international crime of transnational terrorism in February 2011.[2] By recognising a definition of terrorism in customary law, the Special Tribunal neatly side-stepped almost a century of legal deadlocks in (ongoing) treaty negotiations and debates in bodies such as the UN General Assembly and Security Council. The first part of this chapter assesses whether there is now an accepted definition of terrorism in general international law. Concluding that there is no such consensus, the second part of the chapter examines the relative advantages and costs of defining terrorism in particular ways.

4.2 Is There a Definition of Terrorism in International Law?

The definition of terrorism identified by the UN Special Tribunal for Lebanon is a useful starting point for considering whether there is a general definition in international law. The Special Tribunal identified a customary law crime of terrorism consisting of three elements:

> (i) the perpetration of a criminal act (such as murder, kidnapping, hostage-taking, arson, and so on), or threatening such an act; (ii) the intent to spread fear among the population (which would generally entail the creation of public danger) or directly or indirectly coerce a national or international authority to take some action, or to refrain from taking it; (iii) when the act involves a transnational element.[3]

The requirement of a transnational element[4] rules out purely domestic terrorism. While the Tribunal recognised only peace-time terrorism as a crime, it indicated that 'a broader norm that would outlaw terrorist acts *during times of armed conflict* may also be emerging'.[5]

State practice does not, however, support the conclusion reached by the Tribunal. A close analysis of relevant treaties, United Nations resolutions, national laws and

---

[2] UN Special Tribunal for Lebanon (Appeals Chamber), *Interlocutory Decision on the Applicable Law: Terrorism, Conspiracy, Homicide, Perpetration, Cumulative Charging*, STL-11-01/I, 16 February 2011.

[3] *Ibidem* at para. 85.

[4] *Ibidem* at para. 90.

[5] *Ibidem* at para. 107; see generally paras. 107–9.

national judicial decisions[6] confirms the near-universal scholarly consensus that there does not yet exist a customary law crime of terrorism as defined by the Tribunal.

As regards treaties, a decisive point is that numerous efforts by the international community since the 1920s have not produced agreement on a general international crime of terrorism in a treaty.[7] While there are numerous 'sector'-specific treaties which address particular criminal means or methods used by terrorists,[8] none of those treaties – individually or collectively – contains a comprehensive definition of terrorism[9] or establishes a general international crime of transnational 'terrorism'. At most, specific offences in some treaties may have entered into customary law, such as aircraft hijacking or hostage taking.[10]

In the absence of a general crime of terrorism in treaty law, no parallel customary rule can arise out of those treaties. The sectoral approach was adopted precisely because states could not reach agreement on 'terrorism' as such. The decades of

---

[6]Including regional anti-terrorism treaties, General Assembly resolutions, UN Security Council resolution 1566 (2004), the UN Draft Comprehensive Anti-Terrorism Convention, the Terrorist Financing Convention 1999, 37 national laws, and nine national judicial decisions.

[7] See B. Saul, *Defining Terrorism in International Law* (Oxford: Oxford University Press, 2006), chapters 3–4; G. Guillaume, "Terrorism and International Law" *International and Comparative Law Quarterly* 53 (2004): 537; R. Higgins, "The General International Law of Terrorism," in *Terrorism and International Law,* ed. R. Higgins and M. Flory (London: Routledge, 1997) 13, 13–14.

[8] See, e.g., Convention on Offences and Certain Other Acts Committed on Board Aircraft (adopted 14 September 1963, entered into force 4 December 1969, 704 UNTS 219); Convention for the Suppression of Unlawful Seizure of Aircraft (adopted 16 December 1970, entered into force 14 October 1971, 860 UNTS 105); Convention on the Prevention and Punishment of Crimes against Internationally Protected Persons, including Diplomatic Agents (adopted 14 December 1973, entered into force 20 February 1977, 1035 UNTS 167); International Convention against the Taking of Hostages (adopted 17 December 1979, entered into force 3 June 1983, 1316 UNTS 205); Convention for the Suppression of Unlawful Acts against the Safety of Maritime Navigation (adopted 10 March 1988, entered into force 1 March 1992, 1678 UNTS 221); Protocol for the Suppression of Unlawful Acts against the Safety of Fixed Platforms Located on the Continental Shelf (adopted 10 March 1988, entered into force 1 March 1992, 1678 UNTS 304); Protocol on the Suppression of Unlawful Acts of Violence at Airports Serving International Civil Aviation (adopted 24 February 1988, entered into force 6 August 1989, 974 UNTS 177); Convention on the Marking of Plastic Explosives for the Purpose of Detection (adopted 1 March 1991, entered into force 21 June 1998); 1997 International Convention for the Suppression of Terrorist Bombings (adopted 15 December 1997 by UN General Assembly Resolution 52/164 (1997), entered into force 23 May 2001, 2149 UNTS 256); International Convention for the Suppression of the Financing of Terrorism (adopted 9 December 1999 by UN General Assembly resolution 54/109, entered into force 10 April 2002, 2178 UNTS 229); International Convention for the Suppression of Acts of Nuclear Terrorism (adopted 13 April 2005 by UN General Assembly Resolution 59/290 (2005), entered into force 7 July 2007).

[9] Report of the Special Rapporteur (Martin Scheinin) on the promotion and protection of human rights and fundamental freedoms while countering terrorism, UN Doc. E/CN.4/2006/98, 28 December 2005, para. 28.

[10] *US v Yunis,* 924 F.2d 1086 (DC Cir 1991), 1092; (1991) 30 ILM 403; *Burnett* et al. *v Al Baraka Investment and Development Corporation* et al., Civil Action No 02–1616 (JR), US District Crt, Distr Columbia, 25 July 2003, 274 F Supp 2d 86.

deadlock – continuing in the negotiations for a UN Draft Comprehensive Terrorism Convention since 2000 – demonstrate a lack of global consensus on defining terrorism. Even the 1999 Terrorist Financing Convention – sometimes pointed to as a generic definition of terrorism – only defines and criminalises terrorist *financing*, not terrorism per se, and there is no wider practice suggesting that states have extrapolated wider general crimes of terrorism from its definition.

The treaties of regional organisations also do not support the existence of an agreed definition of terrorism. An accurate reading of those conventions establishes exactly the opposite: enormous variation in regional conceptions of terrorism.[11] Some regional treaties focus on specific terrorist methods, without defining terrorism[12]; others contain (often wide or conflicting) generic definitions,[13] or define terrorism only to criminalize ancillary conduct[14]; and yet others do not create offences at all, but serve other purposes (such as extradition or law enforcement cooperation).[15] Some of the treaties do not enjoy wide participation by members of the regional organisation,[16] and even where states are parties, the treaty may not have influenced national practice much at all.[17]

The General Assembly resolutions have repeatedly condemned terrorism as '[c] riminal acts intended or calculated to provoke a state of terror in the general public, a group of persons or particular persons for political purposes'.[18] The value of such resolutions as evidence of a customary law agreement on the definition of terrorism must be cautiously appraised. The key normative resolution which sets out a definition, the 1994 Declaration on Measures against International Terrorism, itself emphasizes the need to progressively develop and codify the law on terrorism[19] – far from reflecting existing rules. In supporting it, many States argued that there was still a

---

[11] See B. Saul, *Defining Terrorism in International Law* (Oxford: Oxford University Press, 2006), chapter 4.

[12] 1971 *OAS Convention to Prevent and Punish Acts of Terrorism Taking the Form of Crimes against Persons and Related Extortion that are of International Significance*; 2002 *Inter-American Convention against Terrorism*.

[13] 1998 *Arab Convention for the Suppression of Terrorism*; *Organisation of the Islamic Conference (OIC) Convention on Combating International Terrorism*; 1999 *OAU Convention on the Prevention and Combating of Terrorism*; 2002 *EU Framework Decision on Combating Terrorism*.

[14] 2005 *Council of Europe Convention on the Prevention of Terrorism*; 2004 *SAARC Additional Protocol to the 1987 Convention*; 2004 *African Union Protocol to the 1999 Convention*.

[15] 2002 *Inter-American Convention against Terrorism*; 1977 *Council of Europe Convention on the Suppression of Terrorism*; 1987 *SAARC Regional Convention on Suppression of Terrorism*; 1999 *Commonwealth of Independent States (CIS) Treaty on Cooperation in Combating Terrorism*.

[16] As with the Organisation of the Islamic States.

[17] As with the Organisation of African Unity.

[18] The 1994 Declaration states that: 'Criminal acts intended or calculated to provoke a state of terror in the general public, a group of persons or particular persons for political purposes are in any circumstance unjustifiable, whatever the considerations of a political, philosophical, ideological, racial, ethnic, religious or any other nature that may be invoked to justify them'.

[19] UNGA Resolution 49/60 (9 December 1994): Declaration on Measures to Eliminate International Terrorism, para. 12.

need to define terrorism and/or to adopt a comprehensive treaty criminalizing it,[20] and to distinguish self-determination struggles[21] – including the 118 States of the Non-Aligned Movement and 56 OIC states.[22] At most the Declaration reflects a political agreement on the wrongfulness of terrorism which falls short of evidencing a customary definition of terrorism, particularly against a background of continuing, inconclusive UN treaty negotiations on a definition since 2000.

Moreover, the Declaration's definition of terrorism (requiring a political purpose) is, in any case, different to that in the UN Draft Comprehensive Convention (which does not require a political motive). It is different again from the definition in Security Council resolution 1566 (which is limited to underlying sectoral offences, and does not catch all forms of terrorism). It is also different from the definitions in the 1999 Terrorist Financing Convention, where the emphasis is on intimidating a population or coercing a government, for whatever purpose. As shown below, it is also different from those many different definitions in national laws and, as shown above, in regional treaties. All of this suggests that the legal definition of terrorism, and such criminal liability as may attach to it, remains deeply contested.

National laws also do not evidence a customary law definition of terrorism.[23] Not all countries have even defined or criminalised terrorism generally in their legal systems, and still prosecute terrorism as ordinary crime or deal with it according to pre-existing legal categories (such as general security or emergency laws). Some countries thus resist the idea that the factual phenomenon of terrorism should be legally conceptualised as 'terrorism'.

While there are now a great many national laws giving legal life to 'terrorism', the picture is highly fragmented and variable. First, some national laws address domestic terrorism, others concern international terrorism, and some states deal with both. The many national laws which address domestic terrorism are irrelevant in evidencing a customary international crime of *transnational* terrorism (which the UN Special Tribunal claims exists).

Secondly, countries sometimes deploy different definitions of terrorism for different legal purposes (whether in criminal law, civil or administrative law), further fracturing any consensus on a core definition across most legal systems.

---

[20]UNGAOR (49th Session) (6th Committee), 14th meeting, 20 October 1994, para. 5 (Sudan), 13 (India), 27 (Algeria), 71 (Nepal); 15th meeting, 21 October 1994, para. 4 (Sri Lanka), 9 (Iran), 18–19 (Libya).

[21]*Ibidem*, 14th meeting, 20 October 1994, para. 6 (Sudan), 20 (Syria), 24 (Pakistan); 15th meeting, 21 October 1994, para. 9 (Iran), 18–19 (Libya).

[22]Non-Aligned Movement ('NAM'), XIV Ministerial Conference, Final Document, Durban, 17–19 August 2004, paras. 98–99, 101–102, 104; NAM, XIII Conf of Heads of State or Government, Final Document, Kuala Lumpur, 25 February 2003, paras. 105–06, 108, 115; NAM, XIII Ministerial Conf, Final Document, Cartagena, 8–9 April 2000, paras. 90–91; OIC resolutions 6/31-LEG (2004), para. 5; 7/31-LEG (2004), preamble, paras. 1–2; 6/10-LEG(IS) (2003), para. 5; 7/10-LEG (IS) (2003), paras. 1–2; OIC, Islamic Summit Conference (10th Session), Final Communiqué, Malaysia, 16–17 October 2003, para. 50; OIC (Extraordinary Session Foreign Ministers), Declaration on International Terrorism, Kuala Lumpur, 1–3 April 2002, paras. 8, 11, 16 and Plan of Action, paras. 2–3.

[23]Cf. STL Appeals Chamber Decision, op cit, paras. 91–98.

More particularly, only national criminal law definitions of terrorism can usefully evidence any customary international law criminal definition of terrorism.

Thirdly, where national laws do define terrorism (for whatever purpose), they reveal fundamental disagreements between states as to what legally constitutes terrorism.[24] Examination of state reports to the UN's Counter-Terrorism Committee clearly evidences such wide variations in approach.[25]

Fourthly, even where national laws converge on the definition of terrorism, they may be inappropriate models for an international definition. Various national definitions have been criticised for violating international human rights law, such as by being too vague to satisfy the principle of legality and freedom from retroactive criminal punishment.[26] Such unlawful acts are not accompanied by *opinio juris* to the effect that rights-violating definitions are permissible or required under international law: they remain simply unlawful.

While certain national judicial decisions have also been invoked to support the existence of a customary definition of terrorism,[27] analysis of national decisions does not sustain such a claim. At worst, some national decisions expressly doubt the customary law status of terrorism[28]; do not concern terrorism at all[29]; mention terrorism incidentally but not dispositively[30]; or refrain from ruling on the issue.[31] At most, some national decisions accept that certain forms of terrorism may have attracted international consensus[32] (for instance, hijacking or hostage taking), but that falls short of support for the existence of a comprehensive, universal definition of terrorism per se.

---

[24] Cf. *ibidem* at para. 97 (citing 37 national laws which it claims converge on a consensus definition).

[25] See analysis in B. Saul, *Defining Terrorism in International Law* (Oxford, 2006), 263–269.

[26] Under article 15 of the *International Covenant on Civil and Political Rights* 1966. For human rights critiques of national laws, see, eg, UN Human Rights Committee, Concluding Observations: United States of America (15 September 2006) UN Doc. CCPR/C/USA/CO/3, para. 11; Algeria (18 August 1998) UN Doc. CCPR/C/79/Add.95, para. 11; Egypt (9 August 1993) UN Doc CCPR/C/79/Add.23, para. 8; Democratic Peoples' Republic of Korea (27 August 2001) UN Doc. CCPR/CO/72/PRK, para. 14; Portugal (Macao) (4 November 1999) UN Doc. CCPR/C/79/Add.115, para. 12; Peru (25 July 1996) UN Doc. CCPR /C/79/Add.67, para. 12; and Report of the Special Rapporteur (Martin Scheinin) on the promotion and protection of human rights and fundamental freedoms while countering terrorism, UN Doc. E/CN.4/2006/98, 28 December 2005, paras. 27–28, 45–47, 56, 62.

[27] STL Appeals Chamber Decision, op cit, para. 86.

[28] *US v Yousef* et al., 327 F.3d 56 (US Crt App, 2nd Cir), 4 April 2003 at 34, 44, 46, 53–60, affirming *Tel-Oren v Libyan Arab Republic* 726 F.2d 774 (DC Cir 1984) at 795 (Edwards J) and 806–07 (Bork J) (USA); *Ghaddafi* case, Bulletin des arret de la Cour de Cassation, Chambre criminelle, mar 2001, No. 64, 218–219; *Madan Singh v State of Bihar* [2004] INSC 225 (2 April 2004).

[29] *Chile v Clavel,* quoted in STL Appeals Chamber Decision, op cit.

[30] *Cavallo*, quoted in STL Appeals Chamber Decision, op cit, para. 86; *US v Yunis,* 924 F.2d 1086 (DC Cir 1991); *EHL* case, Cass. 15 février 2006, RG P.05.1594.F, Pas. 2006, No. 96; RDP2006, 795, cited in *Rapport annuele la Cour de cassation de Belgique 2009.*

[31] *Zrig v Canada (Minister of Citizenship and Immigration)* (CA) [2003] 3 FC 761, para. 180.

[32] *Zrig, ibidem*; *US v Yunis,* 924 F.2d 1086 (DC Cir 1991).

In those few cases which mention customary law, the methodology of analysing custom formation is minimal to say the least and 'rest[s] upon a very inadequate use of the sources'.[33] The position on customary law is ambiguous in a few cases. One matter was a civil case and did not involve criminal liability,[34] while others concerned national law contexts such as extradition[35] or exclusion from refugee status.[36] One decision identifies 'the essence' of terrorism for the limited purpose of interpreting a domestic immigration law statute, but acknowledges that 'there is no single definition that is accepted internationally' and that '[o]ne searches in vain for an authoritative definition'.[37]

While one Italian decision appears to squarely identify a customary crime of terrorism,[38] it then defines such crime quite differently from the notion suggested by the UN Special Tribunal – specifically, by requiring a political, religious or ideological motivation. This is not a trivial or marginal difference of opinion. On the view of the Italian court, terrorism is simply *not* terrorism unless it is defined to include such a motive. Indeed one of the central disagreements in defining terrorism in national and international law is whether a publicly-oriented motive should be an element of the definition.[39]

Such divergence amongst national laws has not been cured by the UN Security Council's edict in Resolution 1373 (2001) requiring states to criminalise terrorism.[40] That resolution failed to define terrorism, and in practice the Security Council's Counter-Terrorism Committee tolerated a wide variety of national approaches to defining terrorism. The Council's subsequent 'working definition' of terrorism in Resolution 1566 (2004) does not require States to conform their anti-terrorism laws to it. Nonetheless, that resolution is understood by States as establishing 'soft' guide-posts in the implementation of earlier Resolution 1373. Over time, sufficient State practice in conformity with the resolution – that is, an *actual* common national law approach to defining terrorism – may provide evidence of a customary law definition. There is, however, a long way to go.

---

[33] Brownlie, *Principles of Public International Law*, 6th ed. (Oxford: Oxford University Press 2003), 22 (speaking of the value of national decisions generally).

[34] *Almog v Arab Bank*, 471 F. Supp. 2d 257 (EDNY 2007)

[35] *EHL* case, op cit.

[36] *Al-Sirri v Secretary of State for the Home Department* [2009] EWCA Civ 364.

[37] *Suresh v Canada (Minister for Immigration and Citizenship)* [2002] 1 SCR 3 at 53, para. 94.

[38] *Bouyahia Maher Ben Abdelaziz* et al., Judgment of 11 October 2006, Corte di Cassazione.

[39] See, eg, B. Saul, "The Curious Element of Motive in Definitions of Terrorism: Essential Ingredient – Or Criminalizing Thought?," in *Law and Liberty in the War on Terror*, ed. A. Lynch, E. MacDonald and G. Williams,(Sydney: Federation Press 2007), 28.

[40] Defined as: 'criminal acts, including against civilians, committed with the intent to cause death or serious bodily injury, or taking of hostages, with the purpose to provoke a state of terror in the general public or in a group of persons or particular persons, intimidate a population or compel a government or an international organization to do or to abstain from doing any act, which constitute offences within the scope of and as defined in the international conventions and protocols relating to terrorism'.

Any emerging global consensus around the definition in Resolution 1566 would reflect a fairly narrow and rights-respecting concept of terrorism, and would not be a bad result. The cumulative elements set out in that resolution define conduct as terrorism only: (a) when it is committed to harm people, (b) with the purpose to provoke a state of terror, or to intimidate a population, or to compel a government or an international organization, and (c) and where such conduct *also* constitutes an offence under the existing sectoral anti-terrorism treaties.

In other words, Resolution 1566 does not criminalize any conduct which is not already criminal under existing transnational crime treaties; rather, it reclassifies as 'terrorism' certain existing criminal wrongs where they are designed to terrorize, intimidate or compel. There is no further 'special intent' or motive requirement of a political, religious or ideological purpose behind the conduct. The relatively narrow scope of that definition complements efforts by the UN human rights bodies and mechanisms[41] to identify and wind-back excessive national anti-terrorism laws which adversely affect human rights.

4.3 Defining Terrorism to Civilize Legal Exceptionalism

If terrorism is not presently defined under general international law, the twin questions arise whether it is worth the effort, and what kind of definition is worth the effort. As briefly noted earlier, numerous 'sectoral' treaties on transnational criminal cooperation, adopted since the 1960s, targeted the common methods of violence used by terrorists (such as hijacking, hostage taking, endangering maritime facilities and so on), but did not create or define a new international crime of terrorism.[42] Such treaties typically required States parties to criminalise certain conduct, to establish

[41] Including the UN Human Rights Committee, various Special Rapporteurs, the Human Rights Council, and the UN High Commissioner for Human Rights. See, e.g., UN Human Rights Committee, General Comment 29, States of Emergency (article 4), 31 August 2001; UN Commission on Human Rights, Resolutions 2003/37 (2003) and 2005/80 (2005); UN Human Rights Council, Resolutions 7/7 (2008), 10/9 (2009), 10/11 (2009), 10/15 (2009), 10/22 (2009). Reports of the Special Rapporteur on Terrorism and Human Rights (Kalliopi K. Koufa): Working Paper, 26 June 1997; Preliminary Report, 7 June 1999, Progress report, 27 June 2001, Second Progress Report, 17 July 2002, Additional progress report, 8 August 2003, Final Report, 25 June 2004, Updated framework draft of principles and guidelines concerning human rights and terrorism: Second expanded working paper, 3 August 2006. Report of the independent expert (Robert K. Goldman) on the protection of human rights and fundamental freedoms while countering terrorism, 7 February 2005. Reports of the Special Rapporteur (Martin Scheinin) on the promotion and protection of human rights and fundamental freedoms while countering terrorism: Report to the Commission on Human Rights, 28 December 2005; Reports to the General Assembly, 16 August 2006, 15 August 2007, 6 August 2008; Reports to the Human Rights Council, 29 January 2007, 21 November 2007, 4 February 2009. Office of the UN High Commissioner for Human Rights, Report to the UN Human Rights Council on the protection of human rights and fundamental freedoms while countering terrorism, 2 September 2009.

[42] See B. Saul, *Defining Terrorism in International Law* (Oxford, 2006), chapter 3.

extraterritorial jurisdiction over it, and to cooperate by prosecuting or extraditing suspected offenders.

This pragmatic approach enabled the repression of terrorism while side-stepping the irreconcilable problem of defining it, at a time when States were unable to agree on the legitimacy of violence committed by self-determination movements or by State forces. The result has been a functional transnational cooperation against terrorism, even if there remain regulatory gaps because of the reactive, ad hoc nature of treaty making (for example, terrorist attacks by small arms, as in Mumbai in 2008, are not prohibited by treaty law).

Despite the wide range of terrorist conduct criminalised by the sectoral treaties and the law of armed conduct, the international community has continued to feel compelled to pursue a more general international anti-terrorism treaty framework. Since 2000, efforts have been underway to negotiate a Comprehensive Anti-Terrorism Convention under the auspices of the United Nations. Draft article 2(1) proposes an offence if a person 'unlawfully and intentionally' causes: '[d]eath or serious bodily injury to any person'; '[s]erious damage to public or private property'; or '[d]amage to property, places, facilities, or systems... resulting or likely to result in major economic loss'.[43] The purpose of any such conduct, 'by its nature or context', must be 'to intimidate a population, or to compel a Government or an international organization to do or abstain from doing any act'.[44] Possible exceptions to the Draft Convention remain contentious, particularly as regards violence by non-State groups and State military forces.

The ongoing effort to define a general international crime of terrorism suggests that the international community places some importance on that effort. At a normative level, defining terrorism as a distinct category of legal harm also symbolically expresses the international community's desire to condemn and stigmatize 'terrorism', as such, beyond its ordinary physical or criminal characteristics. Doing so normatively recognizes and protects certain international community values, and sets legal limits on the acceptable means and methods of political action. At a practical level, the patchy regulation of terrorism in many domestic legal systems can give rise to impunity, as a result of jurisdictional lacunae, differences in the definition of offences, gaps the coverage of the sectoral treaties, and limits on the extradition of political offenders. International agreement on defining terrorism and cooperative measures to deal with it is capable of narrowing those gaps. It would also bring greater precision and certainty in the definition of terrorist offences pursuant to UN Security Council measures, and thus strengthen the rule of law in responding to terrorism.

In the practice of the international community over many decades, concentrated through the United Nations organs and regional organizations, broad consensus has emerged that transnational terrorism is internationally wrongful because it: (1) seriously threatens or destroys basic human rights and freedom; (2) jeopardizes the

[43] UNGA (56th Sess) (6th Cttee), Measures to Eliminate International Terrorism: Working Group Report, 29 Oct 2001, UN Doc A/C.6/56/L.9, annex I, 16 (informal Coordinator texts).

[44] Ancillary offences are found in Draft Comprehensive Convention, *ibidem*, art. 2(2), (3) and (4) (a)–(c).

state and the stability of political life; and (3) threatens international peace and security.[45] While those explanations are not entirely coherent or without criticism,[46] the collective identification of what is wrongful about terrorism aids in explaining both why it is insufficient to leave its regulation to domestic law alone, and how terrorism can be best defined to reflect the underlying international interests and protected values at stake.

This in turn raises important questions about who is entitled to use violence and for what purposes. Depending on the scope of the definition of terrorism and the acceptability of any exceptions to it, the criminalisation of terrorism risks empowering the State – including autocratic ones – at the expense of other (potentially legitimate) political claims to the use of violence. Terrorism may often jeopardize the human rights of civilians; but if terrorism is defined more widely as any violence against the State, then the criminalisation of terrorism itself strips away the human freedom to resist oppressive or authoritarian regimes. Criminalising terrorism may serve to safeguard the stability of the State and its political order; but those political orders which systematically violate human rights may warrant destabilisation and subversion. Protecting democracy from terrorism is one thing, but protecting all States is different matter – hence the understandable political difficulty of reaching international agreement on an acceptable universal definition of terrorism.

One important means of legally distinguishing terrorism is by reference to the motivation of offenders. A compelling reason for including a motive element in an international or domestic definition of terrorist offences is that it helps to differentiate terrorism from other kinds of serious violence which may also generate fear (such as common assault, armed robbery, rape, or murder), while also according with commonplace public understanding of what constitutes terrorism. The core premise is that *political* violence, or violence done for some other public-oriented reason (such as religion, ideology, or race/ethnicity) is *conceptually* and *morally* different than violence perpetrated for private ends (such as profit, greed, jealousy, animosity, hatred, revenge, personal or family disputes and so on).

As such, international law should recognise this distinction in defining terrorism, so as to more accurately express what is considered by the international and national communities to be distinctively wrongful about terrorism. This distinction does not necessarily imply that terrorism is always morally *worse* than organised crime (a mafia hit may cause as much fear as a terrorist act), but it does suggest that it is morally *different*, not least because it aims to disrupt and coerce peaceful political processes through violence.

Until recently, the international community's legal response to terrorism did not focus on motive. From the early 1960s, the 'sectoral' anti-terrorism treaties avoided any general definition of terrorism, including reference to motive. Instead, most of the treaties require States to prohibit and punish in domestic law certain physical or objective acts—such as hijacking, hostage taking, misuse of nuclear material, or bombings—regardless of whether such acts are motivated by private or political

[45] See B. Saul, *Defining Terrorism in International Law* (Oxford, 2006), chapter 1.

[46] *Ibidem.*

ends. Proof of the motive(s) behind the act (as distinct from the *intention* to commit the act) is not required as an element of the offences.[47]

At best, some of the treaties define their offences by inclusion of special intent requirements, but which fall short of requiring a political or other motive as such. For instance, the *1999 Terrorist Financing Convention* prohibits the financing of certain acts where their purpose 'is to intimidate a population or to compel a government... to do or abstain from doing any act'.[48] While this definition partly signals a focus on repressing public-oriented violence – by targeting acts directed at the community or a government– it still does not accurately capture what is most wrongful about terrorism.[49] For it is still possible to intimidate a population or compel a government for a host of private, non-political reasons, including simple extortion.

As a result of their failure to include motive elements, many of the existing anti-terrorism treaties reach considerably beyond common understandings of terrorism, since violence for public and private motives alike is equally criminalized. Thus hostage taking or hijacking for profit or to obtain custody of a child in a family dispute is treated no differently than identical acts committed in pursuit of a political cause. The lack of differentiation arguably fails to capture what it distinctively wrongful about terrorism, which is not inherent in a physical act of violence alone.[50] As Levitt writes:

> Not all hijackings, sabotages, attacks on diplomats, or even hostage-takings are 'terrorist'; such acts may be done for personal or pecuniary reasons or simply out of insanity. The international instruments that address these acts are thus 'overbroad'...[51]

Overreach undermines 'the moral and political force of these instruments as a counter-terrorism measure'[52] and dilutes the special character of terrorism as a crime against non-violent politics and social life. As Habermas suggests, terrorism 'differs from a private incident in that it deserves public interest and requires a different kind of analysis than murder out of jealousy'.[53] Prosecuting an individual for politically motivated 'terrorism', rather than for common crimes like murder or sectoral offences like hijacking, may help satisfy public indignation at terrorist acts, better express community condemnation, and placate popular (but reasonable) demands for justice.

In international practice, there is increasing support for the view that terrorism is *political* or other publicly motivated violence, which is distinguishable, and should be distinguished, from private violence. In its influential and widely supported 1994

[47] J. Lambert, *Terrorism and Hostages in International Law: A Commentary on the Hostages Convention 1979* (Cambridge: Grotius 1990), 49.

[48] 1999 Terrorist Financing Convention, art 2(1)(b).

[49] Human Rights and Equal Opportunity Commission (Australia), Supplementary Submission to the Security Legislation Review Committee (2006), 8.

[50] Lambert, *Terrorism and Hostages in International Law...*, at 50.

[51] G. Levitt, "Is 'Terrorism' Worth Defining?," *Ohio Northern University Law Review* 13 (1986): 97 at 115.

[52] *Ibidem.*

[53] J. Habermas, "Fundamentalism and Terror: A Dialogue with Jürgen Habermas," in *Philosophy in a Time of Terror: Dialogues with Jürgen Habermas and Jacques Derrida*, ed. G. Borradori (Chicago: University of Chicago Press 2003), 25 at 34.

Declaration mentioned earlier, the UN General Assembly distinguished terrorism from other violence because of its motivation 'for political purposes'.[54] In the European Union's 2002 Framework Decision on Combating Terrorism,[55] terrorism is considered a distinctive form of violence precisely because 'the motivation of the offender is different'.[56]

The definitions of terrorism in Britain, Canada, Australia, New Zealand and South Africa similarly reflect a political judgment by those democratic communities that the motives of terrorists set them apart from other criminals. According to the Australian Parliamentary Joint Committee on Intelligence and Security in 2006, 'terrorism is qualitatively different from other types of serious crime' and is perceived as so distinct by the public.[57] For Australia's Human Rights and Equal Opportunity Commission, the aim of terrorists to undermine the political system and institutions 'makes the differentiation between "terrorist" and "non-terrorist" offences meaningful'.[58] As the Canadian government suggests, removing the motive element would thus make terrorism offences indistinguishable from the general law.[59] In a review of British terrorism laws in 1996, Lord Lloyd of Berwick observed that labelling what would otherwise be ordinary crime as terrorism reflects that terrorism attacks society and democratic institutions.[60]

At the same time, the international community has equally recognised the distinctiveness of non-political crime. For instance, the oldest international crime, piracy, is defined as violence on the high seas for 'private ends', indicating that core notion of piracy as common robbery which takes place beyond the reach of national criminal law enforcement. More recently, the *2000 UN Convention against Transnational Organized Crime* defines transnational organised crime as serious crime that is motivated by 'financial or other material benefit',[61] with indications during the drafting that proposals for an international treaty definition of terrorism should take into account what is already covered by this Convention.[62]

---

[54] UN General Assembly resolution 49/60 (1994), annexed Declaration, para 3.

[55] The European Union also distinguishes organized crime for profit: see EU Council, Joint Action 98/733/JHA of 21 December 1998; 1995 Europol Convention, art 2; EU Council Decision 2002/187/JHA of 28 February 2002.

[56] European Commission, Proposal for a Council Framework Decision on Combating Terrorism, 19 September 2001, COM(2001) 521 Final, 2001/0217 (CNS), 6, 7.

[57] Parliamentary Joint Committee on Intelligence and Security (Australia), Review of Security and Counter Terrorism Legislation, December 2006, 57. Australia's independent Security Legislation Review Committee agreed in the same year that the motive element 'appropriately emphasises a publicly understood quality of terrorism': Security Legislation Review Committee (Sheller Report), Report tabled in the Australian House of Representatives, 15 June 2006, 57.

[58] Human Rights and Equal Opportunity Commission (Australia), op cit, 8.

[59] Cited in *R v Khawaja*, Case No 04-G30282, Ontario Superior Court of Justice (Canada), 24 October 2006, para 66.

[60] Rt Hon Lord Lloyd of Berwick, *Inquiry into Legislation against Terrorism*, vol. 1, CMD3420, xi.

[61] 2000 UN Convention against Transnational Organized Crime (adopted by UN General Assembly resolution 55/25 (2000) on 15 November 2000, entered into force 29 September 2003), arts 2 and 5.

[62] UN General Assembly resolution 55/25 (2000), para. 7.

In sum, the expressive function of international law cannot be overstated; a conviction for *political* or *religious* violence sends a symbolic message that certain kinds of violence, *as such*, cannot be tolerated against states, which are duty bound to ensure the safety of their peoples and to legitimately suppress those who wish to influence politics, and interfere in the autonomy of others in peaceful societies, by resorting to violence. Here international law has a role in reinforcing the ethical values of democratic political communities, which are constructed on a shared commitment to peaceful deliberation and participatory dialogue – rather than using the unilateral force of arms against one's fellow citizens or the community at large.

4.4 The Elements of Definition

It is possible to sketch the contours of a rational definition of terrorism based on the policy reasons for definition revealed in state practice and discussed above, to reflect existing agreement on the wrongfulness of terrorism. To fully reflect the consensus on what is wrong with terrorism, each of the elements outlined below is necessarily conjunctive, thus increasing the specificity of terrorist offences.

First, if terrorism is thought to seriously violate human rights, a definition must contain elements reflecting this judgment. In particular, if terrorism infringes the right to life and security of person, a definition should prohibit serious violence intended to cause death or serious bodily injury to a person. The prohibition should also extend to attacks on public or private property where intended or likely to physically endanger people, including acts against essential utilities and public infrastructure.[63]

To increase certainty, the element of 'serious violence' could be qualified by enumerating prohibited violent acts, such as by listing the offences in existing sectoral terrorism treaties, and specifying additional acts not covered by those treaties (such as murder or physical assault by any means and in any context). At the same time, the element of 'serious violence' could remain as an open-ended 'catch-all' category to ensure that offenders do not evade liability by perpetrating violence by new or unanticipated methods.

Certainty could also be increased by qualifying 'serious violence' as that which is already 'criminal' under international or national law, thus excluding violence which is lawfully justified or excused by legal defences. The seriousness of criminal violence could remain a matter of appreciation in individual cases, just as 'serious non-political crime' in exclusion cases under international refugee law is interpreted by reference to comparative national law. This approach may, however, be challengeable for lack of specificity under human rights law and a definition may be more predictable if it particularizes all prohibited physical acts.

[63] Cf the Australian Criminal Code Act 1995 (Cth), s 100.1, which defines a threat to commit a terrorist act as a terrorist act in itself, thus blurring essentially different gradations of criminal harm.

Secondly, there are a number of possibilities for framing a definitional element to reflect the normative consensus that terrorism undermines the State and the political process. A narrow approach would be to criminalize only violence directed at State officials, institutions, or interests. This approach would fail to cover acts directed at individuals, groups or populations unconnected to State interests and would thus omit to address a significant proportion of acts commonly understood as terrorism.

To meet this problem, a number of recent international definitions of terrorism have supported protecting both the State and the broader population, by requiring that the *purpose* of an act, 'by its nature or context', must be 'to intimidate a population, or to compel a government or an international organization to do or to abstain from doing any act'.[64] One difficulty is that mere *intimidation* of a population, or *compulsion* of a government, seems to fall short of the severe impact implied by the term 'terrorism'.[65] This problem is arguably cured by the European Union's solution of requiring an aim to *seriously* intimidate a population or *unduly* compel a government or international organization.[66] Alternatively, New Zealand modifies this approach by replacing the 'intimidation' of a population with a graver intention 'to induce terror in a civilian population'.[67]

The language of 'terrorism' itself implies that the intention to inflict terror, as opposed to mere intimidation, ought to be required. There has been considerable support for including such an element in an international definition of terrorism, commonly formulated in proposals as either an intention 'to create a state of terror',[68] or 'to provoke a state of terror',[69] in particular persons, groups of persons, or the general public. The serious social stigma which attaches to labelling an offender a 'terrorist' should be reserved only for those people who cause the grave psychological harm which is signified by the term terrorism. That label should not be deployed too easily to describe violent offenders who generate other harms.

Still, it remains the case that intimidation of a population or compulsion of a government may be motivated by private concerns such as blackmail, extortion, criminal profit or even personal disputes. Consequently, if a definition of terrorism is to reflect the real nature of the harm that terrorism inflicts on the political

---

[64] 1999 Terrorist Financing Convention, art 2(1)(b); see also UNSC resolution 1566(2004); UN High-Level Panel on Threats, Challenges and Change, *A More Secure World: Our Shared Responsibility* (2004); UN Secretary-General, *In larger freedom: towards development, security and human rights for all*, UNGA (59th Sess), 21 March 2005, UN Doc A/59/2005; UN Draft Comprehensive Convention, art 2(1).

[65] In the UK, it is enough merely to 'influence' a government: Terrorism Act 2000 (UK), s 1(b).

[66] 2002 EU Framework Decision, art 1(1).

[67] Terrorism Suppression Act 2002 (NZ), s 5(2)(a)–(b).

[68] 1937 League of Nations Convention, art 1(2); 1991 ILC Draft Code of Offences against the Peace and Security of Mankind, art 24; 1998 Draft Rome Statute, art 5.

[69] UNSC res 1566 (2004); 1994 UNGA Declaration on Measures to Eliminate International Terrorism.

process, it must differentiate publicly-oriented violence from private violence. As mentioned earlier, a terrorist act is committed not only where there it has a political purpose,[70] but wherever there is a public motive, aim, objective or purpose broadly defined: political, ideological, religious, ethnic or philosophical. The presence of a public motive distinguishes terrorism from private violence which also intimidates a population or compels governments.

Thirdly, if terrorism is thought to threaten international peace or security, an international definition must be limited to acts capable of that result—for instance, because of its cross-border or multi-national preparation or effects, the involvement of State authorities, or injury to other vital international community values or interests. This need not preclude a definition from covering domestic terrorism, where such conduct is thought to injure international values of sufficient gravity and attract international concern.

Historically, the weight of international opinion has only supported the definition and criminalization of *international* terrorism. The offences in the sectoral anti-terrorism treaties adopted since 1963 typically do not apply to purely domestic terrorism.[71] The most recent sectoral treaties have followed a common formula, building on that in the 1979 Hostages Convention. The 1997 Terrorist Bombings Convention, the 1999 Terrorist Financing Convention and the 2005 Nuclear Terrorism Convention all do not apply where an offence is committed in a single State, the offender and victims are nationals of that State, the offender is found in the State's territory and no other State has jurisdiction under those treaties.[72] Article 3 of the UN Draft Comprehensive Convention follows the same formula and is a reasonable approach.

Accordingly, based on the international community's identification of the underlying wrongfulness of international terrorism, terrorism can be deductively defined as follows:

1. Any serious, violent, criminal act intended to cause death or serious bodily injury, or to endanger life, including by acts against property;
2. Committed for a political, ideological, religious or ethnic purpose; and
3. Where intended to:
   (a) Create extreme fear in [or seriously intimidate] a person, group, or the general public; or
   (b) Unduly compel a government or an international organization to do or to abstain from doing any act.

[70] UNGA resolutions 49/60 (1994), annexed Declaration on Measures to Eliminate International Terrorism.

[71] 1963 Tokyo Convention, art 1(3); 1970 Hague Convention, art 3(4)–(5); 1971 Montreal Convention, art 4(2)–(4); 1988 Rome Convention, art 4(1)–(2); 1973 Protected Persons Convention, art 1(a)–(b); 1979 Hostages Convention, art 13; 1980 Vienna Convention, art 2(1)–(2); 1991 Montreal Convention, arts 2–3.

[72] Common art 3 to those conventions.

The cumulative elements of this definition ensure that the stigma of the terrorist label is reserved for only the most serious kinds of unjustifiable political violence. Its limited application also prevents the symbolic power of the term from being diluted or eroded.

4.5 Exceptions to Definition: Democratic Protests, Armed Conflicts

The question remains whether any exceptions to the general definition should be recognised by international law. Agreement on exceptions to any definition of terrorism has proved more difficult than agreement on the definition itself. In particular, two controversies have plagued the debate: whether national liberation or self-determination movements should be exempt, and whether State violence causing terror should be covered. The wider the definition of terrorism, the more likely a broader range of exceptions or defences should be available. If international law is to avoid criminalizing legitimate violent resistance to political oppression, agreement on the lawful boundaries of political violence is an essential first step before agreement on definition can be properly reached. The variety of possible exceptions and defences to, and justifications and excuses for, terrorism under international law has been considered fully elsewhere.[73]

In the first place, it is justified to include an exception acts of advocacy, protest, dissent or industrial action which are not intended to cause death, serious bodily harm, or serious risk to public health or safety – as exists already in some national laws.[74] Such exclusions are useful devices to prevent criminalizing as 'terrorism' comparatively minor harm (limited to property damage), such as when protestors at a union demonstration smashed the foyer of the Australian Parliament House in 1996; when anti-Iraq war protesters painted 'No War' on the shell of the Sydney Opera House in 2003 (requiring expensive repairs)[75]; or when urban rioters cause extensive property damage, as at G8 anti-globalization protests, or in the Paris suburbs in late 2005. While such destruction to property may exceed the limits of freedom of expression and amount to public order offences, they should fall short of being labelled as terrorism. This is particularly important in the construction of an international crime of terrorism, since States that are not democratic or generally rights-respecting are far less likely to exercise prosecutorial restraint in selecting appropriate criminal charges.

---

[73] See B. Saul, "Defending Terrorism: Justifications and Excuses for Terrorism in International Criminal Law," *Australian Yearbook of International Law* 25 (2006): 177.

[74] See, eg, Canadian Criminal Code s 83.01(1)(E); Australian Criminal Code s 100.1(3); Terrorism Suppression Act 2002 (New Zealand), s 5(5).

[75] M. Brown, "'No war' sail painters sent for trial," *Sydney Morning Herald*, 16 July 2003.

Secondly, violence committed in the context of an armed conflict (international or non-international) should be excluded from a general definition of terrorism, and instead dealt with under the specialised regime of international humanitarian law (IHL). In armed conflict, where 'terrorists' commit unlawful violence under IHL or international criminal law, they may be prosecuted for war crimes or crimes against humanity, either in national courts or (where available) in international tribunals. Most terrorist-type conduct committed in connection with an armed conflict is already criminalized as war crimes,[76] including as a special war crime of spreading terror amongst a civilian population.[77] Where terrorism is not connected the conflict, it could be prosecuted under general terrorism offences.

Lawful violent acts committed by State or non-State forces should be excluded from the scope of any general international crime of terrorism, to prevent such a crime interfering in the carefully constructed parameters of permissible violence in IHL. IHL is also the appropriate legal framework for dealing with self-determination conflicts, and for internal rebellions rising to an armed conflict. Those who target military objectives in accordance with the laws of war would thus not be liable to prosecution as international 'terrorists'.

By contrast, if non-State parties to an armed conflict find themselves branded and delegitimized internationally as criminal terrorist groups, the incentive to comply with IHL by those groups evaporates. For it then makes sense to such groups to fight as dirtily and for as long as possible to avoid defeat, since defeat and capture brings severe criminal penalties rather than amnesties, demobilization and social reintegration. The brutal last months of the internal armed conflict in Sri Lanka is a telling case, where international legitimation of the government's cause in rooting out Tamil Tiger (LTTE) 'terrorists' encouraged an escalation of government violence into systematic war crimes or crimes against humanity; while the LTTE used civilian hostages as human shields and executed civilians attempting to flee.[78]

In contrast, if non-State groups are not criminalized as terrorists, but treated as belligerents in an armed conflict, there is greater reason to comply with humanitarian principles, both to enhance the group's own legitimacy and to stake a claim to more dignified treatment as belligerents upon capture. Of course, there may be some extreme organisations which are not, and will never be, interested in playing by any rules; but the broad definitions of terrorism currently in play sweep up many more organisations than only the most extreme or asocial.

---

[76] See H. Gasser, "Acts of Terror, 'Terrorism' and International Humanitarian Law," *International Review of the Red Cross* 84 (2002): 547.

[77] *Prosecutor v Galic*, ICTY-98-29-T (5 December 2003), paras. 65–66; affirmed in *Prosecutor v Galic (Appeals Chamber Judgment)*, IT-98-29-A, 30 November 2006, paras. 87–90. See also B. Saul, "Crimes and Prohibitions of 'Terror' and 'Terrorism' in Armed Conflict: 1919–2005," *Journal of the International Law of Peace and Armed Conflict* 4 (2005): 264.

[78] See, eg, Report of the UN Secretary-General's Panel of Experts on Accountability in Sri Lanka, 31 March 2011; G. Weiss, *The Cage: The Fight for Sri Lanka and the Last Days of the Tamil Tigers* (Australia: Picador , 2011).

Where terrorism is committed in peace-time (or in situations not covered by IHL), in order to maintain moral symmetry[79] and broaden its legitimacy, a definition should cover acts of both State officials and non-State actors. Thus extrajudicial assassinations of political opponents by State officials,[80] or collusion in such killings,[81] might gainfully be qualified as terrorism, as might suicide bombings by non-State actors outside armed conflict. As Primoratz argues, acts which exhibit the 'the same morally relevant traits' should be similarly morally understood.[82]

In other cases not covered by any of the forgoing exceptions—such as in internal rebellions beneath an armed conflict—the international community may still regard some terrorist-type violence as 'illegal but justifiable'. In such cases, consideration might be given to excusing such conduct, and mitigating penalties for it, where it was committed in the 'collective defence of human rights'. Concrete examples might include the assassination of a military dictator, or politicians who forcibly refuse to cede power following defeat in a democratic election. Political amnesties and pardons, as well as ordinary criminal law defences, may also play a role in more sensitively responding to particular instances of terrorism in context.

4.6 Conclusion

The application of international law to terrorism rapidly developed in the 10 year period from 2001–2011, and certainly more rapidly than in the previous 70 odd years. Security Council law-making, sanctions regimes, national law reform and transnational legal borrowing, judicial decisions, and 'soft law' standard-setting by a range of bodies have all increasingly shaped international counter-terrorism practice.

[79] M. C. Bassiouni, "A Policy-Oriented Inquiry into the Different Forms and Manifestations of 'International Terrorism'," in *Legal Responses to International Terrorism*, ed. M. C. Bassiouni, xv, xxxix (Dordrecht: Martinus Nijhoff, 1988).

[80] See, eg, S. Jeffery, "Abbas Accuses Israel of "Terrorist" Attack," *Guardian*, 10 June 2003; AFP, 'Mossad switches from analysis to action', *Sydney Morning Herald*, 4 April 2003; W. Pincus, "Yemen aided CIA strike on 6 Al Qaeda suspects," *International Herald Tribune*, 7 November 2002; J. Risen and D. Johnston, "Bush has Widened Authority of CIA to Kill Terrorists', *New York Times*, 15 December 2002; D. Priest, "Drone Missile Kills al-Qaeda Suspect," *Sydney Morning Herald*, 16 May 2005 (possibly in Pakistan and outside the conflict in Afghanistan). Where committed in armed conflict, the targeting of civilians not taking an active part in hostilities (or after they have taken part) would amount to a war crime: Cassese, A, Expert Opinion on Whether Israel's Targeted Killings of Palestinian Terrorists is Consonant with International Humanitarian Law, prepared for the petitioners in the *Public Committee against Torture* et al. *v Israel* et al., available at www.stoptorture.org.il (21 Dec 2005); but see Kretzmer, D, 'Targeted Killing of Suspected Terrorists: Extra-Judicial Executions or Legitimate Means of Defence?' (2005) 16 *European Journal of International Law* 171.

[81] N. Hopkins and R. Cowan, "Scandal of Ulster's Secret War," *Guardian*, 17 April 2003.

[82] I. Primoratz, "State Terrorism and Counter-terrorism," in *Terrorism: The Philosophical Issues*, ed. I. Primoratz (Hampshire: Palgrave Macmillan, 2004), 113, 114.

Despite these rapid developments, there remains basic conceptual confusion about defining the problem of terrorism which is subject to such deepening regulation. No doubt certain effective measures can be taken to counter-terrorism even whilst the concept remains ambiguous. But quite apart from considerations of effectiveness, there are other costs which should properly concern the international community. Ambiguity of legal concepts allows both states to unilaterally shape their counter-terrorism responses in ways which undermine human rights and other international social interests and values; and terrorists too can take advantage of the gaps.

Bibliography

AFP. 2003. Mossad switches from analysis to action. *Sydney Morning Herald*, April 4.

Bassiouni, M.C. 1988. A policy-oriented inquiry into the different forms and manifestations of "International Terrorism". In *Legal responses to international terrorism*, ed. M.C. Bassiouni. Dordrecht: Martinus Nijhoff.

Brown, M. 2003. "No war" sail painters sent for trial. *Sydney Morning Herald*, July 16.

Brownlie, I. 2003. *Principles of public international law*, 6th ed. Oxford: Oxford University Press.

Cassese, A. 2005. Expert opinion on whether Israel's targeted killings of palestinian terrorists is consonant with international humanitarian law (prepared for the petitioners in the *Public Committee against Torture* et al v *Israel* et al., available at www.stoptorture.org.il. 21 Dec 2005).

Gasser, H. 2002. Acts of terror, "Terrorism" and international humanitarian law. *International Review of the Red Cross* 84: 547.

Guillaume, G. 2004. Terrorism and international law. *International and Comparative Law Quarterly* 53: 537.

Habermas, J. 2003. Fundamentalism and terror: A dialogue with Jürgen Habermas. In *Philosophy in a time of terror: Dialogues with Jürgen Habermas and Jacques Derrida*, ed. G. Borradori, 25. Chicago: University of Chicago Press.

Higgins, R. 1997. The general international law of terrorism. In *Terrorism and international law*, ed. R. Higgins and M. Flory, 13. London: Routledge.

Hopkins, N. and R. Cowan. 2003. Scandal of Ulster's secret war, *Guardian*, April 17.

Jeffery, S. 2003. Abbas accuses Israel of "terrorist" attack. *Guardian*, June 10.

Kretzmer, D. 2005. Targeted killing of suspected terrorists: Extra-judicial executions or legitimate means of defence? *European Journal of International Law* 16: 171.

Lambert, J. 1990. *Terrorism and hostages in international law: A commentary on the hostages convention 1979*. Cambridge: Grotius.

Levitt, G. 1986. Is "Terrorism" worth defining? *Ohio Northern University Law Review* 13: 97.

Pincus, W. 2002. Yemen aided CIA strike on 6 Al Qaeda suspects. *International Herald Tribune*, November 7.

Priest, D. 2005. Drone missile kills al-Qaeda suspect. *Sydney Morning Herald*, May 16.

Primoratz, I. 2004. State terrorism and counter-terrorism. In *Terrorism: The philosophical issues*, ed. I. Primoratz. Hampshire: Palgrave Macmillan.

Risen, J., and D. Johnston. 2002. Bush has widened authority of CIA to Kill Terrorists. *New York Times*, December 15.

Rt Hon Lord Lloyd of Berwick, *Inquiry into Legislation against Terrorism*, vol. 1, CMD3420.

Saul, B. 2005. Crimes and prohibitions of "Terror" and "Terrorism" in armed conflict: 1919–2005. *Journal of the International Law of Peace and Armed Conflict* 4: 264.

Saul, B. 2006a. The legal response of the league of nations to terrorism. *Journal of International Criminal Justice* 4: 78.

Saul, B. 2006b. *Defining Terrorism in International Law*. Oxford: Oxford University Press.

Saul, B. 2006c. Defending terrorism: Justifications and excuses for terrorism in international criminal law. *Australian Yearbook of International Law* 25: 177.
Saul, B. 2007. The curious element of motive in definitions of terrorism: Essential ingredient – or criminalizing thought? In *Law and liberty in the war on terror*, ed. A. Lynch, E. MacDonald, and G. Williams, 28. Sydney: Federation Press.
Weiss, G. 2011. *The cage: The fight for Sri Lanka and the last days of the tamil tigers*. Sydney: Picador.

Cases

Almog v Arab Bank, 471 F. Supp. 2d 257 (EDNY 2007).
Al-Sirri v Secretary of State for the Home Department [2009] EWCA Civ 364.
Bouyahia Maher Ben Abdelaziz et al., Judgment of 11 October 2006, Corte di Cassazione.
Burnett et al *v Al Baraka Investment and Development Corporation* et al, Civil Action No 02–1616 (JR), US District Crt, Distr Columbia, 25 July 2003, 274 F Supp 2d 86).
EHL case, Cass. 15 février 2006, RG P.05.1594.F, Pas. 2006, No. 96.
Ghaddafi case, Bulletin des arret de la Cour de Cassation, Chambre criminelle, mar 2001, No. 64.
Madan Singh v State of Bihar [2004] INSC 225 (2 April 2004).
Prosecutor v Galic, ICTY-98-29-T (5 December 2003).
Prosecutor v Galic (Appeals Chamber Judgment), IT-98-29-A, 30 November 2006.
R v Khawaja, Case No 04-G30282, Ontario Superior Court of Justice (Canada), 24 October 2006.
Suresh v Canada (Minister for Immigration and Citizenship) [2002] 1 SCR 3.
Tel-Oren v Libyan Arab Republic 726 F.2d 774 (DC Cir 1984).
United Nations Special Tribunal for Lebanon (Appeals Chamber), *Interlocutory Decision on the Applicable Law: Terrorism, Conspiracy, Homicide, Perpetration, Cumulative Charging*, STL-11-01/I, 16 February 2011.
US v Yunis, 924 F.2d 1086 (DC Cir 1991).
US v Yousef et al, 327 F.3d 56 (US Crt App, 2nd Cir), 4 April 2003.
Zrig v Canada (Minister of Citizenship and Immigration) (CA) [2003] 3 FC 761.

International Conventions

1997 International Convention for the Suppression of Terrorist Bombings (adopted 15 December 1997 by UN General Assembly Resolution 52/164 (1997), entered into force 23 May 2001, 2149 UNTS 256).
Convention for the Suppression of Unlawful Acts against the Safety of Maritime Navigation (adopted 10 March 1988, entered into force 1 March 1992, 1678 UNTS 221).
Convention for the Suppression of Unlawful Seizure of Aircraft (adopted 16 December 1970, entered into force 14 October 1971, 860 UNTS 105).
Convention on Offences and Certain Other Acts Committed on Board Aircraft (adopted 14 September 1963, entered into force 4 December 1969, 704 UNTS 219).
Convention on the Marking of Plastic Explosives for the Purpose of Detection (adopted 1 March 1991, entered into force 21 June 1998).
Convention on the Prevention and Punishment of Crimes against Internationally Protected Persons, including Diplomatic Agents (adopted 14 December 1973, entered into force 20 February 1977, 1035 UNTS 167).
Convention on the Suppression of Unlawful Acts Relating to International Civil Aviation (adopted in Beijing, 10 September 2010, not yet in force).

International Convention against the Taking of Hostages (adopted 17 December 1979, entered into force 3 June 1983, 1316 UNTS 205).
International Convention for the Suppression of Acts of Nuclear Terrorism (adopted 13 April 2005 by UN General Assembly Resolution 59/290 (2005), entered into force 7 July 2007).
International Convention for the Suppression of the Financing of Terrorism (adopted 9 December 1999 by UN General Assembly resolution 54/109, entered into force 10 April 2002, 2178 UNTS 229).
League of Nations Convention for the Prevention and Punishment of Terrorism (adopted 16 November 1937, never entered into forcé, (1938) *League of Nations Official Journal* 19).
Protocol for the Suppression of Unlawful Acts against the Safety of Fixed Platforms Located on the Continental Shelf (adopted 10 March 1988, entered into force 1 March 1992, 1678 UNTS 304).
Protocol on the Suppression of Unlawful Acts of Violence at Airports Serving International Civil Aviation (adopted 24 February 1988, entered into force 6 August 1989, 974 UNTS 177).
United Nations Convention against Transnational Organized Crime (adopted by UN General Assembly resolution 55/25 (2000) on 15 November 2000, entered into force 29 September 2003).

Regional Conventions

African Union Protocol of 2004 to the Organisation of African Unity Convention on the Prevention and Combating of Terrorism 1999 (adopted by the African Union Assembly, 3rd Ordinary Session, Addis Ababa, 8 July 2004).
Arab Convention on the Suppression of Terrorism (adopted 22 April 1998, entered into force 7 May 1999).
Council of Europe Convention on the Prevention of Terrorism (adopted 16 May 2005, CETS No 196).
Council of Europe Convention on the Suppression of Terrorism (adopted 27 January 1977, entered into force 4 August 1978).
Council of Europe Protocol amending the European Convention on the Suppression of Terrorism (adopted 15 May 2003).
European Union Framework Decision on Combating Terrorism (2002/475/JHA) [2002] OJ L164/3 (adopted 13 June 2002, entered into force 22 June 2002).
Inter-American Convention against Terrorism (adopted 3 June 2002, entered into force 10 July 2003).
Organisation of African Unity Convention on the Prevention and Combating of Terrorism (adopted 14 July 1999, entered into force 6 December 2002).
Organisation of American States Convention to Prevent and Punish Acts of Terrorism Taking the Form of Crimes against Persons and Related Extortion that are of International Significance (adopted 2 February 1971, entered into force on 16 October 1973).
Organization of the Islamic Conference Convention on Combating International Terrorism of (adopted 1 July 1999).
Shanghai Cooperation Organization (SCO) Convention on Combating Terrorism, Separatism and Extremism (adopted 15 June 2001, entered into force 29 March 2003).
South Asian Association for Regional Cooperation (SAARC) Additional Protocol 2004 to the Convention on Suppression of Terrorism 1987 (adopted at the 12th SAARC Summit, Islamabad, 4–6 January 2004).
South Asian Association for Regional Cooperation (SAARC) Convention on Suppression of Terrorism (4 November 1987).
Treaty on Cooperation among the States Members of the Commonwealth of Independent States in Combating Terrorism (adopted 4 June 1999, entered into force 4 June 1999).

Resolutions, Reports and Other Sources

European Commission, Proposal for a Council Framework Decision on Combating Terrorism, 19 September 2001, COM(2001) 521 Final, 2001/0217 (CNS).

European Union Council Decision 2002/187/JHA of 28 February 2002.

European Union Council, Joint Action 98/733/JHA of 21 December 1998.

International Law Commission Draft Code of Offences against the Peace and Security of Mankind 1991.

Letter dated 3 August 2005 from the Chairman of the Sixth Committee addressed to the President of the General Assembly, UN Doc A/59/894, Appendix II 'Draft comprehensive convention against international terrorism'.

Report of the Special Rapporteur (Martin Scheinin) on the promotion and protection of human rights and fundamental freedoms while countering terrorism, UN Doc. E/CN.4/2006/98, 28 December 2005.

Report of the UN Secretary-General's Panel of Experts on Accountability in Sri Lanka, 31 March 2011.

UN Commission on Human Rights, Resolutions 2003/37 (2003) and 2005/80 (2005).

UN General Assembly (56th Sess) (6th Cttee), Measures to Eliminate International Terrorism: Working Group Report, 29 Oct 2001, UN Doc A/C.6/56/L.9, annex I, 16 (informal Coordinator texts).

UN General Assembly GA Resolution 49/60 (9 December 1994): Declaration on Measures to Eliminate International Terrorism.

UN General Assembly resolution 55/25 (2000).

UN High-Level Panel on Threats, Challenges and Change, *A More Secure World: Our Shared Responsibility* (2004).

UN Human Rights Council, Resolutions 7/7 (2008), 10/9 (2009), 10/11 (2009), 10/15 (2009), 10/22 (2009).

UN Secretary-General, *In larger freedom: towards development, security and human rights for all*, UNGA (59th Sess), 21 March 2005, UN Doc A/59/2005.

Chapter 5
Terrorism: Limits Between Crime and War. The Fallacy of the Slogan 'War on Terror'

Mariona Llobet*

Nowadays, one of the greatest problems concerns the boundaries between terrorism and war. Firstly, there is confusion about these concepts, especially in the context of violence in Iraq and Afghanistan. As it is known, governments of different countries and the media have used and use the word terrorism to describe all attacks that have occurred from western invasion, both against civilians and representatives of the new governments, and against the members of the armed forces. In addition, it is not clear whether the Iraqi and Afghan conflicts are still in a state of war, although the end of hostilities was formally declared some time ago (in Afghanistan on November 13th, 2001, and in Iraq on May 1st 2003).[1]

Secondly, since September 11th 2001, the international community, led by the U.S., has labeled the activity with the slogan "war on terror" in order to justify the neutralization of global terrorism. Therefore, we must distinguish between the specific conflicts in Afghanistan and Iraq, as well as the so-called "war on terrorism".[2]

The night of September 20th, 2001, when U.S. President George W. Bush addressed Congress, he made clear the perceptions of his Government on the 9/11

*Translated by Marta Garcia Bel.

[1] Either way, international norms of the *Ius in Bello* serves to establish which situations can be considered state of war and which not. Thus, the determination of whether the conflicts in Iraq and Afghanistan are still wars is beyond the scope of this paper [on this issue, see H. Duffy, *The "War on Terror" and the Framework of International Law* (Cambridge/New York: Cambridge University Press, 2005) at 255 ff.]. In this article, we just want to analyze what are the consequences on terrorism if lived in peacetime or wartime (which previously must be defined by another branch of law).

[2] In this sense, Ackerman, "The Emergency Constitution," *The Yale Law Journal* 113 (2004): 1029 at 1032, shows that the wars in Iraq and Afghanistan were wars. Instead, the fight against *Al Qaeda* is not. Is of the same opinion Duffy, *The "War on Terror" and the Framework of International Law*, at 271.

M. Llobet (✉)
Faculty of Law, Universitat Pompeu Fabra, Edifici Roger de Lluria,
Ramon Trias-Fargas 25-27, E-08005 Barcelona, Spain
e-mail: mariona.llobet@upf.edu

A. Masferrer (ed.), *Post 9/11 and the State of Permanent Legal Emergency*, Ius Gentium: Comparative Perspectives on Law and Justice 14,
DOI 10.1007/978-94-007-4062-4_5,

attacks and the response that would follow. Bush described the attacks as "illegal acts of war" and highlighted their responsibility as the work of *Al Qaeda*. However, Bush stressed that the group was linked to many other organizations in different countries, forming a "radical network of terrorists". Thus, the President concluded that although the "war on terrorism" began with *Al Qaeda*, it was unlikely to end until "every terrorist group of global reach would have been found, arrested and defeated".[3]

Finally, the invasion in Afghanistan by U.S. military forces was based upon the fact that the attacks against the *World Trade Center* and the Pentagon were criminal; but, at the same time, these attacks were also described as acts of war.[4]

Thus, the relationship between terrorism and war must be analyzed from three perspectives. Firstly, that terrorist practices are carried out by armed forces and organized groups of resistance during wartime.[5] However, as a phenomenon, terrorism should not be confused with war or *guerrilla warfare*[6]; although, in the context of armed conflict there are also organizations, crimes and terrorist acts. Secondly, it must be defined whether the threat of international terrorism nowadays is a manifestation of some sort of criminality or, by contrast, represents a new form of warfare. We need to consider that the consequences of taking either approach into account leads to the application of two opposing legal models: if terrorism is a crime, the fight against terrorism must be conducted within the legal mechanisms established by the Rule of Law to prevent and punish any crimes committed during peacetime; but, in case of it being a form of war, the provisions of the *Ius in Bello* should be applied.

---

[3] Cfr. R. M. Chesney, "Careful Thinking About Counterterrorism Policy: Terrorism, Freedom, and Security: Winning Without War. By Philip B. Heymann," *Journal of National Security Law & Policy* 1 (2005): 169 at 170. However, as the author says, at 172, the term "war on terrorism" is so closely associated with the Bush administration that many have forgotten that it has also been used by presidents of both parties over the past twenty years, to invoke its commitment to the fight against terrorism. Moreover, according to Dubber, MD, 'Guerra y paz: Derecho Penal del enemigo y el modelo de potestad de supervisión policial del Derecho Penal estadounidense', in M Cancio Meliá/C Gómez-Jara Díez (coords), *Derecho Penal del enemigo. El discurso penal de la exclusión* I (Montevideo/Buenos Aires, Edisofer, 2006) at 685, "American criminal law has been immersed in the so-called 'war on crime' since the late Sixties". Therefore, the introduction of the word war in the fight against crime is common in the U.S. (cfr. B. Ackerman, "This is not a war," *The Yale Law Journal* 113 (2004): 1.871 at 1.871), especially in the war on drugs.

[4] On this point see Duffy, *The "War on Terror" and the Framework of International Law*, at 186 ff.

[5] P. Wilkinson, "Las leyes de la guerra y del terrorismo," in DC Rapoport, *La moral del terrorismo* (Barcelona, Ariel, 1985) at 136.

[6] J. Avilés, "Democratización y terrorismo en Irak" (www.realinstitutoelcano.org, ARI n 130/2003, 6-11-2006), states that "the guerrilla is a form of unconventional warfare in which irregular units attack by surprise military targets and then leave before having to deal with superior enemy forces. Thus, it represents an asymmetric strategy which can compensate for a significant imbalance of forces". Therefore, note that, in this context, the term "guerrilla" does not refer to criminal organizations that, especially in Latin America, are also defined with the same expression: for example, in Colombia, the FARC – which is a group that has all the characteristics to qualify it as terrorist.

Finally, it must be decided if it is possible to respond to crime with war; that is, cases where a crime (terrorism) can also be seen as an armed attack from abroad that legitimizes the resort to war.[7]

5.1 Delimitation of Terrorist Criminality in Peacetime and in Wartime

The most important consequence of war has been the establishment of international laws that regulate conflict[8] and that distinguish between civilians and members of the armed forces.[9] Although in the context of an armed conflict, combatants often use terrorist methods in acts of war, such as action against civilian populations; such conduct cannot constitute crimes of terrorism.

First of all, under International Law, the use of any means or method of warfare against enemy fighters is not permitted when it causes unnecessary damage or suffering.[10] A violation of these rules constitutes a war crime.[11] However, the legitimate use of arms and explosives, aimed at affecting the members of enemy armed forces, is an act of warfare that does not violate any prohibition, neither (criminal) national law nor international law.[12] Certainly, the messages intended by these deaths and injuries, which is likely to be fear provoking for opposition forces, can even be understood in political sense: namely, every "terrorist act" indicates to the enemy government that, unless their forces lay down their arms, there is likely to be further deaths. However, the fact that this "threat" takes place in a state of war between combatants leaves no room for terrorism as a phenomenon.[13] In summary, acts of

---

[7] We must emphasize that there is a fourth area where criminal law and war are intertwined, namely, in cases in which State officials may be held criminally liable under the crime of aggression because they intervene in a "war of aggression" (on this issue, see K. Ambos, "Derecho penal y guerra: ¿Intervención punible del gobierno alemán en la guerra de Irak?" *Revista de Derecho Penal y Criminología* 15 (2005): 171 at 171 ff.).

[8] See The Geneva Conventions of 1949 and their Additional Protocols.

[9] Arts. 43.2 and 50.1 of the Protocol Additional to the Geneva Conventions of 12 August 1949, for the Protection of Victims of International Armed Conflicts (Protocol I), 8 June 1977, define combatants and civilians. On this issue, see Duffy, *The "War on Terror" and the Framework of International Law*, at 228 ff.

[10] Art. 35.1 and 2 of Protocol I.

[11] Art. 8.2 b) xx) of Rome Statute (RE).

[12] G. Rona, "Legal Issues in the "War on Terrorism" – Reflecting on the Conversation Between Silja N.U. Voneky and John Bellinger," *German Law Journal* 9 (2008): 711 at 722–723, shows that a combatant would not be held criminally liable for acts of war that respect the laws, but may be prosecuted for war crimes if he attacks civilians or uses prohibited methods.

[13] According to S. Tiefenbrun, "A Semiotic Approach to a Legal Definition of Terrorism," *Journal of International & Comparative Law* 9 (2003): 357 at 381, an attack against combatants during an armed conflict with the purpose of inspiring them or the population fear or terror should not be called terrorism. "This is war, plain and simple," he states.

war do not represent crimes of terrorism, but can be behaviors which are legitimate, or that constitute war crimes.

Secondly, in a state of war, armed forces often attack civilians by employing terrorist methods to strike fear amid the community.[14] Combatants can instrumentalize the lives of civilians with political purpose. A typical case is the abduction of citizens of a particular nationality to get a specific reaction from the Government.[15] However, such violent actions are considered war crimes.[16] On the other hand, armed forces usually carry out systematic and indiscriminate killings against civilians. In these cases, war crimes,[17] genocide[18] and crimes against humanity are often performed together. Nevertheless, it is not possible to categorize these behaviors as terrorist acts, though in these contexts terrorist methods are also employed[19] (as by murder and destruction, the whole population or part of it undergoes into a state of terror).

In contrast, attacks by non-combatants against civilians, which are aimed at interfering with the decisions of one or more governments through violence, are considered crimes of terrorism despite being carried out during wartime.[20] Moreover, in the midst of an armed conflict, crimes of genocide or crimes against humanity can also be carried out by non-combatants, usually on ethnical, racial or religious grounds. Finally, a more difficult case arises when subjects who are considered

---

[14] Although, as indicated by F. Gudín Rodríguez-Magariños, *La lucha contra el terrorismo en la sociedad de la información. Los peligros de estrategias antiterroristas desbocadas* (Madrid: Edisofer, 2006), 42, "terrorizing the population through cruelty is not a basic war strategy", the author also admits that "indiscriminate attacks on civilians have become normal in modern wars". In fact, Duffy, *The "War on Terror" and the Framework of International Law*, at 25, emphasizes that international law provides a definition of terrorism in the context of war, prohibiting acts of violence whose purpose is to spread terror among the civilian population. In this regard, Tiefenbrun, 'A Semiotic Approach to a Legal Definition of Terrorism', at 384, proposes that an act of terrorism committed during an armed conflict can be regarded as a specific type of war crime.

[15] In this sense, if the Afghan conflict was characterized as war and Taliban forces were considered combatants, the seizure of 23 South Korean missionaries held by the Taliban militia in July 2007, in order to exchange the hostages for Afghan prisoners, would be a real example of this assumption. In this case, the militia finally agreed with South Korea, and the Asian government agreed to withdraw all its troops from Afghanistan by the end of 2008, and hostages were released.

[16] Art. 8.2 a) viii) RE considers that the taking of hostages protected by the Geneva Conventions is a war crime. On this point, see M. Abad Castelos, "La toma de rehenes como crimen internacional," *Lucha contra el terrorismo y Derecho Internacional* (2006) 133 Cuadernos de Estrategia, at 137 ff.

[17] For the purposes of the Rome Statute attacks against civilians that do not take direct part in hostilities in an armed conflict (see art. 8.2 b) i) in case of international conflicts and art. 8.2 c) i) in case of national conflicts) are considered war crimes.

[18] Think of the genocide committed during the Balkan War between 1992 and 1995.

[19] In this sense, Tiefenbrun, 'A Semiotic Approach to a Legal Definition of Terrorism', at 358 ff., stresses that terrorism as a method is also used to commit crimes against humanity.

[20] Under the International Convention for the Suppression of the Financing of Terrorism, adopted by the General Assembly of the United Nations in December 1999 and entered into force in April 2002, is considered terrorism: any act *"intended to cause death or serious bodily injury* ***to a civilian, or to any other person not taking an active part in the hostilities in a situation of armed conflict****, (…)"* (emphasis added).

non-combatants under international law, attack armed forces during armed conflict. How are these instances compartmentalized: are they war crimes, crimes of terrorism or legitimate acts committed against the enemy? In my opinion, we must distinguish between the two types: if non-combatants respect the rules of war, its actions must be regarded as legitimate. Instead, if non-conbatants use means or methods not allowed by the rules of *Ius in Bello*, such instances need to be qualified as war crimes. However, these are not terrorist acts, since terrorism is characterized by affecting non-combatant targets.[21]

In order to distinguish between crimes of terrorism, war, genocide, against humanity, as well as those acts deemed legitimate within armed conflict, two pairs of variables must be taken into account: the perpetrators, soldiers or civilians, and the type of victims, combatants or civilians. Thus, there are four possibilities:

Combatants vs. Combatants	Legitimate acts or War crimes (depending on whether they respect the rules of *Ius in Bello*)
Combatants vs. Civilians	War crimes and in some cases Genocide or crimes against humanity (when committed as part of a widespread or systematic attack directed against any civilian population)
Civilians vs. Civilians	Crimes of terrorism or Genocide or crimes against humanity (depending on the intended purpose: political, in the first case, or not, in the second)
Civilians vs. Combatants	War crimes or Legitimate acts against the enemy (depending on whether they respect the rules of *Ius in Bello*)

In the context of violence in Iraq and Afghanistan, international law has to determine when such conflicts become a state of war and which subjects can or cannot be considered combatants. With these issues settled, it would be possible to distinguish between crime (terrorism or of a different kind) and war, despite all these incidents employing the same (terrorists) methods. While such situations can be defined as armed conflicts, attacks carried out by fighters against military forces are legitimate acts of war as long as they respect international law. In contrast, the same acts directed against civilians are considered war crimes.[22] Only individuals

[21] In this sense, Avilés ("Democratización y terrorismo en Irak", already cited) believes that terrorism is characterized by attacking "noncombatant targets". In my opinion, we should add a second condition, namely, the non-combatant status of the offender. On this issue, see also A. Valsecchi, "La definizione di terrorismo dopo l'introduzione del novo art. 270-sexies c.p," *Rivista Italiana di Diritto e Procedure Penale* 1103 (2006) at 1108 and 1116 ff.

[22] In this sense, the *Human Rights Watch* organization has accused the Taliban militia for war crimes, as they attacked indiscriminately civilians and combatants. Of the 136 suicide bombings in 2006, 20 were only targeting civilians and the rest military objectives, but in any case causing more deaths among the population, 272, than among Afghan and international troops, 37 (cf. his report 'El coste humano: las consecuencias de los ataques insurgentes en Afganistán').

who are not part of the armed forces, who commit acts of violence against other civilians to cause terror, and who attempt to direct change or alter the policy of a government must be considered terrorists.

Especially with the situation in Iraq,[23] we need to differentiate between terrorist attacks and attacks against civilians by non-combatants, which may often be a crime against humanity. For example, murder and massacres based on ethnicity that have resulted in a systematic confrontation between different groups: the so-called sectarian violence. Indiscriminate killings between Shiite and Sunni in mosques, markets and neighborhoods full of civilians cannot be subsumed in the field of terrorism. Certainly, while these methods use suicide bombers and car bombs, their intended purpose does not include them within the frame of terrorism.[24] Despite this, authorities and the media frequently use the term terrorism to describe these situations.[25]

Finally, those subjects who are not considered to be combatants under international law and who attack military forces during times of conflict, either commit war crimes or legitimate acts of war, depending on whether they respect or disrespect international laws. In this sense, the killing of U.S. soldiers using explosives attached to the body which are not being made visible to combatants is deemed a war crime since the legal methods of warfare are not being respected.[26]

In addition there has recently been a new and compelling reason to clarify the legal term of terrorism, to identify the concept of war and legitimate acts of resistance. In Islam, the recruitment of young Muslims in European countries is a quite common. Religious tenets instruct young Muslims to defend themselves to the death and to enroll for "military" training: referred to as the so-called "mujahideen". However, the recruitment of young people sent to fight in Iraq or Afghanistan against invading military forces must be differentiated from the cases in which individuals engage in "terrorist training" to blow themselves up in crowded civilian areas. Such conduct only can be punished if the training is aimed at the civilian population who

---

[23] In the same sense, H. Olásolo Alonso and A. I. Pérez Cepeda, *Terrorismo internacional y conflicto armado* (Valencia: Tirant lo Blanch, 2008) at 150 ff.

[24] Note that, in early February 2007, had already died about 400 civilians in Baghdad, in several attacks performed on markets and Shiite neighborhoods since the beginning of that year.

[25] For example, the November 7th, 2006, following the announcement of the death sentence of former Iraqi dictator, Saddam Hussein, two attacks on districts of Baghdad caused 25 deaths. On the one hand, several mortar rounds made in a Sunni neighborhood killed seven people. In retaliation, 17 people died in a Shiite neighborhood after a suicide bomber blew himself up inside a coffee shop. However, Iraqi police described that persona as "suicide bomber" and so appeared in the media.

[26] Similarly, we must also qualify as war crimes attacks of non-combatants against military forces where necessary or possible side effect is the killing of civilians.

are not taking part in military conflict. If the so-called "military training" teaches individuals how to fight in a war, it would not be possible to consider it potential terrorism.

This is not a trivial question. In practice, the Spanish Supreme Court Judgment of May 31, 2006 (rapporteur Monterde Ferrer) upholds a conviction for belonging to an armed organization of a group of people because they recruited subjects who took part in the war in Bosnia. However, as the judge de Prada Solaesa stresses in his dissenting opinion to the Judgment of the *Audiencia Nacional* in April 30, 2009 (rapporteur de Prada Solaesa), matching a jihadist or mujahedeen fighter with a terrorist is not admissible. In his view, there are various purposes which may encourage acts of those who decide to travel to Iraq to fight in the armed conflict. Therefore, not all situations are to deserve the same consideration and the immediate qualification of terrorism.

It is important to distinguish between terrorism as a crime, terrorism as a legitimate act of war or acts which may constitute a war crime, and terrorism as a means for other criminal activities.[27] While in the first case it is framed as a criminal phenomenon, the latter two cases demonstrate that it is a method of initiating war, legitimate or illegitimate, or the committing of other crimes.[28]

On the other hand, a second consequence of terrorist acts occurring during wartime has to do with the status of their authors in the case of detention: they may be (alleged) criminals, terrorists of another kind, or prisoners of war.[29] In this sense, the status of the "enemy combatant", developed in the U.S. during the Bush Administration, was fully illegitimate. A week after the 9/11 attacks, Congress passed a resolution authorizing the president to use all necessary and appropriate force against those nations, organizations, or persons that he determined to have planned, authorized, committed, or aided the terrorist attacks that occurred, or had harbored such organizations or persons, in order to prevent any future acts of terrorism from abroad and against the U.S.[30] Under this resolution, Bush had the authority to declare an "enemy combatant" as any individual he suspected to have performed any of the acts described and to detain them indefinitely without due process. These individuals were subjected to a special military jurisdiction: first, under the *Military Order* signed on November 13, 2001; and subsequently, through

[27] In a similar vein, see Tiefenbrun, "A Semiotic Approach to a Legal Definition of Terrorism" at 386–387.

[28] As stated by Tiefenbrun, "A Semiotic Approach to a Legal Definition of Terrorism" at 358 ff., when terrorism is conceived as a means to perpetrate other crimes, is overlaid with crimes against humanity, genocide, war crimes, etc.

[29] Art. 4.A) of III Convention and art. 44 of the Protocol I define who the prisoners of war are.

[30] *Authorization for Use of Military Force*, September 18th 2001 (Public Law 107–40, § 2[a]).

the *Military Commissions Act* of 2006,[31] providing for the establishment of military commissions to try "alien unlawful enemy combatants".[32]

The Obama administration has since replaced the category of "unlawful enemy combatants" with "unprivileged enemy belligerent"; privileged belligerents being those individuals who belong to one of the eight categories listed in art. 4 of the Geneva Convention on the Treatment of Prisoners of War (Military Commissions Act of 2009[33]). However, those individuals who would be included under the heading of "unprivileged enemy belligerents" are not only members of *Al Qaeda*, but all those who were involved in hostile engagements with the U.S. or its allies (§ 948a[7]).

This law still prevents the rules of war applying to those individuals who are or have been taken prisoner during armed conflict (Relative to the Treatment of Prisoners of War). Although, as previously mentioned, it was unclear as to whether the current situation in Iraq and Afghanistan was an ongoing or post-war intervention; at some point, the international community has agreed that this was in-fact an armed

---

[31] Public Law 109-366 (10/17/2006). The history of this Act is interesting (cfr. Kness, AJ, 'The Military Commissions Act of 2006: an Unconstitutional Response to Hamdan v. Rumsfeld' (2007) 52 *South Dakota Law Review* 382 at 383 ff.): in Afghanistan, the U.S. military camp captured thousands of individuals, mainly because of a reward system offering $ 5,000 for every Taliban and $ 20,000 for each member of *Al Qaeda*, of whom about 86% were transferred to Guantanamo. On November 13th, 2001, President Bush signed the *Military Order* in which provided for a special military court system, composed of military commissions, to try those detainees. The U.S. Supreme Court in its Judgment in the case *Hamdan v. Rumsfeld* (05–184) 548 U.S. _ (2006), overruled the decision of the president and said that charges could not proceed without specific authorization from Congress. Thus, only a few months later, Congress passed the *Military Commissions Act* (for more information on this Act, military commissions and the Judgement, see R. J. Araujo, "A Judicial Response to Terrorism: The Status of Military Commissions Under Domestic and International Law," *Tulane Journal of International and Comparative Law* 11 (2003): 117 at 117 ff.; J. Y. Capozzi, "Hamdan v. Rumsfeld: A Short-Lived Decision?," *Whittier Law Review* 28 (2007): 1.303 at 1.303 ff.; B. W. Earley, "The War on Terrorism and the Enemy Within: Using Military Commissions to Prosecute U.S. Citizens for Terrorist-Related Violations of the Laws of War," *New England Journal on Criminal and Civil Confinement* 30 (2004): 75 at 77–78; S. Estreicher and D. O'scannlain, "Hamdan's Limits And The Military Commissions Act," *Constitutional Commentary* 23 (2006): 403 at 403 ff.; C. M. Evans, "Terrorism on Trial: The President's Constitutional Authority to Order the Prosecution of Suspected Terrorists by Military Commission," *Duke Law Journal* 51 (2002): 1.831 at 1.831 ff.; R. O. Everett, "The Role of Military Tribunals Under the Law of War," *Boston University International Law Journal* 24: (2006): 1 at 1 ff.; J. R. Fricton, "The Balance of Power: The Supreme Court's Decision on Military Commissions and the Competing Interests in the War on Terror," *William Mitchell Law Review* 33 (2007): 1.693 at 1.693 ff.; T. M. Gore, "Commission Control: The Court's Narrow Holding in Hamdan v. Rumsfeld Spurred Congressional Action But Left Many Questions Unanswered. So What Happens Now?," *Mercer Law Review* 58 (2007): 741 at 741 ff.; N. K. Katyal, "Hamdan v. Rumsfeld: The Legal Academy Goes to Practice," *Harvard Law Review* 120 (2006): 65 at 65 ff.; D. Stoelting, "Military Commissions and Terrorism," *Denver Journal of International Law and Policy* 31 (2003): 427 at 427 ff.; J. Yoo, "An Imperial Judiciary at War: Hamdan v. Rumsfeld," *Cato Supreme Court Review* 83 (2005/2006): 86 at 86 ff.; and S. Yousef, "Military Tribunals: Cure for the Terrorism Virus or a Plague All Their Own?," *Houston Law Review* 42 (2005): 911 at 911 ff., usually very critical of the establishment of military commissions).

[32] Defined in § 948a[1].

[33] Public Law 111–84 (10/28/2009).

conflict. As the majority of detainees at Guantanamo Bay were captured during the Iraq war, combatants arrested during hostilities should be treated as prisoners of war in accordance to the Third Geneva Convention.[34] Initially, this indicates that if such conflicts have already ended, prisoners should be released and repatriated to their countries of origin [35] – unless they have committed war crimes or any act of terrorism, genocide or crimes against humanity. By contrast, if the conflict is still considered to be ongoing, the arrest and detention of Iraqi and Afghan forces respects the law of warfare. However, if this is so, many of the acts that the U.S. and the international community suggests to be terrorist are, indeed, legitimate acts of war.

In conclusion, a state of war must include a definition on the scope of terrorism as a method, a phenomenon and a status of individuals acting as a terrorist and who have subsequently been detained as prisoners of war, criminals or terrorists.

5.2 Terrorism as a Symbolic Attack on Democracy: Terrorism as a Criminal Phenomenon

Terrorism has been perceived as such a threat to nation-states that it has effectively legitimized the use of extraordinary measures to fight the enemy.[36] Consequently, if we are truly at war with the network led by *Al Qaeda*, it is then legitimate to take exceptional measures in accordance to the rules of *Ius in Bello* to remove the threat posed by terrorism.[37] However, if the attacks and the activities of such armed groups around the world were categorized as a type of organized crime, measures undertaken would then need to comply with the legal and political frameworks of the democratic State where the acts were committed.[38]

---

[34] Or, as war criminals, if accused of committing this kind of crimes.

[35] Moreover, indeed, they should have been at the end of hostilities under art. 118 of the Geneva Convention of August 12, 1949, relative to the Treatment of Prisoners of War, Convention III. In the same vein, Duffy, *The "War on Terror" and the Framework of International Law*, at 257. Thus, the decision in *Hamdi v. Rumsfeld* (03–6696) 542 U.S. 507 (2004) of the U.S. Supreme Court emphasized that, in light of the rules of war, the "vital purposes" of the detention of uncharged "enemy combatants" were preventing those combatants from rejoining the enemy. Thus, the imprisonment can only last as long as hostilities remain active.

[36] On this question see D. Golove and S. Holmes, "Terrorism and Accountability: Why Checks and Balances Apply Even in "The War on Terrorism"," *The NYU Review of Law and Security* 2 (2004): 2 at 3–4.

[37] However, it is not acceptable to argue with criteria of efficacy. W. H. Taft IV, "War Not crime," in *The Torture Debate in America,* ed. K. J. Greenberg (New York: New York University, 2006) at 224 ff., considers that applying the rules of an armed conflict, adapted to the characteristics of *Al Qaeda*, is legitimate, since those allow detaining and interrogating indefinitely uncharged people, and therefore are more effective in combating terrorism. Although that may be, it does not confer legitimacy. This would only be possible if this phenomenon constituted a real war.

[38] However, for some authors (Golove/Holmes, "Terrorism and Accountability...', at 3 and 7), international terrorism is neither war nor crime in the traditional sense of the terms. On the contrary, it is a combination of both, or perhaps a new phenomenon.

In other words, the legislation that will apply in these situations will be dependent on whether the process involves peacekeeping or armed conflict; but "legally speaking there is not a third regulatory domain".[39] During armed conflict, although terrorism is said to be the "new" war, without fronts and involving a complex network,[40] international norms must be accepted. However, if terrorism is not considered an act of war, criminal laws must be applied [41] with its limits defined by constitutional guarantees.[42] Therefore, we cannot permit the initiation of war in the case of terrorism, from either a criminal law perspective or beyond international regulation.[43]

With that said, we must determine whether the conditions that were the basis for the war on terror were a legitimate recourse for war. Only if the current threat of terrorism is so serious that it threatens the subsistence of the nation-state that methods, such as armed conflict, can be justified.[44]

---

[39] J. L. González Cussac, "El Derecho Penal frente al terrorismo. Cuestiones y perspectivas," in *Terrorismo y proceso penal acusatorio*, coord. J. L. Gómez Colomer and J. L. González Cussac (Valencia: Tirant lo Blanch, 2006) at 84.

[40] Thus, for instance, A. M. Dershowitz, *Why terrorism works? Understanding the Threat Responding to the Challenge* (New Haven: Yale University Press, 2002).

[41] González Cussac, "El Derecho Penal frente al terrorismo. Cuestiones y perspectivas," at 84 ff.

[42] However, there are proposals that claim the creation of a third regulatory domain. Ackerman, 'The Emergency Constitution', at 1.030 ff., considers that, in order to face the current threat from terrorism, both Criminal Law and the Law of War are inappropriate. In his view, a third way is needed, namely, the "state of emergency" (for more details on this proposal, see two of the later work of Ackerman, "The Emergency Constitution," at 1871 ff.; and *Before the Next Attack: Preserving Civil Liberties in an Age of Terrorism* (New Haven: Yale University Press, 2006) at 13 ff.); or M. P. Scharf, "Defining Terrorism as the Peacetime Equivalent of War Crimes: Problems and Prospects," *Case Western Reserve Journal of International Law* 37 (2005): 359 at 373, proposes to define terrorism as the peacetime equivalent of war crimes. Thus, he advocates the need to apply the laws of war to the terrorists, so it would be permitted to conduct more vigorous measures that cannot be used if applying of common law.

[43] For example, the *Military Commissions Act* de 2009 expressly provides: "No alien unprivileged enemy belligerent subject to trial by military commission under this chapter may invoke the Geneva Conventions as a basis for a private right of action" (§ 948b[e]).

[44] As stated by L. Ferrajoli, *Derecho y razón. Teoría del garantismo penal* (Madrid: Trotta, 1995, translated by Perfecto Andrés Ibáñez) at 830, only on the assumption that terrorism is a real threat against the foundations of the state an emergency legislation would be legitimate. In addition, we must add to this first premise the following: once the state of war is determined, the regulation provided in case of armed conflict should be applied, or, on the contrary, once the threat is faced with the emergency regulations, we have to go back to normality (in this sense, K. L. Scheppele, "Law in a Time of Emergency: States of Exception and the Temptations of 9/11," 6 *Journal of Constitutional Law* 1 (2004) at 3). Thereby, the proposal of Ackerman, 'The Emergency Constitution', at 1030 ff., consisting of using the emergency law is, in the first place, unnecessary, because of the lack of the major premise, namely, the real threat from terrorism to the survival of democratic systems. But in addition, whether terrorism ever becomes such a risk or not, his model is illegitimate because the state of emergency becomes a permanent situation and ordinary regulation is exceptional. The same author believes that the aim of settling a state of emergency is to show people that the danger is under control and that the Government is taking effective action in the short term to prevent further terrorist attacks that could cause panic. Thus, if the emergency regulation just wants to calm society, but not effectively prevent the dangers which are frightening, and so, it is merely symbolic, the terrorist threat has no end (as the author admits explicitly).

As indicated by some scholars however, the damage that terrorism inflicts on democratic beliefs and ideals is purely symbolic, and so, has no real ability in destroying its foundations.[45] Currently, terrorism is likely to never impact upon the survival of our models of governance and democratic institutions[46]; not in the same way as they did for the Nazis or the Japanese Empire.[47] Generally speaking, terrorist

---

Consequently the time frame of the emergency state becomes final and the exception the rule, because while the dangers from terrorism still remain, the need of calming the population is going to be necessary. Thus, although the solution from Ackerman wants to avoid long term damage that the introduction of the exceptional in the ordinary law inflicts on individual rights, it causes the same effect (see criticism of the proposal Ackerman made by D. Cole, "The Priority of Morality: The Emergency Constitution's Blind Spot," *Yale Law Journal* 113 (2004): 1.753 at 1.753 ff.; and L. H. Triebe and P. O. Gudridge, "The Anti-Emergency Constitution" *The Yale Law Journal* 113 (2004): 1.801 at 1.801 ff.). In short, both exceptional standards as the emergency powers tend to last longer than the state of emergency or the emergency request, and, this way, the exception remains, either in ordinary legislation, either in a state of emergency. Thus, we find ourselves, in the words of Ferrajoli, at 820 and 828, in the "perennial emergency".

[45] In this sense, the following words by Rorty are very illustrative, "Fundamentalismo: enemigo a la vista," in *El País*, 29 March 2004 at 11: "The widespread suspicion that the war on terrorism as potentially more dangerous than terrorism itself seems entirely justified. Because if the direct consequences of terrorism were all we had to fear, there would be no reason to suppose that Western democracies would not be able to survive the explosions of nuclear bombs in their cities. At the end of the day, natural disasters that cause human death and destruction on a scale do not represent a risk to democratic institutions. For example, if the tectonic plates of the Pacific Coast moved and all skyscrapers collapsed, this event would mean certain death for hundreds of thousands of people. But after burying the victims, they would begin again with the reconstruction". In the same opinion, Ferrajoli (*Derecho y razón. Teoría del garantismo penal*, at 829 ff.) noted that there would be an agreement in the fact that terrorism that struck Italy in the 1970s and 1980s should not be qualified as a civil war, as anyone except the terrorists themselves or few prosecutors, could "seriously think that terrorism really threatened the foundations of the state"; M. Ignatieff, *El mal menor* (Madrid: Taurus, 2005) at 81, believes that "there is a huge difference between the threat of an armed attack by another state and a terrorist incident. Even if the plane that crashed in Pennsylvania had beaten the White House or the Capitol, "the 11-S attacks would not have threatened to collapse the U.S. democracy"; and W. Laqueur, *Una historia del terrorismo* (Barcelona: Paidós, 2003, translated by Tomás Fernández Aúz y Beatriz Eguibar) at 19, emphasizes that all terrorism comes to an end and that "radical Islamic groups [that] are now at the forefront of terrorism" will not be an exception.

[46] Cfr. Ignatieff, *El mal menor*, at 92 ff.

[47] As noted by J. Dratel, "The curious debate,", in *The Torture Debate in America,* ed. K. J. Greenberg (New York: New York University, 2006) at 113, *Al Qaeda* does not present a military threat comparable to Nazi Germany or the Empire of Japan during the II World War, since that terrorist organization does not control Europe or dominate Asia. In the same vein, Lord Hoffmann, in the Judgement of the House of Lords on December 16, 2004 ([2004] UKHL 56, A (FC) and others (FC) (Appellants) v. Secretary of State for the Home Department (Respondent), declaring unconstitutional the Prevention of Terrorism Bill, 2001 regarding the possibility of indefinite detention for foreign nationals), states: "I do not underestimate the ability of fanatical groups of terrorists to kill and destroy, but they do not threaten the life of the nation. **Whether we would survive Hitler hung in the balance, but there is no doubt that we shall survive Al-Qaeda.** (...) Terrorist violence, serious as it is, does not threaten our institutions of government or our existence as a civil community" (emphasis added; cfr. M. Cancio Meliá, *Los delitos de terrorismo: estructura típica e injusto* (Madrid: Reus, 2010) at 45; and Ignatieff, *El mal menor*, at 81–82, notes that "although the September 11 is often compared to Pearl Harbor, certainly *Al Qaeda* does not have anything like the resources of the Empire of Japan".

organizations do not have enough power to occupy part of a national territory and provide open resistance to the power of the state. For this reason, they are immersed in illegality and operate in secret.[48] Ultimately, then, the survival of the nation and its democratic ideals is not at risk.[49]

Certainly, we must clarify this assertion. It is not excluded that some terrorist organizations may eventually jeopardize a determined government. For example, the FARC in Colombia (particularly in the past) or radical Islamist groups in some unstable Muslim countries. Thus, if the political system of a particular State was in real danger because of some terrorist actions, it would be legitimate use the rules provided for times of war. However, such situations are exceptional on a global level and very detailed, not to justify the "war against global terrorism" which, Occident in general, is waging today against *Al Qaeda*, and this is neither applicable to the terrorism of ETA.

Tangibly, terrorism can have an effect on the life, integrity and collective security of civilians, but such legal rights are also undermined by other types of crime. Therefore, it is illegitimate to use security as a means to justify war; the fight against terrorism cannot be an armed conflict. We must interpret terrorism as a form of crime[50] which is subject to criminal law, both substantive and procedural, as well as employ the use of other tools for democracy and peacekeeping efforts.[51]

As established above, if the conditions for a state to initiate war in these circumstances are illegitimate, the label "war on terrorism" is then not just a mere slogan with rhetorical and symbolic significance, but a tool of great practical significance.[52] Firstly, the slogan creates the necessary legitimacy to limit individual rights and liberties to a perceived threat which appears to require neutralization.[53] Since war is not primarily between States, but of States against individuals, which Beck[54] calls

---

[48] In this sense, Gudín Rodríguez-Magariños, *La lucha contra el terrorismo en la sociedad de la información*, at 28–29.

[49] Cfr. Ignatieff, *El mal menor*, at 81.

[50] In the same vein, U. Beck, *Sobre el terrorismo y la Guerra* (Barcelona: Paidós, 2003, translated by Rosa S. Carbó) at 35; W. K. Clark and K. Raustiala, "Why Terrorists Aren't Soldiers," *The New York Times* 8-8-2007 (www.nytimes.com); P. B. Heymann, *Terrorism, Freedom and Security: Winning Without War* (Cambridge: The MIT Press, 2003); and Viganò, "Terrorismo, guerra e sistema penale," at 679 ff. Of a different opinion, Dershowitz, *Why terrorism works*, at 21 ff.; and Taft IV, "War Not crime", at 223 ff.

[51] Thus, the European Parliament in its report of February 2, 1994, said that "terrorism is a harm of peacetime, which must be treated with the remedies we have for peacetime".

[52] Heymann, *Terrorism, Freedom and Security*, at 19 and 87 ff., emphasizes that the "war metaphor" diverts attention to the measures that States should take to fight terrorism.

[53] In the same sense, Ackerman, 'The Emergency Constitution', at 1.070 and n 4 at 1.872–1.873; and H. Steinert, "The Indispensable Metaphor of War. On Populist Politics and the Contradictions of the State's Monopoly of Force," *Theoretical Criminology* 7 (2003): 265 at 265 ff.

[54] Beck, *Sobre el terrorismo y la Guerra*, at 31.

"individualization of war", any individual may be a potential terrorist and therefore must be controlled for security reasons.[55]

Consequently, democratic systems are waging this war not only in third countries[56] and against foreign nationals, but also against its own population, since any member of such societies can be an enemy combatant.[57] Thus, the battlefield for the new "war on terror" exceeds all boundaries and reaches every corner of the planet.[58]

Secondly, the use of preventive detention in order to incapacitate dangerous subjects has become an unpleasant consequence of the "war on terrorism" and a large point of discussion in the field of criminal law. If, as Judge Hudson[59] states, "history has proven that America is at war with the international terrorist organization *Al Qaeda*", any of its members may be imprisoned for preventive reasons in order to avoid that they "return to the battlefield",[60] while the "conflict" remains.[61] However, if what he (and others) consider war is, indeed, a crime, then the aforementioned "battlefield" is everywhere. Thus, the indefinite incapacitation of subjects considered dangerous to national security, without any specific charge against them, is justified. And, I say indefinite, not only due to the vagueness surrounding the limits of preventative detention, but also due to its sense of endless. As the time limits on preventive detention have not yet been established for conventional warfare, no one is able to determine the time of release because no one can determine the length of the conflict. As such, the detention of enemy combatants during the war against terrorism, could last a lifetime[62] as, unlike other forms of crime under criminal law, the

[55] Beck, *Sobre el terrorismo y la Guerra*, at 33–34. For him, the individualization of war could lead to the death of democracy because "governments should join with other governments against their citizens to avert the dangers that come from them". And the person used as a mere object of control is what characterizes a totalitarian regime (cfr. Gudín Rodríguez-Magariños, *La lucha contra el terrorismo en la sociedad de la información,* at 176).

[56] For instance, in Iraq and Afghanistan.

[57] See Earley, "The War on Terrorism and the Enemy Within...', already cited; Heymann, *Terrorism, Freedom and Security*, at 32–33, is critical to the expansion of military intelligence at a domestic level.

[58] In this sense, the Bush Administration stated that even the U.S. territory is a combat zone in the "global war on terror" (cfr. Golove/Holmes, "Terrorism and Accountability...', at 4–5).

[59] See his dissenting opinion in the case decision *Hamdi v. Rumsfeld* (03–6696) 542 U.S. 507 (2004).

[60] In the ruling of the case *Hamdi v. Rumsfeld*, the U.S. Supreme Court stated that "captivity in war is neither revenge, nor punishment, but solely **protective custody**, the only purpose of which is to prevent the prisoners of war from further participation in the war" (emphasis added).

[61] In this sense, Stoelting, "Military Commissions and Terrorism", at 435, shows that the qualification "wartime" legitimates indefinite detention by military authorities.

[62] Thus, the judgment of the case *Hamdi v. Rumsfeld* acknowledged that, from this perspective, Hamdi's detention could be extended until the end of his life, since the Bush administration declared that the war on terrorism will not cease, at least for the next two generations. In the literature, see Taft IV (n 38 at 226) who, in order to alleviate the life imprisonment of enemy combatants, proposes a periodic individual review that highlights the intentions of each captured if released, and A. C. McCarthy, "Torture: Thinking about the Unthinkable," in *The Torture Debate in America,* ed. KJ Greenberg (New York: New York University, 2006) at 101, who finds unacceptable the indefinite detention of members of *Al Qaeda*.

conflict it is not expected to end in the short or midterm.[63] Hence, the war on terror has been labeled the "endless war".[64]

Thirdly, this slogan has provided a legitimacy to preemptively engage in war[65] with states accused of collaborating with terrorists, such as in the case of Afghanistan,[66] which has led to international militarization and an antiterrorism campaign.

Finally, the label "war on terror" contains the following paradoxes (although, this would obviously never be accepted by the U.S.). First of all, while the deliberate targeting of civilians is not allowed under international laws of warfare, threatening military installations is legal. Thus, a terrorist attack against the Pentagon, for example, would be legitimate.[67] Secondly, in the case of ending global terrorism – certainly, a hypothetical scenario for the purpose of this discussion- all members would be automatically released and be repatriated. This action would suggest that by agreeing with peace processes and with terrorist groups, a *sine qua non* would be imposed for the cessation of violence and the immediate release of prisoners. In addition, victims of terrorism would see like some of his tormentors are released after a short time since his imprisonment.[68]

5.3 Cases in Which a Terrorist Attack Is Both a Crime and a Foreign Armed Attack

The third area where it is possible to discuss the relationships between crime and war is in the case of terrorists attacks being carried out by a State. International law permits governments to fight "attacks from the outside",[69] which can also be

---

[63] In the same vein, D. Cole, "Enemy Aliens and American Freedoms", *The Nation* 23-9-2002 (www.thenation.com).

[64] In this sense, Ackerman, ('The Emergency Constitution', at 1.033) and Dershowitz (*Why terrorism* works, at 21) show that the war on terrorism could never end.

[65] On this kind of war, see D. Cole and J. Lobel, *Less Safe, Less Free. Why America Is Losing the War on Terror* (New York/London: New Press, 2007) at 70 ff.

[66] In the same sense, J. Lobel, "The War on Terrorism and Civil Liberties," *The University of Pittsburgh Law Review* 63 (2002): 767 at 790. And, as demonstrated by Scharf, 'Defining Terrorism as the Peacetime Equivalent of War Crimes…', at 365), one of the consequences (which for this author is positive) to equate terrorism with a war crime is that, then, the State is entitled to use military force in self-defense against a terrorist group physically located within the boundaries of another State.

[67] Clark/Raustiala, *Why Terrorists Aren't Soldiers*, already cited.

[68] Along with these reasons, finally, as demonstrated by M. Cancio Melià, "Terrorismo y Derecho Penal: sueño de la prevención, pesadilla del estado de derecho," in *Política criminal en vanguardia. Inmigración clandestina, terrorismo, criminalidad organizada*, coord. M. Cancio Meliá and L. Pozuelo Pérez (Navarra: Civitas, 2008) at 317–318, the use of the slogan "war on terror" is offering just what the terrorists intend.

[69] Article 51 of the UN Charter. On this issue, with the specific case of Afghanistan, see Duffy, *The "War on Terror" and the Framework of International Law*, at 188 ff.

considered as acts of terrorism.[70] Therefore, if a "crime" is considered an "external armed attack", it is possible to react to a crime in this instance with warfare. However, "retributive wars" cannot exist, as war of this kind should not aim to punish criminals.[71] This idea should only belong to criminal law, where the purpose of punishment is, in whole or in part, a just dessert.

In this section we take the case of the war in Afghanistan in the aftermath of 9/11. From what has already been said, it is clear that the attacks on the *World Trade Center* and the Pentagon were acts of terrorism.[72] But, was this armed attack[73] justified as a right to self defense? Indeed, answering this question is something that is beyond the scope of this paper. Internationalists are the best equipped to resolve this issue. Support for preemptive warfare was received from the United Nations Security Council, who effectively authorized the armed attacks.[74] However, it seems quite clear that the motive for such military action was primarily of revenge and in this respect, be regarded as an illegal invasion.[75]

Bibliography

Abad Castelos, M. 2006. La toma de rehenes como crimen internacional, in *Lucha contra el terrorismo y Derecho Internacional.* Cuadernos de Estrategia 133: 137.

Ackerman, B. 2004a. This is not a war. *Yale Law Journal* 113: 1871.

Ackerman, B. 2004b. The emergency constitution. *Yale Law Journal* 113: 1029.

Ackerman, B. 2006. *Before the next attack: Preserving civil liberties in an age of terrorism.* New Haven: Yale University Press.

---

[70] Although, as stressed by F. Reinares, *Terrorismo y Antiterrorismo* (Barcelona/Buenos Aires/México: Paidós, 1998) at 199 ff., "there is great controversy among diplomats and lawyers over whether the logistical support or harboring terrorists is enough to place charges against an State and consider that it is involved in terrorist activities performed by the terrorists against other countries, thus justifying the use of force by the latter in the territory of the former". See, also, Prittwitz, C, '¿Guerra en tiempos de paz? Fundamento y límites de la distinción entre Derecho penal y guerra' (2004) 14 *Revista Penal* (translated by F. Navarro Cardoso) at 179.

[71] Cfr. Prittwitz, "¿Guerra en tiempos de paz?...," at 179–180. Perhaps the most devastating effect of a retributive war is the idea of collective punishment (on this issue, see Golove/Holmes, "Terrorism and Accountability...', at 7).

[72] In the same vein, Duffy, *The "War on Terror" and the Framework of International Law*, at 84; B. Garzón, "La respuesta," *El País*, 2 October 2001 (www.elpais.es); and Prittwitz, "¿Guerra en tiempos de paz?...," at 179.

[73] As noted by W. K. Clark, *Winning Modern Wars: Iraq, Terrorism, and the American Empire* (New York: Public Affairs, 2003) at X, it is not an exaggeration to compare the 11-S with an act of war. For the society, for public opinion and the media, the attacks were a crime and a war: "'attack on America' and 'terrorist attack', 'war against USA' and 'monstrous massacre'".

[74] Resolutions 1368 and 1373. Critical to this decisions, Garzón ("La respuesta") and Prittwitz ('¿Guerra en tiempos de paz?...' at 179 ff.).

[75] Garzón (("La respuesta"); A. I. Pérez Cepeda, "El paradigma de la seguridad en la globalización: guerra, enemigos y orden penal," in P Faraldo Cabana (dir)/LM Puente Aba/EM Souto García (coords), *Derecho Penal de excepción. Terrorismo e inmigración* (Valencia: Tirant lo Blanch, 2007) at 111; and Prittwitz ('¿Guerra en tiempos de paz?...', at 176).

Ambos, K. 2005. Derecho penal y guerra: ¿Intervención punible del gobierno alemán en la guerra de Irak? *Revista de Derecho Penal y Criminología* 15: 171.
Araujo, R.J. 2003. A judicial response to terrorism: The status of military commissions under domestic and international law. *Tulane Journal of International and Comparative Law* 11: 117.
Avilés, J. 2006. Democratización y terrorismo en Irak. www.realinstitutoelcano.org, ARI n° 130/2003, 6 Nov 2006.
Beck, U. 2003. *Sobre el terrorismo y la Guerra* (trans: Carbó, Rosa S.). Barcelona: Paidós.
Cancio Meliá, M. 2008. Terrorismo y Derecho Penal: sueño de la prevención, pesadilla del estado de derecho. In *Política criminal en vanguardia. Inmigración clandestina, terrorismo, criminalidad organizada*, ed. M. Cancio Meliá and L. Pozuelo Pérez. Navarra: Civitas.
Cancio Meliá, M. 2010. *Los delitos de terrorismo: Estructura típica e injusto*. Madrid: Reus.
Cappozzi, J.Y. 2007. Hamdan v. Rumsfeld: A short-lived decision? *Whittier Law Review* 28: 1303.
Chesney, R.M. 2005. Careful Thinking About Counterterrorism Policy: Terrorism, Freedom, and Security: Winning Without War. By Philip B. Heymann. *Journal of National Security Law & Policy* 1: 169.
Clark, W.K. 2003. *Winning modern wars: Iraq, terrorism, and the American empire*. New York: Public Affairs.
Clark, W.K., and K. Raustiala. 2007. *Why terrorists aren't soldiers. The New York Times*, 8 Aug 2007. www.nytimes.com.
Cole, D. 2002. Enemy Aliens and American Freedoms. *The Nation*, 23 Sept 2002. www.thenation.com.
Cole, D. 2004. The priority of morality: The emergency constitution's blind spot. *Yale Law Journal* 113: 1753.
Cole, D., and J. Lobel. 2007. *Less safe, less free. Why America is losing the war on terror*. New York/London: New Press.
Dershowitw, A.M. 2002. *Why terrorism works? Understanding the threat responding to the challenge*. New Haven: Yale University Press.
Dratel, J. 2006. The curious debate. In *The torture debate in America*, ed. K.J. Greenberg, 111. New York: New York University.
Dubber, M.D. 2006. Guerra y paz: Derecho Penal del enemigo y el modelo de potestad de supervisión policial del Derecho Penal estadounidense. In *Derecho Penal del enemigo. El discurso penal de la exclusión I*, ed. M. Cancio Meliá and C. Gómez-Jara Díez, 685. Montevideo/Buenos Aires: Edisofer.
Duffy, H. 2005. *The "war on terror" and the framework of international law*. Cambridge/New York: Cambridge University Press.
Earley, B.W. 2004. The war on terrorism and the enemy within: Using military commissions to prosecute U.S. citizens for terrorist-related violations of the laws of war. *New England Journal on Criminal and Civil Confinement* 30: 75.
Estreicher, S., and D. O'Scannlain. 2006. Hamdan's limits and the military commissions act. *Constitutional Commentary* 23: 403.
Evans, C.M. 2002. Terrorism on trial: The president's constitutional authority to order the prosecution of suspected terrorists by military commission. *Duke Law Journal* 51: 1831.
Everett, R.O. 2006. The role of military tribunals under the law of war. *Boston University International Law Journal* 24: 1.
Ferrajoli, L. 1995. *Derecho y razón. Teoría del garantismo penal* (trans: Ibáñez, Perfecto Andrés). Madrid: Trotta.
Fricton, J.R. 2007. The balance of power: The supreme court's decision on military commissions and the competing interests in the war on terror. *William Mitchell Law Review* 33: 1693.
Garzón, B. 2001. La respuesta. *El País*, 2 Oct 2001. www.elpais.es.
Golove, D., and S. Holmes. 2004. Terrorism and accountability: Why checks and balances apply even in 'The war on terrorism'. *The NYU Review of Law and Security* 2: 2.
González Cussac, J.L. 2006. El Derecho Penal frente al terrorismo. Cuestiones y perspectivas. In *Terrorismo y proceso penal acusatorio*, ed. J.L. Gómez Colomer and J.L. González Cussac, 57. Valencia: Tirant lo Blanch.

Gore, T.M. 2007. Commission control: The court's narrow holding in Hamdan v. Rumsfeld spurred congressional action but left many questions unanswered. So what happens now? *Mercer Law Review* 58: 741.
Gudín Rodríguez-Magariños, F. 2006. *La lucha contra el terrorismo en la sociedad de la información. Los peligros de estrategias antiterroristas desbocadas*. Madrid: Edisofer.
Heymann, P.B. 2003. *Terrorism, freedom and security: Winning without war*. Cambridge: The MIT Press.
Ignatieff, M. 2005. *El mal menor*. Madrid: Taurus.
Kaytal, N.K. 2006. Hamdan v. Rumsfeld: The legal academy goes to practice. *Harvard Law Review* 120: 65.
Kness, A.J. 2007. The military commissions act of 2006: an unconstitutional response to Hamdan v. Rumsfeld. *South Dakota Law Review* 52: 382.
Laqueur, W. 2003. *Una historia del terrorismo* (trans: Aúz y Beatriz Eguibar, Tomás Fernández). Barcelona: Paidós. .
Lobel, J. 2002. The war on terrorism and civil liberties. *The University of Pittsburgh Law Review* 63: 767.
McCarthy, A.C. 2006. Torture: Thinking about the unthinkable. In *The torture debate in America*, ed. K.J. Greenberg, 98. New York: New York University.
Olásolo Alonso, H., and A.I. Pérez Cepeda. 2008. *Terrorismo internacional y conflicto armado*. Valencia: Tirant lo Blanch.
Pérez Cepeda, A.I. 2007. El paradigma de la seguridad en la globalización: guerra, enemigos y orden penal. In *Derecho Penal de excepción. Terrorismo e inmigración*, Faraldo Cabana, P (dir)/Puente Aba, LM/Souto García, EM (coords.), 95. Valencia: Tirant lo Blanch.
Prittwitz, C. 2004. ¿Guerra en tiempos de paz? Fundamento y límites de la distinción entre Derecho penal y guerra. 14 *Revista Penal* (trans: Navarro Cardoso, F.).
Reinares, F. 1998. *Terrorismo y Antiterrorismo*. Barcelona/Buenos Aires/México: Paidós.
Rona, G. 2008. Legal issues in the 'war on terrorism' – reflecting on the conversation between Silja N.U. Voneky and John Bellinger. *German Law Journal* 9: 711.
Rorty, R., Fundamentalismo: enemigo a la vista. *El País* 29 Mar 2004, 11.
Sharf, M.P. 2005. Defining terrorism as the peacetime equivalent of war crimes: Problems and prospects. *Case Western Reserve Journal of International Law* 37: 359.
Sheppele, K.L. 2004. Law in a time of emergency: States of exception and the temptations of 9/11. *Journal of Constitutional Law* 6: 1.
Steinert, H. 2003. The indispensable metaphor of war. On populist politics and the contradictions of the state's monopoly of force. *Theoretical Criminology* 7: 265.
Stoelting, D. 2003. Military commissions and terrorism. *Denver Journal of International Law and Policy* 31: 427.
Taft IV, W.H. 2006. War not crime. In *The torture debate in America*, ed. K.J. Greenberg, 223. New York: New York University.
Tiefenbrun, S. 2003. A semiotic approach to a legal definition of terrorism. *Journal of International & Comparative Law* 9: 357.
Tribe, L.H., and P.O. Gudridge. 2004. The anti-emergency constitution. *Yale Law Journal* 113: 1801.
Valsecchi, A. 2006. La definizione di terrorismo dopo l'introduzione del novo art. 270-sexies c.p. *Rivista Italiana di Diritto e Procedure Penale* 1103.
Viganò, F. 2006. Terrorismo, guerra e sistema penale. *Rivista Italiana di Diritto e Procedure Penale*, 648.
Wilkinson, P. 1985. Las leyes de la guerra y del terrorismo. In *La moral del terrorismo*, ed. D.C. Rapoport, 115. Barcelona: Ariel.
Yoo, J. 2005/2006. An imperial judiciary at war: Hamdan v. Rumsfeld. *Cato Supreme Court Review* 83: 86.
Yousef, S. 2005. Military tribunals: Cure for the terrorism virus or a plague all their own? *Houston Law Review* 42: 911.

Part III
Keeping Counter-Terrorism Within the Criminal Law Justice?

Chapter 6
The Impact of Contemporary Security Agendas Against Terrorism on the Substantive Criminal Law

Clive Walker

6.1 Introduction

For several jurisdictions in Europe, the phenomenon of terrorism did not commence on September 11, 2001. Some countries, like the United Kingdom, had been earnestly augmenting and refining counter-terrorism measures, including the criminal law, during several previous decades. But the events on that date did prompt a fundamental reappraisal even in jurisdictions which viewed themselves as experienced and sophisticated, such as the United Kingdom, as well as representing an epiphany for other jurisdictions. Arising from these (re-)appraisals, this paper will explore three questions.

The first concerns the appropriate role to be served by the criminal law in response to terrorism as compared to other potentially coercive exercises of state power. It is evident that 'democracies respond when there is blood on the streets'.[1] There is noble justification for them to do so based on the international law duties to combat terrorism and the duty in national and international law to protect individual life.[2] Thus, it has become fashionable to revive the language of 'militant democracy' and to urge responsible polities not to sit idly by while citizens are slaughtered and

[1] J. M. Collins, "And the Walls Came Tumbling Down," *American Criminal Law Review* 39 (2002): 1261.

[2] See C. Walker, "Clamping Down on Terrorism in the United Kingdom," *Journal of International Criminal Justice* 4 (2006): 1137.

C. Walker (✉)
Professor, Centre for Criminal Justice Studies, School of Law, University of Leeds, Leeds LS2 9JT, UK
e-mail: Law6cw@leeds.ac.uk

A. Masferrer (ed.), *Post 9/11 and the State of Permanent Legal Emergency*, Ius Gentium: Comparative Perspectives on Law and Justice 14,
DOI 10.1007/978-94-007-4062-4_6, © Springer Science+Business Media B.V. 2012

democracies subverted.[3] The question for this paper is what are to be the roles of the criminal law within this militant stance? The second and third questions, which are not easy to disentangle, relate to the modes of application of the criminal law within counter-terrorism and also how far criminal law may be altered from its 'norm' in the pursuit of those functions before its application becomes counter-productive. The latter point assumes that a criminal law 'norm' can be identified. Yet, the potential societal functions served by the criminal law are manifold[4] and certainly extend beyond the due process and crime control models made famous by Herbert Packer.[5] Nor even can it be claimed convincingly that one model is, or should be, wholly dominant within a given system,[6] since selected models depend on societal judgements about rights and other values which may come into play according to the level of the court, the consequences of the decision, the type of offender, and the interests of the victim. In the context of divergent European systems, the European Convention on Human Rights and Fundamental Freedoms will be invoked to offer some sure grounding as to applicable rights, though that choice inevitably confuses 'norm' with 'lowest common denominator', since its standards were set at a deliberately meek level so as to encourage compliance and avoidance of clashes with Contracting States jealous of their sovereignty.[7]

The overall thesis adopted for the purposes of this paper is that the challenge of terrorism can be the subject of legitimate, rational and effective legal responses within criminal law. In this outcome, terrorism might be said to resemble other forms of specialised criminality, such as organised crime, or even broader security threats to democracy and rights, such as fascism or espionage. But criminal law solutions to counter-terrorism are not without costs to the values of criminal justice. Therefore, the state and its critics need to be vigilant and should not assume that a criminal justice preference in counter-terrorism represents an unquestionable victory in all circumstances.

As a final introductory point, most of the examples in this paper will predominantly be based on United Kingdom experiences and laws. This choice reflects the richness of the British anti-terrorism legal catalogue,[8] but the lessons are not solely for British audiences since other jurisdictions are also struggling with these issues. A notable foreign example concerns the travails of President Obama, who, having

[3] See K. Loewenstein, "Militant Democracy and Fundamental Rights" (Pt 1) *American Political Science Review* 31 (1937): 417, 638; A. Sajo, ed., *Militant Democracy* (Utrecht: Eleven International Publishing, 2004); M. Thiel, ed., *The 'Militant Democracy' Principle in Modern Democracies* (Aldershot: Ashgate, 2009).

[4] See M. King, *The Framework of Criminal Justice* (London: Croom Helm, 1981), chap. 2.

[5] H. L. Packer, *The Limits of the Criminal Sanction* (Stanford: Stanford University Press, 1969) at 153.

[6] M. J. Damaska, *The Faces of Justice and State Authority* (New Haven: Yale University Press, 1986) at 241.

[7] See A. Lester, "The Mouse That Roared," *Public Law* (1995): 198.

[8] For a full survey of that catalogue, see C. Walker, *Terrorism and the Law* (Oxford: Oxford University Press, 2011).

set out on a bold course for the closure of the Guantánamo Bay Detention Facilities and for the criminal trial of those inmates who were not to be repatriated,[9] encountered serial rejection of his prescription. The Detention Policy Task Force recognised in 2009 that criminal prosecution under any guise can apply only 'where appropriate', and so it floated in addition the idea of reformed military commissions and even indefinite detention without trial as a residual option.[10] Later, the Guantánamo Review Task Force recommended that 126 inmates be repatriated but that only 36 should be prosecuted by Federal court or military commission, leaving 78 detainees in executive detention (48 for an indefinite period).[11] Even the five 'high value' prisoners (including Khalid Sheikh Mohammed) who were to be transferred to the jurisdiction of the Federal criminal courts for trial in New York were reassigned in 2011 back to the military commissions system. That system, under the Military Commissions Act 2009,[12] resumed operation in 2010 with the trial of Omar Khadr.[13] Federal criminal trials for detainees became impossible with the passage of the National Defense Authorization Act for Fiscal Year 2011, s.1032 ('Prohibition on the use of funds for the transfer or release of individuals detained at United States Naval Station, Guantanamo Bay, Cuba').

Because of their dubious status in international law,[14] their patent procedural unfairness, their discriminatory impact,[15] as well as their limited practical impact, these military style adjudicative processes present a dysfunctional model for terrorism adjudication.[16] For its part, the United Kingdom government has rejected the 'war on terror' concept, which is said to have given 'ammunition to America's enemies, and pause to America's friends'[17] as well as being 'misleading and mistaken'.[18] Yet, this process of contestation over American policies for the determination of facts and punishments in terrorism cases illustrates that criminal prosecution does not always appear to be the most attractive or viable option.

---

[9] Review and Disposition of Individuals Detained at the Guantánamo Bay Naval Base and Close of Detention Facilities and for a Review of Detention Policy Options (Executive Orders 13492 and 13493, 74 FR 4897 and 4901).

[10] Detention Policy Task Force, *Memorandum for the Attorney General and for the Secretary of Defense*.

[11] *Final Report* (Washington DC: Department of Justice, 2010).

[12] PL 111-84. See *Al-Bihani v Obama* (2010) 590 F 3d 866.

[13] See http://www.defense.gov/news/commissionsKhadr.html

[14] See especially C. Zerrougui, et al., *Situation of Detainees in Guantanamo Bay* (E/CN.4/2006/120, New York, 2006); G. Rona, "An Appraisal of US Practice Relating to "Enemy Combatants"," *Yearbook of International Humanitarian Law* 10 (2007): 232.

[15] US citizens could not be held indefinitely as enemy combatants: *Hamdi v Rumsfeld* (2004) 542 US 507. Prosecutions were mounted for example against John Walker-Lindh (227 F Supp 2d 565 (2002)) and James Ujaama (see *US v Kassir* 2009 US Dist LEXIS 83075).

[16] See also the (Israeli) Incarceration of Unlawful Combatants Law 2002.

[17] L. K. Donohue, *The Cost of Counterterrorism: Power, Politics, and Liberty* (Cambridge: Cambridge University Press, 2008), 2. See further B. Wittes, ed., *Legislating the War on Terror: An Agenda for Reform* (Washington, DC: Brookings Institution Press, 2009).

[18] *The Guardian*, January 15, 2009 at 29.

6.2 The Appropriate Role of the Criminal Law in Counter-Terrorism

Consistent with his 'war on terror' paradigm, President Obama's predecessor in office, George W. Bush, asserted that 'it is not enough to serve our enemies with legal papers'.[19] His alternatives to the criminal law as modes of exercise of the states powers in counter-terrorism cohered around a 'war on terror' which, as well as conveying rhetorical power, has entailed tangible measures such as detention and surveillance.[20] However, this extreme alternative to criminal justice has never been emulated within European jurisdictions, as already indicated.

Instead of a 'war on terror', the United Kingdom government has asserted that 'prosecution is – first, second and third – the government's preferred approach when dealing with suspected terrorists'.[21] The most recent affirmation emanates from the Macdonald Report in 2011, which recommends the amendment and curtailment of executive control orders so that 'Where people are involved in terrorist activity, they must be detected and, wherever possible, prosecuted and locked up … [as] a primary purpose of public policy…'.[22] Prosecution has been a pre-eminent tactic for some decades. The trend was decisively signalled during the era when Irish terrorism dominated the official counter-terrorism agenda by the Diplock Report in Northern Ireland as long ago as 1972.[23] The package then created included the juryless 'Diplock court' system and an associated package of specialist criminalisation elements which required pre-trial, trial, and post-trial departures from normal rules.[24] This clarion call for criminal prosecution was not unalloyed or exclusive,[25] but Lord Diplock was sure that[26]:

> … if decisions as to guilt are to be made by tribunals, however independent or impartial, which are compelled by the emergency to use procedures which do not comply with these minimum requirements [of article 6 of the European Convention], we do not think that a

---

[19] President Bush, State of the Union Address 20 January 2004 (http://georgewbush-whitehouse.archives.gov/news/releases/2004/01/20040120-7.html)

[20] US Presidential Order, Detention, Treatment, and Trial of Certain Non-Citizens in the War Against Terrorism, of the 13 November 2001 (66 Federal Register 57831); Terrorist Surveillance Program (see Offices of the Inspectors General, Unclassified Report on the President's Surveillance Program, Report 2009-0013-AS, Washington, DC, 2009).

[21] House of Commons Debates vol. 472 col.561 (21 February 2008), Tony McNulty.

[22] *Review of Counter-Terrorism and Security Powers* (Cm 8803, London, 2011), p. 9.

[23] *Report of the Commission to Consider Legal Procedures to Deal with Terrorist Activities in Northern Ireland* (Cmnd. 5185, London, 1972).

[24] See C. Walker, "The Role and Powers of the Army in Northern Ireland," in *Northern Ireland Politics and the Constitution*, ed. B. Hadfield, 114–115 (Buckingham: Open University Press, 1992) at 112; L. K. Donohue, *Counter-Terrorism Law* (Dublin: Irish Academic Press, 2001). These courts continue in modified form under the Justice and Security (Northern Ireland) Act 2007: C. Walker, *Terrorism and the Law* (Oxford: Oxford University Press, 2011), chap.11.

[25] *Report of the Commission to Consider Legal Procedures to Deal with Terrorist Activities in Northern Ireland* (Cmnd. 5185, London, 1972) para.24.

[26] *Ibidem* at para.12.

> tribunal which fulfils this function should be regarded or described as an ordinary court of law or as forming part of the regular judicial system or should be composed of judges who also sit in the regular criminal courts in Northern Ireland.

While criminal prosecution is given pride of place, it has rarely been exclusive in United Kingdom counter-terrorism laws[27]:

> Our aim throughout has been that our first priority would be to prosecute alleged terrorists; secondly, if we cannot prosecute them, to remove them; and thirdly, failing the opportunity, wherewithal and appropriate circumstances to remove such people, to detain them.

One constant rival involves executive measures, such as detention without trial under the Anti-terrorism, Crime and Security Act 2001 and then its replacement[28] in the form of control orders under the Prevention of Terrorism Act 2005.[29] Another alternative followed the promise of Tony Blair in 2005 that 'the rules of the game are changing'[30] and concerns the application of tighter immigration, asylum, and nationality laws against foreign terror suspects and rabble-rousers.[31] But the growing spectre of 'neighbour terrorism'[32] – the recognition that the prime threat of terrorism is from citizens and not aliens – has reaffirmed the need to resort more firmly to regular criminal prosecution.[33] As a reflection, in 2008/09, 76%[34] of imprisoned terrorists were British citizen 'neighbours'.[35]

This domestic trend towards regular criminal prosecution may be evidenced by four indicators. One is that the most recent United Kingdom anti-terrorism legislation has avoided reliance upon executive measures. Thus, the Terrorism Act 2006 concentrated on the delivery of new crimes (described later). As a result, the parliamentary Joint Committee on Human Rights welcomed the 'possible adaptations of the criminal justice system which are capable of facilitating the effective criminal prosecution of terrorist suspects in ways compatible with the UK's human rights obligations'.[36]

---

[27] House of Lords Debates vol.629 col.459 (29 November 2001), Lord Rooker.

[28] See *A v Secretary of State for the Home Department* [2004] UKHL 56.

[29] See C. Walker, "Keeping Control of Terrorists Without Losing Control of Constitutionalism," *Stanford Law Review* 59 (2007): 1395.

[30] http://www.number10.gov.uk/Page8041

[31] See C. Walker, "The Treatment of Foreign Terror Suspects," *Modern Law Review* 70 (2007): 427.

[32] See C. Walker, ""Know Thine Enemy as Thyself": Discerning Friend from Foe Under Anti-terrorism Laws," (2008) 32 *Melbourne Law Review* 275.

[33] Another consequence is an emphasis on social control through prevention: see Home Office, *Prevent Strategy* (Cm.8092, London, 2011); C. Walker and J. Rehman, ""Prevent" Responses to Jihadi Extremism," in *Global Anti-terrorism Law and Policy*, ed. V. V. Ramraj, M. Hor, and K. Roach, 2nd ed. (Cambridge: Cambridge University Press, 2012).

[34] See Home Office, *Operation of Police Powers Under the Terrorism Act 2000 and Subsequent Legislation* (18/09, London, 2009) at 12.

[35] See C. Walker, ""Know Thine Enemy as Thyself": Discerning Friend from Foe Under Anti-terrorism Laws," *Melbourne Law Review* 32 (2008): 275.

[36] Joint Committee on Human Rights, Counter-Terrorism Policy and Human Rights: Prosecution and Pre-Charge Detention (2005-06 HL 240/HC 1576) para. 7.

Likewise, the Counter-Terrorism Act 2008 establishes enhanced sentences and post-sentence restrictions, which necessarily rely upon prosecution.

The second indicator is the paucity in practice of alternative executive (Ministerial) security measures. Despite the apocalyptic analysis in 2007 of Jonathan Evans, the Director of the Security Service, that 2,000 suspects pose a threat to national security,[37] there were just 10 executive control orders in force in March 2011.[38] There have never been more than 20 detention or control orders at any one time.

The third indicator is a statistical gathering of pace for criminal prosecution following the arrest of suspected terrorists. The 35% average between 2001 and 2008 reached 48% in 2005–2006.[39] This criminalisation approach logically demands that terrorists should not be treated as offenders or prisoners with political motivations which mark them out as extraordinary or afford them special status.[40] Accordingly, homicides, offences against the person, and offences under the Explosive Substances Act 1883 are the common diet of major terrorist trials.[41]

The fourth trend has involved a gradual dismantling of the abnormal criminalisation processes associated with the 'Diplock' court system in Northern Ireland. In particular, the special admissibility rules for confessions in police stations, the mainstay of prosecutions and allegations of abuse for a decade or so in Northern Ireland, were terminated in 2002.[42] Even the centrepiece juryless court has been put on notice of its eventual demise by the Justice and Security (Northern Ireland) Act 2007, which contains an (extendable) sunset clause.[43]

The concentration on deploying criminal law within counter-terrorism has been marked by two trends. One concerns a proliferation of different types of offences (which will be explored in this paper). The second is a stiffening of punishments and related controls; these will not be covered here, save to note that there has been no imposition of disproportionate (rather than just severe) punishments, nor even

---

[37] https://www.mi5.gov.uk/output/intelligence-counter-terrorism-and-trust.html

[38] House of Commons Debates vol. 525 col.26 (17 March 2011), Theresa May.

[39] Source: Home Office, *Statistics on Terrorism Arrests and Outcomes Great Britain 11 September 2001 to 31 March 2008* (04/09, Home Office, London, 2009).

[40] See C. Walker, "Irish Republic Prisoners, Political Detainees, Prisoners of War or Common Criminals?," *Irish Jurist* 19 (1984): 189; M. von Tangen Page, *Prisons, Peace and Terrorism* (Basingstoke: Macmillan, 1998); J. Williams, "Hunger-Strikes: A Prisoner's Right or a "Wicked Folly"?," *Howard Journal of Criminal Justice* 40 (2001): 285.

[41] See *R v Bourgass* [2005] EWCA Crim 1943, [2006] EWCA Crim 3397; *R v Barot* [2007] EWCA Crim 1119; *R v Khyam* [2008] EWCA Crim 1612; *R v Ibrahim* [2008] EWCA Crim 880; *R v Asiedu* [2008] EWCA Crim 1725; *R v Sherif* [2008] EWCA Crim 2653; *R v Ali The Times* 9 September 2008 at 1; *R v Abdulla The Times* 17 December 2008 at 1. The same feature applies in the US: R. M. Chesney, "Beyond Conspiracy? Anticipatory Prosecution and the Challenge of Unaffiliated Terrorism," *Southern California Law Review* 80 (2007): 425 at 495–498.

[42] Terrorism Act 2000 (Cessation of Effect of Section 76) Order 2002 SI 2141. See further *Report of the Committee of Inquiry into Police Interrogation Procedures in Northern Ireland* (Cmnd.9497, London, 1979).

[43] See s.9. The sunset has been postponed at least until 2013: Justice and Security (Northern Ireland) Act 2007 (Extension of duration of non-jury trial provisions) Orders, SI 2009/2090, SI 2011/1720.

the wholesale reduction of the procedural rights of the defendant. On the latter point, it is true that the United Kingdom became the only country in Europe after September 11 to enter a notice of derogation under article 15 of the European Convention,[44] but that step was in connection with the device of executive detention rather than any conception of 'enemy criminal law'.[45] The United Kingdom derogation was withdrawn in 2005, and there is no present intention to issue a new notice.[46] The limited application and availability of derogation gives lie to the wayward ideas of any 'state of exception', as espoused by Agamben[47] That stance evinces ignorance the efforts of national and international legal developments since 1945. Thus, the judges have refused to grant *carte blanche* to the declaration of emergency, from *Lawless v Ireland*[48] onwards, though this has become only an assured stance in the current decade and is especially reflected in the national security jurisprudence in the UK and USA which has refused to accept any legal 'black holes'.[49]

Is criminal prosecution a self-evident good? Criminal prosecution might indeed be viewed as preferable to executive-imposed measures of restraint or supervision because it affirms individual autonomy through the requirement of *mens rea*, whereas collective risk to public or state security predominates in executive measures. The individuation of crime might thus be esteemed as an affirmation of the values of human autonomy and equality.[50] There is affirmation in more open fashion in court than is possible for executive measures of system legality, accountability, and due process.

---

[44] Human Rights Act 1998 (Designated Derogation) Order 2001, SI 2001 No. 3644.

[45] G. Jakobs and M. Cancio Meliá, *Derecho Penal Del Enemigo,* 2nd ed. (Madrid: Civitas, 2006); M. Cancio Meliá, "Terrorism and Criminal Law," *New Criminal Law Review* 14 (2011): 108.

[46] There are doubts as to whether it is possible to derogate from art.6: D. Weissbrodt, *The Right to a Fair Trial Under the Universal Declaration of Human Rights and the International Covenant on Civil and Political Rights* (Hague, Kluwer, 2001); Special Rapporteur on the promotion and protection of human rights and fundamental freedoms while countering terrorism, 4th Report to the General Assembly (A/63/223, 2008) para.12; *Öcalan v Turkey*, App. no.46221/99, 2005-IV, para.112.

[47] G. Agamben, *State of Exception* (Chicago: University of Chicago Press, 2005). Compare: S. R. Chowdhury, *The Rule of Law in a State of Emergency* (London: Pinter,1989); J. E. Finn, *Constitutions in Crisis* (Oxford: Oxford University Press, 1991); J. Oraa, *Human Rights in States of Emergency in International Law* (Oxford: Clarendon Press, 1992); J. M. Fitzpatrick, *Human Rights in Crisis* (Philadelphia: University of Pennsylvania Press, 1994); D. Dyzenhaus, "Schmitt v Dicey," *Cardozo Law Review* 27 (2006): 2005.

[48] App. no. 332/57, Ser A 3 (1961).

[49] J. Steyn, "Guantanamo Bay," *International and Comparative Legal Quarterly* 53 (2003): 1. See also H. Duffy, *The 'War on Terror' and the Framework of International Law* (Cambridge: Cambridge University Press, 2005); C. Walker, "The Threat of Terrorism and the Fate of Control Orders," *Public Law* (2010): 3, "The Judicialisation of Intelligence in Legal Process," *Public Law* (2011): 235; *Al-Skeini v United Kingdom* (app. no. 55721/07, 7 July 2011); *Al-Jedda v United Kingdom* (App. no.27021/08, 7 July 2011).

[50] See M. A. Drumbi, "The Expressive Value of Prosecuting and Punishing Terrorists," *George Washington Law Review* 75 (2007): 1165 at 1170; K. Roach, "The Criminal Law and Terrorism," in *Global Anti-terrorism Law and Policy*, ed. V. V. Ramraj, M. Hor, and K. Roach (Cambridge: Cambridge University Press, 2005) at 137.

Amongst the downsides of a priority for criminal justice is the lesser inability of prosecution to incapacitate in anticipation of a terrorism event no matter how catastrophically deadly or damaging. Thus, the threat to life and political stability from terrorism may justify a different response based on the precautionary logic of neutralising risk rather than punishing sustained misdeeds than, say, in the case of 'normal' crimes such as murder, most of which in the United Kingdom arise from a narrow domestic setting and pose no political threat. As the then Director of the Security Service, Dame Eliza Manningham-Buller, warned in 2005[51]:

> We may be confident that an individual or group is planning an attack but that confidence comes from the sort of intelligence I described earlier, patchy and fragmentary and uncertain, to be interpreted and assessed. All too often it falls short of evidence to support criminal charges to bring an individual before the courts, the best solution if achievable.

The next problem with proof in criminal prosecution arises from the disclosure of secret sources, techniques and data. The beauty of executive procedures is that they can handle 'intelligence information, whose disclosure may involve unacceptable risks.'[52]

The final drawbacks relate to potential negative perceptions of the courts protecting the state and not victims, allied with the appearance of judges being co-opted into the work of the executive, resulting in damage to their reputation for impartiality and independence. The danger is that minority communities, upon whom the anti-legislation unevenly impacts, will feel distrust leading to less cooperation.[53] Authentication that any damage has occurred is disputed.[54] But there is no doubt about the importance to criminal justice of community approval and involvement[55]:

> The Criminal Justice System (CJS) belongs to the people it serves. The public need to believe that to be the case. …. Criminal justice services should be open, transparent and accountable to those they serve. They should help the public understand how they are performing. They should do this collectively and in ways which build the confidence of all sections of the community that the system is fair, effective and, above all, working for them.

Finally, the high security and prolonged imprisonment of dozens of convicted terrorists incur very direct costs, both for those held[56] and for the taxpayer.

---

[51] http://www.mi5.gov.uk/output/director-generals-speech-to-the-aivd-2005.html

[52] *Review of the Operation of the Prevention of Terrorism Acts 1974 and 1976* (Cmnd.7324, London, 1978) para.52.

[53] See House of Commons Home Affairs Committee, Terrorism and Community Relations (2003-04 HC 165) para.153; G. Mythen, et al., "I'm a Muslim, but I'm not a terrorist," *British Journal of Criminology* 49 (2009): 736 at 744; T. Choudhury and H. Fenwick, *The Impact of Counter-Terrorism Measures on Muslim Communities* (Equality and Human Rights Commission Research report 72, London, 2011).

[54] The most comprehensive survey is by the Defence Science and Technology Laboratory, *What Perceptions do the UK Public Have Concerning the Impact of Counter-Terrorism Legislation Implemented Since 2000?* (Home Office Occasional Paper 88, London, 2010).

[55] Consultation Paper, *Engaging Communities in Criminal Justice* (Cm.7583, London, 2009) at 5.

[56] See HM Chief Inspector of Prisons, *Muslim Prisoners' Experiences* (London, 2010); *R (Bourgass and Hussain) v Secretary of State for Justice* [2011] EWHC 286 (Admin).

6.3 Functions of the Criminal Law in Counter-Terrorism

Six functions will be explored in this paper as being served by criminal law in counter-terrorism. First, criminal law can allow for prescient intervention against terrorism endangerment and well before a terrorist crime is completed. Second, there can be net-widening. Third, criminal law can instil a lowest common denominator of rights and so reduce obstructive 'technicalities'. Fourth, the criminal law can be used to mobilise the population against terrorism. Fifth, the criminal law can serve a denunciatory function. Sixth, the criminal law can bolster symbolic solidarity with the state's own citizens and with the international community.

6.3.1 Precursor Crimes

By 'precursor crimes' is meant the criminalisation of acts in preparation of terrorism. The extraordinary threat posed by suicide attacks or chemical biological, radiological, or nuclear weapons has warranted utilisation of the criminal law to avert anticipatory risk from terrorism.[57] Unfortunately, traditional criminal law generally intervenes after, rather than before, a crime event,[58] and there are also process obstacles to early intervention around admissibility, disclosure, and proof.[59]

Precursor offences have long sought to respond to these obstacles, and not only in the case of terrorism[60] or just in recent times. For example, conspiracy charges under the Explosive Substances Act 1883 are still commonly applied to contemporary terrorism. The prime contemporary examples in United Kingdom law are sections 57 and 58 of the Terrorism Act 2000.[61] Section 57 criminalises the possession of materials relevant to terrorism, and section 58 deals with the possession of information relevant to terrorism. The range of materials and actions captured potentially under these offences is broad but the nature of the terrorism being prevented is somewhat abstract. Thus, the possession of batteries and bleach will be the product of a drain-clearing exercise more often than a bomb-making exercise. The downloading from the internet of *jihadi* material is much more often sparked by idle (or even stupid) curiosity or fantasy than the compilation of technical blueprints to commit an outrage. Nevertheless, sections 57 and 58 extend the reach of the criminal law to a point where, often based on equivocal evidence, the prospect of harm is uncertain and where the only immorality has been the imagining of wickedness

[57] See A. Dershowitz, *The Case for Preemption* (New York: W.W. Norton, 2006); R. Suskind, *The One Percent Doctrine* (New York: Simon & Schuster, 2007).

[58] See R. Chesney and J. Goldsmith, "Terrorism and the Convergence of Criminal and Military Detention Models," *Stanford Law Review* 60 (2008): 1079 at 1084, 1088.

[59] Joint Committee on Human Rights, *Counter-Terrorism Policy and Human Rights: Prosecution and Pre-Charge Detention* (2005-06 HL 240/HC 1576) paras.12, 28.

[60] See also Theft Act 1968s.2; Prevention of Crime Act 1953s.1; Firearms Act 1968 ss.16–21.

[61] C. Walker, *Terrorism and the Law* (Oxford: Oxford University Press, 2011), chap.5.

rather than its materialised infliction rather than the traditional predicate of criminal law which is proof of immediate or inflicted harm.

The culmination of this trend towards the pre-emptive may be represented by some of the offences in the Terrorism Act 2006. Sections 1 and 2 contain offences of indirect incitement of terrorism, by which there is 'glorification' of terrorism to an audience albeit in a way which invites emulation by the audience.[62]

Next, by section 5(1) of the 2006 Act, an offence arises if, with the intention of (a) committing acts of terrorism; or (b) assisting another to commit such acts, a person engages in any conduct in preparation for giving effect to that intention. The scope of the preparatory acts is deliberately broad, save that the object of attention must be 'acts' rather than, say, the continued existence of a proscribed organization. Acts of terrorism are also distinct from acts of terrorists, the assistance of whom might comprise, say, shopping. The modes of involvement in connection with those 'acts' can be distinct from conspiracies (requiring an agreement with others)[63] or attempts (the very definition of which demands action which is 'more than merely preparatory').[64] In addition, attempts and conspiracies are in relation to specific 'normal' offences rather than 'terrorism'. There must be intent to commit or assist the acts or to assist acts. The person must have the further intent that the act or assistance must further terrorism. By section 5(2), it is expressly irrelevant whether the intention and preparations relate to one or more particular acts of terrorism, acts of terrorism of a particular description, or acts of terrorism generally. It is not just that the 'exact plans are unknown'[65] but that the offence approximates to 'having criminal thoughts'.[66] There are no specified outlawed activities, no set level of commitment to the enterprise, and no threshold as to the proximity or viability of any terrorism activity.

Next, by section 6 of the 2006 Act, an offence arises through providing instruction or training with knowledge that the person receiving it intends to use the skills in terrorism. It is forbidden under section 6(2) to receive instruction or training. This offence is broader than the outlawing of weapons training under section 54 of the Terrorism Act 2000. Attendance at any place, whether in the United Kingdom or abroad, where instruction or training within section 6 or section 54(1) of the 2000 Act is being provided is forbidden by section 8. It is not part of the *mens rea* that the offender intends or condones the training. There is guilt by presence rather than involvement, and so investigative journalists might fall foul of this offence.[67]

---

[62] Compare the prosecution for sedition in *State of Israel v Kahane* [2000] IsrSC 54 (5) 145, CrimA F.H. 1789/98, at 24 where Kahane's pamphlet not only (setting a climate) depicted Arab villages as 'nests of murderers' but also (as emulation) called for the destruction of Arab villages in response to the killing of Jews.

[63] See Joint Committee on Human Rights, *Counter-Terrorism Policy and Human Rights: Prosecution and Pre-Charge Detention* (2005-06 HL 240/HC 1576) para 54.

[64] Criminal Attempts Act 1981, s 1(1).

[65] House of Commons Debates vol 438 col 999 (3 November 2005), Paul Goggins.

[66] A. Jones, R. Bowers, and H. D. Lodge, *The Terrorism Act 2006* (Oxford: Oxford University Press, 2006) para 3.05.

[67] House of Commons Debates vol 438 col 1015 (3 November 2005), Paul Goggins; *Government Reply to the Joint Committee on Human Rights* (2005-06 HL114/HC 888) p 10.

Terrorist training is a worthwhile offence,[68] but it applies to a wide span of activities, with the result that a conspiracy to commit it can venture into the equivocal realms of attempting to board an aircraft to Pakistan when in possession of night-vision binoculars, medical provisions, two British passports, and nearly £9,000 in cash.[69] Given the allegation that 75% of jihadi training occurs in Pakistan,[70] section 8 could be invoked to cast suspicions on many young male British citizens of Pakistani ethnic origins who commonly attend madrasses in Pakistan.

Another category of precursor crimes builds upon suspicious associations. Rather than await the outcome of the plotting of associates, the association itself is criminalised. This goal can be achieved by the concept of membership of a proscribed organisation under section11 of the Terrorism Act 2000.[71] This offence has some justification in international law[72] but has not been very successful for two reasons. First, it is less relevant to *jihadi* type groups which lack any modicum of formality.[73] Second, proof is often in terms of action which can itself be prosecuted and so the membership offence is superfluous. Therefore, a looser form of personal (rather than organisational) associational offence has been suggested in addition. For instance, the French Penal Code, article 421-2-1 ('*association de malfaiteurs en relation avec une entreprise terroriste*'), forbids 'The participation in any group formed or association established with a view to the preparation, marked by one or more material actions, of any of the acts of terrorism provided for under the previous articles....'[74] However, this offence has in turn been criticised as 'a catch-all offence which in practice is found to be proved on a minimum of objective, independent evidence and a maximum of speculation, innuendo and inference, some of which is supplied by sources of questionable impartiality and integrity.'[75]

[68] According to CSRT proceedings at Guantánamo, at least 317 detainees 'took military or terrorist training in Afghanistan.' (B. Wittes, *Law and the Long War* (New York: Penguin, 2008) at 81). Compare 18 U.S.C. s.2339D (Intelligence Reform and Terrorism Prevention Act 2004, Pub. L. 108–458). This provision is narrower since there must be a link to a designated foreign terrorist organization. *US v. Maldonado*, H-07-125 M (S.D. Tex.) (alleging receipt of training from al Qa'ida while in Mogadishu, Somalia).

[69] *R v Qureshi* [2008] EWCA Crim 1054.

[70] Gordon Brown, *The Times*, December 15, 2008, p. 33.

[71] See C. Walker, *Terrorism and the Law* (Oxford: Oxford University Press, 2011), chap.8.

[72] See *Special Rapporteur on the Promotion and Protection of Human Rights and Fundamental Freedoms While Countering Terrorism, Report to the General Assembly* (A/61/267, 2006) para.26.

[73] See R. M. Chesney, "Beyond Conspiracy? Anticipatory Prosecution and the Challenge of Unaffiliated Terrorism," *Southern California Law Review* 80 (2007): 425, 437–446 (2007). For a rare case, see Rangzieb Ahmed *The Times* 19 December 2008 at 17, 20 December 2008 at 8.

[74] Inserted by Act no. 96-647 of 22nd July 1996 Article 2 Official Journal 23 July 1996. See also the Italian Penal Code art.416-bis ('Association of Mafia type').

[75] M. McColgan and A. Attanasio, *France: Paving the Way for Arbitrary Justice* (Paris: FIDH, 1999) at 35. See also Y. Mayaud, *Le Terrorisme* (Paris, Dalloz, 1997) at 27–29; Human Rights Watch, *Preempting Justice: Counter-Terrorism Laws and Procedure in France* (New York: Human Rights Watch, 2008) Part IV; A. Garapon, "The Oak and the Reed," *Cardozo Law Review* 27 (2006): 2041 at 2055.

These departures from the Millian standard of 'harm to others' in order to accommodate remoter risks are troubling for several reasons,[76] since 'The criminal law has not traditionally been a preventive tool in the UK'.[77]

First, the more remote is the harm, the less certain it is that harm will actually occur. Thus, the criminal law maintains in normal times a distinction between attempts and preparatory acts,[78] but this distinction becomes blurred in the terrorism arena because of the extreme danger of the potential harm and the importance of the interests protected (the lives of others).[79] As a result, it may be simplistic to say that preparatory acts such as the collection of information useful to terrorism are not worthy of moral criticism or legal reaction.[80]

Second, some of the more remote harms, such as the glorification of terrorism, become harms because of the intervening agency of others rather than the speaker *per se* who does no more than influence a climate of choice rather than underwrite a specific outcome.[81] In this way, the culpability of the speaker seems undeserving of a criminal penalty.

Third, the expanded purview of the criminal law inevitably impinges on desired constitutional activities such as expressive and associational rights.[82] The law traditionally protects the words of the extreme and offensive speaker, especially those at the margins of politics who have limited access to traditional media.[83] However, it should be noted that the US Supreme Court upheld as constitutional in *Holder v Humanitarian Law Project*[84] the offence of providing material support, including 'services', 'personnel' or 'training, expert advice or assistance', to a designated

[76] S. Wallerstein, "Criminalising Remote Harm and the Case of Anti-democratic Activity," *Cardozo Law Review* 28 (2007): 2697.

[77] Joint Committee on Human Rights, *Counter-Terrorism Policy and Human Rights: Prosecution and Pre-Charge Detention* (2005-06 HL 240/HC 1576) para.12.

[78] See R. A. Duff, *Criminal Attempts* (Oxford: Clarendon Press, 1996) at 33–75.

[79] See S. Wallerstein, "The State's Duty of Self Defence," in *Security and Human Rights*, ed. B. J. Goold and L. Lazarus (Oxford: Hart, 2007).

[80] Compare V. Tadros, "Justice and Terrorism," *New Criminal Law Review* 10 (2007): 658 at 675; *Special Rapporteur on the Promotion and Protection of Human Rights and Fundamental Freedoms While Countering Terrorism, Report to the General Assembly* (A/61/267, 2006) para.11.

[81] See A. von Hirsch, "Extending the Harm Principle," in *Harm and Culpability*, ed. A. P. Simester and A. T. H. Smith (Oxford: Clarendon Press, 1996) at 267.

[82] See J. Feinberg, *Moral Limits of the Criminal Law: Harm to Others* (New York: Oxford University Press, 1984) at 187–217.

[83] Compare *Redmond-Bate v DPP* [1999] EWHC Admin 732; *Tabernacle v Secretary of State for Defence* [2009] EWCA Civ 23; *Munim Abdul and Others v Director of Public Prosecutions* [2011] EWHC 247 (Admin).

[84] 561 U. S. (2010). For challenges to the designation, see *Humanitarian Law Project v US Department of Treasury* 484 F. Supp 2d 1099 (CD Cal., 2007); *Humanitarian Law Project v Mukasey* 509 F.3d 1122 (9th Cir. 2007), 552 F.3d 916 (9th Cir., 2009). Note also *32 County Sovereignty Committee v Department of State* 292 F .3d 797 (DC Cir., 2002); *Holy Land Foundation for Relief and Development v Ashcroft* 333 F.3d 156 (DC Cir., 2003); *Rubin v HAMAS* 2004 WL 2216489.

foreign terrorist organisation,[85] at least when applied to specified activities proposed by the Humanitarian Law Project. Therefore, the group's intention to advise the Kurdistan Workers' Party (PKK) or the LTTE, both designated foreign terrorist organisations, for example on how to file human rights complaints with the United Nations or how to conduct conflict resolution negotiations with governments, could involve crimes. At the same time, the US First Amendment ensures that there is no offence *per se* of the advocacy of the aims of the PKK, even for the carrying out of terrorist acts, but work with the PKK or LTTE for humanitarian purposes is also excessively forbidden under this ruling.

6.3.2 Net-Widening

The next function of the criminal law in the service of counter-terrorism is net-widening. Of course, pre-emption is itself a form of net-widening, but there are other forms which do not rely on chronology. So this heading will consider activities or degrees of involvement which never could be categorised as criminal even if and when they reach their ultimate fruition.

A principal aspect of net-widening in many jurisdictions arises through the use of the term 'terrorism', as defined by section 1 of the Terrorism Act 2000. It is not intended here to analyse at length the meaning of that term. For present purposes, it can probably be accepted by supporters and critics alike that it deliberately exceeds by some way the bounds of any single criminal offence. Nevertheless, the European Court of Human Rights has recognised that 'terrorism' retains sufficient grounding within the notion of criminality.[86] One can perhaps understand and accept that security and policing agencies should be tasked in terms wider than a concentration upon crimes.[87] But this argument is harder to sustain within criminal offences where legal certainty and formal due process are more solemn considerations. As already mentioned, the post-Diplock approach is to cloak so far as possible the condemnation of the terrorist within the legitimacy of the 'normal' criminal law. In any event, many 'normal' offences – relating to homicides, conspiracy to cause criminal damage, firearms possession and so on – capture well most actions of terrorism, therefore it hardly seems warranted to go beyond them. The deployment of the term within offences in the anti-terrorism legislation is therefore highly significant and

[85] 18 USC s.2339B, as originally enacted by the Anti-terrorism and Effective Death Penalty Act 1996, PL 104–132. See R. M. Chesney, "Beyond Conspiracy? Preventive Prosecution and the Challenge of Unaffiliated Terrorism," *Southern California Law Review* 80 (2007): 425; J. J. Ward, "Note: The Root of All Evil: Expanding Criminal Liability for Providing Material Support to Terror," *Notre Dame Law Review* 84 (2008): 471.

[86] *Brogan v United Kingdom*, App. nos. 11209, 11234, 11266/84, 11386/85, Ser. A 145-B (1988) para.50.

[87] See C. Walker, "The Legal Definition of "Terrorism" in United Kingdom Law and Beyond," *Public Law* (2007): 331.

deliberate. Its broad range reduces the chances that scenarios of threatened terrorism (and still less of perpetrated terrorism) cannot ground a prosecution. At the same time, the term increases the danger that it will criminalise persons who are perceived by the public as being committed primarily to political motives rather than violence.[88]

The reliance on 'terrorism' of counter-terrorism criminal offences has already been evidenced by the catalogue already discussed under the heading of 'Precursor crimes'. However, the trend has not been taken to what might be viewed as its logical conclusion, for a special offence of 'terrorism' *per se* has been resisted. This idea was proposed and rejected in 1975 in the United Kingdom.[89] Not only does it have unhappy resonances with foreign repressive regimes, such as *apartheid* South Africa,[90] but more substantial drawbacks would arise. A universal offence of terrorism of this kind would lack justification in international law, which has been unable to agree a single, precise definition for criminal law purposes.[91] Thus, reliance on such an offence in the United Kingdom might hamper international cooperation and create conflicting jurisdictions. It is preferable to reflect the international sectoral approach, with offences such as hijacking and hostage-taking, as well as some broad multi-lateral agreements as the UN Convention for the Suppression of Terrorist Bombings,[92] the enforcement of which is positively required not only by the UN Counter Terrorism Committee but also, in much of Europe at least, the Council Framework Decision of 13 June 2002 on Combating Terrorism.[93] The only conceivable uses to be served by a United Kingdom offence of terrorism would be jurisdictional – for example, to prosecute the attackers of the hotels in Mumbai or of the Sri Lankan cricket team in Pakistan, assuming some of the perpetrators were ever found within the United Kingdom's jurisdictions. Any gaps left could be viewed as the legitimate province of other jurisdictions and no business of prosecutors within the United Kingdom. These problems of conflict of laws would not arise when dealing with activities in failed states, such as Somalia, where extradition or production for criminal prosecution is pointless. However, complications, such as

---

[88] The argument that 'terrorism' is an unsuitable term because it embodies motive and therefore should relate to sentencing rather than criminality ignores the many other instances where criminal law embodies motive/purpose. See M. S.-A. Wattad, "Is Terrorism a Crime or an Aggravating Factor in Sentencing?," *Journal of International Criminal Justice* 4 (2006): 1017.

[89] See Report of a Committee to consider, in the context of civil liberties and human rights, measures to deal with terrorism in Northern Ireland (Cmnd.5847, London, 1975) para.70; House of Lords Debates vol.611 col.1487 (6 April 2000), Lord Bassam.

[90] See Internal Security Act no 74 of 1982 s.54 as considered by the (Rabie) *Report of the Commission of Inquiry into Security Legislation* (RP90/1981, Pretoria, 1981) paras. 8.3.5., 9.21-9.2.2.3; Protection of Constitutional Democracy Against Terrorist and Related Activities Act, 2004 (no.33), s.2, as considered by the South Africa Law Commission, *Project 105: Report on Review of Security Legislation* (Pretoria, 2002).

[91] See B. Saul, *Defining Terrorism in International Law* (Oxford: Oxford University Press, 2006); M. Lehto, *Indirect Responsibility for Terrorism Acts* (Leiden: Nijhoff, 2010), chap. 2.

[92] A/RES/52/164, Cm.4662, London, 1997.

[93] 2002/475/JHA, OJ L164, article 9.

the impacts of the Geneva Conventions, and the costs of criminal process and imprisonment come into play when the role of world prosecutor is assumed even when other states are content to let others shoulder the burden.[94]

A second aspect of net-widening is the extension of the British criminal law to foreign terrorism. First, by Part II of the Terrorism Act 2000, the power of proscription of terrorist organisations was extended beyond the Irish context, and most of the listed organisations are now non-Irish and relate to *jihadist* terrorism. The Terrorism Act 2000 also reformulated the definition of 'terrorism' in section 1(4)(d) expressly to encompass actions directed against foreign governments. In addition, there is a growing trend of extra-territoriality in criminal offences. For instance, UN Convention based offences of terrorist bombing and finance were incorporated in the Terrorism Act 2000 (and extended by the Crime (International Co-operation) Act 2003). Then, by the Terrorism Act 2006, section 17, a range of other terrorist-related offences were applied to extra-jurisdictional acts. The dangers of excessive criminalisation are perhaps at their apogee when dealing with 'terrorism' activities directed against despotic foreign governments, such as that of Libya[95] which for a time before 2011 was the subject of diplomatic rehabilitation by Western governments.[96]

The policy of net-widening to foreign political dissidents has been moderated in practice by the reticence of the British authorities. Indulgence continues to be shown to Hamas and Hizballah, with fine distinctions made between political and military elements,[97] so that both are only partially proscribed and latitude is given to political activities such as the al Manar broadcasts.[98] Equally, during 2009, the police merely took flags from Tamil demonstrators in Parliament Square, London, some of whom showed open support for the Liberation Tigers of Tamil Eelam, even though it is a proscribed organisation under United Kingdom law.[99] Another moderating factor has been the filter of prosecutorial consent by the Director of Public Prosecutions or Attorney-General on prosecution for many of the offences under the anti-terrorism

---

[94] Such is the case of Somali pirates: M. D. Fink and R. J. Galvin, "Combating Pirates Off the Coast of Somalia," *Netherlands International Law Review* 56 (2009): 367; E. Kontorovich, "A Guantánamo on the Sea," *California Law Review* 98 (2010): 243; D. Guilfoyle, "Counter-Piracy Law Enforcement and Human Rights," *International and Comparative Law Quarterly* 59 (2010): 141; House of Lords European Union Committee, *Combating Somali Piracy* (2009–10 HL 103).

[95] See *R v F* [2007] EWCA Crim 243. But the legitimacy of violence in conflict is recognised in *Secretary of State for the Home Department v DD (Afghanistan)* [2010] EWCA Civ 1407.

[96] See especially Letter dated 15 August 2003 from the Chargé d'affaires a.i. of the Permanent Mission of the Libyan Arab Jamahiriya to the United Nations addressed to the President of the Security Council (S/2003/818) and UN SCR 1506 of 12 September 2003.

[97] But foreign supporters are more actively suppressed; see the cases of Ibrahim Moussawi ("Hezbollah Newspaper Editor Is Refused Visa," *The Times,* March 14, 2009 at 14) and *Naik v Secretary of State for the Home Department* [2010] EWHC 2825 (Admin).

[98] Compare the US conviction of Javed Iqbal (B. Weiser, "S.I. Man Gets Prison Term for Aid to Hezbollah TV," *New York Times,* April 24, 2009 at A22) on charges under the International Emergency Economic Powers Act for providing aid to a designated foreign terrorist organization (see http://www.ustreas.gov/press/releases/js4134.htm).

[99] "Tamil Protesters Block Parliament," *The Times,* April 8, 2009 at 20.

legislation.[100] The involvement of law officers is a 'safety valve',[101] but the chilling effect that can arise for foreign dissidents cannot be wholly answered by the future chance of a Law Officer's intervention. In addition, the breadth of the terrorism offences will require assessments of all manner of delicate disputes, such as the decision not to prosecute Boris Beresovsky for invoking revolution in Russia.[102]

6.3.3 Lowest Common Denominator of Rights

The third function which is served by the criminal law in the service of counter-terrorism, and which in equal measure has tainted criminal law, concerns the attempts to reduce to the lowest possible level the traditional safeguards in the criminal law. The reasons are twofold. First, it is hoped to favour prosecution by reducing obstacles which safeguard the defendant and thereby apparently fail to reduce the risk of non-conviction. Second, an inherent problem with criminal proof arises from the damaging disclosure of secret sources, techniques and data:

> From this might follow the death of the informant. The flow of information which can lead, and in many cases has led to convictions in the courts would be endangered.[103]

The normative boundary for this form of redesign is provided by article 6 of the European Convention on Human Rights. But, as already indicated, the Convention is flexible and deferential in the design of criminal and especially of evidential laws,[104] a weakness which the United Kingdom legislature has readily exploited.

A major aspect of this technique has been played out around the use of reverse burdens in special precursor criminal offences. The problem is relevant to membership offences and to the offences of possession contrary to sections 57 and 58 of the Terrorism Act 2000.[105] In order to boost the prosecution's effort to meet the golden rule of proof beyond reasonable doubt, these offences allow for various presumptions to be made. It follows that two toxic characteristics combine in these cases – a precursor offence which net-widens beyond attempt, plus a reversal affecting the normal presumption of innocence.

---

[100] Terrorism Act 2000, ss 63E, 117; Terrorism Act 2006, ss 19, 37; Counter-Terrorism Act 2008, s 29. See Lord Carlile, *The Definition of Terrorism* (Cm.7052, London, 2007) para. 81.

[101] Lord Carlile, *Proposals by Her Majesty's Government for Changes to the Laws Against Terrorism* (London: Home Office, 2005) para. 49.

[102] http://www.cps.gov.uk/news/pressreleases/archive/2007/138_07.html

[103] *Review of the Operation of the Prevention of Terrorism Acts 1974 and 1976* (Cmnd.7324, London, 1978) para.52.

[104] The point was recently confirmed in *Gäfgen v. Germany*, App no 22978/05, 1 July 2010, para.162.

[105] See L. Zedner, "Seeking Security by Eroding Rights," in *Security and Human Rights*, ed. B. J. Goold and L. Lazarus (Oxford: Hart, 2007) at 259.

The responses by the courts to these features have been complex, but the courts have now clearly insisted in *Sheldrake v Director of Public Prosecutions; Attorney General's Reference (No 4 of 2002)* that 'Security concerns do not absolve member states from their duty to observe basic standards of fairness.'[106] In this light, the court viewed the membership offence in section 11(1) as creating a real risk that blameless conduct could be penalised, so section 11(2), by which a defence arises for inactivity since proscription, should be read as involving an evidential burden only – the defendant must merely raise the issue rather than prove it. A corresponding interpretation was taken in regard to sections 57 and 58 in *R* v *Director of Public Prosecutions, ex parte Kebilene*.[107]

There are a number of other disputes about the fairness of sections 57 and 58. One concerns the boundaries (as distinct from who bears the burden of proof) of 'reasonable excuse' for possession, which is a defence under section 57(2) and 58(3). The meaning under section 58(3) was examined in *R v F*,[108] and it did not encompass the despotic nature of the foreign regime being opposed. In *R v G*, the House of Lords emphasised that the excuse must be reasonable under the wording of section 58(3), based on the intrinsic nature of the information.[109] The 'aim was to catch the possession of information which would typically be of use to terrorists, as opposed to ordinary members of the population ... the information must, of its very nature, be designed to provide practical assistance.'[110] The defendant is thereby handicapped by not being able to show wider circumstances or purpose or even mental illness. The same interpretation against nefarious purposes does not apply under section 57(2) since its focus is the purpose of the defendant without reference to its reasonableness.[111]

Through these interpretations, the courts have stopped a trend whereby sections 57 and 58 were becoming akin to offences of the possession of terrorism pornography,[112] based on revelling in the notion of terrorism but without much link to the production of terrorism. The connection between the content of the article and the implementation of terrorism was clarified in *R v Zafar*[113] and *R v K*.[114] In *Zafar*, the court demanded that there must be proven 'a direct connection between the objects possessed and the acts of terrorism. The section should be interpreted as if it reads ... he intends it to be used for the purpose ...'.[115] There remains no element in section 58(1) that requires

[106] [2004] UKHL 43 at para.21 per Lord Bingham. See S. Treschel, *Human Rights in Criminal Proceedings* (Oxford: Oxford University Press, 2005) at 168–171.

[107] [2000] 2 AC 326. See now Terrorism Act 2000 s.118.

[108] [2007] EWCA Crim 243. See further 'Comment' [2007] *Criminal Law Review* 160.

[109] [2009] UKHL 13 at paras.75, 77.

[110] [2009] UKHL 13 at para.43.

[111] *Ibidem* at para. 74.

[112] Criminal Justice Act 1988, s.160.

[113] [2008] EWCA Crim 184.

[114] [2008] EWCA Crim 185.

[115] *Ibidem* at para.29.

the Crown to show that the defendant had a terrorist purpose. In *K v R*, the defendant mounted the bold argument that section 58 was insufficiently certain to comply with article 7 of the European Convention. In response, the Court of Appeal sought to remedy any imprecision by reading in the requirement of a purpose useful to terrorism. As already explained, it is the purpose of the information rather than the possessor at stake – the information intrinsically 'calls for an explanation'.[116] To illustrate, the A-Z of London could be of use to a terrorist in order to find a target, but that use would not place it within section 58 since that document does not intrinsically arouse suspicion unless one looked at the circumstances of its usage. The ruling in *K v R* was applied in *R v Samina Malik*.[117] The defendant was convicted under section 58, not for her crass poetry such as 'How to Behead', but for her possession of documents about military techniques and of a propagandist nature. She was acquitted on appeal on the grounds that the judge's summing up had failed to isolate those documents capable of founding a conviction under section 58 by satisfying the test of inherent practical utility to terrorism.

Though these judgments reduce the scope of sections 57 and 58, the offences are far from 'almost redundant'.[118] They remain top of the list for charges (32% of terrorist offences charges are under section 57).[119] Nevertheless, the United Kingdom courts have now set some important parameters to the compromises to the presumption of innocence under article 6(2) – virtually ruling out switches in 'legal' burdens of ultimate proof rather than evidential burdens of raising some facts to put specific elements of an offence at issue. It appears remarkably ignorant that the government and Parliament continue to insert 'legal' burdens of proof (for example in the Terrorism Act 2006, sections 1(6) and 2(9)), but these provisions probably face emasculation if they ever reach the courts.

6.3.4 Mobilisation Function

The next facet of the utilisation of criminal law in the service of counter-terrorism resides in the conscription of the public into counter-terrorism work. If, as Bobbitt argues, market-state terrorism takes as its principal target the citizens of its enemy,[120] then it makes sense to mobilise that citizenry to defend themselves. Thus, the market-state might demand of individuals, 'Whose side are you on?', in line with the warning to all nations of President Bush that, 'Either you are with us, or you are with the terrorists.'[121] Rather than leaving individuals to a Manichean debate, the law

[116] *Ibidem* at para.14. See further *R v G* [2009] UKHL 13 at para.44 on reliance upon extrinsic explanations.

[117] [2008] EWCA Crim 1450.

[118] V. Tadros, "Crime and Security," *Modern Law Review* 71 (2008): 940 at 968.

[119] Home Office, *Statistics on Terrorism Arrests and Outcomes Great Britain 11 September 2001 to 31 March 2008* (04/09, London, 2009).

[120] *Terror and Consent* (London: Allen Lane, 2008) at 147.

[121] http://georgewbush-whitehouse.archives.gov/news/releases/2001/09/20010920-8.html

imposes a duty to help themselves and thereby the state. Consequently, special criminal offences might foster a proactive 'informer society' where informers abound, just like the during the operations of the German Democratic Republic's *Ministerium für Staatssicherheit* ('Stasi'),[122] even worse than a passive 'surveillance society'.[123] The consequent dangers include, first, the creation of social tensions, especially if one takes due cognisance of the fact that the threat of *jihadi* terrorism has shifted from the exceptional alien to one's common 'neighbour'. There is, second, a direct threat to the individual human right of informational privacy. The third problem relates to the speculative basis for intervention, so the dangers are heightened of knowing or unwitting false accusations. Criticisms along these lines were equally raised in 2002 in the US in regard to its Operation TIPS (Terrorism Information and Prevention System).[124] Uncontrolled private surveillance proved unacceptable, and TIPS was cancelled and then prohibited.[125] These comparisons do not rule out invitations to report suspected terrorism, whether as a volunteer police informant[126] or for the more venal reasons in the American 'Rewards for Justice Program'.[127]

Notwithstanding these dangers, novel duties backed by the criminal law have been imposed in the United Kingdom.[128] The most common context is financial reporting measures which are demanded by international bodies such as the Financial Action Task Force under its Special Recommendations on Terrorist Financing.[129] It follows that many jurisdictions have enacted requirements for employees in the financial sector to report their suspicions to a central authority. Failure to do so will be an offence. The United Kingdom versions are set out in section 19(1) of the Terrorism Act 2000, (as amended by the Counter-Terrorism Act 2008, section 77), and, for the 'regulated sector',[130] by Schedule 2, Part III of the Anti-terrorism, Crime and Security Act 2001.

---

[122] See D. Childs and R. Popplewell, *The Stasi* (Basingstoke: Macmillan, 1996); J. O. Koehler, *Stasi* (Boulder: Westview Press, 2000).

[123] See *A Report on the Surveillance Society* (Wilmslow: Information Commissioner, 2006); R. Thomas and M. Walport, *Data Sharing Review* (London: Ministry of Justice, 2008); House of Commons Home Affairs Committee, *A Surveillance Society?* (2007–08 HC 58, and Government Reply, Cm 7449, 2008); House of Lords Select Committee on the Constitution, *Surveillance: Citizens and the State* (2008–09 HL 18, and Government Reply, Cm 7616, 2009); M. Scheinin, *Report of the Special Rapporteur on the Promotion and Protection of Human Rights and Fundamental Freedoms While Countering Terrorism* (A/HRC/13/37, 2009).

[124] See L. K. Donohue, *The Cost of Counterterrorism* (Cambridge: Cambridge University Press, 2008) at 251.

[125] Homeland Security Act 2002 (PL 107-296), s 880.

[126] See https://tips.fbi.gov/; http://www.met.police.uk/so/at_hotline.htm

[127] See http://www.rewardsforjustice.net/; Act to Combat International Terrorism 1984 (PL 98-533, 18 USC s.3071). The PATRIOT Act 2001(PL 107-56) increased the maximum reward to $25 m.

[128] See C. Walker, *Terrorism and the Law* (Oxford: Oxford University Press, 2011), chaps. 3, 9.

[129] http://www.fatf-gafi.org/document/9/0,3343,en_32250379_32236920_34032073_1_1_1_1,00.html

[130] Terrorism Act 2000, Sch 3A, as substituted by: Terrorism Act 2000 (Business in the Regulated Sector and Supervisory Authorities) Order 2007, SI 2007/3288; The Terrorism Act 2000 and Proceeds of Crime Act 2002 (Amendment) Regulations 2007, SI 2007/3398. The duty is required by the Third Money Laundering Directive 2005/60/EC, art 22.

United Kingdom law goes further still and obliges private individuals to snitch. The duties so imposed are almost unique to the field of terrorism, whereas the financial reporting is also (primarily) demanded in respect of organised crime and drugs cartels. The relevant United Kingdom offence is section 38B of the Terrorism Act 2000 which is committed if a person, without reasonable excuse, fails to disclose relevant information about terrorism.[131] As for the *actus reus*, a person may commit this offence through total inactivity (by not answering police questions or by not volunteering information). The defence of reasonable excuse under section 38B(4) will often relate to fears of reprisal or reaction going beyond the defence of duress. It does not excuse a person who simply does not wish to 'get involved'. A close personal relationship between the person involved in terrorism and the person with knowledge of it, such as a husband and wife, also offers no defence.[132] Nor are journalists excused from revealing sources.[133]

Justification for section 38B turns on practice and principle. In practice, the main advantage is that it will 'create an atmosphere in which it [is] respectable to provide ... information'.[134] The imparting and sharing of intelligence are key elements of responding to terrorism.[135] Information can then be used to 'Prevent' and 'Pursue' in the language of the United Kingdom Government's Countering International Terrorism ('CONTEST') strategy.[136] In exceptionally dangerous situations, society regularly compels its citizenry to provide succour, and 'in the case of terrorism, which is almost by definition criminal activity aimed at society as a whole, it seems... reasonable that there should be more than a merely moral duty to assist the police'.[137]

Two important drawbacks arise from this tactic. The first is that there is no clear evidence that the flow of information to the police has been increased, and it seems improbable that it will ever do so. It is implausible that section 38B carries much clout with hardened terrorists, so it must be primarily aimed against those on the periphery of terrorism, whether as minor helpers or true bystanders. Yet, even such soft targets are likely either to be more intimidated by terrorists or to be more concerned for the plight of their kinfolk. The second practical drawback concerns the effect of section 38B on the media, as already outlined.

---

[131] See C. Walker, "Conscripting the Public in Terrorism Policing: Towards Safer Communities or a Police State?," *Criminal Law Review* (2010): 441.

[132] *R v Girma* [2009] EWCA Crim 912; *R v Sherif* [2008] EWCA Crim 2653.

[133] See C. P. Walker, *The Prevention of Terrorism in British Law,* 2nd ed. (Manchester: Manchester University Press, 1992), 141–143.

[134] House of Commons Debates vol 882, cols 928-9 (28 November 1974) George Cunningham.

[135] See further C. Walker, "Intelligence and Anti-terrorism Legislation in the United Kingdom," *Crime, Law and Social Change* 44 (2006): 387.

[136] Home Office, *Pursue, Prevent, Protect, Prepare: The United Kingdom's Strategy for Countering International Terrorism* (Cm.7547, London, 2009).

[137] *Review of the Operation of the Prevention of Terrorism (Temporary Provisions) Act 1976* (Cmnd 8803, London, 1983) para101.

In conclusion, any traditional distaste of the enforcement of good Samaritanism[138] and any concerns about creating the sort of 'informer's society which exists in totalitarian states'[139] can be allayed by the limit and seriousness of this exception. The state is right to demand every assistance in preventing the mass murder of fellow citizens but should guard more effectively against undue intrusion into either personal allegiances or undue reliance upon personal prejudices.

6.3.5 Denunciatory Function

The next function of criminal offences in the service of counter terrorism concerns their denunciatory impact. The traditional specialist mechanism by which a state can most vehemently denounce its political opponents is by way of offences against the state, such as treason and sedition. The message is particularly manifest with treason, which carried through most of its history exceptional penalties (not just death, but gruesome death, and the forfeiture of all property). The principal offences of treason are still contained in the Treason Act 1351. However, there has been minimal recent interest in a revival of these offences against terrorists. The principal reasons are, first, that the death penalty for treason was abolished in 1998[140] and, second, that the offences remain largely archaic formulations which entail many complexities and thereby increase the possibilities of acquittal.[141] In addition, the tactic is self-defeating[142] since offences against the state would emphasise the political nature and therefore claims to legitimacy of the attacks.

By contrast, treason has been more actively threatened in the US.[143] In 2006, a Federal grand jury issued an indictment for treason, charging Adam Yahiye Gadahn with involvement in al-Qa'ida videos.[144] Seditious conspiracy was charged against Sheikh Omar Abdel Rahman and others on the basis of 'the waging of the purpose

---

[138] See A. Ashworth, "The Scope of Criminal Liability for Omissions," *Law Quarterly Review* 105 (1989): 424; M. Vranken, "Duty to Rescue in Civil Law and Common Law," *International and Comparative Law Quarterly* 47 (1998): 934; M. Menlowe and A. McCall Smith, eds., *Duty to Rescue* (Aldershot: Dartmouth, 1993); Law Commission, *Report 237: Legislating the Criminal Code: Involuntary Manslaughter* (2005-06 HC 171) paras.2.23, 5.45.

[139] House of Commons Debates vol 904, col 475 (28 January 1976), Ian Mikado.

[140] Crime and Disorder Act 1998s.36.

[141] See G. S. McBain, "Abolishing the Crimes of Treason," *Australian Law Journal* 81 (2007): 94.

[142] See: Fabian Society, *Tract No. 416, Emergency Powers: A Fresh Start* (London: Fabian Society, 1972) at 19.

[143] See S. K. Babb, "Fear and Loathing in America," *Hastings Law Journal* 54 (2003): 1721; T. W. Bell, "Treason, Technology and Freedom of Expression," *Arizona State Law Journal* 37 (2005): 999; C. F. W. Larson, "The Forgotten Constitutional Law of Treason and the Enemy Combatant Problem," *University of Pennsylvania Law Review* 154 (2006): 863.

[144] See D. A. Kash, "The United States v. Adam Gadahn: A Case for Treason," *Capital University Law Review* 37 (2008): 1; M. Head, *Crimes Against the State* (Abingdon: Ashgate, 2011), chap. 4.

of which was "jihad," in the sense of a struggle against the enemies of Islam. Indicative of this purpose, in a speech to his followers Rahman instructed that they were to "do jihad with the sword, with the cannon, with the grenades, with the missile . . . against God's enemies."[145] However, another indication of disinterest in the United Kingdom is that offence of sedition was abolished barely without debate by the Coroners and Justice Act 2009, section 73. The need for reform has been duly noted both in the UK[146] and in Australia,[147] but police and prosecutors have instead simply ignored these offences.

Denunciation is nowadays more routinely achieved through tough sentencing.[148] Dershowitz argues that terrorism is more goal-oriented than crime and so is more open to disincentive and deterrence than the many crimes which are driven by impulse or passion.[149] This viewpoint is not shared by most governments or judges. A potent illustration concerns Zacarias Moussaoui, who was imprisoned for life without prospect of parole and was even taunted by US Judge Leonie Brinkema, who said that he will 'die with a whimper'.[150]

Denunciation of the espousal of opposing viewpoints has been tackled directly through the criminal law by the passage of advocacy offences, in pursuance of Article 5 of the Council of Europe Convention on the Prevention of Terrorism of 2005[151] and United Nations Security Council Resolution 1624 of 14 September 2005. The United Kingdom response is contained in the Terrorism Act 2006, section 1(1), which relates to the publication of statements that are 'likely to be understood by some or all of the members of the public to whom it is published as a direct or indirect encouragement or other inducement to the commission, preparation or instigation of acts of terrorism'. As for the *mens rea*, in section 1(2)(b), the publisher must either intend members of the public to be directly or indirectly encouraged or otherwise induced, by the statement to commit, prepare, or instigate acts of terrorism or specified offences, or be subjectively reckless as to whether members of the public will be so directly or indirectly encouraged by the statement. It is no defence under section 1(5)(b) to show that the dissemination fell on deaf ears – in other words, that no person was in fact encouraged or induced by the statement.

---

145 *United States v. Rahman*, 189 F.3d 88; 1999 at 94.

146 Lord Goldsmith, *Citizenship: Our Common Bond* (London: Ministry of Justice, 2008) para.4.42; M. Head, *Crimes Against the State* (Abingdon: Ashgate, 2011), chap. 6.

147 Australian Law Reform Commission, *Fighting Words* (Report 104, Canberra, 2006), chaps. 8, 9, 11.

148 See C. Walker, *Terrorism and the Law* (Oxford: Oxford University Press, 2011), chap. 6.

149 A. Dershowitz, *Why Terrorism Works* (New Haven: Yale University Press, 2002) at 22.

150 T. Baldwin, "You Will Die with a Whimper," *The Times*, May 5, 2006, at 35.

151 CETS No 196. See further Committee of Experts on Terrorism, 'Apologie du Terrorisme' and 'Incitement to Terrorism' (CODEXTER, Strasbourg, 2004); Joint Committee on Human Rights, The Council of Europe Convention on the Prevention of Terrorism (2006-07 HL 26/HC 247); A. Hunt, "The Council of Europe Convention on the Prevention of Terrorism," *European Public Law* 4 (2006): 603.

The most controversial aspect of the offence is indirect encouragement, and so Parliament sought to apply further clarifications and limits.[152] By sub-section (3), the indirect encouragement of terrorism includes a statement that 'glorifies' the commission or preparation of acts of terrorism or specified offences (either in their actual commission or in principle) but only if members of the public could reasonably be expected to infer that what is being glorified in the statement is being glorified as conduct that should be 'emulated by them in existing circumstances'. The notion of 'emulation' ensures that the words uttered should be understood as more than rhetorical. Consequently, praise for historical acts of violence, such as the armed occupation of the General Post Office, Dublin, in 1916, is not an offence, unless the statements can be readily understood to resonate with the present and to guide future action.

The overall impact is to criminalize generalized and public encouragements – that terrorism would be a good thing, without stating where or when or against whom. In this way, United Kingdom law has fallen into line with the notion of 'apologie du terrorisme' which appeared in the French Law of 29 July 1881 in Freedom of the Press, article 24(4), and the Spanish Penal Code, articles 18(2) and 578. Another effect may be to close channels of communication and to reduce the option of dialogue as a way of resolving conflict.

6.3.6 Symbolic Solidarity

The final purpose of the criminal law in the service of counter-terrorism involves a summation of the impacts of all of the foregoing points. The added cumulative impact is an expression of symbolic solidarity on the part of the state, not only that it stands for the protection of its own population but also that it is a responsible member of the international community. The requirement to support other states is expressed forcefully by the seminal UN Security Council Resolution 1373 of 28 September 2001.[153] Other Security Council resolutions which demand action by way of criminal law against terrorism include resolutions 1456 of 20 January 2003, 1566 of 8 October 2004, and 1624 of 14 September 2005.[154] The European Union Council Framework

---

[152] See House of Lords Debates vol 679, col 136 (28 February 2006), vol 680, col 241 (22 March 2006).

[153] See P. C. Szasz, "The Security Council Starts Legislating," *American Journal of International Law* 96 (2002): 901; E. Rosand, "Security Council Resolution 1373, The Counter Terrorism Committee and the Fight Against Terrorism," *American Journal of International Law* 97 (2003): 333.

[154] See Special Rapporteur on the promotion and protection of human rights and fundamental freedoms while countering terrorism, First Report to the Human Rights Commission, Promotion and Protection of Human Rights (E/CN.4/2006/98,2005).

Decision on Combating Terrorism of 2002[155] has played a role in putting the enactment of criminal offences on the agenda of some European states.[156]

The extent of the expression of solidarity may be evidenced by the volume of legislative activity against terrorism in almost every country, as monitored by the UN Counter-Terrorism Committee. In the United Kingdom, though it already had a comprehensive Terrorism Act 2000 (with 131 sections and 16 schedules), this catalogue has been added to by the Anti-terrorism, Crime and Security Act 2001 (equally as large), the Prevention of Terrorism Act 2005, the Terrorism Act 2006, the Justice and Security (Northern Ireland) Act 2007, and the Counter-Terrorism Act 2008. Not to be outdone, the USA PATRIOT Act 2001 consists of some 158 dense sections and has been followed by dozens of amendments and additions. In Australia, 29 major Acts of Parliament have been passed about terrorism since 2000. Thus, all countries must show symbolic solidarity by passing laws, even if they are largely of no practical effect. Well-crafted and extensive codes in New Zealand,[157] for instance, are worthy enough but are not installed because of any significant terrorist threat. Even in countries, like the United Kingdom, where the threat is real, large swathes of counter-terrorism law are 'symbolic' in the sense that they have never or rarely been invoked.

6.4 Conclusions

Criminal law is experiencing the pressures of late modernity[158] – not only from internationally networked, technologically aware terrorism but also from other forms of criminality, such as drugs trafficking and organised crime, which require sophisticated, anticipatory, and transnational responses. Consequently, the pressures are not unique to terrorism, in part because the formats of terrorism are not entirely novel.[159] But the proposition that terrorism in general poses distinct problems which are worthy of a considered response by criminal law cannot seriously be doubted.

---

[155] [2002] O.J. L164/3.

[156] See K. Nuotio, "Terrorism as a Catalyst for the Emergence, Harmonization and the Reform of the Criminal Law," *Journal of International Criminal Justice* 4 (2006): 998 at 1010. See further Commission Staff Working Document, Synthesis of the Replies from the Member States to the Questionnaire on Criminal Law, Administrative/Procedural Law and Fundamental Rights in the Fight against Terrorism (SEC 2009/225).

[157] See Terrorism Suppression Act 2002.

[158] See M. Castells, *The Rise of Network Society* (Oxford: Blackwell, 1996).

[159] Compare B. Lia, *Globalisation and the Future of Terrorism* (London: Routledge, 2005); P. Neumann, *Old and New Terrorism* (Cambridge: Polity, 2009); E. N. Kurtulus, "The "New Terrorism" and Its Critics," *Studies in Conflict and Terrorism* 34 (2011): 476.

The British experience of using criminal law in counter-terrorism underlines the plasticity of 'normal' and 'special' in criminal justice – that it is relatively easy to recalibrate what is 'normal' and what is 'special'. The resultant adaptations, which are replicated in many other jurisdictions, suggest that it is legitimate to examine how criminal justice might respond to the special challenges of terrorism and that it is wrong to treat criminal justice as a sacrosanct monolith. The difficulty is to ensure that the consequent designs remain within parameters which prize the objectives of both criminal justice and counter-terrorism. The United Kingdom government's counter-terrorism strategy ('CONTEST') seeks 'to reduce the risk from international terrorism, so that people can go about their daily lives freely and with confidence.'[160] This formula modestly suggests that the state has no expectation of the eradication of terrorism and concedes the 'false and extravagant presumptions about the ability of harsh criminal law to stop terrorism'.[161] Instead, the question is how society can co-exist with risk. In the case of criminal law in the service of counter-terrorism, a range of values, rights, constitutional, governance, and democratic accountability, can be either served or imperilled. The fundamental paradox of proof beyond doubt in a climate of precautionary logic remains troubling and encourages a slide towards minimum standards of due process.

To avoid undermining the criminalization project, four checks are suggested. First, prosecutors should consider in priority charges under 'normal' offences. Second, there should be much closer monitoring of the results of the prosecution process, so that its impact can be better understood. Third, the security services should be trained further to produce evidence and to expect to make court appearances as often as executive hearings.[162] Finally, the courts should recognize that they are on their own patch where their expertise exceeds that of the minister. They must act as prime guardians against the infliction of miscarriages of justice on individuals[163] and of abusive processes on their own institution.

Finally, whilst savage alternatives to criminal law, such as executive detention without trial or a 'war on terror', have been largely rejected, criminal law is not a panacea and further work should be undertaken to develop more social controls of terrorism through forms of assessment, counselling, and assimilation of political enemies. Societies are right to engage in the prosecution of their 'neighbour terrorists', but one's unruly and sometimes nasty neighbours should be handled without automatic

---

[160] Home Office, *Pursue, Prevent, Protect, Prepare: The United Kingdom's Strategy for Countering International Terrorism* (Cm.7547, London, 2009) para.0.17.

[161] K. Roach, "Anti-terrorism and Militant Democracy," in *Militant Democracy,* ed. A. Sajo (Utrecht: Eleven International, 2004) at 186.

[162] See K. Starmer, "Setting the Record Straight: Human Rights in an Era of International Terrorism," *European Human Rights Law Review* (2007) 123 at p 131.

[163] See C. Walker and K. Starmer, *Miscarriages of Justice* (London: Blackstone Press, 1999), chaps. 2, 14; K. Roach and G. Trotter, "Miscarriages of Justice in the War Against Terrorism," *Penn State Law Review* 109 (2005): 967; L. Zedner, "Securing Liberty in the Face of Terror," *Journal of Law and Society* 32 (2005): 507 at 524.

reliance upon imprisonment, especially for those who have expressed intent or sympathy but not have not perpetrated any deed. The United Kingdom government increasingly appreciates this approach,[164] but this more variegated response to potential violent extremism awaits effective delivery.[165]

Bibliography

Agamben, G. 2005. *State of exception*. Chicago: University of Chicago Press.
Ashworth, A. 1989. The scope of criminal liability for omissions. *Law Quarterly Review* 105: 424.
Australian Law Reform Commission. 2006. *Fighting words*. Report 104, Canberra.
Babb, S.K. 2003. Fear and loathing in America. *Hastings Law Journal* 54: 1721.
Bell, T.W. 2005. Treason, technology and freedom of expression. *Arizona State Law Journal* 37: 999.
Bobbitt, P. 2008. *Terror and consent*. London: Allen Lane.
Cancio Meliá, M. 2011. Terrorism and criminal law. *New Criminal Law Review* 14: 108.
Castells, M. 1996. *The rise of network society*. Oxford: Blackwell.
Chesney, R.M. 2007. Beyond conspiracy? Anticipatory prosecution and the challenge of unaffiliated terrorism. *Southern California Law Review* 80: 425.
Chesney, R., and J. Goldsmith. 2008. Terrorism and the convergence of criminal and military detention models. *Stanford Law Review* 60: 1079.
Childs, D., and R. Popplewell. 1996. *The Stasi*. Basingstoke: Macmillan.
Choudhury, T., and H. Fenwick. 2011. *The impact of counter-terrorism measures on Muslim communities*. Equality and Human Rights Commission Research report 72, London.
Chowdhury, S.R. 1989. *The rule of law in a state of emergency*. London: Pinter.
Collins, J.M. 2002. And the walls came tumbling down. *American Criminal Law Review* 39: 1261.
Damaska, M.J. 1986. *The faces of justice and state authority*. New Haven: Yale University Press.
Dershowitz, A. 2002. *Why terrorism works*. New Haven: Yale University Press.
Dershowitz, A. 2006. *The case for preemption*. New York: W.W. Norton.
Donohue, L.K. 2001. *Counter-terrorism law*. Dublin: Irish Academic Press.
Donohue, L.K. 2008. *The cost of counterterrorism*. Cambridge: Cambridge University Press.
Drumbi, M.A. 2007. The expressive value of prosecuting and punishing terrorists. *George Washington Law Review* 75: 1165.
Duff, R.A. 1996. *Criminal attempts*. Oxford: Clarendon.
Duffy, H. 2005. *The 'War on Terror' and the framework of international law*. Cambridge: Cambridge University Press.
Dyzenhaus, D. 2006. Schmitt v Dicey. *Cardozo Law Review* 27: 2005.
Fabian Society. 1972. *Tract No. 416, Emergency powers: A fresh start*. London: Fabian Society.
Feinberg, J. 1984. *Moral limits of the criminal law: Harm to others*. New York: Oxford University Press.
Fink, M.D., and R.J. Galvin. 2009. Combating pirates off the coast of Somalia. *Netherlands International Law Review* 56: 367.
Finn, J.E. 1991. *Constitutions in crisis*. Oxford: Oxford University Press.

[164] Home Office, *From the Neighbourhood to the National* (Cm.7448, London, 2008) at 25.

[165] One such initiative is Project Channel (see Home Office, *Channel: Supporting Individuals Vulnerable to Recruitment by Violent Extremists* (London: Home Office, 2010)), but its failings to date are recognised in Home Office, *Prevent Strategy* (Cm.8092, London, 2011).

Fitzpatrick, J.M. 1994. *Human rights in crisis*. Philadelphia: University of Pennsylvania Press.
Garapon, A. 2006. The oak and the reed. *Cardozo Law Review* 27: 2041.
Guilfoyle, D. 2010. Counter-piracy law enforcement and human rights. *International and Comparative Law Quarterly* 59: 141.
Head, M. 2011. *Crimes against the state*. Abingdon: Ashgate.
Hunt, A. 2006. The Council of Europe convention on the prevention of terrorism. *European Public Law* 4: 603.
Jakobs, G., and M. Cancio Meliá. 2006. *Derecho Penal Del Enemigo*, 2nd ed. Madrid: Civitas.
Jones, A., R. Bowers, and H.D. Lodge. 2006. *The Terrorism Act 2006*. Oxford: Oxford University Press.
Kash, D.A. 2008. The United States v. Adam Gadahn: A case for treason. *Capital University Law Review* 37: 1.
King, M. 1981. *The framework of criminal justice*. London: Croom Helm.
Koehler, J.O. 2000. *Stasi*. Boulder: Westview Press.
Kontorovich, E. 2010. A Guantánamo on the sea. *California Law Review* 98: 243.
Kurtulus, E.N. 2011. The "new terrorism" and its critics. *Studies in Conflict and Terrorism* 34: 476.
Larson, C.F.W. 2006. The forgotten constitutional law of treason and the enemy combatant problem. *University of Pennsylvania Law Review* 154: 863.
Lehto, M. 2010. *Indirect responsibility for terrorism acts*. Leiden: Nijhoff.
Lester, A. 1995. The mouse that roared. *Public Law* 198.
Lia, B. 2005. *Globalisation and the future of terrorism*. London: Routledge.
Loewenstein, K. 1937. Militant democracy and fundamental rights (Pt 1 and 2). *American Political Science Review* 31:417, 638.
Lord Carlile. 2005. *Proposals by Her Majesty's Government for changes to the laws against terrorism*. London: Home Office.
Lord Carlile. 2007. *The definition of terrorism*. Cm.7052, London.
Lord Goldsmith. 2008. *Citizenship: Our common bond*. London: Ministry of Justice.
Mayaud, Y. 1997. *Le Terrorisme*. Paris: Dalloz.
McBain, G.S. 2007. Abolishing the crimes of treason. *Australian Law Journal* 81: 94.
McColgan, M., and A. Attanasio. 1999. *France: Paving the way for arbitrary justice*. Paris: FIDH.
Menlowe, M., and A. McCall Smith (eds.). 1993. *Duty to rescue*. Aldershot: Dartmouth.
Mythen, G., et al. 2009. I'm a Muslim, but I'm not a terrorist. *British Journal of Criminology* 49: 736.
Neumann, P. 2009. *Old and new terrorism*. Cambridge: Polity.
Nuotio, K. 2006. Terrorism as a catalyst for the emergence, harmonization and the reform of the criminal law. *Journal of International Criminal Justice* 4: 998.
Oraa, J. 1992. *Human rights in states of emergency in international law*. Oxford: Clarendon.
Packer, H.L. 1969. *The limits of the criminal sanction*. Stanford: Stanford University Press.
Roach, K. 2004. Anti-terrorism and militant democracy. In *Militant democracy*, ed. A. Sajo. Utrecht: Eleven International.
Roach, K. 2005. The criminal law and terrorism. In *Global anti-terrorism law and policy*, ed. V.V. Ramraj, M. Hor, and K. Roach. Cambridge: Cambridge University Press.
Roach, K., and G. Trotter. 2005. Miscarriages of justice in the war against terrorism. *Penn State Law Review* 109: 967.
Rona, G. 2007. An appraisal of US practice relating to "enemy combatants". *Yearbook of International Humanitarian Law* 10: 232.
Rosand, E. 2003. Security Council Resolution 1373, The Counter Terrorism Committee and the fight against terrorism. *American Journal of International Law* 97: 333.
Sajo, A. (ed.). 2004. *Militant democracy*. Utrecht: Eleven International Publishing.
Saul, B. 2006. *Defining terrorism in international law*. Oxford: Oxford University Press.
Starmer, K. 2007. Setting the record straight: Human rights in an era of international terrorism. *European Human Rights Law Review* 12: 123.

Steyn, J. 2003. Guantanamo Bay. *International and Comparative Legal Quarterly* 53: 1.
Suskind, R. 2007. *The one percent doctrine*. New York: Simon & Schuster.
Szasz, P.C. 2002. The Security Council starts legislating. *American Journal of International Law* 96: 901.
Tadros, V. 2007. Justice and terrorism. *New Criminal Law Review* 10: 658.
Tadros, V. 2008. Crime and security. *Modern Law Review* 71: 940.
Thiel, M. (ed.). 2009. *The 'militant democracy' principle in modern democracies*. Aldershot: Ashgate.
Thomas, R., and M. Walport. 2008. *Data sharing review*. London: Ministry of Justice.
Treschel, S. 2005. *Human rights in criminal proceedings*. Oxford: Oxford University Press.
von Hirsch, A. 1996. Extending the harm principle. In *Harm and culpability*, ed. A.P. Simester and A.T.H. Smith. Oxford: Clarendon Press.
von Tangen Page, M. 1998. *Prisons, peace and terrorism*. Basingstoke: Macmillan.
Vranken, M. 1998. Duty to rescue in civil law and common law. *International and Comparative Law Quarterly* 47: 934.
Walker, C. 1984. Irish Republic prisoners, political detainees, prisoners of war or common criminals? *Irish Jurist* 19: 189.
Walker, C. 1992a. The role and powers of the army in Northern Ireland. In *Northern Ireland politics and the constitution*, ed. B. Hadfield. Buckingham: Open University Press.
Walker, C. 1992b. *The prevention of terrorism in British law*, 2nd ed. Manchester: Manchester University Press.
Walker, C. 2006a. Clamping down on terrorism in the United Kingdom. *Journal of International Criminal Justice* 4: 1137.
Walker, C. 2006b. Intelligence and anti-terrorism legislation in the United Kingdom. *Crime, Law and Social Change* 44: 387.
Walker, C. 2007a. Keeping control of terrorists without losing control of constitutionalism. *Stanford Law Review* 59: 1395.
Walker, C. 2007b. The legal definition of "Terrorism" in United Kingdom law and beyond. *Public Law* 331.
Walker, C. 2007c. The treatment of foreign terror suspects. *Modern Law Review* 70: 427.
Walker, C. 2008. "Know thine enemy as thyself": Discerning friend from foe under anti-terrorism laws. *Melbourne Law Review* 32: 275.
Walker, C. 2010a. The threat of terrorism and the fate of control orders. *Public Law* 3.
Walker, C. 2010b. Conscripting the public in terrorism policing: Towards safer communities or a police state? *Criminal Law Review* 441.
Walker, C. 2011a. *Terrorism and the law*. Oxford: Oxford University Press.
Walker, C. 2011b. The judicialisation of intelligence in legal process. *Public Law* 235.
Walker, C., and J. Rehman. 2011. "Prevent" responses to jihadi extremism. In *Global anti-terrorism law and policy*, 2nd ed, ed. V.V. Ramraj, M. Hor, and K. Roach. Cambridge: Cambridge University Press.
Walker, C., and K. Starmer. 1999. *Miscarriages of justice*. London: Blackstone Press.
Wallerstein, S. 2007a. Criminalising remote harm and the case of anti-democratic activity. *Cardozo Law Review* 28: 2697.
Wallerstein, S. 2007b. The state's duty of self defence. In *Security and human rights*, ed. B.J. Goold and L. Lazarus. Oxford: Hart.
Ward, J.J. 2008. Note: The root of all evil: Expanding criminal liability for providing material support to terror. *Notre Dame Law Review* 84: 471.
Wattad, M.S.-A. 2006. Is terrorism a crime or an aggravating factor in sentencing? *Journal of International Criminal Justice* 4: 1017.
Weissbrodt, D. 2001. *The right to a fair trial under the universal declaration of human rights and the international covenant on civil and political rights*. Hague: Kluwer.
Williams, J. 2001. Hunger-strikes: A prisoner's right or a "Wicked Folly"? *Howard Journal of Criminal Justice* 40: 285.
Wittes, B. 2008. *Law and the long war*. New York: Penguin.

Wittes, B. (ed.). 2009. *Legislating the war on terror: An agenda for reform*. Washington, DC: Brookings Institution Press.
Zedner, L. 2005. Securing liberty in the face of terror. *Journal of Law and Society* 32: 507.
Zedner, L. 2007. Seeking security by eroding rights. In *Security and human rights*, ed. B.J. Goold and L. Lazarus. Oxford: Hart.
Zerrougui, C., et al. 2006. *Situation of detainees in Guantanamo Bay*. E/CN.4/2006/120, New York.

Cases

32 County Sovereignty Committee v Department of State 292 F .3d 797 (DC Cir., 2002).
A v Secretary of State for the Home Department [2004] UKHL 43.
A v Secretary of State for the Home Department (no.2) [2004] UKHL 56.
Al-Bihani v Obama (2010) 590 F 3d 866.
Al-Jedda v United Kingdom App. no.27021/08, 7 July 2011.
Al-Skeini v United Kingdom App. no. 55721/07, 7 July 2011.
Brogan v United Kingdom, App. nos. 11209, 11234, 11266/84, 11386/85, Ser. A 145-B (1988).
Gäfgen v. Germany, App no 22978/05, 1 July 2010.
Hamdi v Rumsfeld (2004) 542 US 507.
Holder v Humanitarian Law Project 561 U. S. ____ (2010).
Lawless v Ireland App. no. 332/57, Ser A 3 (1961).
Munim Abdul v Director of Public Prosecutions [2011] EWHC 247 (Admin).
Naik v Secretary of State for the Home Department [2010] EWHC 2825 (Admin).
Öcalan v Turkey, App. no.46221/99, 2005-IV.
R (Bourgass and Hussain) v Secretary of State for Justice [2011] EWHC 286 (Admin).
R v Abdulla The Times 17 December 2008.
R v Ali The Times 9 September 2008.
R v Asiedu [2008] EWCA Crim 1725.
R v Barot [2007] EWCA Crim 1119.
R v Bourgass [2005] EWCA Crim 1943, [2006] EWCA Crim 3397.
R v *Director of Public Prosecutions, ex parte Kebilene* [2000] 2 AC 326.
R v F [2007] EWCA Crim 243.
R v G [2009] UKHL 13.
R v Girma [2009] EWCA Crim 912.
R v Ibrahim [2008] EWCA Crim 880.
R v K [2008] EWCA Crim 185.
R v Khyam [2008] EWCA Crim 1612.
R v Qureshi [2008] EWCA Crim 1054.
R v Rangzieb Ahmed The Times 19 December 2008 p.17, 20 December 2008.
R v Samina Malik [2008] EWCA Crim 1450.
R v Sherif [2008] EWCA Crim 2653.
R v Zafar [2008] EWCA Crim 184.
Redmond-Bate v DPP [1999] EWHC Admin 732.
Rubin v HAMAS 2004 WL 2216489.
State of Israel v Kahane [2000] IsrSC 54 (5) 145, CrimA F.H. 1789/98.
Tabernacle v Secretary of State for Defence [2009] EWCA Civ 23.
United States v. Rahman, 189 F.3d 88 (1999).
US v James Ujaama (referred to in *US v Kassir* 2009 US Dist LEXIS 83075).
US v John Walker-Lindh 227 F Supp 2d 565 (2002).
US v. Maldonado, H-07-125 M (S.D. Tex.).

Other Sources

Act no. 96-647 of 22nd July 1996 Article 2, Official Journal 23 July 1996 (France).
Act to Combat International Terrorism 1984 (PL 98-533, 18 USC s.3071) (USA).
Anti-terrorism and Effective Death Penalty Act 1996, PL 104-132, 18 USC s.2339B (USA).
Commission Staff Working Document, *Synthesis of the Replies from the Member States to the Questionnaire on Criminal Law, Administrative/Procedural Law and Fundamental Rights in the Fight against Terrorism* (SEC 2009/225).
Committee of Experts on Terrorism. 2004. *'Apologie du Terrorisme' and 'Incitement to Terrorism'*. Strasbourg: CODEXTER.
Consultation Paper, *Engaging Communities in Criminal Justice* (Cm.7583, London, 2009).
Council of Europe Convention on the Prevention of Terrorism of 2005 CETS No 196.
Counter-Terrorism Act 2008 (UK).
Crime and Disorder Act 1998 (UK).
Criminal Attempts Act 1981 (UK).
Criminal Justice Act 1988 (UK).
Defence Science and Technology Laboratory, *What Perceptions do the UK Public have Concerning the Impact of Counter-terrorism Legislation Implemented since 2000?* (Home Office Occasional Paper 88, London, 2010).
Detention Policy Task Force, *Final Report* (Department of Justice, Washington, DC, 2010).
Detention Policy Task Force, *Memorandum for the Attorney General and for the Secretary of Defense* (Department of Justice, Washington, DC, 2010).
Financial Action Task Force, Special Recommendations on Terrorist Financing http://www.fatf-gafi.org/document/9/0,3343,en_32250379_32236920_34032073_1_1_1_1,00.html.
Firearms Act 1968 (UK).
Government Reply to the Joint Committee on Human Rights (2005-06 HL114/HC 888).
HM Chief Inspector of Prisons, *Muslim Prisoners' Experiences* (London, 2010).
Holy Land Foundation for Relief and Development v Ashcroft 333 F.3d 156 (2003).
Home Office, *Channel: Supporting individuals vulnerable to recruitment by violent extremists* (London, 2010).
Home Office, *From the Neighbourhood to the National* (Cm.7448, London, 2008).
Home Office, *Operation of police powers under the Terrorism Act 2000 and subsequent legislation* (18/09, London, 2009).
Home Office, *Prevent Strategy* (Cm.8092, London, 2011).
Home Office, *Pursue, Prevent, Protect, Prepare: The United Kingdom's Strategy for Countering International Terrorism* (Cm.7547, London, 2009).
Home Office, Statistics on Terrorism Arrests and Outcomes Great Britain 11 September 2001 to 31 March 2008 (04/09, Home Office, London, 2009).
Homeland Security Act 2002 (PL 107-296) (USA).
House of Commons Home Affairs Committee, *A Surveillance Society?* (2007–08 HC 58, and Government Reply, Cm 7449, 2008).
House of Commons Home Affairs Committee, Terrorism and Community Relations (2003-04 HC 165).
House of Lords European Union Committee, *Combating Somali Piracy* (2009–10 HL 103).
House of Lords Select Committee on the Constitution, *Surveillance: Citizens and the State* (2008–09 HL 18, and Government Reply, Cm 7616, 2009).
Human Rights Act 1998 (Designated Derogation) Order 2001, SI 2001/3644.
Human Rights Watch, *Preempting Justice: Counter-Terrorism Laws and Procedure in France* (New York, 2008).
Humanitarian Law Project v Mukasey 509 F.3d 1122 (9th Cir. 2007), 552 F.3d 916 (9th Cir., 2009).
Humanitarian Law Project v US Department of Treasury 484 F. Supp 2d 1099 (CD Cal., 2007)
Incarceration of Unlawful Combatants Law 2002 (Israel).

Information Commissioner, *A Report on the Surveillance Society* (Wilmslow, 2006).
Intelligence Reform and Terrorism Prevention Act 2004, PL 108-458, 18 U.S.C. s.2339D (USA)
Internal Security Act no 74 of 1982, s.54 (South Africa).
Joint Committee on Human Rights, *Counter-Terrorism Policy and Human Rights: Prosecution and Pre-Charge Detention* (2005-06 HL 240/HC 1576).
Joint Committee on Human Rights, The Council of Europe Convention on the Prevention of Terrorism (2006-07 HL 26/HC 247).
Justice and Security (Northern Ireland) Act 2007 (UK).
Justice and Security (Northern Ireland) Act 2007 (Extension of duration of non-jury trial provisions) Orders, SI 2009/2090, SI 2011/1720 (UK).
Law Commission, *Report 237: Legislating the Criminal Code: Involuntary Manslaughter* (2005-06 HC 171).
Letter dated 15 August 2003 from the Chargé d'affaires a.i. of the Permanent Mission of the Libyan Arab Jamahiriya to the United Nations addressed to the President of the Security Council (S/2003/818) and UN SCR 1506 of 12 September 2003.
President Bush, State of the Union Address 20 January 2004 (http://georgewbush-whitehouse.archives.gov/news/releases/2004/01/20040120-7.html).
Prevention of Crime Act 1953 (UK).
Protection of Constitutional Democracy Against Terrorist and Related Activities Act, 2004 (no.33) (South Africa).
Report of a Committee to consider, in the context of civil liberties and human rights, measures to deal with terrorism in Northern Ireland (Cmnd.5847, London, 1975).
Report of the Commission of Inquiry into Security Legislation (RP90/1981, Pretoria, 1981).
Report of the Commission to consider legal procedures to deal with terrorist activities in Northern Ireland (Cmnd. 5185, London, 1972).
Report of the Committee of Inquiry into Police Interrogation Procedures in Northern Ireland (Cmnd.9497, London, 1979).
Report of the Special Rapporteur on the promotion and protection of human rights and fundamental freedoms while countering terrorism (A/HRC/13/37, 2009).
Report of the Special Rapporteur on the promotion and protection of human rights and fundamental freedoms while countering terrorism, Report to the General Assembly (A/61/267, 2006).
Report of the Special Rapporteur on the promotion and protection of human rights and fundamental freedoms while countering terrorism, 4th Report to the General Assembly (A/63/223, 2008).
Report of the Special Rapporteur on the promotion and protection of human rights and fundamental freedoms while countering terrorism, First Report to the Human Rights Commission, Promotion and Protection of Human Rights (E/CN.4/2006/98,2005).
Review and Disposition of Individuals Detained at the Guantánamo Bay Naval Base and Close of Detention Facilities and for a Review of Detention Policy Options (Executive Orders 13492 and 13493, 74 FR 4897 and 4901).
Review of Counter-Terrorism and Security Powers (Cm 8803, London, 2011).
Review of the Operation of the Prevention of Terrorism (Temporary Provisions) Act 1976 (Cmnd 8803, London, 1983).
Review of the Operation of the Prevention of Terrorism Acts 1974 and 1976 (Cmnd.7324, London, 1978).
Secretary of State for the Home Department v DD (Afghanistan) [2010] EWCA Civ 1407.
South Africa Law Commission, *Project 105: Report on Review of Security Legislation* (Pretoria, 2002).
Terrorism Act 2000 (UK).
Terrorism Act 2000 (Business in the Regulated Sector and Supervisory Authorities) Order 2007, SI 2007/3288 (UK).
Terrorism Act 2000 (Cessation of Effect of Section 76) Order 2002 SI 2002/2141 (UK).
Terrorism Act 2000 and Proceeds of Crime Act 2002 (Amendment) Regulations 2007, SI 2007/3398 (UK).

Terrorism Act 2006 (UK).
Terrorism Suppression Act 2002 (New Zealand).
Terrorist Surveillance Program (Offices of the Inspectors General, Unclassified Report on the President's Surveillance Program, Report 2009-0013-AS, Washington DC, 2009).
Theft Act 1968 (UK).
Third Money Laundering Directive 2005/60/EC.
US Presidential Order, Detention, Treatment, and Trial of Certain Non-Citizens in the War Against Terrorism, of the 13 November 2001 (66 Federal Register 57831).

Chapter 7
The War on Terror and Crusading Judges: Re-establishing the Primacy of the Criminal Justice System

Francesca Galli

Since 11 September 2001, countering terrorism has become one of the biggest priorities of the international community, the common trend among different jurisdictions being the adoption of fierce and authoritarian measures to prevent and suppress the terrorist threat in the name of a widespread call for further security.

The political and academic debate on anti-terrorism law and policies often stresses the need for a liberal democracy to find the right balance between the respect of individual liberties and the protection of national security.[1] Thus, some scholars simply provide a cursory analysis, framed in the language of balance, of the overall human rights impact of the legal measures adopted in the wake of September 11.[2]

7.1 Criminological Developments and Theoretical Framework

The shift toward prevention, surveillance and security, which has substantially expanded in the context of contemporary counter-terrorism frameworks, has been the subject of considerable criminological attention in the last few years. In order to

I would like to express my appreciation to the Fonds de la Recherche Scientifique (FNRS) for its generous financial support over the years of my post-doctoral research at the Institut d'Etudes Européennes (ULB), focusing on "L'Union européenne et la prévention du terrorisme : impact sur le droit pénal et redéfinition de la relation entre le droit pénal européen et les droits pénaux nationaux".

[1] See, e.g. A. M. Dershowitz, *Why Terrorism Works* (London: Yale University Press, 2002).

[2] For an argument against the misleading metaphor of balance which is based on an abstract conception of liberty and security (and their inter-relationship) and might obscure the real interests and issues at stake see D. Moeckli, *Human Rights and Non-discrimination* (Oxford: Oxford University Press, 2008) ch 1.

F. Galli (✉)
FNRS Post-doctoral Researcher, Institut d'Etudes Européennes, Université Libre de Bruxelles, Avenue Franklin Roosevelt, 39, 1050 Brussels, Belgium
e-mail: francesca.galli81@gmail.com

A. Masferrer (ed.), *Post 9/11 and the State of Permanent Legal Emergency*, Ius Gentium: Comparative Perspectives on Law and Justice 14,
DOI 10.1007/978-94-007-4062-4_7, © Springer Science+Business Media B.V. 2012

explain the new approach, sociologists such as Ulrich Beck have described the emergence of a "risk society": industrial society produces a number of serious risks and conflicts – among which those connected with terrorism and organized crime – and has thus modified the means and legitimization of state intervention placing risks and damage control at its centre as a response to the erosion of trust among people.[3] According to Beck:

> Risk may be defined as a systematic way of dealing with hazards and insecurities induced and introduced by modernization itself. Risks, as opposed to older dangers, are consequences which relate to the threatening force of modernization and its globalization of doubt.[4]

On similar lines, Feeley and Simon have described as "new penology" paradigm (or "actuarial justice"): a risk management strategy for the administration of criminal justice aiming at securing at the lowest possible cost a dangerous class of individuals whose rehabilitation is deemed futile and impossible.[5] The focus is on targeting and classifying a suspect group of individuals and making assessments of their likelihood to offend in particular circumstances or when exposed to certain opportunities.

According to David Garland (2001) the economic, technological and social changes in our society during the past 30 years have reconfigured the response to crime and the sense of criminal justice leading to a "culture of control" counterbalancing the expansion of personal freedom.[6] In his view, criminal justice policies thus develop from political actors' desire to "do something" – not necessarily something effective – to assuage public fear, shaped and mobilised as an electoral strategy.

Governments have often claimed that modern international terrorism cannot be handled adequately within the ordinary criminal justice system as there is a lack of evidence to prosecute and bring terrorist suspects to trial and thus a need for exceptional measures. Detailed rules of procedure and evidence are said to be too slow and cumbersome; criminal offences must be redrafted in order to address acts in their preparatory stage and also to punish ancillary participations.

One of the driving forces behind the implementation of new measures is the need to assuage public anxiety and reassure public opinion that resolute action has been taken, thus reinforcing the state's authority. Governments do not seem interested in finding out whether there has actually been an increase in the incidence of serious offences as in public discourse the focus is often on the fear of crime as opposed to actual crime or objective risks.[7]

Particularly after major attacks, there is a shared belief that the existing legal framework is beset by considerable security problems and deficiencies. An enormous role is played by the invasive television news reporting: the broadcasting of literally bloody horror of terrorist incidents creates an overwhelming political need

---

[3] See for instance the ubiquitous use of CCTV cameras.

[4] U. Beck, *Risk Society: Towards a New Modernity* (London: Sage, 1992) at 21.

[5] M. M. Feeley and J. Simon, "The New Penology", *Criminology*, no. 30(4) (1992): 449.

[6] D. Garland, *The Culture of Control* (Oxford: Oxford University Press, 2001).

[7] J. Waldron, "Security and Liberty: The Image of Balance", *Journal of Political Philosophy*, no. 11 (2003): 191 at 209–210; V. Dinh, "Freedom and Security After September 11", *Harvard Journal of Law and Public Policy*, no. 25 (2002): 399.

to be seen to act. This fuels legislative activism and has a great impact on the drafting techniques and on parliamentary scrutiny. Time pressure becomes a predominant element in the ensuing legislative process. Numerous new provisions are drafted in haste with little assessment of whether they are actually needed (or if they will overlap with existing provisions); or of whether such measures could possibly be an effective means to counter the threat; and what their impact would be on the individual rights not only of suspects and defendants but of all citizens.

By contrast, because they impact so negatively on even deeply entrenched rights and liberties, such legislation ought in principle to require deep consideration, wide consultation and careful review by expert committees before being enacted into law. But in many cases due deliberation appears to be sacrificed to other concerns.[8] In addition terrorist incidents have been often used as a catalyst for the implementation of other measures concerning immigration or security at large which would have not been accepted otherwise.[9] Mr Blunkett, former Home Secretary, confessed to using the Anti Terrorism, Crime and Disorder Security Bill as a vehicle to enact a list of repressive measures that the Home Office had long been wanting to get onto the statute book.[10]

7.2 Counter-terrorism Measures and the Broader Context of Current Changes Within the Criminal Justice System

The changes post-2001 in the context of counter-terrorism are to be seen in a larger framework of measures promoted by governments to address an allegedly mounting insecurity and the so-called "justice gap" (or its French equivalent "*laxisme de la justice*") in the need to be "tough on crime". The policy of governments is to reform criminal law and procedure to make it deal more effectively with identified categories of potential offenders. Along these lines, for instance, Tony Blair expressed a profound disapproval for the failed practice of 'fight[ing] twenty-first century crime with nineteenth century methods, as if we still lived in the time of Dickens'[11]; 'the rules of the game', he said, 'are changing'.[12]

On the basis of the findings examined above, a number of features common to the three systems emerge: the normalization of extraordinary measures – *i.e.* the possible leakage of special powers, from time to time, from terrorist legislation into criminal law and procedure generally; a shift from repression to prevention; and the emergence of a new "us and them" approach to criminal justice, called by writers in Germany the "*Feindstrafrecht*".

[8] For instance, the British Anti Terrorism Crime and Security Act 2001 was rushed through Parliament in less than a month.

[9] See for example the enactment of the French *Loi sur la sécurité quotidienne* in 2001.

[10] See S. Pollard, *David Blunkett* (London: Hodder & Stoughton, 2005).

[11] 'Tony Blair's keynote speech to the Labour Party's 2005 conference' *BBC News* (London September 28, 2004), http://news.bbc.co.uk/1/hi/uk_politics/4287370.stm (accessed October 22, 2009).

[12] PM's Press Conference (London August 5, 2005), http://www.pm.gov.uk/output/Page 8041.asp (accessed November 1, 2009).

7.2.1 *The Normalization Process: A Slippery Slope?*

The subsequent introduction of extraordinary anti-terrorism measures has been regarded as exceptional and legitimized by the fact that such measures are temporary and targeting only terrorism-related activities and specific groups of people.

According to the Italian Constitutional Court, an emergency situation legitimizes special anti-terrorism legislation but also places an intrinsic limit on it:

> In a situation of emergency, the Parliament and the government have not only the right and the power, but also the duty to intervene through the enactment of a specific emergency legislation (…) An emergency is certainly an anomalous and serious condition, but also intrinsically temporary. As a consequence, it justifies exceptional measures which lose their legitimacy if unjustifiably extended over time.[13]

When that is the case, Parliament has a parallel duty to repeal them.

The problem is that the current threat is not intrinsically temporary. How do we reconcile the permanent character of the current threat with the need for the response to remain temporary? If the emergency becomes permanent, exceptional limitations cannot be considered in compliance with national Constitutions (or with art. 15 ECHR).

The description of anti-terrorism powers as temporary emergency measures facilitates their acceptance. Then the notion of "normalization" describes a process through which emergency measures prompted by extraordinary events become institutionalised over time as part of the ordinary criminal justice system, long after the circumstances that initiated them have passed. The theory of "normalization" does not claim that the adoption of extraordinary powers is necessarily inappropriate in response to exceptional events. The problem is that the powers introduced are likely to remain limited to the context of the fight against terrorism, or that they have a tendency to be applied beyond their original scope and, thus, become part of, and impact upon, the ordinary criminal justice system and law enforcement policies at large.[14] The normalization of extraordinary powers is also perilous because the new provisions become the standard of reference for the design future policies.

In reality, the story of the temporary legislation adopted in Northern Ireland to deal with the troubles shows that emergency measures tend to perpetuate themselves as they are repeatedly extended although at first designed to be temporary.[15]

The normalization process can take two different forms. On the one hand, the practical application of an existing power, on the initiative of legislators, can be

---

[13] Cost. 14 January 1982, no. 15, in (1982) *Giurisprudenza Costituzionale*, no. 85 note L. Carlassare.

[14] O. Gross, "Chaos and Rules", *Yale Law Journal*, no. 112 (2003): 1011 at 1090; D. Dyzenhaus, "The Permanence of the Temporary" in *The Security of Freedom*, ed. RJ Daniels et al. (Toronto: University of Toronto Press, 2001).

[15] See J. Sim and P. A. Thomas, "The Prevention of Terrorism Act: Normalising the Politics of Repression", *Journal of Law and Society*, no. 10 (1983): 71; P. Hillyard, "The Normalization of Special Powers from Northern Ireland to Britain", in *A Reader on Criminal Justice*, ed. N. Lacey (Oxford: Oxford University Press, 1994).

expanded to a range of situations wider than those originally intended and often remote from them. A significant example of a normalization process at the initiative of the legislator is the development of a parallel track of criminal procedures for the investigation and trial of organized crime offences in Italy. Similarly, in the United Kingdom the use of civil preventative orders – which were originally conceived and "justified" as extraordinary measures – is expanding beyond the domain of serious offences. In France, special procedural measures adopted in the counter-terrorism framework have been applied since 2004 to a newly-defined category of "organized crime" offences. Another and different form of "normalization" is when police practices stretch the limits of what the law enacted with terrorism in mind permits. The controversial use made of s. 44 of the British Terrorism Act 2000 exemplifies the spill-over effect possibly resulting from police practices.

Italian legal writers have used the expression "*doppio binario*" (parallel track) to describe the development since the early 1990s of special procedures as a parallel track to deal with organized crime offences.

In fact, in Italy the normalization process results from the reciprocal influence of anti-terrorism and anti-organized crime legislation during the last 30 years and the subsequent re-enactment of repealed provisions following a new outburst of terrorism and organized crime at different stages. Since 1975 (Law 152/1975)[16] special measures adopted to deal with the domestic terrorist threat have been progressively introduced as derogations to the ordinary principles of criminal law.[17] With the enactment of the new *Codice di Procedura Penale* in 1988, Italian criminal procedure was redesigned in a more accusatorial fashion with an emphasis on defence rights, cross-examination and on the gathering of evidence at trial rather than beforehand, during the investigation phase. The new code was also meant to redress the numerous derogations brought about by the emergency legislation in the previous decade.

However, from when the level of the threat from organized crime increased once again at the beginning of the 1990s, the tools provided by the 1988 *Codice di Procedura Penale* began to seem inadequate and the legislator had to resort once again to old means in spite of their inquisitorial flavour.[18] Major changes in the law came along in the form of subsequent layers of new principles, rules and exceptions and not as a coherent legislative design. These include: special investigative judges, prosecutors and police (*Direzioni Distrettuali Antimafia* and *Direzione Investigativa Antimafia*), relaxed requirements for the interception of communications (and the development of preventive interceptions) and searches, a potential extension of pre-trial detention and preliminary investigations, etc. In addition, Law 203/1991[19]

[16] Law 152/1975 (*Disposizioni a tutela dell'ordine pubblico, detta Legge Reale*).

[17] G. Illuminati, "Reati "speciali" e procedure "speciali" nella legislazione d'emergenza", *Giustizia Penale* (1981): 106.

[18] P. L. Vigna, "Il processo accusatorio nell'impatto con le esigenze di lotta alla criminalità organizzata", *Giustizia Penale* (1991): 462.

[19] Law 203/1991 (*Conversione in legge, con modificazioni, del decreto-legge 13 maggio 1991, n. 152, recante provvedimenti urgenti in tema di lotta alla criminalità organizzata e di trasparenza e buon andamento dell'attività amministrativa*).

re-introduced the mandatory use of pre-trial detention with regard to a large number of offences, a measure that the new *Codice di Procedura Penale* (1988) had conceived as an *extrema ratio*.

With the enactment of Law 438/2001[20] and Law 155/2005[21] the scope of many of these provisions has been extended to cope with the newly-emergent international terrorist threat.[22] Hence, temporary measures adopted in the 1970s for the investigation and trial of domestic terrorism – although temporarily repealed by the 1988 *Codice di Procedura Penale* – are still part of the counter-terrorism framework and meanwhile have been applied to a larger range of offences.

In the United Kingdom the counter-terrorism "arsenal" is only the tip of the iceberg of a broader phenomenon, to the point where administrative measures are no longer exceptional and temporary, nor are they necessarily linked with a genuine emergency.[23] Control orders introduced by the UK Prevention of Terrorism Act 2005 are just one of many examples of preventive orders now in use in England and Wales. These include: Sexual Offences Prevention Orders (SOPO) and Risk of Sexual Harm Orders, introduced by the Sexual Offences Act 2003; Anti-Social Behaviour Orders (ASBOs), introduced by the Crime and Disorder Act 1998[24]; Serious Crime Prevention Orders created by the Serious Crime Act 2007; and Violent Offender Orders launched by the Criminal Justice and Immigration Act 2008. Not all preventive orders require a criminal offence to have been committed.[25] Some of them are used in place of a criminal prosecution where there is insufficient evidence or prosecution is not in the public interest. A similar normalization process of extraordinary means has occurred with regard to Special Advocates, introduced in 1997 to meet national security concerns in immigration hearing and later employed in relation to the indefinite detention of terrorist suspects and control orders within the proceeding of the Special Immigration Appeals Commission. It seems possible that the use of Special Advocates will soon be considered useful in the criminal prosecution of terrorist offences, particularly where the disclosure of sensitive information is at stake.[26]

---

[20] Law 438/2001 (*Conversione in legge, con modificazioni, del decreto-legge 18 ottobre 2001, n. 374, recante disposizioni urgenti per contrastare il terrorismo internazionale*).

[21] Law 155/2005 *(Conversione in legge, con modificazioni, del decreto-legge 27 luglio 2005, n. 144, recante misure urgenti per il contrasto del terrorismo internazionale).*

[22] Interestingly some provisions (such as derogations on cross-examination requirements *ex* Art 190 *bis Codice di Procedura Penale*) had already been applied to sexual offences and paedophilia by Law 268/1998.

[23] W. Hassemer, "Sicherheit durch Strafrecht", *HöchstRichterliche Rechtsprechung im Strafrecht* (HRRS) (2006): 130.

[24] Since April 1999 up to October 2006 there have been 9,853 ASBOs issued. *CDRP survey 2003–6: use of anti-social behaviour tools/powers* (November 2006) http://www.asb.home office. gov. uk/members/article. aspx?id=9822 (accessed November 1, 2009.

[25] Some require the subject to have been convicted or an offence, and others require the civil court imposing the order to be satisfied that he has committed one.

[26] See L. Zedner, "Preventive Justice or Pre-punishment?", *Current Legal Problems*, no. 60 (2007): 174 at 201. The Chilcot Report has already accepted that if intercepted evidence were admitted as

On 9 March 2004 the French Parliament enacted the *Loi Perben II*,[27] which contains the most far-reaching amendments of substantive criminal law and criminal procedure of the last decades.[28] In this context what we have called "normalization" process led to the application of special anti-terrorist procedures (*e.g.* with regard to house searches, identification of individuals, *garde à vue*, surveillance, or interception of communications) to a long catalogue of offences classified as "organized crime". As in the case of the definition of terrorism as a criminal offence, the legislator has not attempted to define "organized crime" and has merely introduced in the *Code de Procédure Pénale* a list of more than 30 offences to which special procedures become applicable. This list also includes a number of less serious offences (such as extortion, procuring or assistance in the illegal entry of immigrants) which do not obviously justify the use of extraordinary powers. The legislator can expand this catalogue at any time.

In addition, under broad definitions of stop and search powers (and of the definition of terrorism in itself) actions which are not terrorism-related have fallen under the scope of s. 44 of the British Terrorism Act 2000, resulting in a spill-over of special measures into areas other than terrorism. More than six-hundred people were stopped in 2005 during the Labour Party conference and as many as 995 anti-war protestors were stopped and searched over 2 months at the Royal Air Force military base of Fairford in 2003.[29] But only a small percentage of terrorism arrests since 11 September 2001 resulted in a charge and the charge, where there was one, was often not terrorism-related. Only in 60% of cases have terrorism-related charges resulted in a conviction.[30]

7.2.2 A Shift Towards Prevention

As already underlined in the introduction of the thesis, policy-making and crime-fighting strategies are increasingly concerned with the prediction and prevention of future risks (in order, at least, to minimise their consequences) rather than the prosecution of past offences.[31] Zedner describes a shift towards a society 'in which the

evidence in court, it should only be disclosed to cleared judges, prosecutors, or special advocates. See Lord Chilcot, "Privy Council Review of intercept as evidence: report to the Prime Minister and the Home Secretary" (the Chilcot Review)(Cm 7324, 2008), [20].

[27] Law 204/2004 (*Loi portant adaptation de la justice aux évolutions de la criminalité, dite Loi Perben II*).

[28] J. Pradel, "Vers un 'aggiornamento' des réponses de la procédure pénale à la criminalité", *Semaine Juridique*, no. 19 (2004): 132 and *Semaine Juridique*, no. 20: 134.

[29] See Hansard HC vol. 404 col. 219 W (28 April 2003).

[30] Home Office, "Statistics on Terrorism Arrests and Outcomes (Great Britain) – 11 September 2001 to 31 March 2008" (13 May 2009) 04/09.

[31] L. Zedner, "Fixing the Future?", in *Regulating Deviance*, ed. S Bronnit et al. (Oxford: Hart Publishing, 2008).

possibility of forestalling risks competes with and even takes precedence over responding to wrongs done',[32] and where 'the post-crime orientation of criminal justice is increasingly overshadowed by the pre-crime logic of security'.[33] Pre-crime is characterised by 'calculation, risk and uncertainty, surveillance, precaution, prudentialism, moral hazard, prevention and, arching over all of these, there is the pursuit of security'.[34] An analogy has been drawn with the "precautionary principle" developed in environmental law in relation to the duties of public authorities in a context of scientific uncertainty, which cannot be accepted as an excuse for inaction where there is a threat of serious harm.[35]

Although they certainly existed prior to September 11, the counter-terrorism legislation enacted since then has certainly expanded all previous trends towards anticipating risks. The aim of current counter-terrorism measures is mostly that of a preventive identification, isolation and control of individuals and groups who are cast as dangerous and allegedly represent a threat to society. The risk in terms of mass casualties resulting from a terrorist attack is thought to be so high that the traditional due process safeguards are deemed unreasonable or unaffordable and prevention becomes a political imperative. In the words of the UK anti-terrorism branch:

> The threat from international terrorism is so completely different that it has been necessary to adopt new ways of working (…). The advent of terrorist attacks designed to cause mass casualties, with no warning, sometimes involving the use of suicide, and with the threat of chemical, biological, radiological or nuclear weapons means that we can no longer wait until the point of attack before intervening. The threat to the public is simply too great to run that risk … the result of this is that there are occasions when suspected terrorists are arrested at an earlier stage in their planning and preparation than would have been the case in the past.[36]

During the last decade Parliaments have been active in enacting new offences in the "inchoate mode" and criminalising preparatory activities even where these stand several steps away from the actual perpetration of the harm.[37] Not only do inchoate offences expand criminal liability, but they also allow the use of enhanced preventive powers and police interventions before the commission of any substantive crime.

---

[32] L. Zedner, "Pre-crime and Post-criminology?", *Theoretical Criminology* 11 (2007): 261 at 261.

[33] L. Zedner, "Pre-crime and Post-criminology?", at 262.

[34] See the previous fn.

[35] See E. Fisher, "Precaution, Precaution Everywhere", *Maastricht Journal of European and Comparative Law* 9 (2002): 7. The analogy is made by L. Zedner, "Preventive Justice or Pre-punishment?", at 187–88.

[36] London Anti-Terrorism Branch (SO13), "Submission in support of three month pre-charge detention" (2005), appendix of Home Affairs Committee, "Terrorism Detention Powers" HC (2005–06) 910-I, 54 as quoted by J. McCulloch and S. Pickering, "Pre-crime and Counter-terrorism", *British Journal of Criminology*, no. 49(5) (2009): 628 at 632.

[37] Academics have traditionally considered it inappropriate to criminalize acts which are merely preparatory to a criminal offence. In defining the scope of criminal law through the harm principle, the dominant concern of legal writers has traditionally been to hinder the increasing expansion of criminal liability. Liberal philosophers have argued that a positive reason in favour of the State's intervention to create a criminal offence is the prevention of a conduct which can cause harm to others.

In relation to terrorism offences, in France and Italy the shift of criminal liability upstream from the commission of any harm has been achieved by the application of 'association for terrorist purposes' offences which have played a central role in the repression of terrorism since the 1980–1990s. The scope of these offences is extremely broad.[38] The United Kingdom anti-terrorist legislation, by contrast, is a particularly controversial example of a current trend in English criminal law, which is to create new offences in inchoate mode over and above the traditional categories of conspiracy, incitement and attempt.[39]

In terrorism cases an additional tension arises between criminal justice, which is supposed to be impartial, and the politically charged concept of national security.[40]

According to Feinberg: 'It is always a good reason in support of penal legislation that it would be effective in preventing (eliminating, reducing) harm to persons other than the actor (the one prohibited from acting) and there is no other means that is equally effective at no greater cost to other values'. J. Feinberg, *The Moral Limits of the Criminal Law* (New York: Oxford University Press, 1987) at 26. On the criminalization of remote harms see A. Ashworth, *Principles of Criminal Law* (Oxford: Oxford University Press, 2006) at 49–50; A. Von Hirsh, "Extending the Harm Principle", in *Harm and Culpability*, ed. A. Simester and A. T. H. Smith (Oxford: Oxford University Press, 1996).

[38] The French provision punishes any kind of participation in a group with a view to preparing a terrorist act, provided this has been demonstrated 'by one or more material actions'. The Italian legislation criminalises the promotion, establishment, organization and direction of terrorist groups (with a possible limit, according to some of the case-law, that the behaviour be evidenced by some form of concrete action) and more recently, a further offence of providing "material assistance" to terrorist activities.

[39] The Terrorism Act 2000 initially introduced only an offence of directing terrorist activities and then s. 5 Terrorism Act 2006 broadly criminalised any preparatory act. Whilst the penalty provided in France is 10 years (increased to 20 years for leaders and organisers of *associations de malfaiteurs*) and in Italy 7–15 years imprisonment (five to ten for the offence of assistance), both offences are punishable in the United Kingdom with a sentence of life imprisonment. By comparison this seems extremely severe. Moreover, the British legislator, unlike his counterpart in France and Italy, has also gone so far as to criminalise the suspicious possession of articles for terrorist purposes and to impose the evidential burden of proof upon the defendant. It is true that a similar offence was created in Italy in the 1970s in the context of an emergency that then existed but it was subsequently abolished and not replaced. New inchoate offences also include: the "encouragement", "glorification" and/or "apology" of terrorism (albeit in an undefined future and at undefined places) as well as the dissemination and the publication of relevant material. Whereas the United Kingdom has recently enacted specific provisions, the criminalisation of the glorification of terrorism in France and Italy is technically possible, but only under old provisions that are rarely used. Most importantly, in the two continental jurisdictions it is only "direct incitement" that can be prosecuted. The requirements set forth by the Council of Europe and the European Union instruments to punish "intentional acts of public provocation" were, it seems, considered to be sufficiently met by the existing provisions. In Italy, the offence of 'indirect incitement' was considered a feature of the fascist era and has been repealed. In the United Kingdom, by contrast, the new provisions are formulated in a very abstract way so as to criminalise an extremely wide range of expressions which could somehow support, justify or condone terrorism. This choice weakens the strong link which is traditionally required in law between the original expression of thoughts and the offence committed.

[40] McCulloch and Pickering, "Pre-crime and counter-terrorism", already cited.

The risk of potential harm is often assessed on the basis of secret evidence and grounded on political considerations, possibly prior to the establishment of any trial. In cases of judicial review, this tension has sometimes led to a certain level of judicial deference towards the executive which is perceived to be better placed to make decisions where national security is at stake.[41]

This paradigm shift towards preventive action poses critical challenges for the protection of individual rights. First, the boundaries of what is a dangerous behaviour are highly contentious and problems arise with the assessment of future harm. Secondly, "suspicion" has replaced an objective "reasonable belief" in most cases in order to justify police intervention at an early stage in terrorism cases without the need to envisage evidence-gathering with a view of a prosecution. Thirdly, there is greater reliance on preventive administrative measures as means of general use instead of seeing them as exceptional and temporary, and necessarily linked with a genuine emergency. They are created for the purpose of early interventions in order to avoid terrorist acts taking place, rather than merely to respond after the event (*e.g.* detention, expulsion and deportation of immigrants, administrative detention, control orders and listing). Governments can thus act on the lower standard of possibility of future harm rather than the higher standard of proof of past criminal activities. This allows a shift towards greater governmental discretion on national security grounds at the expense of judicial scrutiny.[42] Lastly, preventive measures encompass a larger number of activities and affect a broader range of people.

This drift towards prevention raises the question of whether one should see terrorists as criminals, who are both bound and protected, as all citizens are, by the criminal law and due process rights. And, if not, to what rights should they be entitled? The next section will explore this question in the light of the recently developed notion of "*Feindstrafrecht*".

[41] For instance, the House of Lords in the *Belmarsh* case had to consider whether sufficient evidence of a "public emergency threatening the life of the nation" had been provided to justify the issue and continuance of the derogation notice under art. 15 ECHR. The majority of the Court accepted that it was within the government's margin of appreciation to say that after September 11 the terrorist threat amounted to a national emergency which could be said to threaten the life of the nation. See *A and others v Secretary of State for the Home Department* [2004] UK House of Lords 56, [2005] 2 AC 68 as commented by D. Feldman, "Terrorism, Human Rights and Their Constitutional Implications", *European Constitutional Law Review*, no. 1(3) (2005): 531.

[42] In this respect, it is significant to mention that art. 16 of the Italian Law decree 144/2005 would have required the public prosecutor to obtain a specific authorisation from the Minister of Justice in order to proceed in the investigations of international terrorism offences. In order to avoid inappropriate interferences in what are meant to be independent judicial activities, Parliament has fortunately decided not to convert the controversial provision into law.

7.2.3 The Perilous Development of a "*Feindstrafrecht*"

In the words of Carl Schmitt, a specific political distinction to which political actions and motives can be reduced is that between *Freund* and *Feind*.[43] The political enemy is the other, the stranger, existentially something different and alien, so that in the extreme case conflicts with him are possible.

In a similar respect, a large part of the doctrine in continental Europe refers to the development of what is called "enemy criminal law" (*Feindstrafrecht*). This authoritarian model of preventive criminal law is described in the work of the German academic Günther Jakobs. This model would deny human rights and legal guarantees (the "citizen's criminal law")[44] to individuals who are seen as sources of extreme danger because of their suspicious behaviour.[45] The concept of "*Feindstrafrecht*" can be compared with the American concept of "enemy combatants" developed at first by the Supreme Court[46] and then by the Bush administration in order to address the problem of what to do with individuals who are allegedly sources of extreme dangerousness.[47]

Jakobs first formulated this concept in 1985.[48] At that time, he was very critical particularly of the criminalization of preparatory acts and the progressive shift in criminal liability because of the introduction of inchoate offences. Since 2000, however, the author has described the development of an enemy criminal law as inevitable and called for exceptional treatment for non law-abiding citizens who have become enemies. A small minority of "evil" individuals allegedly legitimates the expansion of control and coercive measures, as the vast majority must protect itself. If the enemy intends to negate his opponent's way of life, he must be repulsed or fought. Jakobs affirmed that enemy criminal law is based on the citizens' "right to security" (*Recht auf Sicherheit*) entailing a corresponding "protection duty" (*Schutzpflicht*) by the State.[49] In fact, in Jakobs' view, citizens must enjoy a

---

[43] C. Schmitt, The Concept of the Political (München: Franz Eher Nachfolger, 1927).

[44] "Citizens' criminal law" uses retributive punishment to reintegrate the offender into the society, repairing the damaged relationship with the victim and/or the general public and resume a normal life.

[45] See his "Terroristen als Personen im Recht?", *Zeitschrift für die gesamte Strafrechtswissenschaft*, no. 117 (2006): 839.

[46] Similarly, during the 1970s, the Italian Constitutional Court defined the figure of the "offender for principle": 'a member of organizations characterized not just and not only by a plan to destroy democratic institutions, but also by the effective practice of violence as a means of political struggle'. See Cost. 14 January 1982, no. 15.

[47] C. Gomez-Jara Diez, "Enemy Combatants Versus Enemy Criminal Law", *New Criminal Law Review*, no. 11 (2008): 529.

[48] G. Jakobs, "Kriminalisierung im Vorfeld einer Rechtsgutverletzung", *Zeitschrift für die gesamte Strafrechtswissenschaft*, no. 97 (1985): 751.

[49] The German federal Constitutional Court first formulated this concept. In 1975, in its first abortion case, the Court decided that the combined reading of articles 2 and art. 1(2) *Grundgesetz* gives rise to a comprehensive duty of the state, that each human life has to be protected, especially from illegal interference by others. German Federal Constitutional Court, 39 BVerfGE 1; see Gomez-Jara Diez, "Enemy Combatants Versus Enemy Criminal Law", at 535–38.

minimum of law-abiding behaviour and where they do not, it is legitimate for the state to treat an individual who threatens the basic order of society as an enemy and not as a citizen.

The provisions identified as "enemy criminal law" are characterised by three distinctive features (all three of which are found in the case of terrorist offences, the highest expression of "enemy criminal law"): a significant shift in inchoate liability implies that individuals are not always punished after wrongdoing (retrospectively), but before any actual harm occurs, in order to prevent it (prospectively)[50]; procedural rights are limited or even excluded[51]; and sanctions are disproportionate if compared to similar provisions.[52] The disproportion/inconsistency of sanctions for convicted individuals goes together with significant sentencing discounts for those who accept to cooperate with justice as Crown witnesses (see "*Pentiti* legislation"[53]). Once again the law operates a distinction between "good individuals" who repent and are rehabilitated as law-abiding citizens and "bad individuals" who remain enemies and thus do not deserve any mercy.

The deportation of terrorist suspects is a good example of the development of a "*Feindstrafrecht*" and the policy shift towards preventive measures. Art. 312 of the Italian *Codice Penale* requires the mandatory expulsion of a foreigner convicted of a terrorist offence once he has served his sentence. Similarly, art. 3 of Law 155/2005 allows the Italian Minister of the Interior to expel a foreigner *inter alia* when he has reasonable grounds to believe that his remaining on the national territory is likely to favour in any respect terrorist groups or activity.

---

[50] This would represent an upheaval of the traditional function of the investigation and the trial meant to ascertain the commission of an offence and not to prevent it. After the attacks of September 11, the national legislators have introduced a wide range of new ancillary or inchoate terrorist offences to cope with the terrorist threat as prescribed by international and European instruments. Most importantly, growing significance is recognized to inchoate and preparatory offences disengaged from the actual perpetration of the harm that would be needed to give rise to a charge under the relevant substantive offence.

[51] See long periods of pre-charge detention in the United Kingdom; house searches and the gathering of non-intimate samples without the consent of the individual; deportations where the appeals are non-suspensive, etc.

[52] Particularly severe is the punishment of inchoate offences no matter what the actual or potential harm caused is. The mere participation in a terrorist organization is liable to a maximum charge of 10 years of imprisonment (art. 270 *bis* of the Italian *Codice Penale*). This is even more significant given the fact that according to a strict interpretation of the general rule *ex* art. 115 *Codice Penale* preparatory acts cannot be punished unless the main offence is actually committed. In the United Kingdom the offences of "directing a terrorist organization" and engaging in "any preparatory act" is liable to imprisonment for life; the possession of an article for terrorist purposes is liable to 15 years of imprisonment.

[53] In Italy, in the early 1980s, a series of Laws gave to the judicial authorities the option of offering real incentives to convicted terrorists to collaborate with justice. What was then called "*Pentiti* legislation" was first introduced in relation to terrorism offences and then extended to cover Mafia-related crimes. Judges' discretion ranged from up to 50% sentence reduction with non-application of aggravating circumstances to a simple declaration of 'not liable for punishment'. See Law 304/1982 (*Misure per la difesa dell'ordinamento costituzionale*) and Law 34/1987 (*Misure a favore di chi si dissocia dal terrorismo*).

Another example is the use of "listing" to identify groups or individuals who are deemed to be dangerous and thus deserve a differential treatment, although they are not guilty of a specific offence, nor have they undergone a criminal trial.

The concept of "*Feindstrafrecht*" has provoked heated discussion within academic circles in continental Europe[54] although it has attracted almost no attention in the English-speaking world. Criticisms of this concept emphasise its dubious legitimacy and its potential impact on the criminal justice system. Nobody denies that it portrays accurately significant aspects of current criminal law practice.

In the next paragraphs I propose to explore why the development of a "*Feindstrafrecht*" is perilous and what are the liberal objections to it. I believe its widespread use is deeply undesirable.

First, a problem arises as to defining the category of "enemies" thus deserving of a differential treatment. The "*Feindstrafrecht*" presupposes the identification of a "*Feind*" with serious risks of dreadful injustices in the application of "enemy criminal law" to those who do not belong to this category – supposing that such a category in fact exists! As underlined in the next section there is a risk that the development of the "enemy criminal law" intensifies the politicisation of the law. The ambiguity of the notion of "enemy" – in the absence of any criteria to identify those individuals who belong to this category – is doubtfully compliant with the legality principle "*nullum crimen, nulla poena sine lege*" requiring, *inter alia*, that the law is clear and ascertainable. In addition, contrary to the principle of equality, it would ground policing on prejudice about identity and racial profiling so that criteria such as race, religion and ethnicity are considered and used as indicators of dangerousness under counter-terrorism policies.

Secondly, the question arises as to who has the right to decide which individuals belong to the category of innocence. Such a decision is often a political one, taken outside the courts often on the basis of intelligence sources. Due process rights including the presumption of innocence (no offence has been committed), the right to silence and the right to a fair trial are sidelined. Governments tend to use the notion of 'dangerousness' as a label with a view of criminalisation of individuals often belonging to marginal groups in order to keep them under control.

Thirdly, the principle of proportionality limits the discretion of the legislator in enacting criminal legislation so that the degree of danger posed by an individual should be proportionate to the state's intervention. By contrast to the present situation which only requires "suspicion" to ground preventive measures against dangerous individuals, in principle, a higher standard of proof should be required for the use of intrusive measures to incapacitate "enemies".

Fourthly, what are the limits to the available derogations? What would be acceptable? Jakobs explains that that the expansion of "enemy criminal law" is restricted

[54] See for instance J. M. Silva Sanchez, *La expansiòn del derecho penal* (Madrid: Civitas, 2001); A. Gamberini, and R. Orlandi, eds., *Delitto Politico e diritto penale del nemico* (Bologna: Monduzzi, 2007); M. Donini and M. Papa, eds., *Diritto Penale del nemico* (Milano: Giuffrè, 2007); A. Bernardi and P. Baldassarre, *Legalità penale e crisi del diritto, oggi* (Milano: Giuffrè, 2008).

by the idea that a measure needs to be necessary and useful. The problem is that the identification of an individual as "enemy" legitimates the state to take any measure it considers useful or necessary. Individual rights are no longer to be balanced against public interest and protection, which becomes the overriding objective. In theory this could even legitimate the state to remove the source of danger, *e.g.* covertly assassinating "enemies", shooting them on sight instead of arresting and trying them, and torturing those who are caught to obtain information against others.

In addition, as described above, there is the risk that measures introduced as extraordinary tend to spill into other areas of the law and measures that were originally conceived as temporary derogations, once "normalised" over time, tend to become part of the ordinary system.

7.2.4 "War on Terror", Täterschuld and Crusading Judges

The expansion of the "enemy criminal law" is partially associated with the so-called "war on crime" or the more recent "war on terror".[55] Traditionally, criminal law is said to have a twofold aim. On the one hand, it is a means to combat criminality through the prosecution and conviction of suspects; on the other hand, criminal law is a means to protect the individual rights of suspects and defendants in the context of a due process. However, over the last decades, certain themes have assumed such proportions as to attract the language of battle and governments have increasingly used military language to emphasize the urgency of the situation.[56]

This new approach calls for the demonisation by both the legal and social system of certain individuals who have violated the law, or are likely to do so, on the basis of the law enforcement authorities' suspicions. This leads to the abandonment of an objective legal approach based on the relationship between crime, guilt and punishment in favour of a more pragmatic vision associating national security with social defence. Offenders are deviants, identified as "enemies within" against whom the state must engage a fight. Individual dangerousness remains an unclear concept, often presumed by simple membership in a specific group.[57] Similar trends can be observed both at the national and the EU level, where the language of the battlefield is even used to identify legal instruments.[58]

---

[55] See N. Feldman, "Choices of Law, Choices of War", *Harvard Journal of Law and Public Policy*, no. 25 (2002): 457; J. Huysmans, "Minding Exceptions", *Contemporary Political theory* 3 (2004): 321.

[56] See M. Donini, "Diritto Penale di lotta vs. diritto penale del nemico", in Gamberini and Orlandi, already cited.

[57] See J. Meierhenrich, "Analogies at War", *Journal of Conflict and Security Law*, no. 11(1) (2006): 1.

[58] See e.g. the framework decisions on combating the sexual exploitation of children and child pornography (2003), on combating trafficking in human beings (2002), on combating corruption in the private sector (2003), on combating terrorism (2002), etc.

Criminal law is traditionally concerned with illegal behaviours clearly defined by the law as specific offences grounded on objective and easily identifiable elements according to the requirements of the principle of legality. State punishment is admissible only when an individual infringes criminal law provisions or is likely to do so in the near future. By contrast, the war on terror seems to imply a notion of guilt based on someone's identity (*Täterschuld*) and thus on subjective characteristics. Groups of people are criminalised and prosecuted on the basis of their belonging to a specific ideology/religious belief or originating in a particular region or territory or ascribing to a suspicious network. Hence, there is a tendency to focus on whole categories of people rather than on single individuals.[59] The concept of responsibility is no longer that of a proven culpability in the planning or the carrying out of major attacks or single offences but has shifted towards one of mere dangerousness, either real or regarded as such by law enforcement authorities.[60] And the dangerousness of the individual overrides the potentially harmful impact of an event.

In so doing the "war on terror" – on the pages of popular newspapers – has labeled radical Muslims as the "enemy within", indirectly implying that terrorism had its origin in Islam and religious identity, or that people coming from determined countries and regions of the world are potentially dangerous. In this respect, some authors[61] have argued that the current political discourse has facilitated the construction of Muslims as a new "suspect community".[62]

The re-emergence of racial profiling as a widespread police practice in the wake of September 11 shows the growing relevance of individual characteristics or beliefs in crime prevention strategies.[63]

Offences such as the 'association for terrorist (or criminal) purposes' tend to target people on the basis of whom they know or associate with rather than what they have done in relation to a specific criminal event. In France, the overwhelming majority of people arrested on suspicion of involvement in terrorist activities are

---

[59] The current development is described by the Italian legal doctrine as "*diritto penale dell'autore*" as opposed to a "*diritto penale del fatto*". See the special issue 'Verso un diritto penale del nemico?', *Questione Giustizia*, no. 4 (2006).

[60] This approach has a model in the legal status of foreigners and illegal immigrants, often subjected to special measures where the curtailment of personal freedom results from a combination of criminal and administrative measures (such as the temporary detentions awaiting for expulsion) and is often disengaged from the commission of an offence. An underlying issue today is also the overlap in the eyes of law enforcement authorities and public opinion between illegal immigrants and terrorists who consequently deserve a similar treatment.

[61] C. Pantazis and S. Pemberton, "From the 'Old' to the 'New' Suspect Community", *British Journal of Criminology*, no. 49(5), (2009): 646.

[62] The notion of "suspect community" was first introduced by Hillyard's study of the impact of the PTA 1974 on the Irish community in Northern Ireland. See P. Hillyard, *Suspect Community* (London: Pluto Press, 1993).

[63] For instance, in the United Kingdom the increase in the use of stop and search powers for black people has been staggering, amounting to 322%, compared with a 277% for Asian and 185% for white people. See Ministry of Justice, *Statistics on race and the criminal justice system 2007/2008.*

charged with an offence of *association de malfaiteurs* (art. 421(1) *Code Pénale*). Professor Mayaud has underlined that:

> The offence continues to consist of preparatory participation: participation in a group or an understanding, preparation of a subsequent or ecological act of terrorism. The association therefore remains independent of the actual commission of the offences, which are its object. This is significant, since it means that, as long as it is sufficiently realised, the preparation alone is enough to constitute the punishable offence.[64]

It is noteworthy that in the *Chalabi* case (1998)[65] as in the *Ali Touchent* case (1997)[66] the *réquisitoire définitif*[67] of the public prosecutor followed a long account of recent Algerian history.[68] The underlying idea is that before examining the role and responsibilities of each individual charged of *association de malfaiteurs*, it is appropriate to recall the religious and political context to which these individuals belong.

In Italy, the interpretation of article 270 *bis* of the *Codice Penale* has been particularly difficult as the evidence provided to investigate and then bring an individual to trial tends to prove his association with a terrorist group, rather than evidence of the acts that he has done. In some cases, judges have adopted a relaxed approach to the notion of association and the assessment of individual responsibility[69] to the dangerous extent that, in certain cases, the simple ideological adherence to criminal purposes has been considered enough for a charge under art. 270 *bis*.[70] The use of proscription lists as evidence in support of pre-trial measures (such as remand in custody)[71] has also been particularly controversial and the *Corte di Cassazione* has stated that the use of such lists is acceptable only to encourage further investigations and cannot constitute evidence of terrorist purposes as required by art. 270 *bis* of the *Codice Penale*. The use of proscription lists for evidence purposes, if permitted, would lead to the definition of a specific category of individuals to whom a special regime applies because of their characteristics and prior to any fact finding with regard to their involvement in terrorist activities.

---

[64] Y. Mayaud, *Le terrorisme* (Paris: Dalloz, 1997) at 29.

[65] Crim. 15 June 2000, no. de pourvoi 99–87596 (unrep.).

[66] Crim. 18 February 1997, no. de pourvoi 96–85639 (unrep.).

[67] In French criminal law the public prosecutor at the end of the investigation led by the *juge d'instruction* revises the dossier and writes his opinion concerning the facts established by the investigation, and the elements gathered as of the personality of the suspect and of the *partie civile* (if any). The prosecutor argues whether there are sufficient elements or not to charge the suspect of an offence and requires the *juge d'instruction* to proceed with the committal for trial of the individual. Arts. 80, 82 and 86 *Code de Procédure Pénale*.

[68] See M. McColgan and A. Attanasio, "France: Paving the Way for Arbitrary Justice", (Report) (January 1999) 271/2 http://www.fidh.org/IMG/pdf/271fran.pdf (accessed October 21, 2009).

[69] As in Cass. pen. 13 October 2004 in *Il Foro Italiano*, vol. II (2005): 218 Cass. pen. 9 February 2005, note R. Oliveri del Castillo, in *Dirittoe e Giustizia*, no. 20 (2005): 77.

[70] As in Cass. pen. 25 May 2006 in *Il Foro Italiano*, vol. II (2006): 541.

[71] Trib. Brescia 31 January 2005 in *Diritto e Giustizia*, no. 6 (2005): 92.

Lastly, pursuing a "war on terror" by way of establishing a criminal law based on the potential dangerousness of certain categories of individuals has a potential impact on the criminal process and its different actors and players that is significant and undesirable.[72]

There is an obvious risk that if the defendant became an enemy, prosecutors and judges would tend to perceive themselves as actors in a moral battle against a dangerous offender and engage in a fight against him.[73] In this case, the investigation and trial would not be meant by the judiciary as a neutral means to ascertain the truth as to whether the accused has committed a terrorist offence or not, but to assess whether he is a terrorist, aiding terrorists or belonging to a terrorist network. This trend would endanger the presumption of innocence and the right to be tried by an independent and impartial tribunal (art. 6 EHCR), transforming the criminal process in itself into a machinery *ad usum belli* against individuals who are perceived not to deserve fair treatment or due process rights.

In this respect, NGOs such as the *Féderation Internationale des Droits de l'Homme* are extremely concerned about the functions, powers and attitudes of the anti-terrorism special team of *juge d'instruction* based in Paris.[74] According to them, the existence of this special team is worrying also because of the close link with intelligence service, which represents the primary source of information for investigating judges. When relying uncritically on this information the independence of investigating judges risks turning into "*licence*".

A longstanding criticism of the *juge d'instruction* is that he combines investigative functions with the control of the of the liberty of the suspect while the investigation is taking place, an arrangement that sometimes led to an abuse of pre-charge and pre-trial detention as a means of extracting information.[75] In the light of this, the creation in 2000 of the *juge des libertés et de la détention* to take over from the *juge d'instruction* the responsibility for decisions relating to detention and bail, including in terrorism-related investigations, has been welcomed as a significant improvement.[76] In addition, it would be advisable to increase the number of investigating judges, for a number of reasons. First, the overload of files makes it impossible to try terrorist suspects within a reasonable time as required by arts. 5 and 6 ECHR. Secondly, it would dilute the excessive concentration of power in the hands of a small and intimately connected group of judges.

---

[72] A. Garapon, and D. Salas, *La justice et le mal* (Paris: Jacob, 1997).

[73] To a lesser extent (because suspects and defendant where never denied due process rights) the attitude of Italian prosecutors against corrupted politicians in the context of the big scandal called "*Tangentopoli*" (early 1990s) provides an interesting example of crusading judges pursuing a moral battle. Similar observations arise in relation to the fight against Mafia in southern Italy since the beginning of the 1980s.

[74] The provocative title of the section on *juges d'instruction* in a report on counter-terrorism measures is: 'Quis custodiet custodes?' M. McColgan and A. Attanasio, already cited, at 30–31.

[75] By virtue of Art 81 *Code de Procédure Pénale*: 'The investigating judge undertakes in accordance with the law any investigative step he deems useful for the discovery of the truth (...)'.

[76] Law 516/2000 (*Loi renforçant la protection de la présomption d'innocence et les droits des victimes, dite Loi Guigou*).

7.3 The Way Forward

7.3.1 How Can We Engage with the Current Perilous Trends?

Before exploring detailed policy recommendations and what each country may learn from another, some general suggestions will be made as to what could and should be done to counter the current trends leading to a normalization of extraordinary means, the potentially oppressive shift towards prevention and the emergence of a "*Feindstrafecht*".

7.3.1.1 Emergency Provisions?

An important difference between the situations before and after 2001 is that with the current threat there is no foreseeable end and a negotiated settlement with the authors of it appears to be impossible. The new legislation is thus conceived not as extraordinary but as long lasting and will possibly have a greater impact in reshaping the criminal justice system as a result of the normalization process described above.

Derogations to ordinary provisions are necessary and there is a need in certain circumstances to adjust ordinary rules to the complexity of counter-terrorism investigations and prosecutions. However, as previously argued, derogations should be admissible only if temporary and circumscribed.[77] Therefore, provisions which are enacted as exceptional ones should be formulated in such a way (and subjected to constant scrutiny and review) to avoid that they become part of the ordinary legislative framework.[78]

First, states should engage in a significant assessment of the extent of the threat and of the definition applied to it, as it entails the use of special measures. A clear report of terrorist threat must be presented to Parliament, so as to avoid the tendency to exaggerate it for political purposes. In addition, in order to avoid or at least minimize the spill-over into other fields and because of their strong impact on individual rights, anti-terrorist provisions should provide a clear scope of application for the law and an unambiguous meaning for the concepts used.

---

[77] The recommendations contained in this section elaborate upon the International Commission of Jurists' Report 'Asssessing Damage, Urging Action' (2009) see http://ejp.icj.org/IMG/EJP-Report.pdf (accessed August 2, 2011).

[78] In this respect, the French choice (and the similar one made by the United Kingdom Parliament when enacting the Terrorism Act 2000) to have a separate set of rules within the Codes to be applied to terrorism is controversial. In fact, as explained below, it would on the one hand allow the establishment of a more coherent framework and avoid panic-legislation following major attacks. On the other hand, it introduces a permanent parallel track and so favours the normalization of extraordinary measures.

Secondly, before implementing new counter-terrorism provisions states should ensure that these measures are meant to address a documented gap in the existing legal framework. Instead of adopting merely symbolic (and practically useless) measures to give the impression that they are "doing something about terrorism!" and thus allay fears and build up public confidence, governments should evaluate the prospects of a policy being effective to prevent or suppress terrorist activity.

Thirdly, the introduction of sunset clauses should ensure that derogations are time-limited and subject to periodic review in relation to the enduring need for an exceptional measure and to the proportionality of the provision to its purpose and specific scope of application. In this respect, particularly significant is the creation in the United Kingdom of the Office of Reviewer. By providing an independent scrutiny, the Reviewer is meant to contribute to a fair, efficient and effective use of anti-terrorism legislation. Lord Carlile of Berriew has been formally appointed by the Secretary of State Reviewer of the Terrorism Act 2000, Reviewer of the Anti-Terrorism Crime and Security Act 2001, Part 4 (detention provisions), and Reviewer of the Prevention of Terrorism Act 2005, in which capacity he publishes regular reports.[79] Providing an independent scrutiny of the operation of the Act (scope and continuous need), he is mandated to contribute to a fair, efficient and effective use of anti-terrorism legislation. A Privy Counsellor Review Committee issuing the Newton Report in December 2003 has also extensively reviewed the ATCSA 2001.[80] The UK Parliamentary Joint Committee of Human Rights has equally undertaken valuable inquiries on counter-terrorism policies and human rights issues, seeking evidence from a wide range of groups with relevant interests and experience.[81] Most importantly, these reports are readily available online and anyone can have access to them. By contrast, France and Italy have not been as committed in providing effective and periodic parliamentary oversight or other forms of independent scrutiny of their counter-terrorism legislation.

Finally, derogations submitted by the state to human rights instruments (*e.g.* through art. 15 ECHR) should only be in place for as long as terrorism poses a genuine threat to the life of the nation, in compliance with domestic constitutions and ECHR requirements. When reviewing anti-terrorism legislation, parliamentary committees (as well as courts in individual cases) should have this constraint in mind.

---

[79] Pursuant to s 126 of the Terrorism Act 2000, to (the now repealed) s 28 of the Anti Terrorism crime and Security Act 2001 and to s 14(2) of the Prevention of Terrorism Act 2005.

[80] Privy Counsellor Review Committee, "Anti-terrorism, Crime and Security Act 2001 review: Report" (the Newton Report) HC (2003–04) 100.

[81] The Joint Committee of Human Rights is a joint parliamentary committee which undertakes thematic inquiries on human rights issues and reports its findings and recommendations to the House of Commons. It scrutinises all Government Bills and picks out those with significant human rights implications for further examination. The Committee also looks at Government action to deal with judgments of the British courts and the ECtHR where breaches of human rights have been found.

7.3.1.2 Preventive Measures and Pre-punishment

As explained above, one of the current trends in criminal law is the emergence of a new model of preventive justice in order to avert the risks of serious harm posed by the growth of threats such as terrorist activities. Preventive measures operate in the name of public protection as an alternative to criminal prosecution and stand outside the ordinary safeguards of the criminal process.

The debate about the shift towards prevention in counter-terrorism frameworks should focus on two aspects. First and foremost, concern arises as to whether it is justifiable in any circumstance for the state to incapacitate an individual ahead of any wrongdoing, and hence by definition in the absence of prosecution and conviction.[82] If so, then long-established principles of criminal justice and individual rights would have to be sidelined in the interest of public protection.[83] What are the legal or moral limits the legislator has to place upon the use (and possible abuse) of preventive measures?[84]

Along these lines, control orders represent a significant example of the shift towards a preventive approach in counter-terrorism. The legal debate among academics on these measures has been dominated by their compliance with ECHR requirements.[85] Case-law has oscillated and mostly addressed whether control orders constitute a deprivation of liberty *ex* art. 5[86] and the adequacy of procedural

[82] L. Zedner, "Seeking Security by Eroding Rights", in *Security and Human Rights*, ed. L. Lazarus and B. Goold (Oxford: Hart Publishing, 2007).

[83] A. Ashworth, "Criminal Justice Act 2003", *Criminal Law Review* (2004): 516.

[84] Traditionally, for example, it has been considered "acceptable" to indefinitely detain mentally ill individuals, who might represent a risk of harm for themselves or others, with a view to compulsory treatment. See for instance the community treatment orders introduced by s 32 of the UK Mental Health Act 2007. The enactment of this Act was surrounded by a large public debate. When passing the government's proposal, Parliament imposed safeguards at least on powers to detain mental health patients on public protection grounds. See H. Prins, "Counterblast: the Mental Health Act 2007", *Howard Journal*, no. 47(1) (2008): 81; W. Bingley, "The Mental Health Act 2007", *Archbold News*, no. 9 (2007): 6.

[85] According to art. 5 ECHR, nobody may be deprived of his liberty unless his case falls within one of the listed categories: on sentence following conviction, breach of a court order, arrest on suspicion of crime, infectious disease, mental illness, unlawful entry, pending action to deport or extradite, etc. The ECtHR has underscored that there is no clear divide between a deprivation of liberty and a control on liberty (*Guzzardi v. Italy* (App no 7367/76) (1980) 3 EHRR 533 and R*aimondo v. Italy* (App. no. 12954/87) (1994) 18 EHRR 237) and to decide on the issue it is necessary to look at the realities of the situation as a matter of fact and degree. Moreover, a series of Strasbourg decisions established that 24-h house arrest has been regarded as tantamount to imprisonment and so as depriving the subject of his liberty. See ***NC v. Italy*** (App. no. 24952/94) ECHR 11 January 2001 (unrep.); *Vachev v. Bulgaria* (App. no. 42987/98) ECHR 2004-VIII; *Nikolova v. Bulgaria* (*No 2*) (App. no. 40896/98) ECHR 30 September 2004 (unrep.).

[86] See, e.g. *Secretary of State for the Home Department v. JJ* [2007] UK House of Lords 45 in [2007] 3 *Weekly Law Review* 642; *Secretary of State for the Home Department v. E* [2007] UK House of Lords 47 in [2007] 3 *Weekly Law Review* 720.

safeguards *ex* art. 6.[87] Insisting on the preventive nature of these measures the UK Government has managed to bypass the due process requirements which apply to criminal sanctions. However, it has been suggested that these measures have a punitive quality because of three factors: the seriousness of the harm they are meant to prevent (*i.e.* 'the involvement in terrorism-related activity'), the cumulative impact of the restrictions placed upon the controlees, and the criminal penalty provided for a breach of the order.[88] The Joint Committee of Human Rights has argued that control orders are

> deliberately designed to appear to be civil orders which are intended to be alternatives to criminal prosecution in cases where prosecution is said not to be possible', however, 'in most if not all cases [control orders] amount to the determination of a criminal charge against the individual who is the subject of the order.[89]

In sum, if preventive measures are in effect penal in character and thus better understood as forms of pre-punishment, their use would require the application of higher standards of proof than "suspicion" even where there is a threat of serious harm. As argued in the following section, prosecution should be the most desirable way to deal with terrorism.

In relation to preventive measures, further practical questions arise. Do governments really dispose of any means to assess whether an individual poses a risk to the public? Are they able to appraise the likelihood that an (otherwise only potential) harmful act will occur? What are the criteria to identify whether the measures adopted would effectively prevent an event to occur.[90]

7.3.1.3 Re-establishing the Primacy of the Criminal Justice System

The use of preventative measures might be justified as an extraordinary measure to address current major threats. However, as for the future, surely criminal prosecution should remain the primary response to serious offences, including terrorism.[91] States should make minimal use of administrative measures at the discretion of the executive. From a civil libertarians' perspective the strongest argument to maintain the primacy of criminal prosecution is that it requires formal proof before an

---

[87] See, e.g. *Secretary of State for the Home Department v. MB* [2007] UK House of Lords 46 in [2007] 3 *Weekly Law Review* 681; *Secretary of State for the Home Department v. F* [2009] UK House of Lords 28 in [2009] 3 *Weekly Law Review* 74 as commented by M. Elliott, "Stop the press: Kafkaesque procedures are unfair", *Cambridge Law Journal*, no. 68(3) (2009).

[88] Zedner, "Preventive justice or pre-punishment?", at 192–199. Beyond the context of counter-terrorism see also T. Thomas, "When Public Protection Becomes Punishment?", *European Journal on Criminal Policy and Research*, no. 10(4) (2004): 337.

[89] Joint Committee of Human Rights, "Twelfth Report of Session 2005–2006" HL (2005–06) 122, HC (2005–06) 915, 17 as quoted by Zedner 'Preventive justice or pre-punishment?' at 196.

[90] Zedner, "Preventive Justice or Pre-punishment?", at 190.

[91] L. Zedner, "Securing Liberty in the Face of Terror", *Journal of law and society*, no. 32(4) (2005): 507 at 529–531; C. Walker, "Terrorism and Criminal Justice", *Criminal Law Review* (2004): 311.

individual can be charged and sanctioned for any offence. By contrast, for risk-averse Home Secretaries, the avoidance of the problems of evidence and formal proof are the strongest argument in favour of replacing criminal justice with a system of administrative sanctions. The use of administrative measures allows the government to remove allegedly dangerous individuals from circulation on the basis of mere suspicions or risks. On the other hand, the existing high standard of proof of guilt beyond suspicion aims at avoiding miscarriages of justice and minimising the risk of convicting innocent individuals.

First, the criminal justice system allows legitimate restrictions upon individual rights only where necessary in specific circumstances for legitimate purposes (*i.e.* protection of the public from future harm and deterrence of further offences). Secondly, it minimises the risk of abuses and of "slippery slopes" as its functioning is mostly transparent. Detailed provisions on due process rights allow the individual whose rights have been limited to defend himself against the charges and to challenge the decision taken by the public authority (for example through a more or less developed appeal or judicial review system). In ordinary cases, any limitation of individual rights has to be supported by a reasoned ruling from the judicial authority; the individual (suspect or defendant) has the right to be informed of the charges and of the evidence supporting the prosecution case and to be brought promptly before a judge. Thirdly, judicial authorities cannot normally pursue a fight in the name of a right to security for the neutralisation of dangerous individuals.[92] In fact, judicial discretion is limited by the continuous necessity to justify any decision taken on the basis of reasonable grounds.[93] Finally, a charge will be applied in relation to a specific offence and not because of an individual belonging to a specific category of people. Thorough investigations allow the gathering and selection of appropriate evidence to support the prosecution's case at trial.

Ultimately, as for the limits to available derogations to ordinary rules, there should be a different margin of flexibility not only in relation to the seriousness of the offence but also because of the diverse significance of each safeguard/individual right. Derogations which are likely to affect everybody's rights – such as 'glorification of terrorism' provisions – are particularly controversial.

[92] This is all the more true in the Italian system where the public prosecutor (who not only supports the case against the defendant at trial but is also the master of the investigations) is completely independent from the executive.

[93] This "reasonable grounds" requirement was partially challenged in 2003 with the introduction, promoted by the then Home Secretary David Blunkett, of a new controversial measure by the Criminal Justice Act, the imprisonment for public protection (IPP). This indeterminate sentence had to be imposed upon an individual convicted of a serious offence, carrying a penalty of 10 years' imprisonment or more, where the court considered him to be 'dangerous'. Section 47 of the Criminal Justice ad Immigration Act 2008 amended the IPP regime so that, most importantly, the imposition of this form of indeterminate sentence is no longer obligatory and the sentencing court is given a measure of discretion. See A. Ashworth, "Criminal Justice Act 2003" R. Epstein and B. Mitchell, "Indeterminate Sentence for Public Protection", *Criminal Law and Justice Weekly*, no. 173(20) (2008): 311.

For European countries such the United Kingdom, France and Italy, it would be advisable to follow the specific formal requirements contained in art. 15 ECHR. Under the European Convention on Human Rights there a number of rights from which no derogation is possible, in particular the prohibition of torture. As regards those rights from which derogations are possible, these are justifiable only in time of 'war' or other 'public emergency threatening the life of the nation' and they are subject to a number of further qualifying criteria such as the proportionally to their purposes (suitability, lack of alternative and less coercive means, or limited impact on the individual right in question).

An alternative, but deeply questionable, approach is that of Zedner. She points out that the recourse to preventive measures in the United Kingdom is not at all uncommon: in reality it has now become a central feature of the legal landscape, which could not be readily removed.[94] And in her view, insisting on the conventional tool of prosecution and punishment within the criminal justice system would only lead to a further expansion of inchoate offences and a distortion of due process rights. Instead of attempting to re-establish the primacy of prosecution, legal writers should develop appropriate principles and values to frame the continuing expansion of preventive measures.

The problem is that taking preventive justice as an acceptable feature of a modern criminal justice system risks, as previously argued, its normalization. Preventive orders will no longer constitute an extraordinary measure but a permanent one. Having underlined in the previous section why preventive measures and pre-punishment are not acceptable, it is my view that legal writers should continue to oppose their expansion.

Bibliography

Ashworth, A. 2004a. Criminal justice act 2003: Part 2: criminal justice reform – principles, human rights and public protection' *Criminal Law Review* 7: 516.

Ashworth, A. 2006. *Principles of criminal law*. Oxford: Oxford University Press.

Beck, U. 1992. *Risk society: Towards a new modernity*. London: Sage.

Bernardi, A., and P. Baldassarre. 2008. *Legalità penale e crisi del diritto, oggi*. Milano: Giuffrè.

Bingley, W. 2007. The Mental Health Act 2007. *Archbold News* 9: 6.

CDRP survey 2003–6: Use of anti-social behaviour tools/powers (November 2006). http://www.asb.home office.gov.uk/members/article. aspx?id=9822. Accessed 1 Nov 2009.

Chilcot, Lord. 2008. Privy Council Review of intercept as evidence: Report to the Prime Minister and the Home Secretary (the Chilcot Review) (Cm 7324), [20].

Dershowitz, A.M. 2002. *Why terrorism works*. London: Yale University Press.

Dinh, V. 2002. Freedom and security after September 11. *Harvard Journal of law and public policy* 25: 399.

Donini, M., and M. Papa (eds.). 2007. *Diritto Penale del nemico*. Milano: Giuffrè.

[94] Zedner, "Preventive Justice or Pre-punishment?", at 203.

Dyzenhaus, D. 2001. The permanence of the temporary. In *The security of freedom*, ed. R.J. Daniels et al. Toronto: University of Toronto Press.
Elliott, M. 2009. Stop press: Kafkaesque procedures are unfair. *Cambridge Law Journal* 68(3).
Epstein, R., and B. Mitchell. 2008. Indeterminate sentence for public protection. *Criminal Law and Justice Weekly* 173(20): 311.
Feeley, M.M., and J. Simon. 1992. The new penology. *Criminology* 30(4): 449.
Feinberg, J. 1987. *The moral limits of the criminal law*. New York: Oxford University Press.
Feldman, D. 2002. Choices of law, choices of war. *Harvard Journal of Law and Public Policy* 25: 457.
Feldman, D. 2005. Terrorism, human rights and their constitutional implications. *European Constitutional Law Review* 1(3): 531.
Fisher, E. 2002. Precaution, precaution everywhere. *Maastricht Journal of European and Comparative Law* 9: 7.
Gamberini, A., and R. Orlandi (eds.). 2007. *Delitto Politico e diritto penale del nemico*. Bologna: Monduzzi.
Garapon, A., and D. Salas. 1997. *La justice et le mal*. Paris: Jacob.
Garland, D. 2001. *The culture of control*. Oxford: Oxford University Press.
Gomez-Jara Diez, C. 2008. Enemy combatants versus enemy criminal law. *New Criminal Law Review* 11: 529.
Gross, O. 2003. Chaos and rules. *Yale Law Journal* 112: 1011.
Hansard, H.C. 2003. vol 404 col 219 W, 28 April 2003.
Hassemer, W. 2006. Sicherheit durch Strafrecht. HöchstRichterliche Rechtsprechung im Strafrecht (HRRS) 130.
Hillyard, P. 1993. *Suspect community*. London: Pluto Press.
Hillyard, P. 1994. The normalization of special powers from Northern Ireland to Britain. In *A reader on criminal justice*, ed. N. Lacey. Oxford: Oxford University Press.
Home Office. 2009. Statistics on Terrorism Arrests and Outcomes (Great Britain) – 11 September 2001 to 31 March 2008. (13 May 2009) 04/09.
Huysmans, J. 2004. Minding exceptions. *Contemporary Political theory* 3: 321.
Illuminati, G. 1981. Reati "speciali" e procedure "speciali" nella legislazione d'emergenza. *Giustizia Penale*: 106.
International Commission of Jurists' Report 'Assessing Damage, Urging Action'. 2009. see http://ejp.icj.org/IMG/EJP-Report.pdf. Accessed 2 Aug 2011.
Jakobs, G. 1985. Kriminalisierung im Vorfeld einer Rechtsgutverletzung. *Zeitschrift für die gesamte Strafrechtswissenschaft* 97: 751.
Jakobs, G. 2006. Terroristen als Personen im Recht? *Zeitschrift für die gesamte Strafrechtswissenschaft* 117: 839.
Joint Committee of Human Rights, Twelfth report of session 2005–2006, HL (2005–06) 122, HC (2005–06) 915.
London Anti-Terrorism Branch (SO13). 2005. Submission in support of three month pre-charge detention. Appendix of Home Affairs Committee, 'Terrorism Detention Powers' HC (2005–06) 910-I, 54.
Mayaud, Y. 1997. *Le terrorisme*. Paris: Dalloz.
McColgan, M., and A. Attanasio. January 1999. France: Paving the way for arbitrary justice. (Report) 271/2. http://www.fidh.org/IMG/pdf/271fran.pdf. accessed 21 Oct 2009.
McCulloch, J., and S. Pickering. 2009. Pre-crime and counter-terrorism. *British Journal of Criminology* 49(5): 628.
Meierhenrich, J. 2006. Analogies at war. *Journal of Conflict and Security Law* 11(1): 1.
Ministry of Justice. *Statistics on race and the criminal justice system 2007/2008*.
Moeckli, D. 2008. *Human rights and non-discrimination*. Oxford: Oxford University Press.
Pantazis, C., and S. Pemberton. 2009. From the "old" to the "new" suspect community. *British Journal of Criminology* 49(5): 646.
Pollard, S. 2005. *David Blunkett*. London: Hodder & Stoughton.
Pradel, J. 2004. Vers un "aggiornamento" des réponses de la procédure pénale à la criminalité *Semaine Juridique* 19: 132 and *Semaine Juridique* 20: 134.

Prime Minister's Press Conference (London 5 August 2005). http://www.pm.gov.uk/output/Page 8041.asp. Accessed 1 Nov 2009.

Prins, H. 2008. Counterblast: The mental health act 2007. *Howard Journal* 47(1): 81.

Privy Counsellor Review Committee. Anti-terrorism, crime and security act 2001 review: Report (the Newton Report) HC (2003–04) 100.

Schmitt, C. 1927. *The concept of the political*. München: Franz Eher Nachfolger.

Silva Sanchez, J.M. 2001. *La expansión del derecho penal*. Madrid: Civitas.

Sim, J., and P.A. Thomas. 1983. The prevention of terrorism act: Normalising the politics of repression. *Journal of Law and Society* 10: 71.

Thomas, T. 2004. When public protection becomes punishment? *European Journal on Criminal Policy and Research* 10(4): 337.

Tony Blair's keynote speech to the Labour Party's 2005 conference. *BBC News*, London, 28 September 2004. http://news.bbc.co.uk/1/hi/uk_politics/4287370.stm. Accessed 22 Oct 2009.

Verso un diritto penale del nemico? 2006 *Questione Giustizia 4*.

Vigna, P. L. 1991. Il processo accusatorio nell'impatto con le esigenze di lotta alla criminalità organizzata. *Giustizia Penale* 462.

Von Hirsh, A. 1996. Extending the harm principle. In *Harm and culpability*, ed. A. Simester and A.T.H. Smith. Oxford: Oxford University Press.

Walker, C. 2004. Terrorism and criminal justice. *Criminal Law Review* 311.

Zedner, L. 2005. Securing liberty in the face of terror. *Journal of law and society* 32(4): 507.

Zedner, L. 2007a. Seeking security by eroding rights. In *Security and human rights,* ed. L. Lazarus and B. Goold. Oxford: Hart Publishing; Waldron, J. 2003. Security and liberty: the image of balance. *Journal of political philosophy* 11: 191.

Zedner, L. 2007b. Pre-crime and post-criminology? *Theoretical Criminology* 11: 261–281.

Zedner, L. 2007c. Preventive justice or pre-punishment? *Current Legal Problems* 60: 174–201.

Zedner, L. 2008. Fixing the future? In *Regulating deviance*, ed. S. Bronnit et al. Oxford: Hart Publishing.

Chapter 8
Secret Evidence and Its Alternatives

Kent Roach

8.1 Introduction

One of the many fall-outs from 9/11 has been the increased use of secret evidence to justify detention and other legal sanctions. Before 9/11, secret evidence was associated with countries that were notorious for not respecting human rights and Kafklesque notions of unfairness. This image, however, underestimated the use of secret evidence by democracies especially in immigration law procedures and other forms of administrative detention. Nevertheless, since 9/11 secret evidence has received increased attention and controversy. It has been used in a variety of contexts including detention proceedings at Guantanamo, immigration proceedings resulting in administrative detention in the United Kingdom and Canada and control order proceedings in the United Kingdom. Secret evidence is also used by the United Nations Security Council in its process of listing those associated with al Qaeda under Security Council Resolution 1267.

Much of the debate about secret evidence has centred on correctives such as the use of security cleared counsel or special advocates to challenge the evidence and the use of active and expert judges or Ombudspersons to challenge the secret evidence/intelligence. In Canada, reliance on expert judges was found to be constitutionally insufficient in the *Charkaoui* case and a regime of special advocates was created. At the same time, however, reliance on special advocates in British proceedings has been challenged and narrowed by various requirements imposed by the House of Lords and the European Court of Human Rights that require the gist of the allegations to be disclosed.

K. Roach (✉)
Faculty of Law, University of Toronto, 78 Queen's Park,
Toronto M5S 2C5, ON, Canada
e-mail: kent.roach@utoronto.ca

A. Masferrer (ed.), *Post 9/11 and the State of Permanent Legal Emergency*,
Ius Gentium: Comparative Perspectives on Law and Justice 14,
DOI 10.1007/978-94-007-4062-4_8, © Springer Science+Business Media B.V. 2012

This chapter will take a broader approach to the secret evidence debate in at least two respects. First, it will suggest that political controversies surrounding the use of secret evidence need to be taken seriously. The use of secret evidence can turn terrorist suspects into fairness martyrs. It can also hide the real level of the terrorist threat from the public. The UN's terrorist listing regime risks falling into disrepute in large part because of its use of secret intelligence as evidence. The political controversies created by secret evidence are especially important if it is accepted that the fight against terrorism is in part a public relations battle and that public exposure and criminalization of terrorism might be an effective strategy against terrorism.

The chapter will also attempt to take a broader approach to the secret evidence debate by examining a fuller range less rights invasive alternatives to the use of secret evidence. Much of the debate has revolved around the use of special advocates or security cleared advocates who are allowed to see and challenge otherwise secret evidence. Special advocates are an important alternative to secret evidence, but not the only one. Other alternatives include the use of public interest immunity applications to prevent the disclosure of unused intelligence in criminal prosecutions and allowing lawyers representing detainees and the accused to have access to information on undertakings that they will not disclose the material to their clients without judicial permission. Both of these alternatives accept that some material must remain secret. More radical alternatives include greater acceptance that previously secret intelligence will have to be disclosed. This will require a more critical scrutiny of the traditional claims that sources and methods must be kept secret and with it changes to the organizational culture of intelligence agencies.

8.2 Intelligence and Evidence

The relation between intelligence and evidence is important to understanding the demand for secret evidence. Intelligence refers to secret material collected by intelligence agencies and increasingly by the police to provide background information and advance warning about people who are thought to be a risk to commit acts of terrorism or other threats to national security. Although some forms of intelligence are public, the traditional essence of intelligence has been that it is secret. Secrecy is related to the need to protect the sources and methods used to collect intelligence from disclosure which can threaten the continued collection of intelligence. In addition, intelligence provided by other agencies under the third party rule cannot be disclosed without the consent of the agency that provided the intelligence.

Evidence refers to information used in legal proceedings to impose legal consequences on a person. It can also refer to unused information that is disclosed to the affected person under statutory or constitutional disclosure rules. In common law countries, there are restrictions on the use of hearsay evidence based on the observations or opinions of third parties that are not present in court to be cross-examined. There are also restrictions on the use of opinion and bad character information and requirements that require that the probative value of evidence in proving specific allegations outweigh its prejudicial effects. These evidentiary restrictions are typically not observed in the collection of intelligence about individuals. Intelligence may focus on a person's associations, previous bad acts and character.[1]

As ideal types, the differences between intelligence and evidence are great. At the same time, the relation between intelligence and evidence is changing. Although intelligence can be kept secret if the state only uses the intelligence for preventive purposes, intelligence can also constitute evidence of the many new crimes that have been enacted in many countries in order to prevent terrorism. Intelligence can also constitute evidence that a person is associated with al Qaeda and as such is subject to the terrorism financing ban under Security Council Resolution 1267.

The desire to use intelligence in legal proceedings creates considerable tension between the competing demands of disclosure and secrecy. The disclosure of intelligence will ensure that the accused is treated fairly and that the state conducts public trials. On the other hand, the disclosure of secret intelligence can endanger the gathering of more intelligence by revealing the identity of informers, secret methods of collecting intelligence and ongoing investigations. The disclosure of intelligence can also break promises to foreign countries that shared intelligence would be kept secret.

There are a variety of means to manage the relationship between intelligence and evidence. At one extreme end, intelligence can be used as secret evidence that is not disclosed to the affected person. Both the United States with respect to detention review proceedings at Guantanamo Bay and the United Kingdom and Canada with respect to immigration detention have used secret evidence. The use of secret evidence, however, is controversial and has been frequently challenged because it violates norms of adjudicative fairness.

Even when secret evidence is not used, as is the case in terrorism prosecutions in the regular criminal courts, the accused may seek disclosure of secret intelligence. The state can resist disclosure of such intelligence through two intermediate devices. The first is to restrict its disclosure obligations to all accused and the second is to seek judicial permission for non-disclosure of secret material in the particular case. The latter procedure in the United States is governed by the *Classified Information Protection Act*[2] (CIPA), in Canada by s.38 of the *Canada Evidence Act*[3] (CEA), in Australia by the *National Security Information Act, 2004*[4] and in the United Kingdom by the common law of public interest immunity(pii). Under these procedures, the criminal court trial judge may order that intelligence need not be disclosed or should only be disclosed to the accused in a redacted form. At the same time, the judge may

[1] See generally K. Roach, "The Eroding Distinction Between Intelligence and Evidence in Terrorism Investigations," in *Counter-Terrorism and Beyond*, ed. Nicola McGarrity, et al. (London: Routledge, 2010).

[2] PL 96-456.

[3] RSC 1985 c.C-5.

[4] Act 150 of 2004.

revise such orders and require fuller disclosure at some later point in the proceedings if that is necessary to ensure the fairness of the trial. At that point, the state will have to disclose the material or end the prosecution.

At the other extreme end of the secrecy-disclosure spectrum, intelligence can be disclosed to the accused and used as evidence in criminal proceedings. Such an approach means that the intelligence and the manner in which it was collected will no longer be secret. In some cases, improper methods such as torture used to collect evidence can result in its exclusion from legal proceedings. Disclosure requires those who collect intelligence to accept greater levels of transparency and accountability. It could also in some cases jeopardize their ability to gather more intelligence and may place vulnerable sources and ongoing investigations at risk.

8.3 The Controversial Use of Secret Evidence

Secret evidence was used at Guantanamo Bay, Cuba with respect to Combatant Status Review Tribunals and early versions of military commissions. The rationale for such procedures was that it was more important to gather and protect intelligence than to prosecute detainees. Prosecutions would not allow the use of secret evidence and might require unused but relevant intelligence to be disclosed to the accused. In *Hamdan v. the United States,*[5] the United States Supreme Court held that military commissions violated both Common Article 3 of the Geneva Convention and the Uniform Code of Military Justice in part because secret evidence could be presented without the detainee being present. Secret evidence raised fundamental concerns long associated with the writer Kafka about accused being unable to defend themselves because they do not know the precise allegations and evidence against them.

The *Military Commissions Act of 2006* enacted in response to *Hamdan* did not contemplate the use of secret evidence and provided that the accused should be present in the proceedings unless he was disruptive or dangerous.[6] The *Military Commissions Act of 2009* continues this provision and contains a new chapter providing for the handling of classified information. Military judges are prohibited from ordering the release of classified information,[7] but there are also provisions that ensure that the accused has access to any information that is introduced into evidence in military commissions.[8] There are also provisions drawn largely from CIPA that govern the use and disclosure of classified or secret information. They allow the use of non-classified substitutes for classified information and they provide for the withdrawals or termination of certain counts as a remedy for

---

[5] 548 U.S. 557 (2006).

[6] *Military Commissions Act of 2006* 120 Stat 2611 s.949d(e).

[7] *Military Commission Act of 2009* H.R. 2647-385 s.949p-1(a).

[8] *Ibidem*, s. 949p-1(b).

non-disclosure of classified information.[9] There seems to a growing recognition of the unfairness of the use of secret evidence.

Secret evidence could also be used in the United Kingdom under Part IV of the *Anti-Terrorism Crime and Security Act, 2001.* It provided for the indeterminate detention of non citizen terrorist suspects who could not be deported. Cases were heard by the Special Immigration Appeals Commission which had provisions that allowed security cleared lawyers called special advocates to examine and challenge secret evidence that was not disclosed to detainees or their lawyers. Special advocates are, however, restricted from communicating with detainees once they have seen the secret material because of concerns that they may inadvertently disclose secrets to the detainee. This raises concerns that detainees may not have a fair trial because they are unable fully to assist special advocates in their defence. The fear of inadvertent disclosure by special advocates is related to the Cold War concept of the mosaic effect in which the detainee could potentially fit together the pieces of the puzzle about sources and methods from even innocuous pieces of information.

The provisions for indeterminate detention without trial in Part IV of the *Anti-Terrorism, Crime and Security Act of 2001* were repealed after they were declared in 2004 by the House of Lords to be incompatible with the Human Rights Act, 1998.[10] They were replaced by control orders which also allowed secret evidence to be used. The use of secret evidence has continued to be controversial and the House of Lords, following authority from the European Court of Human Rights, has ruled that the use of secret evidence to support control orders will be unfair if the controlees has not had most of the allegations against them disclosed to them. Although some secret evidence can still be used and subject to challenge by special advocates, most of it must be disclosed to allow persons to defend themselves.[11] The viability of this regime of partial secret evidence remains to be seen and the new UK government has announced its intention to move away from the controversial control order scheme.

The UN Security Council relies on secret evidence in its listing of terrorists under the regime established by Resolution 1267. The European Court of Justice held in the Kadi case that this procedure lacked basic fairness and as such should not be implemented at the European level.[12] The European Court of General Instance subsequently held that a narrative summary designed to provide Kadi with some information about why he was listed while also protecting intelligence sources and methods did not provide enough information to afford a judicial remedy.[13] Canadian and British courts have also made adverse comments about the use of

[9] *Ibidem*, subchapter V.

[10] *A. v. Secretary of State* 2004 UKHL 56.

[11] *Secretary of State v. AF (no. 3)* [2009] UKHL 28 at para 59 following *A v. United Kingdom* App no 3455/05 19 Feb 2009 para 220.

[12] *Yassin Abdullah Kadi and Al Barakaat International Foundation v Council of the European Union and Commission of the European Communities,* Cases C-402/05 P and C-415/05 P, *Yassin Abdullah Kadi and Al Barakaat International Foundation v. Council and Commission*, 3 September 2008.

[13] *Kadi v. European Commission* judgment of the General Court (7th Division) 30 September 2010 available at http://eur-lex.europa.eu/LexUriServ/LexUriServ.do?uri=CELEX:62009A0085:EN:HTML

secret evidence in the 1267 regime and have even compared it with the position faced by Josef in Kafka's *The Trial*.[14]

Secret evidence is also used in judicial reviews of security certificates issued in Canada by the Ministers of Immigration and Public Safety to detain a non citizen on security grounds pending deportation.[15] The judge who reviews the reasonableness of the certificate hears evidence from the government in the absence of the detainee and their counsel if, in the judge's opinion, the disclosure of information would be injurious to national security or the safety of any person. This provision does not allow any balancing between the national security interests of the state and the interests of the detainee in gaining access to the information. This is a broad protection for secrecy. It reflects Canada's status as a net importer of intelligence and its reliance on foreign intelligence in the security certificate process. Material covered by national security or personal safety concerns is used as secret evidence by the judge in determining the reasonableness of the certificate.[16]

In 2002, a judge of the Federal Court made a speech in which he commented that the judges of his Court "do not like this process of having to sit alone hearing only one party and looking at the materials produced by only one party and having to try to figure out for ourselves what is wrong with the case that is being presented before us and having to try for ourselves to see how that witnesses that appear before us ought to be cross-examined." The judge ended his speech with an extraordinary confession- "I sometimes feel a little bit like a fig leaf".[17] He also suggested a more proportionate alternative to the present system, one based on the British system of allowing lawyers with security clearances to have access to confidential information and play the role of the adversary in the national security context. As might be expected, security certificates have been controversial in Canada, often being branded as "secret trials".

In 2007, the Supreme Court of Canada held that the absence of any adversarial challenge to the secret evidence submitted to the judge violated the right to a fair trial under s.7 of the Canadian Charter of Rights and Freedoms.[18] The Court rejected the idea that searching review of secret evidence by specially designated Federal Court judges, many of whom had long experience in intelligence matters,[19] could make up for the use of secret evidence. The Court stressed that the judge only had power to evaluate the secret evidence presented by the government. Combined with the lack of full disclosure to the detainee, this created a risk that the judge would not be presented with all the facts and law that should be

---

[14]*Abousfian Abdelrazik v The Minister of Foreign Affairs and the Attorney General of Canada* [2009] FC 580; *Treasury v. Ahmad* [2010] UKSC 2.

[15]*Immigration and Refugee Protection Act* (IRPA)S.C. 2001 c.27 s.34. as amended.

[16]*Ibidem*, s. 83.

[17]J. Hugessen, "Watching the Watchers: Democratic Oversight," *Terrorism, Law and Democracy*, ed. D. Daubney, et al. (Montreal: Themis 2002) at 384, 386.

[18]Section 7 provides that a person's life, liberty and security of the person can only be taken away in accordance with the principles of fundamental justice (*Charkaoui v. Canada* [2007] 1 S.C.R.). 350. On this case and legislative responses to it see generally the collection of essays in (2008) 42 S.C.L.R.(2d) 251–440.

[19]For further discussion of the judicial management model used in Israel and elsewhere see D. Barak-Erez and M. Waxman, "Secret Evidence and the Due Process of Terrorist Detentions," *Columbia Journal of Transnational Law* 48 (2009): 1 at 20–27.

considered when reviewing the certificate. The court concluded that the fairness of the security certificate process

> rests entirely on the shoulders of the designated judge. Those shoulders cannot by themselves bear the heavy burden of assuring, in fact and appearance, that the decision on the reasonableness of the decision is impartial, is based on a full view of the facts and law, and reflects the named person's knowledge of the case to meet. The judge…simply cannot fill the vacuum left by the removal of the traditional guarantees of a fair hearing. The judge sees only what the ministers put before him or her. The judge, knowing nothing else about the case, is not in a position to identify errors, find omissions or assess the credibility and truthfulness of the information in the way the named person would be.. …Despite the judge's best efforts to question the government's witnesses and scrutinize the documentary evidence, he or she is placed in the situation of asking questions and ultimately deciding the issues on the basis of incomplete and potentially unreliable information.[20]

Although the Court rejected the idea that the reviewing judges were no longer independent and impartial and praised the Federal Court for adopting a "pseudo-inquisitorial role",[21] it clearly had concerns about the factual and legal accuracy of decisions that were made without effective adversarial challenge. The Court held that the right to a fair hearing could only be met by an adequate substitute for disclosure and that there was none under the regime then in place.[22]

All of the above cases from European and North American courts demonstrate that the use of secret evidence is rightly controversial[23] even when the state claims that disclosure of the evidence will harm vulnerable sources and impede their attempts to collect intelligence and ultimately to prevent terrorism. Secret evidence is generally not accepted in criminal prosecutions and there are limits to the ability of security cleared advocates to compensate for the extreme disadvantages imposed on a person when secret evidence is used against him or her.

8.4 Alternatives to Secret Evidence

Having held that the use of secret evidence violated the right to a fair hearing, the Supreme Court of Canada in *Charkaoui* considered whether the government had justified the deprivation of a fair hearing as a reasonable and proportionate limit on

---

[20] *Charkaoui* at para 63.

[21] *Ibidem* at para 51.

[22] The Court concluded on the fair hearing issue: "In the context of national security, non-disclosure, which may be extensive, coupled with the grave intrusions on liberty imposed on a detainee, makes it difficult, if not impossible, to find substitute procedures that will satisfy s. 7. Fundamental justice requires substantial compliance with the venerated principle that a person whose liberty is in jeopardy must be given an opportunity to know the case to meet, and an opportunity to meet the case. Yet the imperative of the protection of society may preclude this. Information may be obtained from other countries or from informers on condition that it not be disclosed. Or it may simply be so critical that it cannot be disclosed without risking public security. This is a reality of our modern world. If s. 7 is to be satisfied, either the person must be given the necessary information, or a substantial substitute for that information must be found. Neither is the case here." *Ibidem* at para 61.

[23] Justice, *Secret Evidence* (London: Justice, 2009).

the right. It concluded that the use of secret evidence had not been justified because there was a range of more proportionate alternatives to the use of unchallenged secret evidence.

The range of less intrusive alternatives included not only the British-based special advocate system, but also (1) a prior system where the security certificates were reviewed by the Security Intelligence Review Committee (SIRC), the watchdog agency over Canada's domestic intelligence agency,[24] (2) the use of security-cleared counsel in public inquiries who were trusted to communicate with affected persons even after they had seen the secret evidence and (3) disclosing secret evidence to counsel for the affected party on undertakings that the counsel will not share that evidence with his or own client. The critical difference between these three alternatives and the British special advocate model eventually adopted is that they allow counsel to have contact with the affected person after counsel has reviewed the closed or secret evidence without anything but self-imposed restrictions on the risk of inadvertent disclosure of secret information.[25]

The Supreme Court was aware of criticisms of the British special advocate scheme, but concluded that it was also a more proportionate alternative to the status quo of no adversarial challenge to the secret evidence. In this vein, it noted that once British special advocates "have seen the confidential material, they cannot, subject to narrow exceptions, take instructions from the appellant or the appellant's counsel; (2) they lack the resources of an ordinary legal team, for the purpose of conducting in secret a full defence; and (3) they have no power to call witnesses."[26]

8.5 The Canadian Special Advocate Scheme

In response to *Charkaoui*, the Canadian Parliament in 2008 enacted a special advocate scheme. With some differences, it follows the British special advocate approach by allowing security cleared special advocates to have access to the secret evidence and to challenge both whether evidence should be secret and its relevance, reliability and sufficiency. It also provides that Minister of Justice has responsibility for ensuring that special advocates have adequate administrative support and resources.

---

[24] Under a previous act, a review of security certificates issued against permanent residents was conducted by the independent review body for Canada's security intelligence agency and security cleared counsel for that agency played an adversarial role in challenging the security certificate. See M. Rankin, "The Security Intelligence Review Committee: Reconciling National Security with Procedural Fairness," *Canadian Journal of Administrative Law and Practice* 3 (1990): 173. The European Court of Human Rights wrongly assumed in *Chahal v. U.K.* (1996) 23 E.H.H.R. 413 that such a special advocate procedure was also used in Canada's Federal Court.

[25] In the first two alternatives, counsel does not owe duties to the affected person but rather to the commission.

[26] *Charkaoui v. Canada* at para 83.

Section 85.4(2) of the amended *Immigration and Refugee Protection Act* provides that once the special advocate has seen the secret evidence, he or she cannot communicate with anyone else without judicial authorization and subject to the judicially imposed conditions. This provision is not an absolute bar, but a delegation to judges of the power to determine how far the special advocate can go in the exercise of his or her duties.

With respect to the secrecy of the information, the secrecy standards were not changed in the 2008 amendments and they still prohibit the disclosure of information that will harm national security or any person with no balancing of the respective harms of disclosure and non-disclosure. Nevertheless, both the government and the special advocates have made more of the secret evidence public since the introduction of the scheme and many special advocates believe that this an important feature of the scheme.

With respect to the sufficiency and reliability of the secret evidence, the law now specifically provides for the special advocates being able to cross-examine witnesses in closed proceedings and to "exercise, with the judge's authorization, any other powers that are necessary to protect the interests of the permanent resident or foreign national"[27] Under this provision, a special advocate could seek judicial approval to call his or her own witnesses, to demand disclosure beyond the secret evidence used by the government in the case or to discuss matters with the detainee and/or his counsel or experts after having seen the secret information. A court that has upheld the new security certificate regime from constitutional challenge has stressed that judges can authorize special advocates to communicate with others after they have seen the secret information when this is necessary to ensure the fairness of the proceedings.[28]

The Supreme Court in *Charkaoui I* has ruled that the use of secret evidence deprives the detainee of a fair hearing. Specifically it presents a risk that reviewing judges will not have access to all the facts and law required effectively to review the reasonableness of the Minister's decisions to certify a non citizen to be a security risk and to detain the person on that basis often for long periods because of the difficulties or impossibility of deportation. The Court has not ruled that the use of secret evidence is inherently unconstitutional but rather that some adequate substitute must be found to protect the accused's right to a fair hearing when secret evidence is used.

The Supreme Court's decisive rejection of reliance on the judicial management model as "pseudo inquisitorial" and inadequate no doubt reflects some bias towards adversarial systems. Nevertheless, the Court's rejection of the model is in my view justified because Canadian judges are not trained in inquisitorial investigations and by the results that special advocates have achieved since being introduced. There is also a danger that specially designated judges may be susceptible to capture or other distortions of the impartial judicial function if they alone must challenge and scrutinize secret evidence submitted by the government. The collapse of the Almrei security

[27] S.C. 2008 c. 3.

[28] *Harkat v. Canada* 2010 FC 1242.

certificate where the special advocate was able to reveal inconsistencies in the secret evidence is a concrete example of the ability of special advocates to make effective adversarial challenges to secret evidence. Another example has been the ability of special advocates to have evidence obtained through or derived from torture or cruel and degrading treatment excluded in the *Mahjoub* case.[29]

In addition, special advocates and other security cleared counsel have also enjoyed considerable success in Canada in responding to the government's overclaiming of secrecy. In three recent public inquiries, security cleared commission counsel have won battles with the government with respect to overclaiming secrecy in large part because they had access to the information that the government claimed must remain secret. Those within government have an incentive to overclaim secrecy to avoid accountability and to minimize risks to sources, ongoing investigations and intelligence sharing relations. Canadian judges are become more aware of the dangers of overclaiming in part because of effective challenges by counsel who have access to secret information. For example, Canadian judges are now becoming more sceptical about government claims that non-damaging information should not be disclosed because of the mosaic effect and are also requiring the Canadian government in disputed cases to also ask foreign agencies whether they are willing to amend caveats to allow the disclosure of information.[30]

At the same time, the Canadian special advocate system is not perfect and could be improved. It is significant that Parliament's response to *Charkaoui I* was to make use of a special advocate system that maximized the government's interest in secrecy[31] while at the same time providing for the new constitutional minimum of adversarial challenge to secret evidence. The SIRC or commission counsel model that allows security cleared lawyers to contact the detainee and his counsel without judicial approval is a more proportionate alternative that responds to some of the deficiencies associated with the British system. It depends on the restraint and discretion of security cleared counsel, but there have been no complaints that these models resulted in inadvertent (or advertent) leakage of secrets.

The lack of interest in Canada for the option of giving security clearances to the detainee's own lawyer as is sometimes used in Australia or the United States discounts the possibility of allowing the lawyers most familiar with the case to have access to the secret evidence.[32] At the same time, such procedures may adversely affect the detainee's ability to select his own counsel because counsel would likely have to be trusted by the state through a security clearance or other means.

---

[29] *Re Mahjoub* 2010 FC 787; *Re Mahjoub* 2010 FC 937.

[30] See generally K. Roach, *The Unique Challenges of Terrorism Prosecutions* (Ottawa: Supply and Services, 2010) at 192–210.

[31] For further arguments see K. Roach, "Charkaoui and Bill C-3," *Supreme Court Law Review*(2d) 42 (2008): 281 and C. Forcese and L. Waldman, "A Bismarkian Moment: *Charkaoui* and Bill C-3," *Supreme Court Law Review*(2d) 42 (2008): 355. For a defence of Bill C-3 that stresses the ability of the judge to give the special advocates additional powers on a case by case basis see D. Dunbar and S. Nesbitt, "Parliament's Response to *Charkaoui,*" *Supreme Court Law Review*(2d0) 42 (2008): 415.

[32] M. Code and K. Roach, "The Role of the Independent Lawyer and Security Certificates," *Criminal Law Quarterly* 52 (2006): 85.

Although the Canadian special advocate legislation is restricted to security certificates, special advocates have also been used in public interest immunity applications and extradition proceedings. The Air India Commission recently recommended that they be used with respect to the review of intercept warrants.[33] This may lead to similar concerns as voiced in the UK about the proliferation of special advocates, but the Commission makes the case that a special advocate will not be at a disadvantage compared to the accused's lawyer when challenging the legality and sufficiency of a warrant.

The special advocate system in Canada seems to be more well- received than in the UK where courts and others have expressed growing concern about the ability of special advocates to ensure fairness in the absence of disclosure of more information to the detainee. This is probably related in part to greater levels of disclosure of underlying material in Canada than under at least some of the UK's control orders.

The main weaknesses of the Canadian special advocate system remain the restrictions on special advocates to call witnesses, seek further disclosure and to contact the detainee and others after having seen the secret evidence. In all these cases, however, the judge retains the ability to authorize such powers if he or she determines that such powers are necessary to protect the detainee's interests. In this way, the Canadian system may effectively combine and maximize the protections of adversarial challenge with a backstop of judicial management in cases where special advocates argue that they need more powers to protect the detainee's interests.

8.6 Protecting Intelligence from Disclosure by Reducing Disclosure Obligations

Another alternative to the use of secret evidence against terrorist suspects is to prosecute them criminally. Criminal prosecutions are generally the fairest response to terrorism and they may also help denounce terrorism by publicly exposing it.[34] It would, however, be a mistake to conclude that the secret evidence problems magically go away when the criminal law is used.

The accused may request and be entitled to disclosure of intelligence material that is relevant to their defence even if the state does not use that intelligence as evidence. In many cases, this non-used material may simply contain irrelevant or incriminating material, but there is a possibility that it could obtain exculpatory material or material that would assist the accused. Non-disclosure of potentially exculpatory material is a leading cause of the wrongful conviction of innocent persons including a series of wrongful convictions in cases involving Irish Republican Army bombings in Britain. In a case that revealed one of these wrongful convictions, the

[33] *Air India Flight 182: A Canadian Tragedy*, vol. 3 (Ottawa: Supply and Services, 2010).

[34] K. Roach, *The 9/11 Effect: Comparative Counter-Terrorism* (New York: Cambridge University Press, 2011) chap. 8.

British courts articulated a broad right that would entitle an accused to information possessed by the state that was relevant and material to the case including material that could lead to new issues being raised at trial.[35] New issues could include state improprieties in obtaining evidence or the unreliability of evidence including human sources or information obtained under duress. Broad disclosure requirements promote adjudicative fairness, but they can also result in the disclosure of much sensitive intelligence to an accused in a terrorism prosecution.

In Britain, broad common law disclosure obligations have been narrowed by legislation. Section 32 of the *Criminal Justice Act 2003* now requires primary disclosure of any previously undisclosed material "which might reasonably be considered capable of undermining the case for the prosecution against the accused or of assisting the case for the accused". As the House of Lords recognized in 2004,

> …section 3 does not require disclosure of material which is either neutral in its effect or which is adverse to the defendant, whether because it strengthens the prosecution or weakens the defence.[36]

Canada has a particularly broad constitutional standard of disclosure that requires the state to disclose all relevant and non-privileged evidence and even to make inquiries to intelligence agencies about whether they possess information that may assist the accused.[37]

The relevant disclosure obligations in the United States are arguably even less onerous than in the United Kingdom though they have a constitutional basis. The main constitutional case is *Brady v. Maryland* [38] which held that "the suppression by the prosecution of evidence favorable to the accused upon requests violates due process where the evidence is material either to guilt or to punishment, irrespective of the good faith or bad faith of the prosecution."[39] The focus in the United States is on exculpatory material and not necessarily material that will weaken the prosecution's case or advance a side issue such as a rights violation. Nevertheless, an associate general counsel of the CIA has written that "close coordination between the activities of law enforcement and intelligence agencies in a particular matter should subject the intelligence files to *Brady* search".[40] Other disclosure requirements relate to material that can be used to impeach a government witness, statements made by the accused, and documents or tangible objects that are material to the defence or belong to the accused.[41]

---

[35] *R v Ward* [1993] 1 WLR 619, 674; *R v Keane* [1994] 1 WLR 746, 752.

[36] *R. v. H and C* [2004] UKHL 3 at para 17.

[37] *R. v. Stinchcombe* [1991] 3 S.C.R. 326; *R. v. McNeil* [2009] 1 S.C.R. 66.

[38] 373 U.S. 83 (1963).

[39] *Ibidem* at 87.

[40] J. Fredman, "Intelligence Agencies, Law Enforcement and the Prosecution Team," *Yale Law and Policy Review* 16 (1998): 331 at 354. But for a more limited approach to the search of an intelligence agency's files for exculpatory material see M. Villarede, "Structuring the Prosecutor's Duty to Search the Intelligence for Brady Material," *Cornell Law Review* 88 (2003): 1471.

[41] F. Manget, "Intelligence and the Criminal Law System," *Stanford Law and Policy Review* 17 (2006): 415 at 423.

One method of protecting intelligence from disclosure is to reduce the state's disclosure obligations to the accused. As discussed above, legislation in the United Kingdom has reduced disclosure obligations and prosecutors in that country have been warned that they need not seek non-disclosure orders for material that is not even subject to disclosure obligations. In some cases, it may be impossible to reduce disclosure obligations beyond a constitutional minimum. In general, it is dangerous to reduce disclosure requirements in all criminal cases as a means to protect intelligence from disclosure. Legislatures make broad rules that may prevent the disclosure of material that would be helpful to the accused in individual cases. As will be seen in the next section, a more proportionate response that is more respectful of trial fairness is to allow judges to order non-disclosure of intelligence in particular cases while still ensuring that the accused has enough information to have a fair trial.

8.7 Protecting Intelligence from Disclosure by Case-by-Case Non-disclosure Orders

In 1980, the United States enacted the *Classified Information Procedures Act*[42] (CIPA) to govern the disclosure and non-disclosure of classified information that the government is taking steps to protect for reasons of national security. National security is defined broadly, to include considerations of national defence and international relations. Section 5 of CIPA places robust requirements on the accused to notify both the prosecutor and the court before trial if they expect to disclose, or cause the disclosure of, classified information.

CIPA is most relevant in cases where the accused might seek access to classified information that is of minimal relevance to the case. In cases where the evidence is very relevant, it is unlikely that courts will hold that the evidence cannot be disclosed to the accused or that they will be able to devise non-classified substitutions that treat the accused fairly.[43] In those cases, the prosecutor may be faced with the stark dilemma of whether to disclose intelligence or not to commence or maintain a terrorism prosecution.

One of the core dilemmas of national security confidentiality is that the process of determining whether the government has made a legitimate claim of secrecy may itself sacrifice secrecy. Section 3 of CIPA protects this anticipatory interest in confidentiality by providing that, upon a motion of the United States, "the court shall issue an order to protect against the disclosure of any classified information disclosed by the United States to any defendant in any criminal case in a district court in the United

[42] PL 96-456.

[43] B. Tamanaha, "A Critical Review of the Classified Information Procedures Act," *American Journal of Criminal Law* 13 (1986): 277 at 305–306; S. Jordan, "Classified Information and Conflicts in Independent Counsel Prosecutions," *Columbia Law Review* 91 (1991): 1651 at 1662–1663.

States." Although CIPA on its face does not contemplate that courts can require defence lawyers to obtain security clearances as a prerequisite to obtaining access to classified information, courts have found this power is an incident to CIPA's procedures.[44] Guilty pleas entered by the so-called 20th hijacker Zacarias Moussaoui were upheld despite arguments that he was denied a fair trial because only his security cleared appointed counsel had access to classified information disclosed by the state.[45] The use of security clearances affects the relationship between the accused and defence counsel because, as is the case with British special advocates, counsel will be prohibited from revealing the classified information to his or her client without the court's permission. Nevertheless, it is a means to ensure that the person other than the accused who is best acquainted with the case can see the information and make submissions about its relevance to the case.

CIPA is designed to give both governments and judges the greatest flexibility possible in reconciling the state's interests in the secrecy of security intelligence with the interests of the accused and the public in the disclosure of evidence. CIPA allows the government to propose substitutions, admissions and summaries for classified information. It allows the trial judge considerable flexibility, when admitting classified information as evidence, to edit the information to minimize harm to national security. The reviews of the operation of CIPA in terrorism prosecutions both before and after 9/11 suggest that it has generally been successful in reconciling the competing interests of secrecy and disclosure. A recent report found a 91.7% conviction rate in post 9/11 terrorism prosecutions involving CIPA.[46]

In Britain, non-disclosure orders can be obtained from trial judges in a manner similar to that contemplated under CIPA. In a 1993 case which overturned a terrorism conviction in part because the Crown had not made full disclosure, the Court of Appeal criticized the prosecution for acting "as a judge in their own cause on the issue of public interest immunity". The Court of Appeal indicated that if the Crown was "not prepared to have the issue of public interest immunity determined by the court, the result must inevitably be that the prosecution will have to be abandoned."[47]

Material over which public interest immunity (pii) is claimed must always be disclosed to the court. Applications for pii should generally be disclosed to the defence, but there may be cases in which the general category of the evidence claimed to be covered could not be disclosed to the accused because it would reveal secrets. There may also be exceptional cases in which no notice at all would be given to the accused because such notice would reveal the nature of the evidence in question.[48] In such cases, only the judge and perhaps a special advocate would see the information that is the subject of the non-disclosure application.

---

[44] *United States v. bin Laden* 58 F.Supp.2d 113, 121; *United States v. Al-Arian* 267 F.Supp 2d 1258.

[45] *United States v Moussaoui* No 06 4495 Jan. 4, 2010 (4th Cir).

[46] Centre on Law and Security *Terrorist Trial Report* Card (2010) at 28.

[47] *R. v. Ward* [1993] 1 W.L.R. 619 at 648.

[48] *R. v. Davis, Johnson and Rowe* [1993] 1 W.L.R. 613.

The House of Lords considered the proper procedures and approaches to pii in *R. v. H. and C.*[49] It recognized the close connections between disclosure and pii when it stressed that there would be no need to claim immunity for material that was not subject to disclosure "if material does not weaken the prosecution case or strengthen that of the defendant, there is no requirement to disclose it." It also warned about the dangers of the accused being "permitted to make general and unspecified allegations and then seek far-reaching disclosure in the hope that material may turn up to make them good. Neutral material or material damaging to the defendant need not be disclosed and should not be brought to the attention of the court."[50] In cases where the material is both subject to the duty of disclosure because it would weaken the prosecution or strengthen the defence and there is a serious prejudice to an important public interest, the House of Lords stressed means to reconcile the demands of secrecy and disclosure through devices such as court-approved editing or summarizing the evidence, or having the prosecution make admissions of facts. This flexible approach is consistent with the orientation of CIPA.

The House of Lords has recognized that in appropriate cases, special advocates can be appointed to assist with pii determinations. It recognized that the appointment of special counsel was not without difficulties. These problems included the lack of explicit authorizing legislation, the delay caused while the special advocate becomes familiar with a complex case and "ethical problems, since a lawyer who cannot take full instructions from his client, nor report to his client, who is not responsible to his client and whose relationship with the client lacks the quality of confidence inherent in any ordinary lawyer-client relationship, is acting in a way hitherto unknown to the legal profession."[51]

Canada has also borrowed from both CIPA and British public interest immunity procedures to give judges an array of flexible options in reconciling trial fairness with protection of secrets.[52] One difference, however, is that only specially designated Federal Court judges in Canada can make non-disclosure orders even though a different trial judge will have to determine if a fair trial is still possible in light of a non-disclosure order. This approach discounts that a critical safeguard designed to ensure that pii does not threaten the accused's right to a fair trial is the trial judge's continuing review of any non-disclosure order. In other words, any such order "should not be treated as a final, once-and-for-all, answer but as a provisional answer which the court must keep under review."[53] The European Court of Human Rights has recognized in *Edwards and Lewis v. The United Kingdom* that:

> The entitlement to disclosure of relevant evidence is not, however, an absolute right. In any criminal proceedings there may be competing interests, such as national security or the need to protect witnesses at risk of reprisals or keep secret police methods of investigation

[49] [2004] UKHL 3.

[50] *Ibidem* at para 35.

[51] *Ibidem* at para 22.

[52] Canada Evidence Act s.38.

[53] *Ibidem* at para 36.

> of crime, which must be weighed against the rights of the accused. In some cases it may be necessary to withhold certain evidence from the defence so as to preserve the fundamental rights of another individual or to safeguard an important public interest. Nonetheless, only such measures restricting the rights of the defence which are strictly necessary are permissible under Article 6 § 1. Furthermore, in order to ensure that the accused receives a fair trial, any difficulties caused to the defence by a limitation on its rights must be sufficiently counterbalanced by the procedures followed by the judicial authorities (ibid, § 52)....[54]

On the facts of *Edwards and Lewis*, which involved pii applications that shielded investigative techniques used by the police in cases in which the accused claimed entrapment defences, the European Court of Human Rights held that the right to a fair trial in Article 6(1) of the European Convention on Human Rights had been violated because the accused had been denied access to important evidence that might have presented a basis for an entrapment defence and because the procedure used did not comply "with the requirements to provide adversarial proceedings and equality of arms or incorporated adequate safeguards to protect the interests of the accused."[55]

The British experience indicates that questions of pii cannot be divorced from the scope of disclosure obligations. Britain has moved away from relying on court decisions to define the prosecutor's disclosure obligations and legislation has both reduced disclosure obligations and made them more certain. The British example also provides some experience with the use of special advocates in pii proceedings. It warns of the danger of increased delay and of the difficulty of the special advocate to take meaningful instructions from the accused after the special advocate has seen the secret and undisclosed information.

Most importantly, both the House of Lords and the European Court of Human Rights have placed considerable emphasis on the ability of the trial judge to revisit initial decisions that the disclosure of sensitive information is not required. The trial judge conducts this ongoing review in light of the evolving trial, including the defence's case and defence cross-examination of witnesses. In Canada, however, trial judges cannot revise a non-disclosure order made on national security grounds even though they can order more drastic remedies such as stays of proceedings that can end a terrorism prosecution.[56]

One the great virtues of criminal trials is that they do not use secret evidence against the accused. At the same time, however, a reluctance to disclose unused but potentially relevant secret intelligence can inhibit the use of the criminal law against suspected terrorists and influence states to use less restrained forms of military and administrative detention that allow secret evidence. This leads us to the last issue, namely whether more secret intelligence can in fact be disclosed.

---

[54] *Edwards and Lewis v. the United Kingdom* Judgment of October 27, 2004 at para 46.

[55] Judgment of October 27, 2004 at para 46.

[56] The Air India commission recommended that the trial judge in the criminal court must as in the UK and US be able to revise the non disclosure order, but Canada's unique and awkward two court scheme has been held to be constitutional in *R. v. Ahmad* 2011 SCC 6.

8.8 Accepting That Some Intelligence Will Have to Be Disclosed and Changing the Culture of Intelligence Gathering

The legal techniques of special advocates and public interest immunity applications examined above have been and will continue to be important means to reconcile the competing demands of fairness and secrecy. Nevertheless, they like secret evidence itself can be politically and legally controversial. The public may not appreciate the subtle and often misunderstood differences between the actual use of secret evidence and public interest immunity non-disclosure orders. The fairness of the special advocate regime will continue to be challenged and contested and concerns have arisen that the Ombudperson introduced to respond to *Kadi* may not even have access to all the secret intelligence relevant to a particular listing under the 1267 regime and in any event does not have the power to provide a judicial remedy to a person who has been listed, perhaps on the basis of flawed secret intelligence used as evidence to justify the listing.[57]

A more radical response to the secret evidence problem is persuade those who collect intelligence that it can more frequently be disclosed. Intelligence collectors are already in the wake of 9/11 being encouraged to disclose intelligence more to other agencies and countries. The remaining task is to convince them that the same intelligence can more frequently be disclosed in legal proceedings.

In the United States, it has been observed long before 9/11 that "[c]ases dealing with classified information often cause friction between the Justice Department and the intelligence agency which has information at stake. The conflict arises because intelligence agencies are uniformly reluctant to disclose classified information, even though this information might be necessary to successfully prosecute a case."[58] Although the United States does not have a separate domestic civilian intelligence agency, administrative barriers known as "the wall" were constructed to regulate the sharing of intelligence with prosecutors working on criminal prosecutions. The barriers played some role in at least one investigation of one of the 9/11 hijackers. One FBI agent working on the intelligence side rebuffed an inquiry from another FBI agent working on the law enforcement side, in part because the file contained signals intelligence. The rebuffed FBI agent replied that "someday someone will die- and wall or not- the public will not understand why we were not more effective…"[59] The 9/11 Commission found that the law enforcement agent had been wrongly denied the intelligence because the suspect was already subject to a law enforcement investigation. It also concluded that more information sharing could have identified

---

[57] C. Forcese and K. Roach, "Limping into the Future: The 1267 Terrorist Financing Listing Regime at the Crossroads," *George Washington International Law Review* 42 (2010):217, 242–270.

[58] B. Tamanaha, "A Critical Review of the Classified Information Procedures Act," *American Journal of Criminal Law* 277 (1986): 13 at 280–281.

[59] 9/11 Commission Report at 8.2.

at least two of the hijackers and possibly disrupted the 9/11 plot.[60] Increased emphasis on information sharing in order to prevent acts of terrorism should also result in a greater willingness to disclose intelligence when necessary to prosecute terrorism cases. The length of time it takes to prosecute terrorism cases may also diminish the dangers of disclosing ongoing investigations. The Obama Administration has taken some steps to prevent the overclassification of documents and the overclaiming of national security confidentiality,[61] though the success of such efforts remains to be seen.

The 9/11 terrorist attacks underlined the importance of sharing intelligence with law enforcement. At the same time, the post 9/11 experience with terrorism prosecutions and detentions suggests that the tensions between the desire to keep intelligence secret and the requirements for disclosure have not gone away. In some respects, they have intensified because prosecutors can argue that it is more important than ever for them to satisfy disclosure obligations in order to obtain convictions, while security intelligence agencies can argue that the need to keep their ongoing operations, methods and sources confidential has increased if they are to prevent another 9/11.

There is a need to rethink the traditional mandates of police and intelligence agencies in light of current conditions where terrorism as opposed to espionage is seen as the prime threat to national security. Security intelligence agencies need to be aware of the evidentiary consequences of their counter-terrorism practices and attempt to adjust to greater disclosure of their intelligence.

Britain's domestic Security Service, MI5, has adjusted some of its activities to better accommodate the need for evidence that can be used against suspected terrorists. MI5 has expressed some willingness to conduct physical surveillance according to evidentiary standards and if necessary even have its agents testify in criminal prosecutions. It has also demonstrated some confidence in the ability of pii applications to protect its most sensitive information from disclosure.[62] At the same time, however, intercepts still cannot be used as evidence in British terrorism prosecutions largely because of the concerns of intelligence agencies that they would have to retain and disclose such material. A recent review has concluded that the use of intercept as evidence was not legally viable because the courts would assume control over what intercept evidence is maintained or discarded in order to achieve equality of arms and assure that the accused had fair access to the intercept material.[63] The reluctance in Britain to use intercept evidence is a testament to the continued reluctance of intelligence agencies to cede control over their work product to the courts and to live with the risk that intelligence may have to be disclosed.

---

[60] 9/11 Commission Report at 3.2.

[61] Executive Order Classified National Security Information December 29, 2009 available at http://www.whitehouse.gov/the-press-office/executive-order-classified-national-security-information

[62] MI5 "Evidence and Disclosure" at http://www.mi5.gov.uk/output/Page87.html

[63] Secretary of State for the Home Department *Intercept as Evidence A Report* December 2009 Cmnd 7760.

Intelligence agencies may be able to learn some important lessons from police forces about preserving the evidential value of intelligence. For example, intelligence agencies often promise human sources complete anonymity whereas police forces are often more circumspect in making promises to sources that revolve around informer privilege. Although witness protection is onerous and expensive, intelligence agencies might in some cases have to become better acquainted with such programs. Canadian courts have started not to take secrecy claims based on the third party rule of control over shared intelligence at face value and require Canadian agencies to request foreign agencies whether they would be willing to amend the restrictions or caveats that they originally placed on the disclosure of shared intelligence.[64] This has not been a comfortable experience for Canadian agencies which rely on foreign intelligence and are worried that such requests might make foreign countries hesitate to share intelligence. Nevertheless, the fact remains that the foreign countries can still refuse to consent to the disclosure of the intelligence. Delay in proceedings may also make it much easier to disclose to intelligence given that the status of ongoing sources and investigations may have changed. There also needs to be a rethinking of traditional claims that disclosure of the methods of intelligence gathering cannot be disclosed given widespread public knowledge about various sophisticated forms of intelligence gathering. To be sure, the disclosure of intelligence will not always be possible, but when it is possible, it can avoid the various political and legal controversies that inevitably and correctly surround its use as secret evidence.

8.9 Conclusion

One of the many effects of 9/11 has been increased use of secret evidence to impose legal consequences on terrorist suspects. The use of secret evidence represents an attempt by the collectors of intelligence to have the best of all worlds: intelligence is used as evidence to impose drastic legal consequences on suspects such as detention or listing as a terrorist even while the intelligence does not have to be disclosed and subject to adversarial challenge that might possibly reveal that it was improperly obtained and/or unreliable.

The use of intelligence as evidence reflects the fact that the relation between evidence and intelligence is dynamic. What was secret intelligence at one point in time, might be evidence at another point in time.[65] There is a need to re-examine traditional distinctions between intelligence and evidence in light of the particular threat and nature of terrorism, the expanded range of preparatory and associational

[64] *R. v. Khawaja* 2007 FC 490.

[65] F. Manget, "Intelligence and the Criminal Law System," *Stanford Law and Public Policy Review* 17 (2006): 415 at 421–422; C. Walker, "Intelligence and the Anti-terrorism Legislation in the United Kingdom," *Crime, Law and Social Change* 44 (2005): 387.

crimes associated with terrorism and the political and legal controversies that often accompany attempts to use secret evidence. Our thinking about keeping secrets should evolve beyond a Cold War paradigm in which counter-intelligence dominated the work of security agencies and secrets about the enemy could be kept perhaps forever. Intelligence agencies must adapt to the new threat environment and the increased possibility that their counter-terrorism investigations may reach a point when it is imperative to arrest and prosecute people. They must resist the temptation to engage in over-classification and unnecessary claims of secrecy. That said, the legal process must also evolve to take account of the particular challenges of terrorism prosecutions and protecting intelligence from unnecessary disclosure. Experiments such as the rise of special advocates and increased use of public interest immunity proceedings suggest that the legal system has adapted somewhat to such challenges, but the collectors of intelligence also should re-evaluate the traditional emphasis that they have placed on secrecy.

Greater disclosure of otherwise secret intelligence is required to treat detainees and others adversely affected by intelligence more fairly. A failure to disclose relevant evidence and information to the accused can threaten the fairness of the legal proceedings and can lead to wrongful convictions or detention of innocent people.[66] It can also lead to the proceedings being discredited as unfair secret trials and it can create sympathy for those who are treated unfairly in the proceedings even if, in some cases, the secret evidence may be accurate and they are or have been engaged in terrorism.

At the same time, the state will continue to have legitimate interests that some intelligence be kept secret. Secrecy may be necessary to protect vulnerable sources, ongoing investigations and promises made to other countries. The interests of justice are not served if the government is forced to disclose secret intelligence and information that is not necessary for the conduct of a fair trial. In such cases, the government will be placed in the unnecessary and impossible position of choosing between disclosing information that should be kept secret or declining to bring terrorism prosecutions. This most difficult choice should only be necessary in cases where a fair trial is not possible without disclosure.

A better tailored and more proportionate means to reconcile the competing interests of disclosure and secrecy in a particular case is to allow a judge to decide on a case-by-case whether intelligence needs to be disclosed or called by the accused in the interests of trial fairness. If secret evidence is ever used, security cleared counsel should have full access to the evidence and the best opportunities possible to challenge both the state's secrecy claims and the reliability of the secret evidence, including exploring whether it was obtained from improper means or other means that may cast doubt on its reliability.

The search for reasonable alternatives which can reconcile the demands of disclosure and secrecy should not be limited to the formal processes of the justice

[66] K. Roach and G. Trotter, "Miscarriages of Justice in the War Against Terrorism," *Pennsylvania State Law Review* 109 (2005): 967.

system under mechanisms such as special advocates or public interest immunity applications. The standard operating procedures of intelligence agencies need to adjust from a Cold War mindset where intelligence can almost always be kept secret to a post 9/11 world where most of the resources are devoted to terrorism and intelligence can often have evidential significance. In some cases, this may mean that confidential informers must not always be promised anonymity and in some cases that they will be protected through witness protection programs. Similarly, efforts must be made to persuade both domestic and foreign agencies to amend restrictions that routinely prohibit the use of their intelligence in court. Greater disclosure of secret evidence and intelligence can lead to fairer legal proceedings and greater accountability for the way that intelligence is collected.

Bibliography

Barak-Erez, D., and M. Waxman. 2009. Secret evidence and the die process of terrorist detentions. *Columbia Journal of Transnational Law* 48: 1, at 20–27.

Code, M., and K. Roach. 2006. The role of the independent lawyer and security certificates. *Criminal Law Quarterly* 52: 85.

Dunbar, D., and S. Nesbitt. 2008. Parliament's response to *Charkaoui. Supreme Court Law Review*(2d0) 42: 415.

Forcese, C., and K. Roach. 2011. Limping into the future: the 1267 terrorist financing listing regime at the crossroads. *George Washington International Law Review* 42. Forthcoming.

Forcese, C., and L. Waldman. 2008. A Bismarkian moment: *Charkaoui* and Bill C-3. *Supreme Court Law Review*(2d) 42: 355.

Fredman, J. 1998. Intelligence agencies, Law enforcement and the prosecution team. *Yale Law and Policy Review* 16: 331.

Hugessen, J. 2002. Watching the watchers: Democratic oversight. In *Terrorism, law and democracy*, ed. D. Daubney et al., 384

Jordan, S. 1991. Classified information and conflicts in independent counsel prosecutions. *Columbia Law Review* 91: 1651.

Manget, F. 2006. Intelligence and the criminal law system. *Stanford Law and Policy Review* 17: 415.

Rankin, M. 1990. The security intelligence review committee: Reconciling national security with procedural fairness. *Canadian Journal of Administrative Law and Practice* 3: 173.

Roach, K. 2008. Charkaoui and Bill C-3. *Supreme Court Law Review*(2d) 42: 281.

Roach, K. 2010a. The eroding distinction between intelligence and evidence in terrorism investigations. In *Counter-terrorism and beyond*, ed. N. McGarrity et al. London: Routledge.

Roach, K. 2010b. *The unique challenges of terrorism prosecutions*. Ottawa: Supply and Services.

Roach, K. 2011. *The 9/11 effect: Comparative counter-terrorism*. New York: Cambridge University Press.

Roach, K., and G. Trotter. 2005. Miscarriages of justice in the War against terrorism. *Pennsylvania State Law Review* 109: 967.

Tamanaha, B. 1986. A critical review of the classified information procedures act. *American Journal of Criminal Law* 13: 277.

Villarede, M. 2003. Structuring the Prosecutor's duty to search the intelligence for Brady material. *Cornell Law Review* 88: 1471.

Walker, C. 2005. Intelligence and the anti-terrorism legislation in the United Kingdom. *Crime, Law and Social Change* 44: 387.

Cases

Abousfian Abdelrazik v The Minister of Foreign Affairs and the Attorney General of Canada [2009] FC 580.
Chahal v. U.K. (1996) 23 E.H.H.R. 413.
Edwards and Lewis v. the United Kingdom Judgment of October 27, 2004.
Harkat v. Canada 2010 FC 1242.
Kadi v. European Commission judgment of the General Court (7th Division) 30 September 2010 available at http://eur-lex.europa.eu/LexUriServ/LexUriServ.do?uri=CELEX:62009A0085:EN:HTML.
R. v. Ahmad 2011 SCC 6.
R. v. Davis, Johnson and Rowe [1993] 1 W.L.R. 613.
R. v. H and C [2004] UKHL 3.
R v Keane [1994] 1 WLR 746.
R. v. Khawaja 2007 FC 490.
R. v. McNeil [2009] 1 S.C.R. 66.
R. v. Stinchcombe [1991] 3 S.C.R. 326.
R v Ward [1993] 1 WLR 619.
Secretary of State v. AF (no. 3) [2009] UKHL 28.
Treasury v. Ahmad [2010] UKSC 2.
United States v. bin Laden 58 F.Supp.2d 113, 121.
United States v. Al-Arian 267 F.Supp 2d 1258.
United States v Moussaoui No 06 4495 Jan. 4, 2010 (4th Cir).

Other Sources

9/11 Commission Report.
Air India Flight 182: A Canadian Tragedy (Ottawa: Supply and Services, 2010) vol 3.
Centre on Law and Security, *Terrorist Trial Report* Card (2010)
Executive Order Classified National Security Information December 29, 2009 (available at http://www.whitehouse.gov/the-press-office/executive-order-classified-national-security-information).
Immigration and Refugee Protection Act (IRPA) S.C. 2001.
Justice, *Secret Evidence* (London: Justice, 2009).
MI5 'Evidence and Disclosure' at http://www.mi5.gov.uk/output/Page87.html.
Military Commissions Act of 2006 120 Stat 2611 s.949d(e).
Military Commission Act of 2009 H.R. 2647-385 s.949p-1(a).
Secretary of State for the Home Department, *Intercept as Evidence A Report* December 2009 Cmnd 7760.
Yassin Abdullah Kadi and Al Barakaat International Foundation v Council of the European Union and Commission of the European Communities, Cases C-402/05 P and C-415/05 P, *Yassin Abdullah Kadi and Al Barakaat International Foundation v. Council and Commission*, 3 September 2008.

Chapter 9
Evolution of British Law on Terrorism: From Ulster to Global Terrorism (1970–2010)

Leandro Martínez-Peñas and Manuela Fernández-Rodríguez

9.1 Introduction: Terrorist Threat and Counter-Terrorism Legislation in Britain

The United Kingdom was one of the first states to develop "belligerent"[1] legislation on terrorism as it was one of the first Western European states confronted with an organized terrorist threat. From the mid nineteenth century Irish Fenian nationalists carried out bloody bombing campaigns against the British government including coordinated explosions in the London Underground which was tragically similar to modern attacks.

Over time threats have changed. In the twentieth and twenty-first centuries the appearance of new and different threats involved a different set of challenges for the British government. Sometimes the new face of the threats were caused by changes in the internal development within the terrorist movements themselves (as in the case of Northern Ireland), others by the rise of new threats such as jihadist terrorism, which replaced Irish nationalism as the main risk confronting Britain.

[1] D. López Garrido, *Terrorismo, política y Derecho. La legislación antiterrorista en España, Reino Unido, República Federal de Alemania, Italia y Francia* (Madrid: Alianza Editoral, 1987), 56. However, this experience, acquired before Northern Ireland's conflict in the fight against guerrillas and terrorists in Malaysia, Kenya, Cyprus and Rhodesia, was wasted. The British did not apply to Ulster the valuable lessons that could have learned from those conflicts. For example, the success of campaigns against the insurgency in Kenya and Malaysia was based on the recognition of the interests of the local population, while in Rhodesia, where repression was made without recognizing any right to the local population, the counterinsurgency fight failed. (B. Hoffman and J. Morrisontaw, "A strategic framework for countering terrorism," in *European Democracies Against Terrorism. Govermental Policies and Intergovernmental Cooperation*, ed. F. Reinares (Aldershot: Ashgate, 2004), 8–9, 12–13).

L. Martínez-Peñas (✉) • M. Fernández-Rodríguez
Facultad de Ciencias Jurídicas y Sociales, Universidad Rey Juan Carlos,
Paseo de los Artilleros s/n, E- 28032 Vicálvaro/Madrid, Spain
e-mail: leandro.martinez@urjc.es; manuela.fernandez@urjc.es

A. Masferrer (ed.), *Post 9/11 and the State of Permanent Legal Emergency*,
Ius Gentium: Comparative Perspectives on Law and Justice 14,
DOI 10.1007/978-94-007-4062-4_9,

This evolution of terrorism has driven important legislative changes and has been linked to the public's perception of the threat regardless of whether it is accurate, mistaken or exaggerated.[2] It's perfectly evident that a large number of legislative reforms – almost all rights restrictive – occurred during periods of intense terrorist activity such as in the case of the 1971 Internment Act or after specific noteworthy attacks such as December 2001 and 2006 laws directly related to the 9/11 attacks in the United States and the January 7, 2006 attacks in London.

9.2 British Counter-Terrorism from the 1970s to 9/11

9.2.1 British Anti-terrorism Legislation of the 1970s: The Internment

At first the British legal framework of counter terrorism was based on the Prevention of Terrorism Acts of 1939 (PTA), which remained in force until 1953.[3] The PTA served as the basis for most of the legislation that emerged after 1973, which was enacted in response to the violence scale in Northern Ireland.

As its name suggests, the PTA and subsequent laws inspired by it, were provisional, conceived as legal texts with special measures for special situations and, therefore, essentially temporary. That is why the validity of the law had to be renewed annually.

Although the emergence of terrorist violence in Northern Ireland took place in the last 1960s and reached a peak during the 1970s,[4] it wasn't the first time British authorities had to take legal measures in response to Irish nationalist terrorism. By the 1970s, Britain had already endured terrorist campaigns, such as those triggered after the American Civil War and Fenian nationalists who committed indiscriminate attacks with dynamite in the London Underground. However, above all, the empire's antiterrorist experience came from British colonial conflicts, where independence movements had often combined the tactics of guerrilla warfare and insurgency with terrorist tactics in urban environments. This was the case in the conflicts in Cyprus against EOKA's nationalists, in Malaysia against the communist guerrillas, in East Africa against the Mau-Maus, against ZAPU in Rhodesia and in Yemen, against the

[2]Thus it has been recognized even by the British courts, concerning certain measures taken under the so-called "war on terror", as will be mentioned in subsequent paragraphs of this chapter.

[3]About the origins of British anti-terrorism legislation see A. Bunyan, *The Political Police in Britain* (London: St. Martin's Press, 1955), 51–56; also L. K. Donohue, *Counter-Terrorist Law and Emergency Powers in the United Kingdom, 1922–2000* (Dublin: Irish Academic Press, 2001).

[4]"The Troubles and their aftermath became the defining national security experience for the postwar generation in Britain – much as the first world war was for Eden and Macmillan, or the Second World War for Heath and Callaghan" (D. Godson, "The Real Lessons of Ulster," *Prospect Magazine*, no. 140 (2007): 1).

separatist insurgency. However, none of these movements sought -or could- take terrorist violence to the territory of the British Isles. So the threat posed by the IRA and other groups in Northern Ireland, although not new at an ideological level, was new to the extent that it brought terrorist violence to the British streets.

Such was the level of violence developed by the IRA that the British government imposed the Direct Rule; in disregard the regional government represented by the Stormont parliament. It was also at this moment when the British authorities, unable to stop the rise of violence, set up the policy known as Internment launched in 1971. The internment was a series of legal measures that led to the arrest and long periods of detention of suspects accused of having connections with terrorism without having to file specific charges or provide judicial hearings until the detention period had expired.

This rule was not new, both the British government and the Republic of Ireland had used it between 1956 and 1962.[5] The success that the measure had in that previous period was undoubtedly one of the reasons why the British re-introduced Internment. The opposition to this measure revealed divergent positions in the fight against terrorism, as Lieutenant General Harry Tuzco, who held at that time the command of British forces in Ulster.[6] The Internment legislation came into force dramatically with the Demetrius Operation. This was a series of massive raids that took place in Belfast on January 9, 1971 and ended with the detention of about 300 prisoners.[7]

The Spanish Professor Rogelio Alonso summarized the problems posed by the Internment: its conceptualization was so broad that it easily permitted the abuse by allowing detention of any "suspect of having acted, being acting or could act in a detrimental manner to the maintenance of peace and public order"; secondly, the lack of reliable information ensured that the vast majority of detainee were not IRA members, but members of the Irish nationalist community, so that the Internment only accentuated the feeling of oppression in that community; thirdly, the large number of allegations of brutality during interrogations alienated policing agencies and civil population and proved detrimental to the image of the government in Northern Ireland and abroad.[8]

---

[5]D. Godson, "The Real Lessons of Ulster," 3; R. Alonso Pascual, *Irlanda del Norte. Una historia de guerra y la búsqueda de la paz* (Madrid: Editorial Complutense, 2001), 152.

[6]M. Burleigh, *Sangre y rabia. Una historia cultural del terrorismo* (Madrid: Taurus, 2008), 387.

[7]Both the reintroduction of Internment as Operation Demetrius were brought about by two heinous actions of the IRA: a murder by a bomb of five engineers who were repairing a BBC transmitter and the execution of three off-duty Scottish soldiers (including two brothers of 17 and 18 years) who were surprised by IRA gunmen in a field (Vv. Aa, *Lost Lives* (Edinburgh, 2004), 270–274). This is not the only opinion on the Internment, one of the most important British civil servant in Northern Ireland during Kenneth Bloomfield's period, said that Internment was not conceived as a response to IRA, but as a way to curb on a wave of loyalist violence (D. Godson, "The Real Lessons of Ulster," no. 140 (2007): 4).

[8]Alonso, *Irlanda del Norte*, 153. Some counterterrorism policies are not only unsuccessful, but counterproductive, as British law Internment (B. Hoffman and J. Morrisontaw, "A Strategic Framework for Countering Terrorism," 4).

The failure of Internment was not just a matter of image, which impugned British integrity while conferring major publicity to Irish nationalism, but was also a law enforcement failure. Far from reducing terrorist activity, the number of fatalities in the second half of 1971, after internment, increased fourfold from the first half, prior to its adoption. The following year, during which the policy of Internment was fully in force, witnessed no reduction in the number of deaths and was, to the contrary, the bloodiest year in the whole Northern Ireland conflict, resulting in a total of 470 people killed.[9]

Eventually the United Kingdom tried to improve its negative image by altering the Internment law.[10] It ultimately adopted the Detention of Terrorist (Northern Ireland) Order of 1972, which clarified some issues relating to Internment and adopting the so-called "Detention Model," replacing the term Internment in favor of detention. According to the 1972 law, the Minister for Northern Ireland was authorized to order detention of terrorist suspects for up to 28 days with extensions if deemed necessary. Extensions were to be reviewed by an independent person with legal experience.[11]

Shortly after the implementation of this law Lord Diplock's launched a report where he was commissioned to consider legislative solutions to the problems posed by anti-terrorism.[12] This report led to the enactment of the Northern Ireland Emergency Provisions Act (EPA) of 1973. The EPA was passed on 25 July 1973 and replaced the Civil Authorities Special Power Acts 1922.[13] It was subsequently amended in 1978.[14]

The EPA established that the detention of suspects should be decided by an impartial authority -a judge- and not by the enforcement branch of the government. However, this law also removed the accused right to a jury in terrorism trials owing to the heightened pressures they might suffer in the politically charged climate of

---

[9]Besides the number of deaths, is significant the escalation in number of bomb attacks, a good indicator of the operational capacity of terrorist groups: in April 1971 there were 36; on May, 47, on July, 78; after implementation of Internment in August there were 131 bomb attacks; in September, 196; and in October, 117 (Donohue, *Counter-Terrorist Law and Emergency Powers in the United Kingdom*, 118).

[10]P. Cumaraswamy, *Cuestión de los Derechos Humanos de todas las personas sometidas a cualquier forma de detención o prisión. Informe del Relator Especial sobre la independencia de magistrados y abogados, Sr. Param Cumaraswamy, presentado de conformidad con la resolución 1997/23 de la Comisión de Derechos Humanos.* Accessed via computer resource http://www.unhchr.ch

[11]Whether this rule abolished Internment or just changed its name and endowed it with certain judicial guarantees for detainees is a subject of some debate. See M. F. Noone, "El Ejército Republicano Irlandés: Soldados ilegítimos," *Military Review* LXXXVI (2006).

[12]J. Diplock, *Report of the Commission to Consider Legal Procedures to Deal with Terrorist Activities in Northern Ireland* (London: HMSO, 1972).

[13]Initially, this rule was renewed annually, but became permanent in 1933.

[14]López Garrido, *Terrorismo, política y Derecho*, 57.

Northern Ireland.[15] Thus, this legislation made an exception of those accused of terrorist crimes from other criminal charges in the United Kingdom, where criminals were provided with the right to a jury trial.[16] These Northern Ireland courts, consisting of a single judge, were known as "Diplock courts."[17]

In Article 12, the EPA approved the admission of confessions, if they had not been obtained under torture, inhuman or degrading treatment. Nonetheless the British government continued to rely upon this type of interrogations, including the use of both physical and psychological pressure. This coupled with the system of trial by a single judge, undermined the rights of defendants. "Judges in Diplock courts applied a lower standard of admissibility, which resulted in many Diplock court cases relying on coerced confession evidence that would have been held inadmissible in a jury trial".[18] At one point, 90% of Diplock cases relied on confessions obtained through "intensive interrogations" as primary evidence.[19] Opportunities to obtain coerced confessions were amplified in the Diplock court context by the Detention of Terrorists (Northern Ireland) Order of 1972, which also precluded the right to a hearing or access to counsel during the initial 28 day detention period.

"Another problem with single-judge Diplock trials is the potential for casehardening, the principle that over time 'judges become more cynical of defense claims of innocence and more prosecution prone in their decisions.'"[20] A judge who sees many similar cases would arguably begin to treat those cases alike, rather than basing his decision on the facts of each case independently. Quantitative data supports this conclusion as Diplock acquittals "decreased from 53% in 1984 to 29% in 1993 [and]... [i]n contrast, acquittal rates for criminal trials by jury remained steady, at 49% in 1984 and 48% in 1993".[21]

---

[15] The adoption of the "Diplock courts" was triggered by the murder of a bus driver named Agnew, occurred in Belfast, the day before he was to testify against several terrorist (Donohue, *Counter-Terrorist Law and Emergency Powers in the United Kingdom,* 123). A full report on the Diplock courts in Vv.Aa, *Replacement Arrangements for the Diplock Court System. A Consultation Paper* (Belfast, 2006b); see also J. D. Jackson, K. Quinn, and T. O'Malley, "The Jury System in Contemporary Ireland: In the Shadow of a Troubled Past," *Law and Contemporary Problems* 62 (1999).

[16] D. Bonner, "The United Kingdom's Response to Terrorism: The Impact of Decisions of European Judicial Institutions and of the Northern Ireland Peace Process," in *European Democracies Against Terrorism. Governmental Policies and Intergovernmental Cooperation*, ed. F. Reinares (Alderhorst: Ashgate, 2004), 45.

[17] Diplock courts were in effect in Britain, one way or another, until 2007; in fact, even in a late time of Northern Ireland conflict, one of each three serious crimes were tried by a court Diplock (L. M. Jacobs, "It's Time to Leave the Troubles Behind: Northern Ireland Must Try Paramilitary Suspects by Jury Rather Than in Diplock-Type," *Texas International Law Journal* (Texas, 2010): 656).

[18] J. D. Jackson, *The Restoration of Jury Trial in Northern Ireland: Can We Learn From the Professional Alternative?* (St. Louis/Warszaw, 2001–2002), 17.

[19] B. McGuiverin, "In the Face of Danger: A Comparative Analysis of the Use of Emergency Powers in the United States and the United Kingdom in the 20th Century," 263.

[20M.] P. O'Connor and C. L. Rumman, "Into the Fire: How to Avoid Getting Burned by the Same Mistakes Made Fighting Terrorism in Northern Ireland," 24.

[21] C. D. Rasnic, "Northern Ireland's Criminal Trials Without Jury: The Diplock Experiment," (1996), 67.

The 1973 law introduced membership in a terrorist group as an offense, with an exception: the members who left the group prior to the date of its banning were not held liable. However, even this exception was unfair because the statute reversed the burden of proof, requiring the accused to show they left the group before it had been declared illegal.[22]

The British government evidently considered these rules rights restrictive and suitable only in exceptional situations (such as Northern Ireland) as their application was restricted to a limited geographical scope (i.e. to the six counties of Ulster under British sovereignty). Initially these measures weren't otherwise applied in the territory of Great Britain.[23] However, this changed the following year. On 21st November in Birmingham a terrorist attack left 20 dead and over a 100 injured. All of the victims were civilians unconnected with the British army or security forces and were killed or injured when bombs were exploded in two pubs of that English city.[24] This attack resulted in the Prevention of Terrorism Act of 1974 (Temporary Provision), which extended the application of the emergency measures included in the Northern Ireland Emergency Provisions Act 1973 to Britain.[25]

This initiative gave way to one of the most controversial measures of the British anti-terrorism legislation known as the Exclusion Orders. These orders consisted in a legal mechanism by which the British government could expel from Britain to Northern Ireland any Northern Irish citizen who had lived in the island for less than 20 years and which the authorities related to terrorism. Not without reason, this measure was sharply criticized because it was considered an executive mechanism in which no judicial intervention occurred which led to a sort of internal exile against which suspects retained no effective defense.

The law also changed the arrest rules.[26] It authorized warrantless arrests, eliminated the need to show probable cause and established a period of detention of 48 h without review. Moreover, the period of review could be extended by the Home Secretary by five additional days in order to complete a maximum of a 168 h of detention without charges. Such were the powers granted by this law that the Home

---

[22] López Garrido, *Terrorismo, política y Derecho*, at 74.

[23] Great Britain is a term that refers to the three regions that form the island: Scotland, Wales and England, but excludes Northern Ireland. In contrast, the term United Kingdom, covers four areas, since its full name is United Kingdom of Great Britain and Northern Ireland.

[24] IRA never recognized the action: only in 2004, a Sinn Fein's spokesman formally recognized the Birmingham bombing was a mistake, declaring that what happened was bad and it shouldn't have occurred. Well known is the case of the six Irish, with no relation to IRA, who were accused and convicted of having organized this attack. After 16 years in prison of their life imprisonment sentences, they were eventually acquitted by a British court. On this case, see C. Mullin, *Error of Judgment. The Truth About the Birmingham Bombings* (London: Poolbeg, 1986).

[25] To get an idea of the climate in those days in Britain, it suffices to know that "The Times" described the action as an act of war and that a deputy stated in Parliament that the Chamber wanted blood (Alonso, *Irlanda del Norte,* 202 note 41).

[26] Until then, the current rule in force was the Magistrates Court Act, 1952.

Officer, Roy Jenkins, described its provision as "draconians" and "unprecedented in peacetime," but "absolutely justified to face the present danger."[27]

The anti-terrorism legislation was broadened in 1976 with the reform of the Prevention of Terrorism Act of 1974 (Temporary Provision). This reform expanded the number of offences that were covered under the statute including failure to report the facts related to terrorists activities, even by innocent third parties who had not taken part in those acts.

The basis of the British anti-terrorist legal system was the Northern Ireland Emergency Provisions Act 1973 (as revised in 1974, 1976 and 1984). However, several complementary laws also came into force. These included the Suppression of Terrorism Act of 1978, which amended British legislation on extradition in order to adapt it to the European Convention for the Suppression of Terrorism (which the United Kingdom had recently signed); the law on the taking of hostages (Hostage Taking Act of 1982); and the Public Order Act of 1986 (which came into force on January 1, 1987), which regulated public order issues designed to prevent disturbances related to Northern Ireland terrorism by imposing greater limitations to the rights of expression and assembly.[28]

One of the most important legal issues confronting the British justice system was the interrogation of detainees. British criminal law established that during the detention period "people (…) can be subjected to interrogation determined persistent and intense." Tortures and mistreatment or degrading treatments were illegal, but confessions obtained by the application of psychological pressure on detainees[29] were considered valid. During the early years of the Detention scheme, the police and British army applied the so-called "five techniques"[30] with full legal backing by the state. These five techniques involved prolonged standing postures,[31] hooding, to subject them to a constant noise, sleep deprivation, and food deprivation (both liquid and solid).

As the application of these techniques led to complaints, several British commissions discussed their application, but despite the finding that they were likely to be considered abuse, it was justified by the extraordinary situation of the Ulster. The issue reached the European Court of Human Rights in Strasbourg in 1976, which

---

[27] P. Hillary, *Suspect Community. People's Experience of the Prevention of Terrorism Acts in Britain*. (London: Pluto Press, 1993), quoted in Alonso, *Irlanda del Norte*, 202.

[28] López Garrido, *Terrorismo, política y Derecho*, at 58. As happened later in the case of nationalist terrorism in Spain, with the so-called strategy of "democratization of violence". In the late 1980s a relative decline of the deadly terrorist attacks was accompanied by a surge in street violence, implemented in a conscious way by terrorist organizations as an alternative and complement to the attacks themselves.

[29] D. Kurff, "Las leyes antiterroristas en el Derecho comparado europeo, con especial incidencia en la situación del Ulster," Vv. Aa, *Democracia y leyes antiterroristas en Europa. Ulster, Italia, Alemania y Estado Español* (Bilbao, 1983), 61.

[30] Alonso, *Irlanda del Norte*, 154.

[31] For example, squat without resting the hands on the floor or standing with arms outstretched and palms turned upward.

ruled that these techniques violate Article 3 of the European Convention of Human Rights – "No one shall be subjected to torture or to cruel or inhuman or degrading." The Court's majority decision was overwhelming with 16 votes to one.[32] Theoretically, the United Kingdom ceased implementing the "five techniques" on March 5, 1972 as a result of a report made by Lord Gardiner who described them as "secret, illegal, morally unjustified and undemocratic."[33]

These measures did great damages to the detainee's legal guarantees. During the years when the Internment legislation was in force, nine out of ten of those convicted had given confessions obtained by the security forces while detained and before formal charges were brought; under prior law many of those confessions would not have been admissible – or at least would not have been decisive – absent corroborating evidence (which was absent). In many cases verbal confessions were a prove enough to be admitted and was considered proven if a police officer testified that it had existed, though there was no written record of it.[34]

9.2.2 1989 Law

The annual renewal systems of the temporary Acts in the UK were until 1989. Thereafter the UK adopted the Prevention of Terrorism (Temporary Provisions) which, despite its name, provided a greater degree of permanence as it did not have to be reexamined every year. This rule was divided into seven sections. The first section contained a list of banned terrorist organizations.[35] This provision criminalized membership in the organization, public support, and fund raising. The list of organizations has been periodically updated to include both domestic and international groups. The February 2009 list reflects a greater concentration of Islamic fundamentalist groups. Moreover, this list includes 42 international organizations. Only three of them don't have primarily a religious character (ETA, the Kurdish PKK and Tamil separatist guerrillas).[36] The focus of the list reflects a change from exclusively Irish organizations to other international terrorist groups and can be explained by the influence of the Lockerbie attack (in December 21st, 1988[37]) which occurred shortly before the statutes passage in 1989.

[32] However, in 1978, the Court rejected, by 14 votes to three that the five techniques constituted torture (Kurff, "Las leyes antiterroristas en el Derecho comparado europeo," 83).

[33] Alonso, *Irlanda del Norte*, 154.

[34] Kurff, "Las leyes antiterroristas en el Derecho comparado europeo," 43.

[35] Fourteen Northern Ireland's organizations were included in this list, which it has been now added 21 international organizations. None of the groups that have been, at some point, included in the United Kingdom lists have been subsequently excluded of them (K. Thorne, "Proscription of Terrorist Groups in the United Kingdom," (2006), www.hdcentre.org, 1).

[36] Of the remaining 39 organizations, the only non-Muslim was the ISYF, a Sikh organization.

[37] Pam Am flight 109 exploded in the air while flying over the Scottish town of Lockerbie, 270 people were killed in the attack, including 11 Lockerbie villagers.

The 1989 law also provided Exclusion Orders, but expanded it to allow the British government to refuse the entry into Britain of all people who posed a security threat. The violation of an exclusion order could lead to a sentence of 5 years imprisonment. The third section of the law articulates prohibited means of financial support for terrorist organizations and the fourth section allowed the arrest and detention for 48 h of people suspected of committing, preparing or instigating a terrorist act.[38] The detention period could be increased to 5 days with authorized from the Home Secretary.

The remaining sections consisted of measures specifically earmarked for Northern Ireland. Among the most important innovations was the renewal of the licensing procedure for possession and use of explosives (previously regulated by an outdated law from 1875, the Explosives Act).

Overall, the Act of 1989 focused on six objectives: Prohibition and identification of terrorist organizations, interrogation and search of terrorist suspects in Northern Ireland and Great Britain, averting the aid and funding of terrorism, widening the governments arrest and detention capabilities and the establishment of executive extrajudicial procedures.[39]

Seven years later, in 1996, Great Britain adopted a provision specifically directed to the violence in Northern Ireland, the Northern Ireland Emergency Provisions (also known as the Good Friday Agreements of 1997). As the violence had not ceased in Northern Ireland this act took shape despite the secondary threat against peace posed by jihadist terrorism or other so-called global terrorism.

9.2.3 *Terrorism Act of 2000*

The Terrorism Act 2000 was the last major British anti-terrorism law enacted prior to the attacks of September 11 in the United States.[40] One of its noteworthy characteristics was its inclusion of a legal definition of terrorism. This was not the first time UK legislation dealt with the thorny task of defining terrorism. The Prevention of Terrorism (Temporary Provisions) Act of 1989 described terrorism as "the use of violence for political ends, and includes any use of violence for the purpose of putting the public or any section of the public in fear."

---

[38] For common criminals, the maximum detention period was 36 h (Bonner, "The United Kingdom's Response to Terrorism: The Impact of Decisions of European Judicial Institutions and of the Northern Ireland Peace Process," 43).

[39] Bonner, "The United Kingdom's Response to Terrorism," 40–41.

[40] An official report entitled "Statistics on the Operation of Prevention Terrorism Legislation 16/01," contains statistics on terrorist activity in Britain in 2000. It reflects the growing importance of international terrorism in front of domestic terrorism, this latter is the associated with the issue of Northern Ireland. The full report is available at http://rds.homeoffice.gov.uk/rds/pdfs/hosb1601.pdf.

In 1993, the Reinsurance (Acts of Terrorism) Act, defined terrorism as:

> Acts of persons acting on behalf of, or in connection with, any organisation which carries out activities directed towards the overthrowing or influencing, by force or violence, of Her Majesty's government in the United Kingdom or any other government de jure or de facto.

In 1996, the Northern Ireland (Emergency Provisions) though not providing a definition of terrorism *per se*, created a list of 70 actions that were considered terrorist conduct which was intended to be exhaustive.

The definition in the 2000 Act aimed to give a more flexible definition that would provide the concept a permanence that previous rules failed to achieve. Thus, Section 1 stated:

> (1)In this Act "terrorism" means the use or treat of action where:
> a) the action falls within subsection (2).
> b)the use or threat is designed to influence the government [or international governmental organisation] or to intimidate the public or a section of the public and
> c) the use or threat is made for the purpose of advancing a political, religious, racial or ideological cause.
> (2) Action falls within this subsection if it
> a) involves serious violence against a person.
> b) involves serious damage to property,
> c) endangers a person's life, other than that of the person committing the action,
> d) creates a serious risk to the health or safety of the public or a section of the public or
> e) is designed seriously to interfere with or seriously to disrupt an electronic system.
> (3) The use or threat of action falling within subsection (2) which involves the use of firearms or explosives is terrorism whether or not subsection (1) (b) is satisfied.

A definition of terrorism is by its very nature a complex matter and it is subject to discussion and opinion.[41] In the British Act of 2000, sections 2b and 2e were sharply criticized, in both the attacks that cause serious damage to property and those whose target are electronic systems. Inclusion of section 2b probably was influenced by the serious attacks by the IRA against economic targets in Britain, setting off huge quantities of explosives in the financial hearts of London and Manchester. These attacks were not intended to cause casualties - although two people were killed in London – but to cause serious damage to the British economy through the destruction of valuable property and the temporary disruption of key economic and financial centers.

Additionally, it is noteworthy that Section 41 of the 2000 Act kept the 48 h detention period for those suspected of preparing or inciting terrorist acts and increased the authority of the Home Secretary by authorizing him to extend this period beyond that allowed under the previous rules. Another controversial provision was Section 44, which increased police competence for the search of motor vehicles and people and eliminated the need for a showing of "reasonable suspicion."[42] In January 2010

---

[41] A reflection on the concept of terrorism in Rodríguez-Villasante and J. L. Prieto, "¿A que llamamos terrorismo?," *Cuadernos de Estrategia*, n. 133, monographic entitled 'Lucha contra el Terrorismo y Derecho Internacional', 8.

[42] Arrest on reasonable suspicion is included in a conceptual debate about the extent to which police action is legitimate in a preventive manner, that is, before the wrongful act has been committed: "*En un sistema democrático deberían establecerse fines en relación con el control penal del Estado.*

the European Court of Human Rights declared Section 44 of the British Act of 2000 illegal. It found that the statute violated Article 8 of the European Convention on Human Rights as it bestowed on the police powers that were not sufficiently defined and therefore did not provide the minimum guarantees required to prevent police abuses.[43] Subsequently, the Criminal Justice Act extended the detention period and authorized the Home Secretary to extend the detention period to 14 days, thus doubling the time provided in the previous Terrorism Act's.

Section 58 of the Act was also innovative as it designated the crime gathering information that could be used to commit or prepare a terrorist act.

Professor Clive Walker considered the law as follows:

> The Terrorism Act 2000 represents a worthwhile attempt to fulfil the role of a modern code against terrorism, though it fails to meet the desired standards in all respects. There are aspects where rights are probably breached, and its mechanisms to ensure democratic accountability and constitutionalism are even more deficient.[44]

9.3 Legislative Reaction to the 9/11 Attacks[45]

The British legislative response to the 9–11 attacks against the Twin Towers in New York and the Pentagon in Washington D.C. took place on 19 November 2001 with the passage of the Anti-Terrorism, Crime and Security Act (came into force December 14, 2001). Despite its name many of the measures introduced by this law

---

De ahí que ya en el siglo XIX, y más aún en el XX, se haya planteado con insistencia -sobre todo con el rebrote de las tendencias utilitaristas por el resurgimiento del liberalismo económico- la idea de la prevención como función de la policía. Si el sistema ha de ser preventivo, lógicamente la acción de la policía al ejecutarlo también ha de ser preventiva. Y de hecho también la labor de la policía ha sido preventiva; más aún, se ha señalado que la prevención efectiva no puede ser de la pena sino solo de la acción policial" (J. Bustos Ramírez, "Las funciones de la policía y la libertad y seguridad de los ciudadanos," *Nuevo Foro Penal* 32 (1986): 165).

[43] In 2008, a report by the BBC stated that London's Metropolitan Police had conducted, during that year, about 175,000 arrests and searches of vehicles based on Section 44 of the Act of 2000 (V. Dodd, "Metropolitan Police Used Anti-terror Laws to Stop and Search 58 Under-10s," *The Guardian*, August 18, 2009. Accessed via computer resource, http://www.guardian.co.uk/politics/2009/aug/18/met-police-stop-search-children (removed December 12, 2009)).

[44] *The Anti-Terrorism Legislation* (Oxford, 2002), 212. An official statistical report of the Home Office on police operations during the term of the 2000 law, see "Operation of Police Powers Under the Terrorism Act 2000 and Subsequent Legislation: Arrests, Outcomes and Stops & Searches," *Home Office Statistical Bulletin*, no. 04/2010 (February 25, 2010).

[45] From first time after 11-S, police and British government were aware that the threat of global jihadism posed terrorist scenarios very different from those it had raised them the IRA. Thus, the jihadist attacks threat with chemical weapons, biological or nuclear weapons became probable hypothesis, as well as attacks by suicide terrorists or the so-called Deadly and Determined Attacks (DADA), that is, those which combined car bombs and commands armed with automatic rifles. Suicide terrorist attack as the one led by the Saudi branch of Al Qaeda in Riyadh in 2003, against a residential complex where were staying Westerners (F. Gregory, "Policía y estrategia contra el terrorismo global en el Reino Unido," in *Las democracias occidentales frente al terrorismo global*, ed. C. T. Powell and F. Reinares (Barcelona: Ariel y Real Instituto Elcano, 2008), 150).

were not specifically aimed at terrorism, which prompted many criticisms. It was said that the law introduced regulations that did not respond to an emergency situation. The specific provisions dealing with counter-terrorism consisted in three sections that reformed the rules on financial prosecution of terrorism stated in the Act of 2000. The main thrust of this law was not used against Al Qaeda. In 2008, Prime Minister Gordon Brown resorted to the rules of the Act of 2001 to freeze British's funds from Landsbanki, an Icelandic financial institution affected by the economic crisis triggered in that Nordic country. The law authorized the government to act if any organization planned actions that might harm the British economy, whatever the nature of that organization may be. Though the intent of the Act was not originally contemplated for non-criminal economic relations (however serious), they nonetheless fell within the legal parameters of the Act and greatly expanded the laws intended consequence. Predictably, Icelandic Prime Minister Geir Haarde protested because of this application of an anti-terrorist law against a bona fide financial institution in a case that had nothing to do with terrorism.

Part 4 of the 2001 law also allowed Home Secretary to indefinitely detain non-British citizens for suspicion of terrorism if deportation to their home country would result in a violation of the British law of human rights.[46] Although indefinite detention had already been declared illegal in the European Court of Human Rights 1996 case Chahal vs. United Kingdom, the Act of 2001 restored this power to the Home Secretary citing the exception under a national state of emergency.[47] The indefinite detention procedure was subject to judicial review, but the effectiveness was assuaged by the reservation of the competence of the Home Secretary to withhold confidential information from the presiding judge. Ultimately, British courts declared the provisions of Part 4 of the Act illegal, based on three arguments: Firstly, the period of detention pending deportation was already temporarily limited by other laws, secondly it was an unjustified as a discriminatory law against foreigners and thirdly, there wasn't a state of emergency in the nation[48] justifying departure from human rights norms. Part 4 regulations were eventually amended by the Terrorism Prevention Act 2005, see infra page 12.

A significant change introduced by the Act of 2001 was the replacement of aggravating circumstance term of "racially motivated" to "racial or religious grounds", a measure directly motivated by the threat of Islamic terrorism. It also allowed the British military police to act outside the military bases, in civil areas, when circumstances were related to terrorism. Finally, the law allowed the Home

[46]For example, if it was thought that, being deported, the individual would be tortured or sentenced to death in their country of origin.

[47]Under Article 15 of the European Convention on Human Rights, certain safeguards and civil rights can be temporarily abolished if the state concerned is under dangers which threaten its own existence.

[48]In fact, British government, in exercising the powers contained in Part 4 of this Act, has been, of all those affected by threats and acts of global terrorism, the only one who has tried to claim that state.

Secretary to detain a foreigner not only for retrospective acts, but also for what an officer from the intelligence agency suspected he could do.[49]

The Criminal Justice Act 2003 not only affected a variety of issues which had little to do with terrorist activities (such as the activities of the "taggers"), it also reformed aspects of the judicial process which could affect terrorist activity. One initiative provided for the possibility of life imprisonment for those who committed two or more murders "with a substantial degree of premeditation or planning." This description was clearly applicable to most of the terrorist acts that involved loss of lifes. At the same time it extended the possibility of life imprisonment for those who committed murders for political, ideological or religious reasons, aims which are inherent to terrorist violence.

Also the 2003 Anti-terrorism, Crime and Security Act of 2001 (continuance in force of sections 21–23) was passed, whose objective was exactly what its name implies: continuation in force of sections 21, 22 and 23 of 2001's law.

A major reform of United Kingdom anti-terrorism legislation took place with the Prevention of Terrorism Act of 2005. It was largely motivated by the Court's declaration of the illegality of Section 44 of the 2001 Act. That declaration left without legal support the arrest of several foreigners held in custody in Belmarsh detention center. The government refused to provide them a hearing in court, claiming that the evidence which incriminated them was inadmissible and its appearance in a public trial would threaten national security. Yet the government still refused to release them.

The legal precept which replaced indefinite detention was "control order" delivered by the Home Secretary, which was applicable to people who were suspected of terrorist activities. Control orders allowed the government to keep terrorist suspects under arrest and restrict their access to telecommunications, whether by telephone, mobile phone or internet.[50] It also limited suspect's access to certain objects or substances, jobs, businesses they could undertake, places where they could live and limitations on when they could move.

The law had reached a crisis point on March 11, 2005 when both British Chambers reviewed the law in an urgency climate before the 2001 Act expired.

---

[49] E. Álvarez Conde and H. González, "Legislación antiterrorista comparada después de los atentados del 11 de septiembre y su incidencia en el ejercicio de los derechos fundamentales," *ARI* 7 (2006): 5. Another important issue the Act stated in Section XI, was on communications and data protection, a subject matter discussed in detail by C. Walker and Y. Akdeniz, "Antiterrorism Laws and Data Retention: War Is Over?," *Northern Ireland Legal Quarterly* 54, no. 2 (2003): 159–182.

[50] One of the characteristic features of the new terrorism is the use of new technologies to publicize their actions. On the nature of "communicative element" that has the terrorist violence of Al Qaeda see M. R. Torres Soriano, "Violencia y acción comunicativa en el terrorismo de Al Qaeda," *Política y Estrategia* 96 (October–December 2006). Profesor Torres says: "*Violencia y comunicación están indisolublemente unidas en el terrorismo llevado a cabo por la organización terrorista Al Qaeda. El carácter religioso de su ideología no implica que sus atentados no busquen la propagación de un determinado mensaje dentro de amplios sectores de la población (…) La realización de espectaculares atentados ha permitido a Al Qaeda convertirse en un ente propagandístico y comunicacional que apunta hacia dos sectores de población bien diferenciados: el occidental y el musulmán. En el primero pretende lograr la erosión del apoyo que ésta presta a sus gobernantes, y en el segundo, la expansión de una ideología fundamentalista de vuelta a los orígenes del Islam*" (83).

This resulted to be the longest session in the history of the House of Lords, lasting 30 continuous hours. Finally, a compromise was reached with a "sunset clause," which provided that the Act should be renewed annually (as done previously with the special anti-terrorism powers in legislation established for Northern Ireland up until 1989). Therefore, the legislature again applied the temporality principle for laws relating to terrorism.

Criticized by non-governmental organizations such as Amnesty International and Human Rights Watch – because of the restriction of rights of the control orders – the 2005 Act also had validity problems. In 2006, Section 3 was declared illegal for violation of the right to a fair trial under the European Convention on Human Rights, Article 6:

> To say that the Act does not give the respondent in this case, against whom a non-derogating control order has been made by the Secretary of State, a fair hearing in the determination of his rights under Article 6 of the Convention would be an understatement. The court would be failing in its duty under the 1998 Act, a duty imposed upon the court by Parliament, if it did not say, loud and clear, that the procedure under the Act whereby the court merely reviews the lawfulness of the Secretary of State's decision to make the order upon the basis of the material available to him at that earlier stage are conspicuously unfair. The thin veneer of legality which is sought to be applied by section 3 of the Act cannot disguise the reality. That controlees' rights under the Convention are being determined not by an independent court in compliance with Article 6.1, but by executive decision-making, untrammeled by any prospect of effective judicial supervision.[51]

The outcry received by the law caused the Home Secretary to commission an independent report regarding to the implementation of the Act the following year (before renewing its validity). This report was drawn up by a team led by Lord Carlile of Berriew and released on February 2, 2006. The report defended the need to renew the law in order to consolidate the usefulness of its measures. Thereafter, the 2005 Act has been renewed year after year in both the House of Commons and the House of Lords. As pointed out by C. Walker: "expedients such as control orders may be acceptable in extremis by providing short-term abeyances from criminal justice but should not be adopted as long-term solutions to troublesome friends or foes."[52]

The 2006 Terrorist Act was the next major British law on terrorism. This law resulted as a direct consequence of the attacks of July 7, 2005 at the underground and several London buses, which took the lives of 56 people and left many others injured.[53] The 2006 Act expanded the number of acts considered terrorist activities.

---

[51] *England and Wales High Court (Administrative Court) Decisions (2006-04-13).*

[52] C. Walker, "Keeping Control of Terrorists Without Losing Control of Constitutionalism," *Stanford Law Review* 59 (2007): 1423.

[53] An analysis of these attacks in F. Gregory, "Los atentados de Londres de 7 y 21 de julio de 2005: ¿Una nueva normalidad o lo ya previsto," *DT*, no. 10 (July 2006). Only 8 days after the attacks on 15 July, the Home Secretary Charles Clarke consulted the liberal and conservative spokesmen in Parliament, Mark Oaten and David Davis, to propose changes in anti-terrorism legislation. In August, Prime Minister Tony Blair announced that there would be new terrorist legislation in autumn of that year 2005.

The harshness of its contents was considered by government as a necessary response to a terrorist threat of such a scale. Some opponents of the law considered that the severity of the law itself may have served to *increase* the terrorist threat against Britain.

Part of the law was devoted to the offence of terrorism support, to prevent the dissemination of publications related to the encouragement of acts of violence, to terrorist training, to provide premises or facilities for terrorist training and other actions related to the preparation, organization and commission of terrorist acts.[54] The rule conceptualized these actions as extraterritorial crimes, that is, those who committed these crimes, even in other countries, could be judged by British courts in relation to those facts.

On 26 October 2005, the Home Secretary Charles Clarke mounted an earnest defense of the Act in the House of Commons, pointing to it as a rule intended to defend the ideals of the State's freedom:

> Its nihilism means that our societies would cease to be a target only if we were to renounce all the values of freedom and liberty that we have fought to extend over so many years. Our only answer to this threat must be to contest and then to defeat it, and that is why we need this legislation.

With amendments, the draft bill was submitted to a vote in the House of Commons on November 9, but was rejected. The cause was the opposition of majority of parliamentarians to fixing a period of detention (without filing criminal charges) for 90 days for people suspected of terrorism-related offenses.[55] The legal time limit for any other criminal offence was only 4 days. The government justified this draconian measure by the high number of mortal victim caused by actions perpetrated by Islamic fundamentalist and the violence advocated by Al Qaeda, thus heightening the need for advance measures as much of the investigation would have to be done prior to the contemplated act and while the suspects were in preventive detention.

While there were negative reactions to this measure in political and legal circles,[56] the police supported this approach. A senior officer of the Metropolitan Police of

[54] "The new legislation also clarifies some of the previous provisions, and makes additional provisions to several offences. In this way, new offences include, as an example, the encouragement of terrorism (maximum penalty of 7 years imprisonment), dissemination of terrorist publications (7 years), preparation of acts of terrorism in any way (life), training in terrorist skills (10 years) and attending training facilities where such skills are being imparted (10 years)" (Thorne, "Proscription of Terrorist Groups in the United Kingdom," at 4).

[55] Previous rule of 2003 fixed the maximum limit of detention without file charge in 14 days for suspicious of murder, rape or serious economic fraud.

[56] "Longer pre-charge detention is not only unnecessary; it is also unjust and potentially counterproductive. Allowing suspects to be held for over a month without charge would inevitably lead to injustice and would fly in the face of our basic democratic principles of justice, fairness and liberty. It would have significant implications for the individuals affected and would certainly not help to win hearts and minds" (Russel, "Terrorism Pre-charge Detention: Comparative Law Study," (2007), 4).

London, Andrew Hayman, wrote to the Home Secretary justifying the implementation of the 90-day detention period citing that it was based on necessity because of terrorist efforts to maximize the number of casualties (unlike Northern Irish terrorist who tried to limit damage to their direct objectives). The new global nature of terrorism threats[57] involved complex investigations usually from different jurisdictions, specialized interpreters (sometimes difficult to find and who in any case slowed down interrogations and other parts of investigation) and the extensive use of computer resources by terrorists requiring law enforcement to analyze computers and mobile phones which slowed down investigations and justified longer pre-trial detention.[58]

These justifications were insufficient to garner the requisite support for the passage of the bill.[59] Owing to its defeat, the government carried out reforms, limiting detention before a hearing to 7 days. Finally, on July 25, 2006, the period of detention without filing charges was established at 28 days.[60] That rule was subsequently applied to those suspects accused of planning attacks on flights between the United Kingdom and the United States by detonating liquid explosives.[61]

In 2008, a new terrorism law was drafted under the name of Counter-Terrorism Act of 2008. This one was passed,[62] but was the subject of intense political debate in Parliament on some of its more controversial provisions. The new law increased the

---

[57] Al Qaeda has been defined as the largest network of global terrorism that has existed in history (Torres, "Violencia y acción comunicativa en el terrorismo de Al Qaeda," 85).

[58] The full text of the letter is posted on the website of the Home Secretary (URL: http://www.homeoffice.gov.uk). On the role of new technologies in terrorism and in the fight against it, both professor Álvarez Conde and González Hortensia reflect on it: "La globalización y el desarrollo tecnológico abren nuevas posibilidades al fenómeno terrorista, pero también deben suponer un avance en la lucha contra el mismo. Hay que elaborar toda una teoría de la gobernabilidad de la globalización, evitando que ésta se convierta en un factor favorable para los terroristas, que parecen encontrarse en un campo abierto para atentar contra los valores democráticos" ("Legislación antiterrorista comparada después de los atentados del 11 de septiembre y su incidencia en el ejercicio de los derechos fundamentales", 1).

[59] Among those who criticized the extension of detention without file charges for 90 days was Archbishop Desmond Tutu, imprisoned by the South African government during the years of Apartheid. He compared the legislation that sought to introduce British government with the South African one in those years when detention without file charge was legally valid for 90 days, exactly the same time. Other British politicians compared this measure with the disastrous internment legislation introduced in Northern Ireland to combat the IRA in the 1970s.

[60] On October 10, 2006, new Prime Minister, Gordon Brown, publicly gave up the purpose, present or future, to extend the detention period without file charge until 90 days. Michael Todd, which held a high position on Manchester Police, backed Hayman's arguments in a series of opinions that were collected by British press (P. Wintour, "Police Support Blair on Terror Detentions," *The Guardian* (London), November 7, 2006; "Who Can We Trust in the Fight Against Terrorism," *The Times* (London), November 7, 2006). The participation of police in the debate over a legislative matter was the subject of criticism from various politicians, reaching even to speak of a politicization of police.

[61] This terrorist plan was responsible for the changes in procedures for passenger access control at airports, as well as limitations on the introduction of liquids on board aircraft.

[62] Received royal assent on November 26, 2008.

length of sentences for crimes related to terrorism and established a control file of people who had been convicted of terrorist acts aimed at tracking them and controlling their actions, similar to the registry of sexual offenders. The law also increased the police power to take fingerprints and DNA samples, criminalizing refusal to submit to such practices and elevating it from an administrative infraction.

Section 76 of the Act criminalized the publication of information on members of the army, security forces, intelligence services,[63] and people who hold public office if it could be deemed to assist in the commission of terrorist attacks. On the strength of this law police could prevent press photographers or TV cameras from taking pictures of their activities.[64] However, efforts to once again extend preventive detention (from 28 to 42 days) failed.[65]

In 2009, a new initiative was drawn up known as the Terrorist Asset-Freezing Act (Temporary Provisions). Passed on February 10, 2010, it imposed restrictions on financial transactions that could be carried out by people linked to terrorist activities. At first, the text was to be passed directly by the executive branch, but it was found to violate the United Nations Act, which stated that no fundamental right could be restricted by a rule which had not been adopted by parliamentary participation. The government referred the rule to Parliament, which ultimately approved it, but not before the government came under attack for its efforts to bypass the Parliament:

> The legislation is before us because the Government has been found to be acting ultra vires and failing to secure proper parliamentary approval… However, the arrogance of this Government and, in particular, the Treasury means that they do not understand what Parliament is for, and they do not understand the proper scrutiny of Bills.[66]

9.4 Conclusion

One of the most common features in the development of anti-terrorism legislation in a time when the threat becomes more visible, whether it is the political terrorism of the 1970s or the religious jihadist terrorism of the twenty-first century is the

[63] A study on the role of intelligence in combating terrorism in *Cuadernos de Estrategia*, no. 141 (June, 2009), monograph entitled 'La inteligencia, factor clave en la lucha contra el terrorismo'.

[64] The predictable reaction from British press made the Home Secretary to draft a circular reminding security forces that legitimate journalistic activity should be permitted and it only had to be limited when the normal journalistic practices as taking pictures or videos, may pose a direct support for the attacks preparation. It was tried, with this circular, to limit abuses that had occurred by the police in order to prevent press from taking pictures in certain contexts of actions of security forces. An analysis of this issue in Vv.Aa., "The Impact of U.K. Anti-terror Laws on Freedom of Expression," in *ICJ Panel of Eminent Jurists on Terrorism, Counter-Terrorism and Human Rights* (London: ICJ, 2006a).

[65] The 42 days were rejected by a group of 36 Labour Members Party. They voted against the government project of his own party.

[66] David Heath's parliamentary intervention (Vv.Aa, *Parliamentary Debates* (London, 2010), 648 column).

increasing efforts by the by government to function outside the judicial process. The British system has not been an exception to this trend.

In order to face terrorism in Northern Ireland the British government applied four processes that did not allow judicial intervention; it refused entry into the country and/or deported foreigners suspected of terrorism (outside the constraints of national immigration laws), it refused entry into Britain of Irish people suspected of terrorism, it expelled citizens suspected of terrorism connections,[67] and the policy of internment without trial, used only on Northern Ireland's soil between 1970 and 1975. These initiatives proved counterproductive to British interests.[68]

In 1975 these laws were amended because of the Gardiner report, which criticized some aspects of them and made recommendations. It recommended the elimination of the status of political crime to terrorism, stated that trial by jury was the best way to judge serious offences and it established that detention without trial could not be seen as a valid long-term measure.[69] Overall, it suggested "normalizing" anti-terrorism legislation and eliminating from the legal system some of the special elements that form the core of the rights restriction measures. The report concluded that restricting rights did not result in an increase in national security, but that scrupulous adherence to rights and freedoms is the best defense and the most effective measure to guarantee national security:

> The greater the threat to society, the more important it is that society as a whole deliberate on and authorise the security measures being introduced on its behalf, and in its name. When, in England, the Police and Criminal Evidence Act (PACE) introduced a range of safeguards for suspects, there was a concern that it might restrict the police's ability to pursue successful prosecutions and secure convictions. In practice, the safeguards have ensured that procedures are properly followed; the rights of the accused, the police, and the alleged victim are more effectively protected; and the police and public have greater confidence in the system.[70]

So "the Northern Ireland experience shows conclusively that human rights safeguards should be maintained, and strengthened. The lessons from Northern Ireland suggest that a speedier move to effective anti-discrimination legislation might have been much more successful in undermining grievances and tackling violence."[71]

However, an echo of these measures is obvious in the rules adopted in the early years of this century. Steps that have bestowed broad powers to government authorities in immigration include the ability to deny entry to suspects and to deport (or detain pending deportation) those already in Britain. This influence is not limited to

---

[67] They were sent back to Ulster, in what has sometimes been defined as a kind of policy of internal exile.

[68] Bonner, "The United Kingdom's response to terrorism", 47.

[69] Alonso, *Irlanda del Norte*, 201.

[70] Committee on the Administration of Justice (C.A.J.), *War on Terror: Lessons from Northern Ireland* (Belfast: Committee on the Administration of Justice, 2007), 7.

[71] C.A.J., *War on Terror: Lessons from Northern Ireland* (2007), 10.

British politics, but as U.S. General Petraeus observed, the lessons of the British counterinsurgency experience were taken into account in Iraq:

> The American commander in Iraq, told an audience at the Royal United Services Institute in September [2007] that his British military counterparts had exerted a big influence on his thinking in how to handle the Sunni tribes in Anbar province. One general, in particular, told Petraeus how he had learned from his time in Northern Ireland that he had to sit "across the table from individuals whose lads had been thumping his men with pipes two years earlier." Yet for all the Americans' alleged shortcomings in counterinsurgency, a senior British military source now acknowledges that they are "streets ahead" of our army in this department. Rather, the British military believe that their real "value-added" is to be found in the para-political realm of negotiating with adversaries.[72]

British anti-terrorism legislation of twenty-first century has exemplified the challenges of balancing traditional criminal legislation with national security interests in a democratic society. These challenges primarily consist of three main issues: first, the criminalization of terrorism and framing them as common criminals rather than freedom fighters or soldiers; secondly, the need of normalizing anti-terrorism legislation, so that it conforms (as nearly as possible) to conventional legislation and rights adherence; and thirdly, the need to avoid extrajudicial executive or police intervention.[73]

Without doubt, at least in the West, the challenge above that has met with the greatest success is the first, where the image of terrorists as martyrs of an ideology or supporting a just belief or freedom for oppressed people has been virtually banished from society's collective association. However, British norms developed after 9–11 are arguably detrimental to judicial scrutiny and for ad hoc applications as witnessed by the frequent legislative resort to "sunset clauses."

Another feature of anti-terrorism laws in the twenty-first century is the expansion of activities that fall into the definition of terrorism. They include not only acts of violence but a series of related activities such as laundering funds, the dissemination of terrorist propaganda or engaging in acts in the furtherance of the commission of terrorism:

> The notion that terrorists engage in a variety of non-terrorist planning activities and criminal conduct prior to the commission of any terrorist act (…) has been noted in previous research. These non terrorist acts include crimes related to the creation of false identities for group members, thefts to procure funding for the group, thefts of weapons or explosive materials and, frequently, crimes related to the maintenance of internal security. These behaviours ultimately culminate in acts of terrorism. If routinized, these preparatory behaviors may serve as pre-incident indicators that may assist law enforcement agencies in early interdiction and prevention of terrorist incidents.[74]

---

[72] Godson, "The Real Lessons of Ulster," 2.

[73] Bonner, "The United Kingdom's Response to Terrorism," 49.

[74] B. L. Smith, K. R. Damphousse, and P. Roberts, *Preincident Indicators of Terrorist Incidents. The Identification of Behavioural, Geographic and Temporal Patterns of Preparatory Conduct* (Arkansas, 2003), 24.

A particularly thorny issue under British jurisprudence is the period of detention prior to filing charges. The United Kingdom has established a higher maximum for this type of detention than any other Western country: British law now sets a limit of 28 days (though substantial government efforts sought to extend them to 56 and 90 days respectively). There isn't any other Western country that provides such a long detention period: Canada allows a single day, the United States two days, Russia five, France six and Ireland seven. Even Turkey, which has come under fire for it's rights regime and particularly with respect to terrorism issues, sets a maximum detention period (without filing charges) of only seven and a half days – approximately a quarter the limit in Britain.[75]

Critics of preventive detention argue that in the case of the terrorists arrested for the attacks of March 11, 2004 in Spain, a country with a maximum preventive detention period of 5 days, the brevity of the time before the filing of charges did not impact the successful police investigation that led to the conviction of the defendants.

The rights restrictions and the extension of powers to the government and security forces made by British anti-terror legislation after the attacks of September 11, similar to what was conducted in other countries threatened by international terrorism, put on the table the eternal dichotomy between security and freedom. Some authors note that the legislative reaction to contain the terrorist threat in recent years, including British law, has gone too far:

> The current threat from Al-Qaida-inspired terrorism is truly international in scope. Since 2001 Islamist terrorists have taken hundreds of lives in the UK, Spain, the US, Turkey and elsewhere. Governments around the world have rightly sought to protect their citizens from these threats. Some have tried to do so while respecting the framework of basic rights and freedoms drawn up by the international community after the horrors of the Holocaust. Sadly, others have been far too willing to cast-aside these basic democratic values as inconvenient "rules" of an outdated "game", in pursuit of a so-called "new normal". Examples of unjust and counter-productive policies from around the world abound: Guantanamo Bay, secret prisons and extraordinary rendition, and, in the UK, control orders, the internment of foreign nationals in Belmarsh prison and, most recently, proposals to detain terror suspects for over a month without formally accusing them of any criminal offence.[76]

[75]Russel, "Terrorism Pre-charge Detention: Comparative Law Study," (2007), 4. Other countries using the figure of detention without file charge are South Africa and New Zealand, limited in both to 2 days; 3 days is the limit set by Denmark and Norway; finally, Italy sets a limit of 4 days. The legislation that is closest to the British is the Australian, whose general rule places the limit at 24 h, but can be raised to 12 days with the intervention of a judge to approve the action.

[76]Russel, "Terrorism Pre-charge Detention: Comparative Law Study," 6; as Bonner states, "in a liberal democracy, antiterrorist policies should comply with the rule of law, not only in the sense of a pure principle of legality, but also in the sense that the rules, legally enacted, should comply with basic human rights and freedoms" ("The United Kingdom's Response to Terrorism," 51).

Bibliography

Akdeniz, Y., and C. Walker. 2003. Antiterrorism laws and data retention: War is over? *Northern Ireland Legal Quarterly* 54(2): 159–182.

Alonso Pascual, R. 2001. *Irlanda del Norte. Una historia de guerra y la búsqueda de la paz.* Madrid: Editorial Complutense.

Álvarez Conde, E., and H. González. 2006. Legislación antiterrorista comparada después de los atentados del 11 de septiembre y su incidencia en el ejercicio de los derechos fundamentales. *ARI* 7.

Bonelli, L. 2008. ¡Ya estábamos pisando a fondo desde 1995! La sorprendente estabilidad del antiterrorismo francés antes y después del 11-S. In *Las democracias occidentales frente al terrorismo global*, ed. C.T. Powell and F. Reinares. Barcelona: Ariel y Real Instituto Elcano.

Bonner, D. 2004. The United Kingdom's response to terrorism: The impact of decisions of European judicial institutions and of the Northern Ireland Peace Process. In *European Democracies against terrorism. Governmental policies and intergovernmental cooperation*, ed. F. Reinares. Aldershot: Ashgate.

Bovard, J. 2004. *Terrorismo y tiranía.* Buenos Aires: Editorial El Ateneo.

Bunyan, A. 1955. *The political police in Britain.* London: St. Martin's Press.

Burleigh, M. 2008. *Sangre y rabia. Una historia cultural del terrorismo.* Madrid: Taurus.

Bustos Ramírez, J. 1986. Las funciones de la policía y la libertad y seguridad de los ciudadanos. *Nuevo Foro Penal* 32: 165.

Committee on the Administration of Justice (C.A.J.). 2007. *War on terror: Lessons from Northern Ireland.* Belfast: Committee on the Administration of Justice.

Cumaraswamy, P. 1998. *Cuestión de los Derechos Humanos de todas las personas sometidas a cualquier forma de detención o prisión. Informe del Relator Especial sobre la independencia de magistrados y abogados, Sr. Param Cumaraswamy, presentado de conformidad con la resolución 1997/23 de la Comisión de Derechos Humanos.* http://www.unhchr.ch.

Diplock, J. 1972. *Report of the Commission to consider legal procedures to deal with terrorist activities in Northern Ireland.* London: HMSO.

Dodd, V. 2009. Metropolitan police used anti-terror laws to stop and search 58 under-10s. *The Guardian*, August 18. http://www.guardian.co.uk/politics/2009/aug/18/met-police-stop-search-children.

Donohue, L.K. 2001. *Counter-terrorist law and emergency powers in the United Kingdom, 1922–2000.* Dublin: Irish Academic Press.

Doyle, C. H. Terrorism: Section by section analysis of the USA Patriot Act. *CRS Report for Congress*, Order Code RL31200.

Godson, D. 2007. The real lessons of Ulster. *Prospect Magazine*, no. 140.

González, H., and E. Álvarez Conde. 2006. Legislación antiterrorista comparada después de los atentados del 11 de septiembre y su incidencia en el ejercicio de los derechos fundamentales. *ARI* 7.

Gregory, F. 2006. Los atentados de Londres de 7 y 21 de julio de 2005: ¿Una nueva normalidad o lo ya previsto. *DT*, no. 10, July.

Gregory, F. 2008. Policía y estrategia contra el terrorismo global en el Reino Unido. In *Las democracias occidentales frente al terrorismo global*, ed. C.T. Powell and F. Reinares. Barcelona: Ariel y Real Instituto Elcano.

Hoffman, B., and J. Morrisontaw. 2004. A strategic framework for countering terrorism. In *European Democracies against terrorism. Governmental policies and intergovernmental cooperation*, ed. F. Reinares. Aldershot: Ashgate.

Jackson, J.D. 2001–2002. *The restoration of jury trial in Northern Ireland: Can we learn from the professional alternative?* St. Louis-Warsaw Transatlantic L.J. 15 (2001).

Jackson, J.D., K. Quinn, and T. O'Malley. 1999. The jury system in contemporary Ireland: in the shadow of a troubled past. *Law and Contemporary Problems* 62: 203–232.

Jacobs, L.M. 2010. It's time to leave the troubles behind: Northern Ireland must try paramilitary suspects by jury rather than in diplock-type. *Texas International Law Journal* (Texas) 45: 655–665.
López Garrido, D. 1987. *Terrorismo, política y Derecho. La legislación antiterrorista en España, Reino Unido, República Federal de Alemania, Italia y Francia*. Madrid: Alianza Editoral.
McGuiverin, B. 2008. In the face of danger: A comparative analysis of the use of emergency powers in the United States and the United Kingdom in the 20th century. *Indiana International & Comparative Law Review* 18(1).
Mullin, C. 1986. *Error of judgement. The truth about the Birmingham bombings*. London: Poolbeg.
Noone, M.F. 2006. El Ejército Republicano Irlandés: Soldados ilegítimos. *Military Review* LXXXVI.
O'Connor, M.P., and C.L. Rumman. 2003. Into the fire: How to avoid getting burned by the same mistakes made fighting terrorism in Northern Ireland. *Cardozo Law Review* 24: 1657.
Portilla Contreras, G. 2005. El retorno del Derecho Penal al estado de naturaleza. *Viento del Sur* 83: 31–44.
Powell, C.T., and F. Reinares. 2008. *Las democracias occidentales frente al terrorismo global*. Barcelona: Ariel y Real Instituto Elcano.
Rasnic, C.D. 1996. Northern Ireland's criminal trials without jury: The Diplock experiment. *Annual Survey of International & Comparative Law* 5: 239–258.
Reinares, F. (ed.). 2004. *European Democracies against terrorism. Governmental policies and intergovernmental cooperation*. Aldershot: Ashgate.
Rodríguez-Villasante, and J.L. Prieto. ¿A que llamamos terrorismo? Introduction to *Cuadernos de Estrategia* 133 ('Lucha contra el Terrorismo y Derecho Internacional').
Russel, J. 2007. *Terrorism pre-charge detention: comparative law study*. London: Liberty.
Smith, B.L., K.R. Damphouse, and P. Roberts. 2003. *Preincident indicators of terrorist incidents. The identification of behavioural, geographic and temporal patterns of preparatory conduct*. Arkansas: National Institute of Justice.
Thorne, K. 2006. *Proscription of terrorist groups in the United Kingdom*. www.hdcentre.org.
Torres Soriano, M.R. 2006. Violencia y acción comunicativa en el terrorismo de Al Qaeda. *Política y Estrategia* 96 (October–December).
Vv. Aa. 1983. *Democracia y leyes antiterroristas en Europa. Ulster, Italia, Alemania y Estado Español*. Bilbao: IPES.
Vv. Aa. 2004. *Lost lives*. Edinburg: Mainstream Publishing.
Vv. Aa. 2006a. The impact of U.K. anti-terror laws on freedom of expression. In *ICJ panel of eminent jurists on terrorism, counter-terrorism and human rights*. London: ICJ.
Vv. Aa. 2006b. *Replacement arrangements for the Diplock Court system. A consultation paper*. Belfast: Northern Ireland Office.
Vv. Aa. 2009. La inteligencia, factor clave en la lucha contra el terrorismo. *Cuadernos de Estrategia* 141, June.
Vv. Aa. 2010. *Parliamentary debates*. London: House of Commons.
Walker, C. 2007. Keeping control of terrorists without losing control of constitutionalism. *Stanford Law Review* 59: 1423.
Walker, C., and Y. Akdeniz. 2003. Antiterrorism laws and data retention: War is over? *Northern Ireland Legal Quarterly* 54(2): 159–182.
Wintour, P. 2006. Police support Blair on terror detentions. *The Guardian*, November 7, London.
Wispinski, J. *The USA Patriot Act and Canada's Antiterrorism Act: Key differences in legislative approach*. http://www2.parl.gc.ca/content/LOP/ResearchPublications/prb0583-e.htm.
Wright Neville, D. 2008. La política del miedo: antiterrorismo y democracia australiana. In *Las democracias occidentales frente al terrorismo global*, ed. C.T. Powell and F. Reinares. Barcelona: Ariel y Real Instituto Elcano.

Chapter 10
Australian Responses to 9/11: New World Legal Hybrids?

Simon Bronitt and Susan Donkin

10.1 Introduction

Our central hypothesis is that the post 9/11 era has spawned a new hybrid form of terrorism regulation. The Oxford English Dictionary defines hybrid as follows: "Derived from heterogeneous or incongruous sources; having a mixed character; composed of two diverse elements; mongrel" (OED 2011). Hybrid for the purpose of our legal analysis is defined as a measure or law containing elements/characteristics of two previously distinct legal entities. The contention is not entirely novel. For example, control orders in the United Kingdom have been described as hybrids between criminal and civil law (Ashworth and Zedner 2007), and melding powers of an executive/judicial nature (Bonner 2007). Equally, in the Australian context, scholars have identified the hybridisation of techniques of power (Pickering, McCullogh and Wright-Neville 2008), as well as the blurring of police and military powers, and crime and war (Fox and Lydeker 2008). Hybrids are not however exclusive to terrorism law. Legal hybrids are also evident in fields such as drug law and public order, where strict liability, reverse onus clauses and civil standards of proof have long been applied (Bronitt 2003). That said, the scale and extent to which regulatory efforts to counter terrorism in Australia span various modes of governance (criminal versus civil measures; judicial versus administrative power) makes legal hybrids a mode of regulation worthy of examination.

S. Bronitt (✉) • S. Donkin
ARC Centre of Excellence in Policing and Security, Social Sciences Building (M10), Mt.Gravatt Campus, Griffith University, Messines Ridge Road, Mt Gravatt, Brisbane, QLD 4122, Australia
e-mail: s.bronitt@griffith.edu.au; s.donkin@griffith.edu.au

A. Masferrer (ed.), *Post 9/11 and the State of Permanent Legal Emergency*, Ius Gentium: Comparative Perspectives on Law and Justice 14,
DOI 10.1007/978-94-007-4062-4_10, © Springer Science+Business Media B.V. 2012

10.2 A New Regulatory Continuum: Transcending the Binaries of Terrorism Law

Law is deeply binary in character resting on fundamental antinomies (Norrie 2005). A moment of reflection reveals that binary distinctions are pervasive. At the level of legal responsibility, distinctions are drawn between fault-based liability and no-fault liability; between reasonable and unreasonable behaviour; between *mens rea* and *actus reus* (the mental and physical elements of an offence); and, more generally between subjective and objective standards. At a broader level, legal reasoning (and legal precedent) rests on key oppositions and distinctions; between matters of fact and law; between rules and exceptions. The purpose of this paper is to explore and contest some of fundamental distinctions (binaries and antinomies) as they apply to counter terrorism measures.

These distinctions, upon closer scrutiny, are inherently unstable and ultimately, in our view, unhelpful to gaining a better understanding of anti-terrorism measures. Why ultimately do we want to do this? Is this not an academic exercise in conceptual mapping, merely replacing the conventional binary typology with a new tripartite typology incorporating hybrids? We believe that this exercise does more than this. By rejecting the binary typology between the "ordinary" (norm) and "extraordinary" (exceptional) legal responses, we redirect debate away from the philosophical fixation on the legitimacy or otherwise of measures against terrorism and whether derogations from the norm are justified.

Much of the existing literature examining terrorism law adopts either a liberal or socio legal critique. In the Australian context, liberal critique focuses on issues of constitutionality, tracking the extent to which these measures deviate from fundamental liberal values of criminal justice, human rights and the rule of law.[1] A sociolegal perspective is less normatively focused, tending to use terrorism law reform as another site of political and social contestation between the state and vulnerable communities. As well as revealing the political context (and political opportunism) of the terrorism law reform, these studies examine how community fear and moral panic has shaped and distorted law reform.[2]

In our view, both liberal and sociolegal perspectives are predicated on the norm-exception binary distinction and thus largely miss the target. Our approach adopts a

---

[1] See for example: Michael Head, "Counter-Terrorism" Laws: A Threat To Political Freedom, Civil Liberties And Constitutional Rights," *Melbourne University Law Review* 34 (2002); Nicole Rogers and Aidan Ricketts, "Fear of Freedom: Anti-Terrorism Laws and the Challenge to Australian Democracy," *Singapore Journal of Legal Studies* (2002): 149; George Williams, "One Year On: Australia's Legal Response to September 11," *Alternative Law Journal* 27, no. 5 (2002): 212. See also A. Lynch, E. MacDonald & G. Williams (Eds.), *Law and Liberty in the War on Terror*. Sydney: Federation Press.

[2] For an edited collection which draws more widely on sociological, psychological and criminological perspectives see M. Gani and P. Mathew, eds., *Fresh Perspectives on the 'War on Terror'* (Canberra: ANU E Press, 2008), chap. 5.

sharper focus on regulation, and in particular recognises that there is a *continuum* of regulation that ranges across the divide between civil and criminal law. Regulation is defined as "the intentional activity of attempting to control, order or influence the behaviour of others" (Parker et al. 2004, 1). A feature of the modern liberal state, as regulatory theorists point out, is the proliferation and pluralisation of regulation – this is somewhat paradoxical because the liberal state purports to favour deregulation with less state intrusion into the lives of its citizens. Terrorism, in common with many other objects of state control, has been the subject of this regulatory trend, spawning an unending cycle of regulation, and re-regulation, as well as experimentation with a range of novel and specialised powers and laws. A regulatory approach in our view, does not conceive hybrid laws as deviations or deficits. Rather it recognises the plural nature of regulation, refocusing attention on the more important issue of whether or not these regulatory efforts are effective (i.e. the extent to which they achieve the desired policy objectives without unintended or counterproductive effects) and uphold legitimacy (i.e. the extent to which they adhere to fundamental rights and values). Applying a critical regulatory perspective offers an alternative framework for analysing law.

Our key contention is that the phenomenon of regulatory hybridity should not be conceptualised as another illustration of extraordinary legal measures or legal exceptionalism, an approach that regards measures as deviant by virtue of their perceived departure from an archetypal 'norm'. Rather, it is our contention, that hybrids should be judged in their own terms as a new mode of regulation, By doing so, we contribute to the call for a separate framework to conceptualise anti-terrorism legislation (Zedner 2009).

Table 10.1 below offers a means of visualising and mapping, through examples, the pervasive and multidimensional nature of regulatory hybridity. It identifies and locates legal hybrids on a regulatory continuum of measures between ordinary and extra-ordinary responses. The table also reveals the multilayered nature, innovation and variation inherent within this hybridity. The table, which is intended to be illustrative rather than exhaustive, is divided into policy, jurisdictional and legislative competence, procedural and enforcement hybrids.

10.3 Policy Hybrids: War on Terror and the Normalisation of Extraordinary Powers

The idea of waging a 'War on Terror' has been a pervasive feature of the post 9/11 policy context (Finnane 2008). The deployment of military metaphors is much more than the mere rhetorical flourish of politicians who customarily wage wars on crime, poverty and disease. The 'War on Terror', much like the preceding 'War on Drugs', has promoted high levels of regulatory experimentation. In Australia, in the immediate years following 9/11 a range of new specialised terrorism offences were enacted

Table 10.1 Regulatory continuum for terrorism – locating hybrid regulations

	Ordinary	Hybrid	Extraordinary
Legal policy	Criminal justice Crime control versus due process (Permanent)	*War on terror* *Balancing liberty and security*	National security War powers Emergency powers (Temporary)
Legal authority	Rule of law Civil power Judicial oversight	*Military power in aid of civil power* *e.g. Part IIIAAA of the Defence Act*	Martial law Emergency powers Executive oversight
Jurisdiction	National Territorial Non-retrospective	*Extraterritorial* *Non-geographic indicators* *e.g. Div 104, Criminal Code - Harming Australians Abroad*	International Universal Retrospective
Legislative competence	State/territory exclusive	*Shared competence* *Referral of powers* *Intergovernmental agreement* *Legal harmonisation*	Federal exclusive
Evidence and procedure	Criminal standard Beyond reasonable doubt	*Modified civil standard* *Control orders*	Civil standard Balance of probabilities
Separation of powers	Judicial power	*Quasi-judicial power* *Administrative powers exercised judicially* *Judicial powers exercised administratively* *e.g. control orders, telecommunications interception*	Executive power
Enforcement actors	Police	*Police assisting intelligence agencies* *Intelligence agencies assisting police*	Military and security intelligence

to criminalise membership, association and incitement of terrorism. These offences were novel in several respects, extending beyond existing inchoate offences of conspiracy, incitement and attempt (McSherry 2009). The offences also employed novel definitions, including the key definition of terrorism itself, which incorporated motive as an aspect of the fault element (Saul 2007). Some of the offences, such as acts done in preparation for or planning of terrorist act (even where the act does not occur) carried life imprisonment (s 101.6), the same penalty that applies to those who carry out a terrorist act! State powers of surveillance were also widened, to the point that counter terrorism surveillance is now a major focus of federal law enforcement activity (AGD 2010).

The most devastating effect of 'war' metaphors is the perceived necessity that society must be prepared to sacrifice some degree of individual liberty for greater collective security. As Clive Walker points out, the rhetoric of war is "conducive to a lack of accountability and proportionality and threatens an everlasting departure from civil society" (Walker 2004, 327). The dichotomy posed between security and liberty is widely regarded as false, much like the one peddled in the 1960s by Herbert Packer between Crime Control and Due Process (Packer 1968). Although the model has been rejected by most (though not all) scholars, the idea of 'balancing' liberty and security continues to guide public policy and law reform (Bronitt and McSherry 2010, 40–43). For example, the Sheller Committee (the Security Legislation Review Committee), which undertook the 5-year review of the first wave of federal terrorism offences, conceived its task in the following terms:

> an appropriate balance must be struck between, on the one hand, the need to protect the community from terrorist activity, and on the other hand, the maintenance of fundamental human rights and freedoms (SLRC 2006, 3).

The principal objection to this approach, in our view, is that it fails to recognise that liberty and security are not inherently oppositional – indeed, liberty and security can be mutually reinforcing. Empirical evidence in relation to police powers suggests that such procedural safeguards may promote more efficient and effective outcomes for law enforcement. An example is the mandatory taping of confessions. Although originally introduced as a due process safeguard against abuse of power by police, the reform has not presented a significant obstacle for the police. Indeed, taping has increased the likelihood of admissibility of confession evidence, and seen a significant reduction in complaints against police (Dixon 1997, 284). As David Dixon concludes "Electronic recording of interrogation is an example of the broader potential for regulation to benefit both police and suspects, both crime control and due process" (Dixon 2007, 263). More recently, social psychology research into procedural justice reinforces this finding, noting that citizens are more likely to comply with police, and with the law, where citizens perceive that their rights are being respected (Tyler and Murphy 2011).

The hybrid nature of the war on terror policy is further revealed in several ways. Although counter-terrorism powers are often presented as being temporary and conditional in nature, there is little evidence that powers are rescinded as security threats dissipate or fail to materialise. Indeed, the absence of any threat is used politically as evidence that the new measures are working. Sunset clauses and mandated legislative reviews of the new powers, though presented as important safeguards against normalisation of emergency powers, have not led to major reversals in legal policy. Indeed, according to some commentators, there is a significant trend towards 'the normalisation of extraordinary powers' (Bronitt and McSherry 2010, 980).

10.4 Jurisdictional and Legislative Competence Hybrids

The default test of territoriality, which operates as the paradigm for jurisdiction in the criminal law, has come under sustained attack in the aftermath of 9/11 (Bronitt and McSherry 2010, 950). Terrorism offences inserted into the *Criminal Code* (Cth) in 2003 were granted broad extraterritorial operation, with some applying the widest scope of 'universal jurisdiction'. This is not controversial in itself, being consistent with many crimes of a transnational character subject to criminalisation through international law, such as crimes against humanity. The strict binary divide between national and international crime however has been sorely tested in the post-9/11 environment by new hybrid offences (see Table 10.1 above).

An example of hybridisation of jurisdiction is the new federal offence enacted in the aftermath of Bali bombings in October 2002. The bombings deliberately targeted nightclubs frequented by western tourists, resulting in 88 Australian deaths and many more tourists suffering serious injury. The bombings of Australian holidaymakers overseas served to reinforce Australia's vulnerability to international terrorism. The Australian government responded swiftly, enacting a raft of new offences into the *Criminal Code* (Cth) that specifically made it an offence to murder, manslaughter or cause serious injury to Australian citizens or residents.[3] Although the perpetrators of the murders were successfully prosecuted (with some being executed) in Indonesia, the symbolic importance of legislating immediately to safeguard Australians overseas from harm was politically irresistible.[4] The offences were novel in two respects: the new offences were intended to have both extraterritorial reach and retrospective application.[5] They were hybrid offences in the sense that they were not geographically linked, but neither were they universal terrorism offences since they applied only to victims who were citizens or residents of Australia. The role of "victim status" as a limiting feature of these offences is

---

[3]There are four offences in Div 104: murder of an Australian citizen or a resident of Australia (s 104.1); manslaughter of an Australian citizen or a resident of Australia (s 104.2); intentionally causing serious harm to an Australian citizen or a resident of Australia (s 104.3) and recklessly causing serious harm to an Australian citizen or a resident of Australia (s 104.4). The offences attract the following maximum penalties: murder, life imprisonment; manslaughter, 25 years imprisonment; intentionally causing serious harm, 20 years imprisonment; and recklessly causing serious harm, 15 years imprisonment.

[4]The Bali bombers were charged under special terrorist offences, rather than simple murder, enacted soon after the bombings. The Constitutional Court held that these laws were invalid, incompatible with the Indonesian Constitution's prohibition of retrospective criminal laws: S. Butt and D. Hansell, "Case Note: The Masykur Abdul Kadir Case: Indonesian Constitutional Court No 013/PUU-I/2003 (Bali Bombing case)," *Asian Law* 6, no. 2 (2004): 176. The outcome of the constitutional challenge however did not quash the convictions or indeed, lead to a stay of execution.

[5]The federal provisions are specified to apply retrospectively, from 1 October 2002, as the drafters intended to use them to prosecute those involved with the 12 October Bali bombings: Parliament of the Commonwealth of Australia, House of Representatives, Criminal Code Amendment (Offences Against Australians) Bill 2002, Second Reading.

another distinctive feature of this response to terrorism. Apart from generating retrospective, extra-territorial, status-based offences, the Bali bombing also expanded the scope of federal legislative power through the referral of powers from the States to the Commonwealth to legislate in respect of counter-terrorism, as in the case of control orders discussed below.

10.5 Judicial and Administrative Hybrids

Judicial oversight of the executive is regarded as a crucial aspect of the rule of law. This is achieved by maintaining some degree of independence or 'separation of powers' between the organs of government (the legislature, executive and judiciary) (Vile 1967). An important feature of separation of powers is the existence of an independent judiciary (with security of tenure) that is free to determine constitutional and other legal questions unaffected by powerful people and groups within or outside government. The separation of powers doctrine has constitutional force in Australia (Stellios 2010). Legal challenges on these grounds are not uncommon due to the dual trends evident in governance in Australia: the vesting of functions typically exercised by judges in executive agencies rather the courts; and vice versa, the vesting of a wide range of executive functions in judges (see Table 10.1 above).

The former trend of transferring judicial powers to the executive has been enabled through the spectacular growth in specialist administrative tribunals in the late twentieth century. These quasi-judicial bodies exercise a wide range of adjudicative functions. While offering advantages in terms of cost, speed and informality, relative to the traditional court system, tribunal members lack the security of tenure of judges and therefore are not immune from political or public pressures. In relation to the other trend towards vesting executive functions in the courts, judicial independence (both actual and perceived) is also threatened. The High Court has sought to address these vulnerabilities by imposing constitutional limits on the power of federal parliament to use the judiciary for non-judicial purposes. By using the structure and organisation of the Australian Constitution into three separate chapters – the legislative, executive and judicial – the High Court implied a doctrine of separation of powers (Stellios 2010, esp Chs 3 and 4). This doctrine has clear implications for the use of federal courts and judges to perform executive roles.[6] These vulnerabilities are further explored below through two examples: (i) telecommunications interception warrants and (ii) control orders.

[6]Another example is the decision by the High Court in *Wilson v Minister for Aboriginal and Torres Strait Islander Affairs* (1996) 138 ALR 220 where the majority of the High Court held that the appointment of a Federal Court judge by the Commonwealth Government to report on matters connected with the construction of a bridge to Hindmarsh Island was invalid as being incompatible with her role as a judge.

10.5.1 Telecommunications Interception Warrants: When Is a Judge Not a Judge?

The High Court has held that the issuing of warrants by federal court judges is an exercise of executive power with respect to both telecommunications interception and listening devices.[7] The rationale for this is that the involvement of judges in the oversight of clandestine investigations by the police and other state agencies threatens the perceived legitimacy and independence of the judiciary. That said, non-judicial functions (that is, those that are not incidental to the exercise of Commonwealth judicial power) may be conferred by parliament upon individual judges their personal capacity (ie, *persona designata*) provided that the judge (a) consents to the performance of that non-judicial function and (b) the non-judicial function is not incompatible with the capacity of the judge or the court to exercise Commonwealth judicial power.[8] In reaching the view that the power to issue a warrant *persona designata* was not incompatible with judicial power, a majority of the High Court in *Grollo* emphasised the desirability of having independent supervision of the investigation process:

> Yet it is precisely because of the intrusive and clandestine nature of interception warrants and the necessity to use them in today's continuing battle against serious crime that some impartial authority, accustomed to the dispassionate assessment of evidence and sensitive to the common law's protection of privacy and property (both real and personal), be authorised to control the official interception of communication.[9]

While constitutionally compatible with separation of powers, few judges have been prepared to compromise their independence. With the supply of authorised judicial officers dwindling, the *Telecommunications (Interception and Access) Act 1979 (Cth)* was amended in 1997 to permit warrants to be issued by members of the Administrative Appeals Tribunal (AAT), who now issue the bulk of warrants. The high rates of approval of warrants by AAT members have led to an assessment that the system of safeguards around telecommunications are largely illusory and operate merely as a 'rubber stamp' for police applications (Bronitt and Stellios 2006). In cases like these, the demand for strict separation of powers is discordant with the need for 'checks and balances' and the desirability of independent judges maintaining a 'watching brief' over the use of covert surveillance by the state.

---

[7] *Grollo v Palmer* (1995) 184 CLR 348, 359; *Hilton v Wells* (1985) 157 CLR; *Coco v The Queen* (1994) 179 CLR 427; *Love v Attorney-General* (NSW) (1990) 169 CLR 307.

[8] *Grollo v Palmer* (1995) 184 CLR 348, 364–365 (Brennan CJ, Deane, Dawson and Toohey JJ). The majority referred, with approval, to the US Supreme Court decision in *Mistretta v United States* 488 US 361, 404 (1989).

[9] *Grollo v Palmer* (1995) 184 CLR 348, 367 (Brennan CJ, Deane, Dawson and Toohey JJ).

10.5.2 Control Orders: Preventive Measure or Judicial Bypass?

Another example of a hybrid administrative measure to combat terrorism is the control order. This measure was introduced in 2005 by the *Anti-Terrorism Act (No 2) 2005,* inserting Division 104 of the *Criminal Code* (Cth). Although based on the control orders introduced earlier that year in the United Kingdom under the *Prevention of Terrorism Act 2005* (PTA),[10] the Australian orders differ in three key areas: first, there is only one type of order, as opposed to the derogating and non-derogating varieties in the United Kingdom; secondly, they leave greater scope for judicial intervention; thirdly, individuals are informed of (most of) the evidence against them and are allowed to be present and give evidence to the contrary at the confirmation hearing. Control orders are also one of the most prominent illustrations of the hybrid nature of Australian anti-terrorism laws. Spanning several procedural hybrid categories, control orders position themselves firmly at the intersection between judicial and executive decision-making, the civil and criminal process, the admission of intelligence as evidence in court, and illustrates the juxtaposition between the reactive and pre-emptive paradigms. Examining each category, we aim to illustrate that control orders ushered in a new era of legal hybridity, one whose intention may have been intelligent design, but whose practical application, or the lack thereof, may soon bring about its extinction.

Control orders are civil orders placing restrictions and obligations on individuals suspected of terrorist involvement in an effort to prevent further involvement to protect the public from a terrorist attack. Being civil in nature, suspicion on the balance of probabilities alone is sufficient to grant such an order. However, breach of an order could result in imprisonment for up to 5 years. Although not officially punitive in nature, these obligations have been described as restrictive and preventing the controlees from living a normal life, leading some observers to label control orders as punitive in nature if not by name. The imposition of restrictions without a finding of guilt has been justified under the guise of public protection. There has been considerable debate over whether this is an appropriate matter for the judiciary to decide upon, especially with its preventative focus in these cases. However, in the *Thomas* case, the majority of the High Court (5 to 2) has observed that judges are regularly called upon by the legislature to perform this role, for example, in relation to serious offenders extending sentences on a regular basis, which clearly did not interfere with any executive role. This civil/criminal overlap has led observers to refer to control orders as quasi-judicial measures, making this hybrid category one of the most controversial (Ashworth and Zedner 2007; Zedner 2009).

In Australia, control orders originate with the Australian Federal Police (AFP) who are obliged to obtain the consent of the Attorney General for the proposed

[10]The British control order scheme was abolished in January 2012 and replaced by Terrorism Prevention and Investigation Measures (TPIMs).

order before seeking approval from a Federal Magistrates Court. Although triggered by the executive, they require judicial approval on the balance of probabilities that making the order would substantially assist in preventing a terrorist act, or that the person has either provided training to or received training from a listed terrorist organisation (*Criminal Code*, s 104.4(1)(c)). Moreover, the court needs to be satisfied that the conditions set out in the order are reasonably necessary, appropriate and adapted for the purposes of protecting the public from a terrorist act (*Criminal Code*, s 104.4(1)(d)). The court also needs to consider the financial and personal impact of such an order on the individual in question. In doing so, the court is not bound by the order as proposed by the AFP, retaining the independence to amend or withdraw certain obligations. Indeed, the judiciary exercised this right in David Hicks' confirmed control order, reducing his curfew and reporting requirements.

Due to the civil nature of the process, individuals do not have access to the same safeguards afforded to criminal defendants. These safeguards were developed to protect against miscarriages of justice and political interference (McCulloch and Carlton 2006), and have since been enshrined in various international human rights conventions, such as the European Convention on Human Rights (ECHR) and the International Covenant on Civil and Political Rights. Of the key procedural safeguards, the right to be heard may be compromised during the interim hearing, which may be conducted *ex parte*, therefore excluding the person of interest or legal representatives from the proceedings. Although the defendant is entitled to be informed of the case against him or her, some restrictions may still apply, thus interfering with the equality of arms and the right to be informed of the accusation principles. The *National Security Information (Criminal and Civil Proceedings) Act 2004 (Cth)* provides for the exemption of disclosing certain information if it is considered to jeopardise national security or ongoing police or security services operations. In this respect the Australian scheme differs significantly from its British counterpart. In the UK, parts of the trial may be conducted 'in camera', where the Home Secretary presents so called 'secret evidence' (security classified intelligence) supporting the case. The controlee is excluded from this procedure, but represented by way of a Special Advocate. Special Advocates represent their clients in closed sessions. However, once they have been privy to the secret evidence, any further communication with the controlee is prohibited. This provision has been successfully challenged on the basis that it violates the right to a fair trial under Article 6 of the ECHR. Indeed, the increased reliance/emphasis on safeguards provided for in human rights provisions have provided the foundations to challenge and amend the British control order scheme. The absence of a federal bill of rights in Australia has caused concern in this regard, leading to calls for its introduction (Williams 2004). Despite Australia's signature on the ICCPR, its international obligations have not been given domestic effect at the federal level (Michaelsen 2005).

Perhaps one of the most serious safeguards affected by the control order process is the presumption of innocence. One of the rationales for introducing control orders was to be able to exert a degree of control over 'persons of interest' against whom there exists insufficient evidence to prosecute. The presentation of the case against such persons to the judge is done by a senior member of the AFP. Much of the foundations giving rise to the AFP's belief of the subject's terrorist involvement are grounded in intelligence. Judges, however, have attached a degree of weight and credibility to the information based on the AFP's belief that it is accurate. Indeed, this scenario is undoubtedly facilitated by the lower (civil) standard of proof in control order cases.

In the next section we examine the emergence of hybrids in the field of evidence and procedure. A critical distinction was made between gathering evidence of criminal conduct (to be admissible at trial) and gathering intelligence for national security purposes (which is inadmissible in any legal proceeding, and indeed whose disclosure may be an offence).

10.6 Evidence and Procedure Hybrids

Intelligence is information gathered from various sources relating to illegal activities or security threats. Intelligence-led policing has been defined as the gathering of information designed for action (Grieve 2004). Intelligence might come from a number of sources. Valuable information may be provided by informants or other covert human intelligence sources. Concerned citizens may alert the authorities by contacting national security or law enforcement 'hotlines'. Alternatively, vital material may be gathered through the use of surveillance devices or wiretapping. Due to its clandestine nature and sensitivities about methods used, intelligence is necessarily shrouded in secrecy. It would be wrong to assume, however, that by virtue of its clandestine nature, intelligence is inherently unreliable or inadmissible. To be sure, there are significant forensic challenges with adducing material as evidence that relies heavily of paid 'professional' informants, dubious hearsay or audacious proactive investigative methods.

Defence lawyers would seek to exploit the full range of evidential rules, in particular the judicial discretion to exclude such material on the grounds of unfairness, illegality or impropriety. Even if the material obtained can overcome the admissibility threshold, law enforcement agencies themselves are extremely reluctant to disclose either their sources or details of intelligence operations. To be admitted as evidence, the authorities must be prepared to present this material in open court, where defendants have the right to contest the accusation against them and test the evidence presented by the prosecution. This right of confrontation is an aspect of the right to a fair trial recognised under domestic law and international human rights law. That said, both common law and statute have recognised that the right of confrontation is not unqualified, and that disclosure of material (revealing the identity of informers and classified information) may be resisted on public interest grounds. As studies in Australia have demonstrated, there is a strong judicial deference to these public interest claims and cases where the right to fair trial has trumped national security or law enforcement interests are few and far between (Mares 2002).

The intelligence-evidence interface came under significant pressure following the revelations in the 9/11 Commission of the failures of law enforcement and security

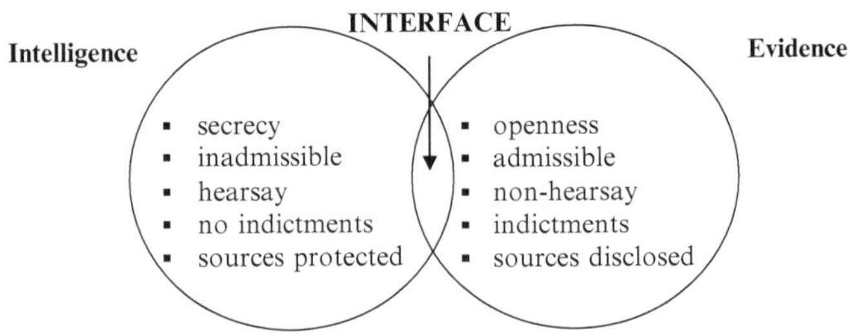

Fig. 10.1 Intelligence-evidence interface

agencies to cooperate in exchange of information (Hawley 2008). These borders between intelligence and evidence-gathering functions are neither impermeable nor immutable. We will explore these issues through further examination of the 'interface' between intelligence and evidence in relation to telecommunications interception and control orders (see Fig. 10.1).

10.6.1 Telecommunications Interception: Melding Tools of Intelligence and Law Enforcement

In the United Kingdom, in common with many countries, interception of telecommunications cannot be used by law enforcement agencies to gather evidence. In Australia, by contrast, the fruits of covert telecommunications interception have been admissible in 'prescribed' legal proceedings for more than three decades provided that the interception lawfully obtained under *Telecommunications (Interception and Access) Act 1979* (Cth) (TIA). Although the warrants under the TIA were initially limited to serious drug offences, they were progressively widened. The TIA now applies to an extensive range of offences, as well extending to access to stored communications (such emails and SMSs). TIA warrants are no longer limited to the Australian Federal Police but can be obtained by 13 law enforcement or anti-corruption agencies (Bronitt and Stellios 2006). Though the TIA was initially presented as 'exceptional' measures in the 'War on Drugs', the incremental annual expansion of these powers is another illustration of the 'normalisation of extraordinary powers' (Bronitt and Stellios 2006). The forensic value of such interception material is now indisputable, playing critical role in prosecution and the securing convictions as revealed in Table 10.2.

10.6.2 Control Orders: Melding Civil and Criminal Proceedings

The system of control orders also involves an interface between evidence and intelligence (see Fig. 10.1). This occurs when the police place their intelligence-based

Table 10.2 Prosecutions and convictions based on intercepted evidence 2007–2010

		Prosecutions			Convictions		
		Intercepts used in evidence			*Intercepts used in evidence*		
		2007/2008	2008/2009	2009/2010	2007/2008	2008/2009	2009/2010
Australian Federal Police	*Terrorism*	7	15	3	0	6	9
	Annual change		114%	−80%		600%	30%
	Serious offences	136	168	96	14	23	31
	Annual change		23.5%	−42.9%		64.3%	34.8%
All agencies	*Terrorism*	7	15	12	0	6	18
	Annual change		114%	−20%		600%	200%
	Serious offences	3,675	3,088	2,872	2,340	1,903	2,043
	Annual change		−16%	−7%		−18.7%	7.4%

Source: The data are drawn from the Annual Reports on the *Telecommunications (Interception and Access) Act 1979*, tabled in federal parliament by the Attorney General for the years ending 30 June 2007–2010.

suspicions in front of a federal magistrate in order to determine whether it is sufficient to warrant imposing an order on an individual. Intelligence is presented as evidence to support the AFP's assertion that the targeted individual has either trained with a terrorist organisation or believes these obligations are reasonably necessary to prevent a terrorist attack. The information adduced has hybrid characteristics in the sense that it is still secret, but nevertheless admissible. Moreover, the secret nature ensures its sources remain protected so as not to jeopardise its sources or any ongoing operations.

In *Thomas v Mowbray* [2007] HCA 33 statements made by Jack Thomas about his involvement in terrorism had been ruled inadmissible on appeal on the grounds that, due to the oppressive conditions in which the interview took place in a military prison in Pakistan, they were made involuntarily. The appeal court consequently quashed his conviction for various terrorism offences. Upon his release, the AFP immediately sought a control order. In those proceedings, the judge allowed the admission by Thomas, which had been judicially determined to be involuntary, to be considered in support the AFP's case for a control order.

In the UK, on the other hand, several cases have challenged the lack of defence access to the intelligence that is being used to obtain a control order. Relying on the ECHR, the courts have 'read down' control orders so as to be compatible with the right to liberty protected by Art 5. In *Secretary of State for the Home Department v AF and another* (2009) UKHL 28, the House of Lords held unanimously that sufficient detail of the allegations must be disclosed to controlees to enable them to give effective instructions to the special advocates representing them. As a result of these rulings, the Home Secretary is now obliged to disclose more information to the controlees so that they might mount a defence. However, the Home Secretary opted to revoke several control orders rather than disclosing additional evidence against the controlees. We have seen that the civil character of proceedings, with their lower standard of proof (balance of probabilities as opposed to beyond reasonable doubt) has facilitated the admission of intelligence as a source of supporting evidence for control orders. While control orders may be characterised as civil orders, the punitive nature and negative impact on the respondent's liberty should not be under-estimated.

The trend toward civil preventive measures is not unique terrorism. New preventative powers are applied to a wide range of individuals who are considered to pose risks to society (McSherry and Keyser 2009). The courts are obviously concerned about the coercive nature of these civil measures, which bypass the criminal justice system and due process safeguards. Indeed, in relation to the analogous civil order – the anti-social behaviour order or 'ASBO' – the House of Lords held that the criminal standard of beyond reasonable doubt should be applied. Their Lordships reasoned that although the relevant proceedings were civil, given the serious consequences of the allegations, fairness to the accused required a higher standard of proof.[11]

[11] *R v Manchester Crown Court* [2003] 1 AC 787.

A similar approach had been taken in Australia with the High Court recognising that the amount of proof necessary for "reasonable satisfaction" in a civil matter varies according to the context. As Dixon J in *Briginshaw v Briginshaw* (1938) 60 CLR 336 held at 361–362:

> But reasonable satisfaction is not a state of mind that is attained or established independently of the nature and consequence of the fact or facts to be proved. The seriousness of an allegation made, the inherent unlikelihood of an occurrence of a given description, or the gravity of the consequences flowing from a particular finding are considerations which must affect the answer to the question whether the issue has been proved to the reasonable satisfaction of the tribunal.

These judicial examples of modifying or upgrading civil standard of proof are further examples of procedural hybridity. Moreover, the civil character of these proceedings adversely impacts on the quality and standard of material adduced in support of the control order, further blurring the boundaries between intelligence and evidence.

10.7 Conclusion

In common with many countries, Australia has significantly altered its legal frameworks for responding to terrorism in the decade since 9/11. Although the risk of attack on Australian soil is comparatively remote, the global and local political imperative to respond has produced a new corpus of terrorism law. Although heavily influenced by reforms in the United Kingdom, as a New World hybrid Australia has developed its own distinctive legal response, one which reflects its complex federal structure (in which criminal law is shared between Commonwealth, States and Territories) and, somewhat unusually for a liberal democracy, the absence of an entrenched bill of rights (Bronitt and McSherry 2010, 126–129).

This chapter has explored the development of Australia's new terrorism laws through a regulatory lens. Our regulatory model moves beyond debates based on binary distinctions of terrorism as crime (ordinary) or terrorism as war (extraordinary), an approach that fixates on the legitimacy or otherwise of derogation from the appropriate norm. Rather than simply positing Australia's terrorism law as deviant, we examine these measures as examples of regulatory hybridity. Regulatory hybrids are manifesting in many fields – indeed, the new serious and organised crime laws in Australia have drawn heavily on the crimes prohibiting association and control orders developed to combat terrorism (Bronitt and McSherry 2010, 1037–1039).

Our core message is that hybrid regulation should not be viewed as deficient simply because it fails to conform to either a criminal or civil law norm. Hybrids are here to stay, and in our view, such laws should be judged from a more substantive perspective. That critical question, which ventures into the field of effectiveness and legitimacy, is beyond the scope of this preliminary essay.

References

Ashworth, A., and L. Zedner. 2007. Defending the criminal law: Reflections on the changing character of crime, procedure, and sanctions. *Criminal Law and Philosophy* 2(1): 21–51.

Attorney General's Department. 2010. Telecommunications (Interception and Access) Act 1979. Report for the year ending 30 June 2010.

Bonner, D. 2007. *Executive measures, terrorism and national security: Have the rules of the game changed?* Aldershot: Ashgate.

Bronitt, S. 2003. The criminal law of Australia. In *The handbook of comparative criminal law*, ed. M. Dubber and K. Heller. Stanford: Stanford University Press.

Bronitt, S., and B. McSherry. 2010. *Principles of criminal law*, 3rd ed. Sydney: Thomson Reuters.

Bronitt, S., and J. Stellios. 2006. Regulating telecommunications interception and access in the twenty-first century: Technological evolution or legal revolution? *Prometheus* 24(4): 413–428.

Dixon, D. 1997. *Law in policing: Legal regulation and police practices*. Oxford: Oxford University Press.

Dixon, D. 2007. *Interrogating images*. Sydney: Institute of Criminology.

Finnane, M. 2008. The public rhetorics of policing in times of war and violence: Countering apocalyptic visions. *Crime, Law and Social Change* 50: 17–24.

Fox, R., and Lydeker, J. 2008. The militarisation of Australia's federal criminal justice system. *Criminal Law Journal* 32:287–302.

Grieve, J. 2004. Developments in UK criminal intelligence. In *Strategic thinking in criminal intelligence*, ed. J. Ratcliffe. Sydney: Federation Press.

Hawley, M. 2008. Consilience, crime control and community safety. In *Handbook of intelligent policing: Consilience, crime control, and community safety*, ed. C. Harfield, A. MacVean, J. Grieve, and D. Phillips. Oxford: OUP.

Mares, H. 2002. Balancing public interest and a fair trial in police informer privilege: A critical Australian perspective. *International Journal of Evidence and Proof* 6(2): 94–124.

McCulloch, J., and B. Carlton. 2006. Preempting justice: Suppression of financing of terrorism and the war on terror. *Current Issues in Criminal Justice* 17: 397–412.

McSherry, B. 2009. Expanding the boundaries of inchoate crimes: The growing reliance on preparatory offences. In *Regulating deviance: The redirection of criminalisation and the futures of criminal law*, ed. B. McSherry, A. Norrie, and S. Bronitt. Oxford: Hart Publishing.

McSherry, B., and Keyzer, P. 2009. *Sex offenders and preventive detention: Politics, policy and practice*. Sydney: The Federation Press.

Michaelsen, C. 2005. *Australia's antiterrorism laws lack adequate oversight mechanisms*. Canberra: Democratic Audit of Australia.

Norrie, A. 2005. *Law and the beautiful soul*. London: The GlassHouse Press.

Oxford English Dictionary, 2nd ed. 2011. Online version. http://www.oed.com/view/Entry/89809 (accessed August 4, 2011).

Packer, H. 1968. *The limits of the criminal sanction*. Stanford: Stanford University Press.

Parker, C., N. Lacey, and J. Braithwaite. 2004. *Regulating law*. Oxford: OUP.

Pickering, S., McCulloch, J., and Wright-Neville, D. 2008. *Counter-terrorism policing: Community, cohesion and security*. New York: Springer.

Saul, B. 2007. The curious element of motive in definitions of terrorism: Essential ingredient or criminalising thought? In A. Lynch, E. MacDonald, and G. Williams (Eds.), *Law and liberty in the war on terror*. Sydney: Federation Press.

Security Legislation Review Committee (SLRC). 2006. *Report of the Security Legislation Review Committee*. Canberra: Commonwealth of Australia.

Stellios, J. 2010. *The federal judicature: Chapter III of the constitution*. Sydney: LexisNexis Butterworths.

Tyler, T. and T. Murphy. 2011. Procedural justice, police legitimacy and cooperation with the police: A new paradigm for policing. CEPS Briefing Paper, May 2011.

Vile, M.J.C. 1967. *Constitutionalism and the separation of powers*. Oxford: Clarendon.
Walker, C. 2004.Terrorism and criminal justice. *Criminal Law Review* May 2004 311–327.
Williams, G. 2004. *The case for an Australian bill of rights: Freedom in the war on terror*. Sydney: UNSW Press.
Zedner, L. 2009. *Security*. Abingdon: Routledge.

Chapter 11
Democratic States' Response to Terrorism: A Comparative Reflection on the Perceived Role of the Judiciary in the Protection of Human Rights and Civil Liberties

Marinella Marmo

But judges – particularly supreme court justices – have a special responsibility to protect democracy. (Barak 2005: 236)

11.1 Introduction

This chapter aims to discuss and evaluate domestic judges' activity in matters related to forms of transnational crime, such as terrorism, to offer an innovative way to approach the debate on democratic state's response to such transnational crimes. The approach adopted in this paper is based on interviews with senior Australian judges during the years 2005–2006, in the years of the so-called global fight against terrorism. The result of these interviews is put into a broader context; in particular with views expressed by judges based in other jurisdictions and involved in cases of terrorism. This approach seeks to explore how judges perceive their role in this context and in comparison to their counterparts abroad at the peak of the fight against global terrorism. Also, the chapter explores how judges are debating these issues in different geographical areas, and whether territoriality in criminal matters remains understood as a fixed legal and judicial environment. And if not, it is noteworthy to map out judicial collaborations and links within their jurisdiction and beyond, to trace down networks, and to observe the different forms of judicial dialogue.

This chapter aims to pin down how judges picture their role as domestic judge in the new world order. It is argued that domestic judges have a role in transnational crime: a role that is now more visible than before; role that has begun to transcend

M. Marmo (✉)
Studies in Criminal Justice, School of Law, Flinders University, GPO box 2100, Adelaide, SA 5001, Australia
e-mail: marinella.marmo@flinders.edu.au

A. Masferrer (ed.), *Post 9/11 and the State of Permanent Legal Emergency*, Ius Gentium: Comparative Perspectives on Law and Justice 14,
DOI 10.1007/978-94-007-4062-4_11,

geographical territorial borders. Slaughter (2004) addresses this innovative role of judges in the New World Order, considering, among other factors, that domestic judges contribute to the construction of a global legal system. This research paper is inspired by her approach, and aims to work towards a more defined role of domestic judiciary in transnational crime, mostly concentrating on Australian judiciary.

Part of the methodology employed for this study is based on an empirical analysis of interviews of a number of judges of Supreme Courts in South Australia, Queensland and New South Wales. I met between three and five senior judges per jurisdiction, a number considered 'remarkable' by a senior judge in South Australia, considering the proportion of judges in a low-populated country such as Australia,[1] and considering the well-debated difficulty in accessing senior judges for social science projects (Pierce 2006; Marmo 2010). Indeed, access is a problem in qualitative studies of elites (Moyser 1988; Stedward 1997). Also I interviewed a (now retired) judge of the Australian High Court, the highest ranked court within the domestic hierarchy in Australia.[2] This judge was the only one, out of seven, from this important court, who accepted to organise a meeting with me. However, among the judges interviewed at lower levels (state's Supreme Courts and Federal Courts) two have been since appointed to the High Court, demonstrating even further the seniority of the judges selected for this project, and consequently the relevance of their opinions.[3]

The main topic discussed during these interviewees is about judicial dialogue across borders, a dialogue about human rights between Australian judges and national and international counterparts, as well as international bodies. The project aimed to check the pulse of an elite group in Australia, spacing and timing the judiciary in a trans-judicial process, mapping out where a sample of significant members of Australia judiciary would place themselves in the New World Order. This methodological approach is combining with experiences of other domestic judges in the field of transnational crime, specifically terrorism. Court cases and senior members of the judiciary's papers form the base of the judicial counterparts' approach to their role as domestic judges, especially across the relevant period. This will serve the purpose to situate Australia judiciary

---

[1]The resident population of Australia is just over 22 million people (ABS 2011a). The number of judges per state and territory is proportional to local population. To offer a couple of an examples, in South Australia there are 13 Supreme Court judges (AIJA 2011) and the local population is over 1.6 million (ABS 2011b); in New South Wales there are 50 judges per over 7 million people (same references). A comprehensive study on Australian judiciary is being undertaken by Professor Mack and Professor Roach Anleu. Preliminary findings can be found here: Mack and Roach Anleu (2008).

[2]The High Court of Australia is the ultimate court of appeal for the Australian system, both via the federal court stream and the state and territory stream. The federal court hears cases of federal matters (for instance, corporations, bankruptcy, immigration; so mostly civil matters). Each state and territory has a court hierarchy of its own, with the Supreme Court as the highest within its state or territory. These courts also have appeal divisions.

[3]In this chapter, I elect the masculine personal subjective or objective pronoun, given that most judges of the sample panel are male.

in an international context of trans-judicial dialogue, and to mark down a moment in time of Australian judiciary.

The initial discussion (a new role for domestic judiciary *against* state power?) aims to place the main argument of the paper in context. This section looks at domestic judges as players in legal matters related to transnational crime seen through the lens of criminology. Subsequently, three main areas will be introduced and discussed: transition in visibility; judges in search of a mission; territoriality as construction of *mental* space. These areas are prompted by the empirical work collected. Even if there is a sense that the judiciary is caught between the changes imposed by reinforced state powers in the fight against terrorism and the protection of human rights, the chapter reveals rather conservative self-reflections on the role and function of judiciary. Most judges interviewed expressed a view about their role that it is not only in contrast with some judicial approach embraced by their counterparts abroad, but also their statement can be considered as a defensive wall to maintain a *status quo*. Insularity of Australian judiciary, a combination of legal imperialism stemmed by socio-legal and historical events, could be a main reason why judges in this geographical area did not see themselves as playing a role in judicial transnational criminal matters. It is questioned whether such insularity is more a state of mind rather than territorial constraints, a comfortable explanation to justify their position.

Yet, the empirical data show that there is some encouraging progress, especially when analysed through the lens of a transitional movement. Generally, geographical isolation and legal upbringing have had an impact on how Australian senior judges see themselves and their role: the idea of a New World Order may have had partial or inadequate influence in their judicial life. There are some exceptions: the self-nominated 'converted' judges do work endlessly to convince colleagues that legal analysis can be approached differently. Further exposure to external pressure and to international counter-parts, combined with internal pushes of 'converted' members of the judiciary may facilitate the movement from one position of isolationism to a more proactive and dynamic approach to these themes, embracing a constructive and parithetical judicial dialogue.

11.2 A New Role for Domestic Judiciary Against State Power?

When considering international criminal justice matters and transnational crime, prevalently the role of national or international policing agencies or offices of prosecution are identified as primary. Domestic judges are systematically excluded. This is due to several reasons. Judges' jurisdiction is territorially limited, above all in the area of criminal law. Their mission and limitation is to apply state law. Judges do not physically move outside their nation-state to execute their daily legal routine; they do not need to 'share intelligence' – actually quite the opposite; they do not need to collaborate with other criminal justice agencies to track down criminals who travel across borders. Their role is seen by themselves and society as static within a jurisdiction that is geographically – and legally – confined.

However, three new elements should be added to this typical analysis of the role of the judiciary. Firstly, crime does travel across borders, and has an impact on criminal activities classifiable as transnational crime which consequences can been traced in domestic judicial activity. Secondly, the traditional interpretation of territoriality in the field of criminal law and criminal justice is shifting, due to the impact in the legal field of more interactive relationship among nation-states at different level; this is part of the effects of globalisation and formation of a New World Order. Thirdly, and as a result of the previous two points, interpretation of human rights is a subject area that is not territorially limited. International and comparative legal analysis is on the increase. This trend should involve domestic judiciary as well. After a long period of stall, due also to a rigid interpretation of the Westphalian concept of nation-state, domestic judges find themselves in a dual situation, whereby national and inter or infra-national levels are more interactive. In this more dynamic environment, judges at national and supranational level are now playing a crucial role. Their pro-active way of dealing with everyday work complements – in fact at times contrasts – the traditional main role of the government in embracing a comprehensive and uniform approach to human rights. Domestic judges (should) look at international and other domestic courts' developments in interpreting human rights in a trans-judicial interactive process; they attend international seminars and conferences during which they may develop a degree of judicial dialogue and legal-cultural exchange of approach and understanding.

Domestic judiciary could fulfil an openly-debated clear-cut role in the area of transnational crime. Their role would involve, among others, giving an interpretation of internal legislation with in mind the legal development of international human rights. In doing so, judges would share a common mission that goes beyond traditional territorial borders in domestic criminal law: judges, in particular senior member of domestic judiciary, have the duty to determine their judgment on the bases on the rule of law. They have a 'special responsibility to protect democracy' (Barak 2005: 236). Through a process of cross-fertilisation, which would include vertical and horizontal judicial dialogue, senior domestic judges would contribute to the development of a 'global community of Human Rights Law' (Slaughter 2004: 79).

This chapter, inspired by positive impact of judicial activism, aims to highlight some aspects and some reasons why it would be beneficial to reject a static and purely territorially-defined understanding of domestic judges' role in this field – a position that is already obsolete in different common law and civil law systems. A more up-to-date vision of judges' role should be embraced, considering that this elite is not secluded in an ivory tower, even if some members of this elite, and the society in general, still persevere to maintain such an untenable status, in the expectation that nothing will change. Invisibility of the judiciary and their unreachability can be described as values of the profession. This is a position that is changing, and changing very rapidly. Today also judges live within a more dynamic, multi-centre, visible and reachable society. The New World Order theory (Held et al. 1999) is not a mere concept that is applicable to economic, politics and social fields. Crime travel fast across borders (Castells 1998), crime policy follows (Sparks and Newburn 2002), and this has an impact on domestic judiciary as well (Slaughter 2004).

Some legal scholars have realised the judges live in a shrinking world too, with obvious consequences on comparative studies, and devote their attention to this area (Markesinis 2006; Tribe 2005). A few social-legal and political scientists started analysing the judiciary as policy-makers and policy-shapers (Shapiro and Stone Sweet 2002; Slaughter 2004; Pierce 2006).

In criminology, the judiciary is simply overlooked within the discipline. There have been some exceptions recently, in the field of terrorism, where suddenly domestic judges have become visible in the international arena and have caught the attention of criminologists, as well as legal and political scientists, politicians, media and general public's attention at national and international arena. Some court cases dated between 2004 and 2006 have been significant for several legal and political reasons:

- in US: *Rasul v Bush* (03–334) 542 US 466 (2004) and *Hamdan v Rumsfeld* (05–184) 548 US (2006);
- in UK: *A and Others v. Secretary of State for the Home Department* HL [2004] UKHL 56;
- in Israel: *Adalah – The Legal Center for Arab Minority Rights in Israel v. GOC Central Comm* HCJ 3799/02 [2005];
- in Australia: *R v Lodhi* [2006] NSWSC 691, and *R v Thomas* [2006] VSCA 165.

For this paper's purpose, these cases are important for three reasons. Firstly, judges became visible in a transnational crime issue. And despite Australian judges, compared to other counter-parts, have maintained a low profile, and have not interpreted laws against executive's intention, the impact of their decisions can be traced in part of the Australian community. Secondly, judges referred to an international or comparative dimension to reinforce their legal arguments – this excludes Australian judges' approach. And thirdly, in these court cases some judges have attempted to define their role within society. Defending basic human rights against the intrusive role of the State in the global war against terrorism has captured judges' attention on their common mission. Judge Q1 (2006) offered the comment below on these cases, and offered a spontaneous reflection on commonalities of duties across jurisdiction, which includes determination of punishment and criminal guilt:

> In criminal law, particularly with the incarceration by the Americans of British or Australian citizens in Guantanamo Bay .. I mean our jurisprudence, the common law view, the view that I think does inform the approach of the United States Supreme Court and of the House of Lords is the same approach as ours which is distrust of the Government, defence of individual rights (..) that does produce the result that the use of the various techniques of statutory interpretation that are deployed in the service of that perspective does produce results like striking down the military commissions, because the common law, the traditional common law view is that (..) in the civil courts [there] are open people charged with crime [who] should be tried by them. In America now we see the Congress being invited to legislate, to

> breath life into, the military tribunals that Bush has established but that will then be, the question then will be the extent to which the American courts will accept the Legislature's word and the last word on that hasn't been spoken yet, because, I think, there will continue to be a strong judicial determination to confine attempts by the Executive or the Legislature to subvert the judicial determination of criminal guilt.
>
> That's a very strong value in the States of course because of the separation of powers and the determination of punishment and criminal guilt is something which is necessarily a judicial function and exclusively a judicial function. In Australia, the separation of powers isn't quite so sharply drawn. [follow example].

This is significant because we can see a senior Australian judge reflecting openly on his role against state power, to protect human rights. It shows a new level of assertiveness, a turning point from the safer and sober approach embraced often by senior judiciary. It indicates there is a self-reflective process about judges' 'mission'; a mission that connects judges of different jurisdictions. And I claim it is the fight against terrorism and against the increasing state powers that have played a key role in this self-reflecting process. Judges are caught in the middle, and those years (2005–2006) are transitory, and reveal a new judicial conscience. And yet, as I argue below, in Australia other factors have been influential and have slowed down a process that has been fast-tracked in the other jurisdictions such as in England and the US.

11.3 Transition in Visibility

The sample group of Australian judges interviewed made it clear, with some exceptions, that they prefer to place themselves outside the debate over national-transnational-international crime: domestic judges, it was commonly argued by the interviewees, deal neither with transnational crimes (with vague ideas about this definition) nor with international crimes. This is a narrow-viewed position inherited by the Westphalian approach to territoriality; also, it is a 'comfortable' and safe position, thereby judges can claim, if and when necessary, their lack of competence and jurisdiction.

Yet, transnational crimes have been recognised as a rising problem that intergovernmental and governmental bodies, and criminal justice policing agencies should fight more systematically, even if they remain, from a jurisdictional viewpoint, a nation-state matter. Therefore, it is clear that terrorism remains, from legal and jurisdictional perspectives, a national matter, in line with the other categories of transnational crime. That means that international judiciary's competence is excluded; as Murphy (1999) emphasises, those transnational crimes that are not included in the jurisdiction of international criminal courts, are prosecuted before national courts, despite arguments against this approach (see, for example, Morris 2004). Nevertheless, it is apparent that domestic judiciaries have been broadly invisible, or simply excluded, not only in discussions and preparation of policies and legislative projects, but broadly also in studies on national impact. The subject area seems to be of particular relevance for a combination of geopolitical circumstances, and domestic judges' role is minimal at these roundtables.[4]

While geopolitical circumstances are complex, and in need of further investigation not within the scope of this chapter, it is relevant to note that we, as academics, are not contributing to the debate as constructively as we can. It is argued that part of the reasons for the omission or insufficient attention to the role of domestic judiciary in transnational matters lies in the fact that the broad discipline of transnational crime is accepted as being a criminological subject (Mueller 2001; Boister 2003), not squarely 'law', either domestic or international.[5] Consequence of such approach is the partial or total exclusion of focus on judges' legal and political role within a society. Boister (2003) suggests that in legal studies 'transnational crime' should have a complementary term, transnational criminal law, to catch the attention and the eyes of lawyers and judges, and therefore to approach the discipline using the usual array of legal focus and analysis on related matters. He criticises the lack of specific terminology to categorise those transnational crimes that are not included in the definition of the core international crimes, through the process of exclusion occurred in recent legal developments. This category of transnational criminal law would be more specific than the label of 'treaty' or transnational crimes. Consequence of this renewed terminology, he claims, would be the legitimisation of the role in this transnational area of national control system, the legal order as well as enforcement issues, attenuating the distinction between transnational and international / national.

While this is in the process of being developed, those working in the area of transnational crimes continue not to pay enough attention to the key role of domestic judges. There is a limbo of discipline which alleviate judges' apprehension from being 'studied' as elite group by social-scientists interested in this subject-area, and from being questioned on a role on transnational issues – a role that, in fact, they already have, and are aware of playing it. Terrorism is becoming the clear exception. Within the parameters of the fight against terrorism – as a transnational issue with domestic impact, judges are already active. This is a role that senior domestic judges, in the timeframe considered, had already acknowledged and accepted (*Hamdan v Rumsfeld*, Justice Stevens' reference to international principles of law), or even acknowledged and rejected (*Hamdan v Rumsfeld*, Justice Scalia' reference to original interpretation of law).

Domestic judges are relevant in this field, and are already committed to play a significant role in creating a system of bottom-up values – the importance of rule of law is a clear example – that shake those governments party of conventions and agreements. This is evident in those years considered in this chapter: in 2004/06, there has been a process of transition in visibility of judiciary in a field dominated by governmental agencies. These agencies have created an exclusive zone, a top-down system of rules over those crimes, especially in the area of fight against terrorism, that has been challenged by the judiciary's bottom-up values.

[4]Even if perhaps this is less so within the EU.

[5]In fact, in the field of international law we see the involvement of judges to policy-focused roundtables more and more routinely.

11.4 Judges in Search of a Mission

Judges' judgments across 2004–2006 in the area of terrorism have had a global impact, or at least an impact within Western legal systems (court-cases listed above). Since the fight against this new form of terrorism is framed in terms of 'global', domestic judges' intervention has been under the reflector of national and international interested parties.

In these court-cases, domestic judges in decision making process have cited and referred to regional and international definitions as well as legal developments and frameworks. In all these cases, the internal link is that senior judges assessing the cases recognised an infringement of constitutional provisions, relevant to human rights enforcement. These judges based their legal reasoning partially on a common understanding and interpretation of human rights as suggested in guidelines contained in different international legal documents or discussed before international or infra-regional courts. Domestic judges showed a similar degree of appreciation of their mission within Western society, producing innovative policy that goes beyond territorial borders and against the national legislator's intentions. This is a most interesting stage in the development of a 'judicial consciousness' that goes beyond borders in the field of transnational crimes. This novel attitude has also been criticised by more conservative judges such as US Supreme Court Scalia, who dismissed it as judicial adventurism:

> For this [US Supreme] Court to create such a monstrous scheme in time of war, and in frustration of our military commanders' reliance upon clearly stated prior law, is judicial adventurism of the worst sort. I dissent. (*Rasul v Bush* (03–334) 542 US 466 (2004) Scalia J., dissenting second part, p. 20)

However, this new level of judicial consciousness that can be traced in the other opinions of the *Rasul* case as well as in the other cases proves to be strongly shared by other judicial parties, and forms a good example of the effects of trans-judicial dialogue, and the existence of a shared mission of purpose and duties.

Most interviewed Australian judges, while on the one hand share the view that their mission is to protect individuals from the State, on the other hand, offer an antagonistic twist to the matter of balance between security and liberty. Specifically, there are a few matters emerging as patterns: the isolation from other geographical regions, the nature of legal upbringing as cause-effect problem, access to (emerging) knowledge, and the lack of, and need of a Bill of Rights in Australia. These patterns, it is argued, reveals a level of resistance to impose their view on their mission, in line with the above-identified new level of judicial consciousness.

Interviewed judges self-complimented themselves on why Australia does not need further and formal discussion on a Bill of Human Rights. In almost all interviews some version of the following has been disclosed: human rights are discussed as foreign, European, Roman-Catholic, unnecessary in Australia, and a 'bandwagon' phrase. In particular, when discussion on 'human rights' was linked to developments in this area within European continental tradition, judges' comments included some negative reference about why in Europe there is a need for further discussion on human rights, as opposite to Australia. The following points were recurrent during the interviews:

- Historically, debate on human right in European civil systems has been rather generic and abstract, not pragmatic and of real application – differently from common law;
- Judges of the civil law system do not form their legal training independently and 'against the state', as opposite to common law judges who would spend years as lawyers fighting against state's abuses;
- Australia is a prosperous country where the protection of Human Rights has been part of primary legal discussion;
- As a consequence of the above points, Australian judges have a general good appreciation of human rights, and therefore:
    - further legislative elaboration on Human Rights can result as redundant;
    - further external judicial influences is not necessary – and anyway not welcomed.

The following are two contrasting examples of why the Australian approach seems fixed in time, while other common legal systems seem to fine-tune their appreciation of judicial role within the theme of fights against terrorism. For this purpose, a court case-study approach will be used, to then return to the interviews.

Former Chief Justice of Israel Barak moved from a more isolated position as a judge to embrace an international appreciation of the matters in hands. He has published papers on the role of domestic judges living within an international (western) community. Recently, in a long-distance debate with the conservative US Supreme Court Justice Scalia (2006) on the role of a judge in a democracy (Fullbright Convention 26/01/06), Barak offered an analysis of his judicial philosophy, which includes a consideration on the role of comparative law and international law in the daily routine of a court of a common law system. This external pressure on him as a domestic judge had a considerable impact in the final years of his career. For instance, when he led his High Court of Israel to decide against previous court-cases and legislation on moderate physical torture in the ticking bomb scenario, Barak claimed:

> We are not isolated in an ivory tower. We live the life of this country. We are aware of the harsh reality of terrorism in which we are, at times, immersed. The possibility that this decision will hamper the ability to properly deal with terrorists and terrorism disturbs us. We are, however, judges. We must decide according to the law. This is the standard that we set for ourselves. When we sit to judge, we ourselves are judged. Therefore, in deciding the law, we must act according to our purest conscience. (*Public Committee Against Torture v. Israel*, HCJ 5100/94 [1999])

His decision to look beyond the reality of his country and to embrace a more similar appreciation of rule of law is yet another example of what is occurring at the moment among domestic judiciaries. These judges are engaging in public highly-specific and difficult discussions on their role in interpreting human rights in transnational criminal matters. Transnational crime has been a subject area that domestic judiciary had to confront their view on: their visibility and impact in this area is now becoming more central.

In contrast with the first example, the second one is the Australian case *R v Lodhi* [2006] NSWSC 691. Judge Whealy talks about his role as a judge:

> 91 The need for substantial sentences to reflect the principles of general deterrence are obvious in relation to crimes of this kind. Such crimes are hard to detect; they are likely to be committed by members of our own community and often by persons of prior good character and favourable background. One has only to consider the tragedy of the London bombings in 2005 to recognise this observation as a sad truism. Moreover, terrorism is an increasing evil in our world and a country like Australia, with its very openness and trusting nature, is likely to fall easy prey to the horrors of terrorist activities.
>
> 92 In those circumstances, the obligation of the Court is to denounce terrorism and voice its stern disapproval of activities such as those contemplated by the offender here. [..]
>
> In my view, the Courts must speak firmly and with conviction in matters of this kind. [..] [I]n offences of this kind, as I have said, the principles of denunciation and deterrence are to play a substantial role. [..]
>
> 93 These are new offences and there is little assistance in decided cases in Australia, which can give the Court guidance as to the appropriate sentence to be imposed. [follow discussion of the Roach's case]

Justice Whealy (2007) later commented the case and the limits of the judiciary:

> As trial judges, we have to respect the legislation that comes into existence from time to time relating to terrorism offences, even if we find it personally distasteful. But the very nature of the legislation to which I have referred may tend to reinforce the potential in the public mind for prejudice animosity and bias. (p. 28)

Justive Whealy's perception of his role within Australian society is in line with most interviewed judges. This may indicate that a judge in a nation-state share similar socio-legal and historical background as well as similar legal upbringing. Therefore the 'mission' as judge may be construed following similar patterns, and may vary from location to location.

Legal upbringing was identified by H1 (2006) as a cause-effect problem, mostly blaming academics, who fail to properly bring their material up-to-date with international legal developments, and therefore to bring a contemporary edge to the legal debate. This position shows the diffident attitude towards academia that many judges often have. It also shows that judges refer back to their university years notwithstanding the fact that their student status belong to a different century – literally.

Access to knowledge should be considered as part of the problem of legal upbringing and further training. As pointed out by Markesinis (2006) understanding foreign law is an art that has to be learned. It should be pointed out that international meetings and judicial exchanges aim to facilitate knowledge-flows.

There is a further element that H1 identified: fear of 'being reversed'. In a hierarchical system where senior judges can reverse a decision, legal behavioural patterns can be traced by looking at most senior judges' model. A conservative High Court projects fear that original, innovative or creative interpretation will be judged as 'wrong', and consequently reversed. Most judges interviewed claimed that either the current Australian High Court is rather orthodox, or is 'different' from the

Mason's High Court that was involved in the *Mabo no 2* case.[6] Some interviewed judges claimed that the current High Court has been dismissive of more progressive legal achievements.

The overwhelming patterNs of the interviews, and the court case cited above, are indicative of an abstract willingness to protect individual rights. Nevertheless, there are a number of concerns or obstacles or justifications as to why the intention cannot be followed by action. In contrast, in other continents, more and more discussion is taking place about judges sharing a mission and having a duty to intervene when the state is not protecting the concept and application of human rights. There are relevant court cases, such as *Rasul v Bush* and *A and Others v. Home Department*, emerging during the years 2004–2006 that sent a clear message: the judiciary is not anymore 'playing with an idea', they have positioned themselves strongly, and against their Governments' principles. The fight against terrorism cannot take place in a vacuum where top-down rules are imposed over a population in discriminatory, but bottom-up principles, such as rule of law, need to be protected.

A minimum number of interviewed Australian judges did refer to external legal developments, and declared they were following those movements with interest. However, within the temporal framework considered, the overwhelming position is cornered in a conservative understanding of their mission. Whether this is transient, such as the one noted in the years 2000–2005 in England,[7] needs to be explored further.

11.5 Territoriality as Construction of Mental Space

During this research project, it occurred several times that issues raised were dismissed by interviewees as being political, and therefore falling outside their range of legal competence. Almost all judges have referred to the notion of 'political will', division between courts and Parliament, and the role of the judiciary. So, political matters are portrayed in opposition to legal matters. Judge's role is to apply the law as it stated by the legislator. Almost all judges have commented on 'judicial influence', but stop short of calling it 'judicial activism' or 'judicial subjectivity'. Judicial influence is talked in reference to interpretation of statutes, so it is masked, subtle and covert, rather than overt. Subjectivity is unacknowledged.

[6]In a nutshell, the High Court under Chief Justice Sir Anthony Mason has been regarded as the most liberal bench, and the *Mabo 2* case on native titles has been often referred as an example of progressive views that challenged more conservative and mainstream positions. See Pierce (2006).

[7]Senior English judges interviewed in 2002–2003 showed levels of resistance towards fighting state power (Marmo 2010); however, the 2005 case *A and Others v. Home Department* shows a different positioning in the protection of human rights against state power.

This understanding of the judiciary's role has major limits, and allow judges to continue being 'invisible' in a multi-interactive society. It allows judges to claim that they do not have a role in the policy-making process. It allows judges to do politics or participate in the policy-making or shaping process without being held responsible and accountable for their discretionary powers on the basis that they only applies law. It allows judges to maintain an untouchable position, sheltered from the realities of increasing transnational crime and international debate on human rights. Judges are hidden away in their *ivory towers*, the court rooms or judicial chambers, where they are difficult to reach, to whom is difficult to talk and with whom is difficult to establish a dialogue. Moran (2006) argues that invisibility of judges goes hand to hand with importancy.

Furthermore, this position favours a perception of the judiciary as being geographically confined in a material space, within a society that moved on from this analysis and construction of space (Scholte 2000). Claiming that the decision and application of criminal law and proceedings is territorially based is a political convention, developed since the Westphalian appreciation and establishment of geographical territorial borders. This position has shifted further (Held et al. 1999). In the 'new world order', the notion of nation-state has been eroded and the effects are visible in different sectors, including the rise and intensification of forms of transnational and organised crime in what Castells (1998) described as the 'perverse connection'. Other fields have a more globalised appreciation of connection and collaboration, to include a more systemic understanding of human rights and basic principles. There is a dichotomy between what the new word order triggered in positive and negative terms, and the position fixed in time into which some domestic judges buried themselves (Slaughter 2004).

This process of reframing the judiciary's position and powers within and outside a geographical setting does not rely on the support of members of the academic community either. Whereas some interests in this area sparked a few papers on judges and politics (Tate and Vallinder 1995; Markesinis 2006), it is a common understanding that domestic judges are territorially confined, and that they communicate to society through their court cases' comments, reinforcing the idea of being inaccessible and invisible.

11.6 Discipline Boundaries

Also, it is a common tacit agreement that domestic judges, if ever they establish a dialogue with the academic community, establish a dialogue with lawyers. However, subject areas are well confined into traditional issues. Besides, within the legal academics, there is an interesting and well-established debate on international core crimes and international courts, but there is little on transnational crime and domestic judges.

Little inter-disciplinary approach is embraced, and echoes of these discussions are barely traceable in social sciences and political sciences. Recently, some emphasis is put on judicial decisions occurring in the area of transnational crime, in particular terrorism. However, empirical work on collecting judges' view other than their decision in court cases are sparse, failing to assess the problem employing the full range of empirical methodologies (Pierce 2006).

11.7 Insularity in a Networked Society

All interviewed judges claimed that they take part in international meetings and conferences. Some of them pointed out that they had been abroad a few times from the beginning of 2006. They all praised the purpose of these meetings as constructive legal environment. For instance, Judge (NSW4) pointed out that he had been abroad four times to international conferences: in China; in Japan; at the Asia-Pacific Judicial Reform Forum Manila; and at the Commonwealth Law Conference London. Slaughter (2004: 99) talk about face to face meeting, either institutionalised or informal exchanges that had become part of an annual routine. The aims, she claims, are multiple:

> they serve to educate and cross-fertilize. They broaden the perspectives of the participating judges. [..] But perhaps most important, they socialize their members as participants in a common judicial enterprise.

Asked to elaborate on the significance and impact of such meetings in the field of human rights and more harmonised interpretation, all interviewed judges agree that exchange of ideas is facilitated. This is very much in line with Slaughter appraisal of such events. H1 refers to a 'Bangalore conversion': how during a particular meeting this judge realised that there was a different purpose and approach either than the usual Australian-focused one. He mentioned the name of another US judge, who in 2006 was at the top of the US judicial hierarchy attempted to push for a stronger interpretation of the *Bangalore Principles of Judicial Conducts* (2002). Both cases should be regarded as successful stories of positive outcomes of trans-judicial networks and judicial dialogue. Remarkably, another judge summarised these meetings as capable to produce some impact in terms of harmonised purpose and aims as part of a process that takes time:

> what you'll find emerging, I think, is a greater commonality of approach than may have been the case in the past .. but it takes time, that's what is happening. (NSW4).

However, further questions about the real effectiveness of such dialogue should be examined. What has emerged from fieldwork is a variety and degree of 'understanding' of such international meetings, which reflects judges' legal upbringing and mental baggage. The 2006 empirical data would suggest the existence of levels and degrees of judicial dialogue which can be linked to effectiveness in terms of investment and return.

The different projects and programme with Asian counter-parts are discussed more in terms of proposing a legal education to 'them', reflecting a unilateral, rather than a bilateral, willingness to learn, teach and share. This topic could be framed as part of discussion on post colonial Australian imperialism; regionally, Australia is the most powerful economy with strategic alliances. The judiciary reflects this attitude, and views its role as a guide on common law values, to help out counterparts living in different geopolitical areas. This itself is extremely positive. However the combination of such an approach with the overall view of unnecessary reform in the field of human rights in a prosperous and fair Australia may indicate that there is not dialogue. It is a monologue.

Also within Australia, an imposed hierarchy of state Supreme Courts could be traced. The courts of New South Wales have a relevant number of cases and judges, besides most High Court judges have been historically selected from this State. There is an unwritten expectation that other courts look at NSW court-cases, but not the opposite. This is certainly not a positive mental training for those judges who move up to the next judicial step of the court ladder. There is a degree of reluctance to go 'outside' that extends to the state level.

Significant is the case of an interviewee (NSW1) who took part to a United Nations Conference in May 2006. During this meeting, an outcome resolution was auspicated. In an absence of a Bill of Rights, Australia appears to be an anomalous case, belonging to the Western legal systems' group. Some pressure was therefore put on the Australian delegate:

> so all the Pacific Islands were there and someone from New Zealand and also South Africa and India and it was only the Australians who didn't have a Bill of Rights. And the organizers of the conference wanted to make what they described as the Suva Declaration, you know at the end of all these conferences they have a declaration that's unanimous and they send it to all the governments and they send it to the United Nations, all part of a means of bringing pressure to bear on different countries to obey human rights and to make human rights part of their legislation.
>
> But, I think they got a little annoyed with me, because I, .. there were many things that I objected to. Because I knew that I could not agree as an Australian to things like 'all judges should try and follow some human rights convention when giving decisions' that was a typical .., and I refused to sign that, I said we don't, we take an oath to apply the law of the land. The law of Australia is not the Human Rights Convention and I'm certainly not prepared to agree to apply human rights when they are, when those human rights are not part of the law of Australia.
>
> Anyway, after a lot of argument and compromise we did arrive at a statement that satisfied everyone, careful wording, but I knew they weren't very pleased, but they wanted to have Australia there and this was inevitable that I don't think any Australian would agree to that, certainly not a representative of Australia.

Through these judicial meetings pressure can be put on members of domestic judiciary to think differently, to embrace a more common vision. However, internal pressure, legal training and cultural elitism may play disadvantageously. Mental insularity and cultural orientation are elements that may change over time, but it is a long term process. Judge Q3 talks about reluctance in many colleagues towards internationalism in the Australian context. This judge refers to the collective recent memory of the Privy Council,[8] abolished in 1986. The reluctance to have external pressure may be link to recent legal history in Australia.

---

[8]Which entitled appeal from any Australian court to a British court. See Mason (1987).

Interviewee SA3 made a case claiming data collected was biased because who had agreed to meet with me were only the 'converted' ones, those who believe that looking outside Australia was constructive in the process of fulfilment of their duty as judge. This is a useful criticism, and is part of constraints of qualitative studies. However, the sample did not reveal to be a homogenous group of *internationalised* judges. Definitely there is a variety of opinion which reveals a variety of position about what judicial dialogue means and could mean in the future.

11.8 Conclusion

This chapter looked at a sample of senior judges in Australia in the years 2005–2006, and compared their experiences and opinions to judicial developments of counterparts in other nation-states. It aimed to offer a reference to a point in time when Australian senior judges were caught between their perceived role and mission, and what achieved abroad by their colleagues. While it is clear that the perceived role is to protect human rights, also in the fight against terrorism, the outcomes are not as radical as in other international cases.

Markesinis (2006) offers an analysis of such judicial view in its historical and political context so as it is better appreciated. Markesinis claims that judicial skepticism towards external pressure is due to the contemporary socio-economic and political situations. He identifies two problems that can be applied to the Australian context as well. Firstly, not sufficient trust is other Western nation-states and their socio-legal development. Secondly, and closely linked to the previous point, the belief in the superiority of own values. This chapter highlights that this analysis can explain partially Australian judiciary's attitude toward a particular discourse on collaboration and exchange of ideas.

Nevertheless, there are other elements to consider. The autonomy achieved in 1986 (Privy Council) goes hand in hand with the idea of Australian values and prosperity cited often by the Howard's Federal Government, which was in place when data was collected. Most interviewed judges refer to this sense of achievement and economic prosperity which has brought fair and just equal opportunity and respect of human rights. From here, a further step to declare unnecessary the introduction of human rights' jargon seems a syllogism. Considering foreign and international law and non-Australian court cases as a source of domestic inspiration and legal development may clash with the above points.

And yet, within the sample group, a few suggested that looking outside Australia is an exercise they have taken more seriously in recent years. This small group is determined to bring home what experienced abroad, and even employs strategies to have their voice heard, like in the case of SA 3 and children's rights; or NSW 2 who was quite proactive (but preferred not to be recorded). The strategy of H1 is to dish out his opinion as extensively as possible, and try to *convert* others.

References

ABS. 2011a. *Population Clock*. Australian Bureau of Statistics, Commonwealth of Australia. http://www.abs.gov.au/ausstats/abs@.nsf/94713ad445ff1425ca25682000192af2/1647509ef7e25faaca2568a900154b63?OpenDocument. Retrieved July 20, 2011.

ABS. 2011b. *Estimated Resident Population*. Australian Bureau of Statistics, Commonwealth of Australia. http://www.abs.gov.au/ausstats/abs@.nsf/Products/1345.4~Jun+2011~Main+Features~Demography?OpenDocument. Retrieved July 20, 2011.

AIJA. 2011. *Judges and Magistrates*. Australasian Institute of Judicial Administration. http://www.aija.org.au/JudgesMagistrates.pdf. Retrieved July 20, 2011.

Bangalore Principles of Judicial Conducts. 2002. *Adopted by the Judicial Group on Strengthening Judicial Integrity*. The Hague, November 25–26, 2002. http://www.unodc.org/pdf/crime/corruption/judicial_group/Bangalore_principles.pdf. Retrieved August 10, 2006

Barak, A. 2005. *Purposive interpretation in Law*. Princeton: Princeton University Press.

Boister, N. 2003. Transnational criminal law? *European Journal of International Law* 14(5): 953–976.

Castells, M. 1998. *The end of the millennium*. Oxford: Blackwell Polity Press.

Held, D., A. McGrew, D. Goldblatt, and J. Perraton. 1999. *Global transformations*. Cambridge: Polity Press.

Mack, K.M., and S.L. Roach Anleu. 2008. The National survey of Australian Judges: An overview of findings. *Journal of Judicial Administration* 18(1): 5–21.

Markesinis, B. 2006. Judicial mentality: Mental disposition or outlook as a factor impeding recourse to foreign law. Centenary Lecture of the Society of Comparative Legislation. *Tulane Law Review* 80 (4): 1325–1375.

Marmo, M. 2010. *The role of judges in European criminal justice: Judicial harmonisation processes in Italy and England*. Saarbucken: VDM Verlag.

Mason, A. 1987. Future directions in Australian Law. *Monash Law Review* 13: 49–163.

Moran, L. 2006. Judicial diversity and the challenge of sexuality: Some preliminary findings. *Sydney Law Review* 28(4): 565–598.

Morris, M. 2004. Terrorism and unilateralism: Criminal jurisdiction and international relations. *Cornell International Law Journal* 36: 473–489.

Moyser, G. 1988. Non-standardized interviewing in elite research. In *Studies in qualitative methodology*, vol. 1, ed. R. Burgess. Greenwich: JAI Press.

Mueller, G. 2001. Transnational crime: Definitions and concepts. In *Combating transnational crime*, ed. P. Williams and D. Vlassis, 13–21. London: Frank Cass.

Murphy, S. 1999. Progress and jurisprudence of the international criminal tribunal for the former Yugoslavia. *The American Journal of International Law* 93(1): 57–97.

Pierce, J. 2006. *Inside the Mason Court revolution: The High Court of Australia transformed*. Durham: North Carolina, Carolina Academic Press.

Scalia, A. 2006. *International influences on national legal system, at law symposium: International influences on national legal systems, Fulbright Convention* (26/01/2006) 1–40. http://www.fulbright.org.il/index.php?id=2644. Retrieved March 28, 2009.

Scholte, J.A. 2000. *Globalization*. Basingstoke: Palgrave.

Shapiro, M., and A. Stone Sweet. 2002. *On law, politics, and judicialization*. Oxford: Oxford University Press.

Slaughter, A.-M. 2004. *A new world order: Government networks and the disaggregated state*. Princeton: Princeton University Press.

Sparks, R., and T. Newburn. 2002. Introduction: How does crime policy travel? *Criminal Justice* 2(2): 107–109.

Stedward, G. 1997. On the record: An introduction to interviewing. In *Surviving the research process in politics*, ed. P. Burnham, 151–165. London: Pinter.

Tate, C.N., and T. Vallinder. 1995. The global expansion of judicial power: The judicialization of politics. In *The global expansion of judicial power*, ed. C.N. Tate and T. Vallinder. New York: New York University Press.

Tribe, L. 2005. On Judicial Review. *Dissent* (Summer vol): 81.

Whealy, A. 2007. The impact of terrorism related laws on judges conducting criminal trials. *The Judicial Review* 8(3): 353–383.

Cases

A and Others v. Secretary of State for the Home Department HL [2004] UKHL 56.

Adalah – The Legal Center for Arab Minority Rights in Israel v. GOC Central Comm HCJ 3799/02 [2005].

Hamdan v Rumsfeld (05–184) 548 US [2006].

Mabo and Others v Queensland (No. 2) [1992] HCA 23.

Public Committee Against Torture v. Israel, HCJ 5100/94 [1999].

R v Lodhi [2006] NSWSC 691.

R v Thomas [2006] VSCA 165.

Rasul v Bush (03–334) 542 US 466 [2004].

Chapter 12
The U.S. Response to Cuban and Puerto Rican Right-Wing Terrorism in the Pre and Post 9/11 Era

José M. Atiles-Osoria

> *Of course, the good terrorists are those who respond to the interests of the State, those who become allied with them. Bear in mind that the governments of Puerto Rico and the U.S. very much feared the development of Puerto Rican independence movements in the 1960s and the 1970s.*
>
> *They were afraid because the independence movements were very strong in those years. Then, these other right wing groups –paramilitary, death squads– that feed off of Vietnam veterans, people from the PNP and Cuban exiles were the base that the State had there, on the street, and obviously they were operating according to the interests of the State.*
>
> *Then, the State looked at them with sympathy because they took a bit of pressure away. Because the State did not have to set the bombs, these people set them against the independence movements.*
>
> (Interviewee)[1]

---

[1]This interview was carried out as part of the field work for my PhD dissertation (the translation is mine); I would like to show my gratitude to various people who assisted me in the preparation and in the writing process of this chapter. First, I would like to thank the editor of this book, Dr Aniceto Masferrer for his invitation to join this project. Similarly, I would like to thank to Gustavo José Rojas Paez and Lusina Yannicelli for their great collaboration in the editing process, and to Dr David Whyte and Pablo Ciocchini for their support in the process of reflection and construction of this chapter.

J.M. Atiles-Osoria (✉)
Centro de Estudos Sociais, University of Coimbra, Colegio de S. Jerónimo,
Apartado 3087, 3001-401, Coimbra, Portugal

Department of Philosophy, University of the Basque
Country, Spain Ave. Tolosa, 70, 20018, Gipuzkoa, Spain
e-mail: joseatiles@gmail.com

A. Masferrer (ed.), *Post 9/11 and the State of Permanent Legal Emergency*,
Ius Gentium: Comparative Perspectives on Law and Justice 14,
DOI 10.1007/978-94-007-4062-4_12, © Springer Science+Business Media B.V. 2012

The September 11th 2001 terrorist events in the United States of America (henceforth U.S.) and the subsequent development of the War on Terror brings us back to a series of discussions and analysis of the concept of terrorism. What is at stake is the role of the State preventing terrorism and the use of international and state law as a response to this threat of political violence. One important discussion that emerged after the 9/11 focuses on the constant tension between the National and Global Security (including the multiple political, legal and military strategies implemented to ensure it) and the protection of the civil, political and human rights in liberal democracies. Various scholars and commentators have tried to provide a possible solution to this tension. Among these theoretical efforts the Orthodox[2] studies on terrorism stand out (Richmond and Franks 2009). Scholars from this approach have developed different levels of response (mainly legal, political and military) to the problem of terrorism based on the guarantee of security and protection of civil and human rights under a terrorist threat within a democratic state. This group of studies have been characterised –in the pre and post 9/11 era– by its particular emphasis on non-state or non-governmental actors who challenge the hegemony of the state with the use of political violence. As a result, the scope of this academic field or approach to terrorism is limited due to two reasons. On the one hand, it mainly focuses on describing the 'terrorist' actors and their organisation, and, on the other hand, it attempts to provide possible answers only within the framework of liberal advanced democracies (Pedahzur 2001; Wilkinson 1986). By so doing so, other political scenarios where terrorism takes place remain unaddressed.

In response to the above described orthodoxian agenda, the Critical Studies on Terrorism (e.g. Jackson et al. 2011) and Jackson (2008) have stressed that orthodox studies on terrorism are limited, because they do not consider the possibility that state can also be a terrorist actor. As a consequence we are left with a theoretical silence that is orchestrated or that operates by the invisibilisation of the state terrorism. Thus, two interesting phenomena arise: a monolithic focus on non-state actors as the only perpetrators of terrorism, and, a stigmatisation of the democracies of the global South (Santos 2002),[3] which are described as the only political space where state terrorism takes place. To this analytical perspective, I would like to add that orthodox studies analyse the political conflict as an encounter between two isolated, radically different and presupposed positions. That is to say, a bipolar phenomenon in which each actor has a certain predetermined space in which there is supposedly no room for dialogue, negotiation or alliance among them.

The aim of this chapter is to challenge the limited view of the above mentioned conflict and the "terrorist threat" by arguing that in the conflicted scenarios

[2]I take the concept of 'Orthodox studies on Terrorism' from O. P. Richmond and J. Franks (2009).

[3]For good analysis of the Global division between Global North and Global South and their effect in socio-politics, legal and economics ambit see Santos (2002).

addressed in this chapter there have been multiple alliances, and interaction among different actors and between both non-state and State actors which have traditionally been silenced. From this standpoint, I may argue that the position assumed by the U.S. during the pre and post 9/11 era has been malleable as there is a constant tension between the support, tolerance and reaction to some mobilisations that resorted to political violence. In this regard, I will focus my reflection on settling the tension implied in the U.S. reaction to some extreme right-wing movements in the pre and post 9/11 era.

Based on this contextualisation, I argue that by carefully reflecting on the U.S. reaction to the Cuban revolution, our understanding of the tension that arises when governments assume a position pro or against certain terrorist activities will be broadened. Moreover, when analysing the response of the U.S. government to extreme right-wing organisations of Cuban exiles and Puerto Rican conservative supporters, attention should be paid to two periods in particular: between 1960s to 1990s and the post 9/11 era. These periods are informed by the exacerbation of political violence and state terrorism orchestrated under U.S. tolerance. This display of violence has a twofold implication. On one hand, the maintenance of the U.S.-Puerto Rican colonial system through violent means; on the other, the repression and criminalisation of Puerto Rican independence movements.

Throughout this chapter, two underlying elements of the Puerto Rican context will be addressed: firstly, the multiplicity of interests that interact in the colonial conflict, and; secondly, the way how the resulting relationship of complicity and support between the State and extreme right wings organisations is articulated with the intention to hamper the Puerto Rican anti-colonial and counter hegemonic mobilisations.

In order to show this particular phase of the Puerto Rican colonial conflict and the duplicity of actions that have taken place in this context, I shall propose a threefold analytical framework. Firstly, a brief description of the historical, socio-political and legal conditions that led to the formation of Cuban exiles extreme right-wing organisations in the U.S. in the pre 9/11 era. Secondly, I will outline some of the terrorist acts perpetrated by Puerto Rican and Cuban extreme right-wing organisations against Cuban citizens and Puerto Rican members of the independent movement and their families, and also against civilians in Puerto Rico (henceforth PR) between the 1960s and the 1990s. Finally, I will show the positions of the U.S. and PR governments to those activities, and how this position has established a precedent for further action in the Puerto Rican colonial case in the post 9/11 era. I will then show that in general, both the U.S. and PR governments have been permissive and sometimes even complicit with the terrorist activities of those organisations. In doing so, I will intend to show how counter-terrorist policies implemented by democratic states in the pre and post 9/11 era are not effectively reinforced when dealing with actions that contribute in their struggle for the control of the left wing and independent movements. This proves, at least in the cases presented, that terrorism is not always equally treated. This complex reality lays the foundations for a new approach to research on democratic states and their effort to guarantee human and civil rights to people who are not directly involved in the political and colonial conflict in the post 9/11 era.

12.1 Cuban Revolution and the Emergence of Right-Wing Terrorism

On 1st January 1959, as a consequence of the Revolution carried out by *26th of July Movement* Cuba entered a new historical and political era. At the same time, the gradual process that led Cuba to adopt the Communist system brought about a radical change in the political and diplomatic affairs of both Latin America and the Caribbean. This transformation was mainly due to the adverse position assumed by the U.S. towards Cuban revolutionary process.

The Cuban Revolution does not only imply the end of the Batista Dictatorship but also the break with more than 60 years of neo-colonial history with the U.S. (Kapcia 2008). Since 1898 Cuba was under a neo-colonial status after the U.S. intervention in the Cuban war of independence against Spain. With this intervention the U.S. transformed the Cuban independence war into the Spanish-American War (Cripps 1979; Kapcia 2008; Lievesley 2004) which has been described by Foner as "Spanish-Cuban-American War" (quoted in Zinn 2005: 11). This intervention also marked the crystallisation of the interests of the U.S. and their economic elites that since early Nineteenth century approved of the idea of annexing the Island to the U.S. (Kapcia 2008). As a result of the Spanish-Cuban-American War and the peace negotiation that was materialised in the *Treaty of Paris,* the U.S. received from Spain four new territories as spoils of war: Cuba, PR, Philippines and Guam. As a consequence of this treaty, the U.S. guaranteed the 'independence' of Cuba but under a neo-colonial situation especially exemplified with the military occupation that lasted until 1903, and thereafter the imposition of the Pratt Amendment in the Cuban Constitution (Hernández 1993; Kapcia 2008; Pérez 1986). In the interim, the Philippines became independent early in Twentieth century, while PR continued under a colonial situation.

At the same time that the Cuban Revolution ended the U.S. 'colonial hegemony' on the Island, Cuba started its transition to political and economic self-determination. The Agrarian reform, the Urban reform, the nationalisation of foreign companies along with the reform towards a communist system on the basis of the Soviet Union exemplify the process of self-determination that the Island underwent. These movements fostered the U.S. to counter the revolution since Cuba challenged the 'Imperial doctrine' that established that the Island was located in the U.S. 'area of influence'. Thus, the U.S. position against Cuba should be understood in economic and political terms. The economic position is exemplified with the imposition of the *Embargo or Bloqueo,* which remains in effect until today (2012), whereas the political position is exemplified by the aid and support given to different Cuban counter-revolutionary and exiles organisations. This chapter aims to analyse the way the political-economic and strategic support given to the Cuban exiles which laid the foundation for the exercise of the political violence against Cuba and the Puerto Rican independence movements.

12.1.1 Cuban Exiles and Its Political Organisations

An important outcome of the Cuban Revolution was the displacement of thousands of Cuban citizens to the U.S. and PR. The massive migration included: supporters and members of the Batista dictatorship; high classes; petite bourgeois; professional or high-skilled workers; businessmen and merchants. This migratory process has been broadly analysed by different scholars. One that stands out and perhaps the most important analysis of migration to the State of Florida –more concretely to Dade County and to Miami City– is that by García (1996). In her work, García traces a depiction of the configuration of the different waves of migration to the U.S. throughout the last 40 years of the Cuban Revolution (between 1959 to the mid-1990s). In Garcia's words: 'most Cubans who arrived after 1959 came in three distinct periods: immediately after the revolution from 1959 to 1962; during the 'freedom flights' from 1965 to 1973; and during the 'Mariel boatlift' of 1980' (García 1996: 1). Also, she briefly presents a fourth migratory group in the 1990s traditionally known as '*balseros*' (rafters). However, García does not analyse this group since she believes their migration was motivated by economic reasons (Duany 2005).[4]

When reviewing the literature on Cuban migration to PR, we could note that the account presented by García (1996) differs from what actually took place in PR. In PR the migratory waves were longer and included a different scale of migration (Duany and Cobas 1995; Martínez 2007). Martínez (2007), by way of example, presents three groups:

> (1) from 1959 to 1973, which consists mostly of professionals and members of the upper and middle class who left the country because of their differences with the regimen; (2)1973 to 1980, which includes members of the working class – especially during the Mariel exodus- so Cuban began to be perceived as economic migrants, not necessarily political ones; and (3) from 1980 to 1995, characterized by being mostly an economic migration, but which had, in terms of numbers, a lesser impact on Puerto Rico, and which included those Cubans who left the country during the rafter crisis of August 1991 (Martínez 2007: 49–50).

In this context of migration to U.S. and PR, García (1996) suggests that the first group of migrants -with U.S support- tried to create a 'Monolithic Identity'. For that Cuban émigré, although they had some serious divergence as regards the political and juridical configuration of the Cuban State in the post-Castro era, their identity was composed by a fundamental consensus: 'a conservative political tendency; an anti-communist and anti-Castro position; and the link to the Cuban Cause (*la Causa*

[4] In that sense, Duany (2005) has done an analysis of the Cuban migratory groups to the U.S. between 1982 and 2005, the so-called 'economical migrant'. In his analysis, Duany agrees with the argument that the new configuration of this migration phenomena is more economic than political or counter-revolutionary, it is a consequence of globalization and of the international division of labour.

Cubana)' (García 1996: 121–22). However, it should be noted that not all the exiles adopted that identity. As we find in our research, dozens of Cuban migrants, second generation and other groups started to feel an affinity with the Cuban process. Thus, it should be stressed that here we are talking about a very particular type of Cuban exiles and not all Cuban immigrants.

Based on the constitution of a 'Monolithic identity', the Cuban émigré manifested themselves against Communism and Cuban Revolution by means of four political strategies: (1) the exercise of lobby in the U.S. and mobilisation in the 'legal context'; (2) international campaigns and mobilisation for recognition of the alleged violation of human rights in Cuba; (3) activation of the Civil Society and 'Dissidence' in Cuba; (4) the exercise of political violence and terrorism against Cuba, supporters of Cuban political system and against Puerto Rican independence movements. As stated earlier, for the purpose of this work, I will intend to explore this last point in detail in the following sections. More precisely I will focus on describing how the U.S. government instrumentalised this mobilisation as a strategy to recover the geopolitical control of Cuba and to thwart the counter-hegemonic and Puerto Rican independence movement who challenged the U.S. hegemony in PR.

12.1.2 The Emergence of Cuban Extreme Right-Wing Terrorism

Following Sprinzak (1995) characterisation of extreme right-wing terrorism,[5] one can argue that Cuban exiles' counter-revolutionary organisations in the U.S. could be described as *Reactive terrorism* while in PR, together with the Puerto Rican right wing organisations, they would fall within Sprinzak's description of *Vigilante terrorism*. Sprinzak describes Reactive terrorism as follows:

> [R]eactive terrorism is resorted to by organizations which have either lost their positions of power and social status or are fearful of such a development.[…] Terrorism is grasped as a means of last resort in order to restore the status quo ante, and is usually applied against organizations which themselves have reached power through the use of violence […] Reactive terrorist may be divided into two types: those who have already lost political power and are fighting an uphill battle to regain it, and those who have not yet been stripped of their power and privileges but are worried about such development (Sprinzak 1995: 26–27).

In that context, Sprinzak describes the strategies adopted by reactive terrorism groups as: 'sporadic revenge attacks and assassination attempts of government officials […] [m]embers live either underground or in exile […]' (Sprinzak 1995: 27). In that sense when analysing the configuration of the Cuban exiles organisation in the U.S., we will notice that these organisations are due to obey the model

[5]Sprinzak divided the use of political violence of the extreme right wing organisations into five different types of terrorism: Revolutionary Terrorism; Reactive Terrorism; Vigilante Terrorism; Racist Terrorism and Millenarian Terrorism.

of 'Reactive terrorism', as their actions are primarily aimed at recovering the 'power or status' that was 'taken' by the revolution. Moreover, the analyses will show how the U.S. supports and instrumentalises these organisations for their own benefit, which means the recovery of geopolitical and economical control on the Caribbean Island.

Another fundamental concept of Sprinzak that serves to explain the PR case is that of Vigilante Terrorism. According to Sprinzak

> Vigilante terror is used by individuals and groups who believe that the government does not adequately protect them from violent groups or individuals and that they must protect themselves. Vigilante movements rarely perceive themselves involved in conflict with the government and the prevailing concept of law. They are neither revolutionary nor interested in the destruction of the authority. Rather, what characterizes the vigilante mind is the profound conviction that the government and its agencies have failed to enforce the law or establish order in a particular area. (Sprinzak 1995: 29)

In this vein, this analysis of the Puerto Rican colonial case and the terrorist action performed by Cuban and Puerto Rican right-wing organisations will show that their position was directed to thwart the Puerto Rican independence movement. This is because they knew that both PR and the U.S. governments were not effective in such actions. Thus, in the next section, we will present a series of events that show how the relationship between State and extreme right-wing terrorism is set as a recurring tension between supporting the mobilisations of the Cuban exiles in the U.S. and protecting human and civil rights of both Cuban and U.S. citizens.

12.1.2.1 Brief History of the Cuban Exile Right-Wing Organisations in the U.S.

Cuban exiles began to organise themselves since the very moment the Cuban Revolution triumphed in 1959. This fast organisation took place thanks to the support from the U.S. government, the CIA and other security agencies (Arguelles 1982; Chomsky 2005; Welch 1985).[6] In this regard, García (1996) presents five periods in the organisation of Cuban exiles since 1959 to 1990 whereas Douglas (2005) identifies approximately seven periods. For the purpose of this chapter, I will use García's (1996) chronological account in tandem with other analyses and interpretations of this process of political actions. García's (1996) account of the Cuban exile organisation is summarised as follows: Firstly, the period called 'Eisenhower, Kennedy and the Exile's War against Castro'. This phase lasts from 1959 to 1963 and it was characterised by an unconditional support of the Presidents

[6] As a result of the Hearings that took place in the US Congress in 1975 following the assassination of John F. Kennedy, we have access to declassified documentation that show the involvement of the CIA in different count-revolutionary activities during the 'Cold War'. These documents are available in "The National Security Archive of the George Washington University", http://www.gwu.edu/~nsarchiv/ and in the "Marry Ferrell Foundation", http://www.maryferrell.org/wiki/index.php/Main_Page (accessed August 3, 2011).

D.D. Eisenhower and J.F. Kennedy to Cuban exile counter-revolutionary and terrorist organisations. García (1996) argues that from 1959 two major groups were formed in the U.S.: the Revolutionary Recuperation Movement and; the People's Revolutionary Movements. This author states that:

> These groups established an underground rebel force that conducted a campaign of violence and destruction in both rural and urban areas hoping to weaken the new government and pressure the population to support a counter-revolution. Their chief target was Cuban economy, and they bombed or torched important sugar and tobacco mills, factories, seaports, and other centres of economic activity. They raided police and government offices, jails, and military installations, destroyed water mains and farm machinery, and sabotaged railways and bridges (García 1996: 122).

It is important to note that these counter-revolutionary activities carried out against Cuba took the South of Florida as a base where the Cuban exiles started to organise and train (Arguelles 1982). By the same token, these activities violated the 'U.S. Neutrality Act' (Arguelles 1982); however, since Cuba had begun to link with the USSR and communism, the CIA and the U.S. government tolerated and supported these terrorist activities. In this context the CIA –under the direction of President Eisenhower– began to look for 'the solution to the Cuban problem' (García 1996: 123). The solution was the implementation of the 'Operation 40',[7] which consisted in organising, training and supplying equipment to the Cuban groups organised in Miami. As Arguelles (1982) has put it,

> Thus, the CIA began recruiting more Cuban agents than ever before in the first months of the revolution. Estimates of the recruitment of Cuba agents in the formal period of CIA involvement in anti-revolutionary of Cuba operation, that is, from 1959 to 1967, vary from 5,000 to 50,000. (Arguelles 1982: 293)

Due to this support to counter-revolutionary activities and the increasing support provided by the CIA in the early 1960s, Cuban counter-revolutionary movements in the U.S. doubled its presence (Arguelles 1982; Bolander 2010; Douglas 2005; Hinckle and Turner 1981).[8] As it is broadly present in the literature regarding this topic, these years were characterised by a high level of counter-revolutionary activities exemplified by some particular and very well-known actions such as: (1) the Bay of Pig (Girón) invasion on 25th April 1961 (Quesada 2009; Johnson 1965); (2) the upsurge of the *Embargo*; (3) the 'Missile Crisis' in 1962 (Chayes 1974), among other periods of tension between both countries.

In this context, there was an emergence of new groups: the Alpha 66; the Cuban Student Directorate; Commands L; among others. All these movements were characterised by the implementation of military strategies of the 'pin-prick raids and flea-bite-operations' (García 1996: 128). The modus operandi of these groups was simple: they leave south of Florida, attack a specific target in Cuba and return

[7]For a detailed analysis of the Operation 40, see the web page: "Terrorism Made in USA", http://www.terrorfileonline.org/es/index.php/Operaci%C3%B3n_40 (accessed August 3, 2011).

[8]Some examples are: Revolutionary Democratic Front; Revolutionary Rescue Movement; Cuban Revolutionary Council.

quickly to the U.S. These types of operation in most cases were performed without any opposition from the U.S. even though they violated the U.S Neutrality Act.

The second phase of the organisation of Cuban exiles identified by García (1996) is: '1960: The Revolutionary Industry'. The author suggests that, as a result of the strategical and economical support provided by the U.S. in the second half of the 1960s Cuban terrorists' organisations increased exponentially. García states that,

> By 1963, there were so many exile political organizations that the Department of Justice was unable to keep track of them all. […]The majority of these organizations were in Miami, but others emerged wherever émigrés settled: Union City, Chicago, New York, Los Angeles, San Juan, Caracas, Madrid, Mexico City. (García 1996: 131)

As a result of the great amount of terrorist organisations in those years, some organisations that tried to unify all of them emerged. Two of them are: Revolutionary Junta of National Liberation and Cuban Representation of Exiles. García suggests that these organisations: 'received between US$3 and US$6 million from the U.S. government to train and equip an army of two hundred men […] they occupied five camps in Costa Rica and Nicaragua, owned four boats and half a dozen planes, and families of its 'commandos' received generous monthly stipends' (García 1996: 132).

Thanks to the support by the CIA and the U.S. government, Cuban terrorist organisations declared 1965 as the 'Year of the Freedom'. That implies the beginning of a huge number of terrorist actions of big scale, such as: planes bombing sugar mills, use of chemical and biological substances in Cuba territory (Bolander 2010),[9] assassination, kidnapping and sabotages. Around the same time, it started to emerge a movement of utmost importance out of the U.S.: Cuban Revolutionary Unity which was founded in PR by Manuel Ray. Thus, despite the effort to unify all these counter-revolutionary organisations by the end of this decade there were many more terrorist organisations, for instance: Abdala; Free Nationalist Commands; Cuban Power in which Orlando Bosch already appears to be active.

The third phase described by García is '1970: A Transition Period'. To her mind, this period is characterised by a confluence between the first group of exiles and new generations of exiles. García (1996) argues that in this decade some political and legal strategies were included for the progress of the 'Cuban Cause', and terrorist activities diminish to a certain extent. Contrariwise, Douglas (2005) and Franklin (1992) argue that the 1970s were the period when the greatest number of terrorist actions was experienced not only in Cuba but extrapolated globally. In other words, we were witnessing the 'Global Terrorism' for the first time.

Some examples of this global terrorist performances are: (1) April 1972, two bombs exploded inside the Cuba Trade Commission in Montreal; (2) 1973, the Cuban Embassy in the city of Santiago in Chile and the homes of Cuban diplomats were bombed six times in a period of 4 month; (3) January 1974, a bomb exploded in the Embassy of Cuba in Mexico City; (4) February 1974, a bomb exploded in the

[9]For a good analysis of the use of biological substances against Cuba see Bolender 2010.

Embassy of Cuba in Peru; (5) March 1974, several bombs were thrown into the Embassy of Cuba in Jamaica; (6) April 1974, a bomb destroyed the Embassy of Cuba in Madrid; (7) May 1974, bombs went off at the Embassy of Cuba in London, and the Cuban Consulate in Mérida, Mexico; (8) July 1974, a bomb exploded at the entrance of the Embassy of Cuba in Paris (Franklin 1992).

In addition to targeting Cuban embassies worldwide, in these first 5 years of the 1970s extreme right wing organisations carried out different actions against Cuban sugar mills, ships in Cubans harbours, civilian population in Cuba and the use of biological weapons on animals and farms. Also, in this period a new number of terrorist organisations emerged: the intensification of Alpha 66, Omega 7, Coordination of United Revolutionary Organisations CORU; Cuban National Liberation Front and Alacrán, to mention a few.

The second part of the decade of the 1970s can be hailed as a milestone when speaking of terrorist activities. Douglas (2005) and many other authors (Chomsky 2007; Frankling 1992; Lamrani 2005) explain, what happened on 6th October 1976 when two bombs exploded on a Cuban airplane that took off from Barbados towards Cuba. In this terrorist action there were 73 casualties (Douglas 2005: 82). This action was re-vindicated by CORU and later on, two of the most known Cuban exiles terrorists, Luis Posada Carriles and Orlando Bosch, were eventually prosecuted by the Venezuelan Justice.

In the same period, the level of political violence and political assassination increased dramatically. Some telling instances are: the political assassination of former Chilean ambassador Orlando Letelier in Washington in 1976; the assassination of Carlos Muñiz Varela in PR in 1979 and; the political assassination of the Cuban diplomat Félix García Rodriguez of the UN Mission in NY in early 1980s. García was the first UN diplomat ever assassinated in NY (Franklin 1992: 151). Undoubtedly, these are the most important actions but nevertheless we must notice that there were hundreds of actions in this decade, ranging from sabotage, kidnappings, and bombings, both in Cuba and against Cuban exiles in Miami who had begun to distance themselves from exile hardliners.

García (1996) called the fourth phase of Cuban exile organisations as '1980: Working within the System'. In her view this decade was characterised for the abandonment of terrorist activities by Cuban exiles in the U.S., yet when we review different literature we notice that in the 1980s there was a high intensity of terrorist actions as well. As described before, in this decade the political assassination of Félix García Rodríguez took place in NY. Likewise, the bombings and political assassinations remained an important strategy for these groups. Especially in the U.S. context where tensions between exiles began to intensify between those who proposed a rapprochement with Cuba as a result of the Antonio Maceo Brigade; and those exiles who continued to support the positions of zero dialogue and terrorist struggle against Cuba.

This tension changed, as Morley (1987) states, during Reagan administration in 1980s. With this administration there was a resurgence of terrorist movements and actions supported by the U.S. During the 1980s, as Agee (2003) demonstrates, the CIA and the U.S. government began to support economically and strategically the so-called civil society within Cuba to 'destroy the system from inside'. This is to say, the U.S. government began to provide economic support to the hereafter known 'Cuban dissidents'.

Since the fall of the Communist or 'Real Socialism' in East Europe and the emergence of the Special Period in Cuba, the fifth period of the organisation of Cuban exiles in the U.S. began. García (1996) refers to this period as '1990s: A Turning Point in the U.S.-Cuba Relations?' Although by that time the U.S. continued to support terrorist activities against Cuba, the author remarks that the most important U.S. strategy of that period was the rise of economic policies. Under the administration of George H.W. Bush the tightening of *Embargo* took place. At the same time, in this period the U.S. continued to support the 'Cuban dissidence'. Finally, in this very moment Helms-Burton Act or the Cuban Liberty and Democratic Solidarity (LIBERTAD) Act was enacted, which tried to organise Cuban transitional process to capitalism (Agee 2003; Domínguez and Hernández 1989). However, it must be noticed that the U.S. government and the CIA[10] continued to support the armed siege and creation of organisations.

All this development of terrorist activities in the U.S. and around the world shows us the strong relationship between the State and the extreme right-wing organisations. Once more we find constant tension between the exercise of terrorism, complicity and, at the same time, the possibility of a radical break with it. In that sense, we must notice that the exercise of terrorism occurs mainly from the perspective of what was earlier called 'Reactive terrorism' and clearly within the State support. Reactive terrorism has its effect on the U.S. politics since terrorism is not against the U.S. but rather against other States. Similarly, from the imperialist perspective, terrorism is brought against a state that challenges U.S. hegemony. This phenomenon explains the laxity with which the U.S. moves to act against right-wing terrorism but, at the same time, it explains why they support counter-revolutionary terrorism. That is, with the support of counter-revolutionary organisations and dissent, it seems that it is the Cubans who are articulating terrorists and armed actions in pursuit of the 'power that was taken', a power that has always been shared with the U.S.

However, when we study the case of terrorism in PR we will notice that there is another turn in the configuration of discourse. In this case, it no longer tries to regain power, but rather to stand aloof from a mobilisation that challenges colonial, class and privilege structures. Therefore, we can argue that Cuban and Puerto Rican right-wing organisations fall into the sphere of 'Vigilante terrorism' but not necessarily into 'Reactive terrorism'. However, in this context definitions are not important but rather the alliances and dialogues between the state and the extreme right-wing movements and how this shaped a new phenomenon with the same actors. At the same time, this element will provide a set of important strategies of actions against the counter-hegemonic and anti-colonial movements for the post 9/11 era. That is, while in the case of Cuba we see an attack against one State and its supporters; in the next section we will see a joint attack against a movement and its members.

---

[10] Some examples of the organisations that emerge in the 1990s are: F-4 Commands and; Democracy Movement.

12.2 Cuban Exiles in PR and the Development of State and Right-Wing Terrorism

As I have previously showed, the relationship between the U.S. government, the CIA, the FBI and the Cuban extreme right wing has been broadly discussed by different scholars from different perspectives. However, literature on this relationship in the case of Puerto Rican is limited. I have identified some articles that, to some extent, address the relationship among Puerto Rican and Cuban extreme right wing, the U.S. and PR government as regards the exercise of terrorism against Puerto Rican independence movements (Álzaga 2009a, b; Torres Rivera 2007). Similarly, there are some texts that address the process of repression and criminalisation of Puerto Rican independence movements (Atiles-Osoria 2009; forthcoming 2012; Nieves Falcón 2009; Paralitici 2011). Also, there are some organisations such as 'Commission for Truth and Justice' which try to develop a project of Historical Memory.[11] Thus, from what seems to be a puzzle of information, I intend to construct a narrative that tries to challenge the existing silence as regards extreme right wing and state terrorism in Puerto Rican colonial case.

Hypotheses about the reason for this silence or theoretical void –on the relationship between the State and extreme right wing as regards acts of terrorism in PR– could be multiple and diverse. However, I will argue that in order to overcome the simplistic understanding of the Puerto Rican situation, attention should be paid to the fact that PR has been a U.S. colony for 114 years, and; what is more problematic, it has been 'administrated' under a permanent State of Exception (Atiles-Osoria 2009; Forthcoming 2012). The implementation of this legal and political figure in PR comprises three strategies: firstly, the criminalisation of the independence movements; secondly the use of Law and Rule of Law as a strategy to de-mobilise independence movements and legitimate colonial violence; thirdly the use of political violence and State terrorism against independence movements.

This colonial condition has made this political conflict a highly polarised one. Broadly speaking, society is divided into various socio-political groups and spheres of influence. Given this context, by spheres of influence we are referring to the colonial state of the U.S., the colonised state of PR, civil society and the church. For the classification of social political groups, I shall propose three: those who advocate for the total annexation to the U.S.; those who support the status quo or a kind of Free Associated State with more autonomy; and those who advocate for the independence of the Island. Naturally, within these three groups there are multiples positioning, division, clashes of interests and conflict.

In what follows, rather than presenting the complete Puerto Rican colonial history, I am interested in the configuration of such history since the Cuban revolution, the strategical alliances between both the U.S. and PR government and the Cuban and Puerto Rican right wing organisations to thwart the progress of the Puerto Rican

[11] See the web page: http://www.verdadyjusticia.net/ (accessed August 3, 2011).

independence movements. In that sense, I will neither consider the events of State Terrorism, what Poynting and Whyte (Forthcoming 2012) have called 'counter-terrorism terrorism' nor the governments of the U.S. and PR prior to 1959 or after 1990. The fundamental focus of my analysis will be the period from 1960s to 1990s when Cuban exiles played a central role in the development of the extreme right-wing terrorism in PR.

It is important to underscore that these three decades I have studied represent the period of highest mobilisation of the independence movements, and therefore, the decades of largest repression against them. In 1958 the mobilisation called 'New Struggle for Puerto Rican Independence' emerged. This mobilisation was the articulation of the nationalist tradition developed in the first half of the twentieth century and the adoption of other strategies and policy proposals circulating around the world, for instance: Latin American tradition, socialism, anti-colonialism, the clandestine armed struggle, syndicalism, among others. Likewise, the Cuban revolution and the new model of struggle in politics had its effects on PR. That is, during this period Puerto Rican independence movements attempted to articulate all levels of mobilisation for the self-determination and decolonisation of PR. In this context of progress in the struggle for the Puerto Rican independence, the U.S. and PR government and Puerto Rican and Cuban extreme right wing were expected to mobilise against them.

The way the U.S. and PR governments countered the rise of independence movements was not only – as it will be discussed below – by way of political violence, state terrorism and support of extreme right wing terrorism, but also by developing several surveillance programmes and emergency laws to participate in independence movements. In the case of the U.S., this process was articulated by the FBI and it was called COINTELPRO; whereas the PR government called this programme '*Carpeteo*' (Bosques Pérez and Colón Morera 1997). Both programmes consisted in creating a 'list of subversive people and movements', infiltrating independence movements, psychological war, distortion of information, creating tension between the movements and its followers as a strategy to avoid the configuration of a unitary project. This process of surveillance and infiltration served as a precedent for the exercise of political violence and, more specifically, state and extreme right wing terrorism against these 'subversive' individuals and movements that 'threat the national security'. As it will be discussed in the following sections, the process of identification and infiltration served to articulate those campaigns against independence movements and their leaders in an effective and well directed way. At the same time, it provided both governments with the necessary symbolic and political legitimacy to criminalise the 'separatists and subversive people'.

12.2.1 Three Decades of Extreme Right-Wing Terrorism in PR

Studies show that between 1960 and 1990 extreme right wing in PR performed 106 acts of terrorism (Álzaga 2009a). These events could be divided into five groups: firstly arson of houses, offices, businesses, headquarters of independence movements as well as the printing and writing centres of *Claridad* newspaper; secondly placement of bombs or explosive devices in these places; thirdly political assassinations; fourthly kidnapping and enforced disappearances; fifthly intimidation and persecution. The vast majority of these actions share the same pattern: impunity. This means that only in rare cases people were prosecuted, imprisoned or even interviewed by a security agency of the U.S. or PR state. How is this relationship articulated? Or even worse, how is it possible that nobody has been prosecuted for these actions? This invisibilisation of the connection and actions of the extreme right wing in PR is outlined by Álzaga in the following lines:

> Two months after the political assassination of Carlos Muñiz Varela, the Superintendent of Puerto Rican Police, Desiderio Cartagena, told the press that "he was not aware of any official information on right-wing terrorism in Puerto Rico". On 2nd May 1979 […] the Secretary of the Department of Justice of Puerto Rico, Miguel Jiménez Muñoz, declared that the so-called "right-wing terrorism exists, but without enough evidence to prosecute anyone or any particular organisation". He also stressed that terrorism was "imported from Miami" and the "seed of terrorism comes from outside". On the other hand, the chief prosecutor at the Puerto Rican Department of Justice, Pedro Fontan Colton, stated that in the country there have been acts which "tend to imply that right-wing terrorism exists in Puerto Rico". (Álzaga 2009a: 2; translation is mine).

As this quote clearly states, from, the existence of the extreme right-wing terrorist acts in PR at the end of the 1970s was insistently and strongly made invisible and, even when it was acknowledged, it was argued that these practices were external to PR. History shows that this was part of the strategies implemented by the U.S. and PR governmental apparatus to cover up the campaigns of political violence and persecution perpetrated against independence movements. One of our interviewee stated that,

> What we have discovered over time was that here since the 60s the state, no matter which party was in power, has always been on the side of the Cuban counter-revolution. In that context, the State has always looked the other way and traditionally they have ignored the terrorist acts of the Cuban counter-revolution. As a matter of fact the big amount of extreme right-wing activities in PR, almost all of them were perpetrated by Cuban exiles and you will see that nobody was prosecuted. This allows me to say they were somewhat tolerant with these terrorist actions.[12]

In this context of tolerance and complicity, there were many organisations of Cuban exiles that were very active in PR during these three decades.[13] Some of the most important ones were identified by Álzaga (2009b) as: Firstly, Cuban National Liberation Front (FNLC)[14] founded in 1973 and composed by three other organisations: Golden Hawks, Abdala and Independent Union Action which Orlando Bosch

---

[12] This is a fragment of the interview done as part of my Ph.D dissertation; translation is mine.

[13] As a telling instance, it is interesting to notice that our interviewee told us that in this period there were many right-wing organisations registered in the Puerto Rican State Department as non-profit organisations. However, the Puerto Rican police argued that there was not such a thing as extreme right-wing terrorism in PR.

[14] FLNC comes from the Spanish *Frente de Liberación Nacional Cubana.*

and Luis Posada Carriles belong to. This organisation would be the one to develop the thesis that, 'Puerto Rico is to be considered 'free territory' and they can place bombs anywhere in so much as the PSP has free reign there' (Álzaga 2009b: 4).[15]

Secondly, the Latin American Anti-Communist Army. Thirdly, the Pedro Luis Boitel Commando. Fourthly, and one of the most important ones, CORU. This organisation was founded on 11th June 1976 in the Dominican Republic and it followed the thesis developed by the FLNC that PR 'is a free territory for placing bombs and for the development of terrorist acts' (Álzaga 2009b: 4). Fifthly, the Commandos Zero. Sixthly, there was Omega 7, which claimed responsibility for the political assassinations of Eulalio Negrín in New Jersey, U.S. in 1979 and the Cuban diplomat Félix García. Seventhly, Friends of Democracy, this organisation was composed mainly by Cuban Exiles from PR. Finally, the JURE[16] or Cuban Revolutionary Union. At the same time, with the development of these terrorist organisations, there was the organisation and publication of the tabloid *La Crónica* (The Chronicle), which played an important role in the propaganda and legitimation of terrorist acts by the Cuban extreme right wing in PR.

In the next section, I shall propose a brief description and analysis of the activities of the Cuban Exiles and Puerto Rican right-wing actions in PR during the pre 9/11 era. To achieve this, I will present different events, moments and situations that signal the connection and articulation of a counter-revolutionary campaign of terror against the independence movements and against those Cubans who distanced themselves from the mainstream position of the Cuban exile community.

12.2.2 The 1960s

Contrary to what happened in the U.S. and Cuba, PR in 1960s did not have a high level of counter-revolutionary and extreme right-wing activity. Broadly speaking, we could point out six events that will establish the pattern of action in the following decades. Firstly, on 19th April 1967 the headquarters of the Pro Independence Movement (henceforth MPI[17]) mission in *Barrio Obrero Santurce* were set on fire. Secondly, on 27th September 1967, a policeman killed a taxi driver after the University Association Pro-Statehood (henceforth APEU[18]) provoking student unrest at the University of Puerto Rico (henceforth UPR). It is important to note that APEU was one of the most important Puerto Rican extreme-right organisations during this studied period. Thirdly, on 7th January 1969 a bomb is placed in the car of the Secretary General of the MPI Juan Mari Bras. Fourthly, on 31st May 1969 an antipersonnel explosive is mailed to the headquarters MPI Río Piedras.

[15] Translation is mine.

[16] JRC comes from the Spanish *Junta Revolucionaria Cubana.*

[17] MPI comes from the Spanish *Movimiento Pro Independencia.*

[18] APEU comes from the Spanish *Asociación Pro Estadidad Universitaria.*

Fifthly, on 7th November 1969 a group of supporters of the New Progressive Party (henceforth PNP[19]), with Senator Juan A. Palerm (PNP Arecibo) tried to attack the MPI and *Claridad* headquarters in Río Piedras causing property damage and several members of MPI wounded. Again, all these actions went unpunished.

These actions established the strategies that will be implemented for those organisations in the next decade. As I will show in the next section, many of these terrorist actions were carried out not to challenge the established system but rather to intimidate important member of independence movements. That is, contrary to what happened in the case of terrorism against Cuba, this is not an attack against the State or people linked to the colonial structure of power, on the contrary, they seek to silence, demobilise or eliminate those subjects who challenge the colonial structure. This element is important as it marks a new configuration of political violence in PR since independence movements not only have to struggle repression, criminalisation and persecution by the governments of PR and the U.S. but during this period they also have to face a new scope of action, right-wing terrorism.

12.2.3 The 1970s

Álzaga (2009a, b) has identified the 1970s as the decade of major intensity in the Cuban exile and Puerto Rican extreme right-wing activities. Given the great amount of paramilitary actions that took place during this period, the author presents three analytical divisions: from 1971 to 1973; from 1974 to 1976 and from 1978 to 1980 (Álzaga 2009a: 3). The author states that in the first period of this decade there were 42 acts of political violence. These actions can be summarised as follows:

> Targeted primarily at newspaper Claridad and the Imprenta Nacional, independence supporter's properties, offices of labour unions and independence political party committees (PS.P. and PIP). In this period firebombs or Molotov cocktails, shooting and placing bombs like "nipple" were mainly used. We could only call high power bombs the one placed to the Cuban exile Alberto Rodríguez Moya on 22nd January 1973, the bomb that destroyed almost the entire fourth floor of the Faculty of Social Studies at the University of Puerto Rico on 11th March 1973 and the powerful bomb outside the basketball game between Cuba and Venezuela in Roberto Clemente Coliseum on 16th September 1973. This marks a transition to a more aggressive and dangerous terrorist activity (Álzaga 2009a: 3; translation is mine).

At the same time that this manifestation of political violence took place, we will see for the very first time the intervention of the U.S., the Puerto Rican Tribunal and the FBI in a right-wing terrorist activity in PR. As regards the role of the Tribunals, in this decade the Cuban exile Luis Fathel Catasu was prosecuted for shooting

[19] PNP comes from the Spanish *Partido Nuevo Progresista*.

the headquarters of the Puerto Rican Independence Party (henceforth PIP[20]). The intervention of the FBI will come later after a powerful bomb exploded on the fourth floor of the Faculty of Social Sciences at the UPR Río Piedras. Although at that time the Puerto Rican right wing organisation APEU and the Progressive Action were suspected to be responsible for this bomb, the investigation never found anyone to accuse formally. This shows that the Rule of Law and Law Enforcement agencies regarded activities of this nature with very little interest.

In the second period above presented, there were 24 terrorist actions. Although in this context there was a reduction in quantity, the quality and the intensity of the actions improved potentially (Álzaga 2009a). Álzaga states that,

> The bombs placed in the Puerto Rican Bar Association, in the Consulates of Argentina, Peru and Venezuela, the one placed in Radio Avance and in the Theatre Modelo of Río Piedras are some examples of the improved aggressive capacity of the right wing in PR. To this we must add the fire in the National Printers, the shooting of the *Claridad* newspaper with 5 wounded people, the bombs placed in PSP political rally in Mayagüez during the commemoration of the birthday of Eugenio Maria de Hostos, with 2 people being killed and 12 wounded. The kidnapping and disappearance of the Nationalist leader Julio Pinto Gandía and the dramatic murder of Santiago "Chagui" Mari Pesquera on 24th March 1976 while his father Juan Mari Bras was the PSP candidate for governor of Puerto Rico. In all these attempts, it is known that the FBI only investigated the attack on the Venezuelan Consulate, which we suspect was the result of pressure from the Consular Corps of the U.S. Department of State in Washington DC for the repeated attacks against diplomatic missions in Puerto Rico. (Álzaga 2009b: 3–4; translation is mine).

It is important to remark that the political assassination of Santiago 'Chagui' Mari Pesquera represents a new stage in the extreme right-wing actions in PR since it was the first political assassination of a son of an independence leader. In that sense, Allard (2010) presents important data to show the relationship and coordination between the CIA, the Cuban exiles and the Puerto Rican right-wing organisations to stop the heyday of the independence movements. He also tries to show that the political assassination of Chagui and the attempts to kill Juan Mari Bras and his eldest son, Raul Mari Pesquera, were all part of a bigger plan to counteract the Puerto Rican Socialist Party (henceforth PSP) mobilisation and its struggle for the independence of Puerto Rico. Allard states,

> Under the convenient pretext of mutual sympathy between fighters for the independence of Puerto Rico and the Cuban Revolution, the U.S. Intelligence Department, in their effort to thwart the legitimate aspirations for independence of the Island, did not hesitate to choose Juan Mari Bras and his family as prime target. Declassified FBI documents show how the United States made the Cuban-American hit men to act with impunity (and in close alliance with Puerto Rican right-wing) in dozens of terrorist attacks against the Puerto Rican independence movement with the purpose of neutralising Puerto Rican independence emergence (Allard 2010: 1; translation is mine).

Naturally, the constant pressure and paramilitary campaigns against the independence movements did nothing but intensify the level of conflict among all parties

[20] PIP comes from the Spanish Partido Independentista Puertorriqueño.

involved in the colonial conflict. In other words, the independence movements not only demanded the clarification of political assassinations and violent acts perpetrated by the right-wing but also developed a series of armed responses against these terrorist campaigns.[21] This element marks the duality of reactions of the U.S. government against political violence. On the one, the U.S. was very tolerant with extreme right-wing actions against independence movements; while on the other side, it was extremely repressive to the point that even today, 30 years later there are Puerto Ricans political prisoners in U.S. prisons.[22]

In the third period there were 32 right-wing actions including many political assassinations. As Álzaga (2009a) states, in this period it is more evident the complicity between Puerto Rican right-wing groups, Cuban exiles, the governments of the U.S. and PR.

> The involvement of right-wing groups formed by Cuban exiles will be present in this period. Documented participation of the U.S. Navy members, although suspected of having participated in terrorist activities before, will be confirmed with the arrest of Lieutenant Alex La Cerda. In this period, it started the practice of carrying out right-wing terrorist activities and attributing them to alleged leftist organisations. As well in this period, it is documented that the Intelligence Division of the Police of Puerto Rico organised and monitored clandestine leftist organisations to conduct terrorist actions (Álzaga 2009a: 6; translation is mine).

About this last element – the creation of alleged clandestine leftist groups– the existence of three of these groups has been documented the Anti-annexationists Patriotic Committee; Armed Revolutionary Command; and Anti-Imperialist Armed Front. The last two groups were organised and directed by the Intelligence Division of the Police of PR and the undercover agent Alejandro González Malavé (Pérez Viera 2000). The same person in charge of the ambush that caused the political assassination of the young independents Arnaldo Dario Rosado and Carlos Enrique Soto Arriví on 25th July 1978 at Cerro Maravilla in Villalba, PR. These political assassinations carried out by the Police of PR, the Intelligence Division and Special Arrests Division marked a new period in the struggle for independence. It is important to note that almost all of those who were involved in this political assassination were prosecuted, with the exception of the corridors of power, for instance, former PR Gov. Carlos Romero Barceló (Pérez Viera 2000).

In this context of repression, political persecution and terrorist activities from Cuban exiles and Puerto Rican extreme right-wing, the assassination of Carlos Muñiz Valera took place. Muñiz Valera was a Cuban exile who began to get closer to the Cuban Revolution. This young man was part of independence movements, he was one of the founders of the *Areito* Journal and the Antonio Maceo Brigade,

---

[21] As Álzaga states: 'Several weeks after the bomb on 11th January 1975 in Mayagüez that killed two people and wounded 12, the FALN place a powerful bomb in the French Tavern on Wall Street'. (Álzaga 2009b:5; translation is mine).

[22] The best example is Oscar Lopez who was jailed in 1980 for the "crime" of seditious conspiracy and his relationship with the FALN and today (2012), after 31 years, still in prison and has been repeatedly denied the Parole.

which went to Cuba in 1977 and started (the *Diálogo*) conversations with Cuban government and some groups of exiles in 1978. Later on, Carlos Muñiz together with Raúl Álzaga Manresa and Ricardo Fraga created the travel agency 'Viajes Varadero'. The offices of this agency were shot, tapped, burned and, on several occasions, various explosive devices were placed there.

The research conducted by the 'Commission for Truth and Justice' suggests that these actions against 'Viajes Varadero' and the political assassination of Carlos Muñiz Varela were carried out by Cuban exiles linked to the tabloid '*La Crónica*' and to members of CORU and Omega 7 (Álzaga 2005). Álzaga (2005) provides a detailed and well referenced explanation that shows that the FBI allowed the political assassination to happen, and furthermore, they did nothing to investigate the facts related to the crime. The case remains unresolved to this day (2012) after more than 30 years.

Finally, in the last part of this decade a large quantity of explosives were placed against a number of independence activists. In addition to this, the practice of placing explosive devices in post offices and places belonging to right-wing organisations continued and independence movements continued to be blamed.

12.2.4 The 1980s

The 1980s are characterised by a significant decline in right wing terrorist activities in PR. There is a wide range of plausible reasons, among these we can point out some of them: for instance, the arrest of Alejo Maldonado and his death squad; and the campaigns of the U.S. Security Agencies to stop the mobilisation of both the extreme right-wing and the Puerto Rican independence movements. On the other hand, we might note that in this decade a number of repressive activities against independence movements came to light as well as the involvement of the governments of the U.S. and PR in these activities. An example of this was the first hearing in the Senate of PR on the Cerro Maravilla political assassinations (Pérez Viera 2000), the discovery of the practice of '*Capeteo*' and the eventual dismantling of the Intelligence Division of the Police of Puerto Rico (Bosques Pérez and Colón Morera 1997).

However, in this period, there were some terrorist activities by the organisations mentioned before. Thus the decade begins with the planting of a bomb at the Puerto Rican Bar Association. As Álzaga puts it:

> The organisation claiming this attack was identified as the "Anti-Communist" Alliance […] and were arrested the Navy lieutenant Alex de la Cerda, René Fernández del Valle Cuban militant of Abdala and Roberto Lopez González Vieques gunsmith. This is the third incident in which the FBI was involved and they were prosecuted but technically found innocent by a federal judge' (Álzaga 2009a: 12; translation is mine).

As it could be seen in the quote, once again, the FBI participates in a right wing terrorist action in PR but the suspects are declared 'non guilty'. The main reason for this declaration, resides on the fact that, there was, supposedly, a mishandling of evidence by the FBI. In addition, on 25th January 1980 a bomb was placed in a Vieques Air-Link airplane which was piloted by Raul Mari Pesquera, eldest son of Juan Mari Bras (Álzaga 2009a: 13). Similarly, José Juan Adorno Maldonado and Jorge Zayas Candal are assassinated for allegedly having participated in the ambush of a military in Sabana Seca Naval Base, PR. This armed action –against the U.S. military interests in P.R –was claimed by the independence underground organisations PRTP-EPB-Macheteros[23] OVRP[24] and FARP.[25] Also, in this period Manuel de Jesus Cortez, the PIP candidate who was running for Mayor of *Trujillo Alto* was assassinated. Similarly, in 1986 the activist Orlando Canales Azpietia was kidnapped and murdered. Likewise, Canales was a member of the Antonio Maceo Brigade, and it should be stressed that other Cuban exiles who belonged to this organisation were also killed in this decade (Álzaga 2009a: 13).

Finally, throughout this decade the siege by the FBI and the Cuban exile organisation of some Cuban immigrants who did not share the positions of the extreme right continued. The most emblematic case is perhaps that of Álzaga Manresa, he lived in constant persecution, throughout 1980s and mid-1990s.

> They [the FBI] were continually looking what we were doing. To the point that they even bug my telephone … I had something like a machine to cut paper and they reconstructed the bits of paper to see if they could find something. So they were for ten years looking for us. Well, there is a document that says that we were being watched from an airplane, and says "the plane determined that they left work at such and such hour and they are located somewhere else". There is a report of two planes saying which place we left and which we arrived at.[26]

As shown by this quote, the state continued its surveillance, persecution and its psychological war against the independence movements and even against those individuals struggling to clarify the political assassinations and the terrorist actions of the Puerto Rican State and right-wing organisations. This quote also exemplifies, to some extent, what I have been trying to argue in this chapter, that is, the tension that exists between the protections of civil and human rights and the exercise of State terrorism and tolerance (or complicity) of extreme right-wing terrorism against some citizens. The Puerto Rican case is interesting for two reasons. One reason is the constant tension between the criminalisation of the independence movements and the attempts to eliminate them. The other reason stems from the complex relationship between Cuban exiles and Puerto Rican right-wing organisations and the governments of PR and the U.S.

---

[23] PRTP-EPB-Macheteros comes from the Spanish *Partido Revolucionario de los Trabajadores Puertorriqueños- Ejercito Popular Boricua-Macheteros.*

[24] OVRP comes from the Spanish *Organización de Voluntarios Para la Revolución Puertorriqueña.*

[25] FARP comes from the Spanish *Fuerzas Armadas de Resistencia Popular.*

[26] This is a fragment of the interview done as part of my Ph.D dissertation; translation is mine.

12.3 The Post 9/11 Era and the Consolidation of State and Right-Wing Terrorism in PR

As it has been shown to this point, the development of U.S. and PR State polices and counter-terrorist measures in the pre 9/11era are informed by a lack of consistency in the regulation of the terrorist activities of extreme right-wing in PR. This can be seen when observing the support of the U.S. and PR governments towards counter revolutionary and extreme right wing organisations in PR, Cuba and the U.S. This support has led to the criminalisation of Puerto Rican independence movement, which has resulted in the consolidation of the state of exception as a strategy of colonial governance and domination in PR, on the one hand, and the reduction of the political and social power of the independence movement on the other. This social and political power has been further curtailed by the state terrorism of the last decades. Here we propose a brief description of both socio-political and legal elements and how these have directly affected PR in the post 9/11 era.

In previous works, I have presented how the state of exception and the use of emergency Laws have been implemented in PR as a colonial strategy of administration and domination since the very moment of the U.S. invasion of PR in the 1898 (Atiles-Osoria 2009; forthcoming 2012). This means, the implementation of the state of exception became a norm of colonial domination. It is here that Agamben's (2005) concept of state of exception can be used as an analytical tool to understand the governance strategy of Bush's administration in the aftermath of the terrorist attacks of 11th September 2001. Contrary in PR the configuration and implementation of the State of exception has a long history.

Notwithstanding, the number of practices of repression and criminalisation of the Puerto Rican independence movements that diminished during the 1990s will intensify significantly in the post 9/11 era. More concretely this new wave of state and right-wing terrorism will be manifested in some specific events, which will be listed as follows: firstly, the repressive campaign against the Civil Society and the social movement who struggle for the end of the USNAVY military practices in the Puerto Rican island of Vieques between the years 2001 and 2003; secondly, the political assassination of the independence leader Filiberto Ojeda Ríos by the FBI and the Police of PR on 23rd September 2005 and; finally the repressive operations against the University of Puerto Rico Student Strike between 2010 and 2011(Atiles-Osoria and Whyte 2011).

All these repressive actions were carried out in the name of national security and the apparent threat that Puerto Rican independence movements represent for the states of the U.S. and PR. Thus, the discourse of security has prevailed over the protection of human and civil rights of these citizens. The most telling example of this argumentation was the use of PR state repressive power against the Student Strike above mentioned. The repression was such that the ACLU[27] made a report (ACLU 2011a, b) and the U.S. Department of Justice started an investigation on the

[27] Acronym for America Civil Liberty Union.

violation of civil and political rights in this context. In this scenario, the use of law and the political violence that the state of exception implies have propitiated the criminalisation and the violation of civil and political rights of those actors who struggle for the recognition of some of these rights. Even when this sounds like an oxymoron, this is the colonial reality in almost all cases when social movements struggle for the recognition of their civil and human rights (Santos 2002).[28]

On other hand, as a product of the years of PR and U.S. state repression, persecutions and the deployment of violence exercised by the extreme right-wing, the Puerto Rican independence movements have been severely decimated and criminalized. As a result of the pervasive use of political violence and the concerted mobilisation between the above mentioned actors, it could be argued that they have achieved their aim: the reduction of dissidence and the counter-hegemony. However, in this process the fundamental rights of hundreds of citizens were violated only because of their ideology. This element allowed us to reflect on the constant tensions experimented by the state between the protection of the humans rights and the so called counter-terrorist practices. As presented above, the counter-terrorist practice in the colonial context must be understood as the counter-terrorist terrorism (Poynting and D. Whyte 2012 forthcoming).

Finally, the presence of the Cuban exiles organisations both in PR and in the U.S. had become stronger in the post 9/11era. Generally speaking, this organisation became more powerful in 2001 after Bush administration included Cuba in the list of 'States supporting Global Terrorism' or in the 'Axis of Evil' (Borght and Strawson 2004). This U.S. repressive policy has favoured Cuban exiles organisations and Cuban dissidents inside Cuba have put forth new arguments against the Government of Cuba. At the same time, the U.S. prosecution of the "Cuban Five"[29] shows again the support of the U.S. government to the Cuban exiles organisations. As it has been stated in Lamrani (2005), the Cuban Five case has been intrumentalised by the Cuban exiles organisation and the U.S. government to argue that Cuba is trying to export the revolution to the U.S. and participate to the U.S. sovereignty. However, as many authors (Lamrani 2005; Landau 2005; Petras 2005; Sharma 2005; Smith 2005) have showed, the so called Cuban Five were trying to thwart possible new acts of right wing terrorism against Cuba. In that sense the strategical mobilisation of the U.S. shows the instrumentalisation, of some organisations and political ideologies in favour of the U.S. geopolitical interest in Cuba.

[28] For a good analysis of this phenomenon see Santos (2002).

[29] The Cuban Five make reference to the five Cuban counter-terrorist agents that were arrester in 12th September 1998 in U.S. Gerardo Hernandes, Ramon Labanino, Fernando Gonzalez, Antonio Guerrero and Rene Gonzalez were arrests for "conspiracy to commit espionage". But the reality is, as Sharma (2005) states that they were infiltrate in the Cuban counter-revolutionary and terrorist organisation trying to collect information about the possible new terrorist act against Cuba. For better develop of this argument see Sharma (2005).

12.4 Conclusion

In conclusion, we must think again what the position of the liberal-democratic State towards terrorism should be like. Naturally, this work shows the tension between the articulation of an effective response to the violent political threat and the articulation of a campaign that supports terrorist activities. Similarly, this chapter shows the duality that the so-called terrorist threat confronts. That is, when we analyse the U.S. case and the role played in the Puerto Rican colonial conflict in both pre and post 9/11 eras, we see a campaign of criminalisation, persecution and delegitimation of independence actors who challenge its colonial hegemony. On the other hand, the U.S. state is extremely tolerant with the extreme right-wing exercise of terrorism and Puerto Rican state terrorism against those independence movements.

Hence, the fundamental challenge is not to know how to react to terrorism but rather to know how far the state could make use of its intrinsic violence. That is, to what extent the state acts in an 'imperialistic' way, imposing the systematisation of political violence or tolerating terrorism against those who challenge its hegemony by no-violent methods. In that context, it is not possible to speak of the preservation of human and civil rights neither inside nor outside the State.

Both Cuban and Puerto Rican cases may be the best examples of this constant Imperialistic and Colonial attitude developed by the U.S. On the one hand, the case of Cuba shows the articulation of an imperial programme against the ideological, political, social and economic development of a country that affects the sovereignty of the people and the right to freely choose the destiny of their own country. The support to the Cuban exile organisations in the U.S., the organisation of those by the CIA and FBI and the complicity to the exercise of terrorism against Cuba and against other Cuban émigré in the U.S. show the direct relationship between both State and right-wing exercise of terrorism. At the same time, it denotes the neglected interests of the Rule of Law, Law Enforcement and Tribunals to solve this problem. Thus, law in this case has not played a central role, but rather the use of violence and strategical alliances between state and right-wing organisation to thwart the social and political mobilisations.

On the other hand, the case of Puerto Rico is even more paradigmatic since it is a colonial territory which endures a colonial conflict. In this case, contrary to the case of Cuba, the U.S. is responsible for 'ensuring' the respect of human and civil rights. However, with the benefit of historical hindsight, we can argue that to this day, the U.S. has consistently violated this principle. This indicates that the U.S. government has not showed the least interest in solving or even stopping the terrorist acts committed by the extreme right wing against Puerto Rican independence movements. On the contrary, we have witnessed the articulation of an intricate corpus such as the U.S. government, its security and intelligence agencies, and the government of PR and the extreme right-wing groups. These groups have stood together in an attempt to thwart the Puerto Rican independence movement. In this colonial scenario the Rule of Law has been very effective as it has criminalised and delegitimised the mobilisations for the independence of PR. It has also been effective in setting a tolerance and 'invisibility' campaign towards extreme right-wing terrorism. In this sense, once more we are faced with the old complicity developed during the pre 9/11 era being repeated and recycled in the post 9/11 era.

References

Agamben, G. 2005. *State of exception: Homo sacer II, 1* (trad.: Kelvin Attell). Chicago: University of Chicago.

Agee, P. 2003. Terrorism and civil society as instruments of U.S. policy in Cuba. *Socialism and Democracy* 17(2): 1–25.

Allard, J.G. 2010. Documentos desclasificados demuestran que EEUU usó sicarios para agredir a Cuba y neutralizar el auge independentista en Puerto Rico. http://www.rebelion.org/noticia.php?id=113242.

Álzaga Manresa, R. 2005. El FBI y su complicidad en el encubrimiento del asesinato de Carlos Muñiz Varela. http://www.terrorfileonline.org/es/index.php/Alzaga_Manres.

Álzaga Manresa, R. 2009a. Puerto Rico: Actividades terroristas de Estados Unidos, 1898–2005. http://www.elcorreo.eu.org/?Puerto-RicoActividades-terroristas.

Álzaga Manresa, R. 2009b. Puerto Rico: Terrorismo de derechas la conexión cubano-puertorriqueña. http://www.elcorreo.eu.org/?Puerto-RicoTerrorismo-de-derecha.

American Civil Liberties Union (ACLU). 2011a. *Human right crisis in Puerto Rico* [online]. Available from: http://es.scribd.com/doc/49936611/Informe-Human-Rights-Crisis-in-Puerto-Rico-de-ACLU. Accessed 19 July 2011.

American Civil Liberties Union (ACLU). 2011b. *Preliminary findings of the ACLU human rights documentation research in Puerto Rico* [online]. Available from: http://www.aclu.org/files/assets/puerto_rico_preliminary_findings_6_13_11_final.pdf. Accessed 19 July 2010.

Arguelles, L. 1982. The US national security state: The CIA and Cuban emigré terrorism. *Race and Class* 23: 287.

Atiles-Osoria, J.M. 2009. *Colonialismo, estado de excepción y resistencia: La criminalización de la lucha armada en Puerto Rico.* Thesis MA, IISL, Oñati.

Atiles-Osoria, J.M. 2012. The criminalisation of anti-colonial struggle in Puerto Rico. In *Counter-terrorism and state political violence*, ed. S. Poynting and D. Whyte. London: Routledge. Forthcoming.

Atiles-Osoria, J.M., and D. Whyte. 2011. Counter-insurgency goes to university: The militarisation of policing in the Puerto Rico student strikes. *Journal of Critical Studies on Terrorism* 4(3): 393–404.

Bolender, K. 2010. *Voices from the other side: An oral history of terrorism against Cuba.* New York: Pluto Press.

Borght, K.V.D., and J. Strawson. 2004. Cuba and the axis of evil: An old outlaw in the new order. In *Law after ground zero*, ed. J. Strawson. London: Glasshouse Press.

Bosques Pérez, R., and J. Colón Morera (eds.). 1997. *Las carpetas: derechos civiles y persecución política en Puerto Rico*. Río Piedras: CIPDC.

Chayes, A. 1974. *The Cuban missile crisis*. London: Oxford University Press.

Chomsky, N. 2005. Cuba and United States: A near-half century of terror. In *Superpower principle: U.S. terrorism against Cuba*, ed. S. Lamrani. Maine: Common Courage Press.

Cripps, L.L. 1979. *The Spanish Caribbean: From Columbus to Castro*. Cambridge, MA: Schenkman Publishing.

Domínguez, J.I., and R. Hernández. 1989. *The U.S.-Cuban relations in the 1990s*. London: Westview Press.

Douglas, R.G. 2005. *Being successfully nasty: The United States, Cuba and state sponsored terrorism, 1959–1976.* Thesis MA, University of Victoria.

Duany, J. 2005. La migración cubana: Tendencias actuales y proyecciones [Cuban migration: Current trends and projections]. *Encuentro de la Cultura Cubana* 36: 164–179.
Duany, J., and J.A. Cobas. 1995. *Los cubanos en Puerto Rico: Economía étnica e identidad cultural*. Río Piedras: Editorial de la Universidad de Puerto Rico.
Franklin, J. 1992. *The Cuban revolution and the United States: A chronological history*. Melbourne: Ocean Press.
García, M.C. 1996. *Havana USA: Cuban exiles and Cuban Americans in South Florida, 1959–1994*. Berkeley: University of California Press.
Hernández, J.M. 1993. *Cuba and the United States: Intervention and militarism, 1868–1933*. Austin: University of Texas Press.
Hinckle, W., and W. Turner. 1981. *The fish is red: The story of the secret war against Castro*. New York: Harper & Row Publishers.
Jackson, R. 2008. The ghosts of state terror: Knowledge, politics and terrorism studies. *Journal of Critical Studies on Terrorism* 1(3): 377–392.
Jackson, R., et al. 2011. *Terrorism: A critical introduction*. New York: Palgrave and Macmillan.
Johnson, H.B. 1965. *The Bay of Pigs: The invasion of Cuba by Brigade 2506*. London: Hutchinson.
Kapcia, A. 2008. *Cuba in revolution: A history since the fifties*. London: Reaktion Books.
Lamrani, S. (ed.). 2005. *Superpower principle: U.S. terrorism against Cuba*. Maine: Common Courage Press.
Landau, S. 2005. Five Cubans in prison-victims of Bush's obsession. In *Superpower principle: U.S. terrorism against Cuba*, ed. S. Lamrani. Maine: Common Courage Press.
Lievesley, G. 2004. *The Cuban revolution: Past, present and future perspectives*. New York: Palgrave and Macmillan.
Martínez-San Miguel, Y. 2007. Puerto Rican Cubanness. Reconfiguring Caribbean imaginaries. In *Cuba: Idea of a nation displaced*, ed. A. O'Relly Herrera. New York: State University of New York.
Morley, M.H. 1987. *Imperial state and revolution: The United States and Cuba, 1952–1986*. Cambridge: Cambridge University Press.
Nieves Falcón, L. 2009. *Un siglo de represión política en Puerto Rico 1898–1998*. San Juan: Ediciones Puerto.
Paralitici, J.C. 2011. *La represión contra el independentismo puertorriqueño: 1960–2010*. Cayey: Publicaciones Gaviota.
Pedahzur, A. 2001. Struggling with the challenges of right-wing extremism and terrorism within democratic boundaries: A comparative analysis. *Studies in Conflict & Terrorism* 24: 339–359.
Pérez, L.A. 1986. *Cuba under the Platt Amendment, 1902–1934*. Pittsburgh: University of Pittsburgh Press.
Pérez Viera, E. 2000. *El juicio de la historia: Contrainsurgencia y asesinato político en Puerto Rico*. San Juan: Editorial Cultural.
Petras, J. 2005. The Cuban five: Nominees for the Nobel peace prize. In *Superpower Principle: U.S. Terrorism Against Cuba*, ed. S. Lamrani. Maine: Common Courage Press.
Poynting, S., and D. Whyte, eds. 2012. *Counter-terrorism and state political violence*. London: Routledge. Forthcoming.
Quesada, A. 2009. *The Bay of Pigs Cuba, 1961*. Oxford: Osprey Publishing.
Richmond, O.P., and J. Franks. 2009. The impact of orthodox terrorism discourses on the liberal peace: Internalisation, resistance, or hybridisation? *Journal of Critical Studies on Terrorism* 2(2): 201–218.
Santos, B.S. 2002. *Toward a new legal common sense: Law, globalization and emancipation*. London: Butterworths and LexisNexis.
Sharma, J. 2005. Real fighters against terrorism. In *Superpower principle: U.S. terrorism against Cuba*, ed. S. Lamrani. Maine: Common Courage Press.
Smith, M.S. 2005. A tale of two law suits. In *Superpower principle: U.S. terrorism against Cuba*, ed. S. Lamrani. Maine: Common Courage Press.
Sprinzak, E. 1995. Right-wing terrorism in a comparative perspective: The case of split delegitimization. *Terrorism and Political Violence* 7(1): 17–43.

Torres Rivera, A. 2007. *Apuntes generales sobre la represión en Puerto Rico en las pasadas tres décadas*. http://www.defensahumanidad.cu/artic.php?item=5070.

Welch, R.E. 1985. *Response to revolution: The United States and the Cuban revolution: 1959–1961*. Chapel Hill: University of North Carolina Press.

Wilkinson, P. 1986. *Terrorism and the liberal state*. London: Macmillan.

Zinn, W. 2005. The roots of United States policy toward Cuba. In *Superpower principle: U.S. terrorism against Cuba*, ed. S. Lamrani. Maine: Common Courage Press.

Part IV
Counter-Terrorism from an International-Law Perspective

Chapter 13
Permanent Legal Emergencies and the Derogation Clause in International Human Rights Treaties: A Contradiction?

Christopher Michaelsen

13.1 Introduction

A decade after the 9/11 attacks, international terrorism is considered by many to remain a significant threat in the years to come.[1] It is thus unsurprising that many governments continue to adopt new legislation to respond to the perceived threat, or, in many cases, extend existing laws. Indeed, over the last 10 years, most countries around the world have enacted specific anti-terrorism legislation. In many instances these laws were initially introduced as temporary legislation, often containing sunset clauses requiring parliamentary renewal after a specified timeframe. Yet, despite their extraordinary and temporary character, anti-terrorism laws have now become a permanent feature of the legislative landscape of most states. What is more, many of these laws continue to raise serious concerns in relation to their impact on human rights and the rule of law. As the Eminent Jurists Panel on Terrorism, Counter-Terrorism and Human Rights, an independent body of experts convened by the International Commission of Jurists, has observed in a major report in 2009:

> Many States have fallen into a trap set by the terrorists. Ignoring lessons from the past, they have allowed themselves to be rushed into hasty responses, introducing an array of measures which undermine cherished values as well as the international legal framework carefully developed since the Second World War. These measures have resulted in human rights violations, including torture, enforced disappearances, secret and arbitrary detentions, and unfair trials.[2]

[1] See, e.g.: P. R. Neumann, *Old and New Terrorism* (Cambridge: Polity Press, 2009); M. Sageman, *Leaderless Jihad: Terror Networks in the Twenty-first Century* (Philadelphia: University of Pennsylvania Press, 2008); G. T. Allison, *Nuclear Terrorism: The Ultimate Preventable Catastrophe* (New York: Times Books/Henry Holt, 2004).

[2] *Assessing Damage, Urging Action*, Report of the Eminent Jurists Panel on Terrorism, Counter-Terrorism and Human Rights, International Commission of Jurists, Geneva, 2009, at 2.

C. Michaelsen (✉)
Faculty of Law, University of New South Wales,
Sydney, NSW 2052, Australia
e-mail: c.michaelsen@unsw.edu.au

A. Masferrer (ed.), *Post 9/11 and the State of Permanent Legal Emergency*,
Ius Gentium: Comparative Perspectives on Law and Justice 14,
DOI 10.1007/978-94-007-4062-4_13,

The question of how to reconcile the interests of 'security' and human rights while countering terrorism has been a central feature of the discourse on the response to the 9/11 and subsequent attacks. On one side the claim is made by those defending incursive counter-measures that terrorists regard liberal democracy itself as the enemy. The unprecedented threat to 'our way of life', therefore, warranted restrictions of civil liberties and human rights. It was imperative to make sure that the very mechanisms protecting the individual from excessive state power did not hamper the government's ability to respond effectively to the threat. In fact, protections like the constitutional Bill of Rights of the United States, for instance, did not, after all, constitute a 'suicide pact'.[3] Civil liberties and human rights, so the argument ran, were political conveniences for enjoyment in times of peace.[4] They should not, however, constitute restraining yardsticks for government in times of emergency and national danger.

On the other side scholars maintain that it is particularly in times of crisis that the liberal democratic state must adhere strictly to its defining principles.[5] Rights would lose all effect if they were easily revocable in situations of necessity. Besides, to believe that restricting human rights and civil liberties was a prerequisite for maintaining security was to put oneself on the same moral plane as the terrorists for whom the end justified the means. When the end justifies the means, however, the 'difference between terror and those fighting it, becomes increasingly indistinct'.[6] Indeed, sacrificing fundamental liberal values such as the respect for the rule of law, civil liberties and human rights would amount to losing the 'war on terrorism without firing a single shot'.[7]

At the international level, the response to international terrorism in the wake of 9/11 has been mainly driven by the United Nations Security Council. Immediately

---

[3]See, e.g., J. Alter, "Time to Think About Torture," *Newsweek* 138 (2001): 45, quoting U.S. Supreme Court Justice Robert Jackson in *Terminiello v City of Chicago* (1949): 'There is the danger that, if the court does not temper its doctrinaire logic with a little practical wisdom, it will convert the constitutional Bill of Rights into a suicide pact'; 337 U.S. 1, 13 (1949) (Jackson, J, dissenting).

[4]See, e.g.: R. A. Posner, "Security Versus Civil Liberties," *The Atlantic Monthly* 288 (2001): 46; V. D. Dinh, "Freedom and Security after September 11," *Harvard Journal of Law and Public Policy* 25 (2002): 399.

[5]See, e.g.: D. Cole and J. X. Dempsey, *Terrorism and the Constitution: Sacrificing Civil Liberties in the Name of National Security* (Los Angeles: The New Press, 2002); see also: C. Brown, *Lost Liberties: Ashcroft and the Assault on Personal Freedom* (New York: The New Press, 2003).

[6]E. Gross, "Legal Aspects of Tackling Terrorism: The Balance Between the Right of a Democracy to Defend Itself and the Protection of Human Rights," *UCLA Journal of International Law & Foreign Affairs* 6 (2001): 167–168.

[7]See, e.g.: the statement by Wisconsin democrat Russell Feingold, the only US senator to vote against the USA Patriot Act, who has pointed out at the time that '[p]reserving our freedom is one of the main reasons we are now engaged in this new war on terrorism. We will lose that war without firing a shot if we sacrifice the liberties of the American people'. Senator Russell Feingold (D–WI), Statement on the Anti-Terrorism Bill, U.S. Senate, 25 October 2001. See also: UN Secretary-General Kofi Annan, Statement to Conference 'Fighting Terrorism for Humanity: A Conference on the Roots of Evil', 22 September 2003.

after the attacks on New York and Washington, the Council adopted resolution 1373 (2001) calling, *inter alia*, on UN member states to 'ensure that any person who participates in the financing, planning, preparation or perpetration of terrorist acts or in supporting terrorist acts is brought to justice and ensure that, in addition to any other measures against them, such terrorist acts are established as serious criminal offences in domestic laws and regulations and that the punishment duly reflects the seriousness of such terrorist acts'.[8] Resolution 1373, however, was also distinctive for lacking references to the need to develop counter-terrorism laws and policy in conformity with international human rights standards.[9] Indeed, it was only in 2003, in resolution 1456, that the Security Council called on UN member states to 'ensure that any measures taken to combat terrorism comply with all their obligations under international law, in particular international human rights, refugee, and humanitarian law'.[10]

In light of the approach taken by the Security Council – an approach that prioritises 'security' over human rights – it is perhaps unsurprising that many states have seemingly paid little attention to their obligations under international human rights law when devising domestic anti-terrorism laws in the aftermath of 9/11.[11] Indeed, human rights obligations were often considered impediments to developing successful counter-terrorism policies. And this in spite of the fact that the major international human rights treaties expressly provide for the limitation of rights as well as the possibility to derogate from certain obligations in times of emergency.[12] Yet, over the last decade, only a very limited number of states have officially made use of those derogation clauses. A prominent exception to this trend was the United Kingdom which, in late 2001, derogated from obligations under both the European Convention on Human Rights (ECHR) and the International Covenant on Civil and Political Rights (ICCPR).

The aim of this chapter is to undertake an analysis of the derogation provisions in the international human rights treaties such as the ECHR, ICCPR as well as the American Convention on Human Rights (ACHR) and to assess whether these clauses remain adequate in an era of international terrorism. To this end, the chapter will first provide an overview of the derogation clauses and relevant interpretations and case law which has developed on the issue before 9/11. It will then examine the derogation rules in post 9/11 case law. In particular, the analysis will critically

[8] U.N. SCOR, U.N. Doc. S/RES/1373 (2001), at para. 2 (e).

[9] There is only a passing reference to human rights in para. 3 (f) of the resolution which concerns the granting of refugee status to asylum-seekers.

[10] U.N. SCOR, U.N. Doc. S/RES/1456 (2003), at para. 6.

[11] See, e.g.: C. Michaelsen, "International Human Rights on Trial: The United Kingdom's and Australia's Legal Response to 9/11," *Sydney Law Review* 25 (2003): 275–303.

[12] Derogations under international human rights law can be distinguished from similar mechanisms in domestic (constitutional) law. For a discussion of domestic derogations in U.S. and Canadian law, se, e.g.: K. Roach, "Ordinary Laws for Emergencies and Democratic Derogations from Rights," in *Emergencies and the Limits of Legality*, ed. V. V. Ramraj (Cambridge: Cambridge University Press, 2008).

review the 2004 *Belmarsh detainees* decision of the House of Lords and the subsequent 2009 judgment on the same matter of the European Court of Human Rights in Strasbourg.[13] The final part of this chapter will provide a critique of the derogation clauses and question their role in the context of a state of permanent legal emergency.

13.2 The International Treaty Rules on Derogation

The International Covenant on Civil and Political Rights as well as the European and American Conventions on Human Rights contain a derogation clause with specific standards for emergencies.[14] While the State parties may not derogate from the entire treaty, they may legally suspend their obligation to respect and enforce specific rights contained in the respective convention during times of war or other public emergency. Article 15 of the ECHR, for instance, provides that:

1. In time of war or other public emergency threatening the life of the nation any High Contracting Party may take measures derogating from its obligations under this Convention to the extent strictly required by the exigencies of the situation, provided that such measures are not inconsistent with other obligations under international law.
2. No derogations from Article 2, except in respect of deaths resulting from lawful acts of war, or from Articles 3, 4 (paragraph 1) and 7 shall be made under this provision.
3. Any High Contracting Party availing itself of this right of derogation shall keep the Secretary General of the Council of Europe fully informed of the measures which it has taken and the reasons therefor. It shall also inform the Secretary General of the Council of Europe when such measures have ceased to operate and the provisions of the Convention are again being fully executed.

Article 4 of the ICCPR reads:

1. In time of public emergency which threatens the life of the nation and the existence of which is officially proclaimed, the States Parties to the present Convenant may take measures derogating from their obligations under the present Covenant to the extent strictly required by the exigencies of the situation, provided that such measures are not inconsistent with their other obligations under international law and do not involve discrimination solely on the ground of race, colour, sex, language, religion or social origin.

---

[13] *A and others v. Secretary of State for the Home Department*, [2004] UKHL 56; [2005] 2 W.L.R. 87; *A and others v United Kingdom*, App 3455/05 (19 February 2009), (2009) 49 EHRR 29.

[14] See generally: R. Higgins, "Derogations under Human Rights Treaties," *The British Yearbook of International Law* 48 (1976–77): 281; T. Buergenthal, "To Respect and to Ensure: State Obligations and Permissible Derogations," in *The International Bill of Rights: The Covenant on Civil and Political Rights*, ed. L. Henkin (New York: Columbia University Press, 1981), 72; J. F. Hartman, "Working Paper for the Committee of Experts on the Article 4 Derogation Provision," *Human Rights Quarterly* 7 (1985): 89; D. J. Harris, M. O'Boyle, and C. Warbrick, *Law of the European Convention on Human Rights* (London: Butterworths, 1995) at 489–507; A. -L. Svensson-McCarthy, *The International Law of Human Rights and States of Exception: With Special Reference to Travaux Préparatoires and Case-Law of the International Monitoring Organs* (Dordrecht/Boston: Martinus Nijhoff, 1998).

2. No derogation from Articles 6, 7, 8 (paragraphs 1 and 2), 11, 15, 16 and 18 may be made under this provision.
3. Any State Party to the present Covenant availing itself of the right of derogation shall immediately inform the other State Parties to the present Covenant, through the intermediary of the Secretary–General of the United Nations, of the provisions from which it has derogated and of the reasons by which it was actuated. A further communication shall be made, through the same intermediary, on the date on which it terminates such derogation.

Similarly, Article 27 of the ACHR provides that:

1. In time of war, public danger, or other emergency that threatens the independence or security of a State Party, it may take measures derogating from its obligations under the present Convention to the extent and for the period of time strictly required by the exigencies of the situation, provided that such measures are not inconsistent with its other obligations under international law and do not involve discrimination on the ground of race, color, sex, language, religion, or social origin.
2. The foregoing provision does not authorize any suspension of the following articles: Article 3 (Right to Juridical Personality), Article 4 (Right to Life), Article 5 (Right to Humane Treatment), Article 6 (Freedom from Slavery), Article 9 (Freedom from Ex Post Facto Laws), Article 12 (Freedom of Conscience and Religion), Article 17 (Rights of the Family), Article 18 (Right to a Name), Article 19 (Rights of the Child), Article 20 (Right to Nationality), and Article 23 (Right to Participate in Government), or of the judicial guarantees essential for the protection of such rights.
3. Any State Party availing itself of the right of suspension shall immediately inform the other States Parties, through the Secretary General of the Organization of American States, of the provisions the application of which it has suspended, the reasons that gave rise to the suspension, and the date set for the termination of such suspension.

Article 15 of the ECHR thus closely resembles Article 4 of the ICCPR. Article 27 of the ACHR, on the other hand, uses slightly different terminology. In contrast to the ECHR and ICCPR formulation which requires a 'public emergency threatening the life of the nation', the ACHR allows for derogation in 'time of war, public danger, or other emergency that threatens the independence or security of a State Party'. However, as Anna-Lena Svensson-McCarthy has observed, the distinctive terminology in the ACHR was most likely chosen to better reflect the emergency terms used in the various constitutions of the American states.[15]

What all three derogation clauses have in common is the fact that they essentially require a derogating state to satisfy two tests. First, the derogating state is required to establish that exceptional circumstances of war or other public emergency do in fact prevail. Second, the derogating state is required to establish that measures taken in consequence of such an emergency are 'strictly required by the exigencies of the situation'. Stephen Tierney has usefully referred to these two steps as the '*designation* issue' and the '*interference* issue'.[16] This terminology will be adopted in the present analysis which predominantly focuses on the ECHR and the ICCPR. In particular, the present chapter focuses on the jurisprudence of the

[15] Svensson-McCarthy, *The International Law of Human Rights and States of Exception*, at 281.

[16] S. Tierney, "Determining the State of Exception: What Role for Parliament and the Courts?," *Modern Law Review* 68 (2005): 668.

European Court of Human Rights. Nevertheless, in light of the fact that the Strasbourg Court tends to examine Article 15 of the ECHR in its natural and common sense (as required by principles of treaty interpretation), and given that many provisions in the ICCPR and ECHR are similar, in particular the derogation clauses, European decisions and findings are relevant to ICCPR cases, and, to lesser extent, in the context of the ACHR as well.

13.2.1 The Designation of a 'Public Emergency'

As to the *designation* issue, the ECHR and the ICCPR both lack a specific definition of a 'public emergency threatening the life of the nation'. Nevertheless, the international monitoring organs established under the treaties, notably the European Court of Human Rights (and previously the European Commission of Human Rights), have interpreted the term and provided jurisprudence valuable for determining its meaning and scope.

The first substantive interpretation of Article 15 of the ECHR was made in the 1961 case of *Lawless v Ireland* which concerned the extrajudicial detention of the applicant from July to December 1957[17] Confirming the determination of European Commission of Human Rights that Article 15 should be interpreted in the light of its 'natural and customary' meaning, the Strasbourg Court defined 'time of public emergency' as 'an exceptional situation of crisis or emergency which afflicts the whole population and constitutes a threat to the organised life of the community of which the community is composed'.[18] The Court found that there was a public emergency due to the existence in Ireland 'of a secret army engaged in unconstitutional activities and using violence to attain its purposes'.[19] The fact that this army was also operating outside its territory seriously jeopardised the relations between Ireland and the United Kingdom.[20] The existence of the emergency was also evidenced by the 'steady and alarming increase in terrorist activities from the autumn of 1956 and throughout the first half of 1957'.[21]

The definition was further developed and clarified in the *Greek Case* of 1969.[22] The case concerned an application against Greece following the *coup d'état* in April 1967. In the wake of the *coup*, the Greek government declared a state of siege and suspended a number of articles of the Greek constitution and various

[17] *Lawless v Ireland* (No 3) (1961) 1 EHRR 15.

[18] *Ibidem* at para. 31.

[19] *Ibidem* at para. 28.

[20] *Ibidem*.

[21] *Ibidem*.

[22] *Greek* Case (1969) 12 Yearbook ECHR 1.

human rights guarantees. The Commission, however, rejected the argument that there was a public emergency within the meaning of Article 15 (1) of the ECHR. Reaffirming the basic elements of the Court's approach in *Lawless*, the Commission emphasised that the emergency must be actual or at least 'imminent', a notion that is present in the Merits judgment in French (authentic version) but not in the English version.[23] In order to constitute an Article 15 emergency, the Commission held that a 'public emergency' must have the following four characteristics[24]:

- It must be actual or imminent.
- Its effects must involve the whole nation.
- The continuance of the organised life of the community must be threatened.[25]
- The crisis or danger must be exceptional, in that the normal measures or restrictions, permitted by the Convention for the maintenance of public safety, health and order, are plainly inadequate.

In the 1978 case of *Ireland v United Kingdom*, the Commission and the Court followed the standards identified in *Lawless* and the *Greek Case* and held that the Article 15 test was satisfied, since terrorism had for a number of years (1971–1975) represented 'a particularly far-reaching and acute danger for the territorial integrity of the United Kingdom, the institutions of the six counties and the lives of the province's inhabitants'.[26] In fact, 'the degree of violence, with bombing, shooting and rioting was on a scale far beyond what could be called minor civil disorder'.[27] The Court reached similar conclusions as regards the continuing security situation in Northern Ireland in the 1993 case of *Brannigan and McBride v United Kingdom.*[28] In the 1996 case of *Aksoy v Turkey*, it accepted that Kurdish separatist violence had given rise to a "public emergency" in Turkey.[29] In neither of these latter cases did the Court develop the Article 15 standards further but merely referred to them as developed in its earlier decisions.

The Human Rights Committee's case law on the issue is rather scarce. In proceedings under the Optional Protocol, the Committee considered the possibility of the existence of a public emergency in the communications *of Landinella Silva v*

[23] The relevant part of the Merits judgment in French reads: 'Une situation de crise ou de danger public exceptionnelle et imminente'.

[24] *Greek* Case, para 153.

[25] Some members of the Commission argued that when the organs of the State are functioning normally, there is no grave threat to the life of the nation and, therefore, emergency measures are not legitimate. However, the majority in the Commission did not follow this reasoning.

[26] *Ireland v United Kingdom* (1978) Series A No 35, at paras. 205 and 212.

[27] *Ireland v United Kingdom*, App 5310/71, ECtHR, Series B, Vol. 23-I (1976–1978), at 117.

[28] *Brannigan and McBride v United Kingdom*, (1993) 17 EHRR 539.

[29] *Aksoy v Turkey*, App 21987/93 (18 December 1996), (1997) 23 EHRR 553, paras. 67–70.

Uruguay, *Weinberger v Uruguay* and *Salgar de Montejo v Colombia*.[30] The Committee found that a public emergency did not exist in any of these cases but, at the same time, did not provide a substantive interpretation of the meaning of the term. However, in 2001, it issued General Comment 29 on Article 4 of the ICCPR.[31] In this Comment, the Committee held that two fundamental conditions must be met before a state can lawfully derogate: 'the situation must amount to a public emergency which threatens the life of the nation, and the State party must have officially proclaimed a state of emergency'.[32] It also stated that 'not every disturbance or catastrophe qualifies as a public emergency which threatens the life of the nation'.[33] Furthermore, any measures derogating from the provisions of the ICCPR needed to be of an 'exceptional and *temporary* nature'.[34]

The definition and scope of 'public emergency' was also the subject of the work of the International Law Association (ILA) as well as of a group of 31 international experts who convened in Siracusa, Italy, in 1984 to formulate a list of principles concerning the limitation and derogation provisions in the ICCPR. The ILA adopted the 'Paris Minimum Standards of Human Rights Norms in a State of Emergency' which contain the following prescription[35]:

> (a) The existence of a public emergency which threatens the life of the nation, and which is officially proclaimed, will justify the declaration of a state of emergency.
> (b) The expression "public emergency" means an exceptional situation of crisis or public danger, actual or imminent, which affects the whole population or the whole population of the area to which the declaration applies and constitutes a threat to the organized life of the community of which the state is composed.

Similarly, Principles 39–41 of the 'Siracusa Principles on the Limitation and Derogation Provisions in the International Covenant on Civil and Political Rights' prescribe the concept of "public emergency" as follows[36]:

> 39. A state party may take measures derogating from its obligations under the International Covenant on Civil and Political Rights pursuant to Article 4 (hereinafter called "derogation measures") only when faced with a situation of exceptional and actual or imminent danger which threatens the life of the nation. A threat to the life of the nation is one that:
>
> (a) affects the whole of the population and either the whole or part of the territory of the State, and

---

[30] *Landinelli Silva v Uruguay* (1981) HRC Comm No 34/1978; *Weinberger v Uruguay* (1980) HRC Comm No 28/1978; *Salgar de Montejo v Colombia* (1982) HRC Comm No 64/1979.

[31] Human Rights Committee, *General Comment 29, States of Emergency* (Article 4), U.N. Doc. CCPR/C/21/Rev.1/Add.11 (2001).

[32] *Ibidem* at para. 2.

[33] *Ibidem* at para. 3.

[34] *Ibidem* at para. 2. Emphasis added.

[35] "The Paris Minimum Standards of Human Rights Norms in a State of Emergency," *American Journal of International Law* 79 (1985): 1072.

[36] "Siracusa Principles on the Limitation and Derogation Provisions in the International Covenant on Civil and Political Rights," *Human Rights Quarterly* 7 (1985): 3.

(b) threatens the physical integrity of the population, the political independence or the territorial integrity of the State or the existence or basic functioning of institutions indispensable to ensure and project the rights recognized in the Covenant.

40. Internal conflict and unrest that do not constitute a grave and imminent threat to the life of the nation cannot justify derogations under Article 4.
41. Economic difficulties per se cannot justify derogation measures.

As Oren Gross and Fionnuala Ni Aoláin have observed, these definitions can be seen as evidence for a broad international consensus on the general contours of the term 'public emergency threatening the life of the nation', particularly with respect to its contingent and exceptional nature.[37] For Gross and Ni Aoláin they 'accentuate the capacity for definitional agreement and the possibility for meaningful and robust oversight and accountability by law over claims of "public emergency"'.[38] At the same time, it is important to note that there are differences in nuance and emphasis. Most important in this regard, perhaps, is the fact that the Human Rights Committee requires the public emergency to be 'temporary'. The Strasbourg Court, on the other hand, has not explicitly referred to this requirement, although various judges have in dissenting opinions.

13.2.2 The Proportionality of the Derogating Measure and the Margin of Appreciation

As to the *interference* issue, a fundamental requirement for any measures derogating from the ECHR or the ICCPR is that such measures are limited 'to the extent strictly required by the exigencies of the situation'. In *Handyside v United Kingdom* the Strasbourg Court differentiated the 'strictly required' standard in Article 15 from the ordinary standard of necessity which the Court translates into the principle of proportionality. The Court articulated three tiers of standards found in the Convention: 'reasonableness' (see e.g. Articles 5(3) and 6(1) ECHR), 'necessity' (see e.g. Article 10(2) ECHR) and 'indispensability'.[39] Indispensability was associated with the phrase 'strictly required' in Article 15 ECHR and the phrase 'absolutely necessary' in Article 2(2). Subsequently the Court has stated in *McCann and Others v United Kingdom* that:

> the use of the term "absolutely necessary" in Article 2(2) indicates that a stricter and more compelling test of necessity must be employed from that normally applicable when determining whether state action is 'necessary in a democratic society' under paragraph 2 of

---

[37] O. Gross and F. Ni Aoláin, *Law in Times of Crisis: Emergency Powers in Theory and Practice* (Cambridge: Cambridge University Press, 2006) at 251–252.

[38] *Ibidem* at 252.

[39] *Handyside v United Kingdom* (1976) 1 EHRR 737, at para. 48.

> Articles 8 to 11 of the Convention. In particular, the force used must be strictly proportionate to the achievement of the aims set out in sub-paragraphs 2(a), (b) and (c) of Article 2.[40]

By contrast to Article 2 ECHR, the stricter standard of necessity is justified in the context of Article 15 ECHR not by the importance of the right at stake but by the nature of the measure, which is to take a State outside the human rights regime altogether. Any derogation measure must thus fulfil the following five basic requirements:

- The measures must be strictly required, i.e. actions taken under ordinary laws and in conformity with international human rights obligations are not sufficient to meet the threat.
- The measures must be connected to the emergency, i.e. they must 'prima facie' be suitable to reduce the threat or crisis.
- The measures must be used only as long as they are necessary, i.e. there must be a temporal limit.
- The degree to which the measures deviate from international human rights standards must be in proportion to the severity of the threat, i.e. the more important and fundamental the right which is being compromised, the closer and stricter the scrutiny.
- Effective safeguards must be implemented to avoid the abuse of emergency powers. Where measures involve administrative detention, safeguards may include regular review by independent national organs, in particular, by the legislative and judicial branches.

As stated by the European Commission in the *Greek* Case, and by the Human Rights Committee in its General Comment 29, the State Parties bear the burden of proof in establishing the existence of a 'public emergency'. [41] However, in assessing whether a 'public emergency' exists and what steps are necessary to address it, the European Court grants states a so-called 'margin of appreciation'. The doctrine of margin of appreciation essentially addresses the difficult task of balancing the sovereignty of Contracting Parties with their obligations under the Convention.[42] As Ronald St James Macdonald, a former judge of the European Court of Human Rights, has observed, it is the doctrine of margin of appreciation which allows the Court to escape the dilemma of 'how to remain true to its responsibility to develop a reasonably comprehensive set of review principles appropriate for application across the entire Convention, while at the same time recognising the diversity of political, economic, cultural and social situations in the societies of the Contracting Parties'.[43]

---

[40] *McCann and Others v United Kingdom* (1995) 21 EHRR 97, at para 149.

[41] Human Rights Committee, *General Comment 29, States of Emergency* (Article 4), U.N. Doc. CCPR/C/21/Rev.1/Add.11 (2001), paras 4 and 5.

[42] R. St. J. Macdonald, "The Margin of Appreciation," in *The European System for the Protection of Human,* ed. R. St. J. Macdonald, F. Matscher, and H. Petzold (Dordrecht/Boston: Kluwer, 1993) at 83.

[43] *Ibidem.*

In the context of derogation in times of 'public emergency threatening the life of the nation', the margin of appreciation represents the discretion left to a State in ascertaining the necessity and scope of measures of derogation from protected rights in the circumstances prevailing within its jurisdiction.[44] In *Ireland v United Kingdom*, the European Court held that:

> it falls in the first place to each Contracting State, with its responsibility for "the life of [its] nation", to determine whether that life is threatened by a "public emergency" and, if so, how far it is necessary to go in attempting to overcome the emergency. By reason of their direct and continuous contact with the pressing needs of the moment, the national authorities are in principle in a better position than the international judge to decide both on the presence of such an emergency and on the nature and scope of derogations necessary to avert it. In this matter Article 15(1) leaves the authorities a wide margin of appreciation.[45]

In *Brannigan and McBride v United Kingdom* the Court held that:

> it falls to each Contracting State, with its responsibility for "the life of [its] nation," to determine whether that life is threatened by a "public emergency" and, if so, how far it is necessary to go in attempting to overcome the emergency. By reason of their direct and continuous contact with the pressing needs of the moment, the national authorities are in principle in a better position than the international judge to decide both on the presence of such an emergency and on the nature and scope of derogations necessary to avert it. Accordingly, in this matter a wide margin of appreciation should be left to the national authorities…".[46]

The margin of appreciation is thus granted to the national authorities both in relation to the existence of a public emergency – the *designation* issue – and in determining whether derogation measures are strictly required by the exigencies of the situation – the *interference* issue.

The Human Rights Committee, too, has confirmed that derogating measures must be limited to the 'extent strictly required by the exigencies of the situation' as well as 'exceptional' and 'temporary nature'.[47] It has clarified that this requirement relates to the 'duration, geographical coverage and material scope of the state of emergency and any measures of derogation resorted to because of the emergency'.[48] Unlike the Strasbourg Court, however, the Committee is reluctant to grant a wide margin of appreciation, if it recognises the application of such a doctrine at all. In *Landinelli Silva v Uruguay*, for instance, the Committee found that 'the State Party is duty-bound to give a sufficiently detailed account of the relevant facts when it invokes Article 4(1)' and that it is the Committee's function 'to see to it that States

---

[44] See, e.g.: T. A. O'Donnell, "The Margin of Appreciation Doctrine: Standards in the Jurisprudence of the European Court of Human Rights," *Human Rights Quarterly* 4 (1982): 474.

[45] *Ireland v United Kingdom*, at para. 78–9.

[46] *Brannigan and McBride v United Kingdom*, (1993) 17 EHRR 539, at para 41.

[47] Human Rights Committee, *General Comment 29, McCann and Others v United Kingdom* (1995), para.4.

[48] *Ibidem.*

parties live up to their commitments under the Covenant.'[49] The *Siracusa Principles* follow a similar line. They explicitly state that the principle of strict necessity shall be applied in an 'objective manner' and, moreover, that 'the judgment of the national authorities cannot be accepted as conclusive'.[50]

13.3 The Derogation Rules in Post-9/11 Case Law

In light of the claims that the 9/11 attacks on New York and Washington changed the world 'forever' and assertions that international terrorism constituted the defining global security challenge of the twenty-first century, it may be surprising to find that the vast majority of states have *not* invoked the derogation clauses of the respective international human rights treaties, at least not formally.[51] Indeed, in the framework of the Council of Europe, only the United Kingdom felt compelled to derogate from the ECHR. This derogation was challenged both in domestic courts in England and in Strasbourg. One of the key issues in the legal proceedings was the question of whether the terrorist threat constituted a 'public emergency threatening the life of the nation', and whether aspects of the United Kingdom's legislative response were proportionate. From an international human rights law perspective, the cases are of particular interest as they deals with both the *designation* and *interference* issues in the context of the *Human Rights Act* 1998 which incorporates the ECHR into domestic British law. The following section will consider the domestic and international judicial findings in more detail.

13.3.1 Terrorism as a 'Public Emergency Threatening the Life of the Nation'

The case – ultimately decided by the House of Lords in the *Belmarsh detainees* decision of December 2004 – was brought by nine foreign (non-United Kingdom) nationals who had been certified by Britain's Home Secretary under section 21 of the *Anti-Terrorism, Crime and Security Act* (ATCSA) (2001) as suspected international terrorists and who had been detained under section 23 of the Act

[49] *Landinelli Silva v Uruguay* (1981) HRC Comm No 34/1978 at para 8.3.

[50] See also: No 54 and 57 of the *Siracusa Principles*.

[51] See, e.g.: P. Kelly, "How 9/11 Changed the World," *The Australian* (Sydney), September 8, 2006; R. W. Stevenson, "Cheney Says 9/11 Changed the Rules," *New York Times* (New York), December 21, 2005. For thoughtful analysis see, e.g.: R. Jervis, "An Interim Assessment of September 11: What Has Changed and What Has Not?," *Political Science Quarterly* 117 (2002): 37.

which allowed for indefinite detention without charge.[52] Section 23(1) ATCSA read as follows[53]:

> a suspected international terrorist may be detained under a provision specified in subsection (2) despite the fact that his removal or departure from the United Kingdom is prevented (whether temporarily or indefinitely) by ((a) a point of law which wholly or partly relates to an international agreement, or (b) a practical consideration.

The claimants challenged the legality both of these provisions and of the government's decision to derogate from Article 5 ECHR in respect of the detention provision. In asserting the existence of a public emergency in the United Kingdom, the British government stated that:

> There exists a terrorist threat to the United Kingdom from persons suspected of involvement in international terrorism. In particular, there are foreign nationals present in the United Kingdom who are suspected of being concerned in the commission, preparation or instigation of acts of international terrorism, of being members of organisations or groups which are so concerned or of having links with members of such organisations or groups, and who are a threat to the national security of the United Kingdom. [54]

The Lords essentially had to address two central issues. The first was whether the government's derogation from the ECHR in respect of the detention measures was lawful. The second was whether the statutory provisions under which the appellants had been detained were incompatible with the ECHR. The Lords thus addressed the *designation* issue as well as the *interference* issue. By an eight-to-one majority, the derogation by the United Kingdom government from the ECHR was quashed and a declaration issued to the extent that section 23 ATCSA (2001) was incompatible with the *Human Rights Act* 1998.[55]

The House of Lords judgments can be divided into three camps. Seven members of the court – Lords Bingham, Nicholls, Hope, Scott, Rodger, Carswell, and Baroness Hale – held that, while a 'public emergency threatening the life of the nation' could be said to exist, the detention provision could not be said to be 'strictly required' by that emergency. It was disproportionate and discriminatory and hence unlawful. One judge – Lord Walker – dissented. He held both that there was a public emergency threatening the life of the nation and that the detention provision of section 23 ATCSA (2001) was neither discriminatory nor disproportionate to the aim the measure sought to achieve.

---

[52] See generally: A. Tomkins, "Legislating Against Terror: The Anti-Terrorism, Crime and Security Act 2001," *Public Law* (summer 2002): 205; H. Fenwick, "The Anti-Terrorism, Crime and Security Act 2001: A Proportionate Response?," *Modern Law Review* 65 (2002): 724.

[53] Section 23 was repealed in the wake of the House of Lord's decision in *A and others v. Secretary of State for the Home Department.*

[54] Human Rights Act 1998 (Designated Derogation) Order 2001, No. 3644, which came into force on 13 November 2001.

[55] *A and others v. Secretary of State for the Home Department*, para. 73 (Lord Bingham).

Lord Hope's speech provided the reason as to why the majority of the House of Lords found that a public emergency threatening the life of the nation existed in the United Kingdom. He held that:

> There is ample evidence within [the open] material to show that the government were fully justified in taking the view in November 2001 that there was an emergency threatening the life of the nation. … [The] United Kingdom was at danger of attacks from the Al Qaeda network which had the capacity through its associates to inflict massive casualties and have a devastating effect on the functioning of the nation. This had been demonstrated by the events of 11 September 2001 in New York, Pennsylvania and Washington. There was a significant body of foreign nationals in the United Kingdom who had the will and the capability of mounting co-ordinated attacks here which would be just as destructive to human life and to property. There was ample intelligence to show that international terrorist organisations involved in recent attacks and in preparation for other attacks of terrorism had links with the United Kingdom, and that they and others posed a continuing threat to this country. There was a growing body of evidence showing preparations made for the use of weapons of mass destruction in this campaign. … [It] was considered [by the Home Office] that the serious threats to the nation emanated predominantly, albeit not exclusively, and more immediately from the category of foreign nationals.[56]

Lord Hoffmann agreed with the majority that the provisions in question were incompatible with the ECHR. However, he was the only judge holding the derogation unlawful on the ground that there was no 'war or other public emergency threatening the life of the nation' within the meaning of Article 15 ECHR. He famously said:

> The Home Secretary has adduced evidence, both open and secret, to show the existence of a threat of serious terrorist outrages. The Attorney General did not invite us to examine the secret evidence, but despite the widespread scepticism which has attached to intelligence assessments since the fiasco over Iraqi weapons of mass destruction, I am willing to accept that credible evidence of such plots exist. The events of 11 September 2001 in New York and Washington and 11 March 2003 in Madrid make it entirely likely that the threat of similar atrocities in the United Kingdom is a real one. But the question is whether such a threat is a threat to the life of the nation…This is a nation which has been tested in adversity, which has survived physical destruction and catastrophic loss of life. I do not underestimate the ability of fanatical groups of terrorists to kill and destroy, but they do not threaten the life of the nation. Whether we would survive Hitler hung in the balance, but there is no doubt that we shall survive Al-Qaeda. The Spanish people have not said that what happened in Madrid, hideous crime as it was, threatened the life of their nation. Their legendary pride would not allow it. Terrorist violence, serious as it is, does not threaten our institutions of government or our existence as a civil community.[57]

Lord Hoffmann's speech is significant in that it engages with the actual nature of the threat by setting it into historical context. However, his conclusions on the matter did not find the support of the other Lords. Lord Hoffmann's approach was also not taken up by the Grand Chamber of the European Court of Human Rights

[56] *Ibidem* at para 118 (Lord Hope).

[57] *Ibidem* at paras. 94–96 (Lord Hoffmann).

which handed down its decision on 19 February 2009.[58] The Court accepted that the 9/11 attacks and the threat of international terrorism constituted an emergency threatening the life of the nation within the meaning of Article 15 (1) of the ECHR. Indeed, the terrorist attacks in London in 2005 had confirmed that such an emergency existed.[59] The Court explicitly rejected Lord Hoffmann's view in the House of Lords that there was no emergency threatening the life of the nation, because the terrorist attacks could not conceivably constitute a threat to the United Kingdom's institutions of government or the United Kingdom's existence as a civil community. The Court held that it had 'in previous cases been prepared to take into account a much broader range of factors in determining the nature and degree of the actual or imminent threat to the "nation" and has in the past concluded that emergency situations have existed even though the institutions of the State did not appear to be imperilled to the extent envisaged by Lord Hoffmann'.[60] It also disagreed with the Human Rights Committee that an emergency, and consequently the derogation measures, can only be 'temporary.' It noted that the Court's own cases on Northern Ireland confirmed that an emergency and a derogation could last for a long while. The duration of the emergency, however, needed to be taken into account in the proportionality assessment, but there was no specific temporal limitation to Article 15.[61]

The Court's treatment of the issue is disappointing, particularly as it lacks any observations in relation to the substantive meaning of public emergency in the era of international terrorism. Rather, the Court simply repeated its findings in earlier cases which, of course, preceded the post 9/11-era. It is equally regrettable that the Court, for the most part, did not engage with the factual question as to why and how international terrorism, or the threat thereof, qualified as a public emergency threatening the life of the nation in the United Kingdom. This is rather problematic as empirical research suggests that contemporary terrorism does generally *not* pose an existential threat to most states.

In the United States, for example, terrorism poses a far lesser statistical threat to life than most other activities. While 1440 US citizens died in terrorist attacks in 2001, three times as many died of malnutrition, and almost 40 times as many people died in car accidents during the same year.[62] Even with the 9/11 attacks included in the count, the number of Americans killed by international terrorism since the late 1960s (when the State Department began counting) is about the same as the number

[58] *A and others v United Kingdom*, App 3455/05 (19 February 2009), (2009) 49 EHRR 29. For a broader analysis of the impact of this decision, see, e.g.: H. Fenwick, "Recalibrating ECHR Rights, and the Role of the Human Rights Act Post 9/11: Reasserting International Human Rights Norms in the "War on Terror"?," *Current Legal Problems* 63 (2010): 153.

[59] *A and others v United Kingdom*, para. 177.

[60] *Ibidem* at para. 179.

[61] *Ibidem* at para 178.

[62] S. Stephen, "Terrorism: Governments Fuel Fear," in *Terrorism*, ed. J. Healey (Balmain: Spinney Press, 2004) at 39.

of Americans killed over the same period by severe allergic reaction to peanuts, lightning, or accident-causing deer.[63] Similarly, the number of annual deaths from Sports Utility Vehicles is reported to be greater than the total number of deaths caused by all terrorist acts combined.[64] Furthermore, it is still to be more likely to get killed by bee stings or DIY accidents than being killed in a terrorist attack.[65]

At the global level, the statistics are equally revealing. Anthony Cordesman and Brian Jenkins have independently provided lists of violence committed by Islamist extremists outside of such war zones as Iraq, Israel, Chechnya, Sudan, Kashmir, and Afghanistan, whether that violence be perpetrated by domestic terrorists or by ones with substantial international connections.[66] Included in the count are such terrorist attacks as those that occurred in Bali in 2002, in Saudi Arabia, Morocco, and Turkey in 2003, in the Philippines, Madrid, and Egypt in 2004, and in London and Jordan in 2005. The lists include not only attacks by Al Qaeda, but also those by its imitators, enthusiasts, and wannabes as well as ones by groups with no apparent connection to it whatever. The total number of people killed in the 5 years after 9/11 in such incidents comes to some 200–300 per year. By comparison, over the same period far more people have perished in the United States alone in bathtub drownings.[67]

The notion that international terrorism is threatening the very basis of power and legitimacy of the liberal democratic state is rather unconvincing, too. Indeed, one may well argue that such an assessment is a classic case of threat inflation. As Andrew O'Neil has observed:

> The idea that extreme, but diffuse, Islamist groups operating loosely under the Al Qaeda banner pose a clear and direct threat to the foundations of Western civilisation and to states that embody Western values (that is, liberal democracy, capitalism) would be laughable if it were not taken with such apparent deadly seriousness by policy makers and non-official observers in the media and academia.[68]

Western values and the political and economic structures that express them are far too robust to be susceptive to destabilisation by terrorist attacks, however horrific and genuinely tragic they may be. Even 9/11, the most audacious and single largest terrorist attack in history, did not compromise the essential workings of government in the United States. Similar observations can be made regarding other terrorist attacks, both past and present, including the Madrid and London train bombings. Historically,

---

[63] J. E. Mueller, "Terrorism, Overreaction and Globalization," in *No More States?: Globalization, National Self-determination, and Terrorism*, ed. R. N. Rosecrance and A. A. Stein (Lanham: Rowman & Littlefield, 2007) at 48. The 3572 people who died in terrorist attacks in 2001 were three times more likely to die from being hit by lightning.

[64] R. Hardin, "Civil Liberties in the Era of Mass Terrorism," *Journal of Ethics* 8 (2004): 79.

[65] R. Jackson, *Writing the War on Terror: Language, Politics and Counter-Terrorism* (Manchester: Manchester University Press, 2005) at 93.

[66] B. M. Jenkins, *Unconquerable Nation: Knowing Our Enemy and Strengthening Ourselves* (Santa Monica: RAND Corporation, 2006), 179–184; A. H. Cordesman, *The Challenge of Biological Weapons* (Washington, DC: Center for Strategic and International Studies, 2005), 29–31.

[67] J. Stossel, *Give Me a Break* (New York: HarperCollins, 2004) at 77.

[68] A. O'Neil, "Keeping the Contemporary Threat Environment in Perspective," *Australian Review of Public Affairs* (2004). http://www.australianreview.net/digest/2004/05/oneil.html.

non-state terrorist activity has neither significantly undermined nor damaged the national cohesiveness or integrity of liberal democracies.[69] Spain, Germany, Italy, the United Kingdom, and many other countries – including Israel – have lived with terrorist activity for many years without such activity seriously threatening their very existence. In fact, it could be argued that previous experiences of political violence posed a somewhat greater threat to the stability states. In particular left-wing and separatist terrorism campaigns in Europe enjoyed a certain degree of popular support or sympathy, at least as far as key political objectives were concerned. This meant that these campaigns had a form of legitimacy to them which was far more threatening to the stability of Western democracies than contemporary Islamist terrorism.

It is also questionable whether contemporary terrorism can qualify as a public emergency threatening the life of the nation when viewed from an economic perspective. The economic destruction of 9/11, for instance, was indeed unprecedented (in terms of terrorist attacks). The attack on the World Trade Center alone and caused billions of dollars in property damage and reportedly destroyed 30% of the office space in Lower Manhattan. Nevertheless, even the extreme events of 9/11 have not had an enduring impact on the world's most powerful economy (despite predictions that the attacks would trigger a recession). A 2002 report prepared for the US Congress, for example, analysed the economic effects of 9/11 and concluded that:

> The loss of lives and property on 9/11 was not large enough to have had a measurable effect on the productive capacity of the United States. For 9/11 to affect the economy it would have had to have affected the price of an important input, such as energy, or had an adverse effect on aggregate demand via such mechanisms as consumer and business confidence, a financial panic or liquidity crisis, or an international run on the dollar.[70]

The report further found that the existing data showed that GDP growth was low in the first half of 2001 and, further, that data published in October 2001 showed that the GDP had also contracted during the third quarter. This led to the claim that 'the terrorist attacks pushed a weak economy over the edge into an outright recession'.[71] However, the report did not find any evidence to back up this claim. At the time of 9/11 the US economy was in its third consecutive quarter of contraction and positive growth resumed in the fourth quarter. According to report, this suggested that any effects from 9/11 on demand were short lived. The report thus concluded that timely action contained the short run economic effects of 9/11 on the overall economy.[72]

---

[69] See, e.g.: A. Roberts, "The "War on Terror" in Historical Perspective," *Survival* 47 (2005): 101. It is essential to differentiate between stable democracies and fragile states. While terrorist attacks may have the potential to destabilise fragile states and states experiencing civil strife, the same cannot be said in relation to stable Western democracies.

[70] G. Makinen, *The Economic Effects of 9/11: A Retrospective Assessment.* Report for Congress, 27 September 2002 (Washington, DC: Library of Congress, 2002).

[71] *Ibidem.*

[72] *Ibidem.* See also: O. A. Jackson, "The Impact of the 9/11 Terrorist Attacks on the US Economy," March 3, 2008. http://www.journalof911studies.com/volume/2008/OliviaJackson911andUS-Economy.pdf; "How Has September 11 Influenced the Global Economy," in the International Monetary Fund's World Economic Outlook Reports, Chapter II, December 2001; http://www.imf.org/external/pubs/ft/wed/2001/03/index.htm.

A study focussing exclusively on the New York area reached similar conclusions.[73] In the aftermath of the 9/11 attacks, New York City's economy contracted briefly but sharply. Many businesses were forced to shut down, mostly temporarily, and tens of thousands of workers were either dislocated for a short time or lost their jobs. However, the study also found that although the attacks caused a sharp temporary disruption in the economy, an advantageous industry mix – one weighted toward high-paying, rapidly expanding industries – kept the city well positioned for growth over the medium term.[74] Similar conclusions were reached by a number of other studies.[75]

The terrorist attacks in Madrid and London also did not have any lasting negative economic impacts in Spain and the United Kingdom respectively, nor on the European economy more generally.[76] For instance, the S&P 500 index dropped 1.5% on the day of the Madrid attacks.[77] However, it recovered most of that loss the next day. Similarly, there were limited immediate reactions to the 2005 London bombings in the world economy as measured by financial market and exchange rate activity. The pound fell 0.89 cents to a 19-month low against the U.S. dollar. The FTSE 100 Index fell by about 200 points in the 2 h after the first attack. While this was its biggest fall since the start of the 2003 Iraq war, by the time the market closed the index had recovered to only 71.3 points (1.36%) down on the previous day's 3-year closing high.

Markets in France, Germany, the Netherlands and Spain also closed about 1% down on the day. US market indexes rose slightly, in part because the dollar index rose sharply against the pound and the euro. The Dow Jones Industrial Average gained 31.61 to 10,302.29. The Nasdaq Composite Index rose 7.01 to 2075.66. The S&P 500 rose 2.93 points to 1197.87 after declining up to 1%. Every benchmark gained 0.3%.[78] The markets picked up again on 8 July 2005 as it became clear that the damage caused by the bombings was not as great as initially thought. By close of trading the market had fully recovered to above its level at start of trading on 7 July 2005, the day of the attacks. These developments led the chief investment strategist at Prudential Equity Group LLC in New York, Edward Keon, to observe that 'the markets reacted the way they often do under periods of great

---

[73] J. Bram, A. Haughwout, and J. Orr, "Has September 11 Affected New York City's Growth Potential?," *Economic Policy Review* 8 (2002) at http://www.newyorkfed.org/research/epr/02v08n2/0211bram/0211bram.html.

[74] *Ibidem.*

[75] See, e.g.: H. Chernick, ed., *Resilient City: The Economic Impact of 9/11* (New York: Russell Sage Foundation, 2005); H. W. Richardson, P. Gordon, and J. E. Moore II, eds., *The Economic Impacts of Terrorist Attacks* (Cheltenham: Edward Elgar, 2005).

[76] R. B. Johnson and O. M. Nedelescu, "The Impact of Terrorism on Financial Markets" (International Monetary Fund, working paper WP/05/60, March 2005). http://www.international-monetaryfund.com/external/pubs/ft/wp/2005/wp0560.pdf.

[77] D. Lawrence, "U.S. Stocks Rise, Erasing Losses on London Bombings, Gap Rises," *Bloomberg News (Online)*, July 7, 2005, http://www.bloomberg.com/apps/news?pid=10000103&sid=aflPCIrU37Ns&refer=us.

[78] *Ibidem.*

stress, initially dropping and then recovering.'[79] The examples of recent terrorist attacks thus suggest that terrorism also does not have a significant *direct* effect on Western economies.

There are thus strong empirical grounds to suggest that contemporary international terrorism does not constitute an existential threat to Western liberal democracies like the United Kingdom. It neither poses a significant objective threat to the safety and physical integrity of individuals, nor to the existence of the institutions of government and the economy of Western liberal democracies. Lord Hoffmann's comparisons to historical emergencies are thus also supported by research on the nature and dimension of the current threat of terrorism. Even extraordinary events like the 9/11 attacks are highly unlikely to threaten the 'life of the nation'. One reason for the European Court's reluctance to engage with factual questions on the terrorist threat, including statistical research, may have been that it has traditionally granted states a wide margin of appreciation in relation to the assessment of whether an emergency actually exists. This aspect of the Court's practice will now be the subject of closer examination.

13.3.2 The Margin of Appreciation

The second key issue at stake before both the House of Lords and the European Court of Human Rights was the question of whether, and to what extent, the British government enjoyed discretion, both in relation to determining the existence of a public emergency and with regard to adopting appropriate measures in response. At the House of Lords, Lord Bingham's lead judgment represented the *ratio decidendi* and had the agreement of six of the Lords. Unlike Lord Hoffmann, Lord Bingham was not prepared to hold that no public emergency threatening the life of the nation existed. Nevertheless he upheld the appeal on the grounds that the detention powers were disproportionate and discriminatory.

In relation to the *designation* issue, Lord Bingham's approach essentially absolved the United Kingdom government from advancing clear and convincing evidence to Parliament (and the courts) to demonstrate that a public emergency threatening the life of the nation actually existed. Lord Bingham approved and applied the case law of the European Court of Human Rights on Article 15 of the ECHR granting a wide margin of appreciation. He found that to hold that there was no public emergency in cases where, 'a response beyond that provided by the ordinary course of law was required, would have been perverse'.[80] This reasoning, however, is illogical as it essentially bases the determination of the question of whether a public emergency exists on the measures taken to address it. As Tom Hickman observed, 'if one is to infer from the fact that exceptional measures have been

[79] *Ibidem.*

[80] *A and others v Secretary of State for the Home Department*, para. 28 (Lord Bingham).

taken that such measures are legitimate then the criteria of legitimacy (i.e. public emergency) is relieved of substance'.[81]

Lord Bingham went on to hold that it was for the appellants to demonstrate that the British government's claim that there was an emergency which required derogation from the ECHR was 'wrong and unreasonable'.[82] The appellants, however, had 'shown no ground strong enough to warrant displacing the Secretary of State's decision on this important threshold question'.[83] Lord Bingham's reasoning is highly problematic. This reversal of the burden of proof in relation to the existence of a public emergency threatening the life of the nation raises serious concerns from a purely practical perspective. It is difficult to see how individuals will ever be able to disprove the government's view that an emergency exists, not least because the relevant evidence will be in the hands of the government.[84] Lord Bingham's view also runs contrary to the approach taken by the European Court of Human Rights. As indicated earlier, the Strasbourg authorities have repeatedly confirmed that the burden is not upon the individual, but upon the government to demonstrate that there exists a national emergency which requires derogation from international human rights obligations. It is noteworthy that the Human Rights Committee in its 'General Comment 29' took a similar view.[85]

The European Court of Human Rights, too, granted the United Kingdom a wide margin appreciation. It acknowledged the fact that the United Kingdom was the only European state to derogate under Article 15 but accepted that it was for each government to make its own assessments about whether the threat of international terrorism constituted a public emergency. It held that:

> While it is striking that the United Kingdom was the only Convention State to have lodged a derogation in response to the danger from al'Qaeda, although other States were also the subject of threats, the Court accepts that it was for each Government, as the guardian of their own people's safety, to make their own assessment on the basis of the facts known to them. Weight must, therefore, attach to the judgment of the United Kingdom's executive and Parliament on this question. In addition, significant weight must be accorded to the views of the national courts, who were better placed to assess the evidence relating to the existence of an emergency. On this first question, the Court accordingly shares the view of the majority of the House of Lords that there was a public emergency threatening the life of the nation.[86]

In granting the United Kingdom a wide margin of appreciation, the Court closely followed its earlier case law. In particular, in *Ireland v United Kingdom* the Court

---

[81] T. R. Hickman, "Between Human Rights and the Rule of Law: Indefinite Detention and the Derogation Model of Constitutionalism," *Modern Law Review* 68 (2005): 655.

[82] *A and others v. Secretary of State for the Home Department*, para 29 (Lord Bingham).

[83] *Ibidem.*

[84] Hickman, "Between Human Rights and the Rule of Law…," at 663. See generally: T. Hickman, *Public Law After the Human Rights Act* (Oxford: Hart Publishing, 2010), especially Chapter 11 (Derogation and Emergency).

[85] Human Rights Committee, *General Comment 29, States of Emergency* (Article 4), U.N. Doc. CCPR/C/21/Rev.1/Add.11 (2001), paras 4 and 5.

[86] *A and others v United Kingdom*, paras 180–81.

had held that it was inappropriate to decide with the benefit of hindsight on issues which a government must necessarily address urgently and on the basis of information that it may not be capable of publicising.[87] This view is shared by some academic commentators. J. G. Merrills, for instance, has argued that the determination that an emergency exists, and what measures are necessary to counter it, was a political judgement in relation to which judges were 'ill-equipped and improper arbiters'.[88] What is more, national authorities, he argued, were in a much better position than a supranational institution like the Court to assess the situation on the ground. The government's discretion thus needed to be respected, especially as it is the government's responsibility to ensure law and order. The Court, on the other hand, serves the public interest in effective government by doing no more than ensuring that the government's conduct in relation to a proclaimed emergency is at least 'on the margin' of the powers conferred by Article 15 of the ECHR and Article 4 of the ICCPR.[89]

A related argument in favour of the Court granting wide margin of appreciation is based on the view that emergencies exert great pressures for governments against continued adherence to the protection of human rights. As Oren Gross and Fionnuala Ni Aoláin have pointed out, governments often consider protecting human rights and civil liberties to their fullest extent as a 'luxury that must be dispensed with if the nation is to overcome the crisis it faces'.[90] Moved by perceptions of physical threat both to the state and to themselves and motivated by growing fear and by hatred toward the 'enemy', the population may support the government in adopting more radical measures against the perceived threats. In these circumstances, notions of the rule of law, rights, and freedoms are legalistic niceties that bar effective action by the government.[91] Exigencies tend to provoke the 'rally around the flag' phenomenon,[92] or, as Mark Nolan has pointed out, a 'siege mentality', in which governmental actions perceived as necessary to fight off the crisis garner almost unqualified popular support.[93] In such, there was no role for a supranational institution like the European Court to play.

In the context of legislation enacted to counter the current threat of terrorism both arguments are unconvincing. The Strasbourg authorities themselves have confirmed that states do not enjoy an unlimited discretion in relation to the determi-

---

[87] *Ireland v United Kingdom*, at para. 214.

[88] See, e.g.: J. G. Merrills, *The Development of International Law by the European Court of Human Rights* (Manchester: Manchester University Press, 1988), 37.

[89] *Ibidem.*

[90] O. Gross and F. Ní Aoláin, "From Discretion to Scrutiny: Revisiting the Application of the Margin of Appreciation Doctrine in the Context of Article 15 of the European Convention on Human Rights," *Human Rights Quarterly* 23 (2001): 638–639.

[91] *Ibidem.*

[92] *Ibidem.*

[93] M. Nolan, "Measuring Support for Australian Counter-Terrorism Initiatives and Human Rights: The Impact of Offence Construal, Perpetrator Motive and Siege Mentality," in *Fresh Perspectives on the "War on Terror"*, ed. P. Mathew and M. Gani (Canberra: ANU E Press, 2008).

nation of a public emergency and that the domestic margin of appreciation is accompanied by 'European supervision'.[94] It is noteworthy that dissenting votes in the Court's own case law repeatedly questioned the practice of granting states a *wide* margin of appreciation. In the *Lawless* case, a minority of the Commission members rejected the margin of appreciation doctrine altogether, arguing that evaluation of the existence of a public emergency ought to be based solely on existing facts without regard to any account of subjective predictions as to future development.[95] They also argued that the Commission ought to review *de novo* the existence of a public emergency in a given situation without assuming an *a priori* deferential attitude towards the respondent government.

It is equally debatable whether the highly politicised discourse on terrorism and counter-terrorism is conducive to rational and calm consideration and an appropriate balancing of the competing interests at stake. Thus, it may well be that a supranational institution like the European Court of Human Rights or the Human Rights Committee, detached and removed from the immediate political debate, is better placed to judge matters more clearly and more accurately. It is the Court or the Committee, therefore, that is in a better position than the national government to decide both on the presence of such an emergency and on the nature and scope of the derogations necessary to avert it.

It is also questionable whether national authorities are in a better position to assess whether circumstances that constitute a public emergency do in fact prevail. Unlike its previous manifestations, contemporary terrorism is hardly attributable to a confined number of terrorist organisations, even though it has been mainly associated with al-Qaeda or 'Islamic jihadism'. In other words, the threat is much more diffuse and abstract. In most circumstances the existence of a 'public emergency threatening the life of the nation' is or will be claimed in relation to a threat. In consequence, there has to be an assessment of the risk of the realisation of the threat, as well as its seriousness. Because the terrorist threat is usually abstract or non-specific, the government's burden of justification in respect of the existence of a 'public emergency' is particularly high. The margin of appreciation granted to individual states in assessing the existence of a 'public emergency' and the proportionality of response measures thus should be reconsidered and adjusted. The more global and non-specific the threat, the less the amount of discretion left to the state. As the threat of international terrorism is global, national authorities are not necessarily in a better position to decide on the imminence of a 'public emergency'. Quite the opposite: other countries might even have superior intelligence on specific terrorist threats.

The Court should be less deferential to a government's assessment that a state of emergency exists where the emergency is possibly a permanent one, given that the concept of an emergency permitting derogation which is embodied in the relevant clauses of the ECHR and ICCPR is necessarily a temporary one, the logic being that

[94] *Ireland v United Kingdom*, at 207.

[95] *Lawless v Ireland*, at 32.

rights may be temporarily suspended, not that they may simply be destroyed.[96] This is particularly the case in the context of international terrorism and the post-9/11 era where the threat that is supposed to constitute a public emergency has become permanent. The Court should refrain from granting a wide margin of appreciation but rather should submit governmental claims to strict scrutiny, in relation to both *designation* and *interference* issues – the longer the emergency, the narrower ought the margin of appreciation to be.

13.4 Concluding Observations on Derogation Clauses in a Time of Permanent Legal Emergency

The previous sections considered rather technical questions about the requirements of the derogation clauses of the ECHR and the ICCPR and how they apply in the context of public emergencies due to contemporary international terrorism. In light of the development over the last decade, however, there is another important question that needs to be addressed. That is, whether derogation clauses are adequate, or indeed needed in a time of permanent legal emergency. This question is not entirely novel, of course. In fact, there are a number of historical examples of quasi-permanent emergencies that engaged obligations under international human rights law. Both the Human Rights Committee and the European Court of Human Rights where confronted with pro-longed states of emergency in states like Egypt, Uruguay, Argentina and the United Kingdom (Northern Ireland).

What set some of these cases apart from the present situation is that states had actually declared constitutional emergencies. In the post-9/11 era, however, states have been reluctant to derogate from their international human rights obligations officially. In the Council of Europe region, the United Kingdom was the only country to do so. The picture is not too different in the framework of the ICCPR. While several Latin American states have derogated from the ICCPR in the last 10 years, a review of the notifications submitted to the UN Secretary-General as depositary of the ICCPR appears to suggest that none of these derogations were directly connected to the threat of international terrorism.[97] Again it seems that the United Kingdom was the only state derogating from the ICCPR with an explicit reference to 9/11 and international terrorism.

The lack of a recent 'derogation practice' may seem surprising at first. Governmental rhetoric across the world, after all, portrayed international terrorism as the ultimate security challenge. Leaders in Western liberal democracies in particular used colourful rhetoric to warn their constituencies about the perils of terrorism.

---

[96] See also: O. Gross, ""Once More unto the Breach": The Systemic Failure of Applying the European Convention on Human Rights to Entrenched Emergencies," *Yale Journal of International Law* 23 (1998): 437.

[97] I wish to acknowledge the research assistance of Angela Kintominas in reviewing the notifications on the UN Treaty Collection database at http://treaties.un.org/.

In Australia, for instance, the then Foreign Minister, Alexander Downer, claimed that Australia was engaged in a 'struggle to the death over values' against 'Islamo-fascists' who were 'convinced that their destiny was to overshadow the democratic West' and who had embarked on a ruthless mission to 'destroy our society by waging a version of total war'.[98] In many instances this rhetoric was consciously adopted to pave the way for draconian anti-terrorism laws. Yet in spite of the doomsday rhetoric and questionable anti-terrorism laws which are unlikely to comply with international human rights obligations the vast majority of states have refrained from invoking the derogation clauses. Even states with a strong rule of law tradition such as Australia have followed this trend.

The explanation for this phenomenon may be simple. Governments may have made a conscious decision against derogation out of a concern that such derogation would implicitly acknowledge that their anti-terrorism laws were inconsistent with human rights obligations. But what are the broader implications of this practice? Is it, perhaps, time for a fundamental re-think of the role of derogation clauses in international human rights treaties? When examining these questions of fundamental importance, it is helpful to consider that the derogation clauses were originally included in the treaties to encourage wide-spread participation. At the time when the ECHR and the ICCPR were drafted, international human rights law was in its infancy and it was considered to be appropriate to allow for suspending obligations in times of serious emergency. As the Human Rights Committee and the European Court of Human Rights have indicated, however, derogation clauses were not designed to allow for a permanent legal emergency.

Interestingly, an analogous line of reasoning can be detected in writings arguing in favour of the Strasbourg Court's practice of granting states a wide margin of appreciation. Commenting on the *Ireland v United Kingdom* case in the late 1970s, Michael O'Boyle, for instance, argued that given their perceived vital interests were at stake, governments could respond to an adverse decision by the Court regarding derogation by denouncing the Convention, or withdrawing recognition of the Court's jurisdiction or competence to receive individual petitions. To avoid losing state support in this way, he argued, the Court should reject derogation only in the most transparently spurious cases.[99]

However, there are strong grounds for suggesting that role of human rights in international politics has changed dramatically. The European Convention of Human Rights and the Court in Strasbourg – as the Council of Europe itself – have become cornerstones of modern-day Europe. As such it is rather unthinkable in the realm of contemporary international politics that a Council of Europe member state would withdraw its recognition of the Strasbourg Court's jurisdiction or competence to

[98] A. Downer, "Transnational Terrorism: The Threat to Australia," (Speech to launch the White Paper on International Terrorism, National Press Club, Canberra, 15 July 2004). http://www.foreignminister.gov.au/speeches/2004/040715_tt.html.

[99] M. O'Boyle, "Torture and Emergency Powers under the European Convention on Human Rights: Ireland v the United Kingdom," *American Journal of International Law* 71 (1977): 705.

receive individual petitions as a result of an unfavourable decision. This argument is supported, *inter alia*, by various unfavourable judgments of the Court in relation to the conflicts in Chechnya and South-eastern Turkey, for instance. A similar argument can be made in relation to the ICCPR which has become a universally accepted core instrument of international human rights law. And it can be extended to calling into question the continued applicability of the original rationale for including a deration clause in the treaty regimes. Indeed, it appears unlikely that states would condition their treaty participation on the existence of a derogation clause.

The analysis in this chapter has revealed that the operation of derogation clauses in international human rights treaties and their interpretation in an era of permanent legal emergency are problematic. In particular, concerns stem from the fact that they effectively allow for indefinite derogation from international human rights obligations. One may thus reach the conclusion that the derogation clauses are ill-suited in an age of international terrorism. To recommend abolishing them altogether may then be a logical consequence.[100] It is clear that such an abolishment would strengthen the overall protection of human rights in the treaty regimes of the ICCPR and the ECHR. It is equally clear, however, that such a development is unlikely to happen in the near future. For the moment, one has to live with the derogation clauses. It is thus particular disappointing that the European Court of Human Rights has not provided a re-interpretation of Article 15 of the ECHR and its definition and application to meet the challenges of international terrorism and corresponding legislative counter-measures. Nonetheless, there is an urgent need for an honest and detailed discourse on the contemporary role of the derogation clauses in international human rights treaties. And it is perhaps in the framework of the Council of Europe that such a discussion could be initiated.

Bibliography

Allison, G.T. 2004. *Nuclear terrorism: The ultimate preventable catastrophe*. New York: Times Books/Henry Holt.

Alter, J. 2001. Time to think about torture. *Newsweek* 138: 45.

Bram, J., A. Haughwout, and J. Orr. 2002. Has September 11 affected New York City's growth potential? *Economic Policy Review* 8 at http://www.newyorkfed.org/research/epr/02v08n2/0211bram/0211bram.html.

Brown, C. 2003. *Lost liberties: Ashcroft and the assault on personal freedom*. New York: The New Press.

Buergenthal, T. 1981. To respect and to ensure: State obligations and permissible derogations. In *The international bill of rights: The covenant on civil and political rights*, ed. L. Henkin. New York: Columbia University Press.

[100] It is interesting to note in this context that the African Charter on Human and Peoples' Rights does not regulate states of emergency, nor does it contain a derogation provision. See generally: F. Ouguergouz, *The African Charter on Human and Peoples' Rights. A Comprehensive Agenda for Human Dignity and Sustainable Democracy in Africa* (Dordrecht: Martinus Nijhoff, 2003).

Chernick, H. (ed.). 2005. *Resilient city: The economic impact of 9/11*. New York: Russell Sage Foundation.
Cole, D., and J.X. Dempsey. 2002. *Terrorism and the constitution: Sacrificing civil liberties in the name of national security*. Los Angeles: The New Press.
Cordesman, A.H. 2005. *The challenge of biological weapons*. Washington, DC: Center for Strategic and International Studies.
Dinh, V.D. 2002. Freedom and security after September 11. *Harvard Journal of Law and Public Policy* 25: 399.
Downer, A. 2004. Transnational terrorism: The threat to Australia. Speech to launch the White Paper on International Terrorism, National Press Club, Canberra, 15 July 2004. http://www.foreignminister.gov.au/speeches/2004/040715_tt.html.
Fenwick, H. 2002. The anti-terrorism, crime and security act 2001: A proportionate response? *Modern Law Review* 65: 724.
Fenwick, H. 2010. Recalibrating ECHR rights, and the role of the Human Rights Act post 9/11: Reasserting international human rights norms in the "war on terror"? *Current Legal Problems* 63: 153.
Gross, O. 1998. "Once more unto the breach": The systemic failure of applying the European Convention on Human Rights to entrenched emergencies. *Yale Journal of International Law* 23: 437.
Gross, E. 2001. Legal aspects of tackling terrorism: The balance between the right of a democracy to defend itself and the protection of Human Rights. *UCLA Journal of International Law & Foreign Affairs* 6: 167.
Gross, O., and F. Ní Aoláin. 2001. From discretion to scrutiny: Revisiting the application of the margin of appreciation doctrine in the context of Article 15 of the European Convention on Human Rights. *Human Rights Quarterly* 23: 638.
Gross, O., and F. Ni Aoláin. 2006. *Law in times of crisis: Emergency powers in theory and practice*. Cambridge: Cambridge University Press.
Hardin, R. 2004. Civil liberties in the era of mass terrorism. *Journal of Ethics* 8: 79.
Harris, D.J., M. O'Boyle, and C. Warbrick. 1995. *Law of the European convention on human rights*. London: Butterworths.
Hartman, J.F. 1985. Working paper for the committee of experts on the Article 4 derogation provision. *Human Rights Quarterly* 7: 89.
Hickman, T.R. 2005. Between human rights and the rule of law: Indefinite detention and the derogation model of constitutionalism. *Modern Law Review* 68: 655.
Hickman, T. 2010. *Public law after the human rights act*. Oxford: Hart Publishing.
Higgins, R. 1976–77. Derogations under human rights treaties. *The British Yearbook of International Law* 48: 281.
Human Rights Committee. 2001. *General Comment 29, States of Emergency* (Article 4), U.N. Doc. CCPR/C/21/Rev.1/Add.11.
International Commission of Jurists. 2009. *Assessing damage, urging action*. Report of the Eminent Jurists Panel on Terrorism, Counter-Terrorism and Human Rights, Geneva.
Jackson, R. 2005. *Writing the war on terror: Language, politics and counter-terrorism*. Manchester: Manchester University Press.
Jackson, O.A. 2008. The impact of the 9/11 terrorist attacks on the US economy, 3 March 2008. http://www.journalof911studies.com/volume/2008/OliviaJackson911andUS-Economy.pdf.
Jenkins, B.M. 2006. *Unconquerable nation: Knowing our enemy and strengthening ourselves*. Santa Monica: RAND Corporation.
Jervis, R. 2002. An interim assessment of September 11: What has changed and what has not? *Political Science Quarterly* 117: 37.
Johnson, R.B., and O.M. Nedelescu. 2005. The impact of terrorism on financial markets. International Monetary Fund, Working Paper WP/05/60, March 2005. http://www.internationalmonetaryfund.com/external/pubs/ft/wp/2005/wp0560.pdf.
Kelly, P. 2006. How 9/11 changed the world. *The Australian* (Sydney), September 8.

Lawrence, D. 2005. U.S. stocks rise, erasing losses on London bombings, gap rises. *Bloomberg News (Online)*, July 7. http://www.bloomberg.com/apps/news?pid=10000103&sid=aflPCIrU37Ns&refer=us.

Macdonald, R.St.J. 1993. The margin of appreciation. In *The European system for the protection of human*, ed. R.St.J. Macdonald, F. Matscher, and H. Petzold. Dordrecht/Boston: Kluwer.

Makinen, G. 2002. *The economic effects of 9/11: A retrospective assessment*. Report for Congress, 27 September 2002 (Washington, DC: Library of Congress.

Merrills, J.G. 1988. *The development of international law by the European court of human rights*. Manchester: Manchester University Press.

Michaelsen, C. 2003. International human rights on trial: The United Kingdom's and Australia's legal response to 9/11. *Sydney Law Review* 25: 275.

Mueller, J.E. 2007. Terrorism, overreaction and globalization. In *No more states?: Globalization, national self-determination, and terrorism*, ed. R.N. Rosecrance and A.A. Stein. Lanham: Rowman & Littlefield.

Neumann, P.R. 2009. *Old and new terrorism*. Cambridge: Polity Press.

O'Boyle, M. 1977. Torture and emergency powers under the European Convention on Human Rights: Ireland v the United Kingdom. *American Journal of International Law* 71: 705.

O'Donnell, T.A. 1982. The margin of appreciation doctrine: Standards in the jurisprudence of the European Court of Human Rights. *Human Rights Quarterly* 4: 474.

O'Neil, A. 2004. Keeping the contemporary threat environment in perspective. *Australian Review of Public Affairs*. http://www.australianreview.net/digest/2004/05/oneil.html.

Ouguergouz, F. 2003. *The African charter on human and peoples' rights. A comprehensive agenda for human dignity and sustainable democracy in Africa*. Dordrecht: Martinus Nijhoff.

Nolan, M. 2008. Measuring support for Australian counter-terrorism initiatives and human rights: The impact of offence construal, perpetrator motive and siege mentality. In *Fresh perspectives on the "war on terror"*, ed. P. Mathew and M. Gani. Canberra: ANU E Press.

Posner, R.A. 2001. Security versus civil liberties. *The Atlantic Monthly* 288: 46.

Richardson, H.W., P. Gordon, and J.E. Moore II (eds.). 2005. *The economic impacts of terrorist attacks*. Cheltenham: Edward Elgar.

Roach, K. 2008. Ordinary laws for emergencies and democratic derogations from rights. In *Emergencies and the limits of legality*, ed. V.V. Ramraj. Cambridge: Cambridge University Press.

Sageman, M. 2008. *Leaderless Jihad: Terror networks in the twenty-first century*. Philadelphia: University of Pennsylvania Press.

Stephen, S. 2004. Terrorism: Governments fuel fear. In *Terrorism*, ed. J. Healey. Balmain: Spinney Press.

Stevenson, R.W. 2005. Cheney says 9/11 changed the rules. *New York Times* (New York), 21 December.

Stossel, J. 2004. *Give me a break*. New York: HarperCollins.

Svensson-McCarthy, A.-L. 1998. *The international law of human rights and states of exception: With special reference to Travaux Préparatoires and case-law of the international monitoring organs*. Dordrecht/Boston: Martinus Nijhoff.

Tierney, S. 2005. Determining the state of exception: What role for parliament and the courts? *Modern Law Review* 68: 668.

Tomkins, A. 2002. Legislating against terror: The anti-terrorism, crime and security act 2001. *Public Law* (summer): 205

Cases

A and others v United Kingdom, App 3455/05 (19 February 2009), (2009) 49 EHRR 29.

A and others v Secretary of State for the Home Department, [2004] UKHL 56; [2005] 2 W.L.R. 87.

Aksoy v Turkey, App 21987/93 (18 December 1996), (1997) 23 EHRR 553.
Brannigan and McBride v United Kingdom, (1993) 17 EHRR 539.
Greek Case (1969) 12 Yearbook ECHR 1.
Handyside v United Kingdom (1976) 1 EHRR 737.
Ireland v United Kingdom (1978) Series A No 35.
Ireland v United Kingdom, App 5310/71, ECtHR, Series B, Vol. 23-I (1976-1978).
Landinelli Silva v Uruguay (1981) HRC Comm No 34/1978.
Lawless v Ireland (No 3) (1961) 1 EHRR 15.
McCann and Others v United Kingdom (1995) 21 EHRR 97.
Salgar de Montejo v Colombia (1982) HRC Comm No 64/1979.
Weinberger v Uruguay (1980) HRC Comm No 28/1978.

Chapter 14
National Self-Defence in the Age of Terrorism: Immediacy and State Attribution

Mark D. Kielsgard

On May 1, 2011 in a residential compound in the Pakistani town of Abbottabad, al-Qaida leader and alleged 9–11 mastermind Osama bin Laden was assassinated by US Special Forces. "The dramatic news closes one chapter in the global turmoil sparked by the September 11 attacks on America that killed 3,000 people in 2001. The event triggered the war in Afghanistan, was used as a pretext for the invasion of Iraq and inflicted grievous damage to America's moral authority after the CIA torture of al-Qaida suspects and detention of more than 700 people at Guantanamo Bay in Cuba."[1] In addition to the cataclysmic impact bin Laden had on policy and executive action, his actions greatly influenced the development of international security law and contemporary understanding of States' right to self-defense.

In 1998, the UN Security Council passed Resolution 1189 in response to the Nairobi and Dar-es-Salaam terrorist bombings and tied the suppression of acts of international terrorism to the maintenance of international peace and security,[2] thus invoking the UN Charter language of Chapter 7 and suggesting that international sanctions under article 41 and 42[3] may be appropriate responses to international

[1] D. Walsh, *Osama bin Laden Killed in US Raid on Pakistan Hideout,* The Guardian News Service, May 2, 2011 at http://www.guardian.co.uk/world/2011/may/02/osama-bin-laden-dead-pakistan/print (last visited May 20, 2011).

[2] S/RES/1189 (1998). Though the connection between international peace and security and counter-terrorism had been forged by the Security Council before resolution 1189 (e.g., Lockerbie resolution) it was reiterated in resolution 1189 at a crucial time in the historic development of international security law, in close proximity to the events of 9–11, and contributed to the expansion into its current form.

[3] United Nations Charter art. 41, 42 at http://www.un.org/en/documents/charter/chapter7.shtml.

M.D. Kielsgard (✉)
City University of Hong Kong, School of Law, City University of Hong Kong,
Tat Chee Avenue, Kowloon Tong, Kowloon, Hong Kong
e-mail: mkielsga@cityu.edu.hk

A. Masferrer (ed.), *Post 9/11 and the State of Permanent Legal Emergency*,
Ius Gentium: Comparative Perspectives on Law and Justice 14,
DOI 10.1007/978-94-007-4062-4_14,

terrorist activity. These acts of terrorism were attributed to the al-Qaida organization. In 1999, the Security Council passed Resolution 1267 directed at Afghanistan and its state sponsorship of terrorism, specifically mentioning "Usama bin Laden" in the text.[4] Resolution 1267 reiterated Chapter 7 applicability to the suppression of international terrorism and ordered sanctions against Afghanistan [for harboring bin Laden] under article 41 of the Charter.[5] These sanctions consisted of prohibitions against Afghan aircraft and freezing Taliban funds.[6]

In 2001, in response to bin Laden's most destructive terrorist act, the Security Council adopted Resolution 1373 which extended counter-terrorism competence to Article 51 of the Charter by "[r]eaffirming the inherent right of individual and collective self-defense."[7] Thus, not only had counter-terrorism initiatives assumed the applicability of UN-ordered sanctions (including military actions), they were extended to provide for unilateral national competence to initiate military responses. These counter-terrorism developments took place over a very few years and have been instigated largely in response to the actions of one person and the organization he controlled. They have changed the landscape of international law and foreign relations and beg the question, how far can sovereign states go to combat terrorism in the name of self-defense in the post-9/11 age? In the context of SC Res. 1373, is article 51 justification only applicable in situations of state-sponsored terrorism or can it be invoked for surgical strikes within neutral third party states? Does this provide greater national discretion in the employment of unilateral military action than otherwise intended in the UN Charter? Finally, in the post-9/11 age during the "Global War on Terrorism," a conflict seemingly without end, will international law trend away from this expansive view or continue down the path suggested by the Security Council? These issues are particularly significant as the so-called doctrine of anticipatory self-defense has taken a parallel course under international law which has arguably further eroded prohibitions against waging war, altered the character of *jus ad bellum* and article 2(4) of the UN Charter.

This essay will examine the nature and history of national self-defense in the context of international law and counter-terrorism. It will recount and analyze state practice, Security Council initiative, international jurisprudence, and scholarship in order to shed light on the limitations imposed by the United Nations Charter. It will explore historic trends in the interpretation of relevant Charter provisions and specifically address the issue of state attribution (or targeting non-state actors) and the degree of immediacy (including anticipatory self-defense) necessary to justify the use of defensive force. Moreover, it will address arguably premature representations that the character of national self-defense experienced organic change in response to the 9/11 attacks. Finally, while the issues of necessity and proportionality are important considerations, a thorough discussion of those concepts is outside the limited scope of this project.

---

[4] S/RES/1267 (1999).

[5] *Ibidem* at 4(a)(b).

[6] *Ibidem.*

[7] S/RES/1373(2001).

14.1 The Early Evolution of National Self-Defense

The concept of a "just war" (*bellum justum*) dates to antiquity and was expressly discussed by such commentators as Aristotle,[8] Cicero,[9] Augustine[10] and others during the time of the Greek and Roman Empires,[11] and later by Grotius in the early modern era.[12] Between the World Wars, Hans Kelsen articulated that war is justified when it is directed as a sanction against a State that has violated international law.[13] After the UN Charter was adopted, "Kelsen adjusted the theory to the evolution of international law. He still regarded war as lawful only when constituting a sanction, but … legitimate war now had to be a 'counter war,' waged in response to an illegal war by the other side."[14] Thus, war could only be legitimately waged in self-defense. Article 2(4) of the UN Charter and, more generally, Chapter VI[15] prohibits non-pacific settlement of disputes or waging war. Article 2(4) prohibits states from "the threat or use of force against the territorial integrity or political independence of any state."[16] The Charter was the first widely ratified international instrument that affirmatively addressed norms *jus ad bellum*, or the propriety of waging war, instead of merely addressing norms *jus in bello*.[17]

---

[8] J. von Elbe, "The Evolution of the Concept of the Just War in International Law," *American Journal of International Law* 33 (1939): 665, 666, n. 9 *citing the Nicomacheon Ethics,*Book X, Ch. VI XVII, 6 and; *Politics,* VII, 14.

[9] W. G. Grewe, *The Epochs of International Law*, 108–111, trans. Michael Byers and revised, 2000; Arthur Nussbaum, *A Concise History of the Law of Nations 35* (revised ed., 1954); cited in M. E. O'Connell, *International Law and the Use of Force*, 2nd ed. (New York: Foundation Press, 2009), 118.

[10] M. E. O'Connell, *International Law and the Use of Force* (New York: Foundation Press, 2009) at 118–119.

[11] See Y. Dinstein, *War Aggression and Self-Defense*, 4th ed. (Cambridge: Cambridge University Press, 2005), *citing* A. Nussbaum, *A Concise History of the Law of Nations* (1954): 10–11.

[12] M. E. O'Connell, *International Law and the Use of Force*, at 123.

[13] *Ibidem* at 67, *see also* H. Kelsen, *Principles of International Law* 311 (1st ed., 1952); H. Kelsen, *General Theory of Law and State* (1945): 331–333.

[14] *Ibidem.*

[15] These provisions were themselves subsequent reiterations of the principles laid out in the Charter of the League of Nations as well as the Kellogg Briand Pact outlawing recourse to war and obliging states to find pacific means to resolve disputes – though they did not forbid recourse to war in self-defense.

[16] UN Charter art. 2(4).

[17] While efforts were afoot to create more definite norms regulating the waging of war in the early 20th century in the treaty of Versailles and the Kellogg Briand Pact, the United Nations Charter was the first International instrument which approached the issue in a practical and enforceable manner. "Until the end of the First World War, resorting to armed force was regarded not as an illegal act but as an acceptable way of settling differences. In 1919, the Covenant of the League of Nations and, in 1928, the Treaty of Paris (Briand-Kellogg Pact) sought to outlaw war. The adoption of the United Nations Charter in 1945 confirmed this trend: the members of the Organization shall abstain, in their international relations, from resorting to the threat or use of force…" On the Prohibition of War, International Committee of the Red Cross, January 1, 2004 at http://www.icrc.org/eng/resources/documents/misc/5kzjjd.htm (last visited June 16, 2011); *also see* McDougal, MS / Feliciano, FP, *The International Law of War*, 138–143 (The Hague: Martinus Nijhoff, 1994).

However, it contained an exception to the general prohibition on the use of force as provided in article 51 which states:

> Nothing in the present Charter shall impair the inherent right of individual or collective self-defense if an armed attack occurs against a Member of the United Nations, until the Security Council has taken measures necessary to maintain international peace and security…[18]

Kelsen's moderated grounds for a "just war" still implies a punitive component for those who would illegitimately launch an armed attack against another state. This is inconsistent with traditional common law theories of self-defense, which require an element of immediacy – sanctions can be imposed at leisure, self-defense must be done without deliberation. Moreover, Kelsen's approach is obviously at odds with the Charter and particularly article 2(4). In any event, Kelsen's theory and article 51 are dependent on a sufficiently well-defined concept of self-defense.

Beginning in the nineteenth century, the concept of self-defense was widened in scope by some to include *self-preservation*[19] and thus "there is hardly an act of international lawlessness which it might not be claimed to excuse. It was, for example, one of the pretexts advanced by Germany in 1914 to justify her attack on Belgian neutrality, although she herself was under no apparent threat of attack either from Belgium or any other state."[20] Self-defense was also argued at both Nuremberg and the Tokyo War Crimes Tribunals in an attempt to establish defenses to the crime of aggression.[21]

An overly expansive definition of self-defense can lead to patently indefensible justifications of aggressive acts, "… as nearly every aggressive act is sought to be portrayed as an act of self defense,"[22] and circumvent the fundamentally pacific aim of the United Nations.[23] Indeed, some scholars have argued that an overly expansive definition of article 51, *inter alia*, has led to the collapse of article 2(4) and that the "… high minded resolve of Article 2(4) mocks us from its grave."[24] Yet the determination

[18] UN Charter, art. 51.

[19] The English Common law case of R v. Dudley and Stevens can be cited to distinguish the concept of self-defense from that of self-preservation. In that case two men conspired and killed a third for the purpose of cannibalism after they were cast adrift in a small dingy for 18 days. They argued the necessity of killing for self-preservation, but their defense was unsuccessful and they were sentenced to hang – subsequently commuted to 6 months penal servitude. R v. Dudley and Stevens, 14 Q.B.D. 273 (1884).

[20] J. L. Brierly, *The Law of Nations: An Introduction to the International Law of Peace*, 6th ed. Sir Humphrey Waldock (Oxford: Oxford University Press, 1963), at 404.

[21] *Ibidem* at 406.

[22] *Ibidem*.

[23] The Preamble of the UN Charter proposes " to ensure, by the acceptance of principles and the institution of methods, that armed force shall not be used, save in the common interest …"

[24] T. Franck, "Who Killed Article 2(4)?," *American Journal of International Law* 64 (1970): 809–810.

of the character of self-defense as it pertains to states is not entirely devoid of content under international law. In response to the early *Caroline* incident (1837), United States Secretary of State Daniel Webster expressed a generally recognized opinion of self-defense that closely corresponds to the traditional conditions for self-defense used in individual criminal cases. Webster stated there must be a showing that it was "a necessity of self-defense, instant, overwhelming, leaving no choice of means and no moment for deliberation, … [and the action taken must include] nothing unreasonable or excessive, since the act justified by the necessity of self-defense must be limited by the necessity and kept clearly within it."[25]

While the *Caroline* incident is often cited in discussions of necessity and proportionality, it is also helpful to consider it in the narrow context of immediacy. Webster's narrow definition was adopted by the Nuremberg Tribunal which stated, "It must be remembered that preventive action in foreign territory is justified only in the case of 'an instant and overwhelming necessity for self-defense leaving no choice of means, and no moment of deliberation.'"[26] Thus, at the time of the formation of the Charter, self-defense required an immediacy of threat that is instant, overwhelming and leaving no time for thought. Therefore, the attack must have been ongoing or immediately pending, not something that was already completed (with time for hindsight) or something anticipated at some vague time in the future. Under this standard, even relative certainty of the attack without knowledge of when it would begin would be insufficient to act with a justification of self-defensive.[27] As an example, if an individual had sufficient certainty, backed by solid evidence, that a second individual was going to kill him at some time in the future, the first individual would not have justification to *sua sponte* ambush and take the second individual's life as an act of self-defense without further provocation. However, if the second individual has struck the first blow or is in the process of doing so, then the first individual may strike in self-defense. The repeated first attacks of the Nazi *blitzkrieg* made this narrow standard sufficiently easy for the prosecution to prove at Nuremberg in the formative years of the Charter.

Taking the early Charter period as the point of departure, there are three corollary issues unsettled. One, whether it is up to the state (or some other entity) to determine if a threat is sufficient (in consequence and immediacy) to establish the necessity of self-defense; two, how immediate the threat must be to assert a valid claim of self-defense; and three, whether national self-defense, the only authorized

[25] *See* Department of State [Mr. Webster to Lord Ashburn], Washington, 6th August 1842, Avalon Project – British-American Diplomacy: The Caroline Case, *at* http://avalon.law.yale.edu/19th_century/br-1842.asp (last visited June 18, 2011).

[26] *Ibidem.*

[27] Naturally, under this scenario, other remedies would be available to the anticipated victim such as restraint on the other party, heightened scrutiny, etc., but justified self-defense calculated to bring death or serious bodily harm would not be available to the potential victim.

justification for unilateral military action in the Charter era,[28] is available when combating non-state actors.

In judging state fitness to assert self-defense, after World War II both Japan and Germany argued that this competence was reserved for the State.[29] While it is, perhaps by necessity, up to the State to make the initial determination on the basis of the immediacy of the threat, the Nuremberg Tribunal found that this decision is nonetheless reviewable in accordance with the rules and customs of international law.[30] Thus, self-defense is not limited to what the State asserting it claims – there is no special State fiat – but consists of a higher threshold, presumably an objective standard. However, beyond citing the language from the *Caroline* incident, the Tribunal didn't address what that objective standard was – it merely found that Germany hadn't satisfied it.

Additionally, the issues of immediacy and against whom the justification of self-defense may be asserted are more convoluted questions that have evolved since the Charter was drafted. These issues are particularly complex because attacks from non-state parties, such as terrorists, typically differ from those by conventional forces as they are usually limited to one strike (or a series of unconnected strikes) without attempts to take and hold enemy territory. Thus, conventional armed attacks and terrorist attacks are distinguishable. Any instant defensive response to a terrorist attack is generally vain as the attack is usually perpetrated *incognito* and the terrorist perpetrators disappear, often killing themselves in the process, before a defense can be mounted. Thus, the traditional military paradigm of conventional forces against like-kind forces attempting to take and hold ground, so prevalent during World War II, are inapplicable with the irregular forces and tactics of modern terrorist activity. This suggests that military counter-terrorism initiatives are incompatible with a coherent reading of article 51 and that these initiatives fall more properly within the province of a domestic or horizontal law enforcement competence.[31] However, this interpretation of article 51 would also only allow for a military response to terrorism under article 42 with the requisite Security Council approval, which is directly contravened by Security Council Resolution 1373.[32] Moreover, this issue becomes even thornier with the phenomenon of state-sponsored terrorism, or the sending of irregular forces (i.e., terrorists) at the behest of a sovereign state, and state harboring of terrorism.

---

[28] The other exception to the use of force in article 42 provides authority to the Security Council to instigate military action in order to maintain international peace and security.

[29] Japan raised this issue on the weight of the US Declaration to the Kellogg-Brand Pact which proposed that "[the State] is competent to decide whether circumstances require recourse to war in self-defense." Germany also raised the self-defense reservations to Brand-Kellogg Pact in defense at the Nuremberg Tribunals. Brierly, *The Law of Nations*, at 407.

[30] *Ibidem* at 408.

[31] For a detailed analysis of counter-terrorism approaches *see generally* M. D. Kielsgard, "A Human Rights Approach to Counter Terrorism," *California Western International Law Journal* 36 (2006): 1.

[32] S/RES/1373(2001).

14.2 Trends in National Self-Defense Prior to 9/11

The language of article 51 is arguably unambiguous; it can be read as a document regulating state-on-state conduct to the exclusion of non-state actors. This interpretation is consistent with a contextual reading under international law as it was understood at the time of the Charter's drafting.[33] In 1945, international law had assumed little jurisdiction over domestic matters, including domestic law enforcement, and was reluctant to intrude upon state sovereignty.[34] This can be seen, *inter alia*, by the League of Nations' failed effort to implement a counter-terrorism convention in 1937[35] and the historic legal emphasis on *jus in bello* under "Hague law,"[36] in contradistinction to *bellum justum*. Furthermore, debate continues to loom over whether article 51 is the definitive norm for self-defense or whether pre-existing customary international law still functions to provide additional grounds such as the protection of nationals abroad and anticipatory self-defense.[37] Those who advocate this wider view argue that the language of article 51 (which describes self-defense as an "inherent right") suggests the continuity of pre-existing customary law coexistent with the Charter provision.[38] Others challenge this view as a misreading of the customary international law of 1945, and as a reading that "deprives article 51 of any purpose; article 51 imposes restrictions on the right of self-defense in response to armed attack and so it would be strange at the same time to preserve a wider right to self-defense unlimited by these restrictions."[39]

---

[33] *See generally*, Brierly, *The Law of Nations*, already cited.

[34] Obviously the exceptions to this general rule were the tribunals at Nuremburg and Tokyo, but they consisted of prosecutions for international crimes that had recently become recognized and arguably differ from the crimes associated with terrorism.

[35] The League of Nations Counter-terrorism Convention never entered into force for failure to receive the necessary number of ratifying signatures. *Convention For the Prevention and Punishment of Terrorism*, 19 League of Nations O.J. 23 (1938), League of Nations Doc. C.546(I).M.383(I).1937.V(1938)(16 November 1937).

[36] By emphasizing jus in bello, or the constraints on tactics of war, and deemphasizing jus ad bellum, constraints on waging war, international law still provided great latitude for state sovereignty. Pre-Charter efforts had been made in the Treaty of Versailles and the Kellogg-Briand Pact, but neither had much impact nor evinced a realistic commitment to interfering with the states right to wage aggressive war.

[37] Dinstein abovr n. 12, at 181–182; *see also* Brownlie, I, *International Law and the Use of Force by States*, 269 (1963).

[38] Id. Among those who believe that national self-defense justifications exist outside the scope of the Charter is Judge Schwebel of the ICJ who, in his dissent in *Nicaragua,* found that self-defense justifications can be found in customary international law even if no armed attack can be shown. See D. W. Bowett, *Self-Defense in International Law* (1958): 187–192; M. S. McDougal and F. P. Feliciano, *Law and Minimum World Public Order* (1961): 232–241; J. Stone, *Aggression and World Order: A Critique of United Nations Theories of Aggression* 44 (1958) cited in Dinstein *War Aggression and Self-Defense*, already cited.

[39] *Ibidem.*

Aside from custom, as the successor body to the League of Nations, the Charter was drafted during the end of the Second World War, the bloodiest conflagration in human history, and was designed to correct the Leagues' failures – namely its inability to prevent the War. It is in this context that the Charter should be interpreted. In accordance with article 32 of the *Vienna Convention on the Law of Treaties* (VCLT) "recourse may be had to supplemental means of interpretation, including the preparatory work of the treaty and the circumstances of its conclusions."[40] The overwhelming circumstances leading to the existence of the Charter was the ongoing World War. In the first line of the preamble the Charter specifically provides, "We the peoples of the United Nations determined to save succeeding generations from the scourge of war, which twice in our lifetime has brought untold sorrow to mankind …"[41] Thus, at the time of drafting, it is logical to infer that the states parties had only intended article 51 application to armed attacks from other states which carried a threat that was immediate, instant and leaving no time for deliberation. Yet, despite its original objective, its implementation has been subject to evolving interpretation under customary international law.

While article 51 provides the right of self-defense to *members,* meaning state parties, it does not explicitly identify *against whom* the right to self-defense may be asserted. That is, whether it can be applied only against other member states or to non-state actors. An interpretation that expands this justification to the defense against non-state actors arguably broadens the authority of states in the use of military force. However, this reading seems consistent with modern evolving concepts of international law, particularly in the twenty-first century, which is relatively obsessed with issues involving non-state actors or terrorism, when compared to the drafters of the Charter.[42] But a flexible interpretation of the original intent of Charter provisions is not without precedent.

In a parallel interpretation, the Security Council enlarged the meaning of the language in article 39 when determining the existence of a threat to international peace and security. As Bruno Simma observes:

> While the concept of threat to the peace in article 39 may have originally referred mainly to threats of inter-state conflicts …, the Security Council soon abandoned such a strict reading. Already the Palestine Conflict in 1948 was no clear cut inter-state war, but the Security Council did not hesitate to regard it as a threat to the peace … Likewise, in 1961, the Security Council determined a threat to the peace with respect to the conflict in the Congo … After the end of the Cold War … the Security Council significantly reinforced such a broader interpretation and it seems by now widely accepted that extreme violence within a state can give rise to Chapter VII enforcement action.[43]

[40] Vienna Convention on the Law of Treaties, art. 32.

[41] UN Charter preamble, already cited.

[42] While "obsession" is a relatively subjective description, it can be inferred by the spate of counter-terrorism initiatives of the early twenty-first century including numerous Security Council and General Assembly resolutions, the formation of the Counter-Terrorism Committee (the sitting Security Council), horizontal law enforcement initiatives from Interpol, Europol, and national law enforcement agencies, additional counter-terrorism conventions and the so-called "Global War on Terrorism" launched by the United States in 2001/2002.

[43] B. Simma, *The Charter of the United Nations: A Commentary*, 2nd ed., vol. 1 (Oxford: University Press, 2002) at 722.

An expansive reading of article 51 is consistent with the treatment accorded article 39. After the formation of the Charter and during the 1950s through the 1970s, there was relatively little development in the concept of national self-defense. As Cold War-fueled proxy wars of national liberation raged in select developing nations and during the period of "mutually assured destruction,"[44] the necessity for expanding self-defense to include non-state actors was superfluous and re-interpretations of the immediacy requirement were in their infancy. In an era where many conflicts were encouraged if not instigated by the *superpowers,*[45] there was little interest or need to expand the definition of self-defense in the Charter because the conflicts were usually internal in nature and often outside the scope of article 51. Alternatively, these proxy wars were waged under the justification of "collective self-defense" with the superpower coming in on the side of the faction whose ideology most closely corresponded to its own.

In determining the meaning of self-defense it is helpful to review state practice. Article 31 (3)(b) of the VCLT provides that the general rules relating to treaty interpretation shall take into account "any subsequent practice in the application of the treaty which establishes the agreement of the parties regarding its interpretation."[46] During the Cold War the United States and the USSR invoked self-defense many times. In 1956 the USSR intervened in the Hungarian revolution at the request of the existing leadership.[47] The Soviets remained after the former government was deposed and installed a new government. In that case the Soviets claimed collective self-defense; its military was already fighting before the original government was deposed, so it was fighting the interim regime and not technically a non-state actor. In 1979 the USSR attacked Afghanistan.[48] Similarly, in that case the Soviets intervened to assist the communist government in Afghanistan against the Muslim revolutionaries during the War (1978–82). Like the situation in Hungary, the Soviets did not intervene against international terrorists, but officially utilized collective self-defense in putting down an internal armed conflict in its *sphere of influence*.

The United States sent military forces to the Dominican Republic in 1965,[49] which, like the Soviet forces in Hungary and Afghanistan, were designed to protect

---

[44] Mutually assured destruction is a "defensive strategy based on the concept that neither the United States nor its enemies will ever start a nuclear war because the other side will retaliate massively and unacceptably." Col. A. J. Parrington, USAF, Mutually Assured Destruction Revisited, (Winter 1997) *Airpower Journal*, at http://www.airpower.maxwell.af.mil/airchronicles/apj/apj97/parrin.html.

[45] A superpower has been defined as "a country that has the capacity to project dominating power and influence anywhere in the world, and sometimes, in more than one region of the globe at the same time, and so may plausibly attain the status of global hegemon." L. Miller, "China an Emerging Superpower?" (2006) *Stanford Journal of International Relations.*

[46] Vienna Convention on the Law of Treaties, art. 31(3)(b).

[47] United Nations General Assembly, Special Committee on the Problem of Hungary (1957) Chap. Ii. C, para. 58 (at 20).

[48] The invasion of Afghanistan resulted in a widespread international outcry that included the US boycott of the 1980 Summer Olympics in Moscow and General Assembly resolutions calling for the withdrawal of the USSR. G/ RES/ES-6/2 (1980) 14 January 1980.

[49] US Department of State, Foreign Relations of the United States, 1964–1968, vol. XXXII, Dominican Republic; Cuba; Haiti; Guyana, Document 43, at http://history.state.gov/historicaldocuments/frus1964-68v32/d43.

the existing government from national revolutionary conflict. Vietnam was a far longer and more costly US military intervention intended to defend the government of South Vietnam from the forces of the North.[50] Self-defense justifications were also used in the US incursions into Laos and Cambodia during the Vietnam conflict.[51]

During the opening decades of the Cold War, Israel cited self-defense when it attacked Egypt (1967) in anticipation of a united attack by several Arab states.[52] This arguably qualifies as self-defense under article 51 as against an armed attack from another state, but calls into question the immediacy requirement and serves as a precursor to the anticipatory self-defense doctrine brought to fruition in subsequent decades.

The opening decades of the Charter era saw article 51 used primarily in a collective self-defense context or in defending existing regimes against conflicts of national liberation. Ideologically, of course, use of this justification was tied to the struggle between Western Democracies and Eastern Marxist states and resulted in the proxy wars of the early Cold War. With both the USSR and the US having permanent seats on the Security Council (and veto power), it was pointless to question their interpretations of self-defense. The problem of proxy war was feebly addressed by General Assembly Resolution 2625 on the *Declaration on Principles of International Law Concerning Friendly Relations and Co-operation Among States in Accordance with the Charter of the United Nations*, which provided:

> Every State has the duty to refrain from any forcible action which deprives people referred to in the elaboration of the principle of equal rights and self-determination of their right to self-determination and freedom and independence.[53]

Moreover, these decades witnessed the trustee period during which most of the world's states won their independence from colonial masters through turbulent and often violent means. These conflicts and the independent states that they produced changed the complexion of the General Assembly, which impacted customary international law. These newly emancipated states, with the ink still wet on their constitutive documents, evinced certain sympathy for freedom fighters and reluctance to fuel state practices that were perceived as contrary to the anti-imperial goals of national liberation. General Assembly resolution 3034 (1973) poignantly expresses

---

[50] The Vietnam War cost the US approximately 58,000 lives (350,000 casualties) and between one and two million Vietnamese deaths. The US price tag for the war was the equivalent of 662 billion dollars (in 2007 dollars). Yassin Musharbash, War on Terror More Expensive than Vietnam, Spiegel Online International, Jan. 16, 2007 at http://www.speigel.de/international/0,1518,460007,00.html.

[51] The United States and South Vietnam justified attacks into these territories on the basis that the North Vietnamese forces were retreating there in order to recover from attacks and stockpile equipment, food and arms.

[52] The Panorama Middle East Archives: Six-Day War, BBC, Feb. 6, 2009, at http://news.bbc.co.uk/panorama/hi/front_page/newsid_7875000/7875655.stm.

[53] GA/8082 24October1970.

this sympathy in its title that emphasizes the causes of terrorism over its effects. The title states:

> Measures to prevent international terrorism which endangers or takes innocent human lives or jeopardizes fundamental freedoms, and study of the underlying causes of those forms of terrorism and acts of violence which lie in misery, frustration, grievance and despair and which cause some people to sacrifice human lives, including their own, in an attempt to effect radical changes.[54]

This application focused on state terrorism rather than non-state terrorism as it articulated condemnation for "the continuation of repressive and terrorist acts by colonial, racist and alien regimes in denying peoples their legitimate right to self-determination and independence and other human rights and fundamental freedoms."[55] During this era of counter-terrorism the international community relied upon a growing set of piecemeal treaties[56] prohibiting terrorist acts, but did not endorse unilateral military action grounded in article 51.

Subsequently however, there were several states that began to invoke article 51 in support of unilateral military action in response to the conduct of non-state actors. Examples of such cases include Israel's use of force in Uganda in 1976 (Entebbe airport)[57]; numerous attacks by South Africa on Angola and Zambia between 1976 and 1979[58]; the US bombing raid on Libya in 1986,[59] on Baghdad in 1993,[60] on Afghanistan in 1998,[61] and on Sudan in 1998.[62] All of these attacks were conducted

---

[54] GA/3034 18 December 1972.

[55] *Ibidem.*

[56] UN Treaty Collection, Conventions on Terror, at http://untreaty.un.org/English/Terrorism.asp.

[57] The so-called "raid on Entebbe" took place in an effort to rescue Jewish hostages hi-jacked on an Air France flight from Athens to Paris. The Idi Amin Ugandan government took no measures against the terrorist group, Popular Front for the Liberation of Palestine, and forced the Israeli commandos to plan for resistance encountered by Ugandan military troops. In the raid 45 Ugandan troops were killed, 11 MIG jet fighters were destroyed, and 3 terrorists, 1 hostage and 1 commando was killed. The Security Council took no action and the raid was applauded by many Western states and condemned by many Middle Eastern states. Terrorism: Vindication for the Israelis, TIME Magazine, July 26, 1976 at http://www.time.com/time/magazine/article/0,9171,914380,00.html.

[58] In 1976 the Security Council adopted resolution 393 that strongly condemned the armed attacks of South Africa against the Republic of Zambia and threatened sanctions against South Africa if it persisted. S/RES/393 (1976).

[59] This raid was in response to a terrorist bombing of a West German discotheque earlier in 1985 and resulted in a General Assembly resolution condemning the United States for its armed attack against Libya and characterized it as a violation of the Charter of the United Nations and international law. G/RES/41/38 (1985).

[60] See generally W. M. Reisman, "The Baghdad Bombing: Self-defense or Reprisal?," *European Journal of International Law* 5 (1994): 120–133.

[61] The bombing missions against targets in Afghanistan and Sudan were in retaliation against the terrorist bombings of American embassies in Kenya and Tanzania earlier that same year. The international response was mixed and the Security Council refused to place the matter on the agenda. See generally, J. Lobel, "The Use of Force to Respond to Terrorist Attacks: The Bombing of Sudan and Afghanistan," *Yale Journal of International Law* 24 (1999): 537.

[62] *Ibidem.*

under the color of self-defense pursuant to article 51. In many of these cases the military action was directed at state governments in reprisal for their condoning or sponsoring terrorist groups inside their territories.[63] Thus, from the waning years of the Cold War to before 9/11, state practice had begun to trend toward a more expansive understanding of article 51. This practice is more consistent with Hans Kelsen's post-Charter definition of *bellum justum* as it included a punitive component.[64]

Other invocations of article 51 during this period evince a more conventional interpretation. Some examples include the UK's intervention into the Falklands in 1982 against Argentine forces who had occupied British territory,[65] Ethiopia's justification for military intervention into Somalia[66] and the US-led coalition to drive Iraq out of Kuwait in 1990.[67] Still other justifications include instances of anticipatory self-defense whereby military action was initiated to prevent a hostile force from striking a devastating first blow.[68] Such attacks include Israel's bombing strike on the Osirak nuclear power station in Iraq in 1981,[69] and multiple attacks against Lebanon beginning in 1978[70]; and the US attack on a chemical plant in Sudan thought to be producing chemical weapons (to be used against the US or its allies).[71]

---

[63] An exception was the US raid in Afghanistan in 1998 in which US forces bombed a terrorist training base on the territory of Afghanistan but without specifically targeting the Taliban government.

[64] The distinction between reprisal and self-defense was presented to the Security Council in 1964 regarding the British air strike on the Yemen Arab Republic. The UK representative claimed their action "was not a retaliation or reprisal. On the contrary, the action was taken in response to an urgent request from ministers of the Federation to protect the interests and integrity of their country. It was a measure of defense." The representative explained that there are punitive attacks and then counter-attacks to repel or prevent an attack. *Repertoire of the Practice of the Security Council, Supplement 1964–1965* (United Nations publication, Sales No. E68, VII.1), chap. XI, part IV, Case No. 7, cited in Reisman, WM / Arsanjani, MH / Wiessner, S / Westerman, GS, *International Law in Contemporary Perspective*, 948–949 (New York, Foundation Press, 2004). The counter-attack might be seen as defensive as otherwise precluding an aggressor from further attacks by incapacitating their ability to launch future attacks.

[65] Argentina, which still maintains that the Falkland Islands are within its sovereign territory, were requested to leave the islands by the Security Council and eventually the Council provided Britain with express authorization to take article 51 defensive measures in Security Council resolution 502. S/RES/502 (1982).

[66] Ethiopia's claim to self-defense was a hybrid of several different bases, including as a defense against terrorist incursions but also based on a claim of aggression. See generally, A. K. Allo, "Ethiopia's Armed Intervention in Somalia: The Legality of Self-Defense in Responding to the Threat of Terrorism," *Denver Journal of International Law and Policy* 39 (December 1, 2010): 139.

[67] Note that this was collective self-defense and with Security Council approval under art. 42, S/RES/0678 (1990) 29 Nov. 1990.

[68] Below n. 87.

[69] Israel's action was strongly condemned by the Security Council later that year. S/RES/487 (1981) 19 June 1981.

[70] The Security Council called upon Israel to withdraw troops from Lebanon in 1978 in UN Security Council Resolution 425. S/RES/425 (1978).

[71] This was justified on article 51 grounds both as pre-emptive self-defense and in retaliation for the terrorist bombings of the US embassies in Kenya and Tanzania earlier that year. J. Lobel. "The Use of Force to Respond to Terrorist Attacks: The Bombing of Sudan and Afghanistan," already cited.

The US also justified the unilateral invasion of Panama in 1989 on article 51 grounds, citing the assassination of a soldier in the Panama Canal Zone,[72] and its invasion of Grenada in 1983, citing fears for the safety of Americans residing in Grenada.[73]

Therefore, by the end of the twentieth century, state practice had begun to trend toward a definition of self-defense under article 51 that included conventional self-defense in the sense of repelling foreign armies; self-defense as a punitive measure (arguably consistent with a Kelsen definition); and emerging anticipatory self-defense. Though the latter justifications could hardly be said to have risen to the level of customary international law, particularly the punitive use of force, state practice has been trending toward a more permissive use of force. This direction has been reinforced by Security Council resolutions 1189 and 1267 tying counter-terrorism to international peace and security and Chapter 7. These developments in international law offer a more expansive reading of the targets of defensive force, and a reduced immediacy necessary to justify its use.

The jurisprudence of this era was more definite. The use of force issue was first raised in the International Court of Justice (ICJ) in the *Corfu Channel case* involving Albania and the United Kingdom.[74] More recently, in the 1986 ICJ case of *Nicaragua v. United States* (Military and Paramilitary Activities in and Against Nicaragua), the Court delineated the requirements for article 51 as regarding unconventional armed bands. In this case the US "conceived, created and organized a mercenary army, the contra force ..." to overturn the Ortega government.[75] The Court ruled that article 51 cannot apply to non-state actors acting alone. The ruling found that the language of an "armed attack" must be read as "the sending by or on behalf of a State of armed bands, groups, irregulars or mercenaries, which carry out acts of armed force against another State of such gravity as to amount to an actual armed attack conducted by regular forces,' or 'its substantial involvement therein.'"[76] Thus, the Court found that non-state actors must be sent on behalf of a State or there must be substantial State involvement in the act that constitutes the armed attack. Writing a few years later, scholar Antonio Cassese concluded:

> The first proposition above--that there must have been an armed attack by the State against which force is used--means, more specifically, that the responsibility of that State must have been engaged in respect of the attack. This may occur in a number of ways: the attack may

[72] The US State Department cited four grounds for the incursion: 1. To protect American lives; 2. To assist the lawful and democratically elected government in Panama in fulfilling its international obligations; 3. To seize and arrest Manual Noriega for drug trafficking; 4. To defend the integrity of US rights under the Panama Canal treaties.' New York Times, A Transcript of President Bush's Address on the Decision to Use Force, Dec. 21, 1989.

[73] J. Quigley, "The United States Invasion of Grenada: Stranger than Fiction," *University of Miami Inter-American Law Review* 18 (1986): 275.

[74] (U.K. v. Alb.) 1949 I.C.J. 4, 29–35 (Dec. 15).

[75] Nicaragua v. United States, ICJ Rep 14 [1986].

[76] *Ibidem* at para 195.

> have actually been carried out by an official State organ (the State must always act through some human agency); or the attack may have been carried out by some unofficial State agent (a person or group in fact acting on behalf of the State); or even by official State organs acting in contravention of their instructions. In all these cases the attack will be attributable or imputable to the State. It will become its act.[77]

Cassese observed that the Court's ruling in *Nicaragua* did not foreclose on peaceful sanctions against the State if it failed to discharge an international obligation in connection with the attack,[78] but unless the attack is attributable to the State it cannot activate article 51 responses. This issue therefore turns on whether the state is a sponsor of terrorism and exercises effective control over it, or if it merely provides safe harbor to the group or if the state is unaware or unable to control the activities of the group. If the former, then defensive measures can be taken against the host country; otherwise only peaceful measures can be used.

The *Nicaragua* case was not without its critics as both Judges Schwebel and Higgins supported an alternative view. Higgins pointed out that "use of irregulars to carry out armed attacks against another state is, 'from a functional point of view,' a use of force"[79] and "[t]he incompatibility of the classical external armed aggression with the present rules regulating international relations, led to the development of other methods of covert or indirect aggression."[80] Thus, Higgins suggests that the inherent functional obsolescence of the original Charter article 51 served as a source for the contemporary irregular aggression taking the form of terrorism and national self-defense should be able to account for this evolution. This conclusion may be a bit fanciful as terrorism and other forms of irregular aggression pre-date the Charter era. The use of covert and indirect aggression is probably more a consequence of disproportionate and overwhelming modern military weapons and tactics, but it does suggest a potential for an evolution in international law.

Naturally, this case did not make allowances for unilateral invasion grounded in retribution or reprisal, nor did it allow for military responses to terrorist groups acting alone. It provided only for self-defense against a state that exercised effective control over irregular forces conducting terrorist activity in another sovereign state.

While the majority decision in the *Nicaragua* case declined to extend article 51 to non-state actors (except as mentioned above), it did not address the immediacy issue intrinsic to a discussion of self-defense. In a line of incidents leading up to

---

77 A. Cassese, "The International Legal Community's "Legal" Response to Terrorism" (1989) 38 *ICQL* 589.

78 State obligation under customary international law is reflected in General Assembly Resolution 2625 (*Declaration on Principles of International Law Concerning Friendly Relations and Co-operation Among States in Accordance with the Charter of the United Nations*) which states, "Every State has the duty to refrain from organizing, instigating, assisting or participating in acts of civil strife or terrorist acts in another State or acquiescing in organized activities within its territory directed toward the commission of such acts, when the acts referred to in the present paragraph involve a threat or use of force." G/RES/2625 (24 October 1970).

79 Nicaragua v. United States, at para 231–232.

80 *Ibidem*.

9/11 the concept of immediacy transitioned beyond a simple reflex action to more controversial strains of anticipatory self-defense.

14.3 The Doctrines of Anticipatory Self-Defense and Pre-emption

The immediacy requirement for self-defense has sustained significant transformation since the formation of the Charter, primarily in the closing decades of the twentieth century and the beginning of the twenty-first. Chief among these changes is the evolution of the doctrine of anticipatory self-defense and pre-emption. Though still relatively rare, anticipatory self-defense was cited by Israel in 1981 when it launched an air attack on an Iraqi nuclear facility at Osirak.[81] "Israel argued that the Iraqi reactor under construction was designed to produce nuclear weapons for use against Israel and therefore it was entitled to take pre-emptive action."[82]

Proponents of anticipatory self-defense argue that it does not make sense for states to wait to be attacked before taking defensive action,[83] that a state need not be a "sitting duck"[84] particularly in an age of weapons that cause mass casualties without warning. On the other hand, anticipatory self-defense is not expressly provided for in the Charter. It is usually impractical to identify specific relevant targets, increases the likelihood of mistakes (and therefore collateral damage)[85] as it is intelligence driven,[86] increases malevolent misuses of force where the state perpetrator can rely on it as a disingenuous justification for advancing national strategic efforts, and arguably circumvents the pacific aim of the Charter.

The ICJ has declined to directly address the issue head-on though it had the opportunity in 1986 in the *Nicaragua* case (after the Osirak strike) and in 2005 in the *Democratic Republic of Congo (DRC)* case (after the US-led invasion of Iraq). Subsequent to Israel's airstrike on Osirak, both the Security Council and the General

[81] S/RES/487 (1981) 19 June 1981.

[82] Christine Gray, *The Use of Force and the International Legal Order in International Law*, 3rd ed., ed. Malcolm D. Evans (Oxford: Oxford University Press, 2010), 628.

[83] *Ibidem*.

[84] *See* M. S. McDougal, et al., *The International Law of War*, at index.

[85] In 1988, the US shot down a civilian Iranian commercial plane and claimed it was in response to a mistakenly anticipated armed attack from Iran.

[86] In a report issued by the United States Institute of Peace, "Potential pitfalls of intelligence analysis include being too reliant on data from clandestine and highly technical sources, being subject to political pressure, and being insufficiently collaborative." L. Woocher, Conflict Assessment and Intelligence Analysis, Commonality, Convergence, and Complementarity, *USIP*, June 2011 at http://www.usip.org/publications/conflict-assessment-and-intelligence-analysis (last visited June 15, 2011).

Assembly condemned the attack,[87] but neither resolution addressed the issue of pre-emption specifically so the future utility of this doctrine remains uncertain. However, the expansive definition advanced by the Bush doctrine seems to be without support.

The Bush doctrine calls for pre-emption rather than specifically anticipatory self-defense which requires a significantly lower level of immediacy or imminence. According to the US National Security Strategy of 2002 and 2006, the requirement of imminence needs to be reexamined.[88] The 2002 Strategy stated:

> We must adapt the concept of imminent threat to the capabilities and objectives of today's adversaries. Rogue states and terrorists do not seek to attack us using conventional means. They know such attacks would fail. Instead, they rely on acts of terror and, potentially, the use of weapons of mass destruction – weapons that can be easily concealed, delivered covertly, and used without warning.[89]

This doctrine reduces the immediacy element on the basis of the unconventional warfare practiced by terrorists (and "rogue states"). Critics of pre-emption argue that eliminating the immediate threat element will only provide a justification for aggressive state conduct. Moreover, it provides for the creation of a permanent state of war – precisely opposite to the stated intent of the UN Charter. Under the Bush doctrine, the US (or any other similarly situated state) could invoke article 51 in justification against any adversary or "rogue state" for so long as the threat of terrorism exists. The threat of terrorism, for all practical purposes, has always existed and always will. Thus, a "Global War on Terrorism" creates a permanent state of war that can be justified on purely speculative grounds.

It also raises a host of other questions such as the seriousness of the anticipated attack and whether it must credibly involve weapons of mass destruction. As to the level of certainty of an anticipated attack, is a generalized speculation sufficient? May the proponent state rely upon the expectation of a future attack based solely on the target group's ideology or history? By reducing the threshold of immediacy, pre-emption risks a permanent state of war as it threatens to grant license to powerful states to practice aggression upon all ideologically opposed groups without the conventional safeguards of immediacy to moderate their national ambitions. In short, a liberal interpretation of pre-emption risks distorting the immediacy requirement to such an extent as to circumvent article 2(4) and default to a pre-Charter *jus ad bellum.*

The interpretation of pre-emption under the Bush doctrine sought to reevaluate the requirement of imminence, but remained vague on the particulars. This view has not taken root and was neither supported as widespread state practice, expressly supported by the Security Council or the International Court of Justice, nor supported by international scholarship. Additionally, it was expressly rebuked in a 2004 report by the UN Panel of Experts on collective security after 9/11 which reaffirmed that

---

[87] S/RES/487 (1981) 19 June 1981; G/RES/36/27 (1981) 13 Nov. 1981.

[88] *Ibidem.*

[89] The National Security Strategy of the United States of America, September 2002, at http://www.whitehouse.gov/nsc/nss.html, at 15.

the threat of armed attack must be imminent.[90] Thus, rather than evoking state practice and changing the course of international law, the Bush doctrine seems to be an aberration.

14.4 Trends in National Self-Defense Subsequent to 9/11

Security Council resolution 1373 tied article 51 to counter-terrorism and therefore impliedly inures this competence to states against non-state actors. Prior to 9/11 the Security Council had a well-documented history with the Taliban government operating in Afghanistan.[91] After the attacks in New York and Washington DC, ratcheting up the stakes to a military response was foreseeable. Though it may be a case of bad facts making bad law, the political ramifications of the attack were unavoidable. Evaluating the Security Council's response and the ensuing so-called "Global War on Terrorism," many scholars have suggested a clear articulation of a change in international law. In 2005 Antonio Cassese reflected on the change and observed:

> … [that] contrary to what the ICJ states in Nicaragua (merits) (at 195) and in Legal Consequence of the Construction of the Wall (at 139) – a holding highly criticized by Judge Higgins in the separate Opinion (at 33) … the aggression need not come from a State; it can also emanate from a terrorist organization or even from insurgents (committing aggression in a state other than the one on whose territory they operate) …[92]

The change in Cassese's analysis from 1989 to 2005 is an illustration of a new articulation of article 51 in the twenty-first century, supported by state practice. In addition to resolution 1373, 2001 saw the full-scale invasion of Afghanistan. The attack against Afghanistan met with nearly uniform state approval. The OAS states, the NATO states, China, Russia, Japan and Pakistan supported the operation on article 51 grounds (only Iraq and Iran contested the invasion).[93] Though it was instigated by the United States, more than 48 nations joined the effort in one capacity or another.[94] Additionally, Israel's use of force against Hezbollah in Lebanese territory is a recent invocation of article 51 in response to attacks by non-state actors.[95]

---

[90] C. Gray, *The Use of Force and the International Legal Order in International Law*, at 631–632.

[91] United Nations Charter art. 41, 42; D. Walsh, *Osama bin Laden Killed in US Raid on Pakistan Hideout,* already cited.

[92] Antonio Cassese, *International Law*, 2nd ed. (Oxford: Oxford University Press, 2005), 354–355.

[93] C. Gray, *The Use of Force and the International Legal Order in International Law*, at 629.

[94] See UN Doc. S/2001/967 (European Union); UN Doc S/2001/1005 (Canada); UN Doc S/2001/1127 (Germany); UN Doc S/2001/1193 (New Zealand); see also Triggs, G, *International Law: Contemporary Principles and Practice* (2006).

[95] UN Doc S/PV.5493 (2006); see also Trapp, KN, 'Back to Basics: Necessity, Proportionality and the Right of Self-Defense Against Non-State Terrorist Actors' (2007) 56(1) *International and Comparative Law Quarterly* 141, 154.

The Security Council "… acknowledged Israel's right to defend itself under article 51 of the United Nations Charter."[96]

Assessing the value of the US-led coalition in Iraq is a little more troublesome. While it could serve as a model for state practice, the US acted conspicuously without express Security Council approval.[97] Acquiescence can be considered when determining state practice, but the world-wide protest[98] against the US incursion into Iraq provides a convincing counter-argument. Thus, the number of objecting states would outnumber those engaged in the practice and destroy its credible claims to customary international law status. Moreover, many of the states that did participate in the invasion were pressured by the US through strategic gain or implied threat. Thus, because states acted out of intimidation instead of *bona fide* belief in the legality of the attack, they fail to satisfy the requisite *opinio juris* to impact customary international law. The invasion of Iraq blurs the discussion of national self-defense against non-state actors as it does the doctrine of anticipatory self-defense.

Nonetheless, state practice in the twenty-first century seems to be trending toward more permissive use of force against non-state actors. Other examples of post-9/11 state practice include Russian bombing missions in Georgia against Chechens[99]; Turkish attacks against the PKK on the territory of Iraq[100]; and Colombia's excursions into Ecuador in March 2008 where it launched a raid on FARC guerillas.[101] However, the legal utility in each of these cases was voided by the invading states claiming alternative factual rationales. In the case of the bombing missions against Chechens, the Russian authorities claim Georgia was a failed state[102] implying exemption to state attribution under those circumstances. The attacks on the territory of Iraq against the PKK were during a time when Iraq did

---

[96] UN DOC S/PV.5493 (2006); see also *Ibidem*.

[97] Secretary General Kofi-Annan stated that the US-led invasion of Iraq was an illegal act that contravened the UN Charter. Iraq War Illegal, Says Annan, BBC News, September 16, 2004 at http://news.bbc.co.uk/2/hi/middle_east/3661134.stm. Others predicted that if the Security Council had voted on a resolution calling for an invasion of Iraq only 4 members would have voted in favor of it. Ronan Bennett, Ten Days to War, The Guardian UK, March 8, 2008 at http://www.guardian.co.uk/world/2008/mar/08/iraq.unitednations…

[98] The level of protests in response to the invasion of Iraq prompted one journalist to observe "that there may still be two superpowers on the planet: the United States and the world public opinion." P. E. Tyler, Threats and Responses: News and Analysis; A New Power in the Streets, *The New York Times*, 17 February, 2003 at http://www.nytimes.com/2003/02/17/world/threats-and-responses-news-analysis-a-new-po…

[99] UN Doc. S/2002/1012 (2002) cited in Teresa Reinhold, "State Weakness, Irregular Warfare, and the Right to Self-Defense Post-9-11" (April 2011) 105 *American Journal of International Law* 244.

[100] *Ibidem*.

[101] *Ibidem*.

[102] Statement by Russian Federation President V.V. Putin, Annex to Letter Dated 11 September 2002 from the Permanent Representative of the Russian Federation to the United nations Addressed to the Secretary-General, UN DOC. S/2002/1012, at 2 (2002), cited in Reinold, *ibidem*.

not enjoy sovereign status. This took place during the US occupation and its efforts were, for all practical purposes, condoned by the US, thereby relieving it of the necessity of state attribution. Finally, in the case of the incursion into Ecuador, state acquiescence was not readily apparent – the incursion led to threats of a referral to the ICC for acts of aggression.[103] Rather than being emblematic of a shift in international law, these actions are more accurately characterized as states taking advantage of temporary international tolerance for US policy, in light of 9/11, in order to further their own national agendas.

If these state practices do tend to push the limits on state attribution, it does not appear to be reflected in the decisions of the International Court of Justice. The jurisprudence of the post 9/11 era has taken a different turn from that of the Security Council. In the *Oil Platforms* case (Iran v. United States) decided in 2003, the ICJ found that while the mining of a single military vessel might be sufficient to constitute an "armed attack" under article 51, the attack could not be shown to be attributable to Iran.[104] Thus, the Court continued to maintain the necessity of the attribution to a state. This case was shortly followed in the ICJ advisory opinion of *Legal Consequences of the Construction of a Wall* ("The Wall Opinion") where the Court found that Israel was in violation of Charter provisions when it constructed a wall blocking it from occupied Palestinian territory and failed to convincingly justify it on article 51 grounds.[105] In both cases the Court maintained its position in *Nicaragua* requiring state involvement for article 51.

In *Cases Concerning Armed Activities on the Territory of the Congo* (Democratic Republic of the Congo v. Uganda) the ICJ found that while the state of Uganda had been attacked by the paramilitary group ADF (coming from the territory of the DRC), there was no involvement of the state government in the attacks.[106] Moreover, since the attack did not emanate from armed bands or irregulars *sent by* the DRC or on behalf of the DRC, there were insufficient grounds for Uganda to exercise its right to self-defense (emphasis added).[107]

The post 9/11 jurisprudence of the ICJ is not without its critics. In the Wall Opinion, Judge Kooijmans critiques the Court for adding a "new element" of state attribution.[108] Likewise in his declaration, Judge Buergenthal states that there are

---

[103] Though international reaction was constrained, the incident threatened to ignite a regional War involving Colombia, Ecuador and Venezuela and was ultimately resolved diplomatically at a Rio Group meeting later that year. J. Glusing, Saber-Rattling in South America, Speigelonline International, March 4, 2008 at http://www.spiegel.de/international/world/0,1518,539294,00.html (last visited June 30, 2011); Ecuador Seeks to Censure Colombia, BBC News, March 5, 2008 at http://news.bbc.co.uk/2/hi/americas/7278484.stm (last visited June 30, 2011).

[104] Iran v. United States, ICJ Rep. 161 [2003] para. 72.

[105] Legal Consequences of the Construction of a Wall (Advisory opinion) [2004] ICJ Rep 136, at para 139 (hereinafter The Wall Opinion).

[106] DRC v Uganda [2005] ICJ 116 para. 131–135 (hereinafter DRC).

[107] *Ibidem* at para 147.

[108] The Wall Opinion, already cited.

two problems with the majority's opinion. One, the Charter does not specify that an armed attack must come from another state; and two, Security Council resolutions 1368 and 1373 do not limit their application to terrorist attacks by state actors only.[109] In the DRC case, Judge Kooijman opines "… [E]ven if one assumes that mere failure to control the activities of armed bands cannot in itself be attributed to the territorial State as an unlawful act, that in my view does not necessarily mean that the victim State is under such circumstances not entitled to exercise the right of self-defense under article 51."[110]

The ICJ's majority analysis is consistent with the customary international law laid out in General Assembly resolution 3314 defining aggression. The relevant provision [of article 3] of resolution 3314 defines an "armed attack" as, *inter alia*, "[t]he sending by or on behalf of a State of armed bands, groups, irregulars or mercenaries, which carry out acts of armed force against another State of such gravity as to amount to the acts listed above, or its substantial involvement therein."[111] Thus, state attribution is required or at least "substantial involvement" which is roughly congruent to the "effective control" test adopted by the Court in *Nicaragua*. More recently, in article 16 of their *Draft Code of Crimes Against the Peace and Security of Mankind*, the ILC also reaffirms state attribution for aggression:

> An individual who, as leader or organizer, actively participates in or orders the planning, preparation, initiation or waging of aggression *committed by a State* shall be responsible for a crime of aggression. (Emphasis added)[112]

Moreover, the definition of aggression was reaffirmed at the 2010 Kampala Review Conference of the International Criminal Court where the national representatives for the ICC State parties (111 at the time, 120 by 4 March 2012)[113] adopted a definition drawn from resolution 3314.[114] At Kampala the States parties adopted the language of General Assembly resolution 3314 with regard to use of terrorists and state attribution.[115] Each state party agreed in principle to accept this definition,[116]

---

[109] *Ibidem*.

[110] DRC, already cited, para. 26.

[111] G/RES/3314, article 3 (g).

[112] Draft Code of Crimes Against the Peace and Security of Mankind, Report of the International Law Commission, 48th Session, [1996] II (2) *International Law Commission Yearbook* 17.

[113] The States Parties to the Rome Statute *at* http://www.icc-cpi.int/Menus/ASP/states+parties/ (last visited March 04, 2012).

[114] The definition at Kampala specified, "Any of the following acts … shall, in accordance with United Nations General Assembly resolution 3314 (XXIX) of 14 December 1974, qualify as an act of aggression." Rome Statute art. 8 *bis* (2)(inserted by RC/Res. 6 of 11 June 2010).

[115] Definition of Aggression, Rome Statute art. 8*bis* (2)(g).

[116] The agreement was subject to limitations imposed under article 15*bis* and 15*ter* requiring additional ratification, ability for states parties to opt out and delay of temporal jurisdiction until 1 January 2017.

even to the extent of assessing individual criminal liability.[117] This provides powerful evidence for maintaining the *Nicaragua* holding and rejecting the applicability of article 51 for non-state actors lacking requisite state attribution.

14.5 Things to Come

In response to a firestorm of criticism that bin Laden was illegally assassinated in violation of international law,[118] Legal Advisor to the US Department of State and recognized international law scholar Harold Hongju Koh defended the assassination on legal grounds.[119] Koh observed that the United States "is in an armed conflict with al-Qaeda … and may use force consistent with its inherent right to self-defense…"[120] Koh further elaborated that the US may use lethal force "by targeting persons such as high-level al-Qaeda leaders who are planning attacks"[121] as belligerents and legitimate military targets in furtherance of military objectives. Koh also identified bin Laden as posing an imminent threat.[122] Finally, Koh asserted that the killing of bin Laden was not an unlawful extrajudicial killing because "a state that is engaged in an armed conflict or in legitimate self-defense is not required to provide targets with legal process before the state may use lethal force."[123]

In reply to Koh's arguments, imminent scholar Mary Ellen O'Connell responded that the raid on bin Laden should have been conducted on the basis of civilian law and, citing the European Court of Human Rights case of *McCann v. The United*

[117] The agreement reached at Kampala, in some ways, exceeds the breadth of the definition of aggression provided for in GA Res 3314 as resolution article 5(2) distinguishes between acts of aggression that create individual criminal liability in the case of a "war of aggression" and just "aggression" which gives rise to international responsibility but not personal liability. The International Criminal Court does not make this distinction.

[118] Noam Chomsky, Bin Laden's Death: Much More to Say, RSN, May 21, 2011 *at* http://readersupportednews.org/opinion2/277-75/6014-bin-ladens-death-much-more-to-say (last visited May 22, 2011); Y. Dreazen, A. Madhani, M. Ambinder, *The Goal was Never to Capture bin Laden,* The Atlantic, May 4, 2011 *at* http://www.theatlamtic.com/politics/print/2011/05/the-goal-was-never-to-capture-bin-laden… (last visited May 22, 2011) quoting former West German Chancellor Helmut Schmidt.

[119] Koh, HH, *The Lawfulness of the US Operation Against Osama bin Laden,* Opino Juris, May 19, 2011 *at* http://opinojuris.org/2011/05/19/the-lawfulness-of-the-us-operation-against-osama-bin-lad… (last visited on May 22, 2011).

[120] *Ibidem.*

[121] *Ibidem.*

[122] *Ibidem.*

[123] *Ibidem.*

Kingdom,[124] concluded that he should have been captured instead of killed.[125] O'Connell stated:

> On May 2, no fighting was going on in Pakistan that would rise to the level of "armed conflict" as defined under international law; Pakistan had to suspend major military operations against militant groups in the country's tribal areas after the floods of 2010. And despite what some commentators have argued, under international law there is no right to engage in cross-border military force based on the argument that a state is unable or unwilling to deal with the threat themselves. The correct choice of law, therefore was peacetime law.[126]

The crux of this disagreement lies in which law should be applied, the law of armed conflict or peacetime law, and whether this initiative should have come under Article 51 (national self-defense) of the UN Charter. The conflicting points of view inherent in this question are foreseeable and stem from the controversy over whom is a legitimate target of national self-defense and how immediate the threat must be. Koh's reliance on *jus in bello* norms as the yardstick for the propriety of action is arguably defensible if the US strategy of pre-emption is adopted. The military conflict transforms from a defensive action foreseen in article 51 to a worldwide war according to almost any definition of the term and the application of "Geneva law."

By reworking the immediacy requirement, US forces are able to continually target its enemies without interruption because it can assert and reassert the threat of terrorism, however vague or speculative that threat may be. Indeed, in the "Global War on Terrorism" it has continually attacked for nearly ten years without visible sign of relenting. On the one hand, article 51 arguably entitles a state to defend its territory by striking at the war-making capability of the aggressor and not just limit its defensive tactics to those actually (physically) prosecuting the "armed attack."[127] On the other hand, the goals of the "Global War on Terrorism" are impossible to achieve as they are self-perpetrating and do little more than escalate violence and war. Moreover, continual military strikes and a state of permanent war are clearly opposed to the object and purpose of the Charter and article 51. The current "Global War on Terrorism" is different from the Israeli anticipatory self-defense bombing on

---

[124] McCann v. The United Kingdom, 21 ECHR 97 GC.

[125] R. Alford, "More from O'Connell on bin Laden Killing as Peacetime Use of Force," *Opinio Juris*, May 4, 2011 at http://opiniojuris.org/2011/05/04/more-from-oconnell-on-bin-laden-killing-as-peacetime-us… (last visited May 22, 2011).

[126] *Ibidem*.

[127] See, 'The Yemen Arab Republic submitted a complaint to the UN Security Council, which on 9 April 1964 passed Resolution 188 condemning reprisals in general as incompatible with the principles of the UN Charter and "deploring" Britain's military action against Harib.' Wm Roger Louis and Avi Shlaim (eds), The 1967 Arab-Israeli War Origins and Consequences (Cambridge University Press: New York 2012) 160. In that case "The Security Council did not accept the wider view of anticipatory self-defence against attacks which were not imminent, condemned punitive action, and rejected the plea of self-defence in cases of a proportionate reaction to a threat or use of force ...There was a long delay between the initial use of force and the response." Stanimir A. Alexandrov, Self Defence Against the Use of Force in International Law (Kluwer Law International, The Hague 1996) 170-171.

the Osirak facility as it was a limited attack with a well-defined objective that did not allow for a permanent state of war.

The inclusion of non-state actors as legitimate targets further fuels permanent war. As non-state actors are mobile and clandestine they cannot be successfully targeted in a military context and so the conflict cannot be won. The character of this conflict provides carte blanche for the states to prosecute the war against terrorism (wherever that may take them) in perpetuity. This seems to be the dispositive feature of the US's "Global War on Terrorism." Moreover, the copy-cat efforts of other states such as Russia, Colombia and Turkey further exemplify the dangers in this approach as the barriers to unilaterally launching attacks become increasingly reduced and justified on a rhetorical basis (i.e., fighting terrorism). Justifying permanent war on the basis of state practice and a self-defeating interpretation of article 51 only serves to concede the hegemonic authority of powerful states, and law through intimidation. It also serves to circumvent the fundamental object and purpose of the Charter to maintain international peace and security. Cherry-picking examples and establishing nuanced interpretations does not justify a result that is otherwise fundamentally opposed to the preemptory norms of global governance, and state acquiescence as a by-product of intimidation is of no utility in determining international law.

In her article *State Weakness, Irregular Warfare and the Right to Self-defense Post 911*, Theresa Reinhold declaims, "… [T]he vast majority of states did not challenge the US's claims to exercise its right to self-defense against both the actual perpetrators of the attacks and the state providing safe haven to the terrorists. … [I] t is probably fair to conclude that as a result of international acquiescence in the US intervention in Afghanistan, the existing rules governing the use of force have been called into question, with the Nicaragua standard losing its validity as the yardstick for what constitutes an armed attack. The rules governing the use of force are indisputably in flux, as … post 9/11 state practice makes clear."[128] This is perhaps an overstatement of the current trend of article 51 in international law. Even though former US President George W. Bush proclaimed that he would hold those who provided safe harbor to the terrorists equally culpable with those who sponsored them,[129] this determination does not rise to the level of international law. It was directly contrary to international law as articulated in *Nicaragua* and consisted more of political rhetoric than binding legal theory.

International acquiescence to intervention into Afghanistan did not amount to changing customary international law as established by the Charter. Firstly, the intervention into Afghanistan did not take place in a vacuum; the Taliban government had been warned and sanctioned by the Security Council under article 41. Secondly, whether the al Qaida forces were sent by the Taliban government, or constituted members of the government of the Taliban, or whether the Taliban exercised

[128] Reinold, "State Weakness, Irregular Warfare, and the Right to Self-Defense Post-9-11", at 251–252.

[129] See S. E. Smith, "Blaming Big Brother: Holding States Accountable for the Devastation of Terrorism," *Oklahoma Law Review* 56 (2003): 735.

some measure of effective control over the al Qaida are issues of fact. As Professor Reisman observes "I retain the adverb 'ostensibly,' even in cases of convictions, because it is in the very nature of international and domestic terrorism that links between the agent and principal are shadowy such that the principal retains a capacity for plausible deniability."[130] If the Taliban helped plan the 9/11 attacks then they would be subject to military invasion under a theory of self-defense in accordance with the standard laid out in *Nicaragua*. The dogged refusal of the Taliban to hand over al-Qaida suspects, a willingness to endure article 41 sanctions rather than stop al Qaida terrorist activity and to court military invasion, and their resistance, fighting shoulder-to-shoulder with al-Qaida forces, evince an intimate working relationship and underscore a strong implication that they did exercise sufficient "effective control" or "state involvement" to activate article 51 self-defense. As regarding the subsequent US-led invasion of Iraq, it clearly fails to have substantial impact on customary international law because acquiescence, such as it was, was anything but uniform and often a product of coercion and because the invasion was subject to widespread international censure.

The 9/11 attacks had tremendous impact on modern international law, culture and society. They resulted in significant loss of life, though modest compared to modern "armed attacks" using conventional weapons, they nonetheless caused massive fatalities compared to most terrorist attacks. They resulted in grave economic consequences and served as a very effective propaganda tool. Visions of cheering crowds juxtaposed with massive destruction will remain indelibly etched in the minds of those who witnessed it. This was a watershed moment politically. Yet, as dramatic as the events were, when viewed in the sober reflection of hindsight, such events seldom permanently shape law, domestically or internationally. Scholars, diplomats and jurists who exaggerate the long-term significance of such events, who claim disproportionate risks or support measures that, in the long run, are more devastating than the harm sought to be remedied – or who take advantage in order to advance self-interested national policy agendas – do a disservice to the international community.

Most of those who deduce that a general organic change has already taken place in international use of force law, or specifically in article 51, may be jumping to unjustified conclusions based on unusual facts and circumstances. Two claims are advanced in support of the contention that article 51 has been permanently broadened in the 9/11 age. They are state practice and Security Council initiative. With respect to Security Council action, while resolution 1373 does cite the article 51 language in response to the 9/11 terrorist attacks, it does not preclude state sponsorship as a necessary prerequisite. Indeed, the language is vague and aspirational and fails to fully articulate the conditions necessary for national self-defense under this resolution in response to terrorist attacks. Does it provide for a military response to de minimis attacks, failed efforts, cyber attacks, or attacks limited to property damage? Resolution 1373 has to be viewed in light of resolutions 1189 and 1267 and the

[130] W. M. Reisman, "International Legal Responses to International Terrorism," *Houston Journal of International Law* 22 (1999): 3.

specific circumstance of the Afghanistan-Taliban franchise. These actions are specific to those groups and an attack against one is an attack against both. Thus, an attack from one is an attack from both. The historic context of resolution 1373 provides a backdrop of Security Council initiative that presupposes a degree of state attribution and is not contradictory to the *Nicaragua* decision (though subsequent acts by the United States in prosecuting its "Global War on Terrorism" may contradict international legal principles and thus lead to justifications sounding in *jus in bello* instead of *jus ad bellum*). However, the Security Council has taken no other steps to reaffirm the competence of article 51 to non-state actors (acting without substantial state involvement). Therefore, the conclusions of the Security Council, though provocative, do little to establish a concrete change in the international law of article 51, or national self-defense generally.

Moreover, even if the Security Council did seek to expand the doctrine of national self-defense by removing the constraints of state attribution and limiting immediacy prerequisites, doing so in a way that brings about a permanent state of [international] war exceeds its mandate, the primary object and purpose of the Charter, and is arguably without legal authority or binding effect. "Even the pivotal text establishing the Council's power to adopt binding decisions – article 25 – proclaims that these decisions are to be accepted and carried out by member states 'in accordance with the present Charter.'"[131] By opening the door to endless war and rewriting the implied state attribution requirement in article 51, the Security Council may be acting outside its authority[132] and theoretically could be subject to judicial review by the ICJ.[133] Moreover, aggression as a *jus cogens* violation is a preemptory norm and "any Security Council decision in conflict with a norm of *jus cogens* must necessarily be without effect."[134] Naturally, proving a broad interpretation of article 51 violates preemptory norms is a heavy burden with little practical hope of success, but endless war predicated on this interpretation could ultimately tilt the scales.

Therefore, the provisions of resolution 1373 are vague in their implementation and legal effect, are bound in a history that makes them context specific in a scenario which already includes state attribution and which has little impact outside that context, and would be an illegal obstruction of the object and purpose of the Charter if it

[131] Dinstein, *War Aggression and Self-Defense*, already cited.

[132] See Advisory Opinion on Certain Expenses of the United Nations (Article17, Paragraph 2, of the Charter), [1962] ICJ Rep. 151, 167.

[133] The issue of ICJ authority for judicial review over Security Council resolutions was tangentially raised in the Lockerbie case and has been the subject of extensive scholarship, see B. Martenczuk, "The Security Council, the International Court of Justice and Judicial Review: What Lessons from Lockerbie?," *European Journal of International Law* 10 (1999): 517, 532; R. F. Kennedy, "Libya v. United States: The International Court of Justice and the Power of Judicial Review," *Virginia Journal of International Law* 33 (1992): 899, 908.

[134] D. Akande, "The International Court of Justice and the Security Council: Is there Room for Judicial Control of Decisions of the Political Organs of the United Nations?," *International and Comparative Law Quarterly* 46 (1997): 309, 322, cited in Y. Dinstein, *War Aggression and Self-Defense*, already cited.

was interpreted in a manner that broadens it beyond the scope of the *Nicaragua* decision. Inasmuch as the Security Council has taken no clarifying steps, *vis-a-vis* a reinterpretation of article 51, since it adopted resolution 1373, Security Council action fails to provide a convincing calculus for change under international law.

Secondly, as a harbinger of changing international norms, state practice is useful in two ways: one, it forms a portion of the manifold requirements for evolving customary international law (along with *opinio juris*) and, two, it can be used to interpret treaty provisions in order to infer the intent of the parties. As an indicator of customary international law, the recent state practice of the invasion of Afghanistan fails to satisfy the *opinio juris* element as laid out above, and it has failed to distinguish predicate state attribution issues with specificity and thus lacks clarity and binding effect.

Additionally, as an alternate means of interpreting article 51, there is a paucity of state practice to support defensive action against non-state actors. Once Afghanistan (or "AfPak"[135]) is removed from the equation (as a conflict involving state attribution), there are relatively few contemporary examples of national self-defense against non-state actors. They include the recent instances of national self-defense against non-state actors in the attacks against the Chechens, PKK and FARC. All of these acts were of a controversial nature, depended on alternative sets of facts and were too few to be of much value in determining changing international legal norm or the interpretation of article 51. They are more accurately depicted as the actions of unscrupulous administrations taking advantage of extraordinary political circumstances to advance national agendas. Nor did state acquiescence play a relevant part as the only demonstrable assent was in the case of Afghanistan with the other instances receiving various levels of censure or disregard from other states or international organizations but little or no support.

Finally, while state practice does seem to be trending toward greater acceptance of anticipatory self-defense (though the ICJ has not made a determination on the issue), it is grounded, at least in part, on the ever-increasing development of weapons with instantaneous delivery systems and greater lethality and the increasing security risk. It does not per se enlarge the subjects of the [defensive] attack and thus only tangentially impacts the operation of article 51. Ironically, the greater development of anticipatory self-defense provides greater latitude on the immediacy issue and thus, in order to preclude a constant state of war and maintain international peace and security, a more scrupulous application of state attribution becomes indispensible.

Bibliography

Akande, D. 1997. The international court of justice and the security council: Is there room for judicial control of decisions of the political organs of the United Nations? *International and Comparative Law Quarterly* 46: 309–343.

[135] Denotes Afghanistan and Pakistan as a single theater of operation.

Alford, R. 2011. More from O'Connell on bin Laden killing as peacetime use of force. *Opinio Juris*, May 4 at http://opiniojuris.org/2011/05/04/more-from-oconnell-on-bin-laden-killing-as-peacetime-us…
Allo, A.K. 2010. Ethiopia's armed intervention in Somalia: The Legality of Self-Defense in Responding to the Threat of Terrorism. *Denver Journal of International Law and Policy* 39: 139–168.
Artistotle, *Nicomacheon Ethics,*Book X, Ch. VI XVII, 6 and; *Politics,* VII, 14.
Bennett, R. 2008. Ten days to war, The Guardian UK, March 8 at http://www.guardian.co.uk/world/2008/mar/08/iraq.unitednations…
Bowett, D.W. 1958. *Self-defense in international law*. New York: Praeger.
Brierly, J.L. 1963. In *The law of nations: An introduction to the international law of peace*, 6th ed, ed. Waldock Sir Humphrey. Oxford: Oxford University Press.
Brownlie, I. 1963. *International law and the use of force by states*. New York: Praeger.
Cassese, A. 1989. The international legal community's "Legal" response to terrorism. *ICQL* 38: 589–608.
Cassese, A. 2005. *International law*, 2nd ed, 354–5. Oxford: Oxford University Press.
Chomsky, Noam, Bin Laden's Death: Much more to say, RSN, May 21, 2011 at http://readersupportednews.org/opinion2/277-75/6014-bin-ladens-death-much-more-to-say.
Dinstein, Y. 2005. *War aggression and self-defense*, 4th ed. Cambridge: Cambridge University Press.
Dreazen, Y., Aamer Madhani, and Marc Ambinder. 2011. The goal was never to capture bin Laden. *The Atlantic*, May 4 at http://www.theatlamtic.com/politics/print/2011/05/the-goal-was-never-to-capture-bin-laden…
Franck, T. 1970. Who killed article 2(4)? *American Journal of International Law* 64: 809–837.
Glusing, J. 2008. Saber-rattling in South America, speigelonline international, March 4 at http://www.spiegel.de/international/world/0,1518,539294,00.html.
Gray, C. 2010. The use of force and the international legal order. In *International law*, 3rd ed, ed. M.D. Evans, 628. Oxford: Oxford University Press.
Grewe, W.G. 2000. *The epochs of international law, 108–111* (trans: Michael Byers and revised). Berline: de Gruyter.
Kelsen, H. 1945. *General theory of law and state*. New York: Russell & Russell.
Kelsen, H. 1952. *Principles of international law.* 1st ed. New York: Rinehart.
Kennedy, R.F. 1992–1993. Libya vs. United States: The international court of justice and the power of judicial review. *Virginia Journal of International Law* 33: 899–925.
Kielsgard, M.D. 2006. A human rights approach to counter terrorism. *California Western International Law Journal* 36: 249–302.
Koh, H. H. 2011. The lawfulness of the US operation against Osama bin Laden, *Opino Juris*, May 19 at http://opinojuris.org/2011/05/19/the-lawfulness-of-the-us-operation-against-osama-bin-lad…
Legal Consequences of the Construction of a Wall (Advisory opinion) 2004 ICJ Report 136.
Lobel, J. 1999. The use of force to respond to terrorist attacks: The bombing of Sudan and Afghanistan. *Yale Journal of International Law* 24: 537–557.
Martenczuk, B. 1999. The Security Council, the International Court of Justice and Judicial Review: What Lessons from Lockerbie? *European Journal of International Law* 10: 517–547.
McDougal, M.S., and F.P. Feliciano. 1961. *Law and minimum world public order*. New Haven: Yale University Press.
McDougal, M.S., and F.P. Feliciano. 1994. *The international law of war*. The Hague: Martinus Nijhoff.
Miller, L. 2006. China an emerging superpower? May 4 at http://www.stanford.edu/group/sjir/6.1.03_miller.html
Musharbash, Y. 2007. War on terror more expensive than Vietnam, Spiegel online international, January 16 at http://www.speigel.de/international/0,1518,460007,00.html.
Nicaragua v. United States, ICJ Rep 14 [1986].
Nussbaum, A. 1954. *A concise history of the law of nations 35* rev'd ed. .

O'Connell, M.E. 2009. *International law and the use of force*, 2nd ed, 118. New York: Foundation Press.
Parrington, A.J. Col., USAF, Mutually Assured Destruction Revisited, (Winter 1997) *Airpower Journal*, at http://www.airpower.maxwell.af.mil/airchronicles/apj/apj97/parrin.html.
Prohibition of War, International Committee of the Red Cross, January 1, 2004 at http://www.icrc.org/eng/resources/documents/misc/5kzjjd.htm.
Quigley, J. 1986. The United States invasion of Grenada: Stranger than fiction. *University of Miami Inter-American Law Review* 18: 271–352.
Reinhold, T. April 2011. State weakness, irregular warfare, and the right to self-defense post-9-11. *American Journal of International Law* 105: 244–286.
Reisman, M.W. 1994. The Baghdad bombing: Self-defense or reprisal? *European Journal of International Law* 5: 120–133.
Reisman, M.W. 1999 International legal responses to international terrorism. *Houston Journal of International Law* 22: 3–61.
Reisman, M.W., M.H. Arsanjani, S. Wiessner, and G.S. Westerman. 2004. *International law in contemporary perspective*. New York: Foundation Press.
Simma, B. 2002. *The charter of the United Nations: A commentary*, vol. 1, 2nd ed. Oxford: Oxford University Press.
Smith, S.E. 2003. Blaming big brother: Holding states accountable for the devastation of terrorism. *Oklahoma Law Review* 56: 735–775.
Stone, J. 1958. *Aggression and world order: A critique of United Nations theories of aggression 44*. London: Stevens and Sons Limited.
Trapp, K.N. 2007. Back to basics: Necessity, proportionality and the right of self-defense against non-state terrorist actors. *International and Comparative Law Quarterly* 56(1): 141–156.
Triggs, G. 2006. *International law: Contemporary principles and practice* Sydney: LexisNexis Buttersworth.
Tyler, P.E. 2003. Threats and responses: News and analysis; A new power in the streets, *The New York Times*, February. 17 at http://www.nytimes.com/2003/02/17/world/threats-and-responses-news-analysis-a-new-po…
von Elbe, J. 1939. The evolution of the concept of the just war in international law. *American Journal of International Law* 33: 665–688.
Walsh, D. 2011. Osama bin Laden killed in US raid on Pakistan hideout. *The Guardian News Service*, May 2 at http://www.guardian.co.uk/world/2011/may/02/osama-bin-laden-dead-pakistan/print.
Woocher, L. 2011. Conflict assessment and intelligence analysis, commonality, convergence, and complementarity. *USIP*, June 2011 at http://www.usip.org/publications/conflict-assessment-and-intelligence-analysis.

Other Sources

A Transcript of President Bush's Address on the Decision to Use Force, New York Times, December 21, 1989.
Advisory Opinion on Certain Expenses of the United Nations (Article17, Paragraph 2, of the Charter), [1962] ICJ Report. 151, 167.
Convention For the Prevention and Punishment of Terrorism, 19 League of Nations O.J. 23 (1938), League of Nations Doc. C.546(I).M.383(I).1937.V(1938)(16 November 1937).
Department of State [Mr. Webster to Lord Ashburn], Washington, 6th August 1842, Avalon Project – British-American Diplomacy: The Caroline Case, at http://avalon.law.yale.edu/19th_century/br-1842.asp.
Draft Code of Crimes Against the Peace and Security of Mankind, Report of the International Law Commission, 48th Session, 1996 II (2) *International Law Commission Yearbook* 17.

DRC v Uganda 2005 ICJ 116.
Ecuador Seeks to Censure Colombia, *BBC News*, March 5, 2008 at http://news.bbc.co.uk/2/hi/americas/7278484.stm.
GA/8082 24October1970.
GA/3034 18 December 1972.
G/RES/36/27 (1981) 13 Nov. 1981.
G/RES/41/38 (1985).
G/RES/3314, article 3 (g).
G/Res/2625 (*Declaration on Principles of International Law Concerning Friendly Relations and Co-operation Among States in Accordance with the Charter of the United Nations*) (24 October 1970).
G/ RES/ES-6/2 (1980) 14 January 1980
Iran v. United States, ICJ Rep. 161 [2003].
Iraq War Illegal, Says Annan, BBC News, September 16, 2004 at http://news.bbc.co.uk/2/hi/middle_east/3661134.stm.
McCann v. The United Kingdom, 21 ECHR 97 GC.
R v. Dudley and Stevens, 14 Q.B.D. 273 (1884).
Repertoire of the Practice of the Security Council, Supplement 1964–1965 (United Nations publication, Sales No. E68, VII.1), chap. XI, part IV, Case No. 7.
Rome Statute art. 8 *bis* (2)(inserted by RC/Res. 6 of 11 June 2010).
S/RES/502 (1982).
S/RES/0678 (1990) 29 Nov. 1990.
S/RES/487 (1981) 19 June 1981.
S/RES/425 (1978).
S/RES/393 (1976).
S/RES/1189 (1998).
S/RES/1267 (1999).
S/RES/1373(2001).
S/RES/487 (1981) 19 June 1981.
S/2001/967 (European Union); UN Doc S/2001/1005 (Canada); UN Doc S/2001/1127 (Germany); UN Doc S/2001/1193 (New Zealand).
Terrorism: Vindication for the Israelis, TIME Magazine, July 26, 1976 at http://www.time.com/time/magazine/article/0,9171,914380,00.html.
The National Security Strategy of the United States of America, September 2002, *at* http://www.whitehouse.gov/nsc/nss.html.
The Panorama Middle East Archives: Six-Day War, BBC, Feb. 6, 2009, at http://news.bbc.co.uk/panorama/hi/front_page/newsid_7875000/7875655.stm.
The States Parties to the Rome Statute at http://www.icc-cpi.int/Menus/ASP/states+parties/.
(UK v. Alb.) 1949 I.C.J. 4, 29–35 (Dec. 15).
UN Charter art. 2(4).
UN Charter, art. 51.
UN Charter, Preamble
UN Doc S/PV.5493 (2006).
UN Doc. S/2002/1012 (2002).
UN DOC. S/2002/1012, at 2 (2002).
UN Treaty Collection, Conventions on Terror, at http://untreaty.un.org/English/Terrorism.asp.
United Nations Charter art. 41, 42 at http://www.un.org/en/documents/charter/chapter7.shtml.
United Nations General Assembly, Special Committee on the Problem of Hungary (1957).
US Department of State, Foreign Relations of the United States, 1964–1968, Vol. XXXII, Dominican Republic; Cuba; Haiti; Guyana, Document 43, at http://history.state.gov/historicaldocuments/frus1964-68v32/d43.
Vienna Convention on the Law of Treaties, art. 31(3)(b).
Vienna Convention on the Law of Treaties, art. 32.

About the Contributors

José M. Atiles Osoria obtained a B.A. in Philosophy and Political Science from the University of Puerto Rico, Mayagüez Campus, PR (2007), an M.A. in Sociology of Law for the Oñati International Institute for the Sociology of Law, in the Basque Country (2008) and is Ph.D. candidate in Sociology of Law and Political Philosophy in the Centre for Social Studies (CES) of the University of Coimbra, Portugal and in the University of the Basque Country.

Simon Bronitt is a Professor at Griffith University, Australia and Director of the Australian Research Council Centre of Excellence in Policing and Security (CEPS). Before assuming this role in 2009, he was a Professor of Law in the ANU College of Law. He has published widely on criminal justice issues, including counter terrorism law and human rights, covert policing, telecommunications interception and international criminal law. His publications include *Principles of Criminal Law* (3rd ed, Thomson Reuters 2010) and *Law in Context* (4th ed, Federation Press, 2011).

Susan Donkin is a Ph.D. candidate in the School of Criminology and Criminal Justice at Griffith University, Australia, affiliated with the ARC Centre of Excellence in Policing and Security (CEPS). Her thesis examines the evolution of pre-emptive anti-terrorism legislation across time and place. Susan has a BA (Hons) in Law and Criminology from the University of Sheffield and an MA in Criminology from the University of Toronto.

Manuela Fernández-Rodríguez is professor of legal history at the Rey Juan Carlos University (Madrid). She is author of near 20 articles and book chapters, including several related to anti-terrorism legislation in the Western Europe. She is member of the research team of the 'Centro de Estudios Europeos Emile Nöel'.

Francesca Galli is a *FNRS* post-doctoral researcher at the *Institut d'Etudes Européennes* of the *ULB* in Brussels. She holds a Masters of Law of the *Institut d'Etudes Politiques* of Paris (*Master en Carrières Juridiques et Judiciaires*) and has completed her Ph.D. in Law at the University of Cambridge entitled "Anti-terrorism legislation in the UK, France and Italy from 1965 onwards", focusing on selected

A. Masferrer (ed.), *Post 9/11 and the State of Permanent Legal Emergency*,
Ius Gentium: Comparative Perspectives on Law and Justice 14,
DOI 10.1007/978-94-007-4062-4, © Springer Science+Business Media B.V. 2012

themes of criminal law and procedures in the area of counter-terrorism legislation and case-law. She works as a private consultant for RAND Europe and is currently involved in a project commissioned by DG Justice on the evaluation of the European Enforcement Order. She has worked in the past as an intern at the UNODC Terrorism Prevention Branch, with the French Liaison Magistrate in London and the Italian Liaison Magistrate at the Ministry of Justice in Paris. Her current research focuses on the impact of EU Counter-terrorism instruments on the legislation and case-law of selected member states. At the ULB she is also a member of the Management Committee of the European Criminal Law Academic Network (ECLAN).

Karl Härter is Legal Historian (Research Group Leader and Senior Research Scientist) at the Max-Planck-Institut for European Legal History, Frankfurt/M., and Professor for Early Modern & Modern History at the University of Darmstadt. He has studied History, Politics and Jurisprudence at the Universities of Darmstadt and Frankfurt and holds several degrees (1st & 2st State Examination, Doctoral degree, Habilitation). The major research interests are on Legal and Constitutional History as well as Early Modern History (Europe) and the History of crime/deviance & penal law/justice. He has published monographs and collected editions on the permanent Imperial Diet, public law, penal law and criminal justice and edited (together with M. Stolleis) ten volumes of the repertory of early modern police ordinances.

Mark D. Kielsgard J.D., L.L.M., J.S.D., is an Assistant Professor of Law at City University of Hong Kong, a Marie Curie Scholar and a former trial attorney in the USA. Dr. Kielsgard has published in the areas of international human rights, terrorism, genocide, international criminal law and authored the 2010 book *Reluctant Engagement: U.S. Policy and the International Criminal Court.* He has also lectured on topics including human trafficking, police oversight, transitional justice, human rights, international humanitarian law and public international law. He has taught law students in the United States, Hong Kong and mainland China and is a member of the International Association of Defense Counsel (licensed to practice before the International Criminal Tribunal for Former Yugoslavia (ICTY)), as well as the District of Columbia and the Commonwealth of Virginia. Dr. Kielsgard is a member of the International Association of Genocide Scholars (IAGS), the American Political Science Association (APSA) and the American Society of International Law (ASIL).

Mariona Llobet is Ass.Professor of criminal law at the University Pompeu Fabra. She is an expert on terrorism. Her doctoral thesis dealt with terrorism and the limits of the 'ius puniendi' in a democratic state (entitled *Derecho penal del terrorismo*, 2010). She has been fellow researcher at the *New York University*. She has also published on other criminal-law fields in specialized law journals and collective books.

Marinella Marmo is Senior Lecturer in Criminology at Flinders University Law School, Australia. She teaches and researches in the area of transnational criminal justice and human rights, and she has published extensively in this area. Previously, she taught in the area of criminology at the University of Leicester and the Liverpool John Moores University in the UK. She earned her Ph.D. in Applied Social Science at Lancaster University, UK.

Leandro Martínez-Peñas is professor of legal history at the Rey Juan Carlos University (Madrid). He is currently the Secretary of the 'Revista de la Inquisición' (Intolerancia y Derechos Humanos) and Treasurer of the *European Society for Comparative Legal History*. He is author of more than 40 publications (monographs, articles and chapter of books). He won the History National Award 2009 in Spain for the collective book 'El Rey. Historia de la Monarquía'.

Aniceto Masferrer is professor of legal history and teaches legal history and comparative law at the University of Valencia (Spain). He is the author of six books and more than 50 articles published in Spanish, European and American law journals. He has published extensively on criminal law from an historical and comparative perspective, as well as on the codification movement and fundamental rights in the Western legal tradition. He has been fellow researcher at the Institute Max-Planck for European Legal History (2000–2003), Visiting Professor at the University of Cambridge (2005), Visiting Scholar at Harvard Law School (2006–2007) and at Melbourne Law School (2008), and Visiting Professor at the University of Tasmania (2010). He is member of the *American Society for Legal History*, the current President of the *European Society for Comparative Legal History*, and vicepresident of the *Fundación Universitas* (www.fundacionuniversitas.org).

Christopher Michaelsen, Ph.D., L.L.M., Dipl. Jur., is a Senior Research Fellow at the Faculty of Law of the University of New South Wales (UNSW) in Sydney, Australia. He teaches and specialises in public international law, human rights and international security. Prior to joining UNSW, he served as a Human Rights Officer (Anti-Terrorism) at the OSCE Office for Democratic Institutions and Human Rights in Warsaw, Poland. He currently is a co-rapporteur on the International Human Rights Law Committee of the International Law Association. c.michaelsen@unsw.edu.au.

Juan A. Obarrio obtained the 'Filosofía y Letras' degree (Alicante, 1986), law degree (Alicante, 1992), and the Ph.D. degree in law (Alicante, 1995). He is professor of Roman law at the University of Valencia. He is an expert on the *ius commne* and the Roman tradition in Europe, field in which he has published 15 books and more than 40 articles (i.e. *Beneficium inventari: origen, pervivencia y recepción en el sistema jurídico español*, 2006; *El proceso por contumacia: origen, pervivencia y recepción*, 2009; *Estudios de tradición romanística: tutela et curatela*, 2011).

Kent Roach is a Professor of Law at the University of Toronto where he holds the Prichard Wilson Chair in Law and Public Policy. He served on the research advisory committee of Canada's Arar inquiry and as research director of its Air India inquiry. He is the author of 12 books including September 11: Consequences for Canada (Montreal: McGill Queens, 2003), *The Unique Challenges of Terrorism Prosecutions* (Ottawa: Supply and Services, 2010) and *The 9/11 Effect: Comparative Counter-Terrorism* (New York: Cambridge University Press, 2011).

Ben Saul is Professor of International Law at the Sydney Centre for International Law, Faculty of Law, The University of Sydney, and a barrister. Ben has published five books, over 50 refereed journal articles and book chapters, and over 150 other publications, and delivered hundreds of public lectures. His work on terrorism has been cited in various international and national courts. He has taught law at Oxford, Sydney, UNSW, and in China, India, Nepal and Cambodia, conducted professional training for numerous governments, been involved in human rights litigation in numerous countries, and is active in numerous international and national legal organisations. Ben is Editor-in-Chief of the *Australian International Law Journal* and President of the Refugee Advice and Casework Service in Australia. Previously Ben was Director of the Sydney Centre for International Law. He has a doctorate from Oxford and two honours degrees from The University of Sydney.

Clive Walker is Professor of Criminal Justice Studies at the School of Law, University of Leeds, where he has served as the Director of the Centre for Criminal Justice Studies and as Head of School. He has written extensively on terrorism issues, and has acted as a special adviser to the UK Parliament and Government. His latest book on terrorism is a comprehensive study of *Terrorism and the Law* (Oxford University Press, 2011).

Printed by Publishers' Graphics LLC